Under the editorship of **Leonard Carmichael**
*Secretary, Smithsonian Institution;
Formerly President, Tufts College
and Director, Tufts Research Labo-
ratory of Sensory Psychology and
Physiology*

The Psychology

A DYNAMIC AND EXPERIMENTAL APPROACH TO

Second Edition

Laurance Frederic Shaffer

Edward Joseph Shoben, Jr.

Teachers College, Columbia University

of *Adjustment*

PERSONALITY AND MENTAL HYGIENE

HOUGHTON MIFFLIN COMPANY

○ *Boston* • The Riverside Press Cambridge

Introduction

Most college textbooks in psychology are written to introduce students to the current state of the subject as a whole or to some aspect of it. In the history of psychology a few notable volumes have appeared which become not only good student books but also landmarks in the evolution of psychology as an organized science. During the last twenty years it has been increasingly recognized that *The Psychology of Adjustment* is just such a history-making book. Its unique status has been attested not only by enthusiastic reviews, but by unprecedentedly large and continuing sales in America and throughout the English-speaking world.

As editor, therefore, it is an especial pleasure to be able to say that this new and completely rewritten edition is an even better book than was the first edition. This is true because psychology has grown in scientific stature during the twenty years that have passed since the first edition appeared. In the present volume a large body of recent research is evaluated. Many of the findings of these investigations throw new and clarifying light on the understanding of adjustive behavior, the make-up of the personality, and mental hygiene.

The student who is well trained in mathematics, physics, chemistry, biology and basic experimental psychology is at first often repelled or even a little amused at some books and articles that attempt to deal with the dynamics of the human personality. Some of these works present unevaluated anecdotes about emotionally disturbed patients or deal with analogies adapted from classical mythology in an attempt to explain behavior. In this book, on the contrary, the reader is systematically introduced to a substantial and organized compilation of scientific fact and theory. This material is presented in so clear and understandable a manner that it illuminates the basis of both man's favorable and his unfavorable adjustments to his total environment. The volume thus gives the

v

reader dependable knowledge about the mental life of normal and abnormal human beings.

The appraisal of psychoanalysis given in this new edition is especially important. Certainly one of the notable intellectual innovations of the first half of the present century has been the rise of the psychoanalytic systems. No one can doubt that the revolutionary insights of Freud, Jung, Adler, and the other pioneers in the study of dynamic psychology have changed in a dramatic way man's understanding of what human nature is. This book recognizes the fact, however, that at the same time that these insightful, but still peculiarly personal psychoanalytic formulations were being elaborated, the psychobiological sciences were also making great progress. Biochemistry, biophysics, physiology and experimental psychology have also been transformed since the end of the nineteenth century. Thus at the same time that scientists were learning more and more about the physics and chemistry of living cells and in a quantitative way about behavior of total organisms, other students were developing new psychoanalytic concepts and dealing with such words as the *superego,* the *id, introversion,* and the *inferiority complex.* Sometimes it has seemed in recent years that these two vital streams — that of psychoanalysis and the objective physiology and psychology of behavior — could never be evaluated together. It is the great strength of the present book, however, that it takes these two at least superficially almost wholly divergent approaches to an understanding of human adjustment, human personality, and mental hygiene and calmly and clearly places them in a single closely reasoned and clearly structured frame of reference. A modern understanding of learning and of human drives and motives is especially important in this synthesis. The present volume thus brings together in a new and positive way the established facts of biology and experimental psychology and the novel and liberating insights of dynamic psychology and psychoanalytic psychiatry. The contributions of cultural anthropology, modern social psychology and sociology also are not neglected in its pages. Others have attempted this modern coordination and synthesis, but in the editor's opinion, it has never before been done as well as in the present book.

The editor also cannot resist a word about the way the present volume is written. This edition, as was true of the previous one, is notable for its clear and concise English. College students who study this book will not only learn modern psychology but they also have before them pages that show that abstract and complicated ideas can be presented in an unambiguous and lucid way.

This edition, like its predecessor, is not intended for only those who are specializing in psychology. It is also well suited for students who expect to become physicians, teachers, nurses, clergymen, lawyers, or businessmen. It would be hard to think of any single book that would be better than this new edition of *The Psychology of Adjustment* to place in the hands of any student or general reader who is seriously interested in learning about his own personality or why other modern human beings behave as they do in adjusting to our complex world.

LEONARD CARMICHAEL

Washington, D. C.

Preface

In the twenty years since the publication of the first edition of *The Psychology of Adjustment*, both psychology itself and the public's awareness of it have undergone great changes. Psychological knowledge has increased in manifold ways, partly as a result of the necessities of wartime and postwar conditions. No part of psychology has grown faster than the area which deals with the intimate, everyday lives of people, with their happiness or unhappiness, with their motivations, frustrations, conflicts, and readjustments. This new knowledge is reflected in the increased professionalization of psychology in clinical, counseling, and personnel services, all responsibly oriented toward helping people solve their problems more effectively. Such developments could not have occurred had there not been a great surge of public interest in the understanding of human conduct. More than ever before, people demand of psychology a functional knowledge of how they deal with the complexities of everyday life, and how the quality of that life may be enriched by greater understanding.

The second edition of *The Psychology of Adjustment* has endeavored to meet psychology's new responsibilities by using psychology's new resources. The improved integration within the science has enabled the authors to approach their task from a point of view which is at once experimental, dynamic, and social. The account presented here is derived from three great movements in twentieth century psychology — the experimental study of behavior, the psychoanalytic approach to psychopathology, and the conceptions of interpersonal relationships developed by social psychology, sociology, and anthropology. This merger of various streams of knowledge and thought, impossible a short generation ago, demonstrates two major trends in the scientific study of human affairs.

First, the emphasis on doctrines or "schools" in psychology, and

the energies spent on polemics condemning one position in order
to bolster another, have proved fruitless and wasteful. New insights,
productive hypotheses, and useful increments to knowledge have
come from many quarters. None need be neglected. Psychology can
be at the same time experimental, dynamic, and social so long as it
maintains a systematic unity.

Second, a basis for unity in psychology may be found in the concept of learning. The experimental study of behavior in the laboratory, psychoanalytic experience with troubled and disordered
people, and social psychology's concern with cultures and groups —
all may be seen as approaches to the problem of how man acquires
his distinctive ways of adjusting to his world. Man's feelings,
thoughts, and actions are constantly being changed by the impact
of his experiences. From this central phenomenon of learning most
of the propositions of general, dynamic, and social psychology
emerge.

Because of psychology's growth, the revision of *The Psychology
of Adjustment* has been a sweeping one. Every chapter has been
entirely rewritten, although here and there illustrative cases and an
occasional paragraph of exposition remain from the first edition.
The level of difficulty of the book remains the same. The authors
have tried to present intrinsically difficult and complex issues as
clearly and simply as possible. But they have equally striven to
avoid the all-too-common oversimplification which leads to blurred
thinking and the neglect of fundamental understandings.

The purpose of the book is to introduce interested persons with a
minimum of previous preparation to the psychology of human personality and adjustment. As a textbook it should prove serviceable,
as did the first edition, in college classes variously titled Psychology
of Adjustment, Psychology of Personality, Mental Hygiene, and the
like. Its predecessor found a number of other instructional uses
ranging from the introductory course in psychology to the graduate
school, and it is hoped that the new edition will continue to fill such
needs.

The usefulness of *The Psychology of Adjustment* has not been
limited to its study in formal classes. Teachers, clergymen, parents,
executives in industry, other persons who want a better understanding of their fellows and of themselves, report that they have read
it with profit. The book was not designed for self-help and contains
few if any exhortations. Yet many people have found that a real

understanding is more personally rewarding than are adm.
to follow some presumed path of virtue blindly.

The theory of human adjustment presented here is by no me.
novel, and the authors have numerous obligations to the many scien
tists and clinicians upon whose work they have built. The book's
deepest roots lie in general experimental psychology, especially in
the psychology of learning. The authors are therefore more remotely
indebted to the foundations laid by E. L. Thorndike, J. B. Watson,
and R. S. Woodworth, and more recently to the ideas and challenges
of C. L. Hull and B. F. Skinner. Among the pioneers who first applied experimentally derived concepts of learning to what we now
call adjustment problems were W. H. Burnham, G. V. Hamilton, and
E. B. Holt.

The experimental sources have been leavened by the authors' own
clinical experiences, and by the impacts of psychoanalysis. The
great contributions of Sigmund Freud and of the movement he
fathered have been slow to merge with the stream of general psychology, perhaps because differences of language long obscured
essential similarities. The rapprochement between psychology and
psychoanalysis has been due in large part to a number of contemporary psychologists whose theories and experiments have brought
the clinic and the laboratory into a close and fruitfully reciprocal
relationship. Among them, the authors are especially indebted to
J. McV. Hunt, N. E. Miller, O. H. Mowrer, R. R. Sears, and K. W.
Spence. They will hardly agree with everything in this volume, but
they will surely recognize their pervasive influences.

The obligations to social science are more diffuse. Modern psychology has been permeated with the concept that human qualities,
including those of personality, are social products to be understood
only in terms of the interactions of man, group, and culture. The
authors are therefore indirectly indebted to the work of social anthropologists including Ruth Benedict, A. Kardiner, R. Linton, and
Margaret Mead. More particularly, they have drawn on the concepts and methods of J. W. M. Whiting and I. L. Child in blending
the cultural approach with the dynamic and experimental.

When a book is a product of joint authorship, it is well to state
the individual responsibilities of the authors as explicitly as possible.
The major part of the revision was written by L. F. Shaffer. Two
chapters were newly prepared for this edition by E. J. Shoben, Jr.,
Chapter 13 on learning and personality, and Chapter 16 on psy-

chotherapy. But the scope of the collaboration goes beyond such a simple enumeration. Five years of almost daily interaction have obscured even to the authors themselves the exact origin of many ideas. Each author read the other's drafts and made many suggestions. As a result, the book is an integration rather than a compilation of their intellectual products.

L. F. S.
E. J. S., Jr.

New York, New York

Contents

xiii

PART FOUR • **Techniques of Mental Hygiene**

PART ONE

Psychological Foundations

CHAPTER **1**

Adjustment

As a human being, you have many needs, and you spend most of your time and energy trying to satisfy them. Several times a day you get hungry, a signal that your tissues lack the nourishment required to keep them functioning. In response to your hunger you eat, and thereby restore the balance between your bodily demands and the food energy available to meet them. Life consists of a series of such sequences in which needs are aroused and then satisfied. This familiar pattern is the process of adjustment.

Many of life's necessities are not obtained so easily but require persistent effort in the face of difficulties. A hungry dog may find food immediately available and be able to restore his inner equilibrium promptly. If food is not forthcoming at once, the dog engages in activities that have brought about success in the past. He looks in the usual places, whines, or seeks a person who customarily feeds him. Such devices failing, the animal is stimulated to further activity by his organic state and runs about exploring until he finds food and reduces his drive, becoming once more at peace with his environment. The behavior of the dog illustrates one of the broadest generalizations of the biological sciences. All living organisms tend to vary their activities in response to changed conditions in their environments. When circumstances change, an animal must modify its behavior and discover new ways to satisfy its wants or it will not survive.

The process of social adjustment is quite similar. Like most people, you want to be recognized and approved by your fellows.

When someone criticizes your actions, that need is thwarted and there is a disharmony between your desire and your ability to fulfill it. You feel that you must adjust in some way. In response to your need for approval, you may act so as to gain favor in the future or you may display other abilities that will bring you recognition. Those are quite sensible things to do under the circumstances. But you might make excuses for your shortcomings, belittle your accusers, or argue that someone else is to blame for the criticized act. You might "feel hurt" and withdraw from the group so as to avoid the risk of further reproaches. Such behavior does not really bring you approval, but it tends to reduce your distress.

In the lives of most civilized people, social adjustments are more significant than responses to physiological wants. Human beings are social persons as well as biological organisms. Social interactions among people and between groups of people are required to fulfill even some of our most elementary needs. On the other hand, people often work in competition or at cross purposes so as to thwart one another's satisfactions. When a child feels insecure and unwanted by his family, when a student feels isolated from his fellows, or when a man is unsuccessful in his work, adjustments are required to mediate between the socially-defined needs and the socially-determined frustrations.

There is one critical difference between adjusting to your physiological needs and adjusting to your social needs. The only successful adjustments to oxygen-want, hunger, or thirst are to breathe, eat, or drink. Compromises are impossible, and the only outcome of complete deprivation is death. But when a man fails to achieve social adjustment he remains alive and keeps on trying, even though he may be ineffective and unhappy. Inadequate adjustments therefore present a continuing and challenging social problem.

PROBLEMS OF ADJUSTMENT

Examples of Social Adjustments

Social adjustments may vary widely in nature and in quality. Most people, quite fortunately, make reasonably successful adjustments to their social groups. Other people develop habits of conduct that hinder rather than aid the eventual solution of their difficulties. A number of illustrations, drawn largely from the experiences of college students, will throw light on some of the issues of social adjustment.

1. Each autumn when thousands of freshmen arrive at colleges and universities, many adjustive problems confront them in their new environment. Most students adjust satisfactorily — they find new friends, develop new interests, and participate in new activities that serve as outlets for their needs. Other freshmen fare less well. A few become homesick, seeking to return to old satisfactions instead of acquiring new ones. A number adjust by showing off or by becoming eccentric, gaining in these ways a certain notice and distinction which they fail to attain in more usual channels. Such variations in adjustive ability are not accidental. There are determiners underlying all types of adjustment, whether the end results are individually satisfying or not, whether the behavior shown is social or anti-social. The study of the origins and development of individually and socially adaptive or maladaptive behavior is the subject matter of the psychology of adjustment.

2. A senior girl has participated in nearly every activity on the campus but has never been elected to an editorship, managership, or office. She does not lack ability. As a reporter for the college paper she could write a very acceptable story, and she was efficient and untiring in her work as a candidate for managership of the rifle team. The trouble is that she has always had an attitude of snobbish superiority. As a freshman she pointed out to the editor the principal errors and shortcomings of the college newspaper. She cannot work with people, has a know-it-all attitude, and an aggressive manner. Now a disappointed senior, she blames campus politics for her lack of success and points out to all listeners how petty college activities really are. She does not recognize that she failed because of her own personality. How can we understand this girl? How did she come to develop the characteristics that annoy other people so much?

3. A young college graduate had eighteen different positions in three years during a period when it was easy to get work. With his attractive personal appearance and reasonably nimble intelligence, he secured positions readily, but each in turn seemed uninteresting and futile. Some jobs he lost because of evident decrease of effort; others he gave up voluntarily because they were not what he wanted. The youngest of several children, he lives at home and is ably defended against accusations of incompetence by his very efficient

mother. So far he has been a conspicuous failure in vocational adjustment.

4. An older woman attempted a difficult graduate course under two handicaps. Her ability and preparation were none too good, and she was struggling with a personal problem that kept her upset emotionally. She failed the course. Unable to acknowledge her failure, she blamed the professor. She asserted that he took a "sadistic" pleasure in making students miserable, that he was unfair, and that he had particularly singled her out for persecution. She was able to cite specific incidents to prove her point. Indeed, everything that happened during the course was interpreted as evidence of the teacher's bias against her. Finally, she left the university because she would not be associated with a school that had such a perverted character on its faculty. The student's beliefs protect her against having to admit her own deficiencies. This too is a kind of adjustment, attained at the cost of a distorted view of the motives and actions of others.

5. A young college faculty member is excessively conscientious. He works day and night, frequently preparing lectures or grading papers until three in the morning. Although he was graduated with highest honors from an eminent university, he constantly fears that he might fall down on the job of teaching. He prepares his lectures three or four times over to be sure that he will make no errors. He assigns daily preparation work to each of his hundred students and grades each paper in detail. Apparently as a result of his absorption in academic duties, he has little time for social activities. He is shy and never initiates a social contact but is eagerly grateful when another faculty member pays some attention to him. Why does he seek his adjustment in so solitary a way? Does he work because he fears failure? Or does he hide behind his work because he fears people?

6. A young woman student comes mournfully to an instructor's office to discuss a low grade. She is worried and distressed about it. She reports that she lies awake at night thinking about her difficulty. In the midst of the interview she bursts into tears. Further inquiry shows that her general scholastic standing is about average and that she is not in danger of any serious consequence such as being dropped from school. The only apparent cause of the outburst is a failing grade on one short quiz. This girl's behavior is quite evidently unadaptive. Instead of working harder, seeking to improve

her methods of study, or making any of a large number of possible good adjustments, she remains tense, worries, and cries. Unlike the people described in the preceding paragraphs, she gets no satisfaction from her conduct, not even of a substitute or inferior sort. Why is she so upset by a difficulty that would seem trivial to most students? How can she be helped to be more constructive in the future?

The psychology of adjustment seeks answers to questions such as these.

Attitudes Toward Adjustment Problems

Inadequate adjustments have undoubtedly been made as long as mankind has existed. Up to the present century the prevailing attitude toward adjustive difficulties has been a *moralistic* one. The essence of such an attitude is that the maladjusted person is "bad." The origin of this popular opinion is not hard to find. First, a person with adjustive difficulties is often a nuisance to his family and friends, as well as no comfort to himself. He is hard to get along with. Second, his behavior does not seem reasonable, and most people cannot understand why he acts as he does, often against his own best interests. His conduct is irrational and lacking in common sense. Those characteristics give us a clue to the basis of moralistic social judgments. To most people, what annoys them or what seems irrational or senseless is "bad." Therefore an inadequately adjusted person is likely to be shunned and scorned.

Even people who would not openly call a maladjusted person bad often act as if they thought him so. A daydreaming boy is described as lazy and is scolded and punished. A worrying girl is told to "snap out of it" and advised that her difficulties exist "only in her imagination." An overaggressive or conceited person is "put in his place" or ostracized. Parents scold and spank, teachers send to the principal, employers discharge, professors tell a student he must "change his attitude," deans expel from college — and all because of an implicitly moralistic interpretation of behavior, a view that is usually unacknowledged and poorly understood by those who hold it.

Lecturing, punishment, and even well-meaning advice have proved to be notably ineffective methods for dealing with adjustment problems. A worrier is not cured by being told he should not worry. A "shiftless" person is aided very little by preaching or threats. Such attempts make matters worse by convincing the maladjusted one of his own weakness and worthlessness. He then has an additional social thwarting to bear.

More recently there has been partial public acceptance of what might be called a *physiological* interpretation of maladjustment, in which the troubled or troublesome person is thought of as sick rather than bad. In its practical implications that attitude is a marked improvement over the moralistic one. Like those who are sick, maladjusted people are ineffective in their life activities. Sick people are not held responsible for their actions and so are regarded more constructively and are not likely to be scolded or punished. However, the concept of sickness has to be stretched to its limit to make it include people whose social relationships are disturbed. In its ordinary sense, the word sickness refers to a disease of some organ or system which can be explained in terms of physiological changes. A maladjusted person is not sick in that sense and his cure cannot be found in medicine or surgery. There are, of course, some intimate relationships between bodily functioning and social adjustment which will be discussed later. As an entire explanation, however, the physiological approach does not give the most revealing account of personal maladjustments.

Another attitude toward people in trouble is the *psychological* viewpoint, which regards both successful and unsuccessful adjustments as the end results of learning processes. In contrast to the moralistic viewpoint, the psychological attitude neither praises nor blames a person for his adjustments. It seeks to understand him. Unlike the physiological approach, the psychological view does not look primarily for germs or injuries. A physically healthy person may learn ineffective ways of dealing with his social relationships, just as a healthy school child may learn the wrong answer to an arithmetic problem. The central issue of a psychological theory of adjustment is to understand how and why people differ in the responses they have learned to make to frustrating social situations.

AN ANALYSIS OF ADJUSTMENT

Psychological study of the adjustment process shows that it can be described as a series of steps, beginning when a need is felt and

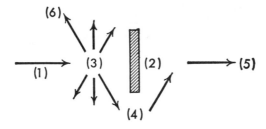

Figure 1. The Adjustment Process

A person proceeding in a motivated course of action (1) is thwarted by some obstacle or circumstance (2) that prevents the fulfillment of his need. He makes varied exploratory responses (3) until some response (4) gets him around the obstacle and he is readjusted (5). In some instances, however, his need to avoid the obstacle (6) is greater than his motive toward the goal and readjustment is not achieved. (Modified from J. F. Dashiell, *Fundamentals of general psychology.* (3rd ed.) Boston: Houghton Mifflin, 1949.)

ending when that need is satisfied. The diagram given in Figure 1 helps to understand the main aspects of many of the simpler adjustments.

You are proceeding in some course of motivated behavior (*1*) when your activity is thwarted or blocked (*2*). You make various exploratory trials (*3*) until one of them (*4*) overcomes the obstacle and you proceed as before (*5*). The principal steps of a normal adjustment process are therefore the existence of a *motive*, the operation of some *thwarting* that prevents its immediate satisfaction, giving rise to *varied responses*, and leading eventually to a *solution*. Unfortunately, a person does not always solve his adjustive problem (*6*) but may become so much preoccupied with avoiding the obstacle that he never satisfies the need that started the sequence.

Some of the examples of human adjustments can be examined in terms of the description of the entire process.

The college freshmen (p. 5) need recognition, approval, and opportunity to gain prestige (*1*). They are thwarted (*2*) by the newness of their environment. Their accustomed ways of securing satisfaction are absent, and they do not yet "know their way around." They try many exploratory responses (3), including, perhaps, daydreaming about home, concentrating on studies, or showing off with proverbial freshman impudence. Eventually, they make new friends and engage in new activities (4) and their problems are readjusted (5).

The aggressively overcritical girl (p. 5) wants success and prestige. She seems to have an uncommonly strong need to excel and to acknowledge no superior (1), the origin of which may be understood by studying her personal history. Any competition represents a threat to her (2), to which she might react in many ways (3) such as by withdrawing from situations involving rivalry or by gaining prestige through her studies. In fact, she readjusts (4) by belittling competitors and by blaming others for her own failures. Such adjustments seem inferior to an outside observer, but they must be satisfying to the girl or she would not make them.

The tearful student (p. 6) presents a somewhat different problem psychologically. Her need for success (1) is common, but her reaction to the small threat of one bad quiz grade (2) is intense. She has not yet found a solution, but worries (3) by fruitlessly mulling over her problem verbally: "What *shall* I do?" She remains anxious and unadjusted (6), since she has failed to find even an inferior way to meet her need.

Some Problems That Need Study

The preliminary description of the adjustment process raises more questions than it answers. In everyday conversation, we use such terms as "motive," "need," "thwarting," and "solution," and in an inexact way we understand what is meant. A psychological understanding requires a more detailed examination of the aspects of human behavior that lie behind these words.

Our first concern is with the concepts of *need* and *motive*. We all understand what it is to need food and water, but it is instructive to examine the exact ways in which these needs operate. Is there a sex need? If so, is it more like needing food or more like needing acceptance and approval? We have spoken somewhat casually of some social motives, such as needs for recognition, security, success, prestige, and for the avoidance of harm or danger. How do these motives work? Are we born with them, and if not, where do they come from?

Thwarting is an idea that requires a great deal of elaboration. People can be thwarted by walls, bars, and other material obstacles, but such thwarting seldom appears in real human case histories. More often, thwarting is social and is due to the demands and competing activities of other people. The most severe type of thwarting comes from the person himself. An individual may want something and at the same time be afraid of the consequences of getting it. In that way he blocks himself from satisfying his own needs. People differ, too, in what they regard as a frustration. A timid person may see threats all around him in situations which others would not perceive as dangerous. Thwarting is not a simple concept, but will require further analysis as we proceed.

The *varied responses* that people make when thwarted will also need extensive study. At first glance it would seem that human adjustive responses are so numerous and so diverse as to defy description and classification. As a matter of fact, a rather modest number of common types of responses account for a major part of all social adjustments. If we know enough about a person's past experiences, we can predict with fair accuracy how he will react to a new frustration.

The concept of an adjustive *solution* is the most perplexing of all. Many normal outcomes of adjustment processes do indeed seem to be solutions of a person's problems, in the commonsense meaning of the term. But how can self-defeating kinds of behavior, such as the college woman's sarcastic superiority or the young professor's seclusive absorption in his work, be adjustive "solutions" at all? Such behavior harms the person in the long run, yet he does not give it up easily. How can we explain this paradox?

SOURCES OF DEPENDABLE KNOWLEDGE

To unravel the complexities of human adjustments requires more than the casual observations and common sense of everyday life. The kind of knowledge that you get from living with people leaves many issues unsolved and usually results in nothing better than moralistic judgments. A scientific approach is needed to achieve a sound understanding.

General Scientific Method

The scientific method of inquiry is basically the same whether it is applied to problems of physics, biology, or psychology. Perhaps the most important aspect of science is the attitude of the scientist. A man who is working in the role of a scientist has disciplined himself to avoid common inaccuracies and errors of observation and thinking. A scientist is engaged in an uncommonly stubborn attempt to observe precisely and to think clearly. He does not set out to prove his preconceptions but is willing to be guided entirely by the evidence he finds by systematic investigation. A scientist is critical of his results and takes special care to define the limitations of his conclusions. No person, of course, is a scientist in all aspects of his life. A man may be entirely a scientist in his laboratory but may be quite like other human beings when he is acting in other roles, as a citizen or a parent.

Several attempts have been made to describe a universal scientific method that can be applied to any field of inquiry. Such descriptions are likely to be oversimplified, but they have some value for teaching the general nature of scientific investigation. One widely used description of scientific method regards it as a sequence of four major steps. The first phase is the accumulation of data, the systematic and precise observation of evidence about the events being studied. Second, the data are arranged in orderly and meaningful sequences and their interrelationships are studied, usually with the aid of mathematics as a tool for quantitative manipulation. Third, the scientist draws tentative generalizations or hypotheses which are short statements of the findings. The final step is the further testing of the hypotheses by new observations, leading to their acceptance or rejection, or to a definition of the limits and conditions under which they hold. Research in all the sciences conforms generally to this sequence of scientific method, but there are many variations. The initial observations usually are guided by some theory or by a preliminary expectation of the results. Many valuable experiments illustrate only the fourth step of the method — the testing of a hypothesis formulated previously by hunch, by deduction from other generalizations, or by observations incidental to another research.

Laymen have one common misconception of science. They often believe that science discovers absolute laws or ultimate certainties that reveal the "truth" about physical, biological, and social problems. A real scientist has no such illusions about ultimate truths. Science is a method of successive approximations, of continuous progress toward both broader and more detailed descriptions and generalizations. Scientific principles are statements of the relationships between observed events. Each well-founded principle may be useful and yet capable of being supplanted by a more precise or a more widely applicable generalization to be discovered in the future. Science believes in continual and gradual progress toward enlightenment, not in the discovery of final and unchangeable laws.

Problems of human adjustment are studied by many types of investigation. Indeed, each research study is a little different from every other, while remaining within the broad framework of science. While it is not possible to place all researches exactly in a small number of classes, two principal methods which are especially pertinent to the study of adjustments can be distinguished. They are the *clinical research method* and the *experimental method*.

The Clinical Research Method

The psychology of adjustment is concerned with persons who are living and acting in their social environments. The obviously suitable research method, then, is the study of the entire lives of people. Relationships may be noted between the antecedent influences in a person's life and his subsequent adjustments. Such observations lead to hypotheses that are helpful in understanding other people.

Most of the major concepts in the psychology of adjustment have come initially from the clinical approach. For example, a concept can be obtained by induction from observations such as these:

> A grade-school boy is a chronic bully. He bosses, pushes, and intimidates smaller children but rarely plays with those his own size. Psychological study reveals him as a spindly youngster who doubts his own physical strength and fears competition with his peers.
>
> A college girl dresses in clothes of brilliant but not always harmonious colors and affects exaggerated hair styles and make-up. Although not really unattractive, she always has been outshone at home by her more beautiful sister, whom her parents favor.
>
> A school custodian has become celebrated for his use and misuse

of long words, by which he tries to show how learned he is. A man of little formal education, he is thrown constantly in the company of people of genuinely scholarly attainments.

A boy is in trouble with the police because of frequent petty thefts. He is also notable for cheating in school, lying, and getting into fights. His classmates regard him with awe as a "tough guy." No one can understand this, since he has been brought up as such a nice child. His mother kept his hair in long ringlets until he was six and has vigorously pursued his cultural education by giving him music lessons, having him recite poetry, and taking him to concerts.

A veritable Don Juan has an unsavory reputation in his community because of scores of tawdry love affairs. In fact, however, he is not a strongly masculine person but is sufficiently effeminate in appearance and manner to excite notice from a casual observer.

A woman had always wanted to be a physician but married early on impulse and through the force of circumstances. Now she is bent on having her daughter enter medicine, and the girl resists. The mother cannot understand the girl's ungrateful conduct, since she feels that she is sacrificing herself for the daughter's advantage.

No conclusion should be drawn from such a limited number of cases and especially not from such sketchy summaries. From a more thorough study of a larger number of similar personal histories, however, a useful hypothesis can be induced. In each instance, there is an exaggeration of what might be a normal kind of adjustment. Everyone likes to succeed and excel in physical, intellectual, sexual, vocational, and other spheres of activity, but each of these persons *overdoes* it. In each case we also find that the person has been thwarted in some desired area of achievement and regards himself as inferior, insecure, or unsuccessful. The hypothesis emerges, then, that one way of adjusting to a sense of deficiency is to overemphasize one's behavior, so as to overcome or hide the defect. In a word, the hypothesis defines a type of adjustment called *compensation.* This concept suggests a very useful approach to the understanding of some people. If a person shows excessively aggressive behavior, we may direct our attention to the discovery of the faults that he is trying to cover up. It is a "working hypothesis," however, rather than a universal principle, since further studies show that not all aggressive conduct can be ascribed to compensation. There is real value in having several such tentative hypotheses to advance when trying to understand a particular case.

The clinical method conforms to an acceptable pattern of scientific method. It clearly illustrates the observation of evidence, the orderly arrangement of data, the making of a hypothesis, and the further testing of the hypothesis on new cases. In addition to being respectable scientifically, the clinical research method is an invaluable way to investigate adjustments, since it studies whole people with maximum freedom.

In spite of its merits, the clinical method has some serious shortcomings when used alone. Its chief defect is in its manner of selecting and obtaining data. A person's whole life is very complex indeed, and no investigator is able to learn all about it. There is always a temptation and an opportunity to see and record the material that proves a point in which the researcher is interested, while other evidence which might lead to different conclusions may go unnoticed. When that happens, the conclusion may show the investigator's bias rather than the facts. An allied fault is that case study data often are obtained retrospectively. It is dangerous to place great faith in an adult's recall of what happened to him or of how he felt when he was a child. Experimental evidence shows that memory over long periods of time is likely to be grossly inaccurate and that it may be distorted by present beliefs and attitudes.

The approach through clinical research is often a more effective method for proposing hypotheses than for testing them rigorously. Many of the concepts of psychology originated from case studies, but we have to look elsewhere for ways to verify dependable principles.

Improving the Clinical Research Method

Most of the earlier clinical research was unsystematic. Hypotheses were often inspirations based on a single case or on a very few cases. At best a worker conceived a hypothesis from his general clinical experience and then explored additional personal histories to confirm the idea or to test its limitations. Only rarely was a planned series of cases studied in such a way as to permit an objective verification of the conclusions drawn.

The clinical method can be improved by blending with it some of the qualities of the experimental method, which will be described more fully in the next section. A study reported by Rogers, Kell, and McNeil [1] * illustrates a clinical-experimental technique. Their research studied some of the factors associated with the successful readjustment of delinquent children. Why do some delinquent adolescents get over their troubles while others continue to be delinquent? One hundred and fifty-one case histories of delinquents were selected impartially from the files of an agency. Each history was then rated on a number of pertinent characteristics, including physical factors, the family record, the family's influence on the child, social influences, education and training, and self-insight. The last factor, self-insight, was defined as the extent to which the child had or lacked an understanding of his own situation and problems. Each factor was rated from —3 (poor) to +3 (good) by the use of comparison scales. By having more than one rater evaluate each child's record, it was possible to see whether raters could agree and hence to judge the reliability or dependability of the ratings.

Later, ratings were made of each child's subsequent readjustment, from —3 (remaining in serious difficulties) to +3 (excellent readjustment). Statistical methods were then used to see which factors of the delinquents' histories were most highly correlated with the later outcomes. The child's self-insight was found to be the best predictor of his later readjustment. His social experiences and his family's record were also significantly related to his success. The economic, physical, and educational factors, on the other hand, predicted the outcome poorly or not at all. These findings were confirmed by a repetition of the study with another group of children.

Such a study is truly clinical, for it takes people as they are and views them as whole beings. By using quantitative methods and by controlling some sources of inaccuracy and bias, it offers a more dependable way to test and verify clinical hypotheses.

The Experimental Method

The experimental method differs from the clinical method most strikingly in one respect. Instead of waiting for an event to happen, the experimenter makes it occur. In studying the effects of frustration, for example, subjects may be deliberately frustrated in a

---

* See References and Bibliography, at the end of the book, for full citations of studies described in the text.

planned way and certain effects can be observed intentionally.

Let us examine one illustration of a pertinent experiment. In discussing the analysis of human adjustments, we have already noted that persons seem to differ in the degree of threat or thwarting that they may perceive in a situation. An event may be very threatening to one person and not so at all to other people. This observation suggests a hypothesis for research: that a person who is under threat or stress from other sources will perceive innocent events as threatening. This hypothesis was investigated in an experiment by Postman and Bruner.[2]

Two groups of subjects were tested for their ability to perceive three-word sentences flashed very rapidly by an exposure device. Then the "experimental group" was "threatened" by being forced to try to describe a complex picture which was presented so rapidly that they could not really see it well. Their sense of failure was intensified by depreciative criticisms from the experimenter. A "control group" was shown the same picture for adequate exposure times and was allowed to succeed in an easy perceptual task. Finally, both groups were again tested for their ability to perceive three-word sentences shown rapidly. In the post-frustration test the experimental group perceived less well than the control group. The effect of their previous failure made them give wild guesses for words they could not see clearly. In general, their ability to perceive was impaired. Even more interesting was the observation that the thwarted subjects tended to misperceive innocent stimulus words as aggressive words. Instead of *rust*, which was shown, some of them saw *bust*, or *burst*, or *hurt*. The unthwarted control group showed no such tendency to see aggressive words which were not there. Although one experiment does not settle the issue entirely, it gives substantial evidence about the effect of threat on how we perceive things.

Some very valuable experiments use laboratory animals as subjects. The experiences of an ape, dog, cat, or rat can be controlled to a degree impossible with human beings. Therefore, it is easier to define an "entirely novel" situation for a rat and to restrict its learning to what we want it to learn. Another important reason for using lower animals is that some especially significant experiments may be harmful to the subject. To secure a real gain in scientific knowledge, we would not hesitate to make a dog "neurotic" experimentally, but we would not expose a child to such a danger. You might think it strange that animals can be used in studying such delicate topics as adjustment and personality, but many aspects of animal behavior, including some learning processes and emotional states, are not too different from those of man.

An animal experiment that helps to clarify a real issue in the psychology of adjustment was carried out by Mowrer and Viek.[3] It is often said that the fear aroused by a physical pain depends on whether or not the pain is under one's control. If the pain is unavoidable, if one feels helpless, the fear is much greater. Once each day for fifteen days, Mowrer and Viek offered food to rats and ten seconds afterward gave an electric shock through a grill on which the rat stood. The shock ended differently for two groups of rats. A rat of the "shock-controlled" group could end the shock by leaping into the air, for as soon as the rat jumped, the experimenter stopped the shock. A rat of the "shock-uncontrolled" group could not itself end the shock, which continued until the experimenter turned it off. The corresponding rats of each group received exactly the same amounts of shock. For example if rat number 6 of the first group jumped and escaped the shock in 14.3 seconds on its first trial, the corresponding rat number 6 of the other group was also shocked for exactly 14.3 seconds regardless of what it did. The effect was measured by noting how many times the rats refused the food when it was presented, since refusal of food by a healthy, hungry rat is a dependable sign of fear. Out of 140 possible opportunities to accept or refuse food, the shock-controlled rats refused only 16 times; the shock-uncontrolled rats refused food 85 times. The experiment supports a hypothesis that a sense of helplessness, a "fear of fear itself," is a major determiner of anxiety.

Experimental studies, whether of human or of animal subjects, yield more precise findings than can be gained from clinical studies alone. A well-designed experiment tries to keep many important determining factors constant, and varies one factor systematically to see what changes will result. The control of an experiment is effected by keeping certain conditions constant physically and often by the use of a control group that is like the experimental group in all respects except for the significant variable being studied.

With all its advantages, the experimental method has some deficiencies for investigating problems in the psychology of adjustment. An experiment deals most successfully with isolated segments of behavior, and therefore is likely to miss important principles that can be found only when many factors interact at the same time, as in real-life adjustments. The very control that is the virtue of the experimental method may even be a handicap in the study of human personality. The most complex and significant features of one's behavior cannot be assigned to any single cause acting alone, but only to a pattern of interrelated causes.

Integration of Clinical and Experimental Methods

Both the clinical and the experimental research methods have faults as sources of dependable information about human adjustments. Their deficiencies, however, are complementary. The clinical method is too inexact and the experimental attack is too restricted. An integration of the two gives the best-balanced approach. An experimental finding that does not hold up in clinical application probably has something the matter with it or has been misapplied. A clinically derived generalization that is contrary to pertinent and well-established experimental evidence must also be regarded with suspicion. The greatest confidence can be given only to principles that ring true both in the clinic and in the laboratory.

THE STUDY OF ADJUSTMENTS

Schools of Psychology

So far nothing has been said about differing schools of psychology and, in fact, it is not necessary to mention them in building a satisfactory psychology of the adjustment process. Until recent years one of the most confusing aspects of psychology was the existence of consciously antagonistic schools whose methods and generalizations seemed to contradict each other. Today the importance of the controversies of the schools has diminished greatly. When faced with a question, most psychologists look to evidence rather than to authority for an answer. The research attitude cuts across all schools and eventually will eliminate them.

In the history of the psychological approach to adjustment problems, two schools have been especially influential, the *psychoanalytic* and the *behavioristic*.

The psychology of adjustment draws many of its concepts and hypotheses from the psychoanalytic school, mainly from the genius of its founder, Sigmund Freud. In the late nineteenth century, when conventional psychology was occupied chiefly with academic problems such as sensation and imagery, Freud pointed out the significance of emotional experiences in human life. He insisted that every act and thought has its causes but that persons are unaware of many of the important determiners of their behavior. These and other great ideas advanced by Freud have influenced not only psychology but also anthropology, sociology, education, and popular thinking. But with all its merits, classical psychoanalysis had one flaw. It was based on clinical studies only and never developed a solid experimental foundation. The result is an object lesson in method. Psychoanalysis today is splintered among a large number of subschools, each adhering to the theories of some leader such as Freud, Jung, Adler, Rank, Horney, Sullivan, and several others. The factions combat each other with words and cases, rarely with experiments. The unbiased observer sees some merit in the contributions of all of the schools and looks for the time when researches, both clinical and experimental, will resolve many of the issues now current.

As a school, behaviorism is dead. Hardly a psychologist today calls himself a behaviorist. The name serves, however, as a convenient label for a great historical movement in psychology which emerged and flourished mainly in the two decades from 1910 to 1930. During that period psychologists made rapid progress in applying objective and experimental methods of study to whole living organisms, investigating their emotions, motivations, and learning processes. Earlier psychologists had been experimental, to be sure, but they had applied precise techniques mainly to the separate features of human life such as sensations, perception, and action. A distinction should be made between the methodological contributions of behaviorism and the dogmatic conclusions that were held by some leading behaviorists back in the nineteen-twenties. The tough-minded experimental and objective attitudes, which are now regarded as the main virtue of behaviorism, have been assimilated into the general body of psychology. No modern experimental psychologist is uninfluenced by them. Many of the detailed conclusions of the early behaviorists, on the other hand, are now out of date. They have been superseded by newer insights obtained through the further application of experimental methods.

The viewpoint of this book is neither psychoanalytic nor behavioristic but is descended from both. If the viewpoint must be named, it might be called *dynamic experimental psychology*. The approach is dynamic because it is interested in the moving aspects of human life — strivings, emotions, and adjustments. It is experimental because it insistently looks at the evidence. The dynamic experimental approach is shared by many psychologists today, perhaps even by most of them, but it has never become a school because it has no authoritarian leader to lay down the line of orthodoxy. It is a joint enterprise of many researchers and thinkers, among whom no one is dominant.

Understanding and Practicing

Some people who are professionally trained in psychology have voiced objections to the study of adjustment problems by students without a medical or a broad psychological background. They point out with justification that, in this field of study more than any other, a little knowledge is a dangerous thing. It is quite true that some harm is done by persons with partial training in psychology who engage in the amateur diagnosis and treatment of their own and their friends' adjustive problems. Whether good or evil comes from studying psychology depends on the attitude of the student.

The professional practice of the specialties that deal with human adjustment problems requires years of postgraduate preparation. A *psychiatrist* is a medical doctor who has undertaken postgraduate study beyond his M.D. degree to learn the theories and skills required to understand and treat disorders of behavior. A *clinical psychologist* has four years of graduate training, leading to a Ph.D. degree, which includes the study of theory, research methods, psychological techniques, and practice under supervision. *Social work*, another profession that uses psychological approaches extensively, demands at least two years of graduate study and supervised casework. Lacking such extensive training, you have to adopt an attitude of humility toward your own psychological knowledge.

It is absurd to suggest, however, that mature and intelligent persons must be kept in ignorance of so important a field of human knowledge. People in almost all walks of life have to deal with human relationships and can do so more effectively if they have some acquaintance with the scientific study of them. Teachers, parents, civic leaders, employers, and many others need an understanding that not only includes well-intentioned common sense and human sympathy but goes beyond these things in scope and precision of knowledge. The aim of this book is to help you to understand and know, rather than to practice and apply. If any applications are made, they must be accompanied by reservations appropriate to the great complexity of human nature.

The Method of Approach

The Psychology of Adjustment is divided into four principal sections, in which the study of social and individual adjustments is pursued in an orderly sequence. Each section is preparatory to the following ones.

At first one has to obtain a clear view of certain essentials. What are the springs of human action, the basic needs and motives? How are those needs modified through social interaction? What are the effects of various kinds of frustrations, and of conflicts between needs? How do we learn to adjust? Such questions are considered in Part I, "Psychological Foundations." Without a careful study of basic issues, the concepts of the adjustments themselves might be only descriptive or biologically unsound. The foundations are based mainly on the results of the experimental studies.

Part II, "Varieties of Adjustive Behavior," describes the many ways in which people respond to the combined demands of their individual motives and their social environments. The chief method here is the clinical approach, interpreted in the light of such experimental evidence as is available and pertinent. Socially inadequate adjustments are emphasized more than excellent adjustments, both because we know more about them and because they present a greater practical problem.

The background of adjustment, an exploration of how some people adjust in one way and others differently, forms the subject matter of Part III, "Personality." Both experimental and clinical types of evidence contribute to the study of individual differences among persons and to the influences on these differences of heredity, physique, development, and social learning.

Part IV, "Techniques of Mental Hygiene," summarizes practical methods for studying and helping people and examines critically the processes of psychological treatment. Most of the material is empirical and is drawn from experience and from clinical research. The section ends with some suggested applications of mental hygiene to education, industry, social work, and family living.

SUGGESTED READINGS

The complete references to books cited in the *Suggested Readings* may be found in the *Bibliography*.

An overview of the problems and processes of adjustment may be obtained by reading the introductory chapters, and browsing generally, in several books on mental hygiene and personality. Among the texts suggested are Katz and Lehner, *Mental Hygiene and Modern Living;* Klein, *Mental Hygiene;* Lehner and Kube, *The Dynamics of Personal Adjustment;* Lindgren, *Psychology of Personal and Social Adjustment;* and Shaw and Ort, *Personal Adjustment in the American Culture.* A consideration of mental health on the college campus, including a number of cases, is available in Fry and Rostow, *Mental Health in College.*

Those interested in the problem of what constitutes "good" adjustments will find challenging and very different ideas in Fromm, *Man for Himself* and Lindner, *Prescription for Rebellion.* May, *Man's Search for Himself* will also appeal to those with a taste for philosophy and ethical issues.

Students who have not had recent preparation in general psychology may wish to review the role of science in the understanding of human conduct in one or more of the broader introductory textbooks, such as Boring, Langfeld, and Weld, *Foundations of Psychology;* Dashiell, *Fundamentals of General Psychology;* Munn, *Psychology;* or Ruch, *Psychology and Life.* More specialized references are Skinner, *Science and Human Behavior;* and the first part of Brown and Ghiselli, *Scientific Method in Psychology.*

On divergent psychological theories, see Woodworth, *Contemporary Schools of Psychology.*

CHAPTER 2

Motivation

When we try to understand any aspect of human behavior, our first and most insistent question is "Why?" The importance of motives, desires, and urges is recognized in many fields, such as industry, law, sports, and education. Why do men work? Economists, political theorists, and psychologists have given various answers. They have suggested that men work because they have an instinct to do so, or because they must earn food and shelter, or because they seek social approval, or because they try to avoid the scorn of their fellows. Why do people play baseball or gather to see others play? Why does the pupil in school learn his lessons? Why does he not just sit there, failing to react to the instructive opportunities the school provides? Such questions indicate the widespread interest in motivation and the need for a thorough study of its problems.

In helping people who have difficulties of personal adjustment, the discovery of motives has been especially fruitful. James is the school bully. On the playground and before and after school he may be found assertively bossing the smaller boys, mauling them, fighting when he is sure to win. Why does he do it? What is there in it for him? Virginia has run away from home three times. Her parents are in good circumstances and seem interested in her welfare, yet she persists in trying to get away. A study of her motives is essential both to understand her problem and to help her solve it. The concrete problems of the psychological practitioner have been greatly clarified by the understanding that all behavior, no matter how strange, has its motives. Only since this dynamic concept entered psychology has much progress been made in the solution of personal adjustment problems.

EXPLANATIONS OF MOTIVATION

What is the source of motivated behavior? What causes a person or an animal to be active and to play an outreaching, examining, and inquiring role in relation to his environment? What determines the direction and strength of a person's wants? Many explanations have been proposed, several of which merit further study, either because they are important today or because they have been widely believed in the past.

Instinct Theories

Years ago the problem of motivation was dispatched neatly by ascribing a motivating power to "instincts." The bullying boy was said to fight because of his "instinct of pugnacity." The industrious man had an "instinct of workmanship," and the ball-game crowd was showing its "instinct of gregariousness." The concept of instinct is no longer regarded as a valid explanatory principle. As a descriptive concept it is only circular. The "instinct of pugnacity" holds that men fight because they have a tendency to fight, which leaves the problem unsolved, as if nothing had been said about it at all. Even worse, some persons have taken instincts to mean forces within a person that cause or compel him to do things. Such a theory peoples the organism with a host of little demons that prod, push, and urge it into activity. That is a very primitive type of explanation indeed, closely akin to the thinking of savage people who for lack of better knowledge ascribe the thunder, the wind, the growth of plants, and the course of the sun to the operation of "spirits." It is far removed from the method of science. While the instinct theory is no longer held by psychologists, it continues to have an effect on popular thinking.

Energy Theories

Somewhat related to instinct theories was a hypothesis that conceived of motivation as a kind of vital energy or inner life force that stirs a person to activity. The life force was supposed to be an entirely "psychic" energy, not synonymous with any physical or chemical energies. The traditional psychoanalytic theories supported the concept of psychic energy as the source of all human action. Examples are Freud's *Eros,* a general life instinct, and Jung's *libido,* a broad drive supplying energy for all behavior. There are a number of objections to the psychic-energy theories. First, it is hard to see how a life-instinct theory is of much explanatory value. All it says is that the function of life is to live, which is pretty obvious. A more serious fault is the need for postulating a different kind of energy, one that lies outside the realm of the energies known to biology, chemistry, and physics. Such a theory should not be considered until we have exhausted all possibilities of explaining motivation in terms of the usual biological processes of organisms.

It is quite true that human and animal activity requires energy or force, but this is the ordinary biochemical energy that comes from the food we eat and the air we breathe. If an organism is amply fed, it will remain active; if it is starved or if its assimilation of food is impaired by illness, the activity will decrease. The concept of nutrition as the source of energy does not shed much light on the practical problems of human motivation, however, especially at the complex level of human social behavior. In fact, a hungry animal or person shows greater activity than a well-fed one. The well-nourished person may be languid and purposeless; the lean and hungry man may be full of ambitions, energies, and activities. Although nutrition is the source of energy, ordinary variations of it are not closely associated with differences in social motivation.

Motivation as Need

An organism that lacks something essential to its survival tends to be stirred to activity. When you have been without food for a number of hours, you become restless and are likely to engage in food-seeking behavior. In many laboratory experiments, motivation is defined in terms of the length of time that an animal has been deprived of something. That a rat has been without water for six hours, or for twelve hours, is often the most objective way to describe its state of motivation. Such observations define *need* as a deficiency of a substance or function that furthers life processes.

Although need is basic to motivation, there are both practical and theoretical objections to regarding need itself as the source of motivated activity. In most instances the degree of need is not proportional to the extent of the activity. For example, up to four days of food-deprivation increases a rat's activity, but the further withholding of food causes a decrease. The need has increased greatly, but the urge to activity does not increase correspondingly. There is also an important theoretical reason why need will not serve as the keystone of a theory of motivation. A need is a lack, a negative kind of an event. The dynamic process of striving seems not to depend on the mere absence of something. We might search for more positive and active agents.

Motivation as Stimulation

The term *stimulus* refers to an energy which acts on a sense organ or other bodily structure so as to initiate new activities in the living tissues. Because stimuli evoke responses, it is evident that we must consider the role of stimulation in motivation. If a baby is pricked by its diaper pin, a most vigorous pattern of activity will ensue. The infant will wail, squirm, and struggle, and, moreover, will maintain these responses until someone relieves his distress. It is quite evident that the stimulation motivates him, for it arouses and sustains activity. The internal motivations such as thirst and hunger are similar in character but more complex. These life processes give rise to elaborate patterns of internal stimulation, mainly chemical in nature, which act on appropriately sensitive tissues of the nervous system.

Motivation has to maintain behavior as well as just to arouse it, and some patterns of stimulation therefore are more motive-like than others. A tap below the kneecap evokes the knee-jerk reflex. Action is aroused but it is not sustained. More motivating are stimuli such as hunger or a pinprick, which require some adjustment on the part of the organism. Responses to such stimuli are maintained until the stimulus is removed. Hunger ends when you have eaten, and the baby's cries cease after someone has removed the offending pin from his skin. Persistent stimuli that require an adjusting response are basic to motivation.

It is an oversimplification, of course, to say that behavior is determined by only one stimulus at a time. Your motivation at any moment is a function of a complex pattern of stimulations, some coming from within your own body and others from your environment as you perceive it. Being moderately hungry plus smelling savory food may motivate responses of approaching and eating that would not be made to either stimulus alone without the added effect of the other. An incipient feeling of nausea plus the same smell of food may lead to aversion. Your perception of a social situation may make the pattern of motivation still more complicated. Hunger plus the smell of food, but also plus the social demands of a dinner party, will evoke no wild rush to the dining room. In that circumstance you will try to talk engagingly with your fellow guests until dinner is announced. All the inner and outer stimuli that bear upon a person at one time constitute his *psychological field* and determine his behavior jointly and in interaction. The psychological field, however, is no mystical relationship between a person and his environment. A human being is a biological organism and is affected only by events within his own skin and by events from the outside that stimulate his own sense organs. However complex the patterns or fields may be, it is still only persistent stimulation that arouses and maintains behavior.

FUNDAMENTAL CONCEPTS

The development of a theory of motivation entails two major issues. The first is to identify the sources of the activities of living things, the springs of action that stir them up. The second issue relates to motivation as a selecting and directing influence, leading an organism to select some courses of action and to reject others. A biological approach to the problem of motivated behavior is aided by two basic concepts, which can now be defined.

Drives

Motivating stimuli are so important to an understanding of adjustment that it is helpful to give them a distinctive name. They are called *drives*. *A drive is a pattern of persistent stimulation that evokes sustained activity.* All drives originate from bodily conditions. Many of the most vital ones are the inner stimuli that signal the existence of the physiological needs of hunger, thirst, and the

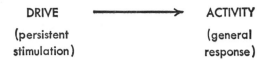

Figure 2. Original Response to a Drive

like. The stirred-up visceral state of emotion contributes many important drives, as we shall see later. External stimuli may be original drives if they are intense enough, as when a loud noise arouses continued restless movement.

Natively, most drives arouse only general activity. An infant cries and moves whether in hunger, in pain, or in other distress. Even a skillful observer cannot tell the exact source of intense activity in a very young infant but only knows that some strong drive must be operating. The mother or nurse tries one ameliorative procedure after another until the cessation of crying shows that the drive has been located and removed. Originally, then, drives evoke an increase in a person's general activity level, as Figure 2 indicates.

Mechanisms

As an individual matures and learns, he discovers ways to reduce his drives. Such adjustive habits are often called mechanisms. Except for a few of the simplest reflex adjustments, such as breathing, swallowing, and some others, mechanisms are acquired through processes of learning. *A mechanism is a response or a sequence of behavior that tends to reduce a drive.* The appropriate mechanism for hunger is to eat. On the more complex level of social behavior, a child who has a motive to secure attention may employ the mechanism of showing off.

When a person has learned how to reduce a drive by a specific kind of response, his behavior sequence can be diagrammed as in Figure 3. The end result of an adjustment mechanism is to remove

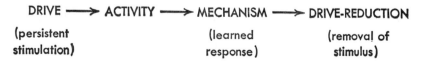

Figure 3. Learned Response to a Drive

the drive-stimulus or to reduce its intensity. When the stimulus pattern no longer arouses him, the person's activity ceases and he is adjusted to that particular drive.

SOME PHYSIOLOGICAL DRIVES

In order to keep on living, you must breathe, eat, drink, excrete, keep warm, rest, and sleep. Such activities therefore define the vital needs whose thwarting leads, not to psychological maladjustment, but to death. Under usual circumstances, these drives do not affect man's psychological and social adjustments directly, but their indirect influence is considerable. The most fundamental social relationship, that of a child with his parents, originates from the child's dependence upon them for the satisfaction of his essential needs. Also, the physiological drives illustrate quite clearly a number of principles that apply to social motivation as well. Hunger will be selected as a representative vital drive, and a few of its most significant aspects will be described briefly.*

Hunger

Nutrition is a biochemical process, and the most probable stimuli for the hunger drive are chemical ones. The precise stimulating substances and the receptors on which they act are not fully understood, but research has revealed much useful information about the process. Blood sugar is one of the body's most essential nutrients. Experiments have shown that a lowered blood sugar level caused by injecting insulin, which controls sugar metabolism, results in hunger.[1] When glucose is injected into the blood, evidences of hunger cease promptly.[2]

In a normal person or animal hunger is accompanied by rhythmic contractions of the stomach. In a classic series of experiments, Cannon had a subject swallow a long thin tube ending in the stomach with a lightly inflated balloon.[3] The variations in air pressure from the balloon permitted a recording instrument to show

---

* For a more complete account of the hunger drive and for descriptions of thirst, temperature regulation, air-getting, excretion, and other physiological drives, see books in general and physiological psychology cited in the Suggested Readings.

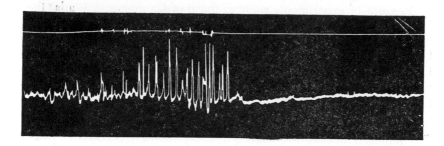

Figure 4. Stomach Contractions and Bodily Movements

The upper line represents bodily movements of a subject who was reading while reclining on a bed. The lower line shows stomach contractions obtained by a stomach balloon. Note that movements coincide with contraction periods. (T. Wada, Experimental study of hunger in its relation to activity. *Arch. Psychol., N. Y.,* 1922, No. 57.)

graphically the contractions of the stomach. Also, Cannon's subject pressed a key whenever he felt a "pang" of hunger, and this information was recorded on the same device as the stomach contractions. The feelings of hunger coincided with the periods of maximum stomach contraction. When you feel hungry, you are feeling the contractions of your stomach.

Further experiments by Wada[4] showed the relationship between stomach contractions and general bodily activity. Four subjects swallowed stomach balloons like those used by Cannon and reclined on beds so arranged that even very slight bodily movements were recorded simultaneously with stomach changes. In one experiment subjects read for nine hours. Numerous body movements appeared during periods of stomach contraction, practically none during quiescent intervals (Fig. 4). In another observation stomach contractions and bodily movements were recorded during sleep, and even then the periods of activity, tossing and turning, coincided with the internal contractions. Other experiments showed that the subjects' strength of grip and even their scores on group intelligence tests were greater when tested during periods of hunger contraction. Evidently the hunger drive intensifies many body activities. Restless activity is increased and learning is facilitated by the presence of the drive.

Because of experiments such as those of Cannon and Wada, the hunger drive was formerly identified with the contractions of the stomach. It was believed that the receptor-aroused neural impulses from the stomach muscles *were* the drive. Further experiments have thrown doubt on the sufficiency of that explanation. Rats with their stomachs removed engaged in as much activity, gnawing through layers of cardboard to reach food, as did normal rats after the same interval of deprivation.[5] One human subject whose stomach had to be removed operatively reported a desire for food at the usual intervals.[6] Other experiments have severed the vagus nerves between the stomach and the brain, preventing sensory impulses from the stomach from reaching the central nervous system.[7] After this operation rats showed the usual rhythm of eating at about two-hour intervals. All these experiments show that the stomach contractions do not constitute the primary or essential hunger drive. In normal organisms stomach movements are probably the source of the *conscious* pangs of hunger. Also, the visceral contractions probably serve as a special augmenting device which is set off by the more basic chemical stimuli for hunger, and in turn strengthens the drive for restless activity. In this respect the stomach contractions of hunger are very similar to the visceral states of emotion which also serve as important drives, as we shall see later.

The function of hunger is further complicated by partial hungers for particular foods. Crude observations of such special appetites are not new. Cattle grazing in country where there is a phosphorus deficiency in the soil will become bone eaters. Laboratory animals or children fed a diet deficient in vitamin B complex (thiamine, riboflavin) will develop an appetite for it.

How do animals and infants choose the foods that are good for them? The best evidence comes from an experiment by Richter.[8] Animals whose adrenal glands have been removed develop an intense appetite for large amounts of salt, without which they will die. Adrenalectomized rats in free-feeding experiments consume much more salt than do normal rats. When the rats' taste nerves are cut, they no longer select salt and soon die from the lack of it. Apparently, some substances essential to the maintenance of life are eaten because they "taste good," and one's taste in many instances is regulated by one's needs. That is not always true, however. Animals deficient in some of the vitamins will not select them in a diet when these vitamins have no distinctive taste to serve as a cue. In summarizing the evidence on partial hungers, Young[9] states that there are special appetites at least for protein, fat, carbohydrate, water, oxygen, salt, phosphorus, sodium, calcium, and vitamin B, and possibly for others. Even as "simple" a need as hunger turns out to be an extremely complex organization of many drives.

Glandular Conditions

The body possesses two great integrating systems, the nervous system and the glands.[10] The latter often act in conjunction with neural innervation and sometimes relatively independently. Glands arouse activity through chemical substances known as hormones, secreted by the glands and circulated by the blood. For example, the thyroid gland, located in the neck, has a considerable effect on the general activity level of a person by its control of the body's rate of metabolism. If the hormone thyroxin secreted by this gland is deficient, the individual may be sluggish and lacking in alertness. An excessive secretion may lead to overactivity, irritability and so-called "nervousness." The adrenal and pituitary glands, and the sex glands to be described shortly, also secrete hormones that govern the general level of bodily vigor and activity.

Hormones interact with appetitive drives. One example of this has been given already, the effect of an adrenal deficiency on the demand for salt. A secretion of the posterior part of the pituitary gland helps to maintain the constant water balance of the body. Where there is an undersupply of water, a hormone is produced that inhibits the kidneys from secreting urine. Damage to that part of the pituitary results in an abnormal loss of fluids, which is compensated by a great increase in the thirst drive. In that way the relationships between endocrine secretions and drives help to maintain the physical integrity of the organism.

Sex

The fundamental sex drives are mainly glandular in origin. The sex glands of both males and females secrete hormones that determine the secondary sex characteristics of the body and also influence the general activity level. The castration of a male animal reduces its alertness and activity, while the injection of male hormones restores the drive. When castration is performed on an immature male the sex drives never develop, but an animal castrated in maturity often continues to show sex activity. The sex hormones are therefore essential to the beginning of sexual drive, but other stimuli for the urge may take over once it is established. Sex drive activates not only specific sexual behavior but increases general activity as well. Much of the active, aggressive behavior of young males of any species, usually vaguely ascribed to "animal spirits," is motivated by sex tension, even though in most cases the individual does not recognize it as such.

The adult female sex drive of animals is cyclic and is related to periods of *estrus* or "heat." A female white rat placed in a revolving cage that measures the gross amount of running will run a mile or two every day, except that on every fourth or fifth day she will show a peak of activity, covering often as much as fifteen miles.[11] The periods of activity coincide with the days on which the rat is in heat and sexually receptive. Males and immature females do not show cyclic activity, and neither do females whose ovaries have been removed. In women the basic sex drives are overlaid by many learned cultural patterns. Several studies, however, have shown a heightened sex urge just before and just after the menstrual period.[12]

In higher animals, including human beings, the sex drive is not governed entirely by glandular secretions. Sex interests and exploratory play in infancy and childhood have been widely observed. Genital responses may occur very early in life. In one study, precise observations of nine male infants, three to twenty weeks old, showed that all of them had frequent tumescence.[13] The onset of tumescence was accompanied by restlessness, crying, and tension, its termination by relaxation. Such observations suggest the presence of a specific genital drive in male infants. Unlike the adult sex urge, however, the infants' tumescence seemed to be evoked primarily by other drives such as bladder and bowel tensions and the frustration of feeding responses.[14]

The strength and frequency of the adult male sex drive, and also its great variability, have been strikingly shown by Kinsey's report of interviews with 5300 men.[15] In the entire group from adolescence to old age, the number of completed sex acts of all types averaged two to three per week. There is great individual variation, from about 15 per cent of men with a frequency of less than one per week, to 8 per cent with frequencies of seven or more. Sex activity is maintained over a wide range of ages. The sex drives are highest in the teen ages and in many instances continue into the eighties. Kinsey interpreted the great range of frequencies as a largely biological variation but recognized that psychological attitudes toward sex may affect the drive. Kinsey's study of 8000 American women showed that more women than men had little sexual urge, and that they were older, on the average, at the time of the first sexual experience.[16] Once established, however, the women's sexual intensity rises gradually and stays at the maximum level until after fifty-five or sixty years of age, while the men's declines much more rapidly. The range of individual variation in sexual behavior and responsiveness is much greater among women than among men.

The effect of learning on sex behavior varies among species. In lower animals, such as the much-studied rat, mating behavior is a native mechanism.[17] Both male and female rats reared in isolation mate when mature in the manner characteristic of their species. The higher animals present a different picture. While controlled observations of human sex development are impracticable, studies of chimpanzees reveal no innate stereotyped mechanism for reducing sex drives.[18] Like human children, chimpanzees of both sexes engage in varied sex play before maturity. As adults, they learn their specific sex responses largely through trial and error and show considerable variation in the final patterns adopted. The evidence suggests that there is a strong human sex drive, but that its mode of satisfaction depends on learning in a particular culture.

CHARACTERISTICS OF MOTIVATION

Homeostasis

The evidence concerning hunger drives, and also the observations about the endocrine glands, conform to a broad and important generalization about the functioning of living things. *All organisms tend to maintain the constancy of the internal conditions essential to their well being,* such as their body temperatures, and their supplies of oxygen, water, and various foods. Cannon[19] gave the name *homeostasis* to the tendency of organisms to maintain an equilibrium of the "inner environment" in which their tissues live. In almost all instances when the balance is disturbed, automatic functions give rise to drives that stimulate the organism to act so as to restore the needed constancy. Homeostasis, then, represents the principle of adjustment at its most primitive level, the adjustment of the body within itself. We will find later that a very similar principle applies to the broader external relationships between a person and his social environment.[20]

"Abnormal" Drives

Even appetites that seem "abnormal" may be only evidences of homeostasis. For a rat to crave huge amounts of salt or for it to drink almost twice its weight in water daily certainly seems to be abnormal behavior. But when we find that these appetites arise from defects of the adrenal and pituitary glands respectively and that they are the only ways to maintain life under the circumstances, even such abnormalities of drive fit the general homeostatic principle.[21] In social adjustments, also, we will find that an over-aggressive or abnormally fearful person may be engaging in a desperate and not altogether successful attempt to restore an equilibrium between himself and his environment.

Tension

A striving organism is often said to be in a state of *tension*, and this term has been used widely to describe and explain motivated behavior. Unfortunately, the term "tension" has been used in two distinct meanings, which must be separated in order to avoid confusion.

One meaning of "tension" is a state of disequilibrium, which leads to a change in behavior tending toward a restoration of equilibrium. That concept of tension is clearly related to homeostasis. A need or lack is said to put an organism off its balance, so that the organism has to be active in order to restore a normal state of affairs. Thus a hunger need makes the whole situation incomplete or unbalanced from the viewpoint of the animal or person who is hungry, and food-seeking activity tends toward restoring the lost harmony. Originally used to signify biological states of unbalance, the term "tension" sometimes has been extended to include inharmonious relationships between persons or groups. You use that meaning when you refer to a "state of tension" between two men or between two nations.

"Tension" also means a contracted, tight, strained, uncomfortably stimulating condition of muscles and other body tissues. When you say that a man is "tense," you are employing this second meaning. So conceived, tension is an intrabodily response that in turn acts as a drive-stimulus. Examples are the stomach contractions that act as a supplementary cue for hunger, the dryness of the throat and mouth in thirst, and the choking and suffocating states arising from the stoppage of free access of air to the lungs. Those states are often called *appetitive tensions,* because they serve as drives in relation to appetitive or survival needs. Tensions are also illustrated by the distentions of the bladder or the large intestine by excretory products, giving rise to restless activity until the source of the tension is removed by emptying the body cavity. Such drives are called *eliminative tensions. Sex tensions* also can be identified. Even more significant in social motivation are the *emotional tensions,* to be described later in this chapter. As stimuli that evoke persistent adjustive activity, tensions constitute a major source of drives.

The two meanings of the word "tension" are equally respectable, and both may be useful if you take care not to confuse them. Unless otherwise specified, the second concept will always be used in this book: Tension is an internal bodily response that acts as a source of drive stimulation.

The Effect of Motivation on Perception

A strong drive has an important influence on what a person will notice or perceive in his environment. At a very basic level, we have already seen that a salt-hungry rat will choose salty water in preference to fresh water. Analogous observations have been made of human subjects. In one study child and adult subjects responded to ambiguous words and pictures that might or might not suggest food.[22] When hungry, the subjects made significantly more food-connected responses than when they were recently fed. For example, they mentioned food or eating more frequently in telling stories based on a set of pictures.

During World War II, thirty-six volunteers lived at a semistarvation level for six months in an experiment to study the effects of a minimum diet and the best methods for rehabilitating seriously underfed people. One striking result of that study was their changed attitudes toward food.[23] Not only did the men react jealously to their small rations, lose their table manners, and lick their plates, but there were broader effects on their attitudes.

Food in all of its ramifications became the principal topic of the
subjects' conversations, reading, and day dreams. More dreams
about food were reported as the stress continued. When subjects
read books and attended movies, they were deeply impressed by
the frequency with which food and eating were mentioned. Cook
books, menus, and information bulletins on food production became intensely interesting reading matter to many of the subjects
who previously had little or no interest in dietetics or agriculture.
Some men went so far as to replan their lives according to their
newly acquired respect for food. . . . A few planned to become
cooks.*

Even the basic and physiological drive of hunger has profound
effects on more complex psychological processes such as perception,
attitude, and interest. Emotionally-toned social motivations have
equally marked effects on the way a person perceives and responds
to the world about him.

The Relative Intensity of Drives

The relative strengths of the simple drives of lower animals have
been measured experimentally. One procedure used is the obstruction method, in which a barrier separates the animal from an object
(water, food, a mate) that will satisfy his motivation. Warden's type
of obstruction apparatus (Fig. 5) contains an electrified grid in the
floor of a passage.[24] An animal's persistence in crossing the grid,
from which he receives a painful shock, is the measure of the intensity of the drive. The strength of a drive, of course, depends somewhat on the length of time since it was last satisfied. After a deprivation of one day the order of the strength of drives in the female
white rat is, first, the maternal or lactation drive to reach her young,
then thirst, sex when in heat, and hunger. After two days' deprivation the hunger drive becomes stronger than thirst or sex.

The strengths of human drives have not been evaluated experimentally. Anecdotes and case evidence about shipwrecked men and
about starving people in concentration camps suggest that there is a
hierarchy of human drives. Thirst and hunger are very strong when
thwarted persistently and soon eclipse the sex drives and the learned
forms of social motivation.

* J. C. Franklin, B. C. Schiele, J. Brozek, & A. Keys. Observations on human
behavior in experimental semistarvation and rehabilitation. *J. clin. Psychol.*,
1948, *4*, p. 32.

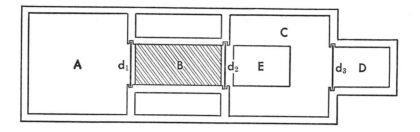

Figure 5. Obstruction Box for Measuring Animal Drives

The animal is placed in compartment **A**. It must cross the electric grid **B** in order to reach the release plate **E** that opens a door enabling it to reach the goal in compartment **D**. (C. J. Warden, *Animal motivation*. New York: Columbia Univer. Press, 1931.)

PERSON-ENVIRONMENT RELATIONSHIPS

Every living organism has to deal with the world outside its own skin as well as to maintain its inner integrity. The environments of organisms contain many material resources that can aid and threats that can hinder the satisfaction of needs. More important for human beings, the world is full of other people whose actions, cooperation, and competition evoke and direct many forms of behavior. Although social motivation is a complex of learnings, as discussed more fully in the next chapter, there are some primary bases of the organism-environment relationship on which the more elaborate social motives are built.

Tissue Injury

An external discomfort may arouse activity as readily as an internal one. The baby's diaper pin, already mentioned as an example of a drive-stimulus, illustrates a very general kind of motivation. Any stimulating pattern that causes the injury or destruction of living tissues tends to serve as a drive to activity. Stimuli that cut, burn, or bruise evoke avoidance responses in an adult. The accurate avoidance shown by an adult's reaction to a hot stove is, however, learned. By nature, a tissue injury inflicted on a young organism sets up only a state of general activity, of writhing, wiggling, and howling. Like other drives, it is nonspecific at first. If his energetic activity takes the child out of the range of the injurious stimulus, the responses subside because they are no longer stimulated. Learning may occur quickly, and the successful "avoidance," first achieved by chance, comes to be made more promptly the next time. The organism originally does not avoid such stimuli because it *knows* that they are harmful, but because the stimuli excite it to intense activity.

In the same class with tissue injury, which may be regarded as an overstimulation of cutaneous receptors, are the drives aroused by the overstimulation of other sense organs. Unless counteracting stimuli are present and prepotent, loud noises, sudden movements or falling, and all too strong tastes, odors, and pressures, tend to arouse violent activity. Too bright a light belongs to this group also if it is so intense and sudden that the adaptive mechanisms of the pupils and eyelids do not have time to act.

Most of the drives so far considered have been "annoying" stimuli — thirst, hunger, eliminative tensions, and bodily harm or overstimulation. In each instance activity is aroused that *persists until the stimulus is removed*. Drives of this class may be termed *avoidant drives*. They are defined objectively in terms of the organism's response to them and there is no need to invoke "pain" or "discomfort" as a principle of explanation.

Adient Drives

Psychological theory has unfortunately rather neglected another class of drive, to which the organism responds so as to *perpetuate the stimulus* rather than to remove it. If you scratch a kitten's neck, it lifts its head, pushes forward, turns, and twists — all activities that tend to bring the stimulus to bear more strongly. Activity is aroused and maintained, and therefore the scratching is a drive-stimulus, but the resulting response moves the organism toward the stimulus instead of away from it.

Such a drive might be called a satisfaction or pleasure drive, but it is no more necessary to use "pleasure" as an explanatory concept than it was to use "pain" to explain avoidance. Instead of using at this point a word that has been employed in many confused and unpsychological meanings, it will be well to follow the lead of

E. B. Holt[25] and introduce a coined term, *adient,* from *ad eo,* to go toward. An adient drive is a pattern of stimulation that results in behavior acting toward the stimulus, increasing and perpetuating its action. Adient responses are more common in child and adult behavior than are avoiding reactions. A child tends to look at, handle, and approach almost all stimulating objects except overviolent ones. Such responses account for much of the outreaching, examining, and inquiring character of all living creatures.

Some stimuli arouse adient responses more dependably than others. Enumerating specific adient drives is speculative, however, because they are affected by learning so readily and so early in an individual's life. A bright color, a sweet taste, a flowery odor, a smooth stroking of the skin, are stimuli to which unsophisticated children seem to react adiently. On the other hand, bitter and sour tastes, foul odors, and harsh scratching usually call forth restless behavior that leads eventually to avoidance. Whether these sensory satisfiers and annoyers are native is open to question. Studies show that a small infant has no marked reaction to a sour substance in the mouth, but that after the age of eighteen months he will quite dependably spit it out.[26] Further changes bring about the enjoyment of some sour foods, usually found only in older children and adults.

Among situations that elicit adient responses, smooth skin-stroking and gentle patting and rocking seem to have special significance for the development of social motives and for interpersonal adjustments. A number of explanations have been suggested for the satisfying nature of that type of stimulation, but the evidence is not conclusive. Perhaps petting and fondling facilitate visceral processes, breathing, and circulation, and therefore inhibit other activity drives that would lead the organism away from the situation. Another hypothesis connects the skin satisfactions with genital stimulation, the infant making a kind of mild and diffuse sexual response to the gentle stroking of any part of his body. A strongly supported theory points to a very early learning process as the origin of such behavior, since a helpless infant is ordinarily touched and held whenever he is fed, kept warm, or otherwise provided with means for reducing his appetitive needs. Whatever their source, the adient responses of infants remain an all-important basis for certain further steps of learning.

It is not impossible that human infants react with native adience to a few other sources of stimulation. A "suckling need" has been suggested by several experiments and observations. Puppies, bottle-fed from nipples with large holes so that they got all their milk with little sucking, continued between feedings to suck on their own paws, on other puppies' fur, and on other available objects.[27] Litter-mate puppies, fed from small-holed nipples that required long-time sucking, showed no such behavior. Case studies of human infants who suck their thumbs and other objects when frustrated by too quick feeding or by early weaning have also been cited to support the theory of a sucking need.[28] Contrary data, however, come from one careful study of infants who were cup-fed from birth.[29] The cup-fed infants did less, rather than more, sucking than a comparison group of breast-fed babies. The evidence so far seems to indicate only that infants who are once accustomed to suckling as a method of getting food will engage in substitute sucking when that activity is thwarted. Although the issue is not entirely settled and an innate sucking need is not impossible, it seems more likely to be a learned adience based on the satisfaction of hunger drives.[30]

Adient drives raise one theoretical issue that is not yet settled by adequate experimental evidence. What ends an adient act? Why does it not go on perpetuating itself forever? The avoidant drives have a clear termination, ending when the annoying stimulus has been removed. The adient drives do not. In many instances young organisms are indeed motivated to have a satisfying form of stimulation continue indefinitely. The kitten can never have enough petting nor the human infant enough cuddling. However, all organisms have multiple drives. Response to an adience-provoking stimulation may continue until some stronger drive of an annoying sort occurs. The kitten or infant gets hungry or sleepy, or its muscles become tense from retaining one position. Such drives may induce a variation in behavior and thereby end the adient response.

The Relationship Between Adience and Avoidance

Although some primary adiences and avoidances may be independent, they become closely related once you have learned a repertory of adjustive habits. After some learning has occurred, an avoidance of one situation almost always becomes an adience toward another one, and vice versa. Hunger is originally an avoidant drive because it gives rise to activity that continues until the stimulus, the hunger drive, is removed. After you have had some experience with food, a learned adience toward it supplements and even to some extent replaces the native restless response to hunger.

The lack of an accustomed adient stimulus is also an annoyance. If an infant has been petted and rocked, he may cry when such stimulation ceases. An older child, or an adult, who customarily receives attention and approval in a certain situation may show restless and annoyed behavior if it is absent. The facts are clear, but their theoretical explanation offers some little difficulty. The nearest experimental analogy is the well-known phenomenon of sensory adaptation. If your hand has been in very hot water, luke-warm water will feel quite cool. When you have been eating a very sweet dessert, normally sweetened coffee may taste too bitter. So, in the larger social contexts of life, a pleasant state of affairs may come to feel normal, so that its absence becomes a genuine annoyance.

EMOTION

Motivation and Emotion

Motives occur in all degrees of intensity. You may observe, for example, a young child who encounters a large strange dog. Perhaps at first the boy is only timid. He does not approach the dog and tends to draw back a little. So far the child shows only a simple avoidant response, though a learned one to be sure, since children have no innate tendency to avoid animals. Then the youngster's behavior may change markedly. He may cry and run toward home as fast as his legs can carry him. If you have an opportunity to examine him now, you will find that his face is pale, his breathing irregular, and his heart-beat rapid. His muscles are tense, and he is likely to tremble. Further physiological study would disclose that the child's salivary glands have stopped secreting, causing his mouth to be dry, and that the gastric glands are also inhibited and digestion is interrupted. His state differs so much from simple avoidant behavior that it seems to fall into another psychological category. You need no formal study of psychology, however, to recognize that the child is afraid and that he is in a state called *emotion*.

Instances can be multiplied easily. A child who wants a toy held by another may reach, grab, and then struggle. If his response continues to intensify, he may become angry and strike wildly at the contesting playmate. Here again, as in the case of the frightened child, your observations would show a strong visceral reaction as well as a muscular one. A simple motivated act has become intensified into an emotional response.

Some of the most important characteristics of emotion can be found even in these simple examples. Emotional behavior is strongly *motivated* behavior, marked by strivings to escape, to attack, or the like. Emotion is noted for its *intensity*, the muscular response — at least in infants and young children — being stronger than that involved in any other kind of bodily reaction. Even though it is modified through learning, emotion exhibits throughout life a *persistence* equalled only by a few of the most basic reflexes. Finally, and perhaps most distinctively, strong emotion includes widespread and violent *visceral changes* affecting the circulatory, respiratory, digestive, and glandular systems as well as the skeletal muscles.

How Many Emotions?

In your own experience as an adult, you recognize a great many emotions such as fear, anger, disgust, distress, love, wonder, elation, grief, jealousy, shame, remorse, and almost countless others. How many emotions are there? The question is not simple, for the answer depends on how you define emotion and on the age of the person whose emotional behavior you are observing. If you base your study on adults and pay attention to the various feelings and impulses that mark emotional states, you will indeed find a large number of emotions. Anger and shame, for example, differ in their conscious feelings and also in the attitudes and behavior that accompany them. There are many reasons to believe, however, that the complex emotions of adults are blends of emotional and intellectual experiences, all greatly modified through learning. When you feel shame, for example, you not only have the basic stirred-up condition of emotion, but you also have an attitude of unfavorable self-evaluation, molded by the culture in which you live and modified by your own particular learning experiences.

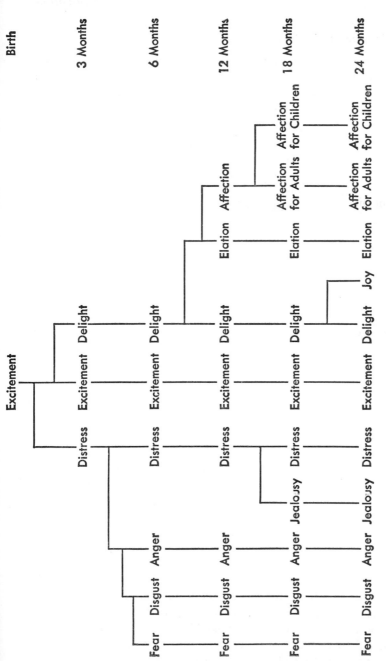

Figure 6. Emotional Development During the First Two Years

At first, the infant shows only the single very generalized emotion of *excitement.* The more specific emotional patterns emerge at approximately the indicated ages, as the infant matures and learns (K.M. Banham Bridges, Emotional development in early infancy. *Child Developm.,* 1932, 3, 340.)

The Development of Emotion

Another way that you can examine emotion is developmentally and objectively. If you observe the emotional behavior of infants and watch their step-by-step development as they mature, you have a different picture of the number of emotions and of their nature.

Many studies have shown that the emotional responses of infants are few, and that they are generalized rather than specific.[31] In one of the most comprehensive studies, Bridges[32] observed some sixty infants daily over a period of several months and used systematic tests to supplement her descriptions of the emotions aroused by the ordinary circumstances of their lives. In the newborn only one pattern of emotion was found, a general state of excitement or agitation. Distress was distinguishable from excitement by three weeks of age, and delight by two or three months. As Figure 6 shows, distress is further differentiated into anger, disgust, and fear, while delight gives rise to elation and affection. Although other studies[33] may require a modification of some of Bridges' detailed findings, the important principle seems to be firmly established that emotional behavior develops by the differentiation of specific emotions from an original matrix of emotion-in-general.

The development of emotion follows the same laws that govern the growth of other aspects of behavior.[34] Studies of the prenatal development of many organisms, and of newborn babies, show that much muscular behavior first appears as undifferentiated activity of the body as a whole. In response to almost any kind of stimulation, the human infant shows diffused and nonspecific activity; he kicks his legs, waves his arms, wiggles, squirms, and vocalizes. Such "mass activity" is due to the as yet incompletely organized character of the infant's nervous system.[35] As the child matures, his most basic motor skills, such as reaching and walking, emerge from his earlier over-all behavior. His behavior grows by the differentiation of more specific patterns from the original mass reaction. Emotion develops similarly.

Our present understanding of the course of emotional development helps us to reinterpret some widely influential earlier studies. John B. Watson in 1919 believed that he discovered three "primary" human emotions in infants: *fear,* evoked by loud noises or by falling; *rage,* elicited by restraint of movement; and *love or sex* in response to stroking and petting.[36] In an apparently contradictory series of observations, Mandel Sherman in 1927 stimulated infants by hunger, sudden dropping, restraint of the head and face, and pricking with a pin.[37] Observers who saw only the infants' responses, without seeing the stimulating conditions, were quite unable to discriminate the supposedly separate "emotions." For example, the response to sudden falling was called "anger" quite as often as it was called "fear." Sherman concluded that Watson's description of "primary" emotions was biased and inaccurate.

One explanation of the disagreement may be found in an experimental error that Watson seems to have made. When an infant was free to move, as when the loud sound stimulus was employed, any general muscular activity was interpreted as "withdrawing movements." If the infant was held firmly, restraint being the stimulus, the identical pattern of muscular movements might have been interpreted as "struggling." In the latter case the infant could not move away or make avoidance movements, simply because of the restraint. The initial difference between fear and rage, therefore, may not lie in the response but in the situation with which the organism is confronted.

Another interpretation suggests that Watson and Sherman both may have reported their observations accurately. Watson made most of his studies on babies four to six months of age, who were old enough already to have acquired some differentiation of their emotions. Sherman used infants under twelve days old, whose responses were still in the undifferentiated stage described as excitement or distress. The disagreement between these studies was therefore due in large part to a failure to recognize the developmental factor in emotion.

That distress and delight are the two earliest differentiated emotions confirms the relationship between emotion and motivation. We have already seen that the two basic patterns of motivated behavior are adience and avoidance, tendencies to approach or to avoid the stimulating event. Distress may be regarded as *excited avoidance,* a blend of primary emotional excitement with a drive to terminate or avoid the stimulus. Delight, similarly, may be considered as *excited adience.* From these beginnings are derived all of the more specific emotional responses of older children and adults.

Distress, Anger, Fear, and Anxiety

Fear and anger do not emerge mysteriously because of processes of inner growth alone but are determined by the learning that an infant gains from living in his world. Rather early in life the baby learns to differentiate between some situations against which he can struggle and other situations that can be terminated only by withdrawing from them. Responses that involve emotion and struggling, perhaps first experienced in connection with restraint by clothing, bed covers, or adult holding, become stereotyped into the response of anger. Other overstimulating situations become connected to emotion plus withdrawing, giving rise to fear. Anger, then, begins with excited emotion plus learned struggling movements. Fear is distress with an impulse to withdraw or flee. There may be vacillation between these two attitudes. Even an adult confronted by an unexpected physical opponent may waver between fighting and flight, between anger and fear, without any appreciable change in the visceral basis of his emotion as he shifts from one to another. In older children and adults it is proper to regard anger and fear as separate emotional responses, but their close relationship and common origin are still evident.

Psychologists of a generation or two ago, who looked mainly at the emotions of adults, believed that fear was aroused natively by many stimuli. William James, typically, stated that fear was stimulated by certain noises, strange men, strange animals, some kinds of vermin, solitude, black things, dark places, holes and corners, high places, certain ideas of supernatural agency, and human corpses.[38] A valuable contribution made by Watson's pioneer studies was his demonstration of the acquired character of the emotional responses to many stimuli. Tests performed with babies four to six months of age showed a total lack of emotional reaction to a black cat, a pigeon, a rabbit, and a large dog. The infants showed no fear of fire or of the dark. Later fears of such stimuli, then, must be learned. Watson's own studies led him to believe that fear in infants was aroused by loud noises and loss of support, but further research has shown that such specific stimuli are by no means uniformly effective.

The conditions that provoke distress and its derivatives, such as anger and fear, probably cannot be defined in terms of simple mechanical stimuli but must be seen in terms of the total adjustive situation faced by the organism. In early infancy distress is probably caused by many sorts of excessively strong stimuli: by internal and external pain, hunger, rough handling, crude restraint and, in general, by sensory *overstimulation*. By the time anger and fear have emerged, the infant's perception of his world has enlarged considerably and he can respond in terms of the meaning of a situation for his adjustment. Anger by that time becomes his response to a simple obstruction of his motivated behavior. The greater the motivation, the greater the anger. Taking away a satiated infant's bottle will evoke little or no response, but the consequences of snatching the bottle from a still hungry infant are dependably more vigorous.[39] Fear comes to be the response to overwhelming situations that cannot be combated directly but to which adjustment can be made only by avoidance, withdrawal, or flight. The stimuli for fear in children and adults cannot be defined entirely in physical terms. Stimuli must be overintense, and also sudden and unfamiliar.[40] Whether a child will fear a loud sound depends not only on how loud it is but also on how unexpected and whether it occurs in a familiar and reassuring context or in a strange setting.[41]

Anxiety is another important emotional pattern that grows out of the primitive distress of infancy. The feeling-tone of anxiety is much like that of fear, but the two emotions can be distinguished in a number of ways. Typically, fear is evoked by a present and external stimulus, such as a ferocious dog or a narrowly escaped accident. Anxiety usually relates to the anticipation of a future situation, an apprehension of a probable pain, loss, or threat. Also, anxiety is most often stimulated by qualities of a person himself rather than by external events. A boy *fears* a larger bully but has *anxiety* about his own strength, competence, or acceptance in the group. Anxiety is therefore a relatively late-emerging emotional pattern, since it depends upon some ability to foresee the future and upon some degree of socially acquired evaluation of one's self. Some writers who have seen anxiety in the behavior of infants have probably confused it with primary distress, making the same error as those who read anger or fear into a baby's early undifferentiated emotion. There is no specific effective adjustment to anxiety. When you are angry you can fight, and when afraid, you can run. When you are anxious, you are merely stirred up, unhappy, and driven to do something when there is really little to do. Anxiety is therefore primary evidence of a lack of adjustment and is a key concept in the study of adjustive difficulties. For that reason, there will be much about anxiety in subsequent chapters.

Grief and depression are sometimes regarded as emotional states. At least, they have the introspective qualities of emotional distress, and literary usage has always regarded them as emotions. But grief and depression lack the excited and drive-like qualities which characterize anger, fear, and anxiety. They are accompanied by slower heart beat and breathing, lowered blood pressure, and a retardation of activity. Normal depression and grief in adults seem to be evoked by losses and deprivations that are perceived as unalterable. They depend, therefore, on some degree of intellectual appraisal of the situation. Babies cry from distress, but they hardly have grief in the adult sense.

Delight, Love, and Sex

If you observe the delighted behavior of a little child who has just been given a much desired but unexpected new toy, you can have little doubt that delight is an emotional response. Certain observations of infants, moreover, may show the close relationship between it and excitement and distress. A baby eight or nine months old being tossed into the air and caught by a familiar adult may squeal with excited delight. Then his perception of the situation may change, perhaps because the tossing gets too rough or because he is caught in a painful way, and his response immediately becomes one of distress accompanied by crying and struggling. Delight, then, is an excited emotion set off by overstimulation in a context that evokes adient behavior. In some degree emotional responses of delight and elation continue throughout life, being seen especially when a highly desired goal is attained unexpectedly.

Whether "love," as Watson defined it, is an emotion depends on the meaning of that much abused word. Gentle stroking, petting, and fondling of an infant or child are calming in their effects and lack the excited character of either delight or distress. On the other hand, the enthusiastic hugging that a two- or three-year-old may give his mother seems to have decided features of emotional excitement. The solution of the apparent dilemma of the emotional status of love, then, lies in a consideration of the intensity of the response. In this respect it is not unlike avoidance, which may vary in strength from calm withdrawal to utter fear. Love and affection may be regarded as adient responses that become emotional when they are very strong.

Love between the sexes, as shown by adolescents and adults, is more clearly a kind of emotional behavior. Not only is the traditional lover strongly adient toward the object of his affection, but he shows the visceral signs of emotional excitement. His blood pressure rises, his heart pounds, and his breathing quickens. Romantic love comes from several sources. In part it is related to the affection and delight responses of early life and the glandular conditions of sexuality. In Western civilization we often overlook another factor, the influence of culture on the approved pattern of behavior for a person who is "in love." Children and adolescents learn the conventions of love from books, from motion pictures, and from observing their fellows. In many cultures different from our own, marriage is arranged by the family and is unaccompanied by the outbreaks of excited emotion that mark the behavior of lovers in our social milieu. Specifically sexual behavior, of course, is a particular kind of excited emotion which includes general visceral changes as well as those relating directly to the sex act.

The Physiology of Emotion

We can understand distressed emotion and also both the calm and excited "love" states more clearly by examining the part of the nervous system that activates the visceral responses.[42] The neural control of most inner responses operates through a special structure of nerve cells and fibers that lie in the body cavity near the spinal column but outside the central nervous system. This network is called the *autonomic system* (Fig. 7) because of its relative independence of voluntary or central control. Fibers from the spinal cord (preganglionic fibers) terminate in ganglia which are the neural centers of the autonomic chain. From the ganglia, secondary (postganglionic) fibers proceed to the smooth muscles and the glands. Anatomically the autonomic system consists of three parts, a *cranial* or upper division whose preganglionic fibers come from lower brain centers, the *thoracico-lumbar* or *sympathetic* division from the middle portion of the spinal cord, and the *sacral* division from the lower part of the cord. Functionally there are two divi-

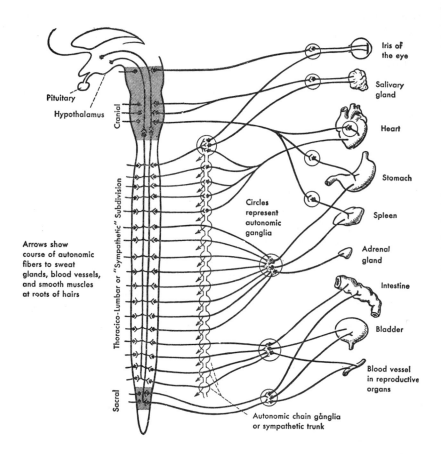

Pituitary

Hypothalamus

Arrows show
course of autonomic
fibers to sweat
glands, blood vessels,
and smooth muscles
at roots of hairs

Cranial

Thoracico-Lumbar or "Sympathetic" Subdivision

Sacral

Circles
represent
autonomic
ganglia

Iris of
the eye

Salivary
gland

Heart

Stomach

Spleen

Adrenal
gland

Intestine

Bladder

Blood vessel
in reproductive
organs

Autonomic chain gânglia
or sympathetic trunk

Figure 7. The Autonomic Nervous System

The brain and spinal cord are indicated at the left. Nerves
from the *cranial* division of the autonomic system go to organs in
the upper part of the body, from the *sacral* to the lower part.
These usually act together and comprise the cranio-sacral or
parasympathetic division. The thoracico-lumbar or sympathetic
division originates from the middle part of the cord, and sends
fibers to all organs through the chains of ganglia shown. The
action of the sympathetic division is ordinarily antagonistic to
that of the parasympathetic. (Adapted from N.L. Munn, *Psychology.* (3rd ed.) Boston: Houghton Mifflin, 1956.)

sions, since the cranial and sacral fibers have similar actions in many instances and are grouped together as the cranio-sacral or *parasympathetic* division.

All visceral organs and most glands have a dual innervation, receiving fibers from both the sympathetic and the parasympathetic divisions. The parasympathetic impulses tend to control and conserve the normal operation of the viscera. For example, the cranial division tends to permit salivation, facilitate the smooth-muscle contractions of the stomach and intestines, and slow the action of the heart. The parasympathetic fibers are capable of some independent action so that these responses can occur separately or in different patterns as required for visceral adjustment.

The sympathetic division evokes quite different effects. It inhibits salivary and gastric secretions and the movements of the stomach and intestines, increases the rate and amplitude of heart beat, constricts visceral arteries and thereby raises blood pressure, dilates the bronchioles of the lungs, makes the liver secrete glucose, and augments the secretion of the sweat glands. The *adrenal medulla,* a portion of an endocrine gland which is located above the kidneys, increases its secretion when it receives sympathetic stimulation. Its hormone, *adrenalin* (sometimes called epinephrine), is secreted into the blood and tends to augment chemically the same effects that the sympathetic innervation evokes by neural action. In fact, sympathetic nerve endings themselves secrete an adrenalin-like substance directly into the organs concerned, which may be a major mechanism by which they accomplish their action.[43]

The coordination of visceral responses by the autonomic nervous system is the neural basis for the bodily changes found in strong excited emotion. In emotion both the sympathetic and the parasympathetic divisions act, but the parasympathetic effects are counteracted or masked by the stronger influence of the sympathetic. The sympathetic acts as a whole — hence the widespread effects of emotion on all of the organs at once. It is also slow to act but persistent, which accounts for the continuation of excited emotional states after the external stimulus has been removed. Further evidence of the action of the sympathetic division in emotion comes from experiments with cats whose thoracico-lumbar ganglia had been removed. After the operation the cats showed normal defensive behavior when stimulated by a barking dog, but the visceral evidences of emotion were absent.

The sacral division of the autonomic system has some specific functions. It is connected to the smooth muscles of the bladder and colon and controls their eliminative reflexes. The preparatory stages of sexual excitement are under sacral domination, but the culmination of the sex act is stimulated through the sympathetic. The neural functions confirm the complex nature of sexual emotion. "Love" is parasympathetic, while "sex" in the more restricted sense is an excited emotion.

The functional antagonism of the two main autonomic divisions has important psychological applications. It has long been recognized that "love casts out fear." A frightened child is calmed by soothing and comforting ministrations that reinforce his parasympathetic responses. Conversely, the sexual functions cannot be excited in the presence of strong fear. Worry or guilt about sex, setting up an anxiety response to sexual stimuli, is the main cause of psychological impotence or frigidity. It is overcome when a changed attitude makes sex no longer a source of fear.

Physiological studies tend to confirm the conclusion that the excited emotional states stem from a common origin. There are no separate and consistent physiological responses by which excitement, fear, anger, and the like can be distinguished from one another. This does not mean that all emotional responses are exactly alike internally. On the contrary, the visceral patterns differ from one person to another and in the same person on various occasions. They also differ from one situation to another, but not consistently enough to serve as dependable indicators of the several so-called "emotions."[44]

The hypothalamus, a brain center just below the thalamus, has much to do with emotional behavior. Impulses from one part of it evoke responses from the sympathetic system, and from another part, the parasympathetic. Direct electrical stimulation of the appropriate part of the hypothalamus of experimental animals produces strong rage-like reactions. When its cerebrum is removed, an animal is readily aroused to an intense but poorly organized rage response. Apparently, emotional responses are coordinated at least in part by the hypothalamus, while the cerebral cortex has some restraining and controlling influence.

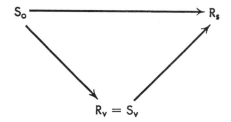

Figure 8. The Relation of Emotional Tension to Drive

An outside stimulus (S_O) may excite both a motor (skeletal) response (R_S) and also an emotional response (R_V). The visceral state is itself an inner stimulus (S_V) that augments the motor response. (Modified from J. F. Dashiell, *Fundamentals of general psychology.* (3rd ed.) Boston: Houghton Mifflin, 1949.)

Emotion as Drive

Emotion is perhaps less important for its own sake than for its relationship to motivation.[45] We have already seen that appetitive tensions and some other strong internal and external stimuli may act as drives, arousing persistent behavior. In many instances persons face situations that require important adjustments even though the external stimuli are not very intense. We may return to the illustration of the child who sees another youngster making off with his favorite toy. The visual stimulation itself is not strong enough to evoke much more than attention, looking, and perhaps reaching. If the sight stirs the boy to an angry reaction, however, his visceral responses are energized, and he is provided with an intense inner condition of unrest that in turn stimulates strong and persistent muscular activity.

An emotional tension is a persistent visceral state, the bodily component of emotion, that stimulates and maintains motivated activity. Figure 8 suggests the way an emotional tension operates. The external stimulus not only evokes some motor response but also arouses emotion. The inner turmoil of emotion constitutes an intrabodily stimulus that strengthens and prolongs the resulting muscular action. In this way emotion serves as a link between external and internal stimuli. Aroused chiefly by situations occurring in one's relationships with other people, emotion provides an inner stimulus as motivating as the strongest appetitive drives.

Emotion in Adjustment

The total life adjustment process has two essential parts, as we saw in Chapter 1. First, it is necessary for the organism to be stirred up when it has a need. Second, the organism has to do something to satisfy the need and to reduce the stimulating condition that served as a drive. The first aspect is as important as the second. If an animal that lacked food and water did not have appetitive drives to arouse it to activity, it would languish inertly and could not survive or reproduce its kind. The function of emotional tension is similar. If we did not have emotion to stimulate us to overcome a threat, to escape a danger, and perhaps also to embrace a mate, we would be ill-equipped for survival.

An early account of the evolutionary value of emotion was Cannon's *emergency theory,* which pointed out that the visceral changes occurring under intense stimulation are of utility in primitive life when brute struggle or flight are adaptive.[46] The increases in blood pressure and in heart rate, the release of sugar from the liver, and the secretion of adrenalin are all reactions that prepare an animal for violent physical exertion in flight or combat. While the emergency theory is of some help in understanding how emotion survived in the course of evolution, the function of emotion as drive is perhaps even more significant. Without it an animal would have to wait for its enemy actually to bite before becoming strongly stimulated. With emotion the organism can be energized to respond to a danger before it strikes, if there is a cue that the threat is approaching. Normal emotion is therefore *adaptive* in the distinct meaning of being valuable for individual and racial survival.[47] It is not, of course, *adjustive* for it stirs up activity, whereas adjustment means the reduction or satisfaction of drives. Adaptive and adjustive are not always synonymous.

The concept that emotion is adaptive seems to be at variance with the common observation that an "overemotional" person is unhappy and ineffective in his adjustments. This discrepancy can be reconciled by considering the strength of emotional drives. Just as the hunger drive can exist at all strengths from a good appetite to intense near-starvation, so emotional tensions can occur at all degrees of intensity. A moderate hunger is a useful drive that stimulates an animal or person to eat before his nutritional resources are exhausted. Starvation, as we have already seen, is too intense a drive, causing the famished person to think about nothing but the seeking of food to the exclusion of all of life's other interests and activities. Various degrees of emotional tension have similar functions. A little fear may make you more cautious, and a little anger may add to your persistence. Both may increase efficiency in everyday life. In one research study many combat aviators in World War II reported that mild fear made them more effective.[48]

Very intense emotional reactions have sometimes been described as "disorganized," a term that requires some further analysis.[49] The emotional response itself is not disorganized; on the contrary, as our study of the autonomic nervous system shows, it is a complex and superbly organized state of the body in which all of the major organs participate intensely but harmoniously. What, then, is disorganized? First, a person's other activities are disorganized by a strong emotion just as they are by any other single strong drive. If you are desperately fearful, your only thought is to fly or escape, and you are incapable of studying a lesson efficiently or of admiring the beauty of a sunset. Second, your intelligent judgments and skillful activities suffer from your overmotivation. The frightened boy may run more strongly, but he is likely to dodge or hide less cunningly. A thoroughly enraged youngster strikes out blindly and will be whipped by a coolly deliberate opponent. In sum, then, intense emotion so fully organizes a person for one kind of activity that he is badly disorganized for anything else. As we shall see later, this fact is one of the salient features of personal-social maladjustment.

SUGGESTED READINGS

Many introductory textbooks in psychology have informative chapters on motivation. Useful collateral readings may be found in Boring, Langfeld, and Weld, *Foundations of Psychology;* Hilgard, *Introduction to Psychology;* Munn, *Psychology;* and Ruch, *Psychology and Life.* There is a fine chapter on "The Needs of Children" in Baldwin, *Behavior and Development in Childhood.*

For more detailed material on the physiological basis of motivation and about hunger and the other appetitive drives, see Morgan and Stellar, *Physiological Psychology,* and Dempsey's Chapter 6 in Stevens, *Hand-*

book of Experimental Psychology. An older but indispensable reference is Young, *Motivation of Behavior.* A classic and charmingly written book on homeostasis is Cannon, *The Wisdom of the Body.*

Those whose interests have been caught by this chapter will find more advanced reading in a number of chapters in McClelland, *Studies in Motivation* and in Stevens, *Handbook of Experimental Psychology.*

On emotion, the elementary textbooks and Morgan and Stellar provide a background of experimental evidence and theory. An older but valuable book of great scope is Young, *Emotion in Man and Animal.* Other advanced references are *Feelings and Emotions* edited by Reymert; Jersild's Chapter 14 in Carmichael, *Manual of Child Psychology;* and Chapter 14 by Lindsley in Stevens, *Handbook of Experimental Psychology.*

CHAPTER **3**

Socially Acquired
Motivation

Your own experience tells you that motivated behavior is set off by many situations beyond the stimuli that directly and physiologically arouse drive-tensions. In fact, the motivations most significant for human adjustment do not arise from simple vital needs but from the social interactions of people. The more complicated motives of a person in his culture are not, however, independent of the drives of bodily states. Social motives originate from the modification of basic drives by learning processes. The learning operates in two principal ways, to extend the range of situations that will evoke the drive and to modify the activity that results.

If, when you are seated at your desk, savory odors arise from the kitchen, you suddenly become aware of hunger. A drive that is natively aroused only by an internal stimulus from nutritional deficiency is now evoked by an external sensory stimulus. Daily throughout your life the odor, sight, and thought of food have occurred at the same time as the hunger drive. As a result of your experiences, these external cues have become capable of arousing an internal drive. The first significant principle in the development of social motivation is the substitution of external stimuli for internal needs as the arousers of drives. The internal states have not lost their importance, of course. If you have just overeaten or if you are digestively unwell, the external stimulus has a different effect. You can lead a horse to water but you can't make him drink — unless his inner thirst drive is to some extent operative.

59

In response to your hunger drive or to some external symbol of it, you now arise from your desk, bathe, dress for dinner, go to the dining room and eat, making definite and skillful movements that convey the food from your plate to your digestive tract. This sequence illustrates the second principle in the development of motive, the acquisition of mechanisms. Instead of making the gross bodily responses to the hunger drive typical of infants or puppies, you make definite and effective learned reactions. The drive, by a learning process, now calls forth specific and differentiated rather than general activity. Exactly what you will do depends on the cultural context in which you have acquired your learning. In your own culture you eat with knife and fork at a table with your fellows; if you were an Arabian, you would dip from the common bowl using only your right hand; if you were Balinese,[1] you would take your leaf-plate of rice to a corner, turn your back on your family, and eat alone in silence.

Emotional tensions are affected by learning even more readily than appetitive tensions. You must overstimulate an infant directly to produce an excited emotion. An adult may show strong emotion in response to sights and sounds that are not themselves painful or overintense. Responses to emotional tension are modified too. An infant squirms and cries whether from pain, rough restraint, or other overstimulation. A three-year-old will withdraw from a painful stimulation, will run to mother when frightened, and is quite likely to have a tantrum when frustrated. Adults show behavior even farther removed from the general activity of infancy. What an adult will do when aroused emotionally depends greatly on his cultural context, which directs much of his individual learning. For example, we express surprise by widened eyes and open mouth, but a surprised Chinese sticks out his tongue.[2]

LEARNING IN RELATION TO DRIVE

The two major problems of acquired motivation require separate study. First, let us consider how drives come to be *evoked* by new situations. Later, we will return to the matter of learning to *do* new things in response to drives.

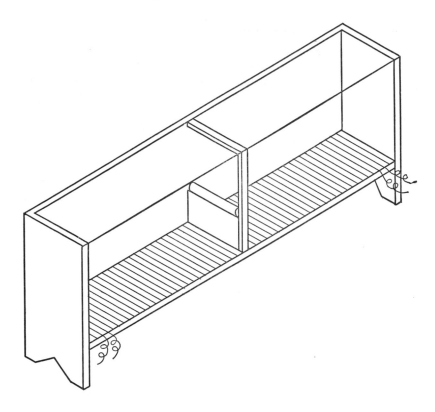

Figure 9. Apparatus for Demonstrating an Experimentally Acquired Drive in Rats

The long narrow alley is divided at the middle by a low barrier with a roller mounted on it to discourage rats from perching. The floor of each half consists of a metal grid through which electric shock can be administered to the rats' feet. The first part of the experiment consisted of training the rats to jump over the barrier to escape the shock. In the second part, in a pen six inches square, rats were stimulated simultaneously by the sound of a buzzer and an electric shock. Third, again in the above apparatus, the buzzer alone produced the drive-initiated response of jumping the barrier. The buzzer had become an *acquired drive*. (Drawn from description in M. A. May, Experimentally acquired drives. *J. exp. Psychol.*, 1948, 38, 66-77.)

An Experimentally Acquired Drive

Real life experiences are ordinarily quite complex, so that it is difficult to separate and identify the factors giving rise to a particular aspect of behavior. Scientific research is often furthered by taking a specialized and simplified part of a problem for study under controlled conditions. An experiment by May [3] provides a clear picture of the essential process through which a drive may come to be evoked by a substitute stimulus. The experiment consisted of three parts. In the first part, rats learned to jump over a low barrier to escape a moderate electric shock. The apparatus (Fig. 9) consisted of a "shuttle box" thirty inches long and six inches wide divided at the center by a low partition. The floor of the box was a metal grid, so arranged that a moderately painful electric shock could be applied to either half separately. The shock was applied to the side on which the rat stood until it crossed the barrier to the "cold" half. After sixty seconds, the shock was applied again and could once more be terminated by crossing the barrier. The rats soon learned to jump over the partition promptly in response to the drive produced by the painful shock.

The second was the crucial phase of the experiment. The rats were divided into an experimental group and three control groups with seven animals in each. Rats of the experimental group were placed in a pen six inches square and exposed simultaneously to the sound of a buzzer and to the shock. The control rats were also placed in the pen one at a time, but the buzzer was never paired with the shock. One control group received shock only, another group the buzzer only, and a third control group was stimulated with buzzer or shock at irregular intervals but never together.

The third part of the experiment was a test of what had been learned in the second phase. Each rat was again placed in the shuttle box, and the buzzer alone was sounded without any shock. If the rat jumped over the barrier within ten seconds, it was evident that the buzzer could now evoke behavior previously aroused only by the shock. The buzzer had become an acquired cue for a drive. Each rat was given twenty-five tests. The experimental group, exposed to paired buzzer and shock in the small pen, responded to the buzzer alone by crossing the partition on 84.5 per cent of their trials. The control rats crossed less often. The shock-only rats responded 34.2 per cent of the time, the buzzer-only, 2.7 per cent, and the unpaired shock-or-buzzer group, 3.4 per cent of the trials. The experimental rats also crossed the barrier more promptly after hearing the buzzer as well as much more frequently.

May's experiment points to the critical factor which permits a new stimulus to evoke drive-induced behavior. If a substitute stimulus and a drive occur together, then that stimulus becomes capable of reinstating the drive. The results of May's experiment are well represented by some diagrams (Fig. 10). In the first phase of the training, the pain of the electric shock arouses a strong visceral

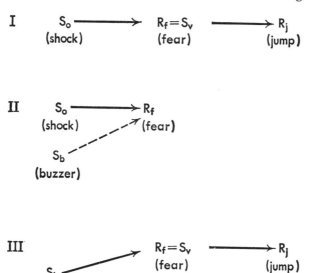

Figure 10. Learning an Acquired Drive

In I, the shock (S_o) arouses fear (R_f) which is a strong visceral drive (S_v) arousing the animal to activity, which is terminated by the successful response of jumping over the barrier (R_j). In the second procedure, II, shock and buzzer are paired so that learning takes place and the buzzer (S_b) becomes capable of arousing fear. In the test, III, the buzzer alone evokes fear in the experimental rats, and the fear again serves as a drive to arouse the escape response. Note that the visceral fear response is the *intervening variable,* the constant factor in each of the three steps, that makes it possible to explain why the rat will cross the barrier in III when it hears the buzzer.

drive, which we may call *fear*, that is reduced upon jumping the barrier. In the second phase of training, the buzzer becomes capable of arousing fear because of occurring simultaneously with it. Third, the buzzer evokes a state of fear and hence the jumping of the partition, even when the shock is omitted. This description does not suppose that the buzzer in some magic way "takes the place" of the shock. The motivated behavior is aroused by the same drive every time, namely by the fear.[4] The visceral state of fear has the intense and persistent qualities that a drive must have, which the buzzer itself lacks. The fear, then, is a kind of "intervening variable" between the cue (buzzer) and the activity (jumping).[5] An intervening variable is any assumed or observed process in the organism which helps to explain the behavior that occurs between the situation we present and the final activity we see. We shall find that human social motivation can be understood in much the same way.

THE CONDITIONED REACTION

In the learning of a new motivation the effect of certain reactions occurring together has been emphasized. For many years, simultaneously occurring reactions have been investigated carefully in laboratories. That kind of learning was first studied experimentally by I. P. Pavlov, a Russian physiologist, beginning about 1904. He called it the conditioned reflex, or more broadly, the *conditioned reaction*. Our store of information about conditioning can be applied to the problem of learning new motives.

Pavlov's Technique

Pavlov, as a physiologist, had long been interested in glands and their secretions. For that reason, the earliest studies were of the conditioned salivary reaction. If a drop of weak acid or a tiny quantity of meat powder is placed on the tongue of a dog, the animal will respond with an increased flow of saliva. The acid or food is an "adequate" or "original" stimulus for the salivary response. If a bell is rung, the dog will not salivate, since the bell stimulus is not directly connected with the salivary response. The conditioning process takes place in the following manner. The bell is rung, and simultaneously or a second or two afterward the acid is placed on the dog's tongue. After a number of paired stimulations with bell and acid, it is found that the bell alone has become capable of arousing a response, salivation, that it could not elicit before. The response of salivation to the bell is termed the conditioned response.

Pavlov's experiments, and many subsequent ones, were carried out under rigorously controlled conditions, and therein lies much of their value. The experimenter with his dog must not be pictured under the old apple tree, ringing the bell with one hand while he administers the food with the other! Pavlov's studies were conducted in soundproof rooms to exclude interfering noises. The dog stood on a table, restrained from moving by a light harness (Fig. 11). A small opening was cut through the dog's cheek, through which a tube was inserted into the duct of one salivary gland, eliminating any losses from swallowing. The saliva was measured drop by drop by a counting device and in bulk in a graduated cylinder. To elimi-

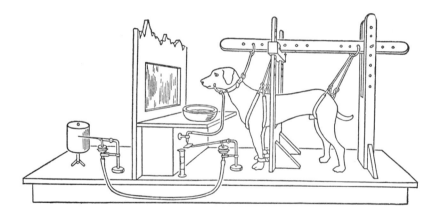

Figure 11. Pavlov's Apparatus for the Conditioned Salivary Response

The figure shows the historic early form of the apparatus, subsequently much improved The saliva flows from the dog's gland through the tube, to a drop-counting device and thence to a graduate. Food was introduced through the window. Special note should be made of the restraining harness, and of the fact that the dog had to be tamed, or made submissive, to stand in it. The restraint and submissiveness are important for some later interpretations of certain phenomena of conditioning. (R. M. Yerkes & S. Morgulis, The method of Pavlov in animal psychology. *Psychol. Bull.*, 1909, 6, 257-273.)

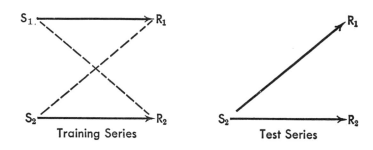

Figure 12. The Conditioned Reaction

Originally, S_1 evokes R_1, and S_2 calls forth R_2. By the simultaneous occurrence of these sequences, either stimulus becomes capable of provoking the entire response.

nate the possibility of the dog's receiving cues from the experimenter, the entire procedure was controlled from outside of the room by means of electrical and pneumatic conductors.[6]

A diagram helps you to picture what goes on when a response becomes conditioned (Fig. 12). The acid stimulus S_1 calls forth the salivary response R_1; the bell S_2 originally arouses only R_2, a response of hearing the bell and probably of postural alertness, pricking up the ears and the like. After the two stimulus-response patterns have occurred together, usually several times, the bell stimulus arouses not only the hearing of the bell but also the salivation. One of the most general ways of describing the conditioned reaction is in these terms: a *part* of a former complex situation may call forth the same *whole* response that was formerly evoked only by the total situation. Of course, something happens in the nervous system when conditioned-reaction learning takes place, but we know all too little about the details of it. A reasonable assumption is that weak or potential neural pathways through the central nervous system exist between all sense organs and all muscles and glands. Adjacent and simultaneously active neural circuits tend to be joined functionally, probably because of a change in conductivity at the synapses, the junction points of neurones. Our use of the empirical fact of conditioning, however, does not have to wait for a complete understanding of its neural basis.

Human Conditioned Reactions

Conditioning is by no means limited to the lower animals. In laboratory experiments, a large number of responses of children and adults have been conditioned, including salivary responses, simple protective reactions such as the eyelid reflex, gross emotional reactions, and many particular segments of emotion including respiratory and circulatory changes and the increased secretion of perspiration. All these responses have been conditioned to a great variety of stimuli. Clinical evidence, too, shows that many real-life human fears can be understood as conditioned responses. You all know people who have some degree of fear of animals, the dark, or crowds. Less commonly, there are people who fear small inclosed places, running water, eyes, and a host of other irrelevant stimuli. Since such fears are not found in tiny children, it is very probable that they are learned.

The classical experiments on the conditioning of emotional reactions were reported by Watson and Raynor in 1920.[7] Typical of their experiments was that with the infant Albert, an eleven-month-old son of a wet-nurse attached to the Johns Hopkins Hospital. Albert, having never been outside the hospital, had been reared in an exceptionally well-controlled environment. It was quite certain that he had never seen an animal prior to the beginning of the experiment. When tested at the outset Albert was found to have only positive approaching reactions to animals such as rats, rabbits, cats, and dogs. The only tested stimuli that elicited fear in Albert were very loud noises and sudden loss of support. At his age, eleven months, fear had probably become differentiated from emotion-in-general, and could be identified correctly. Watson conditioned the infant by presenting a tame laboratory rat simultaneously with a loud noise made by striking an iron bar with a hammer. He describes the experiment as follows:*

> Eleven months, three days old. (1) White rat suddenly taken from the basket and presented to Albert. He began to reach for rat with left hand. Just as his hand touched the animal the bar was struck immediately behind his head. The infant jumped

---

* J. B. Watson, *Psychology from the standpoint of a behaviorist.* (2nd ed.) Philadelphia: J. B. Lippincott Co., 1924. Pp. 232-233.

violently and fell forward, burying his face in the mattress. He did not cry, however.

(2) Just as his right hand touched the rat the bar was again struck. Again the infant jumped violently, fell forward and began to whimper.

In order not to disturb the child too seriously no further tests were given for one week.

Eleven months, ten days old. (1) Rat presented suddenly without sound. There was steady fixation but no tendency at first to reach for it. The rat was then placed nearer, whereupon tentative reaching movements began with the right hand. When the rat nosed the infant's left hand the hand was immediately withdrawn. He started to reach for the head of the animal with the forefinger of his left hand but withdrew it suddenly before contact. It is thus seen that the two joint stimulations given last week were not without effect. He was tested with his blocks immediately afterwards to see if they shared in the process of conditioning. He began immediately to pick them up, dropping them and pounding them, etc. In the remainder of the tests the blocks were given frequently to quiet him and to test his general emotional state. They were always removed from sight when the process of conditioning was under way.

(2) Combined stimulation with rat and sound. Started, then fell over immediately to right side. No crying.

(3) Combined stimulation. Fell to right side and rested on hands with head turned from rat. No crying.

(4) Combined stimulation. Same reaction.

(5) Rat suddenly presented alone. Puckered face, whimpered and withdrew body sharply to left.

(6) Combined stimulation. Fell over immediately to right side and began to whimper.

(7) Combined stimulation. Started violently and cried, but did not fall over.

(8) Rat alone. The instant the rat was shown the baby began to cry. Almost instantly he turned sharply to the left, fell over, raised himself on all fours and began to crawl away so rapidly that he was caught with difficulty before he reached the edge of the table.

In seven combined stimulations, a strong fear of rats had been conditioned. Watson suggests that with more intense stimulation or with a child more sensitively organized (Albert is described as "phlegmatic") the reaction might have been conditioned in one or two trials. Cases are known in which one-trial conditioning certainly has occurred. Further experiments showed that the conditioning was retained over a period of five days without appreciable loss of intensity, and very probably for a much longer time. Furthermore, the fear *generalized* to all furry animals. Although Albert was trained only to fear a rat, tests showed that he now feared a rabbit, a dog, a fur coat, a bundle of cotton wool, and even the whiskers of a Santa Claus mask.

Fears may be learned in ordinary life situations by exactly the same psychological process as that studied in the laboratory. A young woman fears dogs, even though she recognizes her fear as groundless and tries to overcome it. Investigation shows that her mother, too, had a fear of dogs. In childhood, when this girl approached a dog, her mother would shrink back and fearfully call her away. "Get away from that dog," or "Look out, he'll bite you!" The parental warning and the example of her mother's fear caused an emotional reaction, on the basis of previous learning. This fear became conditioned to the sight of dogs. Similar accounts can be given of the origin of fears of mice, rats, and snakes, of strangers, of the dark, and of other situations commonly feared by many persons.

Getting Rid of Conditioned Reactions

Since conditioning occurs so easily, it is a wonder that our lives are not cluttered with a vast number of useless and annoying responses that have been acquired through simultaneous stimulation. How do we get rid of conditioned responses? The laboratory gives an answer.

Pavlov noted that if he sounded the bell a number of times in succession without the food, the salivary response would gradually diminish in quantity and finally cease. To keep the response from disappearing, it had to be *reinforced* from time to time by giving the acid stimulus with the bell. The removal of the response by the unreinforced repetition of the substitute stimulus is known as *extinction*. We are reminded of the boy who cried "Wolf!" when there was no wolf. The response to his cries was quickly extinguished. After a response has been extinguished in one session in the laboratory, it tends to reappear if tested a few days later by what is termed *spontaneous recovery*. The response can then be extinguished again by further unreinforced stimulations, and after several such sessions spaced over a period of time it may be lost permanently.

Extinction suggests a way to cure conditioned fear responses in children. One experiment removed a child's fear of animals by introducing a rabbit into the room while the child was eating.[8] Each day the rabbit was moved a little closer until the child would tolerate its presence tranquilly. In one instance the experiment received a severe setback when the child was scratched by the rabbit, thereby reinforcing the fear. Gradually, however, the fear was eliminated by repeated contact with the rabbit when no adequate stimulus for fear was present. The extinction was aided by other techniques that supplemented the mere repetition of the stimulus. The child saw the rabbit in the reassuring presence of a familiar and trusted adult, was petted, and was engaged in the satisfying activity of eating. The function of all these stimuli was to keep the child from making a fear response, so that the repetition will surely be unreinforced. When a conditioned fear is reduced by evoking it in the presence of comforting stimuli, the process is sometimes given a new name, *reconditioning*. Reconditioning is usually more effective than classical extinction, because the subject learns to make a new response to the conditioned stimulus, a positive or approaching one. Even so, the process may be slow. In the experiment cited, forty treatments over a period of several weeks were required to extinguish a conditioned fear which probably had been learned in one experience.

Common sense seems to say that conditioned responses can be eliminated in another way, by the mere passage of time or the "disuse" of the response. It is true, of course, that we tend to forget unpracticed skills and unreviewed lessons. Research shows, however, that forgetting is not caused by time itself, but by the activities and responses which fill the time.[9] A child who has acquired a conditioned fear of dogs has many other direct and indirect experiences with animals, seeing them under unfearful conditions, noticing the attitudes of his fellows toward them, and hearing favorable stories about dogs. These experiences, rather than the mere passage of time, determine the extinction of his fear. Sometimes a fear continues unabated in spite of such contacts, a matter of great psychological interest which we will take up later. If a strongly conditioned person never has favorable experiences with the feared stimulus the response will survive years of "disuse." A person frightened in an automobile accident will remain afraid of automobiles unless he takes more rides. For the same reason, an aviator is advised to take to the air again immediately after a minor crash or narrow escape, to extinguish his possible fear of flying.

Generalization

Newly learned conditioned reactions are not specific. If a dog is conditioned to respond to a bell of pitch *A*, he will also respond to pitches *B*, *C*, and *D*. The rats of May's experiment, conditioned to fear the buzzer, also showed barrier-jumping responses to the sound of tapping on the glass front of the shuttle box, and to sharp clicks made by a ratchet wheel. A similar observation was made in Watson's experiment. Conditioned to fear the rat, the infant also feared other animals and furry things.

The transfer of a response from the original stimulus to other similar stimuli is called *generalization*, a concept which has great importance in understanding human adjustments. Generalization was demonstrated in an experiment by Miller.[10] Rats were placed two at a time in a box the floor of which was an electrified grid like that of the apparatus shown in Figure 9. The shock was turned on and the rats became active. When by chance the rats struck at each other in the manner that rats use when fighting, the shock was turned off. Soon the rats would start fighting as soon as the shock occurred. (The reinforcement in this experiment was by reward or tension reduction, a matter which is discussed fully in Chapter 5.) In the second part of the experiment, one rat at a time was placed in the box with a white celluloid doll about the size of a rat. When the shock was turned on, the rat struck at the doll. The rat had therefore generalized his "aggression" to the doll, a harmless stimulus object which he had not been taught to strike.

The generalization of emotional drives underlies many prejudices and irrational attitudes. If you have been aroused to emotion by some person or event, the response may be called forth by similar persons or circumstances that are inoffensive in themselves. An antagonistic attitude toward a harsh teacher may generalize to all teachers. One college student reacted with intense emotion to any consumption of alcoholic beverages. If one of his friends as much as took a single drink, he went out of his way to denounce him in most emphatic terms. The explanation, known only to a few, was that the student's father had been a drunkard who treated his mother brutally and finally had deserted her. The intensity of his conditioning made an irrational generalization all the more likely. Such behavior is often called emotional *displacement,* but it is essentially the same process as the generalization of a conditioned response.

The intensity of a response to a generalized stimulus varies with its degree of similarity to the stimulus involved in the original learning. In one series of experiments, human subjects were conditioned to make a response to a tone whose pitch was 153 cycles, and then were tested for their responses to tones of 468, 1000, and 1967 cycles.[11] Generalization occurred and responses were made to all of the tones. But there was a *gradient of generalization;* the intensity of the response decreased gradually as the stimuli became more different from the directly reinforced stimulus. Miller's experiments with the rats also showed a gradient of generalization. A rat placed in the box with both another rat and the doll struck at the other rat. The animal's tendency to strike at the other rat was stronger than the tendency to strike at the doll. But when the doll was presented alone, it received the rat's blows. There was a gradient, or order of preference, from striking at the rat to striking at the doll.

In everyday human behavior, the gradient of generalization is a helpful explanatory principle. If an adolescent is angry with his father but cannot express his feelings directly because the father is absent or, more commonly, because he is afraid to do so, he will generalize or displace his hostility to other persons. Furthermore, the intensity of his anger will depend on how much the other person's role is like that of his father. The adolescent may be hostile to men teachers but not to women teachers; he may vent his anger on adults who are in positions of authority but have no ire toward those who are not. Generalization has constructive effects as well as destructive ones. When a fearful child establishes a warm and secure relationship with one adult, the beneficial change in his attitude may generalize in varying degrees to other adults as well.

Drives as well as other stimuli may be generalized. For example, thirsty rats were trained to run down an alley to get water.[12] Later these same rats were provided with unlimited supplies of water so that they were not thirsty, but half of them were fed and half were hungry. The hungry rats ran down the alley faster, and drank more water at its end, than the non-hungry animals. Their hunger drive had generalized to the response which had reduced thirst. The principle of *drive generalization* helps to understand some human problems. It is not uncommon for an anxious person to eat so excessively that he becomes obese. The drive of anxiety has then generalized to that of hunger. The vague internal discomforts of anxiety are reduced in a measure by satisfying another drive which is also a visceral distress.

Discrimination

A generalized response can be made specific by a further process of learning. In the classical conditioning experiment, if the bell A is sounded again and again, always reinforced by presenting food, and the bell B is repeated without the adequate stimulus ever accompanying it, the response to A will be strengthened and that to B will diminish. Eventually, the laboratory subject will acquire a *discrimination* and will respond to A but not to B.

Discrimination between situations plays an important part in human life. We may learn to respond to the reinforced threats of real danger, but no longer to respond to other cues that have been tested by experience and found harmless.

Inhibition and Disinhibition

What happens to the tendency to respond to discriminated stimuli? When a laboratory dog has learned *not* to respond to the discriminated stimulus B, is his not-responding a passive loss or an active restraining process? The evidence shows clearly that it is a positive process of *inhibition*, which may be seen most readily when the drive is strong and when the stimuli concerned are hard to discriminate. A further type of experiment, which has been performed with both animal and human subjects, gives the most intelligible demonstration of the active character of inhibition. A person or animal is conditioned to respond to a touch at point X on his skin, by simultaneous presentation with an adequate stimulus.[13] If a nearby spot Y is now touched a response is made, due to the typical process of generalization. Training is then given in discrimination by stimulating X frequently with the original stimulus and Y without reinforcement. Differentiation takes place, and the response will be made when *X* is touched, but no longer for *Y*. An important observation may now be made. If *Y* is stimulated and then *X*, no response occurs! The inhibition itself has generalized or "spread," setting up so active a restraining process when the "negative" spot is touched that an immediately subsequent positive stimulation does not overcome it.

Other evidence about inhibition comes from the *delayed* conditioned response. The technique of delayed conditioning may be illustrated from Pavlov's method. The bell is rung and continues ringing; then after a delay of, say, one minute the drop of acid is placed on the dog's tongue. After training is completed, the dog responds to the bell, not when it starts ringing, but after a delay roughly proportional to the delay of the reinforcement during the conditioning trials. The period of delay is one of inhibition rather than of passive waiting. The experimental subject is tense and in a state of readiness during the interval. If some strong stimulation, even though not itself a conditioned stimulus, occurs during the delay, the inhibition is lifted and the dog salivates at once. In one case in Pavlov's laboratory the buzzing of a fly in the dog's ear, and in another a strong odor, were sufficient to precipitate the response. Such a stimulus is said to "inhibit the inhibition." Turning the double negative into one word, it is called *disinhibition.*

Disinhibition may occur in discrimination reactions. Let us return to the experiment in which touching spot *X* on the skin evoked a response, but touching *Y* caused inhibition. If *Y* is touched and immediately afterward a strong extraneous stimulus such as a loud noise is introduced, the response will be made at once. There is a tendency (by generalization) to respond to *Y*, but it is inhibited. When the inhibition is disturbed, the response tendency acts.

The orderliness and effectiveness of your conduct depend as much on what you do *not* do as on what you do. Inhibition is therefore as important as reaction in human adjustments. Practical examples of inhibition and disinhibition are numerous. A young woman is responding with intense grief to the death of her father, but restrains any outward show of emotion and goes about her usual work. At a critical or sarcastic word from her employer, however, she bursts into tears and is uncontrollably emotional. Her colleagues may say that "her nerves are shattered," but experimental psychology offers a simpler and less mysterious account of her conduct. She was making a difficult discriminative response, limiting her expression of grief to times when she was alone or with her family, and inhibiting it elsewhere. The extra stimulation of the scolding inhibited her inhibition. Under many other conditions of excitement or overstimulation inhibitions disappear, and undiscriminative and hence disorganized behavior ensues. The enraged office boy hits the boss and loses his job. The inexperienced driver, in a perplexing traffic situation, steps on the gas instead of the brake and wrecks the car. All these examples involve failures of discrimination because of disinhibition.

Unconscious and Illogical Responses

Many important human drives and responses are *unconscious.* A person has no clear awareness of some of the things he does or of why he does them. The concept of an unconscious response is of such broad significance to the study of human adjustments that it receives repeated attention throughout this book. Some features of the conditioned response furnish a convenient introduction to unconscious behavior.

A conditioned response need not depend on any conscious process or on any voluntary effort. Naive observers of conditioned response experiments might think that the dog salivates because it "expects" food, or that the infant "remembers" the fearful sound that accompanied his first touching of the rat. Nothing of the sort need take place. It is ridiculous to imagine that the dog says to itself, "There's the bell, so the food must be coming and I guess I'll salivate." The salivary response is not controlled by any such conscious processes in human beings who can make so elaborate an introspection, much less in dogs.

Numerous experiments show that conditioning can affect unconscious responses, of which the person is not or cannot be aware through direct experience. One unconscious autonomic reaction that is easily conditioned is the "galvanic skin response," a slight change in the sweat secretion of the hand, originally evoked by any startling or emotion-producing stimulus.[14] The response is measured by electrical means, since a moist surface conducts a current better than a dry one. The galvanic skin response has been conditioned to dim lights and faint sounds in infants under one year old,[15] and in naive adults who did not know the purpose of the experiment.[16] The dilation or contraction of the pupil of the eye in response to changes in the intensity of light,[17] and the small skin temperature changes of one hand which are evoked by cooling the other hand,[18] have also been conditioned to several stimuli. The conditioning of unconscious responses is not at all mysterious. One simply responds to the stimulus without necessarily deliberating, thinking, or remembering. The principle has important implications for human drives and adjustments.

There need be no logical relationship between conditioned stimuli and the conditioned responses, drives, inhibitions, or discriminations they evoke. Nothing could be more absurd logically than for a dog to salivate on hearing a bell. Many human drives and emotional responses are equally irrelevant to the stimuli which arouse them. For a child to fear a harmless rabbit is unreasonable, and for a student to fly into a rage whenever his friend takes a drink is obviously irrational behavior. But such responses are not to be explained by logic or reason. They result from the occurrence together of certain stimuli and responses in the person's past life. The conditioned reaction helps to understand how many features of human behavior are unconscious and irrational.

Some Other Characteristics of Conditioned Responses

The stimulus for a conditioned response can be a *movement of one's own body.* One example is provided by the visceral responses of emotion which act as intervening variables and in turn arouse other activities. Experiments have shown that the kinesthetic stimuli arising from small specific movements may become cues for conditioned responses.[19] In one study, the subjects were first conditioned to blink when a faint light was shown. Then they were stimulated by a tap on the eyelid, which causes blinking, and at the same time by an electric shock which arouses a withdrawal of the finger. Subsequently some of the subjects on being stimulated with the light, were found not only to blink but also to withdraw their fingers, although the light and the shock had never occurred together! The wink and the finger response had been paired repeatedly, however, and the stimuli arising from the *movement* of winking could elicit the finger withdrawal by ordinary conditioning. The light evokes the wink, and the wink in turn evokes the finger retraction. One's own actions, gestures, postures, and the like, can therefore serve as conditioned stimuli. Your conditioned drives and emotional responses are evoked not only by external stimuli, but also by movements and by muscle tension patterns within your body.

The concept of stimulation-from-within-oneself is carried a step farther by other experimental evidence.[20] When one hand is immersed in cold water, the temperature of the other hand drops slightly, because of the constriction of small arteries. By the usual conditioning method of the paired presentation of the cold water and other stimuli, the temperature response of the opposite hand was conditioned in succession to the sound of a buzzer, to a word spoken by the experimenter, to a word whispered by the subject himself, to the visual stimulus of a cross thrown on a screen, and finally to the subject's visual image of the cross. After this conditioning, if the subject whispers a word to himself or "thinks" of a cross, the temperature of his hand goes down! An unconscious autonomic response, ordinarily involuntary and uncontrollable, is arousable by words and thoughts. Since language is the prime medium of social interaction, and since most thinking is talking to oneself, such experiments bridge the gap between the physiology of drives and their social psychology. A word or a thought may stir you to great ambition, or to a panic of fear. These are common observations in everyday life, but they are better understood in the light of controlled experiments.

Conditioning *may affect perceptual responses* as well as motor or glandular ones. A child was once given peach juice with castor oil, supposedly to make it more palatable, but nausea resulted. For many years after that event he suffered an aversion to canned peaches. Not only was avoidance set up, but the peach juice actually *tasted* like castor oil. The perception itself had been conditioned. Similar observations are made in many laboratory experiments that use electric shock as an unconditioned stimulus. When responding to the substitute signal, subjects often report that they *feel* the nonexistent shock. There can be no doubt that perceptual conditioning is also found in the behavior of whole persons as studied by the clinical method. To a person who fears animals, every dog *looks* ferocious; to a boy who has learned an angry antagonism to school, every act of the teacher may be perceived as a malicious attempt to subjugate him. So we learn not only our responses to the world, but concurrently we learn our perceptions of it. In practical problems of adjustment the two are inseparable.

ACQUIRED ADIENT DRIVES

So far, we have been most concerned with learnings based on avoidant drives, especially those derived from negative emotional tensions such as fear and anger. Acquired adience, by which organisms learn to approach, seek, and "like" new situations, are at least equally important.

Experimentally Acquired Positive Drives

The learning of approaching responses to new stimuli has been studied in many experiments, whose subjects have varied from rats to human beings. The studies by Wolfe and by Cowles,[21] performed with chimpanzees, offer instructive illustrations. The chimpanzees were already adient toward food, an acquired though almost universal drive. They would work, seek, and beg for grapes and raisins. The apes were taught to insert tokens, colored poker chips, in a "vending machine" which would deliver food to them. When that primary learning had been accomplished, the tokens themselves became goal objects. The chimpanzees would work for tokens almost as hard and long as for food, would compete with each other for tokens, and would try to beg them from the experimenter.

All the major characteristics of the conditioned reaction were demonstrated with the token rewards. At first, the response to tokens was generalized, and the chimpanzees would work for chips of any color. When one color of token would buy food and another color would buy nothing, a discriminated response was secured and the chimpanzees would work or learn only for the rewarded token. In another experiment, the subjects learned to discriminate between tokens that would earn them one grape, two grapes, water, a period of play with the experimenter, and the privilege of returning to their living cage. When tokens were unrewarded by being no longer exchangeable for anything, the responses to them were extinguished.

The behavior of the chimpanzees toward the tokens was evidently motivated. The sight of a token aroused and sustained activity, and receiving them served as a reward for which the animals would work at difficult tasks and learn new skills. Their attitude toward the tokens was quite analogous to the human regard for money.

Sheep and ducks are notably gregarious, and tend to follow other members of their species. If an orphan lamb is bottle-fed by a person, however, it will tend to follow people and to seek their company to an extent that renders it a nuisance.[22] Farmers call such a lamb a *cosset*, and note that it rarely acquires gregariousness with its own kind. A similar observation has been made of ducks.[23] Newly hatched ducklings, at a certain critical phase of their development, can be taught to follow a person instead of to follow the mother duck. When once established, the response is permanent, and the mature duck so trained in infancy will remain a follower of people the rest of its life. Such observations suggest that adient conditionings early in life, when need is great and past experience is meager, may have especially strong effects. Both anthropological and clinical evidence support the importance of infancy and early childhood in the formation of the pattern of an individual's social relationships.

CULTURE AND MOTIVATION

Members of various human cultural groups may vary considerably in their typical motivations. Some peoples are generally friendly, others suspicious; some are aggressive and striving, others easygoing in their social relationships. There are also similarities. People of each culture work together with some degree of cooperativeness, and all tend to seek the approval of their fellows, though in different ways. What are the sources of these differences and similarities?

The "How" and the "What" of Acquired Drives

One universal similarity among people is *how* they learn. Indeed, humanity shares its basic learning processes with animals much lower in the evolutionary scale. The acquired drives of various peoples are therefore learned in the same fashion, by the substitution of other stimuli for the needs that evoke them originally.

Some other conditions make for a certain degree of uniformity among all human beings. Their physiological needs for air, water, and food, and the most basic aspects of their sex needs, are probably identical. The fundamental emotional patterns, too, seem to be the same for all human infants of whatever race or culture, although emotional behavior begins to vary widely quite early in life because of the influence of learning. The utter dependence of infancy is also a common characteristic of all human beings, and influences many uniformities of behavior, probably including the almost universal tendencies of people to live in groups and to seek one another's support and approval. The innate and intrinsic factors in men mainly tend to make their motives similar rather than different. For the most part, motivational variance between Americans, Russians, Hottentots, and natives of New Guinea cannot be sought in "nature," but in differences between their formative experiences.

People differ because of *what* they learn. The stimuli that will evoke acquired drives are the ones that the environment presents simultaneously with the arousal of primary tensions. To some extent those stimuli are specific to each single person's experience, but in most instances they are greatly influenced by the cultural context in which the learning takes place. In determining learning, "culture" is no simple or unitary force. It is only a convenient term to represent the attitudes, beliefs, and activities of the persons who are in interacting contact with the learner.

The influence of cultural learning on motivation has been appreciated only in recent years, through the impact of objective and thorough studies of cultures differing markedly from our own. A few decades ago, American and European psychologists often prepared lists of "human motives" with little realization that they were describing only their own culture, and usually a limited socioeconomic segment of it, at that. The motives of other peoples, when considered at all, were defined in terms of the deviants of the writer's own culture. Thus a primitive people lacking New England middle-class industry and acquisitiveness were "lazy"; those with different sexual customs were "immoral"; plains Indians whose hygiene was based on a nomadic life in sun, sand, and wind were "dirty" when judged by the standards of people living in small fixed homes. There probably are no intrinsic human motives beyond hunger, thirst, sex, and the like. When different people have similar motives it is because they have had similar learning experiences. When they differ, the causes may also be found in the contexts that have guided their learnings.

Some Cultural Differences in Motivation

Studies by cultural anthropologists have revealed the differing motivations of a number of societies, and have identified some of the learning processes contributing to their formation. Only a few examples can be given here.

Bali, an island near Java, contains about a million people whose old, stable culture has been studied extensively. One outstanding characteristic of Balinese adults and older children is their calm adherence to tradition, and their gentle, relaxed, and unaggressive social relationships.[24] Such behavior defines a pattern of motivation quite different from our own, and is perhaps definable as a low intensity of motives for mastery, pre-eminence, or competitiveness. Numerous observations suggest the origin of this trait.[25] In Bali, infants and very small children are traditionally teased by their parents and by other members of the family, and are stimulated to outbursts of love or anger. As soon as the youngster is thoroughly worked up emotionally, the adults ignore him. They respond neither to his embraces nor to his tantrums. The result seems to be a gradual extinction of the child's strong emotional responses to other people, since they are unresponsive to him. If a little child wanders away, his parents do not chase him in an emotional uproar, but any older child or adult who finds him leads him calmly back. Many other learnings contribute to the learning of the Balinese character. In Bali, it is good etiquette to reach for things only with the right hand. If an infant carried by his mother reaches with the left, the mother pulls back the offending hand gently and extends his right. This is done calmly, monotonously and repeatedly, with no word of scolding. When a girl learns the classic Balinese dances, the instructor sits or stands behind her and gently pulls and pushes her limbs into the required positions. All of these learning experiences, and many others of the same pattern, teach the Balinese child to accept passively the demands of other people and of tradition. Since he learns to conform without being raged at, and without his own early rages being acknowledged, he acquires the easy and unaggressive compliance which marks his culture.

One characteristic of the Sioux Indians of the American plains may be mentioned because of its striking contrast to the Balinese.[26] Like the child of Bali, the Sioux baby is breast fed whenever he demands it, and at least intermittent nursing is often continued until he is three or more years old. Consequently, the Sioux infant rarely cries from helpless need; his parents believe that such crying would make him fearful and a poor hunter. His anger responses are quite another matter. When an older infant is frustrated and has a tantrum, the mother is amused and pleased, and eggs him on to increase the rage. The Sioux believe that such outbursts of anger make the child strong and brave, hence they are to be encouraged. As adults the Sioux are aggressive, very hostile to outsiders, and somewhat quarrelsome among themselves. Their extreme cruelty was notable in the earlier period when they roamed the plains freely. There is certainly a connection between the childhood training of emotion and the adult pattern of motivation. No single aspect of training forms adult character unaided, of course. The one influence cited as an illustration is symptomatic of an attitude of the culture, which gives rise to numerous other training experiences whose cumulative effect is sufficient to produce the traits seen in the adult Sioux.

One does not have to go as far afield as the Balinese and the Sioux to find cultural differences in motivation. They also exist between subcultures in our own society. The motive patterns of middle-class and lower-class children and adolescents in any American city illustrate such differences clearly.[27] Middle-class parents regard physical aggression and early sexual activity as the most dangerous traits that their children can show, and hence suppress them vigorously. The middle-class child's contemporaries, his peer-group culture, also experience the same pressures individually and accept them though not without some resistance. As a result, the youngster's strivings are channeled away from serious fighting, destruction of property, and stealing, into competitive sports played by rules and often even into trying to excel in school. The children and young people from slum areas have fewer restraints placed on them at home. Their parents see aggression and sex as less serious problems, and are themselves more likely to engage in street brawls, domestic quarrels, and unconcealed sexual irregularities. Because of home and community crowding, the slum youngster is thrown more on the resources of his peer-group, which rewards aggressiveness, holds suspicious attitudes about "people putting one over on you," and boasts of early sexual achievements. The slum youth culture is transmitted by punishment and reward from older to younger children and is, to say the least, not effectively counteracted by the culture of the adults who have come through the same training. As a consequence, the acquired motivations of "the American child" are by no means homogeneous. It is necessary to ask "what child?" "from what subculture?" in order to define the motive patterns relating to authority, aggressiveness, school achievement, sex, and property.

Externalizing and Internalizing Drives

Two supplementary processes have special significance for the socialization of drives. The first has already been described and illustrated at length, although it has not yet been named specifically. The *externalization* of a drive is the learning process, through conditioning, by which outer stimuli become capable of evoking inner tensions.[28] That aspect of socialization originates from a person's own drives, which come to be evoked by objects, persons, and social situations, instead of only by his bodily needs.

In the converse process, the demands of the culture are imposed on the individual, so that he adopts and defends them as if they were his own. The *internalization* of cultural requirements starts with a learning process much like that of externalization except for one important difference. The initial distress is emotional, and is aroused by the social acts of other persons. The emotional discomfort thus evoked by social "punishment" can be attached by conditioning to all sorts of external situations and, most of all, to the person's own activities. A simple and perhaps superficial example will make the point clear. A boy's room is in disorder, and his mother makes the youngster uncomfortable in the presence of that disorder. She may do so in various ways, by supervising him in the distasteful task of making it neat, by scolding, by withholding privileges, or by punishment. The mother is the representative of the culture, and evokes tension in the child when he fails to meet a demand that the culture requires.

The first part of the learning process of internalization achieves only one result — it makes one become emotionally uncomfortable in the presence of the cultural demand. The exact "emotion" will depend on the context of the situation. The person affected may call it disgust, annoyance, indignation, anger, anxiety, guilt, or fear, depending on how strongly he has been conditioned and whether the anti-cultural offence is his own or that of someone else. Returning to our illustration, "punishment" of the boy in the presence of his disorderly room will not make him neat; it will only make him stirred up about the situation. He may respond to his arousal in many ways. He may escape from the untidy scene to pleasanter vistas. As often happens, he may under his breath berate the person in authority and only express his anger against her, which means that the learning process has gone in an unintended direction, and the conditioned stimulus has become the punisher instead of the punished act. Or the boy may leave his room in a mess but feel guilty about it. Finally, he may restore the room to the demanded degree of neatness. The last outcome is likely only if one further condition of learning is present, that the neatness of the room has become satisfying, rewarding, or tension-reducing for him.

The full learning sequence involved in the internalization of a drive is therefore a two-step process. First, the punishing culture stirs up an individual's visceral drives in the presence of a situation that the culture abhors, and second, the culture in its rewarding aspects provides tension reduction for the outcomes that it approves. That only the first half is learned in so many instances, and not the second half, is the source of most of the disharmony between a person and his group.

Through learned internalizations, if you are a member of a widely prevalent culture, you are disgusted when you see a person spit on the floor, angry when you see a larger boy bully a smaller one, and embarrassed when an adolescent couple exhibit their love-making too obviously in public. And, in the main, you refrain from doing these things yourself. If you were a member of some other culture, the incidents just cited might concern you very little, but there would be others in their place. Each culture trains its members to experience inner tension when they violate its needs, demands, and customs.

HOW SOME DOMINANT MOTIVES ARE LEARNED IN OUR CULTURE

Motives

So far, we have learned much about the process of motivation without attempting to define "a motive." It has been wise to postpone an attempt at definition, because motive is no simple concept.

Analysis of such motives as "to eat" or "to receive social approval" shows some of the components. To identify any such motive, you must specify the *need* or *situation* that gives rise to it, the *drive* or tension that operates, the behaviors or *mechanisms* that result, and the *adjustment* that will bring the sequence to a close. Any motive involves all of these more elementary concepts. *Motive,* then, is a complex, socially learned pattern involving situation, drive, mechanism, and end-result.

It would be quite possible even to dispense with the word "motive," and to account for all striving behavior in terms of the component categories. In the practical study of human adjustment problems, however, the name of a motive is a convenient brief substitute for a long description. To say that a boy has a motive for approval, or that he strives for mastery, saves us from having to specify the composition of such motives every time we refer to them. It is more economical to describe once for all how some of the dominant motives of the culture are learned, and then to assume a reference to that learning process whenever the motive is mentioned subsequently.

You must be on guard against two dangers that lie in the convenient practice of calling motives by names. First, a named motive is not an entity or thing, but is a way to describe a complex pattern of behavior. The motive of social approval does not *make* a man perform an act; instead it is a description of *how* his acquired drives and mechanisms operate. Second, you must not assume that a named motive always represents the same behavior. The broad motive sometimes called "security" may cover an adult's need to feel sure of continued food and shelter, or his need to feel that he is useful and recognized in the world. In a child, "security" includes the learned need for favorable attention from his parents or from his peer-groups, and his general freedom from hampering anxieties of all kinds. "Security" is therefore no simple motive, but a highly abstract concept of a whole family of more or less related social wants. In spite of these serious objections to the concept of motive, it remains a useful working tool if its complicated meaning is recognized clearly.

No dependable list of motives can be compiled. Even in one cultural segment, the motives are so numerous, so rich in their minor variations, and so likely to differ in degree from one person to another, that they defy enumeration. The following paragraphs give some partial glimpses of the learning processes underlying certain of the more common motives. The selected motives are not an inventory, but only samples that illustrate how motives are acquired.

Approval, Recognition, Affection

Motives to seek the approval of other people, to get attention, to gain sympathy, to be with others rather than alone, and to be recognized as a person of worth, are among the dominant urges of many cultures. The strength of such motivation varies considerably among societies, and seems to be especially strong in the typical American culture. These motives have their beginnings in infancy, chiefly from modifications of the *adient drives* that arise from the satisfaction of vital needs, and from the primary adience-producing stimulations of stroking, fondling, and the like. The infant originally shows adient behavior only to the care and gentle stimulation of its own body. Inasmuch as a mother or nurse is always present when such stimuli are administered, learning soon occurs, and the infant responds favorably to the mere presence of a person who takes care of him. He learns to reach, approach, and facilitate stimulation upon seeing the other person. Similarly, the developing child becomes conditioned to symbolic approvals in the forms of words, gestures and facial expressions. Feeding, petting, and other sought-after stimuli are experienced simultaneously with kind words, a soft tone of voice, and certain gestures and facial expressions. Hence the latter stimuli become potent to call up approaching and maintaining behavior even in the absence of the original direct stimuli. By learning, the child comes to perceive them as satisfying in themselves. The conditionings generalize to other persons in diminishing degrees, as is usual with conditioned reactions. The strength of response is proportional to the similarity between the person calling it forth and the persons from whom the response was learned. A child is more satisfied by the presence or approval of loved (i.e., favorably-stimulating) persons than of others. He is more adient toward the familiar group in which the learning took place than toward strangers.

Infancy and early childhood set the pattern of the socially-positive motives, but learning does not stop then. As adolescents and adults we continue to be rewarded for being in the presence of others and for performing socially approved acts, so that our motivation is reinforced continually.

Case studies of persons who do not act in approved ways, or who seek solitude rather than company, tend to confirm the same account of the learning process. If one's contacts with people are mainly annoying rather than need-satisfying, the opposite responses will be learned. The presence of others will then be avoided rather than sought.

The absence of accustomed adience-producing stimuli, as we have already seen, becomes a positive annoyance and furnishes an emotional drive to activity that ceases when the satisfying stimulus is restored. A baby may cry when petting is discontinued; the child who has been the center of attention "shows off," talks loudly, or turns somersaults when the attention of the group is directed elsewhere; the young man alone for the evening goes out to seek the company of others. Social motives, therefore, are not passive. When you are accustomed to social stimulation you do not wait for it to come to you, but go to seek it. The lack of accustomed companionship or approval evokes increased activity, tending toward the reduction of tension, or adjustment.

Submission, Conformity

A closely related pattern of social motivation is represented by tendencies to submit to the customs of one's group, to conform, to do the expected thing, and to avoid blame and criticism. Motives to submit and conform are the converse of the motives to seek social approval. They seem, however, to have an independent origin. Such motives develop from the *fear* responses of infancy and childhood, which are reactions of emotion and withdrawing made to certain kinds of overstimulation and to the perception of one's helplessness. If painful punishment, either by parents or other adults or by child associates, is accompanied by expressions of criticism, scorn, or blame, a conditioning occurs. In the future, criticism and similar symbolic stimuli become capable of arousing fear tensions. The blameworthy action is inhibited, which may be necessary socially even though the outcome produces tension and therefore distresses the individual. Conformity-conditioning is one of the devices, found in some form in every culture, by which society

maintains its integrity, although often at some cost to the adjustments of individual persons, as we shall see.

If an association between punishment and blame is made very
frequently or very strongly, the conditioning generalizes. A person
so conditioned then comes to react with fear and submission to any
social criticism whatsoever, either expressed or implied. A generalized fear of criticism affects one's perception of other people's
actions, just as all strong motives affect the way the world is perceived. Consequently, a person overconditioned to criticism sees
slights and insults when none are intended, and in popular speech
is said to be "sensitive." We all have a moderate fear of social scorn,
which perhaps is necessary for social control. A stronger degree of
fear is disorganizing, because a person is so preoccupied with
escaping it or combating it that he does not attend to the satisfaction of his other constructive social wants. For that reason, social
training is achieved more effectively by the positive method of
attaching approval to desired responses than by conditioning fear
to undesirable behavior.

Prestige, Mastery, Self-Realization

Our culture gives many examples of motives to excel, to succeed,
to overcome obstructions, to worst a rival, to complete a task once
begun and, in general, to master persons and situations. This is one
of the most variable patterns of motivation from one culture to
another, and is very weak in some societies. Developmentally, mastery motivation seems to originate from *anger* responses. In infants
and young children, anger, or emotion with struggling, is often
aroused by rough restraint, by interference with activity, or by
making demands that thwart a course of action that is under way.
Studies of anger in children show that it occurs more often when
parents are critical of the child and deeply concerned about whether
he is "good" or "bad," and also when they reward a child's anger by
"giving in" to it.[29] Tolerant parents induce fewer anger responses
in their children. Such observations suggest the origin of differences in strong striving responses, both among cultures and
among individuals.

The anger response soon comes to be conditioned to other stimuli,
especially to verbal and other symbolic ones. The parents' saying

"no," frequently accompanied by physical interference with activity, becomes a substitute stimulus for anger. As the child grows older and his circle of contacts widens, other children appear as actual or potential restrainers of his person, his activities, or his possessions. Primitively, the child reacts to such a restraining person or rival by fighting that grows directly from the early struggling responses. Later he responds in a more sophisticated way with increased effort or with planned procedures for overcoming the obstructions offered. All these responses are energized by the inner emotional tension.

As is true for all strong motives in a culture, learning to master or dominate is not limited to the direct conditionings of infancy, but is increased by many other circumstances throughout life. In one study, children from six to thirteen years of age were given a "choice" of two identical pieces of candy, one within reach and one to be attained only by walking around a table or climbing a short ladder.[30] The percentage of children choosing the more distant goal increased sharply with age. The children's reasons for their choices of the harder task showed that many factors influenced the behavior. They had learned that harder tasks are usually better rewarded and more socially approved, or they had learned to enjoy the challenge or adventure, especially of the ladder, for its own sake. Learning to strive develops gradually, since our society rewards competitive success in games, high marks in school, and other evidences of excelling.

The modification of the response of mastery behavior is as important as the extension of the range of stimuli that will evoke it. Originally, the anger response is a random slashing, kicking, and crying. Through learning, the diffuse response is modified into specific activities that are pertinent to various situations. To a parental refusal, the child now responds by pleading, to the rivalry of another child in school by increased effort. The evolution of the response to obstruction is shown in a child's attitude toward a toy that will not work. A younger child may respond with vigorous aggression that will destroy the toy. In an older child the same sort of emotional tension acts as a drive to constructive action in an attempt to discover and remove the difficulty. The most distantly derived form of mastery motivation is seen in the effort and persistence of a scientist or artist toward an abstract problem, on which he may work for years to overcome an obstruction to his understanding or to the achievement of a satisfying product. That motive is often called self-realization, and is shared in some degree by almost all people.

Sex

Certain aspects of the sex drive are modified readily. In lower animals and probably in man in a "state of nature," the sex drive is glandular and physiological and is reduced by direct mechanisms when it arises. In our culture, the direct satisfaction of sexual urges is commonly thwarted at their appearance in infancy and at their strengthening in adolescence by social conventions and other obstacles. The thwarting facilitates the learning of substitute stimuli and responses. By learning processes that are both direct and verbal in nature, the presence of the opposite sex, pictures, books, articles of clothing — in fact an innumerable inventory of objects and events — become sex-arousing stimuli. Many substitute tension-reducing activities such as games, sports, dancing, and even more remotely connected responses become in a broad sense sexually adjustive. Because of their strength, and because direct action is so frequently thwarted or mingled with anxiety and guilt, sex motives are of special importance in many human adjustment problems.

Combined Motives

The strong conditioned emotional motives of social approval, conformity, mastery, and sex are probably too small and arbitrary a sample of human motivation in our culture, important though they may be. Several other categories of motive might have been named as worthily, and their origins traced through learning processes. Furthermore, almost all situations evoke combinations of interacting motives, and all of man's strong motives may be involved in one single act.

If we return to the question of why men work, we find the answer only in many motives. Men work not only to secure food and shelter, but also because work means prestige and self-realization, and because work is applauded by society while idleness is scorned. Men also work because they thus secure the approval and the well-being of individuals to whom they are love-conditioned. To a young man, work means income and therefore money for dates and the possibility of marriage. Work thereby involves the sexual motive.

The *acquisitive* motivation so typical of our culture is complex, and includes subsistence needs, prestige, approval, conformity, and sometimes sex. *Parental love* consists of many components. Although it has its roots in the stimulating effects that nursing, holding, and fondling a baby have on its parents, the factors of social approval and of the sense of accomplishment that comes from the care of a helpless babe are also important. *Security* is one of the most inclusive concepts of motivation, implying the certainty or favorable predictability of the outcomes required by needs for food, shelter, approval, affection, sex, prestige, and self-realization. All these motive patterns are learned, and their form is determined by the culture in which the learning takes place.

Some Other Habits As Motives

The strong, dependable motives of any culture, such as the motive for social approval, are in a sense habits, for they are learned sequences in which drives are aroused and then reduced. Many other habits, less vital and less socially significant, also seem to serve as motives. Let us suppose that a man is in the habit of reading the evening newspaper after dinner. He goes to the door where the newspaper is usually thrown, but fails to find it there. He calls to his wife asking if she has seen the paper, and upon receiving a negative reply he interrupts the play of his children and questions them. They have not seen it either. Then he looks in the shrubbery around the porch to see if the paper could have fallen there, and on his neighbors' porches to determine if it could have been thrown there by mistake. No paper. So, with verbal tension-reducers in the form of uncomplimentary remarks about the newsboy, he puts on his hat and coat and goes forth to buy another copy. When he returns with the paper he sits down to read it with obvious contentment. Must we then postulate a newspaper-reading motive, a cigar-smoking motive, a golf-playing motive and so *ad infinitum?* Such habits are obviously motivated behavior. Activity is aroused and sustained until the stimulus is removed. The parallel between the behavior of the man in search of his newspaper and that of a hungry dog that runs and digs and noses hither and yon, until food puts an end to its drive, is very close and complete. Habits, apparently, may function as **motives.**

One proposed explanation of behavior initiated by habit is that the habits themselves, once they have been well learned, take on an effective driving power, so that they function as autonomous motives apart from organic tensions. Woodworth described that theory in a nicely turned phrase, "the mechanism furnishes its own drive."[31] Allport has named the phenomenon the *functional autonomy* of motives, implying that higher habits operate independently of primitive drives.[32]

As an alternative to "functional autonomy," another explanation may be proposed that is more in keeping with our account of the learned major motives. Most habits are mechanisms of response to fundamental drive tensions. The man reads his newspaper, in the first place, in response to those aspects of approval, conformity, and prestige motives that are satisfied by knowing what is going on in the world and what his neighbors are doing, and by being able to talk about current happenings with his social group. When it is time to read the paper, the tensions underlying those strong motives are aroused. The newspaper-reading situation has become a conditioned stimulus that can evoke an emotional tension as drive. The operation of a habit as a motive is therefore pictured quite adequately by Figure 8 (p. 55). The specific response is determined by the total situation ($S_o - R_s$), but the drive comes from the concurrent emotional tension ($R_v = S_v$).

A supplementary view of the action of habits as motives is that in our culture the interruption of an activity is reacted to as restraint, and hence evokes an anger-conditioned drive of effort. A child who is playing with his blocks reacts with anger if they are summarily removed. An adult reacts with effort, sometimes considered obstinacy, to attempts to change his habits, and not infrequently flies into a full-fledged rage as well. Since most strong habits are acquired as elaborations of strong drives, when the habits are thwarted the strong motives are thwarted indirectly.

THE ORGANIZATION OF MOTIVES

Every one of us responds to his environment as a whole person. Our motives and adjustments do not operate separately, but as interacting systems. Each aspect of behavior is related to and influences every other aspect. In studying motives, we have had to take the whole person apart for purposes of scientific analysis. Let us now put him back together by considering some concepts that emphasize the wholeness of human nature.

Attitudes

An attitude is an organization of motives around an individual's responses to a person, situation, or institution. Attitudes show an evaluative personal reaction. The basic attitudes are acceptance and rejection, which correspond to the elementary drives of adience and avoidance. They are often so defined in practical studies, in which one's attitude toward political liberalism, toward religion, or toward motion pictures means the degree to which these institutions are accepted or rejected. When they are extreme, attitudes of acceptance and rejection may be called "love" and "hate." Such attitudes are not simple emotions or motives because they cannot exist apart from a relationship to a person or object, and because the situation may call forth different emotions at different times, still consistent with the core of the attitude. Someone toward whom you have an attitude of love evokes adient motivation when he is present, fear when he is in danger, and anger when he is threatened. Conversely, a hated person elicits fear or anger or both when present, anger when he succeeds, and joy when he is overthrown.

Experiments have shown that established attitudes have an organizing influence on a person's motivated behavior in new situations.[33] For example, people learn and remember more efficiently the arguments that support their favorite political theory than arguments against that theory.[34] The previously formed attitude is a selective factor to determine what will be perceived, learned, and believed.

No new psychological principles are needed to account for attitudes. Motive patterns are always learned in connection with particular persons or situations, so that it is not at all surprising that attitudes come to be attached to people and events. Because of generalization in learning, we would expect that an established motive pattern would tend to arise in situations similar to the one in which it was learned. Furthermore, conditioned emotions and acquired drives are learned together in complex situations that call forth more than one simple response. The same learning experiences that make you reject a person also make you feel relief when you see that person defeated or removed. Primary learning experiences are themselves complex, and account for the complexity of the motives that are learned. Indeed, the "separate" motives that we studied apart as a matter of convenience really exist only in such organized wholes. The concept of attitude is useful in emphasizing the integrated nature of motivation in real-life affairs.

The Self Concept

While you are acquiring drives and learning attitudes that relate to situations in your environment, you are also learning attitudes about yourself. Every attitude, in fact, involves a relationship between two major aspects, the environmental situation toward which it is directed, and the effect of that situation upon you as a person. Attitudes therefore involve not the situation alone or the person alone, but a "field" defined by the relationship between the two. The common factor in all such relationships is the person himself; the situations vary from one experience to another, but it is always the same "you." Because of more frequent and more intense experiences, you learn more about yourself than you do about external situations, and tend to generalize the common elements of your many learnings. The learned anticipation that you will accept or be accepted in certain circumstances, or that you will reject or be rejected, has been called the *self concept*.

The self concept is a pattern of attitudes and is learned in the same way as other attitudes. There is nothing basic or intrinsic about your self concept. You are not born with it; it is the integration of countless learning experiences. Like other attitudes, the self concept has an influence on perception and motivation in new situations. We have already seen that your attitude toward, say, the Chinese will determine to some extent what you will remember and believe about them. The self concept is no more mysterious, and operates in the same way. A man who conceives himself as a humorist will take every opportunity to clown, and one who conceives himself as unappreciated and scorned will perceive rejection in many innocent acts of other people. Because the self concept shapes new experience to conform to its already established pattern, much behavior can be understood as a person's attempt to maintain the consistency of his self concept, a kind of homeostasis at a higher psychological level.

Some writers have called the self concept the "self" or "ego." [35] To do so involves the danger of confusing a dynamic process of striving, perceiving, and behaving with a thing or entity.[36] The "self" is no entity, except as it means the behavior of the whole person. The "ego," if the concept makes any sense at all, is the integration of one's acquired drives, perceptions, and habits. Although we can get along without these words, they have served a useful end in calling attention to the person-centered nature of motivation.

Goals and Purposes

A *goal* is the end-activity or consummatory response that terminates a sequence of motivated behavior. When hunger is the drive, the goal is to eat. In many circumstances, a motive can be identified only by noting the response that brings activity to a close. In laboratory experiments, you cannot tell whether a rat is hungry or thirsty just by watching its restless movements, but you can observe whether it will choose food or water when offered both. Similarly, a mother confronted with a restless, crying infant often cannot know what drive is operating. She tries one means after another until she locates the cause of the distress, whether a pin, flatulence, cold, or hunger.

Originally, no one has an innate knowledge of his goals. A hungry infant does not "know" that eating will relieve his discomfort; he is merely restless and tense. Many important goals remain similarly unconscious throughout life. An anxious adult who is experiencing difficulties of social adjustment is usually unaware of exactly what is bothering him. His drives tend toward adjustive goals, but he does not have a clear idea of what these goals are. He only knows that certain acts of aggression, defense, or withdrawal make him vaguely feel better. The criterion of a goal is therefore not awareness but drive reduction. Any act or event that satisfies a drive-stimulus is a goal.

Of course, we learn to recognize many of our goals. When such learning has occurred, we strive toward the goal instead of merely away from the discomfort.

A *purpose* is the symbolic representation of a goal. A tiny infant reacts to hunger merely by increased restlessness, but an adult not only responds to the drive but can also state a purpose. He says, "I am hungry. I am going to get something to eat," thereby recogniz-

ing the motive in word symbols and indicating the goal by which
he has learned to satisfy the drive. Purpose involves a knowledge
of the need and of the goal, but does not necessarily imply that one
knows the mechanism by which the end-result may be reached. A
student may purpose to solve a problem in mathematics, but may
not know all the steps needed to reach the solution. Purposes obviously are learned behavior, as are all other behaviors that use
language and other symbols.

The concept of purpose helps to understand behavior that leads
to remote or delayed satisfactions. A well-formulated purpose to
become a physician may involve years of preliminary work, much
of which is not directly satisfying to the motive. Purpose permits
one to set up intermediate subgoals, such as completing courses
and passing examinations, that become satisfying in themselves
because of their relation to the entire sequence. The postponement
of immediate rewards for larger ones to be received at a distant
time is the very criterion of mature and intelligent social behavior.

RESTATEMENT

The study of culturally-derived motives, attitudes, and purposes
has taken us far from the elementary biological drives that impel an
organism to activity. A restatement of fundamentals is needed lest
we be lost in a maze of verbal fancies. Primarily, drives are stimuli,
especially those internal stimuli that occur as visceral tensions.
Visceral drives such as appetites, sex, and emotion are the arousers
of strong persistent activity. By learning, they come to be evoked
by many substitute stimuli. From these tensions, and from primary
adience, come the culturally determined motives of approval, conformity, mastery, and the like. Motives are drives that have been
modified through learning, by the extension of the range of stimuli
that can arouse them, and by the refinement of the activity that
results. The complexity of human motivation, however, cannot be
reduced to any scheme of a few dominant motives. Habits, attitudes, and purposes, all forms of learned behavior, also function
as springs of human action, but they do so *only through the operation of the "lower" fundamental drives of physiological and emotional tensions.*

SUGGESTED READINGS

Much of Shaw and Ort's interesting *Personal Adjustment in the American Culture* is concerned with socially acquired motives. The same topic is discussed instructively and incisively in Dollard and Miller, *Personality and Psychotherapy,* and in Mowrer, *Learning Theory and Personality Dynamics.* Murphy's Chapter 16 in Lindzey, *Handbook of Social Psychology* is another generally useful reference. For experimental evidence on learned motivation, see Miller's Chapter 13 in Stevens, *Handbook of Experimental Psychology.*

Part Four of McClelland, *Personality* is particularly valuable for students who would like to try something a little more advanced than the present treatment, and the chapter on "Anxiety" in O'Kelly and Muckler, *Introduction to Psychopathology* will prove of interest for those concerned with motivation in disordered persons. There are also a number of useful papers in the anthology edited by Kluckhohn, Murray, and Schneider, *Personality in Nature, Society, and Culture.* For an instructive glimpse of motivations in primitive cultures, see Margaret Mead's Chapter 12 in Carmichael, *Manual of Child Psychology.*

CHAPTER 4

Frustration and Conflict

Most of your physiological and social needs are satisfied fairly promptly and completely. In our culture, it is exceptional for a person to go entirely hungry or in need of shelter, and there are also numerous opportunities to achieve a reasonable amount of social satisfaction from having friends, from receiving the approval of people, and from gaining self-realization. In such instances, each adjustment process is brief, although it still shows all the main characteristics of adjustment. A drive is aroused and is then reduced, after more or less delay, by well-learned and effective mechanisms.

There is special interest, however, in adjustments that are achieved only in the face of difficulties. Even though many of our needs are met easily, it is also true that all of us have at least some strong motives that are not entirely satisfied. Few people have all the prestige, approval, or self-realization they might want. It is quite normal for people to encounter some difficulties in their personal adjustments. To be thwarted a little may even be desirable, for it keeps us trying and adds to the zest of life when success finally is achieved. Severe and continued thwarting of motives, on the other hand, often forces a person to accept substitute adjustive solutions that are less satisfying individually and less effective socially. The outcome depends on the intensity and kind of thwarting, and on one's ability to tolerate it.

Two main varieties of thwarting can be distinguished, frustration and conflict. A *frustration* is an external circumstance or an act of another person that prevents the reduction of an aroused drive. An adolescent may want to use the family car to drive to a dance, but be frustrated because the automobile is out of order, or because his father forbids him to use it.

Conflict is somewhat different. A youngster may want to go to a dance because he must do what his friends do in order to be treated as a member of the group and to feel that he belongs. For an adolescent in our culture that is a very strong source of motivation. But the youth may be a clumsy dancer and sensitive to the real or imagined ridicule of his fellows. Therefore, he also has a motive to avoid the dance to escape humiliation. The boy is in a dilemma. Whether he goes to the dance or whether he stays away, he will experience unreduced tension. A *conflict* is the arousing of two or more antagonistic patterns of motivation that cannot be satisfied together.

Frustrations and conflicts are not entirely separate, for many real-life situations involve both. The distinction is a useful one, however. Uncomplicated frustration ordinarily results in more constructive readjustment than do some of the common kinds of conflict.

FRUSTRATION

Our knowledge about frustration and its effects comes from many sources: from observing people in everyday life, from clinical studies, and from a number of experiments.[1]

The most obvious and important effect of frustration is that it ordinarily leads to *varied behavior*. If you are prevented from attaining a goal in one fashion, you will try a different method and then another until some solution is reached. If the original goal is unattainable under the circumstances, you are likely to accept a substitute or compromise one that brings at least partial satisfaction. Varied responses, however, are not solely the result of frustration, but arise from any type of thwarting, including both frustration and conflict. We shall therefore defer the detailed study of them until later. Meanwhile, some evidence should be examined which pertains directly to the effects of frustration.

Frustration and Strength of Motive

When you are frustrated, you will usually try harder to reach the blocked goal. There is evidence, too, that a forbidden satisfaction is often perceived as more attractive than one more easily attained. The grass looks greener on the other side of the fence.

Some information about the effect of frustration on drive strength comes from studies of rats. First, each rat was trained to run down an alley to a first goal box where he received a pellet of food, and then to run down another alley to a second goal box where he was again fed. When the sequence had been learned, the rats were frustrated on alternate trials by giving them no food in the first box. Rats ran down the second alley faster after having been frustrated than after receiving food in the first goal box.[2] It is evident that the frustration had increased the strength of their drive. In another series of experiments, rats were able to learn to make one response when frustrated and another response when not, demonstrating that the frustration drive may serve as a cue.[3]

A milder form of response to frustration has been investigated by studies of the effect of barriers on human motivation. Will people choose a goal just because it is harder to attain? In one experiment, a group of student waitresses who did not know they were being observed were made to choose desserts from a row of plates at the edge of a serving table or from another row of identical desserts placed eighteen inches farther back.[4] When choosing desserts for their own dinners, the waitresses picked from the back row, harder to reach, about 50 per cent more often than from the easier front row. In striking contrast, they selected desserts to serve other people from the front row 97 per cent of the time. When the dessert was a favorite one, as determined by a ranking of preferences, there was a greater tendency to choose for themselves from the back row; when the dessert was less well liked the difference in selection diminished. The stronger the motive, the more it was enhanced by a barrier. Too great a frustration decreased the drive, however. When the back row of desserts was placed thirty-two inches from the table edge, an uncomfortable arm's length away, a dish from the nearer row was chosen almost universally.

Experiments with children have generally shown similar results, but not quite so decisively as the studies of adults. In one study, kindergarten children usually chose toys they could reach only by opening a gate to enter an enclosure, in preference to equated toys on a nearby table. The children also rated toys "nicer" that were shown to them under a wire basket in comparison to similar toys on the open table.[5] Another series of studies has shown that the tendency of children to select a more difficult goal instead of an easier one increases with age (p. 89).

The strengthening of a drive by a moderate degree of frustration is a general characteristic of living organisms as shown by the studies of rats. Such behavior in a human being may be greatly modified by what he learns in his culture. If you learn that harder goals are more desirable, that people praise you for striving toward them, and that such goals may be attained by exerting efforts, then you tend to be challenged by barriers and difficulties. A frustration then evokes your socially learned motives for mastery and prestige. If the original drive is weak or if the barriers are insurmountable, frustration may decrease effort instead of increasing it.

Frustration and Aggression

From the observation that frustration may increase the strength of drives, it is only one step to the next principle, that frustration often results in aggression.[6] Examples are numerous. A young child, when persistently ignored by parents who previously have given him much attention, is quite likely to show his aggression toward them in many ways, by refusing to conform to routine, by marking the walls with crayon, or by wetting his bed. A woman who feels insulted or slighted by her neighbors may be incited to criticize their houses, clothing, manners or conduct, or to assault their reputations by gossip. The aggressions may be direct attacks against the frustrating persons, or may be displaced to innocent objects if the circumstances inhibit overt aggression. A harassed business man may vent his pent-up feelings by thrashing his young son for a minor misdeed.

An experiment by Sears, Hovland, and Miller, designed to study the results of frustration, kept a group of college students awake all night with the excuse that they were measuring the effect of fatigue on certain tests.[7] The men were subjected to a number of planned thwartings, including forbidding them to smoke, breaking up their conversations with periods of silence, and deliberately neglecting to provide them with promised games and food. The aggression shown by the subjects was unmistakable and was directed mainly against the experimenters. The students made derogatory remarks about the sanity of psychologists and belittled the importance and conduct of the supposed experiment. During the night one subject made a number of crude sketches of mutilated and bleeding bodies. When asked what the pictures represented, he replied, "psychologists."

A number of broader social implications have been drawn from the hypotheses that relate aggression to frustration.[8] The persecution of minorities has been attributed to a displaced aggression resulting from social and economic frustrations experienced by the dominant group. The aggression of a warlike nation, such as Germany from 1932 to 1945, has been blamed on internal frustration which results in displaced aggressiveness toward external "enemies." Such generalizations are true to some extent, but they are probably not the entire explanation of complex social phenomena. Exceptions are conspicuous. For example, a persecuted minority is certainly a most frustrated group, but it is generally meek and fearful rather than itself aggressive.[9]

In clinical studies of individual persons, aggression is found to be a frequent response to frustration, but it is only one of several possible responses. A person may react to frustration by withdrawing or by compromising as well as by aggression, depending on the intensity of his thwarted drive, the strength of the frustration, the threat of punishment for aggression, and his past habits of adjusting. Not all aggression comes from frustration. Sometimes it is the rewarded attitude in a social group, as may be seen in certain primitive societies and in some gangs of boys.

Frustration and Regression

Frustration can cause a person's behavior to become less flexible, less constructive, and less imaginative. In brief, behavior under frustration is likely to become more primitive and less mature. For example, an unfrustrated child may play imaginatively and constructively with some toys, showing good ability to organize complex and varied activities. If we frustrate him, the child may revert to

banging the toys together or to repeating a simple activity monotonously. Such a change from better organized to more primitive
behavior is called *regression*. Regression may be conceived as the
opposite of growth, except, quite fortunately, that it is likely to be
temporary and is usually evoked in specifically frustrating situations.

A notable experiment on the effects of frustration on children
was carried out by Barker, Dembo, and Lewin.[10] Thirty children,
two to five years old, were studied in small groups. First, the children were observed in a playroom, playing with a standard set of
ordinarily attractive toys. Observations and ratings were made of
the character of their play. Next a movable partition was raised,
revealing extremely delightful play resources including a large doll
house and a play pond with an island, a lighthouse, and boats to
sail on real water. The children were allowed to play with these
more attractive toys. Then came the frustration period. The children were brought back to the first set of simple playthings and a
wire screen was lowered to prevent them from approaching the
more attractive toys. They could see the doll house and pond but
could not get near them. The situation proved very frustrating, and
the children spent an appreciable part of their time trying to circumvent the barrier, appealing to the experimenter, or trying to
withdraw from the room. Careful behavior descriptions and ratings
showed that their post-frustration play with the simpler toys was
less mature and constructive than it had been prior to the thwarting.
On the average, the children regressed to a play level about a year
and a half younger. There were individual differences, of course.
The children who were most frustrated as judged by the persistence
of their attempts to overcome the barrier also regressed the most in
their play behavior. A few children who showed weak frustration
improved in the constructiveness of their play.

Regression as a response to frustration is not limited to children.
Adults who feel thwarted often display conspicuously "childish"
behavior, becoming peevish and unreasonable in their attitudes.
The regressive response is not incompatible with the aggressive one
described previously. Indeed, regression is probably the broader
concept, for most aggressive behavior can also be described as less
constructive, less flexible, and less mature. The two descriptions
of reactions to frustration go very well together.

CONFLICT

The ongoing course of adjustive behavior may be blocked when two or more incompatible motive patterns are aroused at the same time. A young woman very much in love with a married man suffers from the thwarting of her love and sex motives by conflict with her also well-established tendencies to seek the approval of her cultural group and to conform to its standards. The two conflicting impulses do not cancel each other out, but give rise to increased tension and in turn to restless and vacillating activity.

The concept of conflict is a useful one in psychology if you do not interpret it in animistic terms. It is easy to get an erroneous picture of two motives fighting with each other inside the person as if they were separate and living little demons. Nothing of the sort takes places, of course. Conflict means that a person is confronted by a complicated situation to the different aspects of which he has learned to make incompatible responses. To the love aspect of her situation, the young woman has a tendency to make an approaching response toward the person she loves. Considerations of conformity and approval impel her to make an avoidant reaction. Since the two contradictory responses cannot be made together, the tension remains unreduced and a further adjustment is demanded. In a frustrating situation, a person has no adequate response that will enable him to surmount the barrier. In a conflict situation, on the other hand, he has too many responses and the adjustment must be a selection or a compromise.

An Analysis of Conflicts

A system of concepts and diagrams originated by Kurt Lewin is helpful in analyzing and understanding conflicts.[11] Lewin represents a conflict as an interaction between an individual and the events of his environment. Every person, object, or happening in your psychological environment tends to attract or repel you in some degree. An object's *valence* is the degree to which it evokes approaching or avoiding responses. A positive (+) valence is a goal or an anticipated source of satisfaction. A negative (−) valence is a cue for avoidance. Valences, of course, are not intrinsic in the objects themselves but arise from your attitudes toward those objects.

Your response to every environmental event that has a valence other than zero is either to approach it or to retreat from it more or less strongly. Lewin called such behavior tendencies "forces," but they may be recognized as identical with the fundamental types of motivation previously described as adience and avoidance. The "force" between a person and a situation is proportional to the strength of the valence. It is also inversely proportional to the "psychological distance" of the object. A distant goal is ordinarily approached less strongly than a similar one nearby, and a remote or improbable threat evokes less avoidance than an equal threat that is close or immediate. These "forces" or response tendencies may be represented by lines that show their direction and strength. A shorter line represents a weaker impulse and a longer line a stronger one (Fig. 13).

One possible misunderstanding of negative valences needs clarification. Avoidance has been defined (p. 40) as an action that persists until the distress-producing stimulus is removed. There are

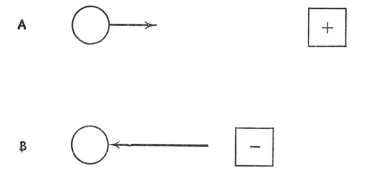

**Figure 13. Response-Tendencies to Situations
Having Positive and Negative Valence**

In A the person, represented by the circle, has a weak approaching tendency toward the distant object with positive valence, indicated by the square. In B, the person has a stronger avoiding response to the nearer object with the negative valence. In general, the intensity of the response depends both on the strength of the valence and on its distance. (After K. Lewin.)

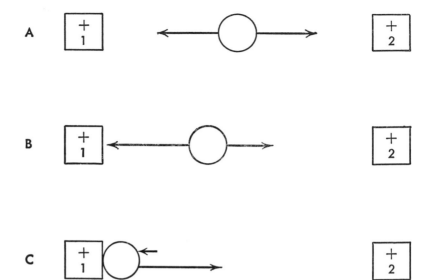

Figure 14. Approach-Approach Conflicts

The approach-approach conflict in **A** occurs when two equally strong valences 1 and 2 are about equally distant.

Some minor variation in behavior or in the environment may bring the person psychologically nearer to 1, as in **B**. Since the impulse to go toward 1 is now strengthened because of decreased distance, and the impulse to go to 2 is weakened correspondingly, the conflict is easily solved.

In **C**, the drive toward 1 has been weakened by satisfaction, making it now weaker than that toward 2. Vacillation then occurs, and the person will approch 2. (After K. Lewin.)

two direct ways for removing a distressing stimulus — to run away from it, or to chase it away from you. Angry and hostile impulses are avoidant drives because their goal is to put an end to an annoyance, even though you may have to approach a person physically in order to assault him or frighten him away. Anger and hostility are therefore classified as negative (—) valences.

Since there are only two kinds of valence, positive and negative, there can be only three basic types of conflict. A conflict may occur between the tendencies to approach two objects that lie in opposite or incompatible directions, or to avoid two threats located so that escaping from one involves getting closer to the other. Or, there may be a conflict between approaching and avoiding tendencies called forth by the same person or object. The three types are called approach-approach, avoidance-avoidance, and approach-avoidance conflicts, respectively.

Approach-Approach Conflicts

When adient drives of about equal strength are evoked togethei by situations that lie in opposite directions and cannot both be satis- fied, you have an approach-approach conflict (Fig. 14). A child may have to choose between watching his favorite television pro- gram and playing out of doors with other youngsters. A student trying to decide between two attractive and practicable careers, and even a woman shopper weighing the merits of two new hats, also illustrate that type of conflict.

Theory, experiment, and clinical observation all indicate that approach-approach conflicts tend to be solved easily, and rarely cause much distress. A minor fluctuation of your behavior or of the environmental context may bring one goal a little nearer (as shown in Fig. 14, *B*), or a new perception may increase the valence of one of the two objects. The boy's friend holds up a bat and glove outside his window, and the boy forsakes the television to join his playmates. The nearer he gets toward one goal, the more attractive it becomes. The balance of the drives is upset and a choice is made.

Vacillation may occur during an approach-approach conflict if circumstances cause the strengths of the almost equal valences to vary. Also, since satiation and fatigue reduce the strength of a motive, a person may return to the alternative that he rejected at first (Fig. 14, *C*). After tiring of outdoor play, the boy may seek his television programs again. The career that one gave up and the hat that one did not buy may also look more desirable in retrospect.

Sometimes what is apparently an approach-approach conflict may give rise to tension and worry. A young woman choosing between two suitors for marriage will often be genuinely distraught. That is because of a concealed negative valence that renders the conflict really an approach-avoidance one in part. Her decision is regarded as irrevocable, and she has to give up the pleasant company of one suitor if she chooses the other. The conflict therefore has a negative aspect of fear or avoidance.

Avoidance-Avoidance Conflicts

A second type of conflict is evoked by two negative valences (Fig. 15). Here both situations evoke tendencies to escape pain,

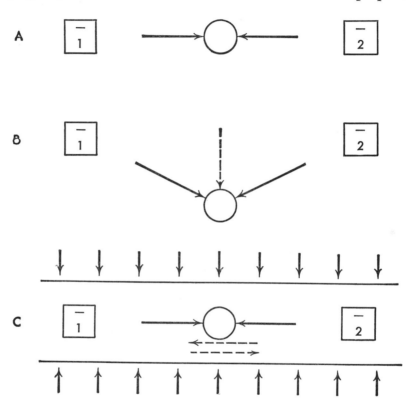

Figure 15. Avoidance-Avoidance Conflicts

A. The avoidance-avoidance situation is a conflict between two negative valences.

B. The usual solution is to "leave the field," escaping both threatening alternatives by some third course of action.

C. If physical or psychological barriers prevent him from leaving the field, a person can only show tense and vacillating behavior at the choice point. (After K. Lewin.)

disapproval, or threat, and you are caught between the frying pan and the fire, or between the devil and the deep sea. A youngster may want to avoid the unpleasant task of mowing the lawn and also escape the threat of his parents' displeasure. The dynamics of an avoidance-avoidance conflict are quite different from those of the first type. If a variation in behavior takes you nearer to one of the negatively charged situations, the strength of the avoidant tendency is increased, and you again withdraw to the middle ground at which the sum of the two threats is minimized.

Many avoidance-avoidance conflicts are solved by *leaving the field,* which is taking another course of action that escapes both the negative valences (Fig. 15, *B*). Applying the principle to a simple conflict, a guilty boy who has been caught stealing apples takes a course that leads equally away from the irate farmer (*1*) and a barking dog (*2*). His path of retreat will be the resultant of the two avoidance tendencies. There are also psychological ways of leaving the field. The boy who wants to get out of mowing the lawn may develop aches and pains in his legs, or discover that tomorrow's school assignments are unfinished. Thus he avoids both the undesired task and his parents' threat of punishment. Another recourse is for the boy to work haltingly and perfunctorily at his job while daydreaming of more pleasant activities. Daydreaming is a very common way to escape from unpleasant conflicts.

If physical, psychological, or social barriers prevent leaving the field, a person can only vacillate in the face of his conflict (Fig. 15, *C*). His freedom of action may be hampered by the presence and pressures of other people. More often, the boundaries are the internalized standards that a person has learned so well from his culture that he feels acute distress when he contemplates escaping by an action that the group regards as inferior or dishonorable.

Some weaker conflicts solve themselves in time by a change in the valences of the alternatives. A negative valence can sometimes become neutral or even positive, as when a boy finds that mowing is not uncongenial labor, or when he begins to take pride in the appearance of the lawn. An increase in one of the negative valences may also resolve a conflict. A negligent student may put off studying until the increased threat of impending examinations forces him to the task.

There are times when a person cannot solve an avoidance-avoidance conflict at all, because of the strengths of the drives and of the boundaries. He then remains in a tense and pent-up state, with a strong unreduced anxiety drive to evoke undifferentiated activity. Aggressive, dependent, or withdrawing responses may then serve to reduce his immediate tension, even though they do not resolve the basic conflict. That is the origin of many apparently irrational forms of adjustive behavior.

Approach-Avoidance Conflicts

Approaching and avoiding tendencies are often evoked together by the same person or situation (Fig. 16). When the negative valence is based on nothing more severe than fatigue, reluctance to exert oneself, or simple avoidance, an approach-avoidance conflict may be no more disorganizing than any other type. A boy is offered a reward to carry out a task that he does not want to do. If the recompense is small he will still refuse, although with some

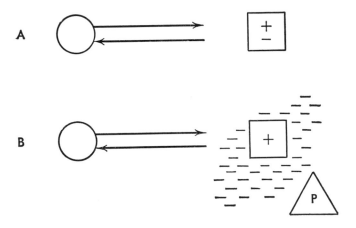

Figure 16. Approach-Avoidance Conflicts

A. An unresolved approach-avoidance conflict causes unreduced tension, since the positive valence holds the person near to the conflict and prevents him from leaving the field.

B. One of the valences of the conflict may be induced by the presence and actions of another person, P. The object has a positive valence for the individual but is surrounded by negative valences arising from the threat or disapproval of the other person. (After K. Lewin.)

regret for failing to receive the gain. If the incentive is enough he will accede, but not without grumbling. Evenly matched valences bring vacillation and maintain the tension.

One of the valences of an approach-avoidance conflict may be "induced" by the presence and attitude of another person (Fig. 16, *B*). A child at the seashore may want to dash into the forbidden waves, but his parent's watchful eye surrounds the desired objective with a field of negative valences. The converse occurs when you are influenced to do something that ordinarily is avoided because it will bring the approval of an esteemed person or group. A boy hesitates on the high diving board, afraid to plunge, but mindful of his prestige before his watching contemporaries.

The most severe of all conflicts arise from approach-avoidance when the negative valence is fear or a derived motive based on strong fear. A boy wants to play active games typical of his age-group to gain approval and mastery ($+$), but he is afraid of being hurt or has formed a concept of himself as clumsy and incapable ($-$). A child is dependent ($+$) on his mother, but fears ($-$) that he will lose her love and support. Such conflicts cannot be solved by leaving the field, because the positive valence attracts the person toward the focus of the conflict. If he withdraws a little his fear is reduced by the greater distance, but his adient motivation brings him back. His approach to the conflict then reactivates the fear and avoidance and a vicious cycle is set up. The opposing impulses do not counteract each other, but leave their unfortunate possessor tense and distressed. The end result is similar to that of an avoidance-avoidance conflict when barriers prevent one from attempting alternative solutions.

The Relation Between Frustration and Conflict

When one person frustrates another, a common outcome is aggression against him. The thwarted child comes to blows with his tormenter or at least is not inhibited from expressing his aggressive feelings in words and thoughts. If the frustrating person is a child's mother, his behavior may be quite different. Past experiences have taught the child that aggression toward his parents will be punished. Even worse, he may have been threatened with the loss of his mother's love and care if he is "bad." Frustration then brings a momentary tendency to aggression which is quickly supplanted by fear. By this process, the boy learns to fear his own aggressive impulses. Simple frustrations become transformed into approach-avoidance conflicts, the conflict arising between his dependence and his fear that his own aggression will alienate the person on whom he is dependent.

Fear of one's own aggression may cause conflict in situations other than the parent-child relationship. People learn to be dependent on teachers, on employers, and on their whole cultural group. Aggressive feelings against any of these may induce a conflict because of the fear of losing good will and support.

EXPERIMENTAL STUDIES OF CONFLICT

Numerous experimental studies have added to our knowledge of conflicts and their effects. An experiment has one main advantage over a clinical observation, that the conflict is produced under defined and controlled conditions so that the effects of various factors can be separated for detailed study. Most of the experiments on conflict have been performed with lower animals, whose lives can be controlled more completely than would be possible with human subjects. It is especially necessary to use animals in studies of artificially induced abnormal behavior, since it would not be wise to expose human beings to the risk of possible harm. Experimental conflicts have been induced in dogs, cats, sheep, rats, and a number of other animals. Some weak and harmless conflicts have also been employed in experiments with people, the results of which confirm the findings of the animal studies.

Conflicts in Cats

In a series of varied experiments, Masserman studied the effects of conflict on cats.[12] His experiments had a "clinical" quality, since the procedure was often varied from one cat to another, and the results were reported as qualitative descriptions of individual behavior, in contrast to the averaged and quantitative data usual in the records of laboratory studies. The originality and imaginativeness of the researches, and their direct applicability to human problems, somewhat offset the lack of formal experimental treatment of the results.

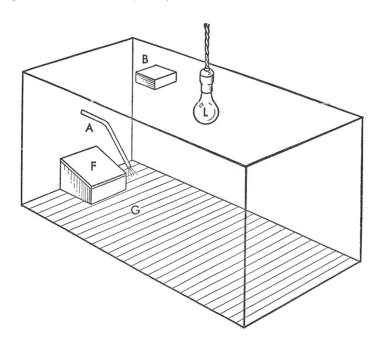

Figure 17. Apparatus for Inducing Conflict in Cats

First, the cat was trained to lift the lid of the food box (**F**) and eat whenever the light and buzzer (**L,B**) signals were given. Conflict was induced by stimulating the cat with an air-blast (**A**) or an electric shock given through the floor grill (**G**), or both, while it was eating. Acute disturbances of behavior resulted. (After J. H. Masserman, *Behavior and neurosis.* Chicago: Univer. of Chicago Press, 1943.)

Each cat was placed in a glass cage 40 by 20 by 20 inches in size (Fig. 17) and equipped with a food box at one end. The cats were trained quite readily to lift the lid of the food box and eat when signals were given by a light and a buzzer. Automatic equipment presented the stimuli at regular intervals, and dropped measured quantities of food into the receptacle. Some of the cats were further trained to step on a pedal that would actuate the food signals. Cats so trained would step on the pedal immediately on being placed in the box and, having "signalled themselves," would then go to the food container and eat.

Conflict was introduced by subjecting a cat to an air blast of ten to fifteen pounds pressure at the moment it started feeding, or by a painful but harmless electric shock from the metal floor grid. In many experiments both the air blast and the shock were used.

Striking effects resulted from the conflict between the responses of approaching the food and avoiding the air blast or shock. The most uniform result was an intense emotional response. The cats' posture, the erection of their hair, the dilation of their pupils, the increased rates of heart beat and breathing, and their frantic mewing, were undeniable indicators of strong emotion. They also showed avoidance responses to all cues associated with the conflict. After only a few conflict-producing stimulations, they crouched, trembled, hid, and tried to escape from the apparatus whenever the light and buzzer signals were given. The cats also resisted being placed in the apparatus, in contrast to their eagerness to get to the food prior to the conflict. In addition to their relatively uniform responses to conflict the cats, like human beings, showed individual differences in behavior. In general, normally quiet cats tended to become agitated, and showed an increase in restless movements. Formerly active cats tended to become passive and to assume rigid but apparently fearful postures that they often maintained for as long as thirty minutes after being stimulated. Some cats also adopted behavior that seemed to reduce tension, such as excessive licking and cleaning of their fur, or seeking attention and petting from the experimenter. Cats trained to step on the pedal to signal themselves now often avoided the pedal as if it were itself a dangerous thing.

The cats' responses to conflict generalized to other aspects of their lives. Many refused to eat even when returned to their living cages, and a few starved themselves to the point where they had to be fed forcibly. Their attitudes toward the experimenter and toward other cats were profoundly affected in varied ways. Some became wild and aggressive, others passive and inert. Removal from the laboratory for rest periods of from two weeks to five months did not cause the responses to die out through so-called disuse. On being placed again in the apparatus, the emotionally toned avoidance responses were reinstated strongly.

Control experiments by Masserman showed clearly the difference between the effects of conflict and responses to mere fear or frustration. Several cats were repeatedly exposed to the air blast in the apparatus, without having it occur at the same time as a feeding response. The initial response to the blast was fear and avoidance, but after a small number of stimulations the animals adapted to the air blast alone and paid little attention to it. Their behavior was in marked contrast to the persistence of the response to the conflict. In other control experiments, some cats were frustrated by locking the food box after they had learned to eat from it, or by confining them behind a glass partition in full view of the food box while the feeding signals were given. Frustration produced vigorous activity and loud mewing for a few trials but the reactions were quickly extinguished and the cat came to ignore the unrewarded signals. In no case did external frustration cause the profound and continued disorganization of behavior that resulted from a conflict of motives. These observations show that neither simple conditioned fear nor imposed thwarting has as great an effect as does a conflict between adience and avoidance.

Experimental Neurosis

Some much earlier experiments from Pavlov's laboratories showed a disturbance of behavior in dogs that can be interpreted in terms of conflict.[13] The first observations were accidental, and occurred in connection with an experiment on discriminative conditioning. By presenting food simultaneously with the visual stimulus, a dog was conditioned to secrete saliva when a circle of light was thrown on a screen. Then, following the usual procedure of discrimination experiments (p. 73), the dog was trained not to salivate for a visual stimulus of an ellipse which was shown repeatedly without food reinforcement. The dog learned readily to salivate for the circle but not for the ellipse, as long as the forms were easily distinguished. As a test of fineness of discrimination, the series of ellipses was made to approach more and more nearly the shape of a circle. The dog succeeded in distinguishing a circle from an ellipse whose axes were as seven to eight. When the experiment was pressed farther and the dog was made to try discriminating an ellipse whose axes were as eight to nine, scarcely different from a circle, very unusual behavior was observed.

When compelled to attempt a discrimination beyond its ability, the dog "broke down." It salivated indiscriminately for either stimulus. More significantly, the dog now made responses to anything connected with the experiment, salivating at the sight of the experimenter or of the apparatus. It was unable to make gross discriminations that had been made easily in the early part of the experiment. The dog also showed a general disturbance of behavior that was evidently emotional. It whined, barked, tore at the restraining harness, and tried to escape from the apparatus. It was useless thereafter as an experimental animal, for it could not learn new reactions in the laboratory situation in which the outbreak had been provoked. Pavlov called the disturbed condition "experimental neurosis," noting that it was similar in many respects to the behavior of people who are termed neurotic.[14]

Not all animals react equally to severe discriminative demands. Although exact numbers were not reported, it seems that only a minority of dogs became "neurotic" when so treated. Others failed to make the difficult discriminations with more or less evidence of tension but without generally disorganized conduct. Experiments with sheep, goats, pigs, and rats have also shown that animals are not all equally susceptible. Among dogs that do develop experimental neurosis, the symptoms vary widely. Pavlov noted that normally quiet and docile animals developed an excited disturbance, while more active dogs seemed to become excessively inhibited, retaining fixed postures and even going to sleep in the apparatus when threatened with unsolvable discriminations. The individual differences were similar to those Masserman observed among his cats.

Experimentally induced abnormal behavior often generalizes widely. In one study, a flashing light was shown simultaneously with a tone that had been used in a discriminative breakdown experiment.[15] Thereafter the flashing light would evoke a general behavior disturbance. Similarly, anxious and maladjusted persons easily displace their emotional responses to situations only slightly associated with their basic conflicts. Animals often generalize even more widely to their normal living environments, remaining restless, shy, and solitary. Instrumental studies show that their heart beat and respiration remain more irregular, even in their living quarters, than those of normal animals.[16] The condition tends to last for a long time. At least one dog and one sheep subjected to experimental conflicts remained "neurotic" until their deaths, in spite of a number of years of rest with no further laboratory reinforcements.

Behavior disturbance has been caused by a number of conditioned response methods other than the requiring of excessively fine discriminations. If the same stimulus is conditioned to a food-evoked salivary response and to a pain-evoked avoidance reaction, emotionally excited behavior may result. Giving a strong conditioned stimulus when the animal has been trained to respond to a weak one, and requiring a long-delayed response involving a prolonged inhibition, have been effective in producing behavior disturbances.[17] In all these instances, the circumstances resulting in disorganization can be described as a conflict between *excitation,* the tendency to make a response, and *inhibition,* the tendency to withhold that response. Normal behavior requires a delicate balance between responding and inhibiting processes. Discriminative strain is therefore essentially the same as conflict.

Another experiment showed quite clearly the identity of the processes of discrimination and conflict.[18] Rats were trained to make approaching responses to the brighter of two lamps and retreating responses to the less bright one, when the two lights could hardly be distinguished. Success was rewarded with food and failure was punished by electric shock. The experiment showed all of the same disruptive effects as the conditioning experiments. When both excitation and inhibition, or approach and avoidance, are evoked inharmoniously at the same time, an animal finds itself helpless in an incomprehensible situation. The plight of a human being facing an intensely motivated conflict is not dissimilar.

In a series of conditioning experiments with sheep, goats, and pigs, Liddell noted another factor that determines the outcome of conflicts.[19] Sheep were readily "broken down" when made to perform difficult discriminations of tones or of the rates of metronomes while strapped in the Pavlov frame (note Fig. 11, p. 65). But when a sheep was placed in a pen five feet square within which it could move about freely, no generalized disturbance could be created by conditioning. Given even that much freedom, the animal becomes hyperactive and makes substitute and diverting responses when the conflict occurs, but does not become "neurotic." Liddell has pointed out that the restraint involved in an ordinary conditioning experiment is itself a disturbing and threatening pressure. The animal is also deprived of freedom by its domestication and taming, which make it dependent on people. The conclusion is confirmed by studies of rats, a notably active and independent species, which can hardly be made "neurotic" except with the aid of extreme restraint obtained by placing them in tight-fitting cages or by taping down their feet.[19] In Lewin's terms, the restrained animal cannot "leave the field" to avoid the brunt of the conflict by effective escaping or distracting responses. People, too, succumb to conflicts when they are hemmed in by actual social barriers imposed by others, or by the boundaries they accept for themselves by internalizing the demands of their cultures.

Experiments on Human Conflicts

Conditioned discrimination techniques can be used to study human reactions to conflict. The Russian laboratories have reported a few such studies with children.[20] A general behavior disturbance was set up in a six-year-old child by demanding a fine discrimination of the rate of beating of a metronome. The child was first conditioned to make a motor response to a metronome beat of 144 beats per minute. He had no difficulty in discriminating between that rate and negative, unreinforced, stimuli of 92 and then of 108 beats. A differential response between 144 and 120 beats was established only with difficulty. General behavior began to be affected at that point, and it was reported that the child was "taciturn," "refuses to go to the laboratory," "walks and mounts the apparatus slowly." Finally, the experimenter tried to set up a differential response between 144 and 132 beats per minute, a very slight difference. The child was entirely unable to discriminate between these stimuli. Moreover, he now appeared to have lost the previously established differentiation between 144 and 120. His conduct was even more disturbed. He was described as "rude, fights, is disobedient, excited," and finally "yawns, closes eyes, falls asleep." In this experiment, the same results were produced as in the animal studies of experimental neurosis: loss of easier discriminations, emotional excitement, and general disruption of conduct. The tendency of the child to fall asleep suggests two explanations. It may be a generalized inhibition similar to the inert behavior already described in some dogs and cats, or it may be regarded as an effective escape mechanism. Sleep is one way to get out of an unbearable situation.

In a milder experiment with American college students, the subjects were instructed to indicate the brighter of two very faint lights, and incorrect responses were punished by electric shock.[21] After having failed at impossibly difficult discriminations, the men were unable to detect differences on which they had previously succeeded. Also, the electrical measurement of the sweating of the palms of their hands showed that they reacted emotionally to the conflict. Even in this experiment with very weak motives, the same phenomena of experimental conflict occurred, but less intensely.

Responses to Lewin's types of conflict were tested by an experiment by Hovland and Sears in which the subjects were told to draw a line on a six-inch square of paper according to signals given by red and green lights (Fig. 18).[22] If a green lamp lighted, the line was to be drawn *toward* it. A red light was a signal to draw the line to the *opposite* corner, away from the red. Conflicts were introduced by lighting two or more lamps, calling for opposed responses, without warning. Approach-approach conflicts, brought about by lighting two differently placed green lamps at once, produced only slight and infrequent disturbances of behavior. When given that type of conflict, 58 per cent of the subjects drew a line to one or the other of the two green lamps, 21 per cent drew first to one lamp and then to the other, and 12 per cent "compromised" by drawing the line half way between the two. Only 9 per cent "blocked" by failing to make any response. The most severe conflict was produced by the double approach-avoidance situation (IV of Fig. 18), which lead to blocking 72.5 per cent of the time. The double approach-avoidance experiment approximates a serious real-life conflict in which a person faces two competing situations both of which have rewarding consequences if met satisfactorily, and punishing consequences if neglected or handled badly. Hovland and Sears give an illustration: "a man has two desirable appointments at the same hour, the neglect of either of which will produce punishment or disappointment." The blocking of the motor response was ordinarily accompanied by emotional or substitute behavior such as giggling, swearing, or appealing to the experimenter. In the main, the study confirmed Lewin's conclusions about the relative severity of the types of conflict.

CONFLICT AND ANXIETY

The Effects of Conflict

The experimental studies reveal the effects of intense conflicts. First, a severe conflict arouses a strong *emotional response*, with

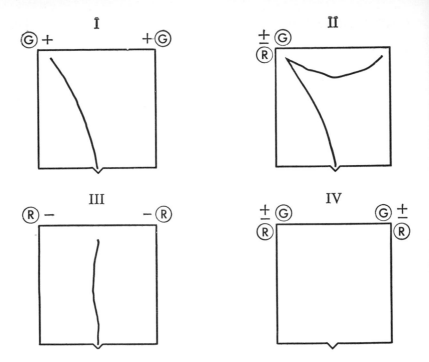

Figure 18. Responses to an Experimental Motor Conflict

First, the subjects received practice in drawing a line to the one green light that was turned on. On the *approach-approach* conflict trial, I, when *both* green lamps were lighted, the typical response was to draw a single line to one lamp. That type of conflict caused little disruption of a habit.

A simple *approach-avoidance* conflict is shown at II. Trained to approach green and to draw to the opposite corner for red, the typical conflict response was a "double response" of doing one, then the other.

The *avoidance-avoidance* conflict, III, led to inhibition of motor response ("blocking") on 46 per cent of trials, but to the "compromise" solution shown above on 29 per cent. Many subjects would have "left the field" but the apparatus did not permit it.

A mixed type of conflict, IV, involved training to respond to one lamp at a time, toward green and opposite to red. Lighting all four lamps at once led to the most baffling conflict, with 72.5 per cent of the subjects blocking. (After C. I. Hovland & R. R. Sears, Experiments on motor conflict. I. Types of conflict and their modes of resolution. *J. exp. Psychol.*, 1938, 23, 477-493.)

many evidences of visceral and muscular tension. Second, the response to a conflict shows wide *generalization,* spreading to stimuli that were only remotely or incidentally associated with the original situation. Easy discriminations that formerly were made without effort can no longer be achieved. Third, the effects of conflict have a notable *persistence.* The behavioral effects of an experimentally induced conflict may last for months or even years, and are not diminished by rest or by lack of further reinforcement.

People who have experienced strong conflicts in real-life situations show effects much like those of the experiments. Conflict throws them into an emotional state, revealed by their visceral tension, their restlessly active behavior, and their subjective discomfort and apprehension. Generalization is also evident. A sufferer from conflict is bothered by petty troubles that a more fortunate person would ignore. He "cannot make up his mind," that is, he cannot discriminate between alternative courses of action. The persistent effects of conflict help us to understand people who seem to deal ineffectively and overemotionally with one after another of life's minor difficulties. A more serious conflict, still unsolved, has predisposed such a person to be less effective in solving his subsequent adjustive problems.

Anxiety

The emotional response that a conflict evokes seems to be the core about which all of the other effects cluster. The emotional pattern is *anxiety,* to which a brief reference was made in Chapter 2.

The characteristics of anxiety show its close relationship to conflict. Anxiety often is described as an apprehension, an unpleasant blend of dread and hope referred to the future.[23] That description fits the picture of conflict very clearly. A conflict is not a present injury, but is a threat of an undetermined future hazard. Anxiety is also sensed as personal and pervasive. It arises from a conflict of one's own impulses and is ascribed to oneself. In this respect it differs from fear, which is referred to some external source of stimulation. Anxiety carries a sense of helplessness, from the fact that a person in conflict is blocked and unable to find a solution to his problem.

Anxiety is readily conditioned to substitute stimuli, a characteristic that it shares with other emotional responses. All conflicts are "real" at first, evoked by a present and genuinely threatening dilemma as perceived by the experiencer. A child who is tied to his parents by dependence, but who is treated coldly and rejectingly by them, may develop a conflict between his incompatible impulses of attachment and hostility. Anxiety results. If the conflict is intense and prolonged, and not offset by other more fortunate experiences, all future situations involving authority and restriction may evoke attitudes of hostility, followed by conflict and anxiety. By such a learning process, a person's own hostility may become a conditioned stimulus for his anxiety. Early and significant conflicts thus shape a person's future anxieties through the understandable process of conditioning.

Anxieties vary greatly in intensity, of course, from a mere qualm in a transient situational conflict to a permeating distress that may affect all of a person's social adjustments. The animal experiments on conflict, and analogous clinical studies of severely anxious people, illustrate anxiety in its most intense degrees. Less severe conflicts and minor anxieties are common enough in the lives of quite normal people.

Anxiety as a Drive

Like other emotional tensions, anxiety acts as a drive.[24] Mild anxiety, like mild hunger, may even be a useful drive. You may develop a moderate degree of anxiety because a low grade on a test is incompatible with your self-esteem, and so be furnished with drive to remedy the academic shortcoming. A young man may react with moderate anxiety because his lack of skill in dancing prevents him from participating fully in social activities. The drive of his anxiety may be enough to motivate him to learn to dance, surmounting such minor obstacles as shyness or inconvenience.

The drive of an intense anxiety tends to dominate a person's behavior. To a person in severe conflict, the reduction of his anxiety is the most powerful urge, to the exclusion of the relatively weaker motivations which lead to most of the positive satisfactions of life. As a result, people with strong, unresolved conflicts often develop mechanisms that have the sole utility of allaying their anxiety, even at the expense of sacrificing richer ultimate rewards.[25] For example, people sometimes withdraw from social contacts or else quarrel aggressively with their fellows in response to their anxiety tensions, although such actions really deprive them of major resources for the fulfillment of their motives. When a person behaves irrationally, and contrary to his own best interests, his need to escape from anxiety is likely to lie at the root of it.

SUGGESTED READINGS

Klein, *Mental Hygiene* contains an excellent discussion of frustration and conflict, as does Cameron and Magaret, *Behavior Pathology*. These topics are also interestingly treated in Dollard and Miller, *Personality and Psychotherapy*. These three books are concerned with frustration and conflict both as aspects of normal experience and as processes associated with ineffective modes of adjustment. A basic work on frustration is *Frustration and Aggression* by Dollard, Doob, Miller, Mowrer, and Sears. For Lewin's influential analysis of conflicts, see his *Dynamic Theory of Personality*, and his Chapter 15 in Carmichael, *Manual of Child Psychology*.

Two books, White, *Lives in Progress*, and Evans, *Three Men*, present cases, in considerable detail and with great literary skill, which illustrate the effects of frustration and conflict on human development. There is also good illustrative material in Coleman, *Abnormal Psychology and Modern Life*.

The chapters by Miller, Rosenzweig, and Saul in the first volume of Hunt, *Personality and the Behavior Disorders* are contributions in themselves, and also review much of the experimental work on frustration and conflict.

CHAPTER **5**

Adjustment
and Learning

Once a strong motive is aroused, it tends to keep a person or an animal in a state of continued activity. Thwarting of behavior by frustration or by conflict delays the fulfillment of the motive temporarily, but does not abolish the drive. In fact, a thwarted motive is usually strengthened. The original drive that initiated the behavior sequence continues to stimulate. In addition, a person's total drive is increased by emotional tensions, such as the anger-type drives which frustration usually arouses, or the anxiety which results from conflict. The organism has a strong urge to be active, and something has to happen.

RESOLVING CONFLICTS AND FRUSTRATIONS

Varied Responses

Confronted with an unsatisfied need or an unavoided annoyance, an organism makes *varied responses,* one after another, until at length some act is discovered that will reduce the drive. This exploratory activity which begins when a drive is aroused and ends when the drive is reduced is one of the most general patterns of human and animal behavior. It is shown by organisms very low in the evolutionary scale.

The very simple organism *Stentor* has a repertory of several adjustive responses that it can make to a noxious chemical stimulus in its environment. *Stentor,* a tiny protozoan, is attached to the

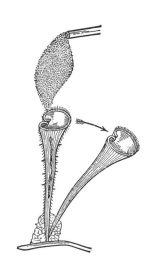

Figure 19. Adjustive Behavior of Stentor

Ink is introduced near the mouth of the tiny simple organism. The first response is bending away from the source of the noxious stimulation. (H. S. Jennings, *Behavior of the lower organisms.* New York: Columbia Univer. Press, 1906.)

substratum at the lower end of its tube (Fig. 19). At the top of the tube are cilia or hairs that draw water containing food particles down into it. If a few drops of red ink are introduced into the water near the animal, a series of responses is initiated. First, the *Stentor* bends to one side, avoiding the ink. If several bendings do not bring relief, the movement of the cilia is reversed, pushing the water away instead of drawing it in. If further adjustment is necessary a third response is made, of contracting into its tube. Finally, when all these responses prove unavailing, the *Stentor* releases itself from its support and floats away. Even a single-celled animal can adjust to an injurious stimulus, and has a sequence or hierarchy of responses that it makes in a preferred order until readjustment is achieved.

One of the classic descriptions of behavior when thwarted was made by E. L. Thorndike, from observations in some of his earliest experiments with animals.[1] Thorndike placed cats in puzzle boxes (Fig. 20), which were cages constructed so that the performance of acts such as pulling loops of string or stepping on pedals would cause the door to open, releasing the confined animal. Young, hungry, and rather untamed cats were used as subjects, since they had enough drive to stir them to activity. Food was placed outside the box where the animal could see it. The cats reacted vigorously to the situation. They tried to squeeze through the bars; they clawed and bit at portions of the cage; they struck at various parts of the

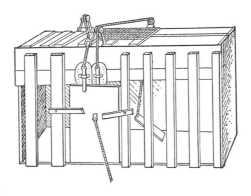

Figure 20. Puzzle Box for Studying the Adjustive Behavior of Cats

The apparatus shown is the very difficult puzzle box K, which required three responses for its solution: stepping on a pedal, pulling a loop of cord, and turning a latch on the door. Other easier boxes required only one response. (E. L. Thorndike, Animal intelligence. *Psychol. Rev. Monogr. Sup.*, 1898, 2, No. 4.)

apparatus. In the course of such varied activities, a cat would in time pull the string, press the latch, or step on the pedal that released the door. The problem was then solved and the animal got out, reducing the drives induced by its hunger and confinement.

Similar experiments have been performed with human subjects. If a problem is very difficult in relation to one's ability, or if it is of a very novel sort so that previously acquired habits are not serviceable, varied motor activity similar to that of the lower animals will result. Mechanical puzzles, assemblies of wire and metal pieces that will come apart if manipulated correctly, have been used to study human adjustments to unfamiliar and difficult tasks.[2] Most people respond to the puzzles by moving the pieces at random, pulling here and pushing there. In fact, varied movements are about the only way to gain success. One of the common causes of failure is the continued repetition of the same useless movement. When easier or more familiar problem-solving tasks are given to human subjects, the amount of varied activity may be reduced, and a solution sometimes is reached in one exploratory trial.

We do not have to go to the psychological laboratory to find evidence of varied responses in the adjustment process. The pattern can be found in innumerable real-life situations. Let us suppose that a boy has kicked his football into the branches of a tree. He may first try to jump from the ground to reach the ball, but it is too high. Then he tries to climb the tree, but there are no low limbs to offer a suitable foothold. He tries to shake the tree, but it is too solid. If the motive to get the ball is sufficiently persistent and if the boy has enough ingenuity he may at length arrive at a solution, such as throwing stones to hit the ball or getting a ladder. If all attempts fail the boy may kick the tree in anger, or blame others for the loss of the ball, or just sit down and cry. These last reactions are not directed realistically to the solution of the problem, but are responses to the boy's own emotional tension.

The varied responses to a thwarted drive are often called *trial and error* behavior. The "trials" that will be attempted in any new situation depend on past experience and previously learned solutions. A cat in a puzzle box has a large number of possible alternative forms of response. When first placed in the box, it scratches, claws, and tries to squeeze through the bars, which are very natural and sensible things for a cat to do under the circumstances. In the past it has escaped from confinement, as when caught behind a fence, by similar means. Only when these habits fail to be effective does a cat show the less directed random activity seen in the experiment. Men behave similarly. At first they are likely to try rational adjustments. If these are thwarted by external obstacles, or inhibited by a man's own conflicts, subsequent trials are likely to become overmotivated, excessively emotional, and hence less effective.

Tension Reduction

What brings to an end the series of varied responses aroused by a drive? From the psychological viewpoint there is only one answer: the solution of an adjustment is *tension reduction*. Any response that reduces the drive tension brings activity to a close because it removes the stimulus that maintained the behavior. When a hungry animal eats, the visceral state that acted as a drive ceases to exist, and the source of the animal's activity is removed. Similarly, when a person is motivated by an emotional tension or by a social motive derived from emotion, any activity that reduces the emotional state is to him a successful response. It terminates the sequence that began with the appearance of the drive.

Various responses may differ in the degree of their effectiveness as reducers of tension. An unattractive girl may experience conflict between her need for masculine attention and her fear of being rebuffed. Her anxiety will be reduced most effectively by actual success in attracting men. But it will also be reduced to some extent by becoming a man-hater, by competing with men in their own occupational fields, or by becoming emotionally attached to members of her own sex. The direct solution is usually most effectively tension reducing, but various substitute solutions also have utility from the point of view of the individual, to the extent that they reduce the drive that initiated the adjustment.

Quite fortunately, most behavior that reduces your drives also serves your long-range welfare. When you are hungry, you eat; when in real danger, you guard yourself or run away. But some very effective reducers of tensions may have ultimately harmful effects. Eating a poisoned food will stay your hunger, but you will become ill later. Fleeing from imagined dangers may prevent you from gaining other legitimate satisfactions. The word *adjustment* does not carry any connotations of goodness or badness, or of ultimate welfare or disaster. Adjustments do vary in quality, an important and complicated issue which is discussed at length later in this chapter. Meanwhile, it is important to remember that adjustment means immediate tension reduction. Some responses to thwarting are inadequate, substitute, or unreal, but if they reduce drives they are adjustments nonetheless.

LEARNING IN ADJUSTMENT

So far, the adjustment process has been described as a sequence of behavior by which organisms overcome obstructions and resolve conflicts. Attention has been directed to the process by which the first solution of a problem is achieved. This approach is very practical, for many problems are met once, solved, and never encountered again.

When you observe a series of solutions of the same problem, however, another important phenomenon is discovered. In his experiments with cats, Thorndike placed an animal in the same problem box again and again and noted the time required for escape on each successive trial. The results of some of these experiments are

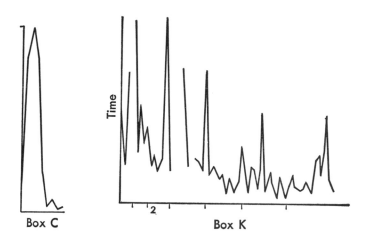

Box C   Box K

Figure 21. Time Improvement in Adjustive Learning

At the left is shown the sudden decrease in time taken to escape from a simple and easy puzzle box **C**. At the right is a record of the times of escape from the difficult box **K**, showing gradual and irregular improvement. The first may be taken to represent learning with "insight," the second, "blind" learning in adjustment. (E. L. Thorndike, Animal intelligence. *Psychol. Rev. Monogr. Sup.*, 1898, 2, No. 4.)

shown in Figure 21. In the series of trials, the animal *learns* to escape from the box. The early trials are characterized by the varied responses previously described. In the later attempts the animal goes directly to the latch, operates it, and escapes at once. In some way or another, the successful solution is selected and perpetuated; the unsuccessful trials tend to drop out and be eliminated.

What is the cause of learning — of this progressive increase in the probability of making the "successful" response? An easy answer that satisfies many laymen is to say that the animal "remembers" the correct solution. However, memory is no more satisfactory an explanation for this problem of learning than it was for the conditioned reaction. In many instances of learning, the words and images that we call memory may not be present at all. A golfer improves from novice to expert by learning processes in which good responses are selected and inefficient ones eliminated, yet if he tries to remember just how to make a stroke nothing but confusion results. In the case of learning by lower animals no evidence of memory is possible except the observation that the animal does learn, and so the explanation turns out to be circular.

The Law of Effect

The explanation of learning by trial, error, and success proposed by Thorndike was that the successful responses were "stamped in" by the satisfaction resulting from the escape and the food. Later, he formalized this principle as the *Law of Effect:*

> . . . when a modifiable connection between a situation and a response is made and is accompanied or followed by a satisfying state of affairs, that connection's strength is increased. . . . By a satisfying state of affairs is meant one which the animal does nothing to avoid, often doing things which maintain or renew it.*

The Law of Effect has been a useful practical principle. Most of the economic processes of our culture and most of our educational methods are based on the observation that people will repeat and learn acts that have satisfying end-results. In the laboratories, countless hungry animals from insects to apes have been induced to learn mazes and to solve other problems when rewarded with food.

The exact processes underlying the Law of Effect have raised many doubts. Some of the earlier statements of the principle implied that the *pleasure* resulting from certain responses tends to strengthen those responses directly. It is hard to conceive how a subjective experience of pleasure can make the changes in the nervous system that must happen when learning takes place. It is more likely that pleasure is the result of certain successful adjustments than that it is a cause. Furthermore, a pleasure-oriented theory of learning fails to account for the observation, especially evident in complex human learning, that many painful responses are selected and learned as efficiently as immediately pleasurable ones. Thorndike avoided the pleasure theory by defining a satisfying state as "one which the animal does nothing to avoid, often doing things which maintain or renew it." Such a theory almost

---

* E. L. Thorndike, *Educational psychology.* Vol. II. *The psychology of learning.* New York: Teachers College, Columbia University, 1913. Pp. 4 and 2.

says that an animal *learns* what it *performs,* and eliminates the concept of pleasure at the risk of approaching circularity. It is evident that further serious consideration must be given to the definition of what is meant by "satisfying."

Reward and Punishment

The original statement of the Law of Effect made it both a law of reward and a law of punishment. In addition to the generalization about the results of satisfaction, Thorndike stated that when a connection is accompanied or followed by an annoying state of affairs, its strength is decreased. Further experiments have led to a reexamination of the effectiveness of punishment in "weakening connections" directly. In a series of human learning experiments with verbal material, Thorndike[3] found that the learning of a correct response word was indeed strengthened by the experimenter saying "Right!" On the other hand, saying "Wrong!" when the subject gave an incorrect word did not appreciably decrease the likelihood of the subject giving that response again on the subsequent trial. Even when the mild punishment of saying "Wrong!" was accompanied by a slight electric shock or by a small monetary fine, it proved not to be a dependable way to eliminate a response. As a result of this experiment, Thorndike abandoned his earlier proposition about the effect of "annoying states of affairs."

In an important experiment with rats, W. K. Estes further clarified the relationships of reward and punishment to learning.[4] The rats first learned to press a small bar projecting into their cage when each pressing of the bar was rewarded with a food pellet. Then one group of rats was punished by being given an electric shock when they pressed the bar, while another group was unpunished. Subsequently, both groups were placed in the apparatus for successive periods, and the number of bar-pressings was recorded under conditions involving neither reward nor punishment. As might be expected, the unshocked rats showed a gradual extinction of the unrewarded response until they no longer pressed the bar at all (Fig. 22). A comparison of the behavior of the shocked rats with the unshocked ones was instructive. In the *earlier* extinction trials, the shocked rats made fewer bar-pressing responses; in the *later* trials they made *more* responses than the unshocked rats. They "made up for" for their slower rate of responding in the earlier tests.

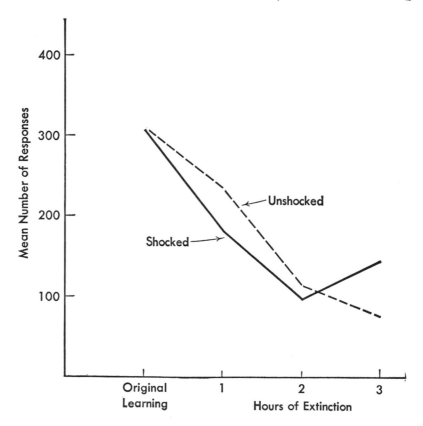

Figure 22. Punishment and Extinction

The experiment shows that punishment suppresses a response but does not extinguish it. Two groups, each of 3 rats, learned a bar-pressing response with food reward. Then the *shocked* rats (solid line) were shocked an average of 9 times when they pressed the bar during a 15-minute period in the first extinction hour. The *unshocked* rats (broken line) were not. During the first and second hours of unrewarded extinction, the unshocked rats made more responses. During the third hour, the shocked rats responded more often. The total number of responses made by the shocked and unshocked rats during the three hours was almost exactly equal. (Data of Experiment A, adjusted for differences in performance before extinction, from W. K. Estes, An experimental study of punishment. *Psychol. Monogr.*, 1944, 57, No. 3 [Whole No. 263].)

In the end, the shocked rats made just as great a total number of responses before the habit was extinguished as did the unshocked animals. The punishment *suppressed* the bar-pressing response temporarily, but did not *weaken* it in the long run.

Some other experiments have shown that a painful effect accompanying a response may even strengthen it under certain conditions.[5] In a study of adult human learning by Peterson,[6] the subjects learned a "mental maze," in which they acquired the ability to recite a sequence of numbers which were presented in successive pairs, one of each pair being "right" and the other "wrong." Subjects learned by three procedures: (1) with only verbal promptings of right and wrong given by the experimenter; (2) with, in addition, an electric shock accompanying each wrong response; and (3) with an electric shock accompanying each *right* response. Far from preventing learning, the painful result of giving the right answer became a positive aid for reaching the goal, and the subjects so shocked learned more quickly than those who received only verbal prompting. In both the animal and the human experiments, reaching a motivated goal was the important determiner of learning. The mild shock served only to signal or emphasize success and therefore was an aid to learning, not a hindrance.

Common observation seems to find some instances in which punishment is related to learning. The once-burned child avoids the fire, and parental punishment sometimes seems to deter a child from disapproved behavior. The best interpretation is that such punishments do not weaken responses directly, but that they set up new drives. A child burned by a hot stove acquires a conditioned fear of it. In the future the sight of the stove will arouse this drive, which can then be reduced by avoiding the stove. Escape from pain is a reward and the child learns from satisfying that need, not directly from the punishment.

The learning situation that occurs when a child is punished by his parent is more complicated.[7] Presumably the child has a motive to perform the forbidden act. Punishment evokes a conflicting drive stemming from the anxiety aroused by the parents' displeasure. The child has to resolve his approach-avoidance conflict as best he can, and does not always solve it in the same way. When the forbidden act is fulfilling a very strong drive, the child may continue it in spite of repeated and severe punishment, to the dismay of his uncomprehending parents. Or he may suppress the punished response, as did the rats in Estes' experiment, without really weakening the tendency. In that case, the conflict continues. Finally, the child may reduce his anxiety by adopting a response that pleases his parents. The punishment seems to work, but the real cause of the learning is the reduction of his anxiety.

The analyses and experiments point to a need for reformulating the Law of Effect. Learning is not determined directly by pleasure or pain, but by the reduction of drives and the achievement of adjustment. The revised Law of Effect is substantially the same as the Law of Primary Reinforcement described by C. L. Hull.[8] It may be stated: *Organisms tend to repeat and learn responses that lead to tension reduction and to the completion of motivated activity.*

Closure and Insight

Other theories of learning have been proposed that are not inharmonious with the interpretation of adjustive learning just stated, although they differ somewhat in their assumptions and implications. The *Gestalt* school of psychology would define the puzzle-box problem in terms of the animal's perception of the total situation, including the needs, the obstructions, and the goal.[9] The situation is described as an "open" system that is incomplete or out of equilibrium from the point of view of the animal. The successful act brings about a *closure* or restoration of equilibrium. Learning proceeds by an improvement of the perception of the situation. At first the latch is part of the perceptual *ground*, while the food is the *figure* or portion of the total field of which the animal is acutely aware. Learning consists of the enlargement of this figure to include the latch as well as the food, which in the end are "seen together" as the significant factors in the attainment of the goal.

Since the Gestalt view of learning is based on perception, the school objects to the notions that definite movements are learned, and that progress in learning is gradual. Their experiments, performed chiefly with chimpanzees, seem to support both these contentions. Typically, the apes learned by a suddenly effective movement preceded by relatively inactive periods. In one experiment a large box was placed in front of a cage so as to make it impossible for the ape to reach a piece of fruit placed outside. After regarding the situation for about two hours the ape suddenly picked up the box, moved it aside, and reached for the fruit. No random responses that in any way concerned the box had been made previous to the final movement. In many experiments learning occurred in one trial. After one successful attempt, the task was performed immediately when presented again. This sudden learning has been ascribed to a *perceptual reorganization* or "insight" that makes the total situation suddenly clearer to the learner. If insight is defined objectively in terms of an abrupt drop in the time taken to solve a problem, it can be found in the learning of animals much lower than apes. Some of Thorndike's learning curves for cats (Fig. 21) showed quick drops when the problem was "simple, obvious and clearly defined," consisting only of pressing a single latch. Other experiments have found evidence of insight in rats.[10] When human subjects solve mechanical puzzles, sudden improvement after long periods of random activity is typical rather than exceptional.

The Gestalt approach has made a valuable contribution by emphasizing that perceptions can be learned as well as movements. People do learn by perceptual reorganization and insight, and the experiments show that lower animals can also learn in that manner. Some Gestalt concepts are useful in describing the processes of psychotherapy through which disturbed people learn to improve their life adjustments. The chief criticism of the Gestalt theory arises from its stress on intellectual understanding as the basis of all learning. The salient fact about maladjustment is that people often learn blindly and stupidly in response to strong thwarted drives. Perceptual theories supplement but cannot entirely replace the principle of learning by tension reduction.

More Than One Kind of Learning

Will the Law of Effect account for all learning? It does indeed seem to explain adjustive learning quite adequately, but there is another type of learning that does not conform to this principle. Tension reduction describes how you learn to adjust to a fear. You can, however, learn to *have* a fear as well as learn to *reduce* it.[11] A child not previously afraid of dogs can learn to fear them through an injurious experience. That is *tension-producing* learning and certainly cannot be covered by a principle of tension reduction.

We have already encountered a law of learning that can be applied to the acquisition of fears and other tensions. The conditioned reaction shows that learning occurs through the *simultaneous oc-currence* of a previously neutral stimulus with the response to which it is to be conditioned. To learn a fear of a new situation it is only necessary for that situation to occur at the same time that the fear response is evoked. Through conditioning you learn to have drives in the face of certain situations; through trial-and-error or adjustive learning you learn to reduce these drives by effective behavior.

The experimental evidence about conditioning confirms the hypothesis that it is a form of learning applying particularly to emotion and drive. Emotional responses and particular aspects of emotion such as the sweating of the palms of the hands are very readily conditioned. Motor responses such as eyelid blinking and finger retraction have also been conditioned, but the resulting learned reactions are usually weak and unstable, quite in contrast with the strength and dependability of emotional conditioning. Many supposed instances of motor conditioning can be reinterpreted in terms of adjustive learning. In numerous experiments, dogs have been "conditioned" to lift a paw upon receiving a light or sound stimulus, the learning being reinforced by the administration of an electric shock as an unconditioned stimulus. These results can be explained more clearly as tension-reduction learning. The real conditioning is that the dog learns to fear the signal that forewarns of the shock. Lifting his paw is an adjustive response by which he avoids the shock and thereby reduces his fear tension.

A number of theorists have attempted to reduce all learning to one principle. Several would explain all learning in terms of drive reduction,[12] while others have tried to reduce trial and error to a special case of conditioning.[13] Scientific parsimony would indeed be grateful for a single law, but not at the expense of ignoring pertinent contrary evidence. Many psychologists today prefer to have several sets of laws each of which applies to clearly defined cases of learning.[14] There is at least associative learning (conditioning), trial-and-error learning (tension reduction), and possibly also the perceptual-organization learning advocated by the Gestalt theory.

Learning in Human Adjustments

Theories of learning have been described at length because of the importance of learning in the acquisition of human adjustive responses. The *personality* of an individual consists of his persistent tendencies to make certain kinds of adjustments rather than other kinds. Some earlier psychological theories assigned the basis of personality to heredity, to constitutional and unmodifiable aspects of temperament, or to an inevitable "growth" process that unfolded as a person matured. None of these explanations have proved very fruitful for understanding, predicting, or modifying personality. Learning theories are more promising.

The formation of personality is a vastly more complicated process than is the acquisition of the habits that have been investigated experimentally. It proceeds over a longer period of time and is the result of a person's adjustments to many situations. It is wrong to oversimplify the problems involved in the acquisition of adjustive habits; it is equally wrong to fail to recognize their origins from simple processes of adjustive learning. If a thwarted child has reduced his tension successfully by withdrawing, he is predisposed to withdraw on other occasions when thwarting occurs. If he has effectively reduced a tension by overaggressive behavior, by a tantrum, or by developing a headache, these successful solutions are learned and are likely to be tried in all future situations of a similar nature.

"Abnormal" personality habits are learned in the same way as normal ones. An experiment reported by Skinner illustrates this quite clearly.[15] A hungry pigeon was placed in a cage constructed so that it received food from a swinging hopper at regular intervals of fifteen seconds. Six of eight birds used as experimental subjects developed extraordinary behavior. One acquired a habit of turning counterclockwise about the cage, making two or three turns between feedings. Another developed a "tossing" response, as if repeatedly lifting up an invisible bar with its head. Two birds showed a pendular swinging of the head and body. The other responses were equally bizarre. The learning process had an obvious source. Each bird happened to be making some movement just before the food was given. The "rewarded" response was repeated immediately, and the reinforcements came at such short intervals that other behavior did not have time to intervene and interfere with the response before it was "rewarded" again. The experimental behavior is analogous to superstitions seen in people who perform rituals "to change their luck." It is also like the repetitious and really useless behavior of some neurotic persons whose responses, however irrelevant, have been reinforced by the reduction of their anxiety.

An example of human learning very much like that of the pigeons is shown in a case that E. B. Holt quoted from Preyer with comments of his own.

> Two children suffered, during their first six months of infancy, from eruptions of the skin. At first, their arm movements were too uncoordinated to enable them to scratch the affected parts. But they soon learned to reach up to their faces, which were accessible because uncovered, and then, "At every moment when they were not watched the hands went up to the head, and the skin, even where healthy, was rubbed and scratched. These scratching movements cannot be inborn and must be acquired. An accidental contact of hand and head resulting in a decrease of the itching sensation must necessarily induce a preference for the hand-to-head motion, over all other movements." That is, the restlessness produced by a mild annoyer led to trial-and-error learning and alleviation of the annoyance. "Now this reflex reaching toward the head led, as a further consequence, to a peculiar association in one of the two cases. (Observations on the other child are lacking.) As, namely, the eczema healed and finally disappeared, the habit of lifting the arms and carrying the hands to the head persisted, and reappeared whenever the child met anything disagreeable or whenever it manifested opposition, as when it did not wish to play or did wish to stop playing. . . . In this way peculiar expressive movements originate from acquired reflexes."[*]

Here a personality characteristic of an unusual sort has been caught in the making. To a less acute observer the tendency of the child to put his hands to his face whenever in need of adjustment would have been inexplicable, or perhaps would have been considered "instinctive." In the same manner other persons acquire tendencies to go away alone, to fight, to pout, to lie, or to twiddle their fingers whenever they are thwarted. These personality and character traits are the residuals of the individual's past experiences and of his past tension-reducing solutions of problems.

Unconscious Adjustments

Most people acquire the characteristics of their personalities without being aware of their origin or significance. Quite normal people lack insight into their own adjustments, and maladjusted persons

---

[*] E. B. Holt, *Animal drive and the learning process.* New York: Holt, 1931, pp. 225-226. Quoting W. Preyer, *Die Seele des Kindes.* (2nd ed.) 1884. Pp. 165-166.

are likely to be even more handicapped in this respect. An adjustive act is impulsive. A person who suffers from strong anxiety may feel vaguely better after some aggressive or evasive act, but he does not know why. Because learning depends more on tension reduction than on understanding, the adjustive response may be reinforced and become habitual, still without insight. Such behavior is properly described as *unconscious*. In Chapter 4 we saw that conditioned responses, including acquired drives, may be unconscious. Adjustment mechanisms, too, may operate without full awareness.

The concept of unconscious learning represents a very great discovery of modern psychology, for which we are mainly indebted to Sigmund Freud. But the concept is often misinterpreted. "Unconscious" is a good adjective but a bad noun. Only an old-fashioned rationalistic theory which believed that normal people reason out their life problems by logical processes in a "conscious mind" had to assume that there is also an "unconscious mind" where inaccessible and often irrational thinking processes go on. Freud made that mistake in his earlier writings, but did not use the concept of "*the* unconscious" in his last book.[16] The wrong notion continues to have some effect on popular thinking. To a layman, the difference between non-conscious processes and a place called "the unconscious" may not seem very important, but the distinction is essential for a sound theory.

Awareness exists in many degrees which merge gradually with one another. Most thoroughly unconscious are many of the basic physiological adjustments, such as the regulation of the size of the pupils of the eyes in response to varying intensities of light. We are unaware of such adjustments because we have no receptors — no sense organs — to receive impressions of the events. Many important features of social adjustment are unconscious in a somewhat different meaning of the word. In these cases, unconscious means *unverbalized;* the person cannot describe what is happening in language symbols, either to other people or, most importantly, to himself. Drives, and the adjustments that reduce drives, may have been learned very early in life before the person's language skills were acquired. The incident of the infant who learned to put his hands to his face when he was in distress (p. 138) illustrates pre-verbal learning. The impulse may last all his life, but he will never understand it.

Other unconscious adjustive behaviors result from *blind trial-and-error learning*. This type of learning, emphasized by Thorndike in his experiments with cats, involves the acquisition of a response by gradual reinforcement without deliberation or insight. Human beings often learn blindly, even in the laboratory, and more frequently in everyday life. A young woman in a class in experimental psychology solved a mechanical puzzle ten times, yet professed still to be ignorant of how it operated. The fact that her time of solution decreased gradually indicated that learning had taken place, but it had occurred without understanding. Very similar psychologically is the case of a young man who has a vaguely anxious attitude and who withdraws from all social contacts. He does not know the origin of his adjustment, although its causes and development could be found in his past experiences if he were studied psychologically. His behavior can be explained in terms of trial-and-error learning without insight. The experimentally oriented approach to problems of adjustment does not assume that all important determiners of behavior are conscious. Far from it! But it explains the unconscious aspects of adjustment by principles of learning, dispensing with any need for the additional hypothesis of a so-called unconscious mind.

SYMBOLIC ADJUSTMENTS

Many human adjustments are unverbalized and are poorly accessible to awareness, as the preceding section showed. It is also true that persons often make extensive use of language and other symbolic behavior in their adjustive processes. Adjustments, whether adequate or inadequate, commonly involve talking and thinking. It is therefore essential to explore the part that symbolic behavior may play in human adjustments.

In the everyday sense of the word, a symbol is an event that stands for or represents some other event, object, or quality. A flag is the symbol of a country, a word is the symbol of the object or concept for which it stands, a certain facial expression is the symbol of some state of emotion. The efficiency of human activity, in comparison to that of lower animals, is largely due to a more extensive use of systems of symbols such as maps, diagrams, mathematics, and above all, language.

Origins of Symbols

The use of symbols is learned, of course, and a study of their origins does not require the formulation of any new psychological principles. If you want to teach a dog to sit up at a verbal command, you say "Sit!" at the same time that some other stimulus makes him sit up, and immediately reward his response with a bit of food. A little child learns the meaning of words by being rewarded when he responds to them correctly. In later childhood and in adult life, after the generally rewarding nature of language has been established, acquired social motives will be enough to motivate the learning of new words. Experiencing a new word in a clear context may then be sufficient to cause learning. Reward is not without significance, however, as shown by the fact that people rarely remember for any great length of time newly acquired words for which they have no use.

Symbols serve not only as substitute stimuli but also as substitute responses. If a dog is always fed in the kitchen, he will learn to run to the kitchen when stimulated by hunger. Similarly, if scratching on the door or sitting up to beg have been followed by the satisfaction of hunger, these actions become symbols to express hunger. A dog can use, as well as respond to, many symbols, and it is ordinarily incorrect to say that it understands more than it can express. By similar processes, people learn symbols that they use to express their needs, to communicate with others, and to manipulate when thinking.

Symbols in Recall

The consideration of symbols brings us close to the problem of memory. What happens when you remember a dentist's appointment, or what you had for dinner yesterday, or the house in which you lived as a child? A description of memory as the "reinstatement of past experience" is a very loose and inadequate definition. Past experience is past, and it is as impossible to bring it into existence again as it would be to reassemble the very food that you ate yesterday, or to reinstate by magic a house that has been torn down. Memory is a present response bearing a relationship to the past because its stimulus has a previously learned relationship with other experiences. The term "recall" is a very apt designation for memory, for in remembering an event you re-call it, that is, you name it again.[17] Nothing is ever remembered without a present sign, which arouses a present response determined by past learning. The present symbol may be very gross and obvious or it may be subtle and difficult to identify. You may recall the dentist's appointment by seeing a note on your calendar or by the twinge of the aching tooth. Or, your remembering may be stimulated by the more remote cues of seeing a person hurrying by, or by a smell of antiseptic, or by looking at your pocketbook. Whether the symbol is gross or subtle the psychological process is the same. A present cue evokes a present response determined by past experience.

Recall can use other symbols than words. You may report your reminiscences in words for the benefit of others or in implicit speech for yourself alone. Or, your recall may be in the form of gestures, attitudes, muscular postures, or visceral states, some of which are impossible for an outsider to detect. Any of these symbols can mean or stand for a more complex pattern of perception.

Symbols in Thinking

Symbols act as convenient short-cuts in thinking. In an algebra problem, x may stand for the amount of lead in a certain alloy of lead and tin. While you solve the problem, the x is used freely without having to verbalize the longer phrase that conveys its entire meaning. The result is an economy of time and effort and an added efficiency, since many problems cannot be solved at all without the use of symbols. Abstract thinking is the manipulation of symbols according to certain rules, and nothing else.

Common problems that arise in everyday living often involve a subtle use of symbols. If a man wants to go from one part of a large city to another, he may think or reason as to the best method of transportation. The subway is most rapid, but the station is inconveniently distant from the destination. A taxicab would be most convenient, but the expense is too great. The bus goes to the destination quite directly, but would be too slow to insure his keeping his appointment. A final solution may be to take the subway for the greater part of the distance, transferring to a bus to complete the trip. In making his decision, the man does not try all routes physically in order to discover the best one. He uses symbols of some sort as his tools of reasoning. These may be words spoken aloud, or words pronounced incipiently, possibly with barely perceptible movements of the larynx of which he may not be clearly aware. The symbols may be still more abridged. A nod of the head may mean the subway, a gesture of the shoulders the bus, and a sigh may indicate the taxi. In any case, thinking is no inaccessible inner process that lies out of the realm of physical events. It consists of making responses to representative symbols.

Distorted Symbols

When you are drowsy, excited, or preoccupied with other matters, you may sometimes use symbols that are mixed up or distorted, or at least are not the public symbols you would use in communicating to another person. People under the influence of some drugs, or who are suffering from some of the more severe mental disorders, tend even more to use symbols that may have meaning for themselves privately, but that are not understandable to others in terms of cultural standards. Two examples of the operation of private symbols, as experienced by a normal person when in a very drowsy condition, will illustrate the process.

(a) Observer played checkers nearly all day on ocean liner. "Retiring to the cabin before sleeping-time, I threw myself drowsily on my berth and fell to ruminating over some projected experiments on the comic, wondering whether to follow the order of merit method or a method of assigning numerical grade to each comic situation. I decide, but in my half-awake consciousness both the deliberation and the decision take the form of moves of checkers on the board. I decide to move my white man up to the king row and mentally watch C— jump it with his black."

. . .

(b) "On board steamship, dressing for dinner in suit purchased abroad. Sitting drowsily on edge of berth and thinking that the suit had turned out to be a bad investment and had been forced upon me by a tricky salesman. Planning to buy cloth abroad this time to be made up in U.S., and wondering if it would pass customs. Thought over the conversation with the salesman and suddenly noticed that the rush of water, heard through the porthole, had become transformed into the voice of the salesman, trying to sell me the suit. Fall to musing in the process, wondering, while he talks, at his husky voice and why he has no more inflection."[*]

---

[*] H. L. Hollingworth, Vicarious functioning of irrelevant imagery. *J. Phil. Psychol. sci. Meth.*, 1911, 8, 688-692.

In both these instances, rational thought processes are in evidence and the conclusions are valid. The symbols, however, are derived from private sources and seem irrelevant to the problems when viewed by an external observer. In the first case the symbols are a perseveration of an immediately past experience; in the second, they are a present perception. The symbols are comprehensible when one knows enough about the private experiences of the thinker.

Symbols in Dreams

The consideration of symbols in drowsy states leads directly to the question of symbols in dreams. Through the ages dreams have been considered occult, but they are now recognized as processes of thinking in the broadest meaning of that term. Some dreams are reminiscences in which the dreamer mulls over the events of the past day. Other dreams are of a problem-solving type in which the dreamer is engaged in finding his way out of a difficulty, either constructively or anxiously and inadequately. Dreams also may express aspirations or desires just as daydreams do. In other instances dreams may simply report a present perception, as when a stomach ache becomes a dream of an animal gnawing at one's vitals. The interpretation of a dream is the determination of the experiences it represents or the problem with which it deals. The interpretation can often be effected with the dreamer's waking help, never without it. An illustration will serve to show how symbols operate in dreams. The dreamer is a male college student.

> I seem to be standing on a street in W—, near the principal corner, with a group of unidentified people. In the group are one or two familiar young women, and I am trying to speak to them without interrupting the others. One of the young women leaves the group. I identify her now as Peg G. and follow her running. As I am nearing the corner, a "hot-rod"* comes around the turn, loaded with young people from P—. Following the automobile are two large busses, also loaded with merrymakers. Then an ox-cart, drawn by five oxen, crowds between the automobile and

---

* This dream was reported some years ago, and the original protocol called the automobile a "cut-down Ford," a type of vehicle now hardly known to our culture. Since slang changes, and lest future readers be baffled, a "hot-rod" may be defined as a distinctive automobile so modified as to meet the demands of youth for individuality and speed!

the busses, obstructing my passage. At the risk of being run down, I push past the ox-cart and try to overtake Peg, who is well down the street by this time.

This dream is silly and meaningless to the dreamer and unintelligible to the psychologist until the dreamer's background and his associations with the dream are ascertained by questioning. A crucial point is the identity of Peg G. The student remembers her as a girl whom he once invited to a college dance. He and Peg quarreled throughout this social function and thereafter regarded each other with mutual dislike. Recently the student had heard that Peg is studying painting in New York. The student meanwhile has been escorting another girl who is also an art student. The progress of this relationship has been unsatisfactory, the student feeling that he lacks the sophistication and social graces of the girl's other companions. In his own words, he is too "slow" for her. The meaning of the dream is now apparent. Peg G. symbolizes the other girl because of two very obvious relationships, her course of study and the unpleasant social contacts. The ox-cart by a very commonplace figure of speech is a symbol of slowness. His personal shortcomings keep the dreamer from the girl and interrupt his pursuit of pleasure. The "slowness" gets in the way of the "merrymaking."

The substitution of one symbol for another in dreams is an example of *displacement* (p. 72). The symbol takes the place of some other person or event. Since dreams are usually narrative sequences in visual form, abstract concepts and qualities are often represented by more concrete symbols. In the dream reported above, slowness was represented by an ox-cart; similarly, effort might be symbolized by climbing a mountain, or fear of failure by falling. Another function of displacement is to symbolize a highly emotionally charged or anxiety-arousing event by another that is less disturbing. For example, it may be supposed that the young man dreamed of Peg G. instead of his more current girl friend because his socially uncomfortable relationship with Peg was in the past, and could be viewed with less anxiety than could the present problem. In that sense, the process of adjustment goes on even during sleep, and displacement serves as an adjustment mechanism to lessen anxiety.

Symbols in dreams, while distorted and mixed up, are derived in the same way as are the more rational symbols we use while awake. Aristotle, 2300 years ago, formulated "laws of association" stating that ideas (symbols) tend to be associated when they are *similar*, or when they *contrast,* or when they have occurred together (*contiguity*). These ancient principles are still useful practical guides for describing the selection of the symbols used in remembering, thinking, and dreaming. The laws of association are essentially the same as the principles of learning. A symbol of an event is learned when it has occurred simultaneously with the event, or in the same perceptual pattern with the event, and has then been reinforced. The same generalizations that account for the symbols used in recall and in thinking also explain the symbols used in dreams.

Some systems of dream "interpretation" have made use of fixed symbols that are always supposed to have the same meaning, regardless of whose dreams they occur in. Modern science gives little support to such a theory. Of course, persons who speak the same language and who have had similar life experiences will frequently hit upon similar symbols in dreams, just as they use like expressions in talking and thinking when they are awake. But beliefs that dreaming of a black dog indicates bad luck (Gypsy dream books) or that all dream symbols have sexual meaning (certain early psychoanalysts) are equally without foundation.

Symbols in Adjustment

Some otherwise unaccountable actions of maladjusted persons may be understood in terms of the displacement of symbols. A business man had an excessive tendency to worry about any situation having an aspect of social disapproval. At one time when he was involved in a minor automobile accident he was frantically anxious for weeks lest the blame be placed on him, and entered a prolonged lawsuit with the sole object of establishing his innocence. When a trivial incident causes so intense an emotional reaction, one may suspect that it is a symbol of some other adjustive difficulty of greater proportions. In the case in question, the man's youth had been a period of struggle to preserve social appearances in spite of comparative poverty. His early business career had been marred by a bankruptcy to which he had reacted with unusual shame. Thereafter any symbol of social disapproval became a stimulus to which he reacted with all the emotional intensity pertinent to the earlier situation. This is an example of a symbol as a substitute stimulus in an adjustment problem. It is the same thing psychologically as a conditioned anxiety reaction.

Symbols also act as substitute responses in adjustment. Pressey[18] describes a case of an unmarried woman thirty-five years old, employed in an orphanage, who was detected stealing baby clothes as they came back from the laundry. She did not try to sell them, and did nothing with the garments but accumulate them in her room. On being accused of the thefts she at first made denials, but finally confessed that she took the articles because of an uncontrollable impulse the source of which she did not understand. A study of the woman's background helps to explain her behavior. Born in an impoverished mountain region in the South, she had been sent to a mission school and then had become a housekeeper. She had never married, whereas marriage and motherhood represented the universal social role of women in the culture from which she came. Now in an environment singularly devoid of matrimonial opportunities, she symbolizes her need by the compulsive thefts. Although other factors of greater complexity are involved in understanding the woman's entire life, the meaning of the symptom is fairly obvious. The baby clothes were a symbolic substitute satisfaction for her motives relating to a husband and children.

While recognizing the importance of symbols in many spheres of human activity, it also is necessary to recognize the normal and commonplace origins of these signs and substitutes. Symbols are acquired in the same manner as are all other learned stimuli and responses. They have no hidden significance except as "hidden" means no more than difficult to discover. If all of a person's past experiences were known, all of his symbols would be distinguished easily. Conversely, a study of a man's symbolic behavior may give clues to his past experiences and present conflicts. Only in that sense are symbols significant to the understanding of behavior disorders.

THE QUALITY OF ADJUSTMENT

Varieties of Adjustment

Most human frustrations and conflicts can be solved in more than one way. If a college student fails a course, he suffers a thwarting of his vocational plans and of his concept of self-esteem. The drives that would have been reduced by the successful completion of the course are undiminished, and are likely to be augmented by anxiety. He *must* adjust in some way. The student may consult his instructor and try to remedy his shortcomings objectively. He may turn to other work in which he is more likely to succeed, and change his curriculum and his life plans. Or he may seek prestige in other fields, as in athletics or extra-curricular activities. He may show preference for situations that bring into play his strong characteristics, such as social skills, and avoid situations likely to result in thwarting. He may claim that the course he failed is useless, or that the instructor was biased, thereby trying to convince himself that he was not at fault. The student may daydream of imagined successes. He may worry chronically, failing to reduce his tensions to any appreciable extent. It is generally agreed that some of these adjustments are better than others, yet not all of them can be classified precisely as good or bad. There is an unbroken continuum of the quality of adjustment, from the best to the worst that a person can make in a given situation.

Defining what constitutes a good adjustment does not lie wholly within the province of science. Good and bad are essentially ethical concepts, resting upon one's basic philosophy of values. A physiologist can study the nature and causes of tuberculosis without making any ethical judgments. A physician who treats the disease, on the other hand, uses not only the scientific findings but also some assumptions of values, such as that it is better to be alive than dead and better to be well than sick. You exclaim "Of course!" yet the fact that everyone agrees with the physician's values does not demonstrate them scientifically. Psychological adjustments can be studied by science as behaviors, the correlates and antecedents of which are to be investigated. To a psychological practitioner, however, a maladjustment is a condition to be remedied. He is called upon not only to understand people but also to help them modify their behavior. Some of the values of psychologists, rarely explicitly stated but always assumed, seem to be that it is better to be happy than miserable with anxiety, better to fulfill all of one's needs than only some of them, and better to act so as to aid rather than hinder the adjustments of other persons.

The Adjustment Paradox

The definition of the quality of adjustments is aided by investigating a paradox or dilemma that arises from the impact of the adjustment process on the principles of learning.[19] According to the theory of learning that we have developed, people repeat and learn the responses that are satisfying or tension reducing. How, then, can anyone become maladjusted? Why does not the learning process automatically reinforce only the good responses and extinguish the ineffective ones? Common observation shows that people may persist for years in behavior that is unfavorable to their real welfare and to their long-time satisfaction. A maladjusted boy who really wants the company of others may become withdrawn and seclusive. Or, he may behave so aggressively, obnoxiously, or sarcastically that the other youngsters avoid him. Why do not such "unrewarded" responses extinguish themselves? Can learning theory account for self-defeating behavior, or must we assume that the

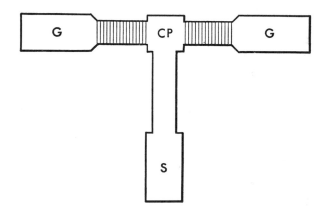

Figure 23. The Effect of Anxiety on the Persistence of "Unrewarded" Learning: Floor Plan of Maze Used by Farber

The hunger-motivated rats were placed in the starting box S, and at the choice point CP had to choose between the right or left food boxes G. The first group, the *unshocked* rats, were given 100 food-reinforced trials to one arm of the maze, but soon readjusted when the food was shifted to the other side. The *shocked* rats received a shock on the shaded grid between CP and G on trials 41 to 100; when the reward was shifted, they did not readjust readily. The *shock-fed* group was fed in an area that included the choice point and the goal-corridor in which they had been shocked. See the text for discussion of the results. (I. E. Farber, Response fixation under anxiety and non-anxiety conditions. *J. exp. Psychol.*, 1948, *38*, 111-131.)

ordinary principles of learning do not hold for some unfortunate people?

Several experiments have shed light on the learning of apparently punishing behavior, and have shown that it can be understood in terms of normal learning theory.

In an experiment designed to attack the problem quite directly, Farber trained a number of rats to go to one arm of a T-maze where they were rewarded with food (Fig. 23).[20] After 100 trials, the reward was shifted to the other arm. As might be expected, the rats soon adjusted to the change, taking an average of only 10 trials to learn to go to the newly rewarded side. A second group of rats, the "shock" group, was trained similarly, but for the last 60 of the 100 practice trials they received an electric shock after passing the choice point and before reaching the food. When the reward was shifted to the other goal box and the shock discontinued, the shocked rats behaved very differently from the unshocked ones. For an average of 61 trials they continued to run to the box with no food, the side on which they had been shocked! Two of 24 shocked rats continued this apparently unrewarded behavior for more than 250 wrong runs, without ever discovering that food could be obtained in the opposite arm.

The behavior of the shocked rats was like that of "neurotic" people who continue an unrewarding symptom indefinitely. Had they ceased to learn? Did the injurious experience of the shock negate the usual principles of learning for them? Farber offered a different interpretation. The choice point, because of its association with the shock, had become a conditioned stimulus for anxiety. For 60 trials the rats had escaped the shock by turning in one direction thereby reducing their anxiety. After the shock was discontinued, they became anxious at the choice point and then reduced the anxiety by making their old response, which had been serviceable in escaping the shock. Instead of contradicting the Law of Effect, the shocked rats merely showed that the anxiety reduction was a stronger reward than the food.

The explanation in terms of anxiety reduction was tested by a third part of the experiment. Another group of rats was trained exactly as were the shocked rats with 40 food-rewarded trials and 60 food-and-shock trials. Then they were fed for two ten-minute periods on the grid at the choice point, with the intention of making that place no longer a conditioned stimulus for anxiety. When tested with the food reward shifted to the other goal box, these "shock-fed" rats readjusted readily. Their behavior was no different from that of the rats who had received no shock at all.

Strikingly similar results were secured in another experiment.[21] Rats that were trained to run down a single alley to a "safety compartment" to escape shock eventually ceased to run when the shock was discontinued. But if a short section of the alley just in front of the safety compartment was always electrified, the rats continued to run for hundreds of trials, even though they were always placed in the farther end of the alley where the grid was uncharged. A "sensible" rat had only to sit still at the starting point to escape the shock, but these rats punished themselves by running toward and over the electrified area to reach a point of safety. They continued to do so because their running was reinforced on every trial by the tension reduction resulting from reaching safety after the shock.

Further light is shed on the problem by considering the factor of *time* in learning.[22] When a boy eats green apples, he receives the reward of immediate enjoyment, but the punishment arising from his stomach ache comes later. Many experiments with both human and animal subjects show that an immediate reward is more effective than a long-delayed one. The prompt relief of anxiety which follows an impulsive act of aggression or withdrawing can therefore outweigh the more remotely unsatisfying social consequences. The anxiety reduction resulting from an adjustive but unconstructive act comes soon after the response and can reinforce it quite strongly. Punishment or lack of reward from an ineffective act is longer delayed — and we have already seen that punishment is not a dependable means for weakening responses in any case. The time factor in reinforcement therefore helps us to understand the learning of behavior that is punishing in the long run.

Integrative, Nonintegrative, and Nonadjustive Behavior

The evidence now permits us to offer some hypotheses about the characteristics of normal or "good" adjustments. Normal behavior may be defined as *integrative*. When a wild animal smells a strong, unpleasantly acrid scent in the air, it may start running and continue until it can no longer smell the scent. Primarily, its response reduces a distressing stimulation and is therefore an immediate adjustment. But the animal's running is also integrative, for it leads to escaping

from a real danger, the forest fire. Similarly, a lonely man who goes
out looking for company feels more comfortable when he finds a
group of friends. Through the social contact, he also gives himself
opportunity for cooperative achievement and enjoyment. In these
instances, the drive-instigated behaviors are adjustive in that they
reduce tensions; they are also integrative because they facilitate
further satisfactions and accomplishments.

When your adjustments are integrative you satisfy all of your
motives as they function in an interrelated system, without the
overemphasis of one drive or the slighting of another. Furthermore,
good adjustments are integrated with respect to time. Representa-
tions of the past and the future are brought into the present by
appropriate symbolic processes, speech and thinking, so that behavior is determined by goals other than the most immediate ones.

In contrast, what we have been calling maladjusted or inadequate
behavior can now be defined more precisely as *nonintegrative*. An
extreme illustration is the legendary behavior of the frightened
ostrich that puts its head in the sand, thereby calming its emotional
drive by shutting out its perception of danger, but without improving its real safety in the least.* Many human adjustments are
ostrich-like. A man develops a strong conflict, for example, because
of an angry antagonistic attitude toward his employer on whose
good will he is also dependent. Perhaps the conflict has roots in
the man's earlier life when he learned his reactions to persons in
authority. Unable to resolve his present conflict, the man finds
other tension-reducing outlets. He may curse under his breath,
imagine what he would do if he were boss, or plan a brilliant retort
that he is afraid to make openly. The employee may also reduce
his tension by soundly and unnecessarily spanking his child when
he returns home, or by bullying his wife. These behaviors are adjustive because they reduce tensions. But they are nonintegrative
because they do not solve any real problem, and because they make
the accomplishment of other adjustments harder instead of easier.

The most marked characteristic of nonintegrative behavior is an
unevenness of satisfactions. A person who is one-sided in his motive
satisfactions, who has to reduce one intense drive at the expense of
thwarting the rest, is just the kind of individual whom psychological
clinics recognize as in need of help. His adjustments are lacking

---

* Reliable information indicates that ostriches do not really put their heads
in the sand. But people do!

in scope or wholeness. Such a person is usually paying so much attention to reducing his immediate anxieties that he is blinded to other considerations bearing on his ultimate welfare.

One type of nonintegrative behavior needs a further designation. The limiting case in the continuum of adjustments is shown by the person who finds no means of tension reduction at all, whether direct or substitute. When affected by a strong conflict, he remains stirred up, in a continuing, restless, unresolved state of anxiety. Such behavior is called a *nonadjustive* reaction.

Integrative, nonintegrative, and nonadjustive behaviors represent classes of responses, not types of people. It is the proper business of a science to classify the phenomena with which it deals, but whole people cannot be pigeonholed so easily. In any person's total behavior, integrative, nonintegrative, and nonadjustive elements may be found. People differ along a scale in the *degree* to which these concepts apply. Even a generally effective person has at least a few attributes of behavior that are nonintegrative in that they are not the best ones for the attainment of his long-term goals. He may even have some residual anxiety and therefore behave nonadjustively in mild degrees on some occasions. At the opposite end of the continuum, quite severely maladjusted people are not entirely ineffective in all respects and at all times.

In defining integrative adjustment, the reciprocal influence between a person and his social group must be emphasized. A person must do his adjusting in a society composed of other people who have their own personalities, motives, conflicts, and mechanisms of behavior. If one person satisfies his own motives without regard for other members of his culture, he not only risks retaliation, but also loses possibilities of cooperation toward the achievement of mutual aims. More broadly, social values hold that other people must be respected for their own sakes, apart from their reciprocal effects on any one individual. The concept of individual integration must therefore be supplemented with that of integration in society. When you can satisfy your motives without undue emphasis or slighting of any one need, and when you do so with constructive consideration for the adjustments of other people, then you are a well-adjusted person yourself.

SUGGESTED READINGS

The most systematic exposition of learning in relation to adjustment, at a relatively simple level, is Dollard and Miller, *Personality and Psychotherapy*. A novel approach is represented by Shaw and Ort, *Personal Adjustment in the American Culture*. LaBarre, *The Human Animal* discusses the ways in which various cultures may affect the adjustments of persons growing up in them.

Menninger, *Love Against Hate*, and Erikson, *Childhood and Society*, are insightful and important for their descriptions of how people develop their ways of behaving. Johnson, *People in Quandaries* is a delightful and nontechnical discussion of adjustments with emphasis on the part played by language and symbolism.

For more complete presentations of the principles of learning, many students will wish to review selected chapters of books in general psychology such as those by Boring, Langfeld, and Weld, by Dashiell, by Hilgard, by Munn, and by Ruch. Discussions of learning more specifically aimed toward problems of adjustment include Mowrer and Kluckhohn's Chapter 3 in Hunt, *Personality and the Behavior Disorders,* and Rotter, *Social Learning and Clinical Psychology*. For other useful material on learning, see Hilgard, *Theories of Learning*, and Guthrie and Powers, *Educational Psychology*.

Several of the research studies cited in the chapter, and others of equal relevance, are in Mowrer, *Learning Theory and Personality Dynamics*. Other advanced references, which are difficult but which will repay the effort spent are Munn's Chapter 7 in Carmichael, *Manual of Child Psychology*, and Chapters 15–21 of Stevens, *Handbook of Experimental Psychology*, especially Spence's Chapter 18.

PART TWO

Varieties of Adjustive Behavior

CHAPTER **6**

Adjustment
by Defense

Adjustment mechanisms are the habits by which people satisfy their motives, reduce their tensions, and resolve their conflicts. In the broadest meaning of the term, every act or thought that satisfies a need is such a mechanism. You are employing mechanisms of adjustment when you eat or sleep, when you attack life's problems directly and planfully, and when you achieve social adjustment by fully cooperative actions with other people. Such direct and entirely integrative mechanisms, however, have not been named, classified, or described in detail. Indeed, it would be quite impossible to do so without enumerating almost every act that you perform. No good purpose would be served by labeling all the major life adjustments as particular mechanisms. The general principle that desirable adjustments are distinguished by their integrative character helps us to understand normal conduct. An enumeration of all the "good" mechanisms would add nothing to our understanding.

In a somewhat narrower sense, mechanisms mean the indirect or substitute habits of adjustment. All persons experience some thwarting, and no one has abilities or qualities that permit a successful frontal attack on all problems. Substitute adjustment mechanisms, therefore, are found in the lives of all normal people. These substitute mechanisms are not "mental disorders" or symptoms of disorder, but are the ways people circumvent frustrations and compromise conflicts. They serve useful purposes in reducing individual tensions, even though they are not optimally integrative. The study

157

of mechanisms is valuable for the understanding of human nature in general, as well as for the treatment of conduct disorders.

One of the great discoveries of modern psychology is that the very same mechanisms are used by normal people in their everyday lives and by people who are affected with the most serious disorders. For example, you tend to get out of unpleasant situations and to justify your failures by making excuses, devising plausible alibis, and blaming other people. That is rationalization, a mechanism used by all of us. A psychotic, or mentally disordered, person may have delusions that there is a conspiracy against him, and that people are trying to poison him. That is rationalization too, and differs only in degree, not in kind, from the rationalizing you do yourself. As we study the various mechanisms, you probably will find that you have used every one of them. You should not be worried, since the substitute mechanisms describe ways that all people behave, normal as well as abnormal.

CLASSIFYING ADJUSTMENTS

All sciences classify the phenomena with which they deal, and try to order them systematically so as to reveal important relationships. In psychology it is customary to name the commonest mechanisms of adjustment and to group or classify them in some way. Naming the mechanisms is an economical procedure, for it often permits us to convey a meaning with a single word in place of a long description. Unfortunately, there is something less than unanimous agreement as to how the mechanisms should be named, and even less agreement on their classification. A survey of the indexes of eight books[1] in mental hygiene and allied fields published between 1945 and 1950 revealed that thirty-two different adjustment mechanisms were named, even after consolidating synonyms and discarding terms that did not designate common means of adjustment. Of the thirty-two mechanisms, only two — rationalization and repression — were cited in all eight books. Three more — identification, projection, and regression — were named by seven of the eight authors, while four — aggression, compensation, fantasy, and negativism — received six votes each. The remaining twenty-three mechanisms were mentioned by from one to four of the authors only. One reason for the lack of agreement in naming varieties of substitute adjustment lies in the complexity of human behavior. A great many habits can serve to reduce tensions. The classification of these habits into groups is inevitably arbitrary, and depends more on the resourcefulness and viewpoint of the classifier than on the almost inexhaustible supply of source material.

The practical problem of describing modes of adjustment remains, however, and must be given some kind of solution, even though an arbitrary one. Several schemes for grouping mechanisms might be suggested. To classify adjustments according to their *cause* would seem desirable, but remote causes are often so complex as to be undetermined, and evidence shows clearly that the same immediate influences may result in many different kinds of adjustment. Conceivably, adjustments might be classified by the *type of person* who employs them. This approach runs into difficulties in the measurement of personality and overlooks the fact that one person uses various adjustment mechanisms at different times. A remaining possibility is to group mechanisms according to the *kind of response* displayed. Such a classification has the advantage of objectivity, although it may be accused of superficiality. Five main groups of adjustive responses may be distinguished on that basis. The groups represent only a convenient arrangement arising from the practical need for making *some* division. They should not be regarded as fundamentally distinct types of adjustment.

1. *Adjustment by defense.* This chapter will describe mechanisms that are mainly aggressive or outgoing. They usually involve some group interaction or communication, but of an antisocial and nonintegrative nature. Such mechanisms have been described as "moving *against* people."[2]

2. *Adjustment by escape.* Certain mechanisms are characterized by withdrawing or escaping from the experiences that incite conflicts. They show a marked lack of social activity, either as passive seclusiveness or active refusal, and ordinarily are accompanied by imaginary satisfactions in fantasy. Seclusive adjustments have been called "moving *away from* people."

3. *Adjustments involving focal fears.* Although fear-like or anxious behavior is a factor in all nonintegrative adjustments, it appears with prominence in phobias, which are irrational specific fears. Repression, a mechanism also found in many maladjustments, can be investigated most clearly in connection with phobias.

4. *Adjustment by ailments.* Some of the most spectacular adjust-

ments are those that seem like physical illnesses and include pains, paralyses, and cramps. Such mechanisms, along with others, are classed as psychoneuroses, which are severely disabling maladjustments.

5. *Anxiety states.* If a person finds no way at all to get out of his difficulties, he remains stirred up, anxious, exhausted, and "nervous." The anxiety states are mainly nonadjustive. They are not mechanisms that reduce tensions but are evidences of unresolved adjustment problems.

DEFENSE MECHANISMS

A Case Study

James G. was referred to a psychological clinic because of severe difficulties in his conduct at school. The principal of his school reported general bad behavior in the classroom, constant teasing and bullying of younger children, and occasional petty thievery. His conduct had been at a very unsatisfactory level for two years. During the current term James, now twelve-and-a-half years old, has been placed under three teachers in succession, the school being a large one with several sections in each grade. The first teacher could not control him and neither could the second, but the third succeeded by repressive measures in keeping him from too greatly disturbing the peace of the school, so he has stayed with her.

A careful inquiry revealed the details of James's conduct. In the classroom he shows no seriously delinquent behavior, but persistently makes small infractions of discipline of an aggressive nature. He stamps on the floor when other pupils walk in the aisles; he talks back to the teacher; he engages in petty trippings and scuffles. None of this conduct is in itself indicative of severe maladjustment, for nearly all schoolboys do similar things. Only the persistent and frequent nature of James's misdemeanors make him the despair of teachers — and of interest to psychologists. Out of school he plays little with other boys of his own age but frequently is found bullying and teasing younger boys. James pushes or hits a smaller boy without provocation, and delights to chase him screaming home to his door. Thefts include taking possessions of little value from his fellow pupils, and some stealing of nuts, fruit, and candy from neighborhood stores. The things stolen are often given to or shared with other boys.

At the clinic, James presented an appearance which gave no indication of his unusual reputation as a trouble-maker. He was a pale, slim boy, rather tall for his twelve years. His manner was friendly and he cooperated well in the tests that were given, seeming delighted to be the center of so much attention.

The physical examination revealed no defects needing correction. His general condition was good, sight and hearing were normal, and no glandular disturbances were suspected. In an individual intelligence test, James obtained a mental age of thirteen years, three months, and an intelligence quotient of 107. He was thus slightly above average in mental ability. The standard tests in school achievement told an even more favorable story. James did as well as the average fifteen-year-old, about 20 per cent better than expectation for his age. He showed superior performance in all subjects, being most able in reading and spelling and least above average in arithmetic. These findings eliminated a conclusion which teachers too often make without evidence, that a disagreeable pupil is stupid.

James's early school history was not available, as he had transferred to his present school two years before. Up to that time the family had lived in a suburb where, according to the parents' account, James had done well in school and had presented no difficulties. He is now in the sixth grade. For three semesters his scholarship marks were good, but for the past term, only passing. Conduct marks have been uniformly unsatisfactory. In the sixth grade, James is not seriously retarded for his chronological age, although his mental age suggests that he could do well in about one grade above his present placement. Educational achievement tests show that his command of school subjects is comparable to that of the average eighth grade pupil. The principal says that James is conspicuous in his classes for lack of attention and concentration. No wonder! He has already mastered the arithmetic of a grade in advance, and reads with the skill of most high-school pupils. James's attendance is now quite regular. Last year there was some trouble about tardiness which made him unpopular with his classmates because of a promptness contest between rooms, but this has been remedied.

The G. family lives in an apartment in comfortable circumstances. Mr. G. is a salesman with an adequate income. He is away from home much of the time, and his influence on James is small. Mrs. G. is a large, strong woman, who was born in Norway, but who came to this country in childhood with an older sister. No grandparents complicate the scene, as Mr. G.'s parents are dead and Mrs. G.'s have never come to America. James has a younger brother, Charles, who is ten years and ten months old. Charles is James's constant companion, and has lately shown some of James's behavior traits.

Mrs. G. furnished the psychologist with a history of James's development. He had always been a rather thin and poorly nourished child. He had measles, chicken pox, and whooping cough before he was six, all rather severely. His start in school was delayed a half-year because of the last disease. His tonsils were removed at age eight. The most striking fact was James's history of accidents. His right arm has been broken twice, at age seven and age eight, and his left leg was fractured at age nine and a half. All these injuries occurred while he was engaged in rough play with other children.

James's play is mostly solitary or in the company of his younger brother. He prefers playing cards and other indoor games to outdoor play, but gets a fairly adequate amount of exercise by roller skating and running around. James's real passion is for the movies. He is allowed to go only once a week, but each movie is talked about for days afterward. His favorite pictures are "Westerns" and other films of adventure. James says that when he grows up he would like to be "a cowboy in the movies." He has no other vocational ambitions, and seems quite unaware of the inappropriateness of his aim for a rather puny city boy. Another recreation is extensive reading. He reads an average of two or three books a week, chiefly of the boy-adventure type. When asked why he does not play football or baseball, James replies that he just doesn't like to, but afterward volunteers that he guesses it is because he was hurt so much. His mother discourages his playing with other boys, partly from fear of his being hurt again, partly because of his inability to get along peaceably in a social group.

The precipitating cause of James's difficulties seems to be his reaction to his physical difficulties. His frequent injuries — breaking an arm twice and a leg once — and also his general lack of physical stamina, have given him an unfavorable attitude toward his own capability. When faced with situations involving the competitive, rough-and-tumble play typical of twelve-year-old boys, James has learned to respond with anxiety. His conditioned avoidance of the usual outlets for activity has led to needs for substitute satisfactions. He fulfills his normal motives for mastery and approval by bullying, showing-off, and petty thievery. He also finds adjustment in the imagined satisfactions of fiction, movies, and daydreams. Since all these mechanisms serve to reduce his anxiety, they have been learned and have become habitual. As in most real-life situations, James's difficulties are complicated by other factors. His misplacement in school, so that his studies provide no challenge and require no effort, prevents school achievement from satisfying his needs, and gives him added opportunity to display his overaggressive attitudes in the classroom.

Another, and probably a more basic, source of James's attitudes is found in his family life. He lacks an intimate relationship with his father, whose work keeps him away from home most of the time. His mother is overprotective, and has not encouraged him to grow toward independence. Both these factors make it harder for James to develop manly qualities.

The clinic at which James was studied did not have resources for working with him directly. Conferences were held with his parents and with his school principal to plan a constructive program for him. James's mother received some enlightenment on the need to encourage him to play with boys of his own age. In order to promote desirable social contacts he was enrolled in a troop of Boy Scouts and in a Y.M.C.A. Consultations with the scoutmaster and the gymnasium director evoked their cooperation in helping James to join in group activities and to avoid initial failure. Boxing instruction was suggested as a way to build up his self-confidence as a manly and physically adequate boy. The school was advised of his superior accomplishment and of his need for more challenging academic standards. As a result, he was given an extra promotion at once. The work of the higher grade proved to be stimulating, and placement in a new group gave James an opportunity to establish different attitudes toward school in the company of pupils who did not expect mischief of him. These remedial measures are quite different from those of an old-fashioned "common-sense" view that probably would have called for suppression and punishment. The treatments of giving boxing lessons to the bully, and of promoting the troublesome pupil instead of failing him, were effective because they were based on an understanding of the boy's needs and of the reasons underlying his unsuccessful adjustments.

Origins of Defensive Behavior

The behavior patterns shown by James G., including attention-getting, bullying, unruly conduct, and certain kinds of stealing, are examples of defense mechanisms. They are among the most common methods for reducing tension. When real achievement in a strongly motivated direction is thwarted, pseudo-achievements, sometimes of an aggressive character and sometimes imaginative, make their appearance as responses to the unsatisfied drives. Defense mechanisms often arise from immediate and temporary frustration. An ignored child begins to show off. When you have been insulted or slighted by an acquaintance, you are likely to talk too aggressively, brag too strongly, and try to belittle your opponent, or else to daydream of imagined successes. Since everyone is thwarted from time to time, all people employ defense mechanisms.

An important observation, however, is that some persons show strong defensive behavior even when confronted with little or no immediate frustration. The sight of a smaller boy usually would not be frustrating to a twelve-year-old, but James G. often reacted to that situation by aggressively chasing the child home. Something in his *past learning* made him behave defensively when the present situation offered little justification for such behavior.

Persistent and intense defensive behavior is evoked by a conditioned *anxiety response* to social situations that imply competition or criticism. In his past life, an individual has experienced pain, punishment, threat, or rejection in connection with situations in which he was evaluated as a person. Anxiety was aroused in such circumstances, and then reduced by some form of defensive behavior. Subsequently, other situations even remotely suggesting evaluation, competition, or the like are capable of stimulating anxiety, an example of the typical generalization of a conditioned emotional response. The anxiety acts as an added drive, and has to be reduced by any adjustive mechanisms that may be available.

The self concept of an overdefensive person is characterized by a generalized *attitude of inferiority*. An attitude of inferiority is a chronic and permeating concept of one's self as incapable or un-worthy; its possessor has an expectation of being unsuccessful and defeated in competitive situations, either in one restricted sphere such as physical effort or in broader areas of his life activities. Like all attitudes (see p. 93), an attitude of inferiority is acquired by a long series of experiences extending in almost all cases into child-hood. Horney calls this same feeling *basic anxiety:* "an insidiously increasing, all-pervading feeling of being lonely and helpless in a hostile world."*

The anxiety arising from an inferiority attitude sets up a conflict whenever an evaluative situation is perceived or implied. A person wants to satisfy his normal culturally-determined needs to succeed and achieve and to receive recognition and approval. In conflict with these needs are his learned expectations of failure or defeat. Defense mechanisms are frantic but nonintegrative attempts to resolve that conflict. One way to end a conflict is to strengthen one of the incompatible motives so that it becomes dominant over the opposed need. So the defensive person tries too hard; he overdoes the attempt to demonstrate his adequacy and strength.

Causes of Unfavorable Self-Evaluation

The most important causes of anxiety reactions to evaluation are home-grown. Attitudes of inferiority can be created by a variety of unfortunate child-parent relationships. Some anxieties originate quite early in childhood, when parents do not respond to a child's needs, or when they do not give him warm recognition as a person. He feels deserted and helpless, because of his real dependence on his parents for psychological as well as physiological satisfactions. In later childhood, inappropriate methods of "discipline" may give rise to anxieties. Some parents blame and ridicule their children, and accompany scolding and nagging with really painful punish-ments and deprivations. In many instances such parental behavior is motivated by the parents' defenses against their own anxieties. A child's immature behavior is perceived as reflecting on their capa-bilities as parents, and by condemning and belittling the child they defend themselves against blame. A vicious circle is set up, for the more a child is made to feel inferior, the more defensively "bad"

---

* Karen Horney, *The neurotic personality of our time.* New York: W. W. Norton & Co., 1937. P. 89.

he may become. A number of adolescent adjustment problems arise from the father and son relationship. Even a quite well-meaning father, by making all his son's decisions for him, by pushing him to succeed in school or in sports beyond his capabilities, or by constantly impressing him with the superiority of adults, may cause a defensive attitude toward himself and a generalized attitude toward all authority that will result either in timidity or in rebellion.

Physical and organic inferiorities have some part in the origin of anxieties, not because of any intrinsic characteristics of physical traits as such, but because of the important role that strength plays in the lives of children in our culture. Among boys, inferiority attitudes are often rooted in weakness, frailness, lameness, and other structural defects, because of the persecution that boys almost always apply to a weak member of their group. Repeated injuries and painful experiences, as in the case of James G., and also clumsiness and lack of skill, often operate in the same way. Among older boys and men some of the same characteristics may result in perceptions of one's own inadequacy. In the case of girls and women the same defects may be important but to a lesser degree, since the social role of girls in our culture does not demand so much strength or such active participation in games. Physical unattractiveness is a stronger cause of inferiority attitudes among girls than among boys. Sometimes defenses against inferior pulchritude are directed only against men. It is proverbial that prudish reactions, a defense against sex, are more characteristic of unattractive women than of comely ones.

Intellectual defects may be precipitating causes of defense reactions, but only when there is invidious comparison of the mentalities of persons who are in close contact, as between brothers or sisters, parents and children, or pupils in the same classroom. A large segment of our society has a high regard for achievement in school, and children who do not succeed are subjected to painful criticisms.

> In one case, a girl of seventeen displayed markedly defensive reactions against members of her family, making remarks obviously intended to hurt the feelings of others, and engaging in eccentric behavior which directed attention to herself. The girl had dropped out of high school after showing little scholastic interest or aptitude, while her two brothers and two sisters had achieved brilliant academic success. An intelligence examination

showed that she was of normal mentality, but the other members of her family undoubtedly were very superior. Thus the girl had no mental defect in relation to the average person, but was inferior to her sisters, with whom she was compared most closely. Inferiority attitudes concerning intellect occur most often in families in which the children vary in ability or in which the aptitude of a child is insufficient for the plans his parents make for him.

The sexual sphere of behavior contributes more than its share of anxieties. Among older boys and men, real or imagined inferiorities of sex organs or functions may precipitate defensive behavior. Adolescents often feel very guilty about their sex experiences and fantasies. Studies such as those of Kinsey have shown that some form of sexual activity is almost universal, in childhood and adolescence as well as in the adult years. The standards of middle-class culture, directly enforced by most parents, hold that sex is unmentionable, guilty, or sinful. Young people reared in homes in which morality is closely bound to narrow religious beliefs are especially likely to suffer from this difficulty. They may come to believe that their normal curiosity and interest concerning sex is a sign of depravity, that is, of their moral and religious inferiority. Boys often have intense anxiety about masturbation, strengthened by unfounded but widely held superstitions that they will become insane or lose their manhood. The guilt and inferiority arising from sex may lead to defense mechanisms, sometimes of an aggressive nature but more often of the withdrawing sort.

Failure to achieve one's expectations in social status may be another source of attitudes of inferiority.

> One eleven-year-old boy was quite a problem to his family and to his school because of moody, aggressive, sarcastic conduct and occasional truancy. The boy's family had occupied a position of social prominence in a small town, but his father's early death and subsequent financial reverses had led to a sharp reduction in circumstances. They still occupied the large and well-located ancestral house, but it was in poor repair. They lacked an automobile and other signs of status. The crowning indignity to the boy was that his mother made him wear the readily-recognized discarded clothes of his classmates which their parents sympathetically gave him.

In the case of social status, as also in physical and intellectual inferiorities, the objective defect itself is not the problem. The

anxiety arises from the discrepancy between expectation and realization.

Symptoms of Inferiority Attitudes

A person who has acquired a conviction of his own inadequacy
shows this attitude in many incidents of everyday life as well as in
the more obvious mechanisms of defense. Bagby gave a useful
inventory of the symptoms of attitudes of inferiority.[3] A person full
of anxiety about himself shows marked *sensitiveness to criticism*.
He resents any direct or implied evaluation of his personal qualities
and cannot react constructively to criticism. A student with this
habit is likely to devote much effort to prove that his solution to a
problem is a correct one, when he might more profitably search for
a better method of attack. The inferiority attitude is characterized
by *ideas of reference*, in which a person applies all criticism to himself. He supposes that the chance laughter or the whispered comments of others that he overhears are directed toward him and that
his actions are being observed by everyone. *Seclusiveness* is likely
to be noted. Persons with attitudes of inferiority will cross the
street to avoid meeting people and will hesitate to join a group
gathered informally in the school corridor or on the street. They
think they are not wanted.

An apparently contradictory but really consistent trait is *over-
response to flattery*. Since the person feels a great need to prove
his own adequacy, anyone who supports it will be given a welcome
reception. Hence he will be led easily by those who gratify his need
for praise. Another symptom is *poor reaction to competition*. All
contests are entered for the purpose of winning, and the individual
plays in dead earnest. He is not a good loser. Often he will be
willing to compare his skill only with those he can defeat easily or
else he will compete only in obscure games, little practiced by
other people, in which he has developed a high degree of competence. A *tendency to derogate others* is another indication of an
attitude of inferiority, for in pointing out the faults of other persons
an individual minimizes his own defects.

In moderate degrees, all of the signs of anxiety about personal
adequacy are characteristic of human nature in general. You probably can recognize several of them in your own conduct. All persons
react with some degree of anxiety to interpersonal evaluations.

Differences between normal and markedly anxious states are of intensity and scope, not of kind.

The Development of Defense Mechanisms

When an attitude of inferiority is in process of formation, a person is learning to react with anxiety to social criticism, competition, and authority. His first response is likely to be simple withdrawing, but soon a number of defenses will appear that are characteristic of the early *varied response stage* of adjustment. In the beginning stages of defense, the mechanisms usually are numerous, varied, and relatively temporary. The affected person's behavior is that of trial and error. Any response that will reduce the tension may be tried, and markedly different forms of behavior may be found in the same person from time to time. In one instance he will be blustering and overaggressive, in another he will try to explain away his shortcomings, and on another occasion he will be shy, seclusive, and submerged in imaginary satisfactions. James G. was in the primary stage of adjustment, as he showed almost all forms of defense mechanisms.

As various forms of defense are tried, some are found more satisfactory or more applicable to a person's situation than others. The mechanisms that reduce the person's tensions more successfully are selected in the course of adjustive learning and others are abandoned. Eventually, without any sudden change, a *fixed response stage* of adjustment will be evolved. In the fully developed adjustment, the defense mechanisms are well-organized habits, few in number, consistent, and likely to be enduring. When complete defensive habits have been established, the primary evidences of an attitude of inferority may be submerged and hard to detect. The individual is no longer anxious; on the contrary he may be very aggressive and egotistical. Since well-fixed defense mechanisms are more difficult to extinguish, constructive mental hygiene is furthered by discovering and treating attitudes of inferiority in their early stages in childhood. When, as occasionally happens, a catastrophe breaks down the complicated defenses of a mature man, seriously disorganized behavior may result, usually in the form of severe anxiety or depression.

Defense mechanisms are not acquired deliberately. For the most part, they are unconscious and unverbalized. An individual does not show overaggressive or withdrawing behavior because of a reasoned decision to satisfy his motives with such devices. Instead, he finds himself aroused to activity by a drive the nature of which he does not understand. He is just restless and unhappy. In the course of trial and error he discovers some responses that reduce his tensions and afford relief. Defensive behavior develops through blind learning and does not involve conscious choice.

VARIETIES OF DEFENSE MECHANISMS

Defense mechanisms have been classified into a number of common types. An understanding of each of the mechanisms enriches your conception of defensive behavior as a whole, but you should not regard the categories as entirely separate or mutually exclusive. Many of the mechanisms overlap, and behavior that one observer would call by one term may be named differently by another equally competent psychologist. The mechanisms of defense are often combined, and a single sequence of human behavior may illustrate several of them at once. In spite of these objections, the mechanisms offer useful descriptions of typical adjustments and valuable insights into the ways in which drives are reduced.

Attention-getting

Attention-getting is perhaps the most primitive of the defense mechanisms. To receive approval from people, or to gain mastery over them, a person first has to make them notice him. Attention-getting is any act that makes a person the focus of other people's behavior. Attention-getting devices are used in infancy and early childhood. A baby's cry is its first interpersonal mechanism of adjustment, and is integrative in early life when the infant has no other way to summon help when in distress. For a baby to cry is normal and useful. When an older child has unfulfilled needs or unresolved conflicts and has not learned to get adult help in other ways, he may remain a "crybaby." His crying is then a special adjustive technique, less mature and less integrative than one might expect for his years. Little children have many other attention-getting habits, such as getting in the way, making noise and asking interminable questions. Refusal to eat is a common way of attracting attention, when the child discovers that he can arouse his parents' concern and make every mealtime a lengthy ritual of which he is the center. Deliberate disobedience is often an attention-getting mechanism, since to be scolded is more satisfying than to be ignored entirely. The inventory of behaviors that have attention-getting value to some children is almost inexhaustible, including bed-wetting, thumb-sucking, running away, complaining of injuries and ailments, and many others.

All normal children try many attention-getting behaviors, which reach a peak at the "questioning age" of from three to five years. That attention-getting is normal does not mean that it is not an adjustive technique resulting from thwarting. A small child has limited capabilities and is constantly hampered and controlled by his parents and by the other adults around him. In turn he seeks to control them, and gaining their attention is the simplest and most successful means of exercising a rudimentary amount of control. As the child grows older and acquires greater competence in dealing with his adjustive problems independently, the immature types of attention-getting will become less frequent, although they never disappear entirely, even in adults. There can be no set formulas by which parents can deal with attention-getting, since each child's needs and conflicts differ somewhat and require individual study. In normal cases, it is a good general principle to give warm and genuine attention to the child as a person, and to ignore his antic behavior as much as possible.

Attention-getting is often carried into the school years, to the extreme annoyance of teachers and classmates. The child with excessive needs for attention asks too many irrelevant questions, interrupts, foments disorder, and seeks in every way to be unusual. Teachers all too often react to such a child with defensive behavior of their own. A clash ensues, and the child is put in his place. A more constructive approach to the attention-getting child is to give him special duties that will bring socialized recognition. In persistent cases, the attention-getting symptoms cannot be treated in isolation; the whole child needs study and help.

Social-status frustration sometimes evokes attention-getting behavior in older children and adolescents, and in adults too.

One high school girl, Alva B., was notably unattractive because she was overweight and had large, coarse features. Her father was a bartender, an occupation not esteemed in a conservative

small town's social scheme. All these circumstances barred her
from desired social relationships. In response, Alva took to an
excessive use of make-up. She appeared in school well coated
with cosmetics, her eyebrows plucked and penciled, and her lips
drawn in a most exaggerated manner. The painting did not render
her beautiful, but it made her noticed, and this was an effective
substitute for social recognition. Later Alva became a cheer leader
and was an excellent one, the position being perfectly suited to
her need for attention.

Compensation

Compensation is the overemphasis of a type of behavior, which
serves to reduce tensions resulting from frustration or conflict.
Compensatory habits serve purposes of adjustment in two ways.
First, they are rather close substitutes for real achievement, and
hence reduce quite directly the drives that have been thwarted.
Second, compensations serve to divert attention from personal shortcomings and defects, thereby eliminating some of the expressed or
implied criticism that produces anxiety. Compensation reduces
self-criticism more than it eliminates criticism from other people.
Through his preoccupation with the success of his substitute accomplishments, a person finds himself less concerned with anxieties
about his inferiority.

The simplest and most common compensations are those in which
an individual overreacts in the same general area of functioning as
that in which he perceives himself to be inferior. A boy who is
adjusting to a sense of physical inferiority is somewhat more likely
to exhibit defenses of a physically aggressive sort than to seek compensation in other fields. Even his daydreams are of muscular
accomplishments. James G. illustrates this tendency quite clearly.
A physically frail boy, he compensates by bullying and trouble-
making. The very criticisms that his parents, teachers and playmates
direct at him are satisfying, for he is now condemned as a "tough
guy" rather than as a weakling.

Direct compensations also are found in children whose experiences have made them feel insecure in intellectual and scholastic
achievements.

Sidney H., a sixteen-year-old boy repeating the seventh grade
for the third time, illustrates that type of compensation. He was
of very limited intellectual capacity, with an I.Q. of 75 on a group

intelligence test, yet a visitor to the classroom would not guess his test score from his behavior. When the teacher was talking he leaned forward on his desk, his eyes alertly on the blackboard example. His whole manner fairly popped with attention and interest. When a question was asked he was the first to raise his hand, although his answers were sadly deficient in almost every instance. Outside the classroom he was always busy. He rushed from one activity to another with the air of one who has many important duties to perform. Sidney had developed conspicuous scholastic compensations for his intellectual weaknesses. His appearance of alertness not only fooled the casual observer but also, and perhaps more significantly, aided Sidney in his self-deception about his intellectual powers.

Also fairly common are displaced compensations, in which the trait overemphasized is not the one focal to the anxiety. The mental-physical relationship offers many examples. A dull child, over-age in school, is being thwarted in the attainment of recognition and mastery in school performance, and has unreduced needs which lead him to trial-and-error adjustment. Since he is older and larger than most of his classmates, physical mastery provides an easily discovered outlet. He may become a bully or a gang leader. If the compensation can be guided into socially constructive channels, such as excelling in athletics or in manual activities, a more integrative adjustment may be achieved. A compensation displaced in the opposite direction is shown by the pupil who substitutes intellectual superiority for physical achievements that are thwarted by an attitude of inferiority. If the youngster has good intellectual ability the added drive may lead to real scholarly accomplishment. If he is less ably endowed, he may become a grind or a pseudo-scholar, or his defense may be diverted to other mechanisms because his scholastic compensation fails to prove satisfying.

More remote and less obvious compensations are found in everyday life in almost endless variety. Among the most common is the compensation sought by parents through the achievements of their children.

The case of Paul J. is illustrative. Paul's father was a successful drugstore owner who had worked his way to achievement without much formal education. His lifelong desire had been to become a physician, but he had been unable to realize that aim. From early childhood it had been decreed that Paul should enter the medical profession. After completing his college courses without distinction, Paul gained admission to a medical school, but in the first semester failed in anatomy and chemistry. Investigation showed that his ability was in the lowest 5 per cent of his class and that his interests, measured by a relatively objective technique, were not at all those of physicians. Both tests and interviews showed that the young man's interests and abilities were in the business field. His failure released him from medical school, which probably was best for his ultimate welfare. The readjustment had been achieved, however, at the cost of years of lost effort and, more significantly, of creating in Paul a sense of personal inadequacy that will be difficult to overcome in any field of endeavor.

Many failing students in colleges have been pushed into inappropriate programs of study to satisfy the compensatory needs of their parents. In other cases the result may be more integrative. The drive of parental compensation may support the youngster and spur him to achievement if his ability and interests are compatible with his parents' ambitions.

Identification

Identification is a method of tension reduction through the achievement of another person or of a group of people. An individual employing this mechanism is said to "identify himself" with the person, organization, or activity concerned. Identification appears early in life in the relationship between a child and a parent. Since a young child achieves many of his adjustments only through the help of his parents, he establishes a habit of regarding their qualities as assets of his own. A boy's strongest identification is usually with his father, who satisfies many of his needs for strength and knowledge. Many traits, ranging from inconsequential mannerisms to important social attitudes, are learned through the operation of the identification mechanism. In that sense, identification is one of the basic factors in character formation.

Group participation often illustrates the motive-satisfying values of identification. Men join clubs, fraternities, and lodges through which individual aspirations are achieved collectively. Such societies are often valued in proportion to their exclusiveness, which satisfies motives for recognition and self-esteem. A youth identifies with his school and favorite baseball team, a business man with his organization, a housewife with her home and family. The extent to which people speak of "*my* group," and refer to it as "*we*," indicates the individually-centered nature of the satisfactions derived from group identification. People also identify themselves with their possessions. Men take pride in their homes, automobiles, or clothing, and gain tension reduction from exhibiting these material objects or merely from contemplating their excellence.

Like other defense mechanisms, identification is not adopted deliberately, nor is a person usually aware of its adjustive significance to him. It is a deeply ingrained habit arising through trial-and-error learning. For most people, identification is a constructive and integrative mechanism, but it is an adjustment nonetheless.

While usually a superior adjustment, identification may in some instances be associated with personal difficulties. If a person is too fawningly imitative of acquaintances who have prestige, and is too eager to join societies and support causes, you may suspect that he is using identification as an anxiety-reducing mechanism in the same way that he might use compensation or attention-getting. Unfortunate identifications may lead to maladjustments. Instances in which a boy has drifted into delinquency because of his identification with an antisocial person are frequent and obvious. Conflicts of identifications are more subtle. If a boy's father is dead or divorced, or if circumstances or the father's attitudes prevent frequent and warm contacts with his son, the boy may form a strong identification with his mother and adopt many feminine characteristics. Later, his gang of boy peers will demand different attitudes and identifications and will reject him if he continues his feminine outlook. Conflict and anxiety will result, which may be resolved by aggressive compensatory behavior. The neighbors interpret the boy's trouble as due to the lack of a father's "strong hand"; more often it is caused by a lack of father identification.

Reaction Formation

A conflict sometimes may be resolved by strengthening one of the conflicting motives. A mechanism serving that purpose is reaction formation, which is defined as the adoption of an attitude opposite to one that produces anxiety. Like other varieties of defense, reaction formation can be seen in many small incidents of everyday life. The proverbial behavior of a boy passing a graveyard at night is to whistle in the dark, thereby expressing a nonchalance that is the opposite of his real feelings and helping him to inhibit a tendency to flee in terror. Some timid persons whose past experience has caused them to feel anxiety in relationships with other people hide behind a gruff facade and assume a hostility against others that protects them from fear.

Quite a number of the adjustment mechanisms have been demonstrated by experimental as well as by clinical evidence. Some of the experiments have used animals as subjects and show that the common mechanisms are not limited to human behavior. An experimental observation of reaction formation will serve as an example. In one part of a study of responses to conflict, Mowrer placed rats in a compartment in which they received a gradually increasing electric shock through a grill of metal rods that constituted the floor.[4] The rats could end the shock by pressing a metal pedal at one end of the box. As the shock increased, the rats became more active and eventually would touch the pedal. In a few trials all rats learned to press the pedal promptly to terminate the shock. Then, the pedal itself was charged so that the rat received an electric shock upon touching it. Subsequent trials yielded an interesting observation. As the shock from the floor grill became stronger, some rats would move to the end of the box *opposite* to the pedal. These rats acted as though they "wanted" to press the pedal, but retreated from it so as to protect themselves from performing a desired but punishing act. Their behavior was analogous to the mechanism of reaction formation, in which a person expresses the opposite of an impulse which he really feels, but which also arouses anxiety. The rats that fled from the pedal might be described as "resisting a temptation."

A person who has strong motivation in a socially disapproved direction often displays reaction formation. He may have aggressive or sexual motives which his training has led him to view with anxiety. Less common and more remotely derived urges, as for alcohol or gambling, sometimes operate similarly.

> Morgan[5] described a young clergyman whose sermons developed into frenzied tirades against sin, which to him was synonymous with anything suggesting sexual conduct. He alienated his congregation by denunciations of dancing, new styles of dressing or of hair arrangement, cosmetics, and vice, which he considered all in the same category. He forbade the boys and girls of his

congregation to walk home from church together. This young minister was trying to live a celibate life which he believed essential to his calling. His quite normal sexual impulses and thoughts aroused severe anxiety in him, which he controlled by strengthening his defenses against any evidence of sex in others.

Although the clergyman's adjustment is best classed as reaction formation, it also resembles compensation, and has more than a trace of projection — which illustrates the degree to which defense mechanisms overlap. Prudish attitudes may arise in the same way as did the defenses of the clergyman. Many observers have noted that the most fervent reformer is a man who has been tempted strongly by the evil he seeks to combat.

The mechanism of reaction formation offers a hazard to clear and scientific thinking because it is possible to hypothesize that either of two opposite motives underlies the same behavior. If a mother loves and protects her child with great zeal, one can suppose that she does so because of normal socialized motives. Or, it is sometimes said that she really hates and rejects the child and that her great show of love is a reaction formation. You have to guard against the attractive snare of adopting the explanation that fits your theoretical preconceptions or your prejudices about the particular case. Human behavior is very complex, however, and we cannot discard the concept of reaction formation because it is sometimes abused. Highly moral attitudes and intense preoccupations with socially approved objectives *sometimes* arise from reaction formation but they do not *always* spring from that source. Decisions about the adjustments of one particular person require a careful study of his unique experiences and learnings, and cannot be reached from broad general principles.

Rationalization

Rationalization is a form of defense in which a person gives socially acceptable reasons for his behavior. Rationalization is not a process of logical reasoning but an attempt to make conduct *appear* sensible and in conformity to social expectations; "irrationalization" perhaps would be a more appropriate term. When you rationalize you give "good" reasons that serve to conceal from yourself and from other people the *real* reasons which are in conflict with learned social standards. Rationalizations may be spoken aloud to other people, expressed in private thoughts to oneself, or shown in non-verbal actions.

A man contemplating the purchase of an automobile that he really cannot afford may persuade himself by a host of good reasons. He points out that rides in the country will benefit his wife's health; that he can take the children to school in the car and thereby keep them from getting wet feet in rainy weather; that the recreation afforded by the car will keep him more fit for his job. He may even convince himself that if he does not have the car he is likely to suffer a breakdown and lose his employment entirely. So the man argues that the automobile, far from being an extravagance, will be an economy in the end. Behind such good reasons for buying the car may lie many unacknowledged real reasons. That the car is a badge of success in the community necessary for full social approval, that mastery is involved in the form of outdoing his neighbors, may be strong motives behind his expressed desires.

Rationalization, perhaps more clearly than any other mechanism, illustrates a response to conflicting demands in the culture. Most people in Western culture learn competitive and aggressive patterns of motivation that make them want to succeed and excel, and to secure recognition and approval. At the same time, the training given in the dominant culture teaches children that direct and naive forms of hostility and self-aggrandizement are inferior and punishable. At least, to state openly that one is seeking personal power is not "in good taste." Perhaps the group has to enforce such a rule to keep itself from being dominated too easily by strong persons. People who have learned their social lesson well cannot acknowledge their aggressive motivations. Such needs may be quite unconscious. Another relevant social custom is a high regard for reasonable and logical thinking. Everyone is expected to give a reasonable account of himself, and the impulsive nature of most behavior is given no public recognition. These three trends in socialized behavior, which make us aggressive, make us conceal our aggressions, and make us give logical accounts of our actions, cause all of us to become victims of rationalization.

Several types of rationalization have been described which serve as defense mechanisms to protect people from anxiety arising from an expectation of social criticism. *Blaming the incidental cause* is a common variety. A child who stumbles over a stool turns and kicks it. Here is rationalization in action, defending him against imputations of clumsiness or carelessness. It was the stool's fault. The defeated tennis player must have his racket restrung, and the poor workman proverbially blames his tools.

The *sour-grapes* mechanism is another popular rationalization. Unable to reach the grapes, the fox declares that they are sour. Similarly, we find a person proclaiming that the job he lost was no good anyway. The young man finds that the girl who refused him has a million faults. A highly organized rationalization of the sour-grapes type is the "doctrine of balances," that if a person is superior in some way he must be inferior in some other respect. Many people believe that an intellectually gifted child is especially likely to be weak and puny, or that he is inevitably highstrung and nervous. A belief is prevalent that a quick learner will not remember as well as a slow learner — "easy come, easy go." "Beautiful but dumb" illustrates another common rationalization that comely girls are especially likely to be stupid. In all three of these illustrations, well-established psychological research contradicts the popular beliefs. Gifted children are stronger and less likely to be nervous than are average children; quick learners retain better; beautiful girls are slightly more likely to be bright than to be stupid. The doctrine of balances is a rationalization of the mediocre. That it is undesirable for a child to be bright is very consoling to the parents of a stupid child. The rationalization concerning pulchritude and brains is an invention of the unattractive. The converse of the sour-grapes rationalization often accompanies it. This *sweet lemon* mechanism asserts that one's fates and fortunes, however humble, are just what one wants or just what is best for one in the end.

Projection

A person who employs the mechanism of projection perceives in other people the motives and traits about which he is sensitive and anxious himself. Thus a student who has anxiety about cheating on examinations, perhaps because of a guilty reaction to having cheated in the past, may adopt a scrupulously honest attitude by reaction-formation. Being particularly sensitive to this evil, as he conceives it, he *projects* it upon his fellow students by accepting evidence of very low objective validity as an indication that everyone around him is cheating. Any glance, word, or gesture on the part of his fellow students is interpreted as a sign of dishonesty in the examination.

In an experimental study of the projection mechanism, Sears secured self-ratings and ratings of one another from about one hundred college fraternity men, on traits such as disorderliness, obstinacy, and stinginess.[6] A man's "true" character was assumed to be the average of the ratings given to him by his fellows. That rating could be compared to his self-rating and to the ratings he gave others. The subjects who lacked insight, that is, who did not recognize in themselves the qualities that others saw, were especially likely to project. For example, they tended to attribute "stinginess" to other students who were not stingy, when they were stingy themselves but could not admit it. The research showed that projection can be discovered in measurable amounts in normal young men, and that it operates chiefly with respect to unacknowledged or disowned qualities.

> The case of Mrs. C. and her daughter Sally provides a clinical illustration of projection. Mrs. C. appealed to a guidance clinic for help in dealing with her twelve-year-old daughter, who was described as nervous, overactive, and unmanageable. "She is much too active for a girl so near puberty," wrote Mrs. C. "I keep telling her about the terrible things that will happen to her if she doesn't take care of herself at this age." An examination showed that Sally was a very healthy child, although a little underweight. She had an active interest in sports and was a bit of a tomboy, perhaps because of her close association with her two slightly older brothers. A further study of Mrs. C. revealed the real root of the trouble. Mrs. C. was fifty years old and was undergoing the menopause. She had been depressed and anxious about her health. The conclusion was quite clear that Mrs. C. had projected her own concern upon Sally, attributing to the girl's puberty the characteristics really residing in her own menopause. The family problem was solved successfully by medical treatment and personal counseling for Mrs. C.; Sally needed no outside help beyond the cessation of her mother's nagging.

More Serious Aspects of Rationalization and Projection

Rationalization and projection are common mechanisms of defense among normal people, but they are also prominent in certain patterns of thinking and acting found in much more seriously maladjusted persons. *Blaming failure on a conspiracy of others* offers a transitional example. In four years of study a college student had completed courses that comprised a minimum program for a degree, but with grades so low that he did not have a scholastic average equal to that required for graduation by the rules of the university. He became convinced that the professor at the head of the department in which he had studied was prejudiced against him. The student appealed to the dean and to the president of the university in turn, and having no success in convincing them that he was being treated unfairly, he came to believe that they too had entered a conspiracy to keep him from getting his degree. He then wrote letters to the trustees of the university and to the newspapers, protesting against his treatment. By a belief that others were to blame he spared himself the anxiety of contemplating his own failure.

Unfounded defensive beliefs shade by imperceptible degrees into delusions. A *delusion* is a belief so obviously false that its absurdity is apparent to any alert observer, and so persistently held that no logical arguments can break it down. In the case of another college student, feelings of persecution developed into full-blown delusions.

> Gregory E., as a preparatory school student, had distinguished himself by excellence as a track athlete. He entered college with the expectation of a brilliant career as a runner, but seemed to have a streak of bad luck. Frequent injuries and ailments kept him out of races or prevented him from doing his best. Furthermore, Gregory was outshone both in athletics and in scholarship by his slightly older brother who was in college at the same time. Although a good athlete, Gregory had always been seclusive, unfriendly, and suspicious of the motives and actions of other people. His delusions developed in his senior year. He began to complain of feeling ill, and eventually expressed a belief that someone must be poisoning him. His delusions centered on the fraternities, of which he had not become a member. He stated that the fraternity men were poisoning his food, and that they made secret signs to waiters in restaurants to point him out as the man to be poisoned. Finally, he fled to another city to escape the persecution. His queer behavior attracted attention and he was placed in a psychiatric hospital.

Two mechanisms can be seen in Gregory's delusions. First, the belief that he is ill rationalizes his failures, and the illness itself is explained away by the delusion that he is being poisoned. Both these false beliefs, like the rationalizations of normal people, protect him from having to assume blame or responsibility. The mechanism of projection is also in evidence. For a long time, Gregory has nourished suspicious and hostile attitudes toward other people. By projection, he believes that others are hostile to him to such an extent that they single him out for persecution.

The reader may well ask, "Isn't there something else wrong with a person who develops delusions, in addition to mere projection and rationalization?" The answer, of course, is "yes." Persons like Gregory show a general weakness of integration, and an inability to understand the meaning of other people's behavior and to criticize their own actions. Such shortcomings of personality may arise from physiological causes or may be due to a lifetime of unfortunate adjustive learning. The case illustration does not entirely explain the personalities of psychotic individuals who harbor delusions, but only shows that the delusions are extreme forms of defense mechanisms such as rationalization and projection. Delusions occur because they enable a mentally disordered person to arrive at an understanding that explains away his difficulties and frees himself from blame.

RESULTS OF DEFENSIVE BEHAVIOR

The primary result of any defense mechanism is the reduction of drives. People use defensive behavior because it satisfies immediate needs and helps them control their anxieties, regardless of the remote consequences. Adjustment through defense often is achieved, however, at the cost of bringing discomfort or even harm to other people, and of failing to provide the most enduring satisfaction to the person himself.

Delinquencies as Defenses

Since defensive behavior often takes the form of an aggressive assertion of a false and antisocial superiority, it is not strange that many delinquencies originate in mechanisms such as attention-getting and compensation. Although James G. was not in trouble with the law, and therefore was not classed as a delinquent, his bullying and petty stealing might have been described legalistically as "assault" and "larceny." Many juvenile offenders who have been in court present similar life histories. In a clinical research on causes of delinquency, Merrill has described a number of instances of defensive adjustments in delinquents.[7]

> Tommy, for example, had no basis for maintaining his self-esteem. His widowed mother depended on an older brother as the "man" of the household, and showered affection on a younger child. Tommy, the middle child, was left out. He started stealing gum from a store, progressed to an attempted extortion, and then to a series of burglaries. Stealing was his life of thrill and adventure, a compensation for his lack of satisfaction at home. He gained not only the material rewards, but also the awed admiration of four intimidated boys of his own age who helped him. Two terms in a reformatory, and parole in the home of a relative who did not really accept him, did not wean Tommy from an adjustment that he had found so individually satisfying. Tommy was shot and killed at the age of eighteen in an attempted hold-up.
> Harry started on a similar career. Multiple conditions gave him strong needs for aggressive defenses: he was puny physically; a stepfather had taken the place of his own father at home; a sister two years his senior excelled him in every way and received an undue share of his mother's affection. Harry began by taking money from home and by playing truant from school. The constructive work of a court clinic was directed toward removing the sources of tension at home and at school, and toward finding more acceptable outlets for his needs for attention and prestige. Harry achieved a successful readjustment, and a follow-up study after five years showed no further delinquencies.

Not all adjustments that result in delinquency show the same pattern or serve the same needs. Some delinquents are motivated to secure recognition and admiration, usually from youngsters of their own age who are impressed by the apparent daring and independence of the deviant boy. A youth who has a good relationship with his parents rarely has a need to seek approval and prestige in that fashion. Other delinquents have anxieties originating from physical, social, and intellectual inferiorities, and gain satisfaction from the feeling of mastery that their aggressive behavior gives, without having to display their prowess to their fellows. When a child has developed a deep hostility toward his parents, often not without justification, his delinquency may be a way to hurt and punish them. Flagrant sexual delinquency among girls is almost always a response to an unsatisfied need to have someone love them and pay attention to them. All these need-reducing sequences found among delinquents are adjustive, but the revelant one for a particular child can be discovered only by a study of his attitudes and his history.

Reactions to frustration and conflict are not the only causes of delinquency, of course. Otherwise, all thwarted people would become delinquent. There are other factors that determine whether the outcome of conflict will be delinquency or some other form of adjustment. Perhaps the most significant determiner is a person's degree of socialization, the extent to which he has internalized as his own the ethical standards of a law-abiding culture. That in turn depends on his parents' attitudes, and on the quality of the relationship that he has with them. A strong, mutually understanding parent-child relationship almost excludes the possibility of delinquency, unless the parents themselves have and teach criminal attitudes. A second basic factor in delinquency is the culture pattern of the other persons in a youth's immediate community. If the main sport of youngsters of an area is to fight, steal, and run from the police, a youth will fall in line with the practices of his fellows. The family and community socialization factors are related to a number of variables that have been studied statistically: the effects of broken homes, of parental criminality, of gangs, and of "delinquency areas" in cities. The psychology of delinquency is a complex subject with a large literature of its own. No attempt can be made to present it fully here, but only to show some of its relationships to the psychology of adjustment.

Individually Nonintegrative Defenses

Even when strongly defensive adjustments are not so antisocial as to constitute delinquencies, they tend to make it more difficult for a person to secure well-rounded satisfaction of his needs. Like other habits driven by anxiety, defense mechanisms tend to be excessively specialized. A defensive person is so intensely engaged in proving his adequacy that he does not attend to the satisfaction of broader motives of self-realization. Another shortcoming of defensive behavior is that it limits social interaction. With the exception of identification, all defense mechanisms increase the social distance between a person and his fellow men. Defense mechanisms therefore illustrate the concept of nonintegrative adjustment that was developed theoretically in the last chapter. The cure of defensive behavior, of course, cannot be effected by suppressing the mechanisms, but requires a more fundamental reduction of the anxiety that sets them off.

Some Positive Values

Although defense mechanisms have many shortcomings as ways of dealing with one's life problems, they may have integrative values when they serve long-range objectives. Simple compensations, for example, are among the relatively least harmful methods for combatting frustrations. They are active and outgoing, and less hampering to social adjustment than some of the more serious disturbances that might ensue. It is better to reduce distress by a not too unsocial compensation than to remain miserable with chronic anxiety.

The *peculiar-abilities* adjustment is a rather harmless variety of defense often found in the later or more fixed stages of reaction to an attitude of inferiority. This adjustment consists in developing a high degree of skill in some obscure line in which competition will be at a minimum. It may be a game, perhaps ping-pong, that is infrequently played in the locality, or it may be a collection of stamps, shells, butterflies, old glass, or many other things. Several defense mechanisms are involved. The peculiar ability is attention-getting, is a compensatory form of mastery, and usually is rationalized as much more important than nonparticipants would believe. Not all hobbies and collections are defense mechanisms, but when the field of endeavor is an uncommon one and the accomplishment is overvalued, a defensive adjustment may be suspected. Even so, a peculiar-abilities response is often the most comfortable adjustment for a person with relatively irremediable defects, and even may be encouraged for that purpose.

Although most defensive reactions hinder social adjustment, there may be instances in which their long-term outcome is socially constructive. The greatest orator of ancient Greece, Demosthenes, is said to have been a stutterer in his youth. So great was his drive for compensation that he not only overcame the speech defect but became renowned for his eloquence. It has been suggested, although without conclusive evidence, that the deafness of Thomas

A. Edison provided the incentive that directed his inventive genius to the discovery of the phonograph and the microphone, and that Theodore Roosevelt's advocacy of "the strenuous life" sprang from his physical weakness in boyhood. The efforts of some research scientists may well be defensive forms of behavior, shown by their seclusiveness in retiring to the solitary work of their laboratories and by their zeal to discover new knowledge. In spite of the attractive plausibility of these instances, they probably account for only a minority of cases. The greater part of eminent achievement is motivated by drives of normal social origin acting in conjunction with exceptionally high ability. The large number of unsuccessful aspirants to fame, who continue their efforts in spite of rational evidence of their lack of aptitude, better illustrate the anxiety-driven processes of defensive behavior.

SUGGESTED READINGS

A nontechnical but sound discussion of defense mechanisms, and how they may be effectively used and controlled, is the substance of Morgan, *How To Keep a Sound Mind*. Other introductory descriptions are in Lehner and Kube, *The Dynamics of Personal Adjustment*, and in Chapters 5–7 of Lindgren, *Psychology of Personal and Social Adjustment*. Klein, *Mental Hygiene* contains some novel and stimulating ideas, especially in Chapters 13–16. The characteristic defenses used in different cultures are dealt with in Nadel, *Foundations of Social Anthropology*.

On aggressive behavior which acts out impulses and often constitutes delinquency, see Chapter 3 of Hamilton, *Psychotherapy in Child Guidance*, and Merrill, *Problems of Child Delinquency*. Faris, *Social Disorganization* treats delinquency and crime from the viewpoint of sociology.

An old but irreplaceable reference on rationalization and wishful thinking is Robinson, *The Mind in the Making*. The concepts of rationalization and projection are applied to the development of delusions in Cameron and Magaret, *Behavior Pathology*, Chapter 13, and in White, *The Abnormal Personality*.

CHAPTER **7**

Adjustment
by Escape

Many people adjust to frustrations and to self-devaluating conflicts by retreating from the situations in which they experience
difficulty. Adjustment by withdrawing is a primary and often
useful form of response. You adjust to an anticipation of bodily
harm by getting out of the way, and often it is the only course of
action that will permit your survival. Similarly, escape mechanisms
are frequently the most available means for dealing with overwhelming threats and insoluble conflicts. As long as withdrawing
is a response to realistically appraised threats and to specific situations, it is a sound and integrative method of adjustment. Only
when the technique is overgeneralized, so that an individual comes
to avoid social interactions with all people and to withdraw from
many types of situations, does the mechanism become nonintegrative. At the extreme, deep and continued withdrawal from the
realities of life and from contacts with other people characterizes
the most serious behavior disorders.

WITHDRAWING AS A DEFENSE

Seclusiveness or Isolation

The mechanism of seclusiveness or isolation is an habitual adjustment to tension, which results from the generalization of simple
withdrawing responses. This type of adjustment develops in the
same way as other adjustive techniques. When confronted with the

thwarting of some strong motivation, a person makes varying responses until some form of behavior is discovered that will reduce his drive. In many instances, circumstances favor the selection of withdrawing responses, because they are the most easily made, or the most strongly and immediately rewarded. Seclusive behavior is individually adjustive, for by avoiding the attempt to cope with the difficulties of his environment a person escapes the tension-producing effects of defeat. If you never try, you cannot fail. In the early or varied-response stage of adjustment, isolation often alternates with more aggressive types of defense. For a person to be timid and shy at one moment and to be bold and overbearing in the next may seem inconsistent, but the alternation has psychological coherence because both forms of response indicate the presence of anxieties about his own self-competence and social adjustment.

Because shy and withdrawing people are not as much of a nuisance to those around them as more aggressive persons, their adjustive symptoms often escape notice. The withdrawing adjustments of children are especially likely to be misunderstood. Parents and teachers quickly discover the annoyingly overaggressive child who demands attention, compensates, or rationalizes, but a seclusive child is often considered a model of perfect deportment. Several studies have inventoried the attitudes of teachers, parents, children, and psychologists toward various conduct symptoms.[1] In a research study reported by Thompson, 2315 teachers, apprentice teachers, parents, and school children ranked the "seriousness" of a list of twenty-four symptoms of conduct. They were asked to rank the "very worst" behavior problem number 1, the "next worst" number 2, and so on. Some results are shown in Table 1. Thompson's total group included Negro children and parents as well as whites, and both white and colored apprentice teachers, but the racial differences were inconsequential. As the table shows, children, parents, and teachers agreed in considering stealing, cheating, untruthfulness, and disobedience among the most serious problems. In sharp contrast, forty-two child psychologists ranked those behaviors as of no great importance, but regarded depression, unsocialness, fearfulness, and suspiciousness as the most serious types of conduct. It is evident that the laymen defined "seriousness" from a frame of reference quite different from that of the psychologists. Children and parents held a moralistic viewpoint and were most concerned with aggressive actions against persons and property and with sexual behavior. The child psychologists held a mental hygiene viewpoint instead of the traditional cultural one and were most concerned with behavior that has unfortunate implications for the individual child's future adjustments. The teachers' attitudes, on the whole, resembled those of the parents more than those of the psychologists. However, the departures of the teachers' from the parents' evaluations were in the direction of the attitudes of the psychologists. In a study twelve years earlier, Wickman[2] had found that teachers rated un-

Table 1

Attitudes of Children, Parents, Teachers, and Child Psychologists Toward Behavior Problems*

Behavior Problems	Average Rank Order of Seriousness of Behavior, as Rated by				
	2315 Children, Parents and Teachers	468 White Children	300 White Parents	514 White Teachers	42 Psychologists
Stealing	1	1	1	2	11
Cheating	2	2	3	3	16
Untruthfulness	3	3	2	1	14
Disobedience	4	6	5	6	21
Cruelty	5	5	4	16	5
Destroying school property ...	6	4	15	11	18
Bullying	7	7	8	14	10
Impertinence	8	10	14	7	19
Resentfulness	9	14	13	5	9
Domineering	10	9	10	10	12
Obscene notes	11	11	7	18	20
Truancy	12	8	17	23	17
Defiance	13	15	11	12	13
Masturbation	14	†	9	20	22
Overcriticalness	15	12	18	17	15
Unsocialness	16	18	12	4	2
Suspiciousness	17	13	16	21	4
Heterosexual Activity	18	23	6	22	23
Depression	19	20	20	13	1
Sensitiveness	20	19	21	9	6
Shyness	21	22	22	8	7
Fearfulness	22	21	19	19	3
Dreaminess	23	17	23	15	8
Puppy Love	24	16	24	24	24

* C. E. Thompson, *J. abnorm. soc. Psychol.*, 1940, 35, 120-125.
† Children were not asked to rank masturbation.

socialness and sensitiveness among the least serious symptoms of conduct; the Thompson data show they have approached the psychologists' attitudes with respect to these two traits. The change seems to indicate an increased understanding of mental hygiene concepts by teachers.

Psychologists agree that the withdrawing modes of defense are more insidious than the more aggressive responses because they often escape detection, because they are more difficult to overcome in treatment, and because they may in some cases indicate the beginnings of serious behavior disorders. Although they are subtle, the signs of withdrawing mechanisms can be distinguished by alert teachers and parents. A seclusive child shuns the company of other children, often remaining by himself during recess or play periods when most children are engaged actively and socially. He does not participate in games and sports, but prefers solitary amusements such as reading or games he can play by himself. He may tend to associate with younger and smaller children, avoiding those of his own age. In the classroom he is likely to participate only when called on, seldom volunteering answers or services. The timid child sits on the sidelines; he would rather watch than do. When circumstances compel him to display himself he may blush or turn pale, these autonomic responses being evidences of an emotional state. A seclusive person often appears "absent-minded," for he is not responding vigorously to external social stimuli, since they are either excluded by inhibitory processes or overshadowed by daydreaming, which usually accompanies withdrawing. Somewhat more serious are the symptoms of loss of interest and ambition, shown in listless attitudes toward work, school, or play. For the sake of positive mental hygiene, it must be emphasized that almost all persons show some of these signs to a moderate extent at some times in their lives. A little seclusiveness is a symptom of a moderate maladjustment that is likely to be overcome by changing circumstances or through a person's own resources. A marked and continuous tendency toward withdrawing signifies a need for psychological study and treatment.

Causes of Withdrawing

Like all other adjustment mechanisms, withdrawing reactions are caused by a variety of factors that differ from one person to another and are seldom uncomplicated even in a single individual. A tendency to use withdrawing mechanisms may be established by habit formation through a long sequence of relatively mild experiences. Some people develop a seclusive and isolated style of life because of the rewarding character of their individually centered experiences. A child who is reared with few contacts with other children and who associates chiefly with adults will be predisposed toward solitary rather than social forms of adjustment. If his parents' interests are in reading and quiet hobbies in contrast to parties and athletics, the child may follow their example. There is some indication that children of good mental ability develop more interest in reading, in individual play, and in collections that require complicated symbolic terminology, than in competitive games and sports.[3] Physical weakness or prolonged illness may also lead to the development of seclusive adjustments, selected through trial-and-error learning as the most satisfying response that a weak person can achieve. All these many factors — physique, health, intelligence, parental example, and environmental circumstance — may contribute to the formation of withdrawing habits of adjustment.

A person whose withdrawing, socially isolated character is due to a prolonged and reward-determined series of learnings is not necessarily maladjusted. Perhaps he misses some of the good things of life that come from social participation, but he may be free from anxiety and tolerably satisfied with his manner of living. The only danger from seclusive habits of adjustment appears when circumstances change and the old satisfactions cannot be maintained. An unsocialized adjustment often is accompanied by overdependence on parents or on a very limited circle of other people. Changing conditions may throw such a person into a larger and more actively competitive social group. Since he does not have skill in dealing with people, he responds to them with anxiety and withdraws even more than before, using his only adjustive resource.

The more severe seclusive mechanisms are based on strongly emotionally-toned avoidance responses resulting from anxiety or fear. Case studies of children with markedly withdrawn behavior frequently show abusive treatment on the part of their parents, whose physical punishments, threats, and loud scoldings arouse a persistent state of fear in the child. If the experiences that lead the child to fear the people on whom he is most dependent are intense and prolonged, his response becomes generalized and he will react with retreat and fear to all situations that involve authority or evaluation.

A severely punitive treatment of compensatory or other aggressive behavior in children often results in withdrawing. An over-aggressive child is usually trying to control anxiety by the too-vigorous assertion of his own competence. His defensive behavior shows that he is insecure and that he has special adjustive needs. Many parents, teachers, and peers do not recognize the source, however, but regard aggressive behavior only as an outbreak against authority that must be put down. An impasse develops. The more parents and teachers suppress him, the more anxious the youngster becomes and the more in need of adjustment. Some children turn to seclusiveness as a defense, since this reaction is quiet and orderly and will not bring down disciplinary wrath. The danger of a suppressive type of discipline is that it drives a child or adolescent either to rebel completely or to adopt mechanisms of escape. A constructive treatment of behavior problems encourages more desirable forms of active adjustment instead of merely eliminating the undesired forms.

Acute Withdrawing

Sometimes a child withdraws from social communication to such a marked degree that he no longer makes any active attempt to secure adjustment. Several names have been given to degrees or varieties of extremely seclusive behavior. In very young children it has been called *infantile autism*.[4] Its resemblance to a serious adult mental disorder has led to the term *childhood schizophrenia*.[5] Because a withdrawn child often fails to learn in school, he may be regarded, quite incorrectly, as feebleminded, hence the term *pseudo-feeblemindedness* is sometimes employed to describe the apparent mental deficiency.[6] A good illustration of how a severe withdrawing adjustment set off by parental harshness may be confused with feeblemindedness is given by Morgan.[*]

> A boy of six and a half years of age was brought to our clinic by his mother, grandmother, and the school nurse with the complaint that he was feeble-minded. They requested an examination so that they could be sure of this assumption and thus be guided

---

[*] J. J. B. Morgan, *The psychology of abnormal people.* (Second Ed.) New York: Longmans, Green & Co., 1936. Pp. 514-515.

in their treatment of him. An examination of the boy's intelligence revealed the fact that he was normal in this respect.

Why did they think he was feeble-minded? They reported that he sat listlessly in the classroom, paying no attention to what the teacher said, or what the other children did.

On the playground he was just as indifferent. He could be found off in a corner all alone, not even watching what the rest were doing. If the teacher or anyone else spoke to him he would answer mechanically. He seemed drawn into his shell and no one had been able to penetrate his defenses or get him out.

When we talked to the boy these facts were verified. If we asked some question that could be answered mechanically he would respond. Since most of the test situations were of this sort he made a normal record. We discovered, in spite of his apparent cooperativeness, that, when a question had even a remote personal bearing, he would not respond. He would either fail to answer at all, try to divert our attention, or simply remain in total indifference. Here was a boy who showed at this early age the symptoms that are often attributed to beginning schizophrenia. What was back of it?

It was discovered that his mother had unwittingly started this tendency. Before he began to attend school, she informed us, he had been much more alive and playful. After much coaxing she confessed what happened two months after he began his school career. A neighbor boy informed her that her son had done something on the playground that was quite a shock to her sensibilities. When he came home she quizzed him about it, but he at first denied any knowledge of the affair. She coaxed him and teased him to confess to her and, after two hours of continual persuasion, he did acknowledge his guilt. Whereupon, she informed us, with a gleam in her eye and her fists clenched, she gave him the "whipping of his life." She wound up her tale with the remark, "And he has not done it since."

She had successfully conditioned him against the repetition of an act which was distasteful to her, but in doing so she had made him distrustful and started him on the path toward introversion and withdrawal from others.

We worked with the boy for six weeks, trying to break down this attitude and replace it with one of trust. We made known to him that we knew what he had done. We made him feel that we did not care, that we were his friends and would not punish him for anything he did or said, all in an endeavor to win back his confidence. It was a long, hard struggle but eventually we won. He

grew less and less suspicious when he found we had no ulterior
motive in trying to get him to talk. When at last he was convinced, he changed his attitude entirely. He brightened up in
school, he made his grades easily and again joined his comrades
in play. The mother was delighted with the result and succeeded
in winning back the child into her confidence.

Persistent failure to learn in school is a frequent part of a picture
of maladjustment. Sometimes such children are not withdrawn in
all aspects of their social behavior, but only with respect to their
school work. They will not try to learn, and teachers and other
relatively untrained observers often think of them as feebleminded.

Violet M., a seven-year-old girl, was referred to a psychologist
with the complaint that she was mentally deficient. Her teacher
reported that the girl paid little attention to school work and
made slight progress in the first grade. Instead of learning to
write normally, she developed mirror writing, using her left hand
and making the letters in reversed form from right to left. She
was in constant conflict with the teacher and with other children,
getting into fights, calling obscene names, and having intense
rage tantrums. The psychologist found that Violet was of normal
mentality, her Intelligence Quotient on a verbal test being 92 and
on a nonverbal test, 98. Her school difficulties arose from multiple
causes. Her mirror writing, sometimes found in extremely left-
handed children, required special methods of instruction both in
reading and in writing. Neither at school nor at home had Violet
found any secure relationship with an adult. Deserted by her
parents, she lived in a squalid tenement with an elderly aunt
who was away from home most of the day. Her personal and
school problems reflected difficulties of adjustment, not mental
defect.

Expertly administered psychological examinations, and careful
professional observation, will distinguish most of the extremely
withdrawn and other nonlearners from the true mental defective.
To a skilled examiner, the behavior of a child who will not try differs considerably from that of one who tries but cannot succeed.
However, a small number of the pseudo-feebleminded are so withdrawn that they even make low scores on mental tests, as well as
show a lack of intellectual adequacy in everyday life. From time
to time, sensational studies have been published of apparently
"feebleminded" children who have been cured by special educa-

tional methods. The most spectacular of such cures probably do not involve children who are really mentally deficient, but potentially normal ones who have made seclusive adjustments.

Schizophrenia

The most acutely nonintegrative withdrawing reactions are found in a group of psychoses or serious mental disorders called *schizophrenia*. The same conditions also are known as *dementia praecox*, a synonymous older term. Schizophrenia accounts for about one-fourth of the admissions to mental hospitals. Although the symptoms have considerable variety, the relatively constant and characteristic indications are a loss of interest in normal occupations, an inability to communicate with other people, emotional responses inappropriate to the situations that arouse them, and a tendency toward peculiar mannerisms of speech, action, and gesture which seem to arise from the patient's reveries and to have no connection with the outside world. These conditions are an exaggeration of some aspects of the withdrawing behavior shown by many less seriously maladjusted people.

Some of the typical signs of the early stages of schizophrenia can be seen in the case of Angela B. This sixteen-year-old Italian girl had aroused the concern of her parents and of a social worker who was interested in the family by her persistent refusal to leave her home. At the time the case was referred to a psychologist, Angela had not stepped outside the house for five months. She steadfastly refused to do even the simplest errand and was immune to such inducements as the movies. At home she sat most of the time without apparent occupation and stubbornly refused to do her share of the housework. Once when she was given new and attractive shoes and a dress in an effort to persuade her to go out, she destroyed the gifts, cutting the shoes to pieces with a knife. The social worker asked a psychologist to interview Angela, and to give a psychological examination since there had been some suspicion of mental deficiency. The interview was held in the kitchen of Angela's home. When the psychologist entered the room, the girl retired behind the stove and refused to leave this position or to sit down. She was dressed in a very dirty cotton house dress, a dilapidated sweater, no stockings and very run-down shoes. She had better clothing, but refused to change or to wash her present garb. At first she would not talk. After she became more familiar with the psychologist's presence she spoke of commonplace matters freely, but refused to reply to any personal question. Queries were met sometimes with silence, sometimes with stereotyped answers of "I'm all right" or "It's all right," which were often quite irrelevant to the question. She resisted any attempt to administer a mental test, frequently saying, "I can't be bothered with that." During the course of the interview, however, a number of intelligence test items were given as informal questions. Angela's answers showed normal intelligence and entirely dismissed the suggestion of feeblemindedness. Angela wore a silly smile through most of the meeting and seemed delighted to be the center of attention. Since the symptoms of seclusiveness, negativism, slovenliness, refusal to work, and superficial cheerfulness suggested an early schizophrenia, the girl was referred to a psychiatric clinic for diagnosis and help. Psychiatric interviews and placement in a girls' residential home seemed to brighten her for a time. In a few months, however, Angela returned to her withdrawing behavior, which grew so much worse that she was admitted to a mental hospital.

Schizophrenia is divided into four conventional types, but the classifications are universally regarded as unsatisfactory. The *simple* form is said to be characterized only by extreme seclusiveness. The *hebephrenic* form is more sudden in its onset and the symptoms of emotional confusion and silly behavior are more marked. The *catatonic* type displays a notable stereotypy of behavior either in repeated mannerisms or in a rigidity of posture, the patient often remaining motionless for hours. The *paranoid* form shows some delusions of a compensatory nature, usually delusions of persecution, such as were briefly described in the preceding chapter. These so-called types are not separate entities, however, as they are based merely on the preponderance of symptoms, not on the differentiation of causes. Many cases cannot be classified as to type; others may be differently classed at various periods in the development of the disorder.

The causes of schizophrenia are unknown. The best current estimate is that several causal factors operate, some physiological, some psychological, and all very obscure indeed. Up to the present time neither anatomical nor physiological research has succeeded in identifying specific bodily conditions that will differentiate schizophrenics from other people. Future research with more refined techniques may, of course, solve the problem. Some evidence to be discussed in a later chapter points to an hereditary influence in schizophrenia, but there is far from universal agreement on the importance of that factor.

Psychological approaches to schizophrenia have, in general, regarded the disorder as the result of unfortunate adjustive learning processes. To cite one influential psychological theory, Norman Cameron regards a schizophrenic as a person who has never learned how to understand other people.[7] He lacks skill in taking culturally determined social roles, that is, in putting himself in other people's places so as to grasp their motives and the meanings of their behavior. When he is under stress, he cannot share his anxieties with others because he cannot trust them or communicate with them. As an adjustment to his lack of socialization, a schizophrenic invents in fantasy a pseudo-world inhabited not by real people but by people as he mistakenly imagines them. One of the salient features of a schizophrenic, that his thinking and language have private meaning for him but not social meaning that other people can understand, is well handled by Cameron's theory. So far, psychological theories of schizophrenia have not pointed the way clearly toward its prevention or cure. Still, some theory based on concepts of conflict, adjustment, and learning will probably make permanent contributions to our understanding of schizophrenia, either as a sole theory or in combination with some as yet undiscovered physiological explanation.

People without broad psychological and medical training should avoid making sweeping conclusions about the withdrawing adjustments that they see in the community. Most mildly seclusive adjustments remain minor in degree, and it need not be too greatly feared that a slightly withdrawing person will progress toward profound mental disorder. Even so, a socially isolated child is in greater need of sound professional guidance than is the much more troublesome aggressive child. When an adolescent or adult becomes apathetic, seems to misinterpret other people grossly, and shows mannerisms or impulsive behavior that cannot be understood culturally, he needs immediate help. Even in the serious conditions of schizophrenia, a good proportion of cures can now be affected by psychiatric treatment, especially if the disorder is discovered while in an early stage.

NEGATIVISM

Refusal as a Defense

Withdrawing is not always of a quiet and passive nature. Some people withdraw with vigor and even with violence, their reaction being as aggressive as an attention-getting mechanism or a compensation. When withdrawing is shown as active refusal, stubbornness, contradictory attitudes, and rebellion against external demands, it is called *negativism*. This adjustment is partly seclusive and partly aggressive, and shows the futility of trying to classify all mechanisms tightly into a small number of categories.

Negativism in varying degrees is frequently encountered in school children. A rather striking instance is the case of Mariana F., an eleven-year-old girl in the fourth grade.

> Mariana had a history of trouble throughout her school career. The typical reports concerning her told of stubbornness, lack of inclination to obey, and quarrelsomeness with the other children. The principal described her as nervous, uncontrollable, resentful of any criticism, and easily upset. Her academic progress had also been poor, for she had succeeded in completing only three grades during her five years of school. The precipitating outbreak, which caused Mariana to be referred to a psychological clinic, was one of violent negativism. For a period of about two weeks she refused to take off her coat in the classroom, refused to sit down, and would do nothing she was told to do. The teacher used the disciplinary device of making her stand in the corner (an ingenious method, since she refused to sit!), and made some rather inadequate attempts to reason with her. Her extremely negativistic phase passed before the clinic was well started in its investigation, and Mariana's behavior became fairly normal.
>
> A clinical study disclosed several factors which helped to understand the girl's behavior — a severe physical defect, relatively low intelligence, and an unfortunate home condition. Mariana suffered from a very pronounced curvature of the spine, probably congenital in origin, which caused her to walk queerly. She was a very unattractive child, and the additional infirmity made her the butt of much comment and ridicule. The physical defect had been noted before and orthopedic treatment had been recommended, but Mariana's mother had neglected to carry out the

instructions. Mentally, the child was very dull, an Intelligence Quotient of 74 indicating borderline ability. Since the death of the father two years before, Mariana's mother had been out of the home much of the time doing housework. She was an over-emotional woman who had given no consistent thought to the needs of her children, if, indeed, she was capable of it. Mariana was the eldest child, there being two younger girls, both of whom seemed normal in conduct and in school work. The mother complained that Mariana was not a good helper at home. She would not do as she was told and did not accomplish tasks that she started. She did not help as well as her two younger sisters, with whom the mother compared Mariana very unfavorably. Doubtless she made this invidious comparison very clear to the child and had thoroughly convinced her of her own incompetence. Mariana's mother was a severe but inconsistent disciplinarian, and had no comprehension of the child's difficulties.

The basis of the conduct problems seemed to lie in Mariana's dullness, in her feelings in regard to her physical condition, and in her mother's attitude toward her. She had been scolded and nagged into the outbreaks of negativism that were the only defenses her dullness could devise against her lack of success in school and with other children and her lack of security at home. The treatment recommended included immediate and thorough attention to her physical disabilities at a medical clinic, placement in a special class in school, and interviews with the mother which attempted to establish more sympathetic home attitudes.

Origins of Negativism

Negativism seems to be an emotional response of the anger type, closely related to temper tantrums. The basic situation that evokes negativism is interference with a child's self-initiated activity, resulting in strong anger responses. Negative behavior is so common in young children that it must be considered quite normal in the statistical sense.[8] Research studies show that some resistant behavior can be found in children only a few months old. Negativism usually becomes quite common by the age of eighteen months, reaches a peak at about three years, and declines noticeably by the age of four. The negativism of children at these ages is due to an increasing range of independent activity that makes them prone to assert themselves, together with a lack of understanding and of language that leaves them few degrees of compliance between a complete "yes" and an absolute "no."

Children vary in the use of negativism as a defense. Its frequent use, or its persistence beyond the expected years, may be due to any one of a number of causes. If parents pull and haul a young child, hurry him before he has had time to assimilate a request, or often interrupt his activities unnecessarily, they will quite regularly evoke negativism. Another factor, common to all adjustment mechanisms, is the degree of success or satisfaction that a child receives from its use. If his resistance constantly gets a child what he wants, frees him from unpleasant tasks, or makes him a center of attention, it will be learned as a habitual adjustive technique. Wise parents have to steer a middle course, not interfering excessively with a child's activities, and inviting his cooperation in necessary household routines in such a way as to minimize resistance. Yet they must be quietly firm in real essentials, so that the child does not learn to control the family by his temper outbursts.

Older children, adolescents, and adults sometimes show negativism in less violent forms, by resistance to requests, arguing every small point of routine, pretending not to hear or understand undesired demands, performing unpleasant duties perfunctorily, and by many similar techniques. In some instances, such negativism is carried directly from childhood because it has been reinforced. In other cases, negativism is a last resort in which insecure persons take refuge when confronted with unbearable restraints or interferences.

FANTASY

Daydreaming

Fantasy or daydreaming is the imaginary representation of satisfactions that are not attained in real experience. Because fantasy is always available and requires so little effort, it is not surprising that it is one of the most common adjustment mechanisms. Seclusive people do not obtain the many satisfactions that come from social participation and are therefore likely to develop habits of fantasy as their major method of tension reduction. Most people do not talk extensively about their fantasy life, because they regard it as private and are somewhat ashamed of it as childish and inferior. Consequently, the frequency of daydreaming among normal children and adults is usually underestimated. A maladjusted person often feels quite guilty about his fantasies and is surprised to find that other people daydream too. In well-adjusted persons and in the early trial-and-error stages of maladjustment, daydreaming alternates with many other mechanisms. In a later or fixed stage of maladjustment some people select fantasy as their principal means of satisfaction and use it to the exclusion of more active adjustive efforts.

Fantasy is a normal part of the imaginative play of childhood. In the earlier years, a child acts out his play and often verbalizes it aloud. By the age of two, he can distinguish in some degree between real events and "make-believe."[9] Studies of children's talk have shown that it consists largely of self-assertion and self-expression, by which the child manages and subdues his environment and his fellows. As he grows older, a child finds that open self-assertion is disapproved socially. He may then develop active and socially oriented interests or continue self-centered play in the covert form of fantasy. Most people use both outlets. The extent to which fantasy is employed is inversely proportional to the success of the more active attempts.

Although no one can give a precise definition of what is an "excessive" amount of fantasy, practical criteria can be applied to individual cases. Too great a dependence on daydreaming seems to be caused by the same factors that underlie the seclusive form of defense. When fear, anxiety, or persistent frustration prevents active adjustment, daydreaming will be used. Fantasy plays a dual role as a direct satisfier of basic motives and as a compensation for thwarted attainments. School situations are especially likely to contribute to the development of daydreaming. The school, unlike other segments of a child's experience, requires him to keep quiet. Very bright children find close attention unnecessary because they grasp the work quickly. Dull children are often repelled by instruction they cannot understand and are therefore likely to give up the hopeless task of trying to learn. In either case, daydreaming may offer the most convenient escape from the dreary classroom. Educational practices that pay attention to each child as an individual and adapt the curriculum to his abilities and needs can counteract the prevelance of daydreaming in school.

Varieties of Fantasy

Since daydreams express the imaginative fulfillment of motives, they are always satisfying. Usually they are also pleasant in the ordinary meaning of that word, although not always so. The commonest form of daydream is the *conquering hero* type, in which a person pictures himself doing the deeds or possessing the things he most desires. Throughout life, people's fantasies have a constant quality in representing the attainment of love, security, approval, mastery, and other strong and persistent motives. The detailed content of daydreams varies considerably with age and individual experiences. The daydreams of young children tend to deal with the enjoyment of specific amusements and the possession of particular objects.[10] As they grow older, children add plot to their fantasies and often daydream of gaining prestige or of playing an heroic role. Adolescent fantasies concern the approval or conquest of the desired partner of the opposite sex, and often portray the acclaim received from athletics or other activities highly esteemed by their social group. Adults as well as adolescents daydream of possessing great physical strength and bravery, attractiveness, success in work, wealth, and power and importance. Because of their naive character, quite uncensored by considerations of practicality or social expediency, daydreams offer useful data on people's common motives. If daydreams represent what people in our culture want most, the importance of the motives of mastery, social approval, and sex receives strong confirmation. Daydreams are notably irrational even among well-adjusted persons. It is not unusual for an entirely normal man or woman to daydream of an heroic encounter with a burglar or to plan imaginatively the expenditure of a million dollars. The fantasies of the normal are as absurd as the delusions of grandeur met in some mentally disordered patients, and undoubtedly are related to them psychologically.

The conquering hero daydream has been subdivided into four other categories.[11] In the *display* fantasy, the dreamer gains applause for some act of ability or daring. Another form is the *saving* daydream: the dreamer rescues someone by great bravery under impossible difficulties. In the fantasy of *grandeur*, a person pictures himself as a great person, a king or a god. The daydream of *homage* represents the rendering of a difficult service for another person whose favor or sympathy is sought. These four varieties of fantasy are useful descriptions of common daydream experiences, but the classes are neither complete nor mutually exclusive.

Another fantasy that is fairly common is the *death* or *destruction* daydream, which springs from hostile attitudes. The death or defeat of someone who stands in the way of preferment is imagined. A child may fantasy the removal of a brother who is more the parent's favorite; an adult may imagine the death of a person who will leave him money or open the way for professional advancement. A death or destruction daydream is often disguised because of the dreamer's inhibition against admitting such antisocial desires. The displacement may take the form of imagining that the person to be killed or removed has met with an accident. When both affection and resentment are felt toward the same persons, the daydream may be accompanied with anxiety because of the conflict between loving and hostile impulses.

An unpleasant type of daydream in which the dreamer imagines himself thwarted, injured, or dead is only apparently an exception to the principle of the satisfying nature of fantasy. The *suffering hero* or *martyr* daydream is an expression of self-pity. In the more naive varieties employed in childhood, a youngster who believes himself ill-treated may imagine that he runs away from home, becomes lost in a storm, and is killed by wolves. His body is brought back amid the universal mourning of his family and friends. His parents are repentant, the neighbors tell of his many good qualities, and a certain little girl is especially sorrowful. Adults not infrequently invent more sophisticated versions of this fantasy, in which self-injury brings sympathy. Hypochondria, preoccupation with one's own ills, may be an acting out of the martyr daydream. This fantasy may be unpleasant but it is none the less satisfying to an individual's motives. The imagined pity and sympathy are close substitutes for acclaim and approval, and thus are satisfying to important culturally-derived motives.

Another classification divides fantasies into *casual* and *systematic* types.[12] Casual daydreams vary with a person's immediate experiences and his transient interests. Systematic fantasies are repeated and consistent, often comprising an elaborate plot which is imagined again and again. Systematic daydreams are more likely to reveal the dreamer's needs and conflicts and may even influence his reactions to his real experiences. It is clear that systematic fantasies are concerned with more chronic adjustment problems, but they are so common among normal people that they cannot be said to indicate an alarming maladjustment.

Borrowed Fantasies

The world is full of ready-made daydreams that people can adopt without going to the trouble of inventing new ones for themselves. Such fantasies are found in novels, detective stories, adventure fiction, "comics" of the adventurous sort, motion pictures, and radio and television serials. This "escape literature" is produced in varieties that appeal to a wide range of persons, from six to senility and from the illiterate to the distinguished. The plots of many stories, motion pictures, and radio narratives are highly improbable, designed to represent the attainment of satisfactions that are absent in real experience. The reader or spectator participates by the use of the identification mechanism described in the preceding chapter. When the principal character of the story rises to success against great odds, the reader partakes of the satisfaction, picturing himself in some degree as the person in the imaginary situation. When the stalwart star of the motion picture holds the lovely heroine in his arms, the lovelorn movie fan, of either sex, feels vicariously an attenuated form of the love satisfaction. Stereotyped plots such as the Jack-the-giant-killer motif and the Cinderella theme are repeatedly successful in popular fiction and in the moving pictures, indicating the adjustive value these situations have for millions of normal people.

Borrowed fantasies are commonly used to reduce conflicts that involve self-devaluation or attitudes of inferiority. James G., whose case was described at length, identified himself with the heroes of western movies so thoroughly that they were his chief interest, and his vocational ambition was to be one of them. James's ardent reading of boy-adventure books, in which adolescents little older than himself perform extraordinary feats of daring or accomplishment, points to the same adjustive end.

Hero-worship acts as a form of fantasy. Youngsters attach exaggerated values to persons who are prominently associated with some notable achievement within their comprehension. They read avidly of soldiers, aviators, explorers, and prominent baseball players, play at being these people, and daydream of duplicating their accomplishments. Souvenirs of these individuals and personal contacts with them have satisfaction value through a mechanism closely related to fantasy. Similarly, less prominent children and adults seek the notice and approval of those who are more conspicuous, and gain personal satisfaction by basking in the light of their reflected glory.

Daydreaming Among Normal People

To study the scope of daydreaming among normal people, a questionnaire was administered to a group of undergraduate college students and, a few years later, to a somewhat older group of graduate students. Twelve types of common daydreams were described and questions were also asked about worry, about repeated or systematic daydreams, and about other types in general. A full description of each variety of fantasy was read to the students, who responded by indicating if they had *ever* had that sort of daydream, and whether they had done so *recently*, within the past thirty days or so. The questionnaire was anonymous, the papers being identified only as to sex, age, and college year. Other conditions were conducive to truthful answers. The undergraduate group consisted of 64 men and 131 women, whose median age was 21, with a range from 18 to 30 years. The graduate students were spread over a wider age range, from 19 to 50, with an average age of 28 years; there were 83 men and 112 women.

The principal results are shown in Table 2. The very frequent occurrence of many types of daydream is striking. The average person reported that he had experienced about 12 or 13 types of daydreams in his life, and about 4 or 5 types within the past thirty days. There were no conspicuous differences between the undergraduate and graduate groups, although they were questioned at different universities, in 1935 and 1946 respectively, and also represented dissimilar age samples. In neither group was there any significant relationship between age and daydreaming. For example, as large a proportion of the graduate students over 40 years of age reported recent sexual daydreams as did the younger undergraduates. Only two men and nine women, about 3 per cent of the entire sample studied, reported no recent daydreams. Sex differences were not very marked, except for a tendency for more men to daydream of physical strength and for more women to prefer the fantasy of physical attractiveness, which is quite in keeping

Table 2

The Occurrence of Types of Daydreams Among
Two Groups of Students

Type	Ever? Undergrad. M	Ever? Undergrad. W	Ever? Grad. M	Ever? Grad. W	Recently? Undergrad. M	Recently? Undergrad. W	Recently? Grad. M	Recently? Grad. W
1. Physical feat	91	60	96	58	30	3	13	2
2. Physical attractiveness	89	95	94	96	34	63	17	56
3. Mental feat	88	92	89	90	48	42	47	61
4. Vocational success ..	100	98	99	93	81	69	78	64
5. Money or possessions .	100	97	94	95	69	66	51	52
6. Display	78	76	90	83	22	16	19	19
7. Saving	89	63	90	66	14	5	14	8
8. Grandeur	67	48	63	39	11	7	6	0
9. Homage	81	72	81	66	16	13	24	18
10. Sexual	97	96	96	89	74	73	63	71
11. Death or destruction .	39	44	60	46	9	9	10	9
12. Martyr	70	79	64	62	9	15	10	12
13. Worry	92	89	87	91	45	56	49	50
14. Other types	63	53	52	51	30	20	24	23
15. Repeated daydreams .	89	93	83	87	48	51	36	47
Median number of types .	13	12	13	11	5	5	4	5

with the cultural roles of the sexes. That nearly half of the students reported recent repeated or systematic daydreams minimizes the pathological significance that has sometimes been imputed to that type of revery.

Although the results of the questionnaire experiment cannot be assumed to be valid in all details, they certainly show that daydreaming is a common experience of normal people. Daydreaming alone cannot be regarded as a maladjustment. Only great absorption in fantasy, which was of course not measured by the experiment, is indicative of a seriously nonintegrative adjustment.

Values of Fantasy

Fantasies can serve integrative as well as adjustive purposes. In many instances it is impossible to draw a sharp line between daydreaming and planning. For a young person to daydream of vocational success or of creative activities may be a step toward the accomplishment of these aims in reality. Today's daydreams often become tomorrow's achievements. A great scientist is distinguished not so much by the laborious collection of data as by seeing the facts he gathers in strikingly new arrangements and meanings. Creative thinking is an imaginative act and its processes lie quite near the realm of fantasy. In a broad meaning of the term, fantasy underlies all art. A world without fantasy would be one without music, painting, literature, or drama and therefore a much less pleasant place in which to live.

Aside from its practical utility, normal fantasy has ameliorative and recreational values that may serve integrative ends in adjustment. Fantasies may act as a balancing factor to give a sufficient proportion of satisfaction to a person in periods of his life when social adjustment is unusually difficult. The prevalence of daydreaming indicates that all persons need such a compensation, and most of them use it without becoming too deeply immersed in unreality. The extremely unimaginative person is perhaps as one-sided and poorly integrated as one who depends too much on his daydreams.

Fantasy in Maladjustment

Daydreams do not in themselves constitute a maladjustment, but they are a symptom and a contributing factor found in many maladjusted persons. Fantasy is a mechanism much used by people who are prevented by circumstances or by their own characteristics from making the more active kinds of adjustments. The part that fantasy may play in a maladjustment is shown by the following case of a college student:*

> Edith Perry was badly overweight, poorly dressed, and generally tousled looking. She had the messy, almost dirty appearance that many fat people develop if they do not spend a good deal of time taking care of themselves. From a physical point of view there was nothing wrong with Edith except her obesity, but this condition was unusually effective in causing other maladjustments; indeed, the girl's whole social and emotional life was badly warped in consequence.

---

* Luella Cole Pressey, *Some college students and their problems.* Columbus, Ohio: Ohio State Univ. Press, 1929. Pp. 28-30.

Edith's own complaints were chiefly that she had no friends, that she was not popular with boys, and that she had frequent sexual daydreams. Her social isolation had been increasing ever since she was about thirteen — at which time she first began to acquire her flabby fat. She said that she never looked well dressed, even though she bought the best of materials; that she was always in the way because she was so big; and that both girls and boys made fun of her. In this day of slim feminine shapes she felt particularly conspicuous and was sure that boys would never care about her. As she was a distinctly capable student, she had plenty of leisure, and this time she used chiefly in day-dreaming about boys. By the time she came to the writer's attention she had substituted an imaginary masculine society for real society so thoroughly that she was fairly well satisfied with her existence. Still, she had moments of feeling that she was not "normal" and that she needed friends.

It seemed clear that this girl's fatness was the underlying cause of her social and emotional maladjustments. Therefore a natural first step was to put her on a reducing diet. A second step consisted in having some clothes selected for her in which she looked very well, in spite of her size. Soon the effects of the diet began to show, and the comfort and style of her new clothes began to give her greater self-confidence.

She was told not to worry about her daydreams, even though they were sexual in character, on the assumption that they would largely disappear of their own accord as soon as her social isolation and other emotional difficulties could be remedied, and that anyhow anxiety about sex matters would not help but hinder the total process of social rehabilitation and the development of self-confidence. As soon as Edith was presentable in appearance, efforts were made to have her make friends. She joined one or two clubs, went to shows with some of the girls in her classes, and tried to make people like her. In the course of six months she had succeeded in building a few friendships among girls. At about this time she went away into a new environment for a summer vacation for a few weeks. Here she was so encouraged by her improved appearance that she was willing to try to attract boys — and was in some measure successful. She went to several dances, to shows sometimes, and even on one or two mild "petting" parties. She was enormously "set up" by these experiences, and was willing to take more exercise and maintain better control over her diet than heretofore. As a result, she lost some forty pounds.

Edith's problems are not over by any means. It is quite unlikely that she will ever be thin, but she has learned to dress at-
tractively and to take care of her body so that she is not offensive.
She is still not as popular as she would like to be. She does not
yet have a sufficient number of boy friends to keep her entirely
happy and prevent some daydreaming. Her fantasies have very
considerably diminished both in frequency and satisfaction, however, and it is reasonable to suppose that they will be no more
troublesome than are those of the average individual, if she can
achieve a still better social adjustment. Thus far no one has
fallen in love with Edith, and she will never be completely happy
until someone does. In the meantime, however, she is proceeding
with her college work, making new friends from time to time,
going out with boys occasionally, watching her appearance with
a critical eye, and getting along much better than she did.

Her daydreaming provided this student an important substitute
satisfaction that she needed because of the frustration of strong normal motives. The daydreaming itself was not "treated"; indeed,
only an increase of anxiety would have resulted from making the
girl pay direct attention to her fantasies, or from trying to convince
her of their wastefulness and ineffectiveness. She had to have some
way to relieve her tensions, and fantasy happened to be one within
her power to adopt. When her fundamental difficulties were remedied the tendency to daydream soon returned to a normal level.

Fantasy as Nonintegrative Behavior

In normal fantasy, you make your dreams serve as an end to real
accomplishment, or else you recognize that they play a special role
in life, in the enjoyment of the arts, or in temporary escape from
practical problems. To the extent that these conditions are violated, fantasies interfere with gaining other adjustive satisfactions,
and are therefore nonintegrative.

The first and simplest indictment of daydreaming is that it is a
waste of time. When a person with a habit of fantasy encounters
a difficulty, especially in quiet work such as planning or studying,
he is likely to wander from the task into a maze of imagined pleasures or achievements. Many students could accomplish their work
with twice or thrice their present efficiency if they could avoid
daydreaming. The time saved could then be spent in whole-hearted
enjoyment that would be more satisfying than the stolen hours

used for daydreaming, which often leave a sense of frustration or guilt after them.

Another nonintegrative result of fantasy is that it provides tension reduction without real accomplishment. It is a head-in-the-sand adjustment that does nothing about the seeking of positive goals or the avoidance of genuine dangers. Since the dreamer's wants are fulfilled imaginatively, his drives are less likely to spur him to real effort. Persons who daydream to a great extent often are inert in character and lacking in adjustive vigor. They have little need to adjust outwardly because their drives have been reduced by inner revery.

When daydreaming has built up romantic attitudes toward a career, a marriage, or some other future undertaking, the actual realization may be a keen disappointment. The daydreamer is accustomed to the extreme satisfactions of his imagined successes and so finds the rewards of reality pale by comparison. Many young people form rosy misconceptions of the occupations they plan to enter. The law student imagines himself orating before the Supreme Court; the prospective nurse pictures herself soothing the fevered brow of illness. If too much dependence is placed on such romantic fantasies the drudgery and unpleasantness that form a large part of most occupations will cause serious disillusionment. A large number of marriages fail for a similar reason when actuality does not measure up to the unrealistic dreams of romance.

Nonintegrative daydreaming cannot be attacked directly. An excessive daydreamer usually feels guilty about his fantasies already; scolding and preaching only add to his anxiety. Moralistic approaches to daydreaming, as indeed to all other adjustment problems, tend to aggravate the trouble they are trying to remedy. Daydreaming is best approached by considering the adjustive difficulties of the whole person, not by treating his symptoms. In mild cases, parents, teachers, and counselors can help a dreamy child by building up his self-confidence and by making it easier for him to adjust through social participation. Normal adults without crippling anxieties who feel that they daydream too much can also help themselves by planned attacks on their frustrations and by taking steps toward more socialized kinds of satisfactions. When motives are reduced by more overt means the need for daydreaming will be lessened.

REGRESSION

The mechanism of *regression* has been defined both in a broad and in a narrow meaning. In its widest sense, regression refers to an almost universal characteristic of behavior under threat, stress, or anxiety: that it is less flexible, less constructive, and hence less mature. This meaning of regression has already been described in Chapter 4. It is a quality found in all nonintegrative adjustments rather than a specific means for tension reduction. Regression in its more limited sense refers to a tendency to solve difficulties by returning to a type of behavior that was satisfying at some earlier time in a person's life, but which had been outgrown or abandoned for more effective types of adjustment. The latter definition identifies a common mechanism of adjustment.

Adjustment by Retreating

When a person is thwarted in an attempt to reduce his drives, he often tries again the mechanisms of adjustment which he found satisfying in the past. A number of experiments with animals have shown that they also tend to return to an older habit when a newer and more efficient one is thwarted.[13] Regression may be considered as a withdrawing type of defense because a person retreats to an inferior type of adjustment instead of attacking his frustrations directly. The retreat, of course, may take the form of any type of behavior, verbal or muscular, active or inert.

Regression is so common in early childhood that it is almost an expected form of behavior at two or three years of age. An anecdote is told of a two-year-old girl who no longer received the undivided attention of her parents because of the advent of a new baby brother.[14] One day she fell and remained on the floor crying and saying, "I can't get up, I'm too little." She thus sought the parental aid and attention to which she had been accustomed as an infant. An older child often loses previously well-established toilet habits upon the arrival of a new infant in the home. This regression is a bid for special consideration as a young and helpless individual. A busy and thoughtless mother often meets such situations with scolding and punishment which make matters worse because the child perceives himself as rejected. The basis for the constructive treatment of regression in a young child is to relieve his anxiety by showing him that he is loved and wanted. It also helps to emphasize the privileges of greater maturity by tangible actions, not merely by words.

"Homesickness" is a regressive reaction frequently encountered in children, adolescents, and young adults. Every college has a few severe cases each year. Homesick students have a deep emotional dependence on their families, which may be the result of various causes in individual cases. Sometimes the youngster has great anxiety about being deserted by his family, reinforced by threats over a long period of time; sometimes he has been overprotected and deprived of an opportunity to grow up into an independent person. An anxious and overattached young person finds a new environment unsympathetic and lacking in security. He is likely to suffer from physiological evidences of persistent emotion, such as indigestion, with secondary symptoms of headaches and loss of appetite. If finally he convinces himself and others that he is physically ill, the regressive attitude has won its point and the student returns to the safety of his home. Homesickness is very prevalent, and few have escaped at least a twinge of it. The more pronounced cases occur in people who are predisposed by their formative experiences.

The Conditions of Regression

The basic condition underlying regression is anxiety arising from conflicts and from failures to cope with one's adjustive problems. Every person tends to fall back on old habits when frustrated in a new situation. If the habits prove unrewarding they will be discarded in the normal course of trial and error, unless the person is so driven by threat and anxiety that he is unable to take active steps toward trying new adjustments.

One important factor that leads to the selection of regression instead of other mechanisms is the character of the parent-child relationship. Extremes in either direction seem to foster regression. The parents' attitudes may be extremely hostile during a child's early years because of their own adjustive difficulties. The child then perceives his situation as insecure and clings to his parents, afraid to assert his independence lest he lose them. A contrasting cause leading to the same result is parental overprotection that enslaves the child in dependence. Some parents resent the growth of their children into mature persons and keep them infantile as long as possible. Such parents do little to encourage their children to cope with the social world and hence increase the likelihood of regressive behavior.

Another general condition that favors regression is the tendency to remember only the pleasant experiences of one's past, forgetting the unpleasant.[15] Adolescents regard childhood as a period of bliss before they were troubled with the need for growing up; adults think of adolescence as a time of irresponsible happiness.[16] This characteristic of memory has been called the "Old Oaken Bucket delusion," after the sentimentally reminiscent song:

> How dear to this heart are the scenes of my childhood,
> When fond recollection presents them to view!

Some further evidence about the selective forgetting of the pleasant and the unpleasant will be reviewed in the next chapter. Selective forgetting contributes to the regressive attitude, for the successful adjustments tend to be remembered and cherished while the accompanying difficulties of an earlier developmental period are forgotten.

SUGGESTED READINGS

Klein, *Mental Hygiene* is a penetrating reference on adjustments by escape, particularly in Chapters 7 and 8, devoted to schizophrenia. Some rather new ideas are advanced in Shaw and Ort's chapter on "Protective Interaction" in *Personal Adjustment in the American Culture.* Coleman, *Abnormal Psychology and Modern Life* contains a good description of the mechanisms of escape, as does Cameron and Magaret, *Behavior Pathology.*

Readable chapters on schizophrenia can be found in White, *The Abnormal Personality,* and Noyes, *Modern Clinical Psychiatry.*

An important and not too difficult little book about types of adjustment, including the adjustment of "moving away from people," is Karen Horney, *Our Inner Conflicts.* Another volume which many will find informative and surprisingly easy to read is Hall, *The Meaning of Dreams.* Fromm, *The Forgotten Language* is also an important contribution to the psychology of dreams and fantasy.

CHAPTER **8**

Fear and Repression
in Adjustment

Life without fear is one of mankind's highest ideals, but it seldom is realized fully. Moderate and occasional fear is a very common human experience, and perhaps serves a useful purpose in spurring us to activity in the face of dangers and threats. In contrast, intense and persistent fear underlies some of the most disabling maladjustments. A fearful person is so much concerned with reducing his distress that he cannot attend to his other needs.

NORMAL AND ABNORMAL FEARS

Normal Fears

Almost everyone experiences fear from time to time when really dangerous situations are encountered. You slip at the top of a flight of stairs. Your automobile seems about to collide with another vehicle. To such situations, you tend to respond fearfully because you have learned their possibly injurious outcome by direct experience, by observing other people, or by learning through social communication. Even the bravest men feel fear in realistically threatening circumstances. A study of about five thousand military aviators in World War II revealed that 99 per cent of them were afraid when under enemy fire in combat.[1]

Normal fear also occurs in situations that may not be really dangerous but that are threatening because of their unfamiliarity and intensity. Suppose, for example, that a young man unaccustomed to the woods is walking on a lonely forest path and suddenly hears a strange loud noise, a cross between a shriek and a groan. He starts; his heart begins to pound; he looks about frantically; his knees tremble. He vacillates between flight and investigation but cannot control his strong fear. Eventually he may discover that the cause of his distress is the sound made by the trunks of two trees as they are rubbed together by the wind. As this example shows, fear responses are aroused most readily in adults by *intense* stimuli that occur very *suddenly* under circumstances that permit the use of *no habitual adjustment* for coping with them. The suddenness and unfamiliarity of the situation are important factors in determining the emotional response. If the same sound had been heard in a reassuring situation, as on a familiar city street or when accompanied by a group of friends, it would have evoked a less strong reaction. The young man had no ready response to make to the noise, but if he had encountered it many times before he would have been prepared to react to it in a definite way and would have been spared the emotion.

Studies of combat aviators and of ground troops in battle confirm the generalization that fear is a response to a situation to which a person can make no effective adjustment.[2] Being attacked when one cannot fight back, being idle when in danger, and feeling insecure of the future added to soldiers' fears. The most important factors that counteracted fear were confidence in equipment and leadership, keeping effectively busy when in danger, and being able to communicate with one's fellows. The war studies are important because under no other circumstances have data been available on the realistically fearful behavior of such a large number of normal people.

Directly Conditioned Fears

Many normal people are afraid of specific situations that are not really dangerous or intrinsically overstimulating. Directly conditioned fear reactions account for some of these fears. Perhaps a person has been frightened by a dog's attack, or by being thrown into deep water, or by an automobile accident, or by a childhood panic on a roller-coaster. Thereafter he may avoid contact with dogs, lakes, automobiles, or amusement parks, and may respond with panic when circumstances force him close to the object of his fear. Such fears may even persist when the person remembers and understands the earlier experience in which the fear was learned. An essential condition for the continuation of a directly conditioned fear is the lack of experiences that could bring about relearning. A man with a conditioned fear of dogs, for example, will never unlearn it if he always avoids dogs. He prevents himself from undergoing a process of re-education that would change his attitude toward the animals.

Socially Learned Fears

Fears also may be learned by the indirect and symbolic processes of social communication. A certain young man fears airplane travel, although he has never been in an airplane or witnessed an accident. His aversion dates from an accident some years ago in which an acquaintance was killed. He did not see the fatal crash; his sole experience was reading about it in the newspapers and hearing accounts of it from others. It is quite clear that words and ideas may mediate the learning of a fear.

Whole cultures often show an unrealistic fear of some "tabooed" object or action, reinforced by social learning rather than by any overtly injurious stimulation. Although the best-known instances of such cultural fears are found in primitive societies, we do not have to go to the South Seas for examples. Studies of American children have shown that they have little fear of snakes in their earlier years, but that the proportion of children who fear snakes increases reliably as they grow older.[3] Children from two years to six years old show a gradually decreasing fear of noise, pain, and of strange objects, because they have many re-educative experiences with these stimuli. In contrast, their fears of imaginary creatures, of robbers, and of death increase during those years.[4] Few if any children have had direct experiences with such situations. They learn these fears from their culture by the same processes that underlie other aspects of socialization.

Sometimes a cultural fear may be limited to one segment of a social group. In our culture, girls and women very commonly fear rats and mice, while boys and men rarely do. Both sexes learn the role expected of them by the society.

Both directly conditioned fears and socially learned ones are understood readily, not only by psychologists but also by laymen.

They are entirely comprehensible, and no one feels a need to investigate each case to find an individually significant explanation. Such fears rarely hinder a person's general life adjustments severely, because they are limited to a small segment of his experience. Only when a fear becomes so pervasive that its effects are generally nonintegrative does it become a personal maladjustment.

Fears as Maladjustments

Other instances of fearful behavior do not yield so readily to common-sense explanations. In any large group of people a few will be found who have fears that are inexplicable to themselves and to other laymen. The stimuli for such fears are almost innumerable. Various people have fears of water, of eyes, of high places, of closed rooms, of the street, of knives, and of countless other things. In many such cases, unlike the simpler fears already discussed, the fearful person is unable to account for his behavior. He cannot recall any past experience that might have caused his fear. Moreover, his fear tends to have a generalized effect on his whole life, interfering in some degree with his other activities and adjustments. Such reactions are known as *phobias,* which are often defined as "irrational" fears. Phobias are irrational only in the sense that they cannot be understood easily in terms of the person's remembered past experiences or of the traditions of his culture. When the appropriate evidence is brought to bear, phobias are no harder to understand than many of the other maladjustments. Phobias deserve extended study for two reasons. First, they are a common and significant human problem. Second, they lead quite directly to some important general concepts that are broadly applicable to many varieties of adjustments.

PHOBIAS

A Case of Phobia

Mildred K. had an intense fear of eyes. Her friends noticed that she never looked at anyone directly but always glanced away while talking. Her reason, the young woman explained to a psychologist, was that the sight of an eyeball caused her to feel an uncontrollable emotional panic. She was unable to remember when the phobia started, for it seemed to her that she had been afraid of eyes all her life. Recently the phobia had become intensified and some related symptoms had appeared. Mildred had frequent nightmares of persons whose eyes were horrible and staring and whom she took to be insane. The young woman was also obsessed with the verbal phrase, "fear looking out of her eyes," which she repeated over and over to herself in auditory imagery and in subvocal speech, unable to stop. Because of her concern about her phobia and because of the accompanying state of more general anxiety, Mildred's efficiency was seriously impaired. She found it increasingly difficult to study and could not concentrate on what she was reading. Her phobia also made her avoid her friends. As a result, her academic standing was affected and her social relationships were approaching ruin.

The psychologist explained to Mildred that such fears often may be traced to a forgotten incident associated with the stimulus for the phobia, and that the recall of that experience might be helpful. Since the psychologist was unable to have frequent long consultations with her, Mildred was taught how to facilitate the recall of such memories by herself. She was told to try to reinstate her fear clearly, and then to try to recall any past experience that might have some connection with it. She should do this while lying down in as relaxed a state as possible, or when drowsy and about to go to sleep at night. For several weeks, Mildred's attempts at recollection were fruitless; she could recall no vivid incident associated with the fear. On the fourth consultation she reported a memory of a motion picture that she had seen when she was about twelve years old. In this picture, an alleged comedy, an escaped insane person steals an airplane and ascends with a passenger, who does not discover the character of his pilot until in the air. The crude motion picture represented the insanity by the wild and staring eyes of the player. Mildred identified this character as the wild-eyed person of her dreams. Since phobias ordinarily originate from experiences of much greater personal significance than a motion picture, the psychologist considered the strong reaction to the film as an early symptom of the phobia rather than its source. He therefore recommended that Mildred continue her efforts to recollect.

A week later Mildred returned saying that she had recalled another experience connected with eyes. As a child of about seven she had gone to visit relatives, one of whom, an aunt, was blind. Little Mildred set out to explore the house and, with considerable excitement and some guilty fear of being caught in the act, she was peeping in the bureau drawers. As she opened one drawer, out of it stared two horrible eyes, eyes perfectly real but without a face. They were glass eyes belonging to the blind aunt. Mildred fled in terror. Even in telling the story to the psychologist years later she showed evidence of strong emotion and wept. She reported that she had never told anyone before. At the time she was afraid of parental censure, and then she "forgot" the incident. Mildred was urged to tell the story several times, and on each repetition she was less emotional in her reaction to it. She came to recognize that there was nothing unusual or shameful in her childish curiosity. Telling about the experience gave her some relief at once and in subsequent weeks the phobia of eyes diminished greatly and seemed to be disappearing.

A few other pertinent facts about Mildred's problem should be noted. In the first interview the psychologist made the obvious inquiry about blind persons in her family. Mildred told calmly of the blind aunt, but did not recall the fear-producing incident at that time. After she had remembered the motion picture, the psychologist explored the possibility of a fear of insanity, but no basis for it could be discovered. A reason for the recent greater intensity of the phobia was found in Mildred's home situation. Her father, to whom she was much attached, was in danger of losing his position and might have to leave home to find work elsewhere. The girl had reacted with considerable anxiety which added to her tension and was expressed in terms of the old phobia. Further consultations were held to help her work out her emotional attitudes toward the home problem.

Phobia as Conditioned Fear

The main features of many other cases of phobia resemble those of Mildred's fear of eyes. Three selected instances will be summarized briefly. The first two are among the most "classical" cases of phobia in the literature; the third has not been reported previously.

A phobia in a medical officer of the British army in World War I was described by Rivers.[5] The officer suffered from a "claustrophobia"* so intense that he preferred to spend the night in an open trench under fire rather than to remain in a dugout. He also showed many other symptoms of tension, including battle dreams and stammering. The fear of closed places had existed since boyhood. Under the guidance of a psychiatrist he eventually recalled a critical incident that had occurred when he was three or four years old. He had been caught in a narrow passageway from which he could not escape, and terrorized by a growling dog that threatened him from the other end of the corridor. He had never told of the incident. The phobia was intensified in later childhood by many nights of intense fear when he had to sleep in a "box-bed" set deep into a tiny alcove. Upon the recall of these experiences, the officer was relieved of his particular phobic symptom. The other evidences of anxiety, which did not stem from the childhood experience, remained unmodified.

Bagby cited a case of a young woman who suffered since childhood from an intense fear of running water, particularly if it made a splashing sound.[7] Her phobia interfered with her life in many ways, causing difficulties in traveling and even in taking baths. When the girl was twenty years old, a visit of an aunt whom she had not seen for thirteen years evoked the recall of an earlier experience. At the age of seven, the little girl had gone on a picnic with her family. She had wandered off contrary to the orders of her parents and had fallen into a waterfall from which she was rescued by the aunt. Fearing punishment for disobedience, she never told anyone else of the escapade, and the aunt departed immediately for a distant city leaving her without a confidante. The incident was "forgotten" but the fear persisted. After she recalled her childhood experience, the phobia diminished and eventually disappeared.

Less intense phobias that interfere little with a person's other adjustments occur very commonly.

For as long as she could remember, a woman college student had been afraid of locomotives. It was difficult for her to go to a

---

* A *claustrophobia* means a fear of small, inclosed, or confining places. Years ago it was customary to name phobias by long Greek-derived terms indicating the thing feared. A few of these words remain in fairly common use, including *acrophobia* (fear of heights) and *agoraphobia* (fear of open spaces or streets). A table in one recent medical dictionary listed no fewer than 344 phobia names,[6] which is enough to give anyone *onomatophobia* (fear of words)!

railroad station to see a friend off on the train, and even the whistle of a locomotive in the distance caused her some mild discomfort. When she took a course in psychology, the student heard of phobias for the first time and was surprised to learn that other people had such fears also. She had never admitted her phobia to her family because she regarded it as childish and silly, but now she discussed it with her mother. The mother immediately recalled an event that had happened when the girl was eight years old. The child and mother were walking near a railway crossing. As a locomotive went by noisily, the mother fainted and fell in the street. The little girl was intensely frightened and had the impression that the locomotive had done something terrible to her mother. In fact, the mother was pregnant and had had other fainting spells; the locomotive was only a coincidence. When her mother told the young woman of this childhood experience she had a vague sense of remembering it herself. The phobia weakened immediately, and a further inquiry after ten more years showed that she no longer had any timidity concerning locomotives.

From an examination of a large number of cases of phobia of this type, certain uniformities can be discovered. These generalizations are worth enumerating, but with the warning that *not all* phobias can be understood in such terms alone. In the next section some phobias will be described that require the application of additional principles.

1. The phobia dates from an intense fear-producing episode that occurred in childhood, usually before the age of ten.

2. The sufferer, astonishingly, is unable to recall the frightening experience. It is said to be *repressed*. He may recall it later by the aid of special psychological techniques, or with the help of another person who remembers the earlier episode.

3. The circumstances of the fear producing incident are such as to evoke shame, guilt, or anxiety in the child, whose resources are too immature to overcome such anxiety easily. In some cases the sources of the shame or guilt are evident from the history; in others they can only be inferred. Because of his anxiety, the child does not tell other people about his experience. He does not even think of it or tell it over to himself in inner speech.

4. The later recall of the fearful experience usually causes the phobia to diminish or disappear. This is clearly evident in the four cases cited. In all of them the source of the original fear was child-

ish. An adult could readjust to it easily when he was able to re-examine it from a mature perspective. He was no longer alarmed at the situations — disobedience, snooping, confinement, and the like — that were potent arousers of anxiety in childhood.

The first of these observations is the least difficult to explain. At their outsets, all these phobias were conditioned fear reactions. The same process occurred as when the burnt child fears the fire or Watson's experimental subject feared the rat.

It may be objected, however, that many children have fearful experiences that do not give rise to phobias. For example, when the writer was four years old he fell into a creek when warned not to go near the water, under circumstances quite like those of Bagby's case. No phobia developed. The distinguishing feature seems to have been the absence of repression. He was caught in the act, duly punished, and the incident was much talked about. Therefore the experience was shared with other people, was re-peated verbally, and was remembered. Phobias seem more likely to arise when the fear-conditioning episode is followed by repres-sion. This concept is an important one and must be investigated thoroughly.

Phobia as Displaced Anxiety

The phobias described so far are understood quite adequately as conditioned fears, with the added feature of repression. In each instance a childhood experience conditioned a fear response to a situation. The later phobia is evoked by the very stimulus — eyes, confinement, running water, locomotives — that had aroused the original fear.

Certain other cases of phobia do not follow so simple a pattern. The present phobia is evoked, not by the same stimulus as the earlier fear, but by some *symbol* associated with it.[8] In a sense, two learning processes take place: first, a fear conditioning; and second, the further substitution of a new stimulus for the one originally fear-conditioned. The examination of several more cases will make this essentially complicated process clearer.

> Masserman described a phobia in an eighteen-year-old girl, Anne A., who was afraid of cats, dogs, and other small pets.[9] She also had many other symptoms of tension and anxiety. When

Anne was four years old her mother gave birth to a son. Up to that time the girl had been the center of her parents' attention and affection, but now she felt herself supplanted. At first she was openly hostile to the baby brother but such conduct only increased her parents' rejection. She gave up her direct hostility toward the baby, but continued to be destructive of his clothes and toys. At that point, the parents gave Anne a kitten, presumably to help her learn to love and care for a small and helpless charge. At the outset she was delighted with the kitten but soon abused it so that it died. Her parents punished her severely for the kitten's death, and she soon afterward developed a generally anxious attitude, with a particular phobia for small animals.

A displaced phobia is well illustrated by Morton Prince's famous case of a young woman who suffered an uncontrollable fear of church towers and church bells.[10] She was unable to account for her phobia, but at length a psychiatrist was able to induce the recall of an event earlier in her life, which had caused it. The girl's mother had undergone a serious operation while at a health resort recovering from an illness. The girl felt guilty about her mother's illness and believed, although without real justification, that her lack of care had caused the mother's turn for the worse. While waiting in a hotel room, uncertain of her mother's fate and in an intense state of anxiety, the girl's view from her window had been chiefly of a church tower across the street whose bells chimed every quarter hour. The mother died. In this case, the recall of the earlier experience did not cure the phobia. The young woman still felt guilt and remorse about her mother's death. Even as an adult she could not regard her experience as a petty childish episode, as could the young women who feared running water and locomotives. Further psychiatric treatment was needed to help her to see her mother's death as unavoidable and in no way due to her neglect. When she assimilated this viewpoint fully the phobia disappeared.

A pioneer study of a phobia in a child was Freud's case of "little Hans," first reported in 1909.[11] Five-year-old Hans showed a strong phobia of horses. Freud's interpretation was that Hans really feared his father, a fear that he could not face because of the inevitable dependence of childhood. Several incidents in the boy's life made clear the basis for the substitution. A black horse's muzzle had reminded him of his father's mustache; he had "played horse" with his father; he saw a horse fall in the street and struggle to get up, an incident that had much impressed him.

An even more remotely substituted fear was reported by Bingham.[12] Fanny was a bright little twelve-and-a-half-year-old girl
who had an intense phobia of open places. The fear was discovered by her gymnasium teacher to whom Fanny had complained that she became dizzy in large, high rooms and hence
could not do gymnasium work. In addition to her phobia she
suffered from a rapid heart beat and a "weak feeling," typical
signs of anxiety. Her concern about her heart dated from an incident several years before when she had been reading *The Man
Without a Country* in a library. When she reached the passage
describing the death of the chief character of the book she became
very much excited, found her heart pounding rapidly, and became very dizzy. From that time she believed that she had a
weak heart and was destined for an early death, although medical
clinics found nothing organically wrong. At this time her fear
of open places increased, until she disliked passing by a park or
other large place, and could not enter one. Further study showed
that Fanny had long had a morbid fear of death. Several incidents involving death, including a "Jack-the-Ripper" scare in her
neighborhood and a street-car accident in which there had been a
panic, had made very vivid impressions. A fear of death was disclosed as the fundamental source of the girl's behavior. She had
always thought of heaven as a large place and had engaged in
many fantasies on that theme. The phobia disappeared after psychiatric consultations had cleared up Fanny's unfounded fear of
death. The case was followed for three years and no further difficulties were reported.

Cases of phobia such as these require an amplification of the principles that were drawn from the simpler conditioned phobias.

1. The phobia dates from an early experience involving intense
anxiety, often arising from the parent-child relationship. The conflict causing the anxiety is of an abstract sort: fear of rejection by
one's parents, guilt over a parent's death, fear of one's own death,
and the like. Such stimuli, unlike running water or locomotives,
provide no tangible objects on which to focus the fear or from
which to flee.

2. Closely associated with the anxiety is some concrete object
such as a cat, a bell tower, a horse, or an open space. Through a
learning process, the person comes to react fearfully to this substitute stimulus with all the intensity appropriate to the original
anxiety. The process is *displacement,* which is a kind of symbolic

learning (p. 72). In this learning process, a substitute stimulus occurring at the same time that a response is evoked becomes able to arouse the response.

3. The recall of the original anxiety-producing experience is *repressed,* as in all phobias.

4. Merely recalling the episode that conditioned the phobia sometimes causes the fear to be weakened, and sometimes it does not. Even when the recall removes the specific phobia, the anxiety and tension are likely to remain. A real cure occurs only when the person achieves a full readjustment to the conflict that set off the original anxiety.

In many instances it is proper to think of a displaced phobia as a *conditioned anxiety.* Several cases of fears of the street, of street cars, and of elevators have been traced to associative learning.[13] A woman with a conflict that aroused intermittent panics of anxiety had a strong anxiety attack while riding in a street car. Thereafter, a street car would again arouse her anxiety, resulting in a phobia. In large part, the phobias of pets, horses, and bell towers that have been described may be regarded as conditioned anxieties.

The case of Fanny, who feared open spaces, illustrates a more subtle kind of symbolic learning. Much human learning is based on words and thoughts, which are less concrete experiences than objects, animals, and the like, but no less real. Normal people in everyday life represent abstract notions by words and other symbols, and it is not at all surprising that victims of phobias should do the same. The symbol is connected with its meaning by learning processes of a common type, sometimes occurring in culture-agreed social contexts and sometimes in private experience. "Open places" becomes a symbol for death by a process not very different from that by which "pi" becomes a symbol for the ratio of the circumference to the diameter of a circle.

Learning by sheer contiguity and learning by symbolic meaning are not entirely separate, for both may influence the development of a particular phobia. Why, for example, did the church bells symbolize the mother's death in Prince's case? Why did not the young woman develop a phobia for red carpets, or for open windows, or for some other feature of her perceived environment as she grieved for her mother? It is probably significant that the tolling of bells is a conventional symbol of death in our culture, and that her cultural learning caused her to react to that segment of her experience rather than to some other aspect. Similarly, Anne's kitten, in Masserman's case, was not only the occasion for her parents' severe punishment, but was also a symbol for her baby brother whom she would have liked to harm as she did the little animal. Displacement therefore involves the occurrence-together that is essential for learning, and also involves meanings that come from language and other symbols learned in the culture.

Too sharp a separation must not be made between the two patterns of phobia that have been described. Only in selected instances is it possible to find pure types. The running-water phobia as described by Bagby is an almost pure instance of a conditioned fear. The open-places phobia is almost entirely symbolic, a displaced anxiety. Intermediate examples that involve both factors are more common. In Mildred's fear of eyes both the conditioning childhood incident and her present anxiety about her father were significant. You should not, therefore, think of two separate types or classes of phobia but of two factors, both of which may influence a phobia in varying degrees.

Adjustive Values of Phobias

It seems strange that so painful and inconvenient an experience as a phobia can have an adjustive value. Careful reflection, however, reveals that phobias are adjustment mechanisms. Even the simplest phobias are avoidance responses by which a person keeps away from situations that would arouse his fear. If the feared subject is one not commonly encountered in an individual's culture, his adjustment may be very successful and he may be little inconvenienced. If you have a phobia of elephants, for example, you can control it easily by staying away from zoos and circuses. When the stimulus for the phobia is almost unavoidable, or when a radical rearrangement of one's life is required to avoid contact with it, the phobia becomes seriously nonintegrative. The tension reduction resulting from each escape from his fear is highly rewarding to the sufferer, however, and determines his behavior prepotently in spite of his loss of other satisfactions.

The displacement process found in symbolic phobias has an even stronger adjustive value. An avoidable and therefore somewhat controllable object is substituted for an uncontrollable anxiety. Anne A. could not escape her fear of parental rejection nor her horror that she might actually injure her baby brother, but she could avoid cats and dogs. Between the two evils, therefore, the overt fear is less uncomfortable than the pervasive anxiety. When the real anxiety is evoked by an abstract concept, the only immediate adjustment is to represent it concretely. There was no possible way for Fanny to run away from death, but she secured some drive reduction by avoiding large rooms and open spaces, which symbolized death to her. Displaced phobias are perpetuated because they represent a person's last desperate attempt to deal with an overwhelming anxiety. They are nonintegrative in their considerable interference with other life adjustments.

An additional adjustive function is served by some cases of phobia. Let us first take up an example.

Maslow and Mittelmann tell of a twenty-five-year-old girl who was afraid either to go more than a short distance from her home, or to remain home alone.[14] She was excessively attached to her widowed father, who she feared might remarry and thereby abandon her. Although the phobia had other features, attention can be directed to its utility as an adjustive device by which the young woman was able to control her father. Her father had to stay with her at home, or to accompany her on their infrequent excursions. He accepted her status as a "nervous" young person who needed extra care and protection.

Numerous other cases of phobia show the same feature, often in less transparent form. A person affected by a phobia sometimes secures a direct, even an aggressive, satisfaction by getting attention and sympathy from other people and by controlling their actions for his own benefit. A similar characteristic is found in some psychologically determined illnesses, which will be described in the next chapters.

A minor adjustive value obtained from an otherwise uncomfortable state of affairs is called a *secondary gain*. The term emphasizes that the primary source of the phobia or other maladjustment arises from more significant causes, but that it has in addition a subsidiary or secondary satisfyingness. Popular opinion often regards secondary gains with suspicion, believing that the affected person counterfeits his symptoms to deceive others for his own ends. There is no reason to hold, however, that secondary gains are any more malicious, deliberate, or conscious than any other types of adjustment. They are like the mechanisms of attention-getting and compensation in obtaining satisfactions naively and directly, and usually without conscious intent. A secondary gain, superimposed on another type of maladjustment, illustrates the complexity of the adjustive processes. Behavior is rarely simple, and multiple explanations are often necessary in order to understand all the aspects of even one person's adjustments.

The most important and spectacular adjustive feature in phobias, and also in many other maladjustments, has been left until last. The mechanism of repression, that strange forgetting of intense and personally significant experiences, is a powerful adjustive device for escaping anxiety.

EVIDENCE CONCERNING REPRESSION

Selective Forgetting

Our ordinary concepts of memory seem inadequate to account for the peculiarly active kind of forgetting involved in phobias. The forgetting of unreviewed lessons, infrequently used telephone numbers, and the like seems comprehensible, but repression is a strange kind of forgetting. Indeed, the concept of repression forces us to re-examine the phenomena of remembering and forgetting as a whole, to see what part dynamic factors such as motives, attitudes, and anxiety may play in the selection of what will be remembered.

A commonplace example of repression is the failure to recall well-learned names, engagements, and places which by all usual criteria should be remembered. This is a very frequent experience in people's lives, and almost everyone is bothered by it from time to time. Of course, many examples of such forgetting are due to inattention and to inadequate initial learning. You cannot expect to remember a name that you heard only in one mumbled introduction, and that you did not perceive clearly even at the moment. In other instances you may find a very well-learned response peculiarly elusive. Your failure to remember it seems absurd and inexplicable and quite unlike ordinary forgetting. William James described in striking terms how it feels to have such a failure of recall.

> Suppose we try to recall a forgotten name. The state of our consciousness is peculiar. There is a gap therein; but no mere gap. It is a gap that is intensely active. A sort of wraith of the

name is in it, beckoning us in a given direction, making us at moments tingle with the sense of our closeness, and then letting us sink back without the longed-for term. If wrong names are proposed to us, this singularly definite gap acts immediately so as to negate them. They do not fit into its mould. . . . The rhythm of a lost word may be there without a sound to clothe it; or the evanescent sense of something which is the initial vowel or consonant may mock us fitfully, without growing more distinct. Every one must know the tantalizing effect of the blank rhythm of some forgotten verse, restlessly dancing in one's mind, striving to be filled out with words.*

Sigmund Freud, in his *Psychopathology of Everyday Life,* was one of the first to attempt an explanation of the forgetting of well-learned names and the like as something more than a mere accident or a failure of association. An anecdote similar to those cited by Freud offers a convenient first approach to the problem of repression.

A graduate student of psychology had made a number of contacts with another student who was employed as a night clerk in the university dormitory. He talked with this young man a number of times and heard his name mentioned frequently, yet he never could remember it. This was all the more remarkable since the student was pursuing a course in optometry and had assisted the young psychologist in having an eye examination made by one of the instructors in that department. By all ordinary considerations, the name should have been remembered, but it was most elusive. Deciding that the forgetting was of the type described by Freud, the graduate student secured the name from a mutual acquaintance. The name was Bishop, surely not one of intrinsic difficulty. Using this name as a starting point, a study was made of the associations involved. After nearly an hour of reverie on associations with the name, a significant incident was remembered suddenly and vividly. The student recalled that when about ten years old he had set out for a Sunday afternoon walk alone, his usual companions on such an excursion being out of town. Walking along a road on the outskirts of the town he saw two boys sitting on a fence at some distance and waved to them, thinking that one of them was a boy he had known at camp. The boys called back, and came running. They proved to be total strangers and

---

* William James, *Principles of psychology.* New York: Holt, 1890. Vol. I, Pp. 251-252.

informed the youngster that he had asked them to fight, and that the challenge had been accepted. The odds looked too great and the ten-year-old resorted to flight, only to be caught and ignominiously beaten. The disgracefulness of this situation for a boy of ten is apparent. To have been beaten in a fight was bad enough, but to have been beaten after having run away was unthinkable. The incident was never disclosed to anyone. It was repressed, and recalled with difficulty even when an adult. The name of the camp acquaintance, for whom one of the tormentors was at first mistaken, was Bishop. The name had somehow been tied to the incident, and had been repressed with it. The student suddenly realized that he could not remember ever having had any other male acquaintance of this name. Possibly many Bishops had been met — and forgotten. The mechanism did not operate in the case of women and girls, and no difficulty was experienced in recalling the name when applied to them.

Freud's theory of repression involved the concepts of conscious and unconscious forces. Painful and anxiety-provoking material could not be tolerated in consciousness and hence was rejected forcibly into the unconscious condition. Any associated names or ideas that would tend to bring up the disavowed thought were repressed also. The harm done by repression was supposed to arise from two sources. First, it was conceived that a certain amount of "mental energy" had to be expended in order to keep the painful memory repressed, so that less energy was available for dealing with other problems. Also, the repressed memory was supposed to remain active in the unconscious and to seek to come out in disguise, resulting in various eccentricities of behavior including phobias.

As a descriptive analogy, Freud's account was not without merit. No one feels a need to deny the observations on which it was based. Indeed, psychologists of all theoretical persuasions recognize the fact of repression and agree that a repressed memory certainly is not conscious. Modern experimental psychology, however, wants to go beyond Freud's early theoretical explanation. Some aspects of his theory are not in accord with a scientific biological approach to the understanding of behavior. An important objection is that the theory postulates special mental "forces" that repress an idea and keep it repressed, which are incompatible with what we know about the physiology and chemistry of the body. Also, the theory pictures the repressed events as separate entities within a person, which have forces of their own and "strive" to get back into con-sciousness. A sounder approach regards a person as one whole functioning organism. The psychologist's task is to arrive at an explanation of repression in terms of experimentally verifiable con-cepts.

Experimental Studies of Repression

Since a purely clinical method is a notoriously unreliable way to obtain data, especially when reminiscences of long-past events are concerned, it is important to seek more conclusive evidence about selective forgetting.[15] If repression exists it should be dis-coverable in the ordinary behavior of normal people as well as in clinical cases, although probably in less marked degree. Well-designed experiments using quantitative methods should not only verify the existence of repression but should also reveal additional facts about the conditions under which it will occur. Some 58 experiments have been reported that deal with repression directly, and many others have some relationship to the topic.[16] No other problem in the field of dynamic experimental psychology has been investigated more widely. Among the 58 studies, 40 have found positive evidence for repression and 18 have been negative or in-conclusive. The negative experiments have not refuted the concept of repression, however, but have been constructive in pointing out certain conditions under which it does not occur.

Some of the most relevant experiments have studied the selective forgetting of real-life experiences. A study by Meltzer is typical.[17] On a day following Christmas vacation, 132 college students were asked to list and briefly describe all their experiences during the vacation. Each experience considered pleasant was marked P; each unpleasant recollection was marked U. The students reported 2231 experiences of which 62 per cent were pleasant and 38 per cent were unpleasant. These percentages give no sound evidence of selective forgetting, as it is quite probable that college students experience a greater number of pleasant events during a vacation. The important part of the experiment was the subsequent attempt to recall these same experiences. Six weeks later, without warning, the subjects were asked again to recall all of their vacation experi-ences. The "new" recalls, events remembered on the second recall but not on the first, were eliminated from the calculations. On the average, 53 per cent of the pleasant experiences were retained over the six-week interval but only 40 per cent of the unpleasant experiences. The difference of 13 per cent was more than six times its probable error, indicating that the difference was probably not due to chance factors. Meltzer's experiment, on the whole, confirmed the clinical evidence. Even with the relatively mild emotional tones of such ordinary experiences, there is a general tendency to remember the pleasant better than the unpleasant after only a short interval of time.

Meltzer's and other experiments have found individual differences among people in their tendency to forget the unpleasant. When individual records were analyzed, 56 per cent of the students were found to have remembered more P than U experiences, 8 per cent showed no difference, while 36 per cent (termed the "pessimists" by Meltzer) retained a greater proportion of U than of P memories. In another research, Alper made a clinical study of the personalities of the subjects of an experiment on repression.[18] The results suggest that the "pessimists" tend to blame themselves rather than others when things go wrong, to be idealistic, and to lack strong motives to strive for power, seek recognition, or justify their actions. The clinical and experimental evidence indicates that not everyone uses the mechanism of repression equally. There are individual differences in the mechanisms that people employ for adjustment, just as there are in all other human traits.

An experiment by Stagner carried the evidence further.[19] A group of college students was asked to recall the most pleasant event of the preceding fifteen days and then to write as many associations as possible, either trivial or important, connected with that event. A similar procedure was followed for the most unpleasant event in their recent experiences. Fifteen days later, without warning, the records of the two events were returned and the subjects were asked to reproduce the associations previously given. The results showed that 54 per cent of the P associations were retained and 43 per cent of the U associations. The difference of 11 per cent was reliable statistically. This study showed that the repression of the associations of an unpleasant event, as well as of the event itself, is verifiable experimentally.

What Kind of Unpleasantness Causes Repression?

Most of the experiments on repression, including those of Meltzer and Stagner, permitted the subjects to use their own understandings of the terms "pleasant" and "unpleasant." These vague words have many meanings. It is unpleasant to smell a bad odor; it is also unpleasant to have your friends appraise you as stupid or ill-bred. Just what kind of unpleasantness causes repression most dependably?

The negative findings of some of the earlier experiments help to answer a part of the question. In a number of studies, the subjects were required to memorize materials that seemed to be pleasant or unpleasant in content, such as words with happy or disgusting meanings, gratifying or depressing passages of poetry, and handsome or ugly faces. About half of such studies found weak evidence of repression; the rest found little or none. Studies of the permanence of memory for pleasant versus unpleasant odors and colors have been least positive. Only a minority of researches using such stimuli has found any evidence for repression. In general, repression is not evoked often or strongly by impersonal or unthreatening kinds of "unpleasantness."

A sequence of research studies by Wallen and by Shaw has given a more revealing picture of the kind of unpleasantness that does underlie repression.[20] In his experiment, Wallen first required a group of students to rate themselves on each of 40 traits, including qualities such as "adaptable," "fickle," "punctual," and "rash." The subjects marked a plus beside each word they regarded as descriptive of themselves, and a zero beside each word they thought did not describe them. About a week later, each student was given a sheet bearing his name and 40 numbered spaces each marked plus or zero.

He was told that he had been rated by someone who knew him well, and that the sheet gave the other person's ratings. The list of 40 descriptive words was then read aloud twice slowly while the subjects looked at the marks. After a further forty-eight-hour interval the students were given the list of traits and asked to recall the ratings given to them by the other rater. That was the memory task: to remember how the other persons had appraised them.

As a matter of fact, the "other's" ratings were not genuine. These "bogus ratings" had been invented by systematically changing half the ratings the subjects had given themselves. However, the experiment was conducted in such a way that all subjects believed they had really been rated. Many expressed concern about the "rater's" opinions of them.

In a still further part of the experiment, the subjects indicated whether each word described a desirable or an undesirable trait. For example, most students thought that "adaptable" and "punctual" were desirable attributes, and that "fickle" and "rash" were undesirable ones.

The experiments permitted an analysis of the effects of three factors on the ability to remember the "other person's" ratings: (1) the rater's agreement with the subject; (2) the rater's favorable or unfavorable evaluation; and (3) the qualities conveyed by the words themselves. The results were as follows:

1. The strongest determiner of remembering was the "rater's" agreement with the subject's own evaluation of himself. If the "rater" agreed, his rating was likely to be remembered; when he disagreed, his rating was more often forgotten.

2. The favorable or unfavorable character of the evaluation made by the supposed "rater" was also a significant determiner of remembering. The evaluation was favorable when the "rater" said that the subject possessed a desirable trait, or that he was free from an undesirable one. An unfavorable evaluation was the reverse.

When the first and second factors occurred together, the difference in forgetting was large indeed. In Shaw's study, for example when the student attributed a desirable trait such as "friendly" to himself and the rater agreed, the forgetting was only 14 per cent.[21] But when the "rater" denied that the student had the desirable trait, the bogus rating was forgotten 45 per cent of the time.

3. The qualities of the trait names themselves had no effect on forgetting. Other things being equal, it was as easy to remember one's rating on "fickle" as on "adaptable." The mere unpleasantness of the word did not cause repression.

The Wallen-Shaw studies made explicit the basis of repression that was probably implicit in many of the other researches. If an event is in disagreement with your social evaluation of yourself, and especially if it represents a derogatory appraisal, it will arouse conflict and anxiety. One way to adjust to such a threat is to forget it, or to distort it into agreement with your self-evaluation based on the social standards you have learned. In the case studies cited, persons suffering from phobias repressed their remembrances of events that were disobedient, unworthy, shameful, or guilty. The evidence from the case studies is in good agreement with the best experimental findings.

THE PSYCHOLOGY OF REPRESSION

An Objective Account of Repression

The mechanism of repression can be explained quite satisfactorily by the use of concepts drawn from experimental studies of learning, without requiring any unique hypotheses to account for the "abnormal" cases. As a first step, it is instructive to contrast repression with the more common sort of forgetting.

Ordinary forgetting occurs mainly through a process very much like the *extinction* of a conditioned reaction. In the conditioned reaction experiment, if the bell is rung again and again without the presentation of the food, the dog will cease to salivate for the bell. The unreinforced repetition of the stimulus leads gradually to extinction. Similarly, if the episode relating to the name "Bishop" had occurred without the strong anxiety that led to repression, the name for a while would have recalled the incident. But after the young man had met many people of that name and had used it in many varied situations, "Bishop" would no longer have served as a stimulus for the particular memory unless assisted by additional and more specific cues. Extinction would have occurred by the repetition of the name without its original reinforcement. Similarly, we forget unreviewed lessons and other bits of information, and our routine life experiences are less likely to be remembered as time goes on, because we have associated the cues for such memories with a host of subsequent and unrelated responses. It is not mere "disuse" that causes ordinary forgetting. Active further learning interferes with the recall of unreinforced earlier responses. Of course, extinguished memories are not totally lost. When a response has once been established and then extinguished, it can be relearned more quickly and easily than an entirely new response. For example, a moderate amount of review will reinstate your skill in a foreign language that was once well learned but later forgotten.

A repressed response is not extinguished, for it can sometimes be recalled under appropriate conditions without any relearning, as is shown by the techniques used to recover the repressed memory underlying a phobia. The failure to recall a repressed experience is an example of the more positive process of *inhibition*. At the time of the original traumatic experience basic to a repression, some event, object, or name occurs simultaneously with a response of anxiety or guilt. Consequently, a recall of the event would tend to evoke anxiety. One way to prevent the anxiety from occurring is to inhibit the recall of the memory that might arouse it.

The inhibition of recall offers no more theoretical difficulty than does the inhibition of a motor response. If a dog is whipped when he jumps on a table to grab a piece of meat, he will soon learn to inhibit jumping, even though he has a strong tendency to do so. An inhibition of recall is quite similar. Recall is a response to a stimulus, and a person can learn to avoid making the response, to "not-recall," in order to escape the pain of anxiety.

Where does the repressed memory go? In one sense, it does not go anywhere, for it simply does not occur. One might as well ask where the dog's jump goes when he does not jump. Only a misconception of memory that supposes it to be the "filing away" of past experiences needs to make an hypothesis as to where the repressed response goes. It is not conscious, but this does not mean it is "in" some place called "the unconscious," as an earlier, now discarded psychoanalytic theory supposed. When it is inhibited it is nonexistent at the moment. Of course, there are processes in a person's nervous system in connection with everything that he does or learns. An inhibited response presumably is prevented by counteracting nervous-system processes that keep the neural circuit from being completed. These neural processes are very complicated and we know very little about them.

Repression as an Adjustment

It is quite evident that repression serves as an adjustment mechanism, just as does the inhibition of a simple motor act that would have a painful result. You adjust to a hot stove by not-touching it. Analogously, you can adjust to an anxiety-provoking segment of your past experience by not-remembering. In many instances, the adjustment of repression is not achieved at once. At first, many stimuli will suggest the recall of the traumatic experience, but the person learns to make avoidant responses to them. He turns away from any outer stimulus that might arouse the recall, and inhibits responses to any inner verbal stimuli that would tend to evoke it. Initially, the adjustment may be only partially successful but in time the person becomes more and more skillful in this form of defense, and repression is achieved. Each successful act of repression is reinforced by the resulting reduction of immediate anxiety.

Recent experimental evidence confirms an observation long suspected from clinical studies, that a person can repress his response to an anxiety-arousing stimulus even before he becomes clearly enough aware of it to make a verbal report as to what the stimulus is. Several experiments dealing with the effect of attitudes upon perception have measured how quickly a word can be perceived, by the use of a short-exposure apparatus called a tachistoscope.[22] A favorably toned word can be perceived when it is exposed very briefly; to perceive an unfavorably toned word that presumably arouses anxiety may require twice as long an exposure. One experiment showed that subjects made an emotional response, as indicated by electrically measured sweating of the palm of the hand, to anxiety-arousing words even when a word was exposed so briefly that the subject was "unable" to give a verbal report of it.[23] Such experiments show that perception itself is selectively influenced by repression. A person can make some kind of a discriminative response to a situation, accepting or rejecting it according to his adjustive needs, even before he can give an intellectual report of what he is perceiving.

Repression is one of the least constructive forms of adjustment. It is less integrative than most of the other mechanisms of defense or escape. First, repression gives no opportunity for the reduction of normal socially derived motives. Compensation or fantasy have real drive-reducing values for a person, even though they are asocial or even antisocial. Repression solves nothing, but only serves to keep anxiety within bounds by inhibiting responses to situations that tend to evoke it. Second, repression often adds to a maladjusted person's burden of woe. He is afraid without knowing why he is afraid. His own behavior therefore seems queer and baseless, and he is likely to develop a secondary anxiety about himself. Sometimes he fears that he is not normal or that he is going insane. Finally, repression keeps a person from having new experiences in the area of his anxiety, and thereby prevents him from taking steps toward more constructive readjustment through learning.

Some people have a greater tendency to repress than others. Individual differences in the habit of repressing seem to stem from childhood experiences, particularly from circumstances that create a strong fear of social disapproval. Serious phobias rarely if ever occur in persons who had free and confident relationships with their parents during childhood. If a child receives unsympathetic treatment, so that his early confessions of anxieties and feelings of guilt are met with rebuffs or punishment, he will learn not to confide. He is then more likely to develop a habit of meeting his adjustive problems by repression. There is no sharply distinguishable "repressed type" of person, but this tendency occurs to the extent that it was reinforced during the early trial-and-error stage of adjustment. Persons who have learned to use repression as their major means of adjustment are likely to suffer throughout their lives from fears and anxieties, because they have no adequate means for permanently reducing these emotional tensions.

Culturally Determined Areas of Repression

The traditions of a culture play a large part in determining what kinds of adjustment problems will be subjected to repression. In the typical middle-class American and European culture, two behavior impulses not tolerated in children are overt *hostility* and *sex*. Open aggressiveness toward parents or siblings is usually met with punishment and the withdrawal of affection. As a result, a child usually learns early in his life to repress behavior and thoughts that are hostile toward his family group, even though many frustrating incidents are adequate stimuli for aggressive responses.

A case already described illustrates the relation between family hostility and repression. Anne A. (p. 222) learned to repress her hostility toward her baby brother. Her own hostility evoked strong anxiety, which was displaced to a fear of cats and dogs, since she could not even admit to herself the source of her concern.

Many anxieties and repressions are concerned with the sexual functions. Some of these are manifested directly in conduct as fear of sex, frigidity, and impotence. Not all sexual maladjustments are expressed directly, however, since sex is especially productive of displaced anxieties which, on the surface, seem related to quite different problems.

The main reason for the prevalence of sex as a factor underlying anxiety is that sex problems are more commonly subjected to repression than any other areas of adjustive difficulty in our culture. Children who seek enlightenment on matters relating to sex are usually put off with indefinite answers, are told that such things are not discussed by nice people, or are even scolded or punished for their natural interest. Although the present generation has shown a more open attitude toward sex than did the past few generations, the cultural suppression of talking or thinking about sex is by no means overcome entirely. As a result of such childhood experiences, most people have an inhibition against seeking help on sexual problems even when they are moderately well adjusted in this respect as adults. The sex drive itself is not repressed, but there is a repression of responses to this drive, and an inhibition against thinking about it and against admitting the sexual nature of a problem. These attitudes seriously hinder readjustment when difficulties are encountered. Two cases of sex adjustment problems will be described.

> Hamilton gave the history of a young married woman who was frigid and who felt disgusted and repelled by normal sex relations with her husband.[24] She recognized the undesirability of her condition and strove to overcome it, but was unable to control her feelings. When techniques for overcoming repression were applied, a series of incidents was at last recalled, dating from her early adolescence. The young woman had lived with an uncle and aunt while attending high school. The uncle often came to her room after she had retired and had made frequent sexual advances which she had partially repelled. One night she awoke to find her uncle in bed with her about to attempt sex relations. She screamed and aroused the household, but the uncle had fled. She explained the commotion by saying that she must have had a bad dream, and did not reveal or discuss the incident even at the time. The memory of the fear-producing episode was subsequently repressed. When she recalled the experience and readjusted to it, her frigidity disappeared.

It is probable that only a few cases of fear of sex are due to such specific conditioning experiences. In many more instances, indirect social training causes a youngster to regard sex as nasty, fearful, or disgusting. Men often have unjustified doubts of their own virility which they cannot resolve because of inhibitions against seeking information or help, and which arouse anxiety when they confront a sexual situation. All these learnings lead to sexual maladjustments, because the nature of the autonomic nervous system prevents the arousal of fear and sex simultaneously. Psychological impotence in men and frigidity in women may be regarded as sexual phobias. Displaced anxieties are very common in the sexual sphere of adjustment. A case described by Morgan is illustrative.[25]

> A young man complained of a serious stomach disorder, which had been treated without benefit by several physicians. He blamed his trouble on smoking cigarettes, although his use of tobacco was really very moderate. He described with great anguish his struggles against smoking, but professed that he was unable to overcome the habit. Psychological investigation disclosed that his whole trouble was a displacement of anxiety about masturbation. His father had advised him to take up smoking as a means of overcoming an auto-erotic habit. Later, through reading quack literature, he came to believe that his masturbation would cause him severe mental and physical harm. Repressing his real problem, he displaced his anxiety to the smoking. When the source of the difficulty was discovered, and when he was helped to readjust to his sexual problem, the stomach symptoms disappeared.

The Role of Repression in Maladjustments

Enough clinical and experimental evidence has now been cited to enable us to evaluate the central part that repression plays in phobias and in many other maladjustments. A person with a phobia developed, much earlier in his life, a generalized habit of adjusting by repression. Because of his general tendency to repress, the individual is likely to be broadly maladjusted, and to show other anxiety symptoms in addition to the phobia itself. Phobias are found mainly in persons who are "a bit queer anyway." Such persons have an unfortunate background that predisposes them to repress anxiety-provoking experiences.

The event underlying a specific phobia represents a double process of learning. First, an uncontrollable fear or anxiety is attached to a stimulus by conditioning. That fear is the phobia itself. Second, the situation arouses anxiety, shame, or guilt, to which the person adjusts by repressing certain responses to the situation, in keeping with his established habit.

Phobias differ from simpler learned fears in this respect: *the repression prevents the extinction of the fear reaction.* In Pavlov's experiments, the dog was "cured" of responding to the bell by ringing it repeatedly without adequate reinforcement by food. In phobias, the actual unreinforced repetition of the stimulus is impracticable. No one would suggest, for example, dunking the young woman who feared running water again and again into the stream under reassuring circumstances! Phobias, and other anxiety disorders involving long-past events, are treated by a substitute kind of repetition, that is, by talking about them. A phobia does not disappear because the repression of recall prevents the underlying incident or conflict from being remembered, repeated in word symbols, re-examined in the light of more mature experience, and otherwise subjected to readjustment. Repression makes inaccessible certain cues that are essential for relearning.

The process of psychotherapy, as will be described more fully in a subsequent chapter, establishes a type of social communication between therapist and client in which the latter's anxiety is reduced so that he can dare to think and talk about things he has hitherto been unable to conceive or mention. The client's old fears and conflicts are therefore brought into the present in a verbal form, and the client is able to re-educate his responses to them. In that sense, repression underlies most maladjustments, and its release is instrumental in extinguishing, or unlearning, nonintegrative emotional attitudes generally.

OBSESSIONS AND COMPULSIONS

Obsessions

An obsession is a recurring thought or desire that a person regards as false, useless, or annoying, but from which he cannot free himself. One example of an obsessional thought has already been encountered. Mildred (p. 218) could not help repeating the phrase, "fear looking out of her eyes," even though she tried desperately to avoid it. Obsessions are often associated with phobias; indeed, phobia has sometimes been regarded as a special kind of obsession, in which a person is obsessed with an absurd fear.

Obsessions are not all of the same sort, and do not always serve the same adjustive ends. Some obsessive thoughts are merely overt expressions of an anxiety induced by a conflict. It is perhaps a little more consoling to put the anxiety into words, instead of experiencing it only as a nameless fear. The person gains a slight reduction of tension also by disowning the offending thought. He does not "want" to think that thought, but finds himself verbalizing it in spite of his attempted resistance.

Some obsessions are displaced anxieties. For example, a man suffered from an obsessive thought that he might take a knife and cut his wife's throat.[26] Superficially he was on excellent terms with his wife, but he had a strongly repressed hostility toward her because of her interference with his career. The obsession was an adjustment to his disowned hostility: he could guard against it by avoiding all contact with knives. The obsession was therefore less anxiety-producing than his repressed hostility, which he could not avoid because he carried it with him all of the time. Psychologically similar is the obsession of a mother that her children are in danger, which leads her to make countless telephone calls to the school and to the neighbors to make sure that they are safe. Such obsessions have an adjustive value similar to that of the symbolic, or displaced, phobias.

Compulsions

A compulsion is an irresistible tendency to perform some action, even when it is known to be unnecessary or absurd. A person with a compulsion usually feels a tension of anxiety which continues to mount until he relieves it by performing the compulsive act. Compulsions are closely related to obsessions. The arbitrary distinction is that an obsession is a thought or desire, while a compulsion is an action. Phobias are often accompanied by compulsions that serve to reduce the fear tension. Bagby cited a typical case.[27]

> Miss B. was a teacher of quiet and retiring disposition. Whenever she was alone in her room she became troubled with a fear that someone was behind her. The compulsion to look around would soon become uncontrollable, and her fear usually would not subside until she had made an inspection of the entire apartment. She recognized the absurdity of this performance, but it was the only way in which she could relieve her intense emotional discomfort. A psychological study of Miss B.'s past life revealed what is usually found in cases of phobia: a repressed per-

sonality, and a severe fear-conditioning experience in childhood. When a little girl, she had been locked in a closet by her sisters who went away and forgot her. Her fear at the time was of some horrible thing in the blackness behind her. After she had recalled this experience and readjusted to it, Miss B.'s compulsive tendency disappeared.

Hand washing is another very common compulsive symptom. Since a large proportion of all motor acts are done with the hands, feelings of guilt or anxiety are easily displaced to them. The excessive hand washing is at first a response to an urge to do something about these guilty parts. The common phrase, "I wash my hands of it," and the ritualistic use of hand washing as a purification rite are evidences of the widespread appeal of this mechanism, and at the same time serve as cultural reinforcements of its use by individual persons. Shakespeare effectively dramatized the hand washing of Lady Macbeth, which served as an atonement for her murders. A hand-washing compulsion is also a common result of repressed anxiety about masturbation.

The adjustive value of a compulsive act is quite evident. The compulsion enables a sufferer from a phobia or from anxiety to do something direct and active about the source of his distress. The compulsion is strongly reinforced by the immediate reduction of anxiety, a reinforcement that causes it to be repeated and learned in spite of its manifest absurdity. In the long run a compulsion is nonintegrative, for it reduces tension only temporarily and has to be employed again and again. Practical experience seems to show that it is harder to cure a compulsion than a phobia or an obsession. A compulsive person has worked out his own way to reduce his anxiety, and is perhaps less amenable to the help a psychotherapist might provide.

The Compulsive Character

Some persons show an all-pervading compulsiveness in their behavior, distinct from the limited compulsions so far described which affect only one segment of experience. A compulsive housewife, for example, cannot tolerate any trace of dirt or disorder in her home. She keeps herself busy from morning to night scrubbing, dusting, and arranging, and often prevents her family from enjoying any normal use of their house, lest they upset its perfect order.

Similar psychologically is the compulsive professor, who must always have his books and papers in a predetermined order, and who will not permit himself or anyone else to depart from an invariable schedule.

Cleanliness and neatness are ordinarily esteemed as virtues in our culture and it is necessary to distinguish between a useful orderliness and a compulsive rigidity. As a matter of fact, there is no strict line between the two, but common sense has little difficulty in discriminating between extreme cases. If an author searches several minutes for just the right word, he is probably a more effective writer because of it. But if he spends hours or days writing and rewriting one paragraph, striving compulsively for a perfection he cannot attain, it is evident that his behavior is nonintegrative.

Compulsive people often have little or no open anxiety, but a study of their life histories reveals experiences which have made them feel very insecure. The particular background varies from case to case. Perhaps an insecure parent taught the child to be anxious about all interpersonal relationships, and to cling to a routine order of life to feel safe. A parent who makes heavy demands on a child and who gives affection only in return for good, conforming behavior may also cause the child to suppress all spontaneity and to adhere for security to a tested regularity of behavior. The compulsive person is basically an insecure person, who in the trial-and-error process of adjustment has hit upon the response of being excessively orderly as a way to avoid anxiety and achieve safety. Compulsive behavior also has other adjustive functions. A compulsive person is usually inefficient because of his over-attention to detail, and requires a longer time to get his work done. His absorption in work may protect him from social contacts of which he is afraid. It thus serves as a withdrawing mechanism, defended by the noble rationalization that he is too busy to bother with frivolities. A thoroughly fixed compulsive pattern is usually a very well-reinforced adjustment. The underlying conflict is well repressed, and the dominant drive is continually reduced by the compulsive activities. As a result, compulsive persons are hard to help. The very nature of their maladjustment makes them "set in their ways," and psychotherapy is likely to be prolonged and not often successful.

SUGGESTED READINGS

The discussion of fear and repression in Klein, *Mental Hygiene* is readable and valuable. Chapters 3 and 4 of Lindgren, *Psychology of Personal and Social Adjustment* offer another good introduction to these topics. Bagby's old *Psychology of Personality* is rich in case material about irrational fears and obsessions, and is still well worth reading.

Dollard, *Victory Over Fear* is a nontechnical book which many students have found not only informative but helpful with personal problems. *The Locomotive God* by Leonard is an autobiographical account of a phobia by a poet and scholar.

For more systematic and experimentally grounded approaches to fear and repression, see Part IV of Dollard and Miller, *Personality and Psychotherapy*, and Chapters 3–6 of Prothro and Teska, *Psychology: A Biosocial Study of Behavior*. Rapaport, *Emotions and Memory* is a systematic review of the theories and evidence on repression.

CHAPTER 9

Adjustment
by Ailments

Pain, weakness, paralysis, blindness, and deafness may be caused by psychological processes. Upon meeting this observation, many unsophisticated people are surprised, even incredulous. They may deny that such symptoms can arise psychologically, or they may jump to the opposite extreme and adopt a "psychic" explanation. The so-called psychic hypothesis, supported by the popular thinking of naive people and also by some outdated psychological theories, held that "mind" had a powerful effect on "body." Such a theory breaks the human organism into two parts, mind and body, and postulates inner mental forces which have no biological foundation. Experimentally oriented psychology gives no support to a psychic theory.

It is hardly necessary to say that pains, paralyses, and the like are ordinarily caused by anatomical or physiological defects, and are studied and treated by the profession of medicine. Paralyses are due, in the main, to diseases or injuries of the brain or of the nerves which serve the affected parts of the body. Blindness is usually caused by damage to the eyes or to the areas of the brain concerned with visual functions. Our observation is that such symptoms *may* arise from psychological causes in some instances. No well-informed person believes that they are always psychological.

How can we attempt an explanation of psychological disorders which have apparently physical symptoms? The best approach is to regard such conditions as basically similar to the other non-integrative adjustments. They are responses of the organism as a whole to various kinds of frustrations and conflicts. The psychological theory is not the same as the psychic one, for it views a person as an intact biological and social organism, not as a mind and a body. All adjustments involve physiological changes, which are the ordinary modifications of the nervous system that occur when any learning takes place. The ailment adjustments are therefore as physiological as compensations or phobias, but no more so.

PSYCHONEUROSES

The ailment adjustments fall within a broad class of behavior disorders known as *psychoneuroses,* which have received much attention since the latter part of the nineteenth century. The term psychoneurosis should not be regarded as the name of a disease, but as an indication of a certain range of severity among maladjustments. A psychoneurosis is more serious and incapacitating than a simple maladjustment such as a compensation, but is milder in degree than a psychosis or "insanity."

Psychoneurotic behavior patterns are not all alike, but vary considerably in their symptoms. Because of these differences, it has long been customary to classify and name them. The practice of giving names to the various psychoneuroses is a part of the medical tradition. To identify and name a physical disease is a genuinely constructive step in medical science, and it is easy to see how the custom has been carried over to the psychoneuroses, because most cases are treated by physicians. There is much doubt, however, that the practice of "naming diseases" is applicable to the psychological and social adjustments of whole persons.

The classification of the psychoneuroses that has had the longest historical usage divides them into four types: psychasthenia, hysteria, neurasthenia, and anxiety neurosis. The term "psychasthenia" formerly had wide use to designate severe phobias, obsessions, and compulsions. We have already met these psychoneuroses in Chapter 8. Since these conditions are now understood more thoroughly, the usefulness of the word "psychasthenia" has declined almost to zero. "Neurasthenia" and "anxiety neurosis" referred to states of anxiety often accompanied by restless activity, subjective discomfort, fatigue, and vague visceral symptoms. "Hysteria" is the historical term for psychoneuroses involving more localized physical symptoms of pains, paralyses, and the like, together with some allied conditions characterized by a pronounced loss of personal integration. Many other schemes for classification have been proposed, but none has added much to our understanding of the psychoneuroses. Perhaps the best solution for the future will be to discard all such classifications. All psychoneuroses are either evidences of anxiety, or else severely nonintegrative mechanisms for controlling anxious reactions to conflicts.

Among the old terms for psychoneuroses, *hysteria** has continued in widest use, perhaps because no more rational word to replace it has gained common acceptance. Hysteria has designated a rather wide range of maladjustments, many of which are seriously disabling. The most common is "conversion hysteria," which shows symptoms of localized pains, paralyses, and sometimes deficiencies of sensation termed anaesthesias. The name comes from an outworn theory that a mental difficulty was "converted" into a physical symptom. Psychologically akin to hysteria are certain *motor psychoneuroses* including occupational cramps and tremors, and stammering and stuttering. Hysterical mechanisms differ from other maladjustments mainly in the end-result, not strikingly in the nature of the processes that produce them. In describing these ailment adjustments it is often convenient to use some of the old medical terms, but this usage does not imply that they are "diseases," and does not indicate any agreement with the discarded theories from which the words originated.

HYSTERICAL DISORDERS

An Ailment Adjustment

Ronald B.'s ailment consisted of a persistent sore throat. Aged twenty-two, intelligent, and handsome, he was a student of voice with an eminent private instructor in a large city. Ronald had started singing at the age of seventeen and had been regarded as exceptionally promising by his first teacher in the small town in

---

* *Hysteria* is derived from the Greek word for uterus. An ancient and medieval theory held that hysteria was caused by the uterus wandering about in the body. Such an explanation limited the condition to women, and only late in the nineteenth century was it generally accepted that men could also be subject to it.

which he then lived. Probably the estimates of his vocal ability were considerably enhanced by his charming personal qualities. Everyone liked Ronald and wished him well. His widowed mother strongly believed that he had a great future in opera or on the concert stage. With his ambitions raised far beyond his probable ability to fulfill them, Ronald went to a large city at the age of twenty-one and secured a part-time position by which he earned a portion of his expenses. His move involved a considerable financial sacrifice on the part of his mother.

The change in teachers and in the system of instruction caused an actual decrease in the quality of his singing. Ronald was discouraged, but clung tenaciously to the belief in his ability. At this time a slight cold interrupted his practice. When all other symptoms of the cold had disappeared, a peculiar soreness and stiffness of his throat muscles persisted. His speaking voice was not affected, but any attempt to sing resulted in excessive effort and strained tones. Ronald's teacher referred him to a throat specialist who painted and sprayed the throat without effect. Another specialist was consulted, who could find nothing physically wrong. A third physician to whom Ronald appealed said that the disorder was "nervous," and recommended exercises and diet to build up his vitality, and six weeks' rest for his throat during which period he was not to sing. At this point in the course of his ailment, Ronald consulted a psychologist at one of the city's universities.

The psychologist arrived at an understanding of Ronald's problem in terms of the adjustment process. Ronald was strongly motivated to become a great singer, a desire that had been encouraged by his teacher, his home community, and especially by his mother. For him, the need to excel in singing involved all of the socially learned motives for approval, achievement, and success, so strongly reinforced in his culture. His drive to continue his musical studies conflicted with his opposed tendency to give up the struggle and thus to avoid an anxiety-producing failure. Since it was impossible for him to admit that he was failing, he adjusted in some degree by repressing any open thoughts about his lack of success. Although his poor progress had been apparent to others, Ronald professed to believe that nothing was wrong with his singing except for the unfortunate sore throat.

The course of any adjustment is guided by a person's past experiences and by the adjustive habits he has learned to employ.

Ronald's history gave adequate evidence of earlier adjustive tendencies similar to his present ones. He had no intimate confidants and talked little about himself. Even close friends seldom knew much of his ideas and aims. Such characteristics indicate a general tendency to adjust by repression, often found in those who adopt hysterical mechanisms. As a child he had been sickly, although he was fairly strong as a young adult. He had experienced the sympathy and attention that comes with illness. Most significantly, it was discovered that he had reacted to past conflicts by some form of ill health. About a year before his move to the city, when he had been jilted by a girl to whom he felt strongly attached, he had developed a hacking cough which disappeared when his social relations were restored by the acquisition of another sweetheart. The young man's mother showed similar tendencies. When Ronald was fifteen he had a great desire to go away to school, in which he was opposed by his mother. At that time she had a series of fainting spells which convinced Ronald that he was needed at home. It is not suggested that Ronald inherited his hysterical traits from his mother, but that it was easier for him to learn a type of adjustment which he saw used at home.

With such a background, it is not surprising that Ronald should solve his adjustment problem with a physical symptom. Other persons with different histories might have compensated, rationalized, projected, or daydreamed, but for Ronald an ailment adjustment was the reinforced mechanism. His sore throat, which at first was of the ordinary physiological variety, was very effective in reducing his anxiety. It prevented him from working at the vocal lessons in which he felt himself a failure, and gave an excellent and socially acceptable reason for his not singing. The sore throat therefore provided a way out of his difficulties. He did not recognize the utility of his symptom, since any overt consideration of his failure was inhibited. The hysterical symptom was hit upon blindly, and was retained because it was reinforced by the reduction of drives. It is perhaps also significant in this case that a tightening of the throat muscles is one of the common physiological responses occurring in strong emotion. The slight constriction of the throat felt in anxiety aided Ronald in his belief that the sore throat was a persistent ailment. The hysterical symptom acted as a sort of a rationalization expressed in conduct. It excused him from admitting failure and was satisfying to Ronald's self concept, to his mother, and to society in general. If he had a throat ailment, of course he could not sing, and no one could accuse him of being a failure or a quitter.

The psychological treatment of Ronald necessarily involved his readjustment to the underlying conflict. If the symptom alone had been treated, by convincing him it was a defense mechanism, the cure would have been superficial and temporary. Talks with the psychologist led Ronald to re-examine his vocational aims and satisfactions. Fortunately, the part-time work in which he was engaged interested him and he was succeeding well in it. His life purposes became redirected into the business field and he found adequate satisfaction there. When he returned to singing as an avocation some years later, there was no trace of the throat contracture.

Other Cases of Hysteria

The mechanism of conversion hysteria is not rare; it is about as common as any other form of adjustment. All of us can find at least a trace of it in our own lives if we examine our adjustments diligently and without bias. The "nine o'clock headache" is frequent in children who escape school by being ill, only to recover with surprising rapidity as soon as it is too late to go. A frustrating or conflict-arousing school situation, often not overtly recognized by the child himself, may be at the bottom of such reactions. Adults often fall into petty illnesses that serve to get them out of distressing situations. The symptoms, such as gastric upsets or headaches, may first arise as physiological results of emotion, and then may be intensified and prolonged because they serve some adjustive end. The common sayings that a distasteful task "gives you a pain" or "makes you sick" are not entirely figures of speech. Like other mechanisms, ailment adjustments are found in everyday life, and the more severe cases of this sort are no more than exaggerations of a relatively common kind of behavior.

Hysterical mechanisms often occur in conjunction with illnesses that have an adequate organic basis. An illustration is the case of a young woman who was recuperating from an abdominal operation. She was beginning to feel fine and to go out of doors when her physician injudiciously remarked that he did not expect her to be out of bed yet. The young woman at once developed pains and weakness, with the result that her recovery was considerably delayed. The fact that organic illness is so often overlaid by hysterical symptoms makes diagnosis difficult even for experienced physicians. Also, the combination of physical and psychological symptoms has implications for treatment. Physicians are learning that they have to treat the whole human being as a person, and not merely his diseased organs or injured limbs. The wise old horse-and-buggy doctor was often more effective in this respect than the specialist with his more efficient laboratories but narrower outlook. Modern medicine is rediscovering that a psychological approach is applicable to all patients, not solely to "mental cases."

The wide variety of localized physical symptoms employed as adjustive mechanisms can be sensed only by examining a large number of cases. A few of the symptom pictures that appear in cases of hysteria will be cited as illustrations, without any attempt to trace the histories fully. In each case, the personal background, the development of the symptom, and the adjustive satisfaction achieved are not very different from those described in the case of Ronald.

> A young woman suffered a paralysis of both legs, dating from an attack and attempted rape by a relative in her early adolescence. In the intense fear of the experience her legs gave way, and she was put to bed by her sympathetic family. A few days later, when she tried to get up, it was discovered that her legs were limp and that she could not stand. The paralysis persisted over a period of more than ten years, while she was the center of the devoted attention of her family and neighbors who accepted her illness as a real one akin to "infantile paralysis." Typically, she showed less atrophy of her legs than would be expected of a patient bedridden for so long, as she was able to move them in bed. She was unconcerned about her disability and seemed to have little motivation to get well.*

Anaesthesias, or insensitivities, were common hysterical symptoms some fifty years ago. They included hysterical blindness, deafness and, more often, skin anaesthesias of areas insensitive to touch. In the early period of the scientific study of hysteria, about 1900, an anaesthesia was *the* classical symptom. When a patient was

---

* This case and the three which follow are abbreviated, respectively, from Cameron (1947), pp. 328-330; Brown (1940), pp. 75-76; Burton and Harris (1947), pp. 185-200; and Watkins (1949), pp. 239-248. For a more complete history and interpretation of each case, the original sources should be consulted.

suspected of being an hysteric, his body was often explored thoroughly with a tactile stimulator, in a search for insensitive areas, which were very frequently found. We now know that many such anaesthesias were evoked by the diagnostic search. A psychoneurotic is suggestible, and is likely to develop a cutaneous anaesthesia if an authoritative person acts as though he expects to find one. Although hysterical anaesthesias are now less common, occasional cases appear.

> A young woman complained of a loss of sensation in her right thigh from her hip to her knee. Medical examination showed that she had no organic disease which could have produced such a symptom, and a psychological study traced it to a past experience. The girl's father had been mortally ill, and she had fallen in love with the young physician who was attending him. One day when she and the physician were standing by her father's bed, she touched the physician with her thigh and became very much excited erotically. She was deeply guilty about her conduct, especially of having sexual feelings while her father lay on his deathbed, and repressed her memory of the incident. The thigh anaesthesia originated from this episode. By a symbolic adjustment, she "disowned" the guilt-producing sensations, and by her anaesthesia made sure that the thigh would not again tempt her sexually.

Fainting, having "spells," or falling asleep at inappropriate times are also reported as adjustive techniques of an hysterical nature.

> An attractive young married woman sought help for an uncon- trollable tendency to fall asleep from time to time, and for occasional fainting spells. Her childhood had been marked by her parents' discord and finally by their divorce when she was six. Both parents remarried, and the girl was shuttled between them, having no opportunity to acquire any secure and affectionate relationships. She always placed great emphasis on outer appearances, social prestige, and a shallow kind of conformity. Her sleepy spells began in her fourteenth year, when she was living with her father and stepmother. Apparently, the symptom developed as a way out of an unpleasant relationship, as a withdrawing adjustment of going to sleep to avoid conflict. Later she continued to use the same mechanism to escape other burdens, in college, in her work, and when her baby was born. Other hysterical symptoms were also used from time to time in her life: vomiting spells, chronic diarrhea, and an abdominal cramp which once was almost mistaken for appendicitis.

Both World Wars disclosed cases of psychoneurosis precipitated by the stresses and psychological conflicts of combat. In World War I, such breakdowns were often misnamed "shell shock" because of an early theory that they were due to brain concussion. Subsequent studies made clear the adjustive character of these disorders. Terms often used in World War II were "combat fatigue" and "traumatic neurosis," the latter indicating a condition caused by injury or stress. Although the war neuroses appeared in all forms, cases of conversion hysteria were fairly common among them.

A twenty-three-year-old combat veteran had spent more than a year in hospitals which had treated his paralyzed right hand without success. Only the thumb and forefinger of the hand could be moved; the other three fingers were painful, contractured, immobile, and atrophying from disuse. Because he had received a small shell wound in his forearm, it had been assumed that his paralysis was due to a nerve injury. In one hospital, however, a decision was made to explore the possibility that the symptom was hysterical. Under psychological treatment, he was led to recall a crucial battlefield incident. His best friend had been killed in action, and he felt with intense guilt that his own negligence had caused the friend's death. He had failed to give warning of the approach of an enemy patrol, and had neglected to throw a grenade which might have stopped its attack. A grenade is held in the same position as that in which the soldier's hand became paralyzed, with three fingers grasped tightly around it. His paralysis had arisen from this repressed incident. Psychological treatment cured the soldier's difficulty quickly through having him recall and relive the battlefield experience and re-evaluate his guilt. Such rapid recoveries are usual only when the hysteria is based on a recent and intense experience. Those coming from a lifetime of adjustive learning take longer to cure.

In all these cases, the major characteristics of conversion hysteria may be observed. Hysteria develops only in persons who are prepared for it by a lifetime of habit formation, in which they have learned to adjust to conflicts by repressing and by developing protective physical disabilities. The particular symptom arises at a time of personal crisis, from any of a number of sources: from the physiological effects of emotion, from a real but transient physical disorder, or from a sensation or an action connected with a catastrophic emotional experience. The symptom is perpetuated because of its utility in resolving a conflict or gaining an adjustive advantage.

More Serious Hysterical Disorders

A number of quite serious disorders of behavior are classed as hysterical, because they have certain features in common with conversion hysteria. An adequate description and interpretation of these more severe hysterias would take us too far into the field of abnormal psychology, but they will be enumerated briefly. *Hysterical seizures* are spells or "fits" in which a person is unconscious or nearly so, or at least is in poor contact with his environment. Some seizures resemble conversion hysteria. By having a "fit," the patient gets out of a difficult adjustive situation, gains protection and sympathy, and often frightens parents or spouse into compliance with his wishes. Such seizures are often confused with epilepsy. In some more complex hysterical seizures, the person goes into a trance-like state in which he re-enacts an episode focal to a conflict. For example, a young woman who had a severe conflict about an attempted rape screamed, writhed, and struggled in her seizures as if she were trying to repel an attacker.[1] After returning to contact with the social environment, the person does not remember what occurred during the seizure. This complete repression of a segment of experience is called an hysterical *amnesia.*

Also obviously adjustive are hysterical *fugues,* in which the patient forgets his identity and his experiences for a time and runs away from his usual locale, often "coming to himself" in a distant city with no knowledge of how he got there. The forgetting during the period of the fugue seems to be an extreme instance of repression; the traveling, a form of flight from a conflictual situation. When a fugue is investigated adequately it is usually found to be determined by some crisis that a person with hysterical habits of adjustment is unable to face. Persons with fugue are the "amnesia victims" of which you read in the newspapers. There are, of course, some fraudulent persons who pretend to have a loss of memory, but there are also genuine cases of fugue.

From hysterical seizures and fugues, it is only a step to *multiple personality,* a relatively rare disorder, of which only about one hundred and fifty cases have been reliably reported. Multiple personality involves the functioning of two or more patterns of personal organization which usually alternate irregularly. For example, in the earliest reported American case of Mary Reynolds, described in 1817, the first personality was shy, melancholy, and religious; the second state was gay, witty, sociable, and presumably free from the anxieties which beset the primary personality.[2] The personality states usually show reciprocal amnesia, that is, in one state the person has no memory of the experiences that occurred in the other. Multiple personality seems always to be the result of a long process of habit formation in which the individual is unable to reconcile or to select between two opposing sets of response tendencies. The earlier life of a person who later shows multiple personality is usually marked by faintings, sleeping spells, seizures, and conversion symptoms. For a long time he (or more often she) is learning to separate the parts of experience that can and cannot be endured. Finally, some crisis precipitates the total abandonment of one set of habits and the repression of the knowledge associated with them, in favor of the alternative set.

Several psychological concepts have been used to describe the more serious hysterias and to show their relationship to conversion hysteria. The hysterical mechanism is often called *dissociation*, which emphasizes the striking lack of unity or integration so apparent in fugues and multiple personality and also seen in conversion hysteria. An hysteric is an extreme example of the proverbial "let not thy left hand know what thy right hand doeth." Cameron has described hysteria with the aid of the concept of *overexclusion*. A normal person is able to exclude, or inhibit, his response to many irrelevant competing stimuli, and indeed, his efficiency depends on his being able to do so. When you are deeply absorbed in reading or study, you adjust to your task by excluding distracting noises, irrelevant stimuli, or tendencies to get up and stretch your posture-stiff legs. The hysteric uses the same mechanism, but he overdoes it. He adjusts to his conflicts by excluding movements, sensations, memories, and even whole patterns of personal habits, that would arouse his anxiety or that have been associated with intensely conflict-producing experiences. Concepts such as dissociation and overexclusion do not explain how the hysterical mechanism develops, but they help understand it by relating it to the familiar and normal behavior of which it is an exaggeration.

The Development of Hysteria

An hysterical reaction seldom appears for the first time in an adult, but almost always has a history of gradual development in his earlier life. The most important factor in the genesis of hysteria and other psychoneuroses is not the present adjustive crisis that precipitates the reaction; it is the nature of the past learning experiences that predisposes a person to become neurotic rather than to make some other or better kind of adjustment. The underlying causes of hysteria are not simple, and it is probable that the same result may be brought about by any of several different circumstances. One person may be led to an hysterical response by one set of habits, while in another, a quite different set of experiences may be the source. In spite of this complexity, some common predisposing factors have been identified with sufficient certainty to justify describing them.

Three observations frequently made about the personalities of hysterics are that they tend to be *socially immature,* that they are *externally oriented,* and that they lack *integration* or unity of behavior. These are not isolated characteristics, but fit together into a consistent pattern. The hysteric's social immaturity has two facets: he is selfish and egotistical in motivation, yet he is overconcerned with external appearances and with justifying his behavior to other people. Such a combination of traits points to defective socialization. An hysteric expects to be controlled and rewarded externally; he is deficient in thoughtful social convictions of his own. He has never internalized the ethical standards of his culture to the degree expected of normal people. The hysteric's lack of internal standards and his dependence on the momentary approval of other people are detrimental to sound integration.

For many years, another observation concerning the personality of hysterics has been widely believed: that they are more *suggestible* than other people. In the early classic period of the study of hysteria, suggestibility was often cited as the one most distinctive characteristic of the hysterical personality. Indeed, some earlier psychologists defined hysteria as a state of heightened suggestibility.[4] Practical clinical experience seems to confirm the observation that hysterics are especially suggestible. More recent research, however, has cast doubt on this generalization.[5] In a series of experiments, Eysenck gave objective tests of suggestibility to normal people, and to psychoneurotics who could be classified into two broad groups: those with hysterical symptoms, and those suffering from disorders involving anxiety and depression. In brief, he found that all groups of psychoneurotics were more suggestible than normal people, but that, among the psychoneurotics, the hysterics were no more suggestible than the nonhysterics. Eysenck's challenging findings have not been widely verified by other experimental studies, but the rigorously controlled nature of his research gives confidence in his conclusions. Therefore, while hysterics are more suggestible than normal individuals, it is best not to base an understanding of their condition on an assumption that they are more suggestible than other psychoneurotics. Eysenck's studies did confirm the observations that hysterics are imperfectly socialized and externally oriented.

Socialization, as we have already seen, is largely a product of certain learnings that occur early in life, mainly in the parent-child relationship. One looks for the foundations of hysteria, therefore, in the relations between a person and his parents. An hysterical predisposition often arises from parental overprotection or overindulgence during childhood. A child who is badly "spoiled" has a well-learned expectation that people will give in to him and that he can have his own way even though it is disadvantageous to others. At the same time he is dependent because everything is done for him and he has little opportunity to learn to think independently. The conflict between selfish motivation and dependence leads him to a nonintegrative adjustment in which he satisfies his own needs, but in such a way as to make his behavior appear acceptable to others. An overdominant parent can provide the background for hysteria as fully as an overindulgent one. The dominated child is made to be dependent, but is anxious and insecure in his dependence. Of surprising frequency in the childhood histories of hysterics is a strong conflict of loyalties, as when the individual learns to love and to fear the same person, or when he is torn between quarreling or separated parents. Vacillating and conflicting control by parents, who approve or ignore a form of behavior at one time and punish the same act at another time, also prevents the formation of an integrated and internalized set of values. Through such experiences, an hysteric is trained to act in one manner while thinking or feeling in a way opposite to his overt responses.

The relationship between overdependence and hysteria throws some light on the tradition that it is a woman's psychoneurosis. Although no reliable statistics are available, it does seem true that more women than men suffer from hysterical complaints. If so, the sex differential is probably due to differences in home training and social status: in our culture, women tend to be both more over-indulged and more overdominated. The increasing emancipation of women should have an interesting effect on the relative incidence of hysteria.

Another observation is that hysteria flourishes on ignorance and superstition. Although some hysterical symptoms occur in people at all levels of educational attainment, they are more common among those whose cultural background is naive about human physiology, and who are more credulous about mysterious "visitations" of illness. Some objective data show that hysterical disorders are more prevalent among persons of below-average educational and cultural levels.

An obvious antecedent factor in many cases of hysteria, which seems to influence the use of conversion symptoms instead of other mechanisms is an earlier satisfactory experience with illness. Often some genuine illness or injury of a minor nature, occurring at a time when an adjustive difficulty is present, acts as a solution and is therefore of drive-reducing value. By the ordinary process of adjustive learning, a person with this experience will tend to resort to illness when a similar conflict affects him in the future. If parents who are otherwise distant or rejecting shower a child with over-protection when he is ill, the child will exaggerate his illnesses or pains when he needs attention again.

Psychological illness can serve several adjustive needs. Most often it is an escape mechanism, by which a person withdraws from conflict and excuses his failures. It can also be used aggressively as a means for compelling the submission of the patient's family. In our culture, physically impaired persons are treated with special care and sympathy, so that it is an easy role to assume when con-flicts become overwhelming. An implication for mental hygiene can be drawn. Sick children really do need extra support and consideration psychologically as well as physically, but a wise parent avoids excesses of anxiety or of indulgence. A positive em-phasis on the pleasures of recovering good health will prevent illness from becoming too exclusive a satisfaction.

The particular symptoms that appear in cases of conversion hysteria often seem obscure and irrational, but they can be traced to psychologically comprehensible sources. In many cases, the initial symptom is nothing more than the physiological effects of emotion, as in the case of the rancher's daughter whose legs felt weak when she was attacked. A real but minor physical disability can be enlarged and prolonged as an hysterical adjustment. Ronald's sore throat was such a reaction. In a number of cases a passing numbness of a limb, "one's leg going asleep," has been accepted by an hysteric as a basis for a long-continued paralysis.[6] A third source of symptoms is found in the cases that date from a vividly conflictual incident. A focal response being made at the time of the episode — a movement, a pain, a paralysis, or even an anaesthesia — seems to become conditioned to the anxiety of the moment, so that the reinstatement of the anxiety again evokes the same response. Examples are the soldier's contractured hand and the anaesthetic thigh of the girl who fell guiltily in love with the physician, as described earlier in this chapter. Such symptoms are retained because they have lasting adjustive value, but the particular response is determined by the conditioning at the moment of the crisis.

Many hysterical reactions involve considerable *secondary gain*, a concept that you have already encountered in Chapter 8. The primary adjustive value of a hysteria may be to get out of a difficulty or to escape from the dilemma of a conflict. The hysteric finds, however, that he is given a high degree of attention and protection by his family and by society generally. Perhaps he receives a greater satisfaction of his needs for love and security than he ever enjoyed before. Even after the original conflict is past, he has a secondary motivation to continue to be disabled. A similar mechanism is encountered in many victims of industrial accidents, automobile collisions, and the like, in which there is an expectation of monetary compensation for injuries. Most such disabilities begin with a physically identifiable complaint, which may be exaggerated hysterically. When the case is settled and no more compensation is due, the change in motivation often makes for a rapid recovery.

In some persons, hysterical symptoms remain long after their original utility has ceased to exist, and even after secondary gains are negligible. These persistent hysterias are *consistency reactions*. The patient cannot adjust to the fact that his ailment is psychological, which would leave him open to the accusation of malingering. He retains the defenses that were assumed against a past problem, but which now protect him only against having to admit that the disorder is not organic. Many patients in veterans' hospitals suffer from such residuals of combat stress. They no longer have to face the real conflicts of war, but retain their symptoms partly as consistency reactions, and partly for the secondary gains that accrue from continued hospitalization and government support.

Hysteria and Malingering

When assured that hysterical symptoms are not due to physiological illness in the ordinary sense, laymen often ascribe them to deliberate and mischievous invention. If a wife has a gastric disturbance of a hysterical nature, her husband's first assumption is of organic disease. If it is then proved that the condition has no gross organic basis and that, furthermore, it lets her off from housework she detests, the husband's next belief is that she is feigning the symptoms in order to deceive him! Is the hysterical patient deliberately malingering to gain his or her own ends? The evidence says "no." There is every reason to believe that a hysterical headache hurts as much as any other kind and that hysterical paralyses defy any ordinary attempt to move the affected member. In the descriptive sense of the term, a hysteric is quite unconscious of the purpose and origin of his symptoms.

An illustration adapted from Clendening is helpful.[7] Let us suppose that an inexperienced actor walks upon the stage to say his lines. He faces the audience and is struck speechless. It is to be noted that he is suffering from a purely physical disability: he cannot move the muscles of his larynx. Two explanations might be offered, analogous to those held by the husband just mentioned. One is that the actor has an organic disease of the larynx; the other is that he refuses to speak out of pure devilment. Neither is true, for the larynx will soon be functioning perfectly, and no one is more anxious than the unfortunate actor that he should perform his part well. He is the last person who could explain his disability, for he is undergoing a psychological process over which he has no control and into which he has no insight. The plight of any hysteric is very similar.

It cannot be denied, of course, that malingering does take place. There are some people who lie, and assert that they have a pain, a weakness, or some other disability they know very well to be nonexistent. Lying to gain an end or to escape the consequences of an action is in itself a form of adjustment. Psychologists regard malingering objectively as a form of human behavior, not moralistically as something to be condemned. The boundary between hysteria and malingering is an indefinite one, and no one can say exactly where one ends and the other begins. A deliberate liar is at one end of a continuum. In the middle are the cases in which a person partially convinces himself of the reality of his ailment, or has some slight insight into his condition. At the other extreme is the true hysteric, who in the ordinary sense is entirely sincere and honest in believing in his ailment. Hysterical symptoms have utility to their possessor, and get him out of adjustive difficulties. The young man avoided singing by means of his sore throat; the girl gained her family's undivided attention because of her paralyzed legs. Such observations, however, point to adjustment, not necessarily to malingering. All adjustive reactions are useful to a person in reducing his anxieties or other drives, and hysterical reactions merely conform to this general principle.

The Treatment of Hysterical Reactions

The treatment of hysteria offers special problems because of two characteristics peculiar to this type of psychoneurosis. First, the complaints of a person who suffers from conversion hysteria are so specific and so clearly localized that there is a severe temptation to treat his symptoms instead of his entire personality. A person with an anxiety neurosis is unhappy-all-over, and there can be no doubt that he needs consideration as a whole person. In contrast, it is easy to fall into the error of treating an hysteric's pains or paralyses as isolated phenomena.

Second, the problem of treatment is complicated by the fact that it is relatively difficult to change the basic personality habits underlying an hysteria, because a well-learned hysterical mechanism is such a profoundly drive-reducing adjustment. It is often noted that hysterics have little motivation to be cured, since their anxiety is so fully reduced by the mode of adjustment they have adopted. A classic characteristic of hysteria, described in Janet's pioneer studies, is *la belle indifférence,* the utter unconcern of the hysteric about his symptoms.[8] An hysteric with a paralyzed arm often nonchalantly asks that it be amputated. Although he may be greatly handicapped by his symptoms, he usually shows little or no anxiety about them. The hysteric's indifference has psychological meaning:

he very completely represses any recognition of the conflict underlying his difficulties, and receives relatively full reduction of his
anxiety because of his symptoms. An hysteric likes his adjustment
and has no urge to get rid of it. For that reason, it is often difficult
to bring about a really fundamental cure.

Formerly several superficial methods were widely used to treat
hysterical symptoms. One of these was *suggestion.* Although hysterics are perhaps no more suggestible than other psychoneurotics,
they are more suggestible than normal people. In keeping with
their excessive emphasis on social approval and their immature dependence, they readily believe what they are told with a tone of
authority.

> McDougall reported a typical instance of the use of suggestion
> in the treatment of a soldier of World War I who had hysterically
> paralyzed legs and a "stocking anaesthesia," which is a loss of
> superficial skin sensitivity over an area that would be covered
> by a pair of stockings.[9] Incidentally, a "stocking anaesthesia" is
> a clear sign of hysteria, since it does not conform to the anatomical
> distribution of nerves and cannot be due to an organic nerve
> injury. McDougall explained to the soldier that his anaesthesia
> would recede day by day, and that when it was gone he would
> have full use of his legs. He ostentatiously mapped the upper limit
> of insensitivity on both legs each morning, and "drew off" the
> anaesthesia like a pair of stockings, two or three inches a day.
> The soldier seems to have been a gullible and superstitious man
> to have been susceptible to such a treatment, and it has been
> widely noted that an hysteric is often that kind of a person.

Physicians in general practice often use suggestion in treating the
hysterias that come to their attention in the guise of organic disorders. They give the patient pills, often "placebos" of no real
medicinal value, with the grave assurance that he will get well
after taking them. Since suggestion only removes the symptom,
leaving the underlying adjustive conflict unsolved, it is not an
adequate cure.

Closely allied to suggestion is the treatment of making a patient's
hysterical symptoms unsatisfying to him. A physician will sometimes give an evil-tasting medicine or a painful injection with the
assurance that the treatment will be continued and will become
progressively more unpleasant until the symptoms disappear. After
a series of alarming or painful "treatments," an hysteric often aban-

dons his symptoms quite suddenly. This process is very undesirable psychologically, however, because it succeeds only by setting up a new conflict for the patient to resolve. When he is frightened out of his original symptom, he may develop a different one.

In a few instances, the mere clearing up of an hysterical symptom may have constructive value. If the symptom is a consistency reaction which originated in a conflict no longer significant in the patient's life, a symptomatic cure may be all that is required. In some other cases, suppressing an hysterical symptom may bring the basic conflict to the fore. When deprived of his hysterical defense, a person may show open anxiety that makes him uncomfortable enough to want treatment. This procedure sometimes works fairly well in military psychiatry.[10] A soldier is under external controls and has to stay in the army hospital, where his anxiety can be treated after his hysterical symptoms are suppressed. The danger in abruptly terminating an hysterical symptom is that a patient may be made so acutely uncomfortable by his anxiety that he will flee from treatment. A civilian hysteric whose defenses are broken down often discontinues treatment, and later develops new symptoms to resolve his conflicts.

The fundamental treatment of hysteria by psychological methods is not very different from the treatment of other psychoneuroses and maladjustments. In addition to avoiding the temptation of producing a quick but transient cure by eliminating only the symptoms, a therapist needs to take another precaution when dealing with hysteria. An hysteric is basically a dependent person, and the therapist must keep the patient from becoming strongly and lastingly dependent on him. The psychotherapy of hysteria is not easy, and frequently is a prolonged process. Like other psychological treatments, it involves the readjustment of the patient to the particular conflicts that precipitated his present difficulties and, harder to achieve, his re-education in new habits of adjustment which will function when he confronts new problems. As will be described at length in a later chapter, the process of psychotherapy consists of establishing a warm interpersonal relationship between the therapist and the patient, in which the latter will feel free to think, tell, and relive the past experiences and attitudes that underlie his conflicts and his inadequate modes of resolving them. Through his communication with the therapist, the patient re-educates himself, a process often involving the learning of socialization that he failed to acquire in childhood. Because of the time and labor involved in the complete re-education of such maladjustments, the prevention of hysteria in childhood is a more economical mental hygiene procedure than its treatment in adults.

Hysteria and Miracles

Intelligent persons have long been puzzled by the apparent cures of physical disorders achieved by means which seem outside the bounds of rational explanation. The cures claimed by the makers of some patent medicines and by the proponents of various medical quackeries seem incredible. The miraculous healings that occur at religious shrines or under the ministrations of religious cults or faith healers seem equally incomprehensible. An impartial observer seems to be faced with two alternative explanations: either such cures are fraudulent or nonexistent, or they are due to supernatural forces. The concept of the ailment adjustment explains them fully. Hysterical symptoms often include lameness, blindness, paralyses, and all sorts of weaknesses and pains. Since it is difficult to distinguish between some psychological and physical disabilities, many cases are incorrectly diagnosed as organic. Miraculous cures are cures of hysterical symptoms. An act of faith, supported by the reassurances and rituals either of a medical fallacy or a religious observance, may remove the hysterical ailment by suggestion. At shrines, the cure of one person is often followed by a number of other recoveries on the part of spectators. When an adjustive ailment is a consistency reaction the original utility of which is past, a faith cure may offer an attractive way to get rid of it without loss of self-esteem. Only in these latter cases is the miraculous cure likely to be permanent. When the recovery is based only on belief and suggestion, the benefit will usually be temporary.

Some groups that combine religious beliefs with the healing of ailments, notably "Christian Science," operate on principles somewhat more fundamental than suggestion. There is a great emphasis on a routine of reading and study and on a unified outlook on life. Although differences of opinion may exist as to the value and truth of such doctrines, they are a concern of religion and philosophy, not science. From a psychological point of view, a person's integration seems to be improved by the sincere practice of some faith. He may effect a genuine readjustment of his personal problems on a religious basis and thereby eliminate the need for an ailment adjustment.

While various systems of faith-cure are somewhat effective in treating hysterical and other adjustive disorders, there is no very good evidence that they have an appreciable influence on physical diseases. The great harm done by all faith or religious cures is that they almost universally claim to cure organic disease. Not understanding the difference between an adjustive pain and one due, say, to cancer, a person may depend futilely on magical methods until it is too late for medical aid.

MOTOR PSYCHONEUROSES

Closely allied to conversion hysteria, although they are often considered separately from it, are a number of disorders of motor functioning which affect a limited muscle group or appear only in relation to certain tasks and situations. These may be brought together as _motor psychoneuroses_, although, of course, many other hysterical reactions also show motor symptoms. Motor psychoneuroses are characterized by cramps, localized muscular weaknesses, tremors, or specialized inhibitions of movement. Of particular interest in this group are the occupational psychoneuroses, and stammering and stuttering.

Occupational Psychoneuroses

Occupational cramps and tremors have been noted in almost all the common vocations that involve manual skill. Probably no profession or trade exists that does not have its own peculiar symptoms. Here are two examples.

A pianist complained that his arm became rigid when he tried to play soft, slow music. His cramp occurred only when he was playing a concert before an audience, never when he was practicing alone. Psychological study revealed that he was an outwardly meek and dependent man, but with an intense repressed hostility toward his mother and his wife who, he felt, had pushed him into his career. Playing in public aroused anxiety in him, and his symptom expressed his hostility and his need to escape. Prolonged psychological treatment cured his cramp and improved his relationship with his wife.

A young woman developed a tremor of her left hand that compelled her to give up her job as an elevator operator. She had
been working to save money to be married, but her fiancé jilted
her. Humiliated by this rejection, she returned to her job, but
soon developed the tremor which prevented her from operating
the elevator controls properly. She responded well to brief
psychological treatment and to a change in occupation.*

Many of the characteristics of occupational psychoneuroses may
be seen in telegraphers' cramp, which has been investigated extensively in England.[11] At first the affected person notes difficulty in
manipulating the telegraph key; it "sticks" and he cannot release
the pressure of his hand in time to give the next signal. The muscles
of his hand and arm become tense, movement is often painful, and
finally a contracture of his hand appears that renders any sending
impossible. A psychoneurotic cramp can be distinguished from a
cramp due to fatigue. In the latter case, rest restores the function
entirely. A psychoneurotic symptom can appear when the person
first grasps the key after a rest, before any ordinary fatigue could
be present.

A common occupational neurosis is writers' cramp, which consists of muscular contractures, spasms, or lack of coordination when
any attempt is made to write. It usually is found in people to whom
writing is an occupational essential, but has also been reported in
foremen, gardeners, and others who suffer no occupational disability
because of it. It is probable that more unreported cases of the
latter class exist, as a man is more likely to consult a physician if
his vocational competence is affected.

The psychoneurotic nature of occupational cramps is confirmed
by a number of observations. The disorder usually appears only in
the occupational situation, and is not in evidence when the same
muscle groups are tested with laboratory apparatus which measures
motor skill. Culpin, who conducted extensive research in England,
described a telegrapher who could send perfectly when he knew his
key was connected to a testing machine, but who developed an
immediate cramp when placed at a main line key. Such observations
rule out the possibility that the cramp is caused by an organic defect
of the musculature or nervous system. Persons affected with writers'

---

* More complete accounts of these two cases may be found in Maslow and
Mittelmann (1951), pp. 442-443; and Cameron (1947), pp. 352-353, respectively

cramp often show the irrational variations of symptoms typical of ailment adjustments. One person has cramps only when he tries to write his name, another has trouble with certain letters, while a third is unable to write figures. In one case a man could write when holding the paper against the wall, but developed cramps when he tried to write at a desk. Most occupational cramps are intensified if the individual is closely observed. Such instances suggest the condition of the stammerer who can speak perfectly when alone but cannot prevent his stammer when other people are listening. In fact, a victim of writers' or telegraphers' cramp has sometimes been described as having a "stammering hand." Many persons with occupational cramps show other psychoneurotic symptoms as well. In a study of 41 cases of telegraphers' cramp, Culpin found other signs of adjustive ailments in 31 cases, which was over 75 per cent of the group. Nine of the remaining ten had only the occupational symptom, while one case was due to a definite organic cause.

The interpretation of the occupational psychoneuroses is essentially the same as that of hysteria. At the outset, the person affected has some deep dissatisfaction with his work or has associated it with an intense personal conflict. The condition occurs more frequently when the worker is not free to quit, as when he is in the army, or when giving up his work would mean the loss of a pension, or when he has a chance of receiving compensation for his disability. Some transient fatigue may start the symptom, or the behavior of another affected person may suggest it. As in hysteria, the symptom is adopted and enlarged upon because it provides the resolution of a conflict. In some cases, an individual has a need to secure the status of a physically impaired person, and may develop symptom after symptom as his circumstances change. Thus, some men who were transferred from the telegraph to the telephone service because of cramp developed laryngitis which barred them from the latter occupation also. Only a general readjustment of the patient's personal and vocational problems effects a permanent cure of a persistent occupational psychoneurosis.

Stammering and Stuttering

The terms stammering and stuttering are now used interchangeably, but originally stammering meant a tense stoppage of speech in which no sound can be uttered, while stuttering referred to the involuntary repetition of a speech sound. The two classes of speech defect are closely allied and are almost always found together. It is estimated that about 1 per cent of the population stutters, which means there are about one and one-half million stutterers in the United States. Stammering and stuttering are much more frequent among boys than among girls. The disorder never starts when a child first learns to talk — every stutterer talks normally at first and then later begins to stutter. Most stuttering has its inception between the ages of three and five years, and 80 per cent of the cases begin before six. In a few cases, an adolescent or adult will start to stutter after a catastrophic emotional experience. Quite a few child stutterers overcome the defect without treatment and good speech clinics give substantial aid in many more instances, but there is no one method of treatment that will positively cure all cases.

Theories that stuttering and stammering are the result of various anatomical and physiological defects have long been held and are still the subject of some research. One physiological theory that continues to receive support ascribes them to a lack of balance between the neural activities of the two cerebral hemispheres, or to a lack of complete dominance of one hemisphere over the other. This theory seems to be upheld, at least in some cases, by studies of neural action currents.[12] In right-handed persons, the left half of the cerebrum coordinates the control of the dominant and more skilled side of the body and also contains the brain centers concerned with speech. The issue of whether a change in a child's handedness may cause stuttering is crucial to the cerebral dominance theory. Unfortunately, this apparently simple problem has not been solved. One authority who favors a neurological theory says that half of all stutterers have been changed from left-handedness to right-handedness;[13] an opponent of the theory writes that he knows of not one case caused by a shift of handedness.[14] Data from schools, indicating that 90 to 95 per cent of the children whose handedness is changed do not stutter, give poor support to the dominance theory.[15]

Other physiological studies have found disturbances of breathing rhythm, blood pressure, pulse, and metabolism in stutterers. Such changes are more likely to be a result or concomitant of stuttering than to be its cause. A stutterer is tense, and has a strong emotional reaction to his disability. It is therefore not strange that he should have the visceral reactions which are the usual accompaniments of anxiety.

Some well-known characteristics of stammering and stuttering lead to the conclusion that they may be caused by psychological processes. Stammering is erratic and freakish, just as hysteria is. It is found more frequently in individuals whose personality is of a generally hysterical sort.[16] Most stammerers can speak well when alone but not when communicating with another person; they can sing words they cannot say; the disorder disappears temporarily when they are distracted from paying attention to it. When a stammerer reads the same passage aloud repeatedly, he stammers less on each successive reading.[17] Such features suggest that stammering and stuttering constitute a common psychoneurosis; that they are to be understood in terms of adjustment and learning. Although several psychological theories have been proposed, their main points can be synthesized coherently.[18] Primarily, a stutterer has a fear of social communication, a subtle anxiety evoked by social contacts and by the potential criticism or rejection he expects from his auditors. Secondarily, he is afraid of stuttering itself. His social anxiety involves a tension that interferes with fluent speech, and his apprehension that he will stutter intensifies the interfering anxiety. As a result, the victim is bound in a vicious cycle which is hard to terminate.

Some observations of the development of stuttering in childhood are revealing. As has already been noted, stutterers begin to speak normally in early childhood and are diagnosed as stutterers only after from one to several years of normal talking. But the normal speech of all small children is full of repetitions and hesitations. A history of stuttering commonly begins when an overanxious or dominating parent assumes that the child's normally nonfluent speech is stuttering and tries to correct it. In such a situation, the parent usually does everything that he should not do. He hounds the child to speak more slowly and clearly, and to say again the words with which he has trouble, so that the child grows more and more tense. The vicious cycle starts, for the child becomes anxious whenever he speaks, for fear that he will stutter. An important discovery is that sound repetition (stuttering) always precedes the tense explosive stoppages (stammering), in childhood development.[19] The latter is an attempted inhibitory adjustment to the fear that when he does speak he will be wrong. Stutterers are found mainly among the children of parents who are strict, anxious, and insistent on high standards. Such parents are also the ones who would view with alarm any sign of left-handedness on the part of their child, and would rush to change his handedness. Since all children show some confusion of handedness during the early years, the parents may be unduly concerned even when the child is not really left-handed, and may later report that they changed his handedness. Perhaps the apparent correlation between stuttering and a change of handedness arises from parental anxieties rather than from more physiological causes. There are no stutterers among the American Indians, who treat their children leniently, have relaxed standards of cleanliness and conduct, and accept a child's imperfect speech without comment.[20] There are, of course, other parent-child situations that can and do cause stuttering to begin. In a few instances, it may have its origin in a school situation, or even one in adult life. All cases, however, involve a tense, inhibitory response to an anxiety-loaded interchange of speech communication. No single experience is sufficient except in rarely intense instances, but cumulative anxiety-conditioning over a period of time will fix the habit of stuttering.

Although stuttering is nonintegrative, it is still an adjustment. The most available resource of a person who fears to talk is to inhibit speech. Stuttering therefore has a strong momentary reinforcement that fixes it as a habit, even though it is more punishing in the long run. In this respect it is like other nonintegrative adjustments whose strong instantaneous reinforcement through anxiety reduction causes them to be learned, outweighing the more remotely punishing consequences. Sometimes stuttering also brings substantial secondary gains. Parents may regard the stutterer as a "poor nervous child," and give him attention that otherwise they withhold. A stutterer may be excused from reciting in school and from other social obligations.

Two direct methods for treating stuttering meet with moderate success. One technique is to give the stutterer something else to think about other than his manner of talking. Many systems have been devised, centering on how he holds his tongue, on how he breathes, on talking rhythmically, or on thinking of speech as if it were chewing.[21] The rationales behind such methods are usually absurd, but they serve a real purpose as distractions. By thinking of these things as he talks, a person is prevented from attending to his own deficiencies, and his anxious expectation that he will stutter is reduced. The other direct method for treating stuttering is the development of self-confidence, which is good adjustment to social relationships. Public speaking, reciting passages learned by rote, and similar methods give both practice and confidence. Good speech clinics, such as those operated by a number of universities, tend to use all resources in an integrated effort to aid stutterers. Direct training methods are used together with general psychotherapy to relieve social anxieties. Treating a child's anxious parents is often essential.

Since stuttering is a cumulatively reinforced habit which can in time become almost as unalterable as a reflex, it is often harder to cure in adults than to prevent in its incipient stages in childhood. The nonfluent speech of preschool children should not be mistaken for stuttering. Even when stuttering seems really to be evident, calmly and warmly accepting the child as a person, waiting with genuine patience for him to complete what he has to say, and relieving him of all unnecessary sources of anxiety and tension, are the best procedures. Anything that calls a child's attention to his stuttering is likely to be of more harm than benefit.

SUGGESTED READINGS

On hysterical mechanisms, see Chapters 11 and 12 of Cameron, *The Psychology of Behavior Disorders;* Chapter 6 of Landis and Bolles, *Textbook of Abnormal Psychology;* and Chapter 11 of Klein, *Abnormal Psychology.* Interesting cases are presented in Chapter 10 of Burton and Harris, *Case Histories in Clinical and Abnormal Psychology.*

An easy but helpful introduction to speech and language disorders is found in Johnson, *People in Quandaries.* Hahn, *Stuttering: Significant Theories and Therapies,* and Johnson, *Stuttering in Children and Adults,* provide more extensive overviews of this puzzling problem of behavior.

CHAPTER 10

Anxiety and
Its Effects

Anxiety is the foundation of almost all forms of nonintegrative human behavior. To reduce or control unbearable anxiety, people use the adjustment mechanisms we have considered in the four preceding chapters. In response to the tensions engendered by his conflicts, a person may compensate, rationalize, withdraw, displace his anxiety to a substitute phobic stimulus, or develop hysterical symptoms. All such behavior tends to relieve anxiety, and is therefore personally adjustive, even though it may be nonintegrative in the long run. If his mechanisms are successful in reducing his tensions, a person may show little or no open anxiety.

NONADJUSTIVE REACTIONS

Responses to Baffling Difficulties

In many instances, a person does not succeed in reducing his anxiety. Confronted with an insistent and baffling conflict, he cannot discover any effective solution, or else is inhibited from using the common mechanisms of defense. Consequently, he remains futilely stirred up, and shows the effects of anxiety openly in his conduct. Such an end-result of conflict is called a persistent *nonadjustive* reaction.[1]

The two alternative consequences of human conflicts are analogous to the two possible results of confining a highly motivated rat in a very complicated maze. First, the rat may find some way to get out. Human adjustment mechanisms are like the rat's first alternative; they are "ways out" of life's difficulties. Second, the rat may be unable to discover an exit, and must remain in the maze, restless and thwarted, until it drops from exhaustion. Persons, too, are sometimes prevented from finding any way to cope with their conflicts, and hence are impotently stirred up, or exhausted by their fruitless attempts to adjust. The course of a nonadjustive reaction can be represented by a simple diagram, as shown in Figure 24.

DRIVE ⟶ ACTIVITY ⟶ LACK OF ANY ⟶ UNREDUCED ⟶ MAINTAINED
                    ADEQUATE   DRIVE   EMOTIONAL
                    MECHANISM   (Anxiety)   TENSION
                                                      (Nonadjustive
                                                      Reaction)

Figure 24. Nonadjustive Reaction

When a strong drive, usually arising from conflict, is unreduced by either constructive or substitute mechanisms, a person remains in an unadjusted condition and shows direct evidences of his maintained emotional tension. Compare this diagram with Figure 3 (p. 29), and with alternative (6) of Figure 1 (p. 9).

Although adjustment and nonadjustment are important concepts which help us understand human behavior, you must not suppose that all responses to conflict can be classified exactly as either adjustive or nonadjustive. Many reactions consist partly of one and partly of the other. To separate them too sharply is to commit the "either-or error," that everything is either black or white when in reality many things are in various shades of gray. A youngster whose main mechanism is overaggressive compensation may also have periods of self-devaluation and conscious distress — he vacillates between adjustment and nonadjustment. Even in hysteria, which ordinarily is the most fully tension-reducing of the substitute adjustments, an occasional patient may show open anxiety concurrently with his symptom, combining partial adjustment and partial nonadjustment simultaneously. People who withdraw, regress, or suffer from phobias generally show unreduced anxiety along with their partially successful adjustments.

Certain responses to conflict are more nonadjustive than adjustive. These reactions, popularly identified as "worry," "nervousness," "nervous exhaustion," "nervous breakdown," and the like, are considered in this chapter. Even such conditions are not entirely nonadjustive, however, for they may have incidental and minor tension-reducing values, as we shall see.

The nonadjustive components of behavior may vary greatly in severity. A nonadjustive response is not always catastrophically serious. Worry, for example, is a nonadjustive reaction, but a very common one. Worry afflicts almost everyone from time to time, and must therefore be considered a statistically normal feature of human life. At the other extreme of severity, some nonadjustive states of anxiety and exhaustion are the most complete breakdowns of the adjustive process short of the psychoses.

Symptoms of Unreduced Anxiety

Since an unreduced drive must give rise to some kind of a response, a nonadjustive state is characterized by a number of active behavior symptoms. All these symptoms usually occur together, but with varying degrees of prominence in various persons. The most obvious symptom of nonadjustment is *anxiety* itself, an intensely unpleasant emotional experience, with a sense of uncertainty and helplessness.[2] It may vary in scope from a simple worry about a fairly specific problem to a broadly generalized anxiety which concerns the entire status of the person and envelops all the social situations with which he has contact. A second result of unreduced emotional tension is a persistent *visceral response,* through the action of the sympathetic division of the autonomic nervous system, which interferes with normal vital processes and gives rise to bodily symptoms ranging from vague discomfort to exhaustion. The third effect is diffused *motor activity* and a heightened readiness to make all sorts of muscular responses. A tense person is likely to chew his nails, drum on the table, and make repeated restless movements. He overreacts to stimuli that most people would ignore, being unduly startled by sudden noises. The motor behavior arises from the facilitation of responses by the general state of tension. It is the basis of much of so-called "nervousness."

Nonadjustive anxiety reactions have conventionally been included among the psychoneuroses, along with phobias, obsessive and compulsive mechanisms, and hysteria. One early and widely used system of classification lumped together all the nonadjustive reaction patterns as one type of psychoneurosis, called *neurasthenia*. This term was suggested in 1869 by Beard, an early American psychiatrist, to label a neurotic condition which he ascribed to "the stress and strain of modern life!" The classical symptoms of neurasthenia include vague aches and pains, digestive disturbances, lassitude, a pessimistic attitude, and sometimes diffused fear and anxiety, a list of complaints that corresponds almost exactly to the evidences of a nonadjustive response to baffling conflicts. In recent years, the term neurasthenia has fallen into disrepute, because it has been defined in so many different ways by various authorities, and because it has become a catch-all classification for many otherwise unaccountable psychoneurotic reactions.

Several other classifications of the psychoneuroses have been proposed. One recent and rational scheme was adopted by the Medical Department of the United States Army near the close of World War II.[3] Making no attempt to sort the psychoneuroses into a small number of types, the Army classification used nine categories. Four of these correspond to the psychoneurotic adjustment mechanisms described in the preceding two chapters — phobic reaction, obsessive-compulsive reaction, conversion reaction (hysteria), and dissociative reaction. The remaining five classes contain large nonadjustive components. *Anxiety reaction* designates conditions of diffuse anxiety, often characterized by periodic attacks of more acute panic. *Asthenic reaction* (*neurasthenia*) is retained to indicate responses of general fatigue with vague visceral complaints. *Hypochondriacal reaction* is an overconcern about one's health, without an adequate organic basis. The *neurotic depressive reaction* is anxiety in the form of extreme pessimism and discouragement. The fifth class, *somatization reaction,* involves visceral symptoms arising from emotional tensions which are so severe that actual tissue changes occur. Psychologically caused stomach ulcers illustrate this fifth type of neurosis, which has been recognized and studied widely only in quite recent years. The Army system divides the psychoneuroses objectively in terms of their dominant symptoms, and is perhaps as satisfactory a classification as has yet been devised.

Any strict separation of these psychoneuroses into types has one major defect, however. Many symptoms are common to all of them. Cases of "pure" anxiety reaction or asthenic reaction are relatively uncommon; most asthenics also have some anxiety, and most anxiety neurotics also have some visceral symptoms. Perhaps the old blanket term "neurasthenia" to cover all these disorders was not so bad after all, for it called attention to their unity. It is even better to regard them as behavior disorders whose major component is a nonadjustive response to difficulties.

We have already noted that a single feature of behavior may be somewhat adjustive and somewhat nonadjustive at the same time. The symptom patterns differentiated by the Army classification scheme may be arranged in a scale, according to the degree of non-adjustment they represent. The anxiety and somatization reactions are almost wholly nonadjustive; they have little or no tension-reducing value. The asthenic and hypochondriacal reactions are somewhat more mixed. While mainly nonadjustive, they may help a person to withdraw from conflicts and rationalize away his failures with the excuse that he is physically ill.

ANXIETY REACTIONS

Cases of Anxiety

When the emotional experience — the obvious and explicit misery — of a nonadjustive response is its most conspicuous feature, the psychoneurosis is usually called an anxiety reaction. Most persons who suffer from severe anxiety also have visceral and motor symptoms superimposed upon their overt distress, however. "Pure" anxiety is rare.

An anxiety reaction is well illustrated by the behavior of Thomas R., an eighteen-year-old high school senior who was referred to a counselor because he was failing in his studies, and had an attitude of apprehension and despair which was readily noticed by his teachers. Interviews showed that the boy's anxieties were not limited to any definite situation, but widely generalized. He was concerned about his academic standing, and especially about his father's reaction to it. Referring to his possible school failure, he said, "It will be the end for me." He felt an acute social incompetence, and said in a vague manner that he did not know much about the world, and that he had many things to learn. Thomas had little association with girls and appeared to be afraid of them, or rather of his inability to impress them as favorably as the other boys. During the preceding year he had had a few dates with a girl a little older than himself, on which he placed a high value, considering himself in love. The girl went away to college, and Thomas felt afraid of "losing" her. He was utterly unable to make decisions. The simplest problem caused him to seek advice or to feel incompetent to face the difficulty.

In addition to his anxiety, Thomas had visceral symptoms, centering around his heart. At times his heart beat very rapidly and his pulse pounded in his ears. Although several physicians examined him carefully and reported that he had no organic disorder, Thomas often rested in bed from early Saturday evening until Sunday noon because of his supposed heart disease. The intensity of Thomas' anxiety was best revealed by notes he scribbled from time to time and gave to the counselor. He wrote, "I can never be at rest and am never satisfied. I fear of not being able to control my mental and physical actions. Something is always elusive. I am more afraid of life than the basest coward. Why can't I understand people? Why can I remember only my fears, the vacant mental situations and the lonely places in my life? I seem to exist isolated. All the clean wholesome desires which make a man want to live seem to be crushed. Will I snap out of this, or will I never be a man?"

Thomas' anxiety reaction may be interpreted as a nonadjustive response to all the principal problems of late adolescence. He faces the issues of establishing his independence as a sufficient person, of financial self-support, of the choice of a vocation, and of social and sexual adjustment, quite unable to achieve a satisfactory course of action in any of them. Such an inability to adjust must have its roots in his past learning experiences. In Thomas' case, as in most, the basis was found in the attitudes and personalities of his parents. His father, a successful owner of a small factory, is a large, dominating man who has always made Thomas' decisions for him. When the boy was asked about his hobbies and interests, he said that his father had him study the violin when he was ten, that his father had arranged for him to join the Boy Scouts. The father also chose his studies in high school and made definite plans for his higher education. Thomas apparently had never made an independent decision in his life. He had no open hostility toward his father, but was overwhelmed by his domination. In the interviews he constantly asserted how good his father had been to him. In fact, he seemed to protest too much, and there was good ground for suspecting a thoroughly repressed, and not at all unjustified, resentment against his father. Thomas' mother was a small subdued woman, utterly dominated by the father and described as very "nervous" and weak. It seems that she, too, reacted nonadjustively to her life problems, and that her example influenced Thomas considerably. The mother was extremely religious, and from her Thomas acquired a deep sense of sin and a conviction that dancing, dating, the movies, and in fact almost all of the usual adolescent diversions, are very immoral. Thomas therefore had a substantial set of home-grown conflicts, with weak resources for dealing with them. His relationships with his father created a conflict between the need for independence typical of his age group and culture, and his need to continue the dependence in which he was trained. His mother's attitudes set up a conflict between his social and sex motives and his narrowly religious conception of morality. His adjustive resources were handicapped in two ways: His father's dominance gave him little opportunity to learn how to solve life problems independently, and his mother's anxious behavior tended to suggest to him an anxious reaction to his difficulties.

The counselor did not have an opportunity to help Thomas by extended psychological treatment, and the community had no other agency to offer him aid. A little progress was made in one direction. When the effect of emotion on heartbeat and on other visceral functions was explained to him, Thomas felt greatly relieved. and reported that he had no further "heart spells." The basic anxiety state would be much harder to cure. Sometimes such adolescent anxiety reactions disappear through changes of circumstances. When Thomas has a job, an independent income, and has moved away from home, he may readjust successfully. In many cases, however, long psychotherapy is required to relieve an anxiety reaction that is the result of a lifetime of conflicts and of inadequate adjustments.

Anxiety states usually occur in people who, like Thomas, have been prepared for them by a long history of unsolved conflicts. In some instances, however, a severe anxiety reaction may be precipitated in a previously stable person by an event of catastrophic intensity. In wartime, combatants are called upon to endure stresses almost unknown in civilian life, and to perform acts that are in sharp conflict with all their preceding social learning. Therefore it is not surprising that psychoneurotic breakdowns sometimes occur among combat soldiers. An example of a nonadjustive anxiety reaction may be cited from Hastings' report of psychiatric experiences in the Air Force.[4]

> While on a practice mission, a heavy bombardment plane suffered a severe accident in which its tail section was entirely sheared off. The tail gunner, caught in the severed and falling tail, succeeded in kicking his way through the metal skin of the plane and parachuted to the ground unharmed. The burning body of the plane fell near him, and there was only one other survivor. He tried to extricate some of his fellow crew members from the wreckage but was driven back by the flames. Following this accident, the gunner developed severe anxiety symptoms. During the day he was restless, tense, and could not eat. The nights were worse; he either lay sweating and shaking in his bed unable to sleep, or had recurring dreams of plane crashes. In spite of his anxiety, he completed five more combat missions, two of which were unusually difficult. His plane was badly damaged by anti-aircraft fire, and had to come home on two engines with a torn wing. On one of these missions he shot down an enemy fighter plane, which increased his anxiety because he felt he had made another man suffer the experience he himself had endured. Up to this time, the gunner had not reported his symptoms to a medical officer, but kept on forcing himself to fly for fear he would be regarded as a "quitter." His anxiety finally became so noticeable that he was relieved from further flying duty. Psychiatric interviews showed that he had a stable background, with no adjustive difficulties prior to his catastrophic experience. His anxiety state was regarded as a reaction that exceptional stress had produced in an essentially normal person.

The situations that most obviously precipitated combat anxiety were those of great personal danger, of the continued day-after-day threats of pain, permanent disability, or death. Psychiatric experience in World War II showed, however, that the anticipation of personal injury was by no means the only conflict which evoked anxiety. Groups of combat soldiers were closely knit, and intense reactions of grief and guilt on the part of survivors often followed battle casualties. Anxiety reactions were provoked by situations in which a man felt he had not done everything possible to protect the lives of his comrades, in which he had gained shelter and safety when his fellows had been unable to do so, or in which he felt that he himself should have been killed instead of his closest friend.

Action against the enemy, killing and destroying, frequently evoked conflicts of guilt, because it was at odds with a lifetime of socialized training. There was some relationship between a man's past adjustive experiences and his ability to resist succumbing to the strains of military life. Those who broke down early, under the relatively mild frustrations of training experiences and of separation from home and family, almost always had prior backgrounds of anxiety reactions to conflicts. On the other hand, some very well-adjusted men became anxiety ridden when subjected to uncommonly disastrous situations, as in the case of the aerial gunner.

The Origins of Anxiety Reactions

What causes a person to make nonadjustive reactions when he is faced with a baffling conflict? The determiners are many, and vary somewhat from one case to another. Basic to all nonadjustive behavior is anxiety itself. Childhood experiences that predispose a person to make anxious responses to his conflicts, instead of constructive ones, are the remote causes of nonadjustive reactions. The most significant of these factors lie in the parent-child relationship: cold or rejecting parental behavior toward children, overdominant and belittling attitudes that make a child feel helpless and incapable, or severe conflicts between dependent and hostile impulses that a child cannot resolve with his immature resources. When such conflicts are acute and prolonged, the child's anxiety may generalize to many situations that involve relationships with people, or imply an evaluation of his competence. He perceives the world as hostile, and regards himself as incapable of coping with it. Such a sequence of development may lead to more than one outcome. Sometimes, fortunately, the person's anxiety may be overcome through subsequent processes of readjustment. In other cases it may be reduced by nonintegrative defense mechanisms. Finally, the anxiety may remain and be evidenced in nonadjustive behavior.

Case studies of persons who suffer from anxiety reactions point to some of the differential determiners that make them behave nonadjustively, instead of developing tension-reducing mechanisms. One factor that leads to anxiety is a poverty of adjustive resources caused by a lack of skill in solving problems independently. Overdominating parents often subjugate their children so thoroughly as to prevent them from learning how to adjust to difficulties. When a dominated child tries aggressive defenses, he is suppressed; if he tries to withdraw, his parents force him into activity. Thwarted at every turn, he develops no adjustive resources of his own and must simply remain unadjusted. Case studies of children of dominating parents describe them as unhappy, fearful, and suffering from feelings of inferiority. Anxiety can also be created by parents who are themselves overanxious. Unwittingly, they teach a child to doubt his own capability and to be anxious about his relationships with other people. An overindulged child, in contrast, tends to use over-aggressive defenses or hysterical mechanisms when unable to resolve his conflicts more satisfactorily.[5]

Evidence from clinical studies gives the impression that many culturally and educationally superior people develop anxiety because they reject the less rational means for resolving conflicts such as compensation, projection, or hysterical symptoms, which might be accepted as solutions by persons with less critical judgment. Persons who show anxiety reactions tend to be more self-contained, better integrated, and more individually oriented, in contrast to hysterical patients who are externally oriented and dependent on the opinions of others. The less well-integrated hysteric develops the partial reaction pattern of the localized adjustive ailment. A more reflective and thoughtful person is driven into the whole reaction pattern of anxiety and nonadjustment. Some objective evidence, to be reviewed in the next chapter, suggests that persons with anxiety reactions are, on the whole, more intelligent, better educated, and from a better cultural background than are those who become hysterics. These differences are suggestive, but there is no sharp boundary between the personalities found in anxiety and in hysteria, save in the life histories that have taught each person to adopt his distinctive way of reacting to conflicts.

The Treatment of Nonadjustive Reactions

Treating persons who have anxiety is not essentially different from the psychotherapy of other maladjustments. There are, however, a few pitfalls peculiar to anxiety states which have to be avoided. Since an anxious person is so obviously miserable, it is only human for one to feel sorry for him and to rush in with reassurance and comfort. Parents, teachers, and other relatively untrained people often try to persuade the sufferer that things are not as black as they seem, and that he really has no adequate cause for despair. Such advice has little effect on an anxiety reaction, because an anxious person is not responding to real threats but to his own mistaken perceptions of the world and of himself, formed through the experiences which taught him to be anxious. He knows that he is miserable and that he cannot control his misery voluntarily. If someone advises him otherwise, it is only evidence that the other person does not understand him. He then feels even more isolated from other people, and despises himself because he cannot control his feelings by logic. Advice and reassurance therefore make his anxiety worse instead of decreasing it. Another superficial approach to anxiety states pays attention only to particular symptoms. As is also true of conversion hysteria, the bodily complaints which accompany anxiety reactions can often be relieved by suggestion or explanation. That is illustrated by the counselor's work with Thomas R. in reducing his "heart spells" by showing him they were emotional in nature. Curing a symptom perhaps does little harm, but it fails to get to the core of the anxiety.

Persons in anxiety states often repress any recognition of the conflicts basic to their distress. The repression itself is an adjustment, even though the residual anxiety is nonadjustive. Repressions vary in their completeness. Sometimes the repression is relatively weak, so that the patient remembers all his relevant experiences but does not put them together in such a way as to permit him to understand the cause of his anxiety. In other cases, the repression may be very thorough, so that a person suffers from "free-floating" anxiety, that is, he feels stirred up without knowing why. An objectless panic is itself disturbing to the person; he must regard himself as very queer indeed to be so much aroused for no apparent reason.

In the treatment of anxiety, techniques for overcoming repression are appropriate, just as they are for phobias. When the anxiety is precipitated by an intense recent experience, and not deeply grounded in the person's past history, short-cut methods for reducing repression may be effective. One technique used in World War II was to induce a dreamy state, by the administration of a drug such as sodium pentothal, in which inhibitions are greatly reduced. Under the influence of the drug, the anxious patients recalled, and frequently acted out with dramatic intensity, the fearful incidents that had evoked their anxiety.[6] The patient was kept alert and talking as he came out of the influence of the drug into his normal waking state, and was thereby helped to remember his fears, integrate them with the rest of his life, and eventually to readjust to them. This method was useful for treating conversion hysteria and other combat neuroses, as well as anxiety reactions. It is much less applicable to persons whose anxiety is due to the cumulative effect of many experiences extending back into their childhood.

Chronic anxiety states ordinarily require prolonged psychotherapy, in which the patient recalls and re-examines the bases of his conflicts, and learns to re-evaluate his estimates of his own resources, and of the threats offered by the external world. One favorable factor in the therapy of anxiety is that the patient's misery is open and unreduced, so that he feels a real and continuing need for help. This need motivates him to seek assistance and to persevere until relief is obtained.

Common Worry

Ordinary worry is the most common of the nonadjustive responses. It differs only in degree from an anxiety reaction, but this distinction is important, for almost everyone worries to some extent and yet is able to achieve a passable adjustment. In worry, the nonadjustive behavior is chiefly verbal, in the form of a continuous preoccupation with an unsolved conflict. The worrier thinks over his predicament again and again, but not constructively. It is an ineffective form of trial and error, not leading to a goal. At times a worrier will speak his meditations aloud and gain some tension-reduction by sharing them with others, but usually he mulls his difficulties over in implicit speech, talking only to himself. Worry often involves a circular reaction which aggravates the persistent nonadjustive response. The original situation arouses emotion and implicit speech together, hence by the ordinary process of conditioning the verbal activity itself becomes a substitute stimulus for the emotion. Thus fear arouses worry, and worry in turn arouses more fear, the physiological state of emotion being constantly stimulated anew. The visceral components of emotion act so as to interfere with appetite and digestion. In chronic cases, a person may quite literally "worry himself thin."

Situations that arouse worry vary from quite specific problems to broadly generalized concerns. When the worry centers on a particular issue, such as financial reverses or the illness of a member of one's family, it usually subsides when the direct causal problem is solved. In other cases, the situation to which the worrier seeks an adjustment is not an external one, but concerns his own concept of himself and of his interpersonal relationships. A devaluating self concept or attitude of inferiority is usually combated by defense mechanisms, but these alternate with periods of worry. Among adolescents and young adults in our culture, worries about the choice of a vocation and of success in it, about acceptance by other people, and about sex, are probably the most common.

A worrier generally has an inhibition against sharing his problem and against seeking advice. He feels that his difficulty is private or shameful and attaches to it a fear of social disapproval. The fear of insanity offers a good example. Uninformed people frequently have strange notions about mental disease, particularly in regard to its inheritance. The very fact that a young person is anxiously disturbed may make him believe that he is "going crazy," especially if some other member of his family has suffered a mental disorder. He inhibits seeking advice because of the cultural tradition that insanity is shameful, and he does not know how common his worry is among all people. The giving of information gives substantial help in allaying the unfounded fears in such cases, and paves the way for constructive counseling to overcome the real personal problems which underlie the fear. Other areas in which young people most often worry needlessly because they cannot seek aid are those of sexual morality, of sex potency, and of venereal disease.

A more profound repression than a mere inhibition against seeking assistance operates in some cases. Chronic worriers do not confine their concern to any specific issue, but worry indiscriminately about many aspects of their life experience. Often they seem to go out of their way to find something to worry about. Such cases verge upon fully developed anxiety reactions. Sometimes worries spring from long-established tensions acquired from experiences in an anxiety-ridden home. In other cases, worry over a series of trifling matters indicates a displacement or generalization of anxiety over a deeper issue, the recognition of which is repressed. In such instances superficial treatment is ineffective. To argue against the present trivial worries is futile, and even to do away with them is not permanently effective. Psychotherapeutic help like that given for anxiety reactions offers the only way to readjustment.

How To Relieve Worry

Since worry is a very common human problem, some practical hints concerning the handling of ordinary situational worries will not be out of place. These procedures will not cure all cases, but they will relieve many of the less severe anxieties so frequently encountered by nearly all people. (1) Set a time for the consideration of the problem. One of the most nonintegrative aspects of worry is the tendency to gain a transient relief by putting off unpleasant acts and thoughts. Meanwhile the fundamental tension remains unreduced. (2) Confide in someone, confess all about the worry, and talk it out. Anxieties that seem insurmountable when contemplated alone often become trivial when discussed with an impartial observer. (3) Get information and seek assistance. Many worries are due to misconceptions and misinformation, or to the inability of the worrier to discover enough different ways in which a problem can be attacked. Someone with broader knowledge or experience may be able to help. (4) Do something active about the source of the worry. In worries concerning school marks, a good session of study is tension-reducing even when it will not meet all your academic needs completely. For social worries, participation in any group activity is helpful. Since worry is a nonadjustive reaction, any active attitude will tend to reduce it. (5) If the situation worried about is external and really impossible to remedy, the development of "balancing factors" which are individually satisfying and socially acceptable will be desirable. Balancing factors are activities such as hobbies, sports, amusements, and the like, which give temporary distraction and tension-reduction in times of emotional stress. These interests help one to return to a normal emotional tone, after which another attack on the worry-producing problems may be more effective. (6) If direct measures are not successful, and especially if the intensity of worry seems disproportionate to its recognized cause, seek professional help. Guidance clinics, counseling centers, psychiatrists, and psychologists recognize the needs of normal people who are anxious, and are prepared to give effective help.

HYPOCHONDRIACAL
AND FATIGUE REACTIONS

The reaction to baffling conflicts that most nearly approximates the old concept of "neurasthenia" includes vague visceral symptoms, overconcern about bodily functions, lassitude, and a pessimistic attitude. In more modern terminology, such conditions are often broken down into asthenic, hypochondriacal, and fatigue reactions, but they overlap greatly. The asthenic-hypochondriacal-fatigue pattern is mainly nonadjustive, but it includes some minor adjustive values, as we shall see.

A Case Study

Helen T. was a twenty-year-old college senior with an excellent academic record. In her senior year she developed an illness with an imposing array of symptoms that made her feel she could not continue in college. Helen had little appetite, experienced digestive pains after every meal, was underweight, and was overconcerned about constipation. She suffered from insomnia to the extent that she was seldom able to sleep before two or three o'clock in the morning, but once she fell asleep she was quite likely to sleep until noon, missing her morning classes. Throughout the rest of the day she felt dull and tired; any little exertion fatigued her excessively. In addition to her physical symptoms, Helen was melancholy, avoided the company of her friends, and was given to periods of solitary brooding. She ate at odd hours or missed meals, avoided activity, and neglected her work.

Helen was the only child of parents both of whom were professional workers. Her childhood had been somewhat overprotected and pampered, but she had made remarkable school progress due partly to her good ability and partly to the bookish emphasis of her home which placed a great premium on intellectual accomplishments. Helen's childhood play was largely solitary. She avoided active muscular games and developed a self-centered and unsocial attitude. In adolescence she found herself awkward, not very attractive, and distinctly lacking in social graces. She developed an anxious attitude toward social demands which was partly compensated by her success at school. A severe illness when she was fifteen years old kept her in bed most of the time for five months and contributed to her withdrawing tendencies. Helen was deeply religious. Her one continuing social activity had been in church and Y.W.C.A. affairs, and these interests continued in college. Her social attitudes were highly moralistic, especially in regard to sex.

Six months before the onset of her ailment, Helen had fallen violently in love with a man ten years her senior whom she had met in her church work. Her affections were reciprocated for a while and there was sufficient demonstrativeness that, while the affair did not really go very far, Helen experienced a severe conflict between her aroused sex desires and her highly moralistic attitudes. Her behavior was alternately ardent and yielding, and then ex, tremely prudish. The man, who was a very matter-of-fact person, grew tired of her vacillation between amativeness and preaching, and broke off the relationship. Since Helen had few other social outlets she reacted very seriously to the break. The love affair had been her first satisfying social and sexual adjustment, and its end was a catastrophe to her.

At about the same time two other adjustment problems were developing. Through discussions in student groups and through her studies in some science courses, Helen's immature religious conceptions were shaken, and as yet she had no philosophy of life with which to replace them. Also, her graduation approached and, having no specific vocational aim and being prepared in no special field, she did not know what to do after leaving college. Both these problems added to her emotional tension.

Helen reacted to her difficulties with a diffused set of visceral symptoms. The only treatment she received was from the physician of the college health service who gave her pills of unknown prescription, and reassurances. He also recommended active physical exercise, cold baths, and a strict adherence to a routine of rising, eating, and going to bed.

The symptoms disappeared in another month or so. Although the physician treated only her symptoms, his method was not totally without value. The solution of Helen's adjustment problem was a more decisive factor in her recovery. She decided on the vocation of teaching and on continuing graduate studies in that field. She was elected to an honorary society, which gave her social recognition and some active duties. Of even greater importance was the fact that she attracted the interest of another young man, whose attention to her provided social and, broadly speaking, sexual satisfactions.

The Origins of Physical Symptoms

The asthenic-hypochondriacal-exhaustion pattern of behavior looks like the result of a generally run-down physical condition, as indeed it is, but it is better explained in terms of the effects of a persistent anxiety reaction to unsolved conflicts. Just as a temporary strong emotion disrupts digestive processes, a long-continued emotional tension causes, through the action of the sympathetic division of the autonomic system, a chronic and widespread interference with normal vegetative functioning. The sustained emotion results in loss of appetite, indigestion, vague visceral aches and pains, failure to maintain an adequate level of strength through nutrition, and even in constipation. Normal emotion is an emergency condition, and all of us find it an exhausting experience. An emergency state cannot be maintained for long without exhausting the energy resources of the whole body. Consequently, an asthenic person's nutritional reserves are used up; he shows continuous weakness and is too readily fatigued when he makes any physical effort. His insomnia is a direct indication of emotional tension, of an inability to relax enough to go to sleep, and his daytime lassitude is in part a secondary result of his lack of rest at night. Headaches are very common in the asthenic reaction, and are probably due to mixed and varying causes. Some headaches may be the result of digestive dysfunction, others may be adjustive pains like those found in hysteria.

Many attempts have been made to find physical bases for these disorders which seem so much like bodily illnesses, but most of the findings have been negative. Persons with chronic hypochondriacal or exhaustion reactions do not differ significantly from normal people in blood pressure, blood sugar level, or oxygen metabolism.[7] There is evidence of a higher adrenalin level in the blood during anxiety, a direct consequence of the emotional arousal. A British research found that anxiety neurotics had an elevated secretion of choline esterase, an enzyme that plays a part in the transmission of neural impulses. Hysterics, whose anxiety is reduced by their mechanisms, did not differ from normals in their secretion of this enzyme.[8] Although further research may show that organic pathology has some role in predisposing a person to asthenic reactions, the present evidence suggests that the bodily symptoms are the results of excessive emotion and not its cause.

Some nonadjustive reactions result in symptoms much more severe than those described in Helen's case. The affected person may complain of such extreme exhaustion that he takes to bed, and remains there for a long time in a state of psychological invalidism in which he has to receive care as if he were suffering from a chronic disease. In these cases, the ailment is likely to show great fluctuation in severity, becoming worse when attention is paid to it or when adjustive demands have to be met, and much improved when the patient is distracted from his symptoms or when he thinks he is unobserved. Instances have been recorded of bedridden hypochondriacs who have sat up for long periods to write in diaries, who have climbed stairs to secure food when there was no one to wait on them, and who have even danced about in their rooms when they believed that no member of their family was nearby.[9] Such observations suggest malingering, of course, but the reaction is not usually determined at so deliberate a level. A psychological invalid is responding to a conflict; any added strain makes his symptoms worse, while any distraction from his troubles makes them less severe.

The factors that predispose a person to suffer an asthenic-fatigue reaction are much the same as those underlying an anxiety state. The anxiety neuroses and the visceral-nonadjustive reactions are not two separate kinds of disorder. The difference between them is only one of emphasis. Both involve anxiety and both are likely to show visceral symptoms, but one or the other may be more prominent. In each person's history, of course, factors can be found that determine just what reactions he will make to a baffling conflict. A hypochondriacal attitude in a family, which teaches a child to be overconcerned about his health, may cause him to notice and exaggerate the visceral signs of emotion when he is stirred up. Excessive experience with illness may have the same effect. If a person develops a concept of himself as weak, delicate, and unusually subject to illness, he will be more likely to emphasize the visceral aspects of his experience if he falls into a generally nonadjustive state. Another determinant of the asthenic reaction is a feeling of loss of love, which can be observed both in children and in adults. Parents who treat a child inconsistently, sometimes over-indulging him and sometimes threatening to withdraw their love, often engender feelings of insecurity and unhappiness. When one has an expectation of love and then finds it withdrawn, one "feels very much abused," by a sort of contrast effect. The moping, woe-begone attitude of the rejected young lover is also close to the classical picture of neurasthenia.

Secondary Gains

The hypochondriacal and fatigue reactions are notable blends of adjustive and nonadjustive behavior. As we have seen, their symptoms arise primarily from the pent-up emotion of unsolved conflicts. In a minor degree, however, they may contribute an inferior, highly nonintegrative, solution of such conflicts. Asthenic conditions are serviceable in reinforcing a person's repressions. They help him to avoid a recognition of the genuine psychological causes of his misery, because he can blame his condition on his poor health. Closely related is their rationalization value. If a person is ill he feels himself excused from having to compete, and has a socially acceptable reason to justify his failures. He exaggerates his aches and pains, and talks and thinks about them to the exclusion of other interests. He thus dwells on his bodily symptoms both to distract himself from his real problems of adjustment, and to impress other people of his need for their sympathy and protection.

Hypochondriacal symptoms can also be used aggressively. They serve as a very primitive attention-getting mechanism, based on the special consideration that most cultural groups give to the immature, the weak, and the incapacitated. Psychological invalidism may be a person's last resort to compel the sympathetic attention of his family and to frighten them into submission. Because women assume a less competitive role in life, and because a cultural tradition condones their weakness, it is probable that more women than men escape from their conflicts by means of vague emotionally-determined ailments. Persons who use hypochondriacal reactions to help solve their adjustment problems may truly be said to "enjoy poor health."

SOMATIZATION REACTIONS

"Psychosomatic" Illnesses

In recent years, an entirely new branch of medicine has emerged from a recognition of the part that psychological conflicts may play in causing or aggravating illnesses.[10] Some diseases have been identified in which the psychological component is especially prominent. These have become known as "psychosomatic" disorders, a term which implies that the mind (psyche) determines the disease of the body (soma). The term "psychosomatic" is unfortunate because it implies a dualistic separation of psychological and physiological functions rather than their essential unity. The name *somatization reactions*, used by the psychiatric classification scheme of the Army, is much better. The somatization reactions have two main characteristics: (1) they are brought about by an interaction of psychological and organic factors; and (2) they cause real damage to the structures of the body.

In a broad sense, we have already met a number of somatization reactions. The rapid heartbeat of an anxiety attack and the profound fatigue of an asthenic reaction are truly physiological, and also can readily be identified as the results of emotional conflicts. The disorders more narrowly classified as psychosomatic — peptic ulcers, for example — go somewhat further than these. In a somatization reaction the visceral effects of emotion are so pronounced that actual and irreversible damage may be done to the body's structure. A psychological illness becomes a "real" illness with identifiable tissue pathology.

Hysterical mechanisms also involve bodily symptoms, but they can be sharply distinguished from somatization reactions, at least in theory. Conversion hysteria produces physical disabilities that lack an adequate organic basis, while in the psychosomatic disorders the "adequate organic basis" is present, itself a product of an exaggerated visceral reaction of emotion.

Somatization reactions may involve all the major functional systems of the body: digestive, circulatory, respiratory, glandular, or reproductive. In fact, any organic function that can be disturbed by strong emotion can become the basis of a psychosomatic disorder. Because they are so numerous, whole volumes are required to describe all the somatization reactions. We will cite one well-known disorder at some length, and refer briefly to a few others.

Peptic Ulcer

A peptic ulcer is an inflamed wound caused by the corrosive action of the acid gastric secretions, in the stomach, or in the duodenum, the part of the intestine immediately below the stomach. In a sense, it is a wonder that we do not all develop ulcers, because we digest tough pieces of meat by the action of the acid secretions in our stomachs, and one's stomach is itself a bag of muscle tissue! A normal stomach does not digest itself because it is coated with a mucous secretion that resists the action of acids. If the mucous lining is harmed, or if the gastric juice is secreted in excessive amounts or in too strong an acid concentration, ulcers may ensue. Gastric ulcers vary greatly in severity. The relatively least serious ulcers consist only of inflamed and diffusely painful areas. More severe ones also bleed, and may even become perforated through the wall of the stomach or duodenum. They arise from many causes, one of which is an intense and prolonged emotional reaction to psychological conflict.

The physiological mechanisms of peptic ulcer have been made clear by a number of experimental studies. Wolf and Wolff had an opportunity to make systematic observations of a man who had a gastric fistula, an external opening cut into his stomach through which he was fed, because a childhood scalding had closed his esophagus.[11] When the man had feelings of resentment, hostility, and anxiety, as on one occasion when he was discharged from a job for reasons that he felt unjust, his stomach mucosa were engorged with blood, and he complained of gastric distress. While in that condition, his stomach wall was unusually susceptible to pain and was readily damaged. The experimenters were able to create small gastric ulcers which did not heal readily so long as the man remained emotionally upset, but which subsided when he became calm. The factors that led to ulcer formation were the engorgement of the tissues, the loss of the protective mucous lining, excessive stomach motility, and an increase in the amount and acidity of the gastric juice. Wolf and Wolff found that anxiety, hostility, and resentment produced all these conditions, leading to ulceration. Fear, grief, and depression, to the contrary, caused paleness of the stomach tissues, a decrease in stomach movements, and a lessened gastric secretion. These emotions brought about the distress of "nervous indigestion," but did not result in ulcers.

Mittelman and Wolff measured the stomach motility and gastric secretions of normal persons, of people in anxiety states, and of patients with peptic ulcers.[12] Emotional stress, chiefly of anxiety and embarrassment, was induced by discussing the subjects' psychological conflicts with them. All subjects showed an increase in stomach movements and in gastric secretions, but the reactions tended to be more pronounced in the persons who suffered from peptic ulcers.

The classic ulcer patient is described as an active, aggressive, business or professional man who is always under pressure and unable to relax, but who often shows neither open anxiety nor signs of psychoneurotic mechanisms.[13] This is a typical case history:

> An ambitious, hard-working young executive of twenty-six came to the hospital with a bleeding duodenal ulcer. His father had died in the patient's early childhood, and he had grown up in an atmosphere of personal, family, and economic insecurity, but with marked overdependence on his mother. He married and was overdependent on his wife also. They had to live with his wife's parents, which added to his feeling of insufficiency. His apparent aggressiveness and independence in the business world were probably compensatory; underneath he seethed with hostility against his wife, mother, and mother-in-law. He felt really insecure and dependent, but was unable to accept his own dependent needs. He hated those to whom he felt tied emotionally, but could not express his antagonism against them openly. Earlier family conflicts had caused him gastric distress. After a quarrel in which his wife ordered him out of the house, he developed a severe hemorrhage of his ulcer.*

Not all peptic ulcer patients show the aggressive pattern of compensatory behavior. Some are meek and compliant, and seem to have repressed almost completely their hostility against people. Here is another case:

> A seventeen-year-old boy had been extremely close to his mother and dominated by her. He was a model child at home and

---

* For a more complete description of this case and of the one that follows, and for accounts of several similar cases, see Kapp, Rosenbaum, and Romano (1947).

a "teacher's pet" at school. Gastric distress first appeared when he entered high school and was unable to come home for lunch. Later, he left home for a temporary summer job in a nearby city, was homesick, and overate prodigiously. (Overeating can be one adjustive response to the increased stomach tension caused by emotional states of hostility.) The climax was dramatic. The boy received a telegram summoning him home because of a serious illness of his mother, but his employer harshly refused to pay him unless he finished the week's work. He reacted to the employer's unreasonable demand with an abnormally submissive attitude and with no show of hostile feeling, but immediately developed a severe perforated peptic ulcer.

Evidence from both clinical and experimental sources shows quite clearly the psychological and physiological steps in the formation of a peptic ulcer. A strong and sustained conflict evokes a chronic emotional response, usually of hostility or anxiety. Because of over-dependence or other similar inhibiting factors in his life history, the person is unable to reduce his emotion adequately through mechanisms of defense or escape. Indeed, in most instances he shows little open anxiety, and may be regarded by his fellows as a well-adjusted person. The emotional pattern causes the stomach or duodenum to be susceptible to injury by its own acid secretions, and the susceptibility continues for a long time, in the absence of other mechanisms to reduce the emotional tension. The result is a break-down of the digestive tissues caused by a weakening of the mucosa, and the added mechanical and chemical stimulation of hypermotility and hyperacidity. It is perhaps significant that "aggressive, success-ful" men get peptic ulcers. If their conflicts took any other form than the psychosomatic, they would be tied up with open anxiety or disabling defenses. Overtly neurotic people can seldom be ener-getic or successful.

As yet, there is no well-established explanation of why some people develop peptic ulcers in response to their conflicts, while other people have different psychosomatic complaints, and still others adjust by various mechanisms of defense without damage to their own tissues. Two hypotheses have been proposed. One holds that so-called constitutional factors determine the type of response a person will make to his conflicts. Inadequacies or weak-ness of some organ or system, stemming from defects of structure or from earlier illnesses, may dictate what part of the body is most vulnerable. That part succumbs under stress. A second theory suggests that a particular psychosomatic symptom is determined by the kind of conflict a person faces, not by his constitution. For example, case studies of peptic ulcers show that they occur in people who are both dependent and hostile, and who reject their own needs for dependence and suppress open demonstrations of their hostility. According to this theory, then, a suppressed conflict between hostility and dependence is specific to the causation of peptic ulcers. The two theories are not mutually exclusive and both may be true in part. Future research will almost surely lead to better validated knowledge of the origins of peptic ulcers and of other somatization reactions.

Some Other Somatization Reactions

A number of somatization reactions affect the circulatory system, which is not surprising in view of the effects of strong emotion on heartbeat and blood pressure. Numerous experimental studies have shown that anxiety or anger tends to raise the blood pressure of quite normal people. When a person's emotional state is chronic, and is not reduced by any effective adjustment mechanisms, one result may be *essential hypertension,* a condition of high blood pressure not due to identifiable bodily pathology. Somatization reactions can also imitate all sorts of heart disorders. A large proportion of people who seek medical aid for supposed heart ailments do not have any organic disease of the heart, but are evidencing the physiological accompaniments of unexpressed and uncompensated anxiety or resentment. One cardiac malfunction that is clearly psychosomatic is the *effort syndrome,* in which even a slight physical effort causes an undue heart acceleration, accompanied by difficulty in breathing and feelings of faintness. Psychological studies of persons with the effort syndrome show that it is basically a fear of physical activity, often arising from the guilt or anxiety a person may feel about his own aggressive impulses.

There is a marked relationship between allergic reactions and psychosomatic disorders. Physiologically, allergies are sensitivity reactions that occur when certain substances come in contact with body tissues. The substances, mainly certain proteins, set up a disturbance when taken into the stomach in the case of food allergies, or when inhaled or brought into contact with the skin, as in the sensitivities to pollens, dust, animal hair, and the like. Among the common allergic reactions are *bronchial asthma,* a severe difficulty in breathing due to the constriction of the small air passages in the lungs, *vasomotor rhinitis* or "hay fever," and a number of skin disorders, including *urticaria* ("hives") and *eczema.* It is probable that all allergies are due initially to physiological sensitivities, but when once established, they can be affected by psychological conflicts. Asthmatic attacks are often precipitated by attitudes of hostility or anxiety. Many case studies have shown that susceptible persons may suffer acutely from rhinitis or from skin eruptions when faced with an emotion-laden conflict, and that the physiological symptoms can disappear abruptly when calm attitudes are restored through changed circumstances or by psychological treatment.

The reasons for the relationships between allergic and psychosomatic disorders are not yet known fully, but one frequently repeated experimental observation helps to understand them. Suppose that a sufferer from hay fever who is sensitive to the pollen of goldenrod comes into a room in which there is a spray of goldenrod in a vase. He is free from symptoms until he sees the plant, when he immediately is taken with a spell of sneezing; his nose runs and his eyes are red and watering. Now he is shown that the goldenrod is artificial and made of paper. Within a few minutes his symptoms subside and he is normal again.[14] His reaction is indisputably physiological and malingering is out of the question. How can his behavior be explained? It becomes no mystery when the concept of conditioning is applied. In the man's past experience, the sight of goldenrod has been associated with a response of vasomotor rhinitis, evoked originally by its pollen. Now, as in the case of other conditioned reactions, the response can be elicited by a substitute cue, even in the absence of the stimulus that was required to arouse it when the learning took place. As we have emphasized before (see pp. 75-77), learning processes can involve all the body's responses, even deeply unconscious physiological ones that are not ordinarily subject to voluntary control. The production of asthma, eczema, and other allergic reactions by emotional stress may well follow a similar pattern. An asthmatic attack is a very frightening experience to the patient who is gasping for his breath. After anxiety and asthma have been associated a few times, anxiety from some other source may reinstate the entire physiological response. Through this mechanism, an allergic reaction can be perpetuated as a response to chronic emotional distress, even in the absence of the protein agent that first caused it. Also significant is the observation that many allergic reactions are closely related to the physiological responses produced by emotion. The resemblance between asthma and the heavy breathing of anger has often been noted. The circulatory and glandular structures of the skin normally participate in emotion, as seen in the responses of flushing, paling, and perspiring. These reactions serve as links between psychological conflicts and allergic skin eruptions.

Although certain illnesses have been identified as the ones most profoundly influenced by psychosomatic considerations, modern medicine is coming to hold an even broader view of the relationships between psychological attitudes and bodily sicknesses. This wider conception regards "mind" and "body" as inseparable aspects of the whole functioning organism, and finds that all diseases are to some extent influenced by psychological factors. Even in such an indisputably germ-caused disease as tuberculosis, the attitude of the patient affects his likelihood of recovery. All physicians observe the value of a "fighting spirit," of the effective mobilization of positive motives and psychological resources in recovering from serious diseases and accidents, and conversely, the depressing effect of anxiety and hopelessness on patients who do not believe they can get well or even do not want to recover. The effect of disease on psychological attitudes is equally notable. Persons with dangerous or painful illnesses develop anxiety and pessimism that they readily displace to other situations, and that color all their interpersonal relationships and adjustments. The holistic concept in medicine avoids the "either-or error" of regarding some ailments as physiological and others as psychological. Instead, there is a continuum of disorders with respect to the dominance of physiological or psychological causes. At one end of this continuum lie the defense mechanisms, which are primarily psychological but not entirely uninfluenced by the person's state of health or illness. Mechanical injuries such as a broken leg would seem to be at the opposite pole, but experience shows that a patient's attitude may help to determine the speed and completeness of his recovery even from a fracture. The so-called psychosomatic disorders are in the middle of this continuum, since both organic and psychological factors are conspicuously significant in their origin and in their treatment.

The Treatment of Somatization Reactions

The somatization reactions are handled most successfully by combined medical and psychological treatment. Medical measures, of course, vary with the character of the disorder. Peptic ulcers are aided by appropriate medication and diet, and surgical intervention is usually necessary when the ulcer has perforated.

It is unfortunate that most physicians have only a physiological orientation to their tasks, and hence see psychosomatic disorders only in terms of medication, management of regimen, or surgery. They give advice and reassurance to patients but such measures are as ineffective for psychosomatic conditions as they are for psychoneuroses. If only medical aid is given, the patient's ulcers may clear up temporarily, but recur when he meets stress again.

Although psychotherapy is essential in their treatment, the somatization reactions, and also the more severe psychoneuroses, do not offer an appropriate field for the independent practice of psychologists, social workers, or other nonmedical counselors. First, they face the diagnostic problem of distinguishing the relative weights of the psychological and organic factors that have produced the disorder. Second, nonmedical workers cannot use the combination of physiological and psychological resources that provide the optimum treatment.

The best handling of psychosomatic illnesses is done by persons who have both medical and psychological skills. At present there are all too few physicians who are also qualified in psychological understandings and techniques, but the number is growing. There is a serious need for an increased recognition of the psychosomatic viewpoint in the curricula of medical schools, and for the preparation of a larger number of physicians who can use medical therapy and psychotherapy together. Another good resource for the treatment of psychosomatic disorders, and an economical one, is the clinical team. A team is a group of specialists each practicing his skill in coordination with the others. A physician takes responsibility for the patient's medical welfare, while a closely associated psychologist or social worker treats the psychological aspects of his life adjustment.

SO-CALLED "NERVOUS" CONDITIONS

"Nervousness"

No term descriptive of human behavior seems more widely and at the same time loosely used than the word "nervous." Properly, nervous means "pertaining to the structure or operation of the nervous system." In that sense, it is proper to say that general paresis (the most serious form of central-nervous-system syphilis) is a nervous disease, because it is one in which there is specific pathology of the neural structures.

Since the eighteenth century, however, an essentially incorrect use of the word "nervous" has been current, to designate an irritable, "jumpy," anxious, nonadjustive state. This application of the term is almost entirely a popular one; one looks in vain for any disorder called "nervousness" in textbooks of psychiatry. Even so, physicians and psychologists are guilty of contributing to the popular misconception, for they often use the term to describe a certain pattern of symptoms, and even more often as a convenient euphemism to put off a patient who demands to know the nature of his condition. A physician may tell an insistent patient that his nonadjustive reactions are "nervous," either because he does not know what else to say, or because by doing so he avoids a long discussion of the real nature of the problem. Since "nervous" is used in so many inexact senses, it cannot be said to have any precise meaning. In popular speech it is sometimes used to describe an organic disease of the nervous system, while sometimes it refers to a psychoneurosis. Most often, however, "nervousness" designates a certain aspect of nonadjustive reaction in which motor tension and its effects are the most prominent features.

The typical symptom of ordinary nervousness is a tendency to make varied and generalized *motor responses*. A nervous person cannot sit still, but twists, moves, and fidgets even when he is in a comfortable position, a relatively unboring situation, and free from definite external annoyances. Stereotyped motor acts, which are often called nervous habits, include persistent nail-biting, nose-picking, hand-rubbing, finger-drumming, and innumerable other useless muscular responses. A similar symptom is the nervous *tic,* a spasmodic contraction of some muscle group, most often seen as a twitching of some part of the face. While some tics can be caused by organic pathology of the nervous system, most of them are evidence of a diffused response to emotional tension. Tics that become worse when attention is paid to them are almost always of psychological origin. Another type of behavior commonly described as nervous is an excessive *readiness to react* to chance stimuli. Sharp noises elicit an unusually strong startled response. Persistent sounds, such as those of traffic or of domestic machinery, may be unbearably annoying. Slight dangers or grievances elicit unjustifiably intense emotional outbursts. "Nervous" symptoms seldom occur alone, but are combined with other evidences of unreduced anxiety. A nervous person is often described as irritable, which is another component of the too ready arousal of his emotional reactions upon slight provocation. Indecision, dread of the future, and other evidences of anxiety are usually present.

The pattern of nervousness just described has only one psychological meaning. It is a nonadjustive reaction to unsolved personal conflicts. The conflicts of a nervous person arouse persistent visceral tensions. Lacking any definite outlets, either in direct action or in defense mechanisms, he continues to be stirred up by his emotional tension, and hence to make diffused motor responses. His tense state also explains his irritability or excess of readiness to react. The persistent visceral and muscular tonus facilitates and intensifies responses to various other stimuli. In sum, nervous behavior is tense behavior, a manifestation of continued stimulation from intrabodily sources. Both petty, transient, nervousness and the more chronic varieties have the same underlying causes. A young man who is about to have an important conference with his employer is nervous as a result of a situational anxiety which subsides as soon as the event is past. Chronically nervous people are reacting tensely to a personal conflict of broader scope and longer duration. A habitual life pattern of nervousness may be established, so that all sorts of minor frustrations and conflicts reinstate the tension originally provoked by a more serious personal difficulty.

There is a very prevalent popular misconception of the cause of ordinary nervousness. Most people consider it a subtle organic complaint, ascribed to "weak nerves." A typical nervous person believes that his condition is due to a general weakness of the nervous system, entirely analogous to his conception of an "upset stomach" or a "weak heart." Such a notion is absurd, for the nervous system is not a muscular organ like the heart or the stomach. What is weak in a nervous person is not his "nerves," but his resources for dealing effectively with conflicts. The popular error concerning nervousness is reinforced by several apparently confirming observations that are true in fact, but which are misinterpreted. It has already been noted that organic disorders of the nervous system are called nervous diseases. Most of these are serious illnesses that no one would confuse with ordinary nervousness. Some of them, such as chorea (popularly, St. Vitus dance) result in tremors, tics, and muscular incoordination which have some slight resemblance to nervousness, but the similarity is superficial and confuses only grossly uninformed people. Another misleading observation is that certain glandular conditions, notably overactivity of the thyroid gland, cause a degree of excessive responsiveness which closely resembles common nervousness. A few so-called nervous persons are undoubtedly so because of glandular imbalances, but the great majority of cases are due to purely psychological reasons. It is also noted that nervousness accompanies many painful or dangerous chronic organic diseases, including arthritis, gallstones, heart disorders, and many others. In most such cases, however, the organic disease is not a direct factor in causing the nervousness, but an indirect one. A person suffering from such diseases is in pain, and also is understandably anxious about his future, especially if treatment is prolonged and the results uncertain. Therefore he reacts nonadjustively to his personal handicaps, and his anxiety is the source of his nervousness. This pattern of reaction is very common. In a pioneer survey of two hundred consecutive "nervous" cases in a small city, Hamilton diagnosed forty-six of them as suffering from "persistent nonadjustive affective reaction to baffling physical discomforts and disabilities," a group larger than any other in his study.[15] In such cases, curing the threatening physical disorder usually abolishes the nervousness also.

Another reason for the popular belief that nervousness is an organic disease is that it seems to be relieved by certain drugs. The medicines most often used are known as sedatives or depressants, and include the bromides, the barbiturates, and other drugs. The effect of a sedative is to reduce the body's level of functional activity. Its use to quiet restlessness is analogous to the use of an analgesic drug to relieve pain. Sedatives do not "cure" or "strengthen" the nerves, but only lull them into inaction. When properly prescribed by a physician, such drugs may have value. They relieve the severity of a person's nervous symptoms which are themselves a source of anxiety, convince him that he is improving, and sometimes help him to make a more rational attack on his problems. While drugs alone cannot cure anxiety, they may be an adjunct to psychotherapy. Some years ago, many patent medicines that claimed to be "nerve tonics" were on the market, containing harmful amounts of sedative drugs. They are now banned by federal and state regulations. The remaining patent medicines are generally innocuous preparations which either have no value at all, or else work only because of suggestion and reassurance.

While nervousness is mainly evidence of a nonadjustive reaction, it can have some secondary adjustive functions, just as do the hypochondriacal and fatigue states. A person's "nervousness" may be his excuse for his life failures, or his device for tyrannizing over his family. When the baffling problem that evokes nervousness is an external one, its removal will effect a cure. Changes in mode of living, in occupation, in marital status, in associates, all may be helpful if they take the nervous person away from the stimuli for his nonadjustive behavior. Overcoming chronic nervousness is not so easy a matter. The patient carries the stimulus for his anxiety around with him in the form of a generalized tendency to react emotionally to a wide variety of real or symbolized threats. General psychotherapeutic treatment is as likely to be helpful for nervousness as for any other derivative of anxiety.

"Nervous Breakdown"

Even more vague and variable than the category of nervousness is that of the so-called "nervous breakdown." This term has no exact meaning whatsoever. It is a popular catch-all, used to designate all sorts of nonintegrative conditions of a marked degree of severity. Sometimes a nervous breakdown means an acute organic illness. Sometimes the term is used as a euphemism for a major psychosis, because, due to traditional fears and prejudices, to have a nervous breakdown sounds more respectable than to be called insane. In other instances nervous breakdown is used to signify a psychoneurotic reaction of acute asthenia or nervousness. That is probably the most common meaning of the term. In still other cases, "broken-down" means no more than "fed-up," and implies an hysteria-like mechanism for escaping from an unpleasant situation.

In spite of its vague meaning, or perhaps because of it, nervous breakdown is a diagnosis frequently reported by physicians, and even more used by patients and their families, to describe some serious kind of adjustive difficulty. The frequency of use of the term, and also the variability of its application, are well illustrated by a mental hygiene survey of certain industries in Great Britain.[15] In five concerns investigated, the proportions of long sick-leaves ascribed to nervous breakdown were 36.9, 20.3, 10.6, 0, and 0 per cent, according to the companies' own records. It is inconceivable that a disorder accounting for more than a third of all long illnesses in one plant would be entirely absent in two others. The explanation of these perplexing data lies in the diagnostic habits of the physicians who did the classifying. Some tended to use the term; others did not. When a more objective survey was made of all the employees, 18.0 per cent of those in one plant which had no "nervous breakdowns" were found to have symptoms of nervousness, while 16.6 per cent of the workers in the factory reporting the highest percentage of "nervous breakdowns" were so affected; the difference between the two concerns was really negligible. These observations emphasize the meaninglessness of "nervous breakdown," for it does not stand for any specific or reliable datum in relation to mental health.

Nervous breakdowns and other more securely classified psychoneurotic reactions are very frequently ascribed to overwork. In almost every case in which a student drops out of school because of psychoneurosis, the assertion is made that "he studied too hard and fatigued his brain." This is a ninety-nine per cent falsehood. It is possible that in a very few cases overwork does have some indirect relevance to a psychological breakdown. If overwork causes loss of sleep, irregular eating habits, and lack of hygienic activity, a state of physical disability may be brought about, not by the overwork itself, but by the neglect of positive principles of living. In the overwhelming majority of cases, however, the cause and effect relationship is of a different character. When confronted with a real or imagined threat of failure in school, a student's first adjustive impulse may be to study diligently. In many instances this course of action is effective and the difficulty is removed. When study will not eradicate the fear of failure, the student may give up and lapse into a nonadjustive response of the anxiety or asthenic types which may popularly be called a nervous breakdown. Note that the overwork does not cause the breakdown. Instead, the excessive application to studies is an adjustive attempt; the so-called breakdown is a reaction to the failure to achieve an adjustment. The same pattern often appears in adults in their occupational situations. A person who is reacting strongly to a conflict may find that work is anxiety-reducing. A perplexed business man puts in long hours at his office, in response to his tense visceral state. His anxiety, of course, need not concern his vocation. It always has its roots in his total life history, and may be precipitated by any sort of present conflict. His absorption in his business is a distraction, or a technique for withdrawing from the focus of his difficulty. If he continues unable to adjust, a "breakdown" ensues which is not due to the overwork, but to the same factors that evoked the overwork. Of course, to believe that one's breakdown is due to overwork is highly respectable, since work is so well regarded by our culture, and the rationalization value of this belief helps to perpetuate the misconception. In general, it is not overwork but overanxiety that causes "breakdowns," as persistent nonadjustive reactions to conflicts.

Some Doubts About Labels

The wide use of such indefensible labels as "nervousness" and "nervous breakdown" may make us reconsider the usefulness of labels in general. Even the more widely accepted diagnostic categories, such as hysteria, obsessive-compulsive reaction, anxiety reaction, and the like, do not represent clear and mutually exclusive "types" of reaction to conflict, but only modalities of behavior. All normal people show every one of these responses in slight degree and from time to time. When an individual is severely disturbed, he usually shows a number of responses to his difficulties, even though one sort of reaction may be more prominent or more persistent than the others. The most important consideration is the person, and not his pattern of symptoms.

In any case of human perplexity the crucial questions are these: To what conflicts is the person adjusting inadequately? By what means is he making his partial or nonintegrative adjustments? What factors in his past learning have defined his conflicts for him, and led him to his present behavior? How can he be helped to achieve a better level of adjustment? If we can answer these questions, we can have a real understanding of a person and of his problems, without the need for classifications or diagnostic labels of any kind. You must regard the names and concepts of the mechanisms as necessities for teaching, designed to help you understand the phenomena they encompass. In clinical practice the problem of classification assumes a subordinate place. The troubled person is not considered as a type of case, but as a human being who can be understood in terms of his specific conflicts and adjustments.

SUGGESTED READINGS

Anxiety and the maladjustments which arise from it are considered in Chapters 7, 8, and 9 of Cameron, *The Psychology of Behavior Disorders;* Chapters 10 and 11 of Cameron and Magaret, *Behavior Pathology;* and in Chapter 7 of Landis and Bolles, *Textbook of Abnormal Psychology.* For illustrative cases, see Chapters 11, 13, 14, and 15 of Burton and Harris, *Case Histories in Clinical and Abnormal Psychology.* May, *The Meaning of Anxiety* is a well-written review of theories of anxiety.

Dunbar, *Mind and Body: Psychosomatic Medicine* is a relatively nontechnical and readable discussion of the psychological components in many forms of illness. Grinker and Robbins, *Psychosomatic Case Book* provides many illustrations that the interested student can study profitably. Alexander and French, *Studies in Psychosomatic Medicine* is more technical, and surveys comprehensively the various types of somatization reactions.

PART THREE

Personality

CHAPTER **11**

Personality
Measurement

A fundamental thesis of the psychology of adjustment is that behavior deviations are evoked by frustrations and conflicts. The nature and quality of a person's adjustments are therefore, in a sense, determined by the kinds of situations that life presents to him. If you could live in a hypothetical environment in which no stresses or conflicts could occur, you would inevitably be "well adjusted." Such a formulation, however, is only an incomplete account of the origins of integrative or nonintegrative adjustments. When confronted with equally baffling external situations, people show wide variations in their ability to adjust integratively. In wartime, for example, vast numbers of young men are subjected to the same situational conflicts, such as the conflict between their need for group approval and the guilts and fears that arise from military experiences. Most soldiers remain well adjusted, or develop relatively harmless defenses such as frivolous compensatory attitudes. A few become seriously disturbed. In civilian life in our culture, almost every person has conflicts between his aspirations and his achievements and yet is able to maintain at least a passable level of adjustment. These instances make it clear that the quality of one's adjustments cannot be ascribed solely to the presence or absence of conflicts, since most people can retain a good degree of integration in spite of adverse circumstances.

ADJUSTMENT AND PERSONALITY

The Concept of Predisposition

We can gain a more complete understanding of the origins of individual differences in adjustive behavior by distinguishing between *precipitating factors* and *predisposing factors.* The immediate situation that a person faces is the precipitating cause of his adjustive behavior. A conflict determines *when* a person has to adjust but plays a less crucial part in deciding *how* he will do it. The predisposing causes of a person's behavior lie farther back in his history. How he will adjust to his conflicts depends on what kind of a person he is when the stress occurs. People differ greatly in their tolerance of frustrations and conflicts, and in the types of adjustment mechanisms that they habitually employ. Such differences are variations in *personality.* The personality of an individual may be defined as his persistent tendencies to make certain qualities and kinds of adjustment.

The predisposing and precipitating sources of adjustments are by no means independent, but interact in complex ways. A certain intensity of stress will precipitate a nonintegrative adjustment on the part of a person who is unfavorably predisposed, while causing no disturbance in another person whose life history has been more fortunate. Of course, a predisposition to maladjustment is not an all-or-none affair. One man may be little disturbed by economic or vocational crises, but seriously upset by threats of disharmony within his family. Thus personality varies quantitatively with respect to various intensities of stress, and also qualitatively with respect to particular areas of adjustment.

Problems of Personality

The concept of personality does not lend itself to concise description, for it corresponds to no single or simple attribute of human life. Personality does not depend on one or a few characteristics only, but upon the interplay of practically all of an individual's qualities. Physical structure, chemical functioning, learned motives, and habits of adjustment all contribute to personality, and not as separate entities but as interacting aspects of an organized system.

In spite of this complexity, the problems of personality are those of individual differences. Personality depends upon individuality. If all people were alike in their adjustive tendencies, the problem of personality would hardly exist. In all fields in which individual differences are studied, two basic issues present themselves: *the description and measurement* of the qualities, and the discovery of their *sources or causes*. The principal problems of personality, therefore, are the measurement of its variations, and the investigation of its origins and development.

The differentiation and measurement of personality is not easy, since so many attributes of an individual are involved. For a few components of personality — "intelligence," for example — fairly satisfactory practical tests are available, but most personality characteristics cannot be measured on a single scale or expressed in numerical terms. The difficulties in the measurement of personality have caused this field to lag far behind many other areas of progress in psychology. Crude and unquantified descriptions based on interviews and general impressions still predominate, although more exact methods are gradually being evolved. A number of studies have attempted to identify the major dimensions of personality by which normal people differ from one another. Other investigations have sought to discover characteristics in which well adjusted people differ from maladjusted ones, or in which one variety of maladjustment differs from another. The two trends of research, the identification of the vectors of normal personality and the differentiation of varying qualities of general adjustment, overlap at many points and cannot be considered separately. The present chapter describes some of the problems, methods, and findings emerging from attempts to measure personality.

The second problem of personality, and the significant one, is that of tracing the origin and development of individual differences in adjustive tendencies. If techniques for personality measurement were more highly refined, they would lead inevitably to the solution of this second problem. We would need only to measure people as they develop, and ascertain the effects upon them of various formative influences. Unfortunately, only a small beginning has been made in this desirable direction. In spite of relatively crude methods, however, our understandings of personality development that are in accord with sound learning theory are of substantial value, and will not lead us far astray. The two chapters which follow trace the influences of structure and of learning, respectively, upon the formation of characteristics of personality.

PERSONALITY ''TYPES''

Doctrines of Types

Since the differentiation of personalities involves the identification of "what kind of a person" an individual is, a very natural tendency is to classify all mankind into various *types*. Our cultural traditions of language and thought tend to make us notice extremes and differences — we are much given to "either-or" thinking. Hence we are likely to regard people as either tall or short, bright or dull, and good or bad. That such qualities really exist in a continuous gradation from one extreme to the other, without any abrupt separation into classes, is often a difficult concept to grasp. An "either-or" concept is given up most easily when we have a precise and clearly understood method for quantitative measurement, as in the case of tallness. In the field of personality, where quantitative evaluation has been slow in developing, the habit of dividing people into types has been prevalent and persistent.

The classification of personality types was one of the earliest activities within the field of psychology. Theophrastus, a contemporary of Aristotle, wrote sketches of thirty types of personality still remarkable for their freshness and clarity. The most influential of the ancient concepts of personality types was that of the four temperaments, ascribed to Hippocrates (400 B.C.) and developed by other early writers. The *sanguine* temperament was described as active and quick but lacking in strength and permanence. The *choleric* was easily aroused and strong but irascible; the *melancholic* was slow and pessimistic; the *phlegmatic* was slow and also weak and stolid. The four temperaments were attributed to an excess of one or another of the bodily fluids or "humors," which were blood, yellow bile, black bile, and phlegm, respectively. Normal personality was believed to result from a balance of all of the humors, an interesting forecast of the concept of integration. During the Middle Ages and well into the modern period, the doctrine of the temperaments was accepted without question. Centuries of belief in the notion that personalities can be classified into distinct types have left enduring marks on cultural traditions. The ready acceptance which has greeted more recent attempts to define personality types is undoubtedly due in part to the persistence of ancient and medieval ways of thinking.

So many ways of classifying personality types have been proposed in recent times that it is impracticable to enumerate all of them. One to which reference is often made is William James's classification of the *rationalist* and the *empiricist*.[1] The rationalist or "tender-minded" person is guided by principles and abstract ideas, and tends to be idealistic and religious. An empiricist is a "tough-minded," practical person, influenced most by facts and expediency. These two types correspond closely to those of Jung, which will be described shortly.

Several type classifications have been based on the characteristic differences between persons who suffer from the two most common forms of mental disorder, schizophrenia and manic-depressive psychosis. The *autistic* or *schizoid* type of person is described as shy, uncommunicative, given to fantasy, having few external interests, and not mixing well with people. The *cyclothymic* or *cycloid* personality, in contrast, is outgoing, talkative, overemotional, and given to unstable fluctuations of mood. It is at least true that patients who develop these two psychoses often have a history of such behavior in their earlier lives, and that similar qualities of personality can be seen in a lesser degree in many normal people.

Jung's Types

No classification of types has aroused more interest, research, and controversy than the one proposed by Carl G. Jung.[2] His best known distinction is between the "general attitude types" of *extravert* and *introvert*. Briefly stated, an extravert is one who is dominated by external and social values, while an introvert takes a subjective view and is governed by the relationship of things to himself. The characteristic differences between the two types, as described by Jung, are shown in Table 3. The enumeration represents the extravert as the man of action and the introvert as the man of deliberation, a conception that has had wide influence on psychological discussions of personality.

Jung's own complete picture of personality types is not quite so simple, and the usual condensations are perhaps somewhat unjust to his entire theory. In addition to the general attitude types so far

Table 3
Characteristics of Jung's Personality Types

Extravert	Introvert
1. Directly oriented by objective data	1. Subjective determinants are the more decisive ones
2. Conduct governed by necessity and expediency	2. Conduct governed by absolute standards and principles
3. Accommodates readily to new situations	3. Lacks flexibility and adaptability
4. Is negligent of ailments, not taking care of self	4. Is overattentive to ailments and careful of self
5. Adjustments are compensatory	5. Adjustments are made by escape and fantasy
6. Typical psychoneurosis is hysteria	6. Typical psychoneurosis is anxiety or obsession-compulsion state.

described, Jung also distinguishes four special "function-types" based on his analysis of the chief varieties of human expression. These are stated as *thinking, feeling, sensation* and *intuition*. According to Jung, one or another of these four processes is especially differentiated or well developed in a given individual and hence plays a dominant role in his adaptation or orientation to life. Since the extravert-introvert classification overlaps the four special types, eight principal classes of personality are indicated. The "extraverted thinking type" is concerned with facts and their classification, the "introverted thinker" with theories and with their application to himself. The "extraverted feeling type" wishes to be in harmony with the outside world and is able to achieve close sympathy with others, while the "introverted feeling type" is chiefly concerned with his internal harmony and tends to depreciate the influence of outer factors. The "sensation" types, principally influenced by pure pleasure and pain, and the "intuitive" types, dominated by indirect judgments or "hunches," are also either extraverted or introverted. This doctrine is further complicated by Jung's assertion that more than one of the four main functions may be important, and that an individual may be extraverted in one function but introverted in another. Also, if the "conscious" is extraverted in any one line, the "unconscious" attitude is introverted and *vice versa*. Jung's complete theory counteracts the excessive simplicity of the primary extravert-introvert classification, but does so by plunging into complications bordering on obscurity.

Jung, like most of the strong proponents of definite types, considers all persons to belong definitely to one or another class, and assumes these differences to be inborn. He states that they can be modified, as when a natural-born introvert is forced by circumstances into extraversion, but believes that such transformations are superficial and that an abrupt change is likely to result in a psychoneurotic condition.

An Evaluation of Concepts of Type

A major fault of all theories of personality types is the assumption, directly asserted or implied, that every person fits exactly into one of a limited series of classes. Such a rigid classification is not in keeping with some widely observed facts. It is obvious that all persons are not either tall or short; most of them lie between. Height varies continuously from one extreme to the other. The concept of a continuum, rather than of separate types, should also apply to "good" and "bad," and to the manifestations of personality. In Figure 25, I represents the extreme stand of those who uphold a doctrine of types. Diagram II depicts an inadequate compromise which is often suggested, such as the existence of a mixed class of "ambiverts," intermediate between the introverts and the extraverts. Although II represents a nearer approach to a correct observation than does I, it is still only a crude approximation. By analogy from exactly measured traits such as height, and from some measurements of personality to be described shortly, it becomes evident that the variations of an aspect of personality are more nearly like diagram III. Most of the important characteristics of personality vary in *degree* rather than in kind. The bulk of people possess a personal quality in an intermediate degree, and gradually decreasing numbers of them tend toward the extreme in either direction.

Another valid criticism of a type theory is that it leads to a partial and one-sided view of personalities. Even if some people are at an extreme with respect to a characteristic, according to the conception conveyed by diagram III of the last figure, to designate them as "introverts," "schizoids," "rationalists," or what not, tends to hide the other important differences which may exist among them. An "introvert" may be bright or stupid, ambitious or lazy,

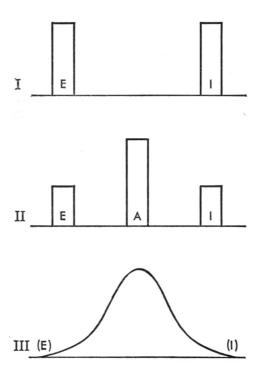

Figure 25. Concepts of Personality Types and Traits

Part I of the figure shows an incorrect conception that all people are of one type or another, as introverts or extroverts. Diagram II is an inadequate compromise which places a class of "ambiverts" between. The best conception is shown in III, which is a continuous distribution with no gaps. Most people lie near the center with smaller numbers toward both extremes.

altruistic or self-seeking, hence merely to label him an "introvert" without consideration of his other characteristics conceals significant facts and hinders a real understanding of him.

The only justification that can be found for a doctrine of types lies in its application to a small minority of persons who have acquired fixed habits of adjusting by one or another of the major mechanisms. If some aspect of such an individual's personality has become so extreme as to be conspicuous to all observers, and so important to him that it prepotently influences all of his adjustments, then there is some excuse for describing him as belonging to a certain "type." In keeping with this suggestion, the compensating, rationalizing, projecting, escapist, phobic, hysterical, and anxious types might possibly be defined. Great care must be taken, however, to avoid confusing cause with effect. If a man persistently withdraws from many situations that demand adjustment, it is not because he "belongs" to an introverted or withdrawing type, but because his past learning has reinforced that kind of response. A person's "type" may therefore have some little value for describing him, but it does not explain his behavior.

PERSONALITY TRAITS

Dimensions of Personality

The critical appraisal of type theories has led to one valuable result: a recognition that personality is multidimensional. No single variable can do justice to the complexity of personality, for it needs to be described in terms of its many aspects or components. One approach to the comprehensive description of personality uses the concept of traits. A trait is a dimension or aspect of personality, consisting of a group of consistent and related reactions that characterize a person's typical adjustments.

Everyone agrees that personality has many traits, but there are differences of opinion as to the number that have to be cited in order to describe a person thoroughly. One study found that nearly 18,000 words in the English language refer to personal qualities or conduct.[3] Many of these words define common attributes which can be found in some degree in almost all people, such as "active," "affectionate," "aggressive," and "alert." Other terms designate rarer styles of conduct — "alarmist," "anarchistic," "atavistic," and the like — which can be used to describe only a few people. Do all these thousands of words define personality traits? We can probably get along with a decidedly smaller number. One important requirement of a trait is its consistency. If a person consistently shows a certain level of activity in comparison to other people, which is characteristic of his own individuality and not primarily dependent on the external situation, then he possesses a trait on the activity-inactivity continuum. In contrast, if his degree of activity fluctuates unpredictably or if it is determined mainly by external circumstances, the person may not have that trait at all. A trait, therefore, may be shown by some people and not by others. *Common traits* are qualities that can be found in most people in some degree from high to low. Since common traits can be studied statistically, they are most applicable to the task of describing general differences among people.

We must not lose sight of the individual person, however. Only a few people can be rated as to the extent to which they are "alarmist," or "chauvinistic," or "quixotic," but when such an *individual trait* is prominent, it may be the most important feature of a person's character. Individual traits are hard to study statistically, but they are highly significant in informal descriptions of specific personalities.

The Organization of Traits

The description of personality would be an endless task if we had to cite every one of the hundreds of traits that may exist. Psychologists have therefore sought more economical methods that will give a good approximation. One fruitful approach is to look for groups or clusters of traits that ordinarily vary together. For example, clinical and statistical evidence shows that people who are dominant in their relationships with others tend also to be assertive, egotistic, tough, vindictive, and hardhearted.[4] The opposites of these qualities also tend to occur together. Some years ago, the grouping of personality characteristics in order to reduce them to a practicable number was done subjectively, on the bases of clinical observation, general experience, and logical reasoning. The resulting speculative lists of personality traits were generally unsatisfactory. Some lists were long and repetitious, others were short and incomplete, and no two were in agreement.

More recently, experimental and statistical methods have been used to discover the patterns of traits that tend to cluster together. The most refined statistical technique used for this purpose is *factor analysis*. In its mathematical theory and in the computations required, factor analysis is very complicated, but its results can be understood in fairly simple terms. Factor analysis depends on the more elementary statistical concept of correlation. If two traits — dominance and egotism, for example — vary together so that most people have about the same degree of one as of the other, they are said to be positively correlated. The extent to which they are associated can be expressed quantitatively as a coefficient of correlation. Now if several traits are studied, it may be found that traits *A, B, C,* and *D* are all significantly correlated with one another, while three other traits, *E, F,* and *G,* are not correlated appreciably with any of the first four. The four intercorrelated traits have something in common. Some broader or more basic factor underlies *A, B, C,* and *D,* but this factor is not present in *E, F,* and *G.* Factor analysis determines how many factors are needed to account for all of the relationships found among a number of traits. The nature of each factor can be identified by examining the traits in which it appears.

The application of factor analysis to the study of personality is illustrated by an investigation carried out by R. B. Cattell.[5] He started with a list of 4,000 trait names, which was reduced to 171 by eliminating overlapping and rare qualities. A preliminary correlation study further reduced the list to 35 clusters of traits, represented by pairs of opposed qualities such as "sociable-seclusive." Each of 208 adult men was then rated on every trait. The correlations among the traits were computed, and the underlying factors were determined. Similar methods of statistical analysis were applied to data drawn from personality questionnaires, from clinical case studies, and from objective tests. Twelve factors or "primary traits" were discovered, which are summarized in Table 4. The table identifies each trait by a pair of terms which indicate the extremes of a scale of measurement. Each trait is accompanied by several descriptive words that illustrate it.

Sophisticated experimental and statistical methods have made notable contributions to our knowledge of personality. There are, however, two dangers in a purely statistical approach. A piecemeal analysis of personality may fail to reveal its integration, and may hide the interaction that each trait has with each other. A man who is "dominant" and "friendly" is a very differently organized person than one who is "dominant" and "hostile." Another shortcoming is that statistical studies can deal only with common traits, and may miss the rare or individual traits so crucial in some particular cases. Even so, such dangers will not be overcome by a return to speculative and subjective methods, but by increasingly subtle and refined techniques for objective research.

Table 4
Cattell's Formulation of Primary Traits of Personality*

I. Cyclothymia	**vs.**	**Schizothymia**
Outgoing		Withdrawn
Good-natured		Embittered
Adaptable		Inflexible
II. Intelligence	**vs.**	**Mental Defect**
Intelligent		Stupid
Painstaking		Slipshod
Deliberate		Impulsive
III. Emotionally mature	**vs.**	**Demoralized**
Realistic		Evasive
Stable		Changeable
Calm		Excitable
IV. Dominance	**vs.**	**Submissiveness**
Assertive		Modest
Headstrong		Gentle
Tough		Introspective
V. Surgency	**vs.**	**Melancholy**
Cheerful		Unhappy
Placid		Worrying
Sociable		Aloof
VI. Sensitive	**vs.**	**Tough Poise**
Idealistic		Cynical
Imaginative		Habit-bound
Grateful		Thankless
VII. Trained, Socialized	**vs.**	**Boorish**
Thoughtful		Unreflective
Sophisticated		Simple
Conscientious		Indolent
VIII. Positive Integration	**vs.**	**Immature, Dependent**
Mature		Irresponsible
Persevering		Quitting
Loyal		Fickle
IX. Charitable, Adventurous	**vs.**	**Obstructive, Withdrawn**
Cooperative		Obstructive
Genial		Cold-hearted
Frank		Secretive
X. Neurasthenia	**vs.**	**Vigorous Character**
Incoherent		Strong-willed
Meek		Assertive
Unrealistic		Practical

* Each trait is defined by a pair of opposed qualities, with descriptive words to clarify the meaning. (After R. B. Cattell, *Description and measurement of personality.* Yonkers, N. Y.: World Book Co., 1946. Pp. 313-316, 475-497.)

Cattell's Formulation of Primary Traits of Personality * (continued)

XI. Hypersensitive	vs.	Frustration Tolerance
Demanding		Adjusting
Restless		Calm
Self-pitying		Self-effacing

XII. Surgent Cyclothymia	vs.	Paranoia
Enthusiastic		Frustrated
Friendly		Hostile
Trustful		Suspicious

APPROACHES TO MEASUREMENT

From early times, the traits of human personality have been esti- mated by three principal methods: by *observing* an individual's conduct, by *asking others* their opinions about him, and by *questioning him* about his present behavior and his past experiences. A fourth method has also been used intuitively for many years, although it has not been recognized explicitly until clarified by recent psychological research: that of finding how the person *perceives others.* The informal use of this fourth method is illus- trated by an employment interviewer asking an applicant how his previous bosses treated him; the interviewer is not interested in "the facts," but in what the answer may reveal about the man's own character. These four very sensible methods have not been displaced in the course of the development of modern psychology, but have only been elaborated and refined.

Progress in the measurement of personality has come about mainly through the improvement of *control* and through the *quan- titative treatment* of results. Casual and uncontrolled observations do not permit an accurate comparison of one person with another because the situations in which various people are studied are not uniform. Control means the restriction of the situation and of the conditions in which the observations are made so that the results are not unduly influenced by irrelevant circumstances. The situa- tions presented to people are uniform, and their responses are recorded and interpreted consistently. Quantitative methods allow traits to be represented numerically, which is an aid both to in- dividual diagnosis and to research. They help to measure one person more precisely, and to determine the relationships that exist among traits.

When the refinements of control and of quantitative treatment are applied to the common-sense method of questioning people, the result is the *personality questionnaire*. Although questionnaires have serious limitations they have been used widely for evaluation and research. The systematic improvement of the old method of asking others about a person has yielded the *rating scale*. The refinement of the method of observing a person as he performs a task has developed chiefly as the *test*. Relatively new among techniques for personality appraisal is the study of how an individual perceives the world, for the sake of what it reveals about him as a person. This subtle method is called the *projective technique*. These four methods, whose description will occupy the rest of this chapter, are not wholly new creations of modern science, but are inevitable developments from procedures long used by all men in their everyday affairs. Perfection is not claimed for them, but they are markedly more effective than the crude beginnings from which they evolved.

QUESTIONNAIRES

One very natural method for studying a person is to ask him questions about his beliefs, his present behavior, and his past experiences. The informal face-to-face interview is a fundamental method for the appraisal and treatment of a maladjusted person, and will continue to be used in intensive work with individuals. Freedom and flexibility are regarded as essential qualities in a clinical interview. Today's best practice avoids the use of probing questions, and finds that the most valid results are obtained by letting a person tell his own story under conditions that enable him to reveal himself most fully. In a later chapter on the clinical study of individuals you will find a further discussion of that kind of interviewing.

For many survey and research purposes it is necessary to sacrifice the freedom of the interview for the sake of a better control of the questions asked and of the range of answers that may be given. A standard series of questions can be asked orally, but it is often more economical to print such questions in a booklet. A standard form has certain advantages, too. The same questions are asked of many persons, and a permanent record of their responses is preserved for future analysis. A printed series of relevant questions, each answered by marking one of a limited number of responses, often only "yes" or "no," is a personality questionnaire.

Screening Questionnaires

Personality questionnaires have been used extensively for "screening," that is, for rapidly and approximately identifying persons who are in need of more thorough psychological study, or who might be poor risks for exposure to exceptionally stressful conditions such as wartime military service. The first screening questionnaire was the Psychoneurotic Inventory constructed by R. S. Woodworth in 1918.[6] In World War I, a need was felt for an instrument that would classify men according to their stability of personal adjustment, analogous to the Army mental tests which classified them according to their intellectual abilities. Woodworth and his collaborators made a list of 200 symptoms of maladjustment drawn from case studies. The symptoms were cast in the form of yes-no questions, and were tried with college students to discover questions that were so often answered in the unfavorable direction as to be of doubtful value as indicators of maladjustment. The remaining 116 items have served as a model for many subsequent questionnaires. Some of the common types of items, with illustrations, were:

> Somatic complaints: "Do you ever feel an awful pressure in or about the head?"
> Social adjustment: "Do you make friends easily?"
> Fears and worries: "Does it make you uneasy to cross a wide street or open square?"
> Fatigue and sleep disturbance: "Do you feel tired most of the time?"
> Obsessive ideas: "Do you feel like jumping off when you are on high places?"
> Personal history: "Did you have a happy childhood?"

The score on the questionnaire was the number of questions answered in the obviously unfavorable direction. Subsequent research showed that the Woodworth inventory has some discriminative value. A diagnosed group of psychoneurotics gave an average of

36 unfavorable answers, while the average score of normal men was only 10.

Early questionnaires such as Woodworth's rested on an *a priori* assumption of validity, that the inherent content of the items justified the meaning of the scores. More recently, statistical methods have been used to select questions that have known predictive values. Questionnaires whose items are pre-selected experimentally are known as *validated* questionnaires. In general, they are more trustworthy than the subjectively compiled lists. The process of item validation is carried out by giving a preliminary version of the inventory to groups that have been differentiated according to some independent criterion. For example, a screening test may be administered to normal men and to diagnosed psychoneurotics. Questions that discriminate successfully between the groups are retained, and the unsatisfactory ones are dropped. One good item in a questionnaire used in World War II was answered unfavorably by 61 per cent of a group of combat veterans suffering from anxiety reaction, and by only 15 per cent of soldiers who had also been through combat but who showed no emotional disturbance.[7] Combining a number of such single items yields a questionnaire whose total score has greater value than any one question alone. A set of pre-selected items is more economical to administer because of its brevity, and is also more valid as a whole. To a layman, a personality questionnaire often looks like a hodgepodge of unrelated questions, but much research has gone into its construction, and its value is known before it is put to practical use.

In World War II several screening questionnaires were used which had a moderate but useful over-all validity. An example is the Cornell Index, which was used mainly at induction stations.[8] On that blank, a "cut-off score" of 23 or more unfavorable answers identified 50 per cent of men subsequently rejected for service on psychiatric grounds, and misidentified as unstable only 4 per cent of acceptable men. A lower cut-off score of 13 points screened 74 per cent of the neurotics, but caught 13 per cent of normal men in the net. No questionnaire was effective enough to be used as a sole measure of personal adjustment, but they were economical and valuable adjuncts to the process of selection.

Questionnaires that follow the early tradition are so obvious in their content that most people recognize immediately which answers are "good" and which are symptomatic. Considerable research has been devoted to improving the value of questionnaires by making them more subtle. One technique, introduced in Shipley's Personal Inventory, is the forced-choice form, in which the examinee is made to choose one of two alternatives, neither of which is flattering to him, but only one of which is really symptomatic of maladjustment.[9] Items were of this type:

I often have a feeling that things are not real.
I often have trouble making up my mind.

Both choices may seem equally "bad" to a naive person, but the first statement is symptomatic while the second is not.

An even more subtle method was developed by Wallen in his Food Aversion Test.[10] This questionnaire is a list of twenty common foods, and the examinee indicates the foods he dislikes so much that he refuses to eat them. The task does not obviously reveal that it is a test of adjustment, but investigation shows that it is almost as good a screening device as some of the longer questionnaires. On one form of the Food Aversion Test, two or more foods were disliked by 62 per cent of a group of psychoneurotics, and by only 11 per cent of a group of normal men. Incidentally, the test gives us an interesting bit of information about neurotic persons — they dislike things generally.

Diagnostic Questionnaires

Screening tests are "blunderbuss" instruments intended to detect maladjustment in general. Other questionnaires have been devised with the intention of measuring more specific aspects of personality. Soon after Jung described his extravert and introvert types, several introversion-extraversion inventories were published. In the main, they were based on a theoretical analysis of introvert and extravert qualities, and were not validated against any independent behavioral criterion. These questionnaires were not very successful and are little used today. At least, they showed that people do not fall into types, but vary continuously from one extreme to another. Later research has shown that introversion-extraversion is a composite of several fairly distinct traits.

One older questionnaire that has held up well with the passage of time is Allport's Ascendance-Submission Reaction Study,[11] which measures the tendency to dominate one's fellows in face-to-face relationships or to be dominated by them. The questions are stated in multiple-choice form, and the examinee checks his most typical response to each described situation. A representative item is:

Have you haggled over prices with tradesmen or junk men?

    Frequently _____

    Occasionally _____

    Never _____

The A-S Reaction Study was validated against an independent criterion. Each of a group of students that took a preliminary form of the blank was rated on his ascendance-submission qualities, by himself and by four classmates who knew him well. The average rating was taken as the criterion of a man's status with respect to this trait. The scoring key for the questionnaire was then prepared by giving positive numerical values to the answers given by students judged to be ascendant, and negative weights to the answers most often marked by the submissive ones. The use of the criterion relieved the author from dependence on his own subjective opinion, and probably made the questionnaire a more valuable instrument.

One way to validate a personality questionnaire is to compare the responses of persons suffering from one type of maladjustment with those of people who have other disorders or who are normal. For example, if patients with conversion hysteria tend to respond "yes" to the statement "I feel weak all over much of the time," while both normal persons and persons with other forms of psychological deviation tend to respond "no," then that item is symptomatic of conversion hysteria. A questionnaire constructed by this method is the Minnesota Multiphasic Personality Inventory — the MMPI, for short.[12] The MMPI consists of 550 statements, each printed on a card, to which the examinee responds by indicating whether each item is true or not true for him. By comparing the responses of people with psychiatric diagnoses to those of normal people, keys have been constructed to measure Hypochondriasis (abnormal concern about bodily functions), Depression, Hysteria, Psychopathic Deviate (disregard for social standards of conduct), Paranoia (suspiciousness and delusions), Psychasthenia (phobias and compulsions), Schizophrenia, and Hypomania (elevated level of activity). There is also a Masculinity-Femininity scale, made up of items that

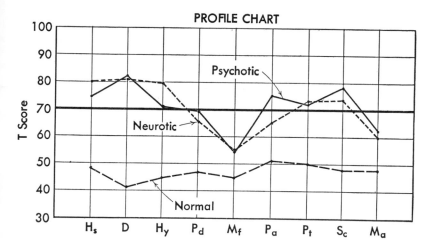

Figure 26. Psychotic, Neurotic and Normal Profiles on the Minnesota Multiphasic Personality Inventory

The symbols below the graph indicate the nine scales of the MMPI: **Hs**, hypochondriasis; **D**, depression; **Hy**, hysteria; **Pd**, psychopathic deviate; **Mf**, masculinity-femininity; **Pa**, paranoia; **Pt**, psychasthenia; **Sc**, schizophrenia; and **Ma**, hypomania. The normal score on each scale is 50, and 70 is regarded as clearly abnormal. The lowest line is the average profile of 98 normal soldiers. The middle broken line represents 26 soldiers with mild psychoneurosis (note typically elevated **Hs**, **D**, and **Hy**). The upper profile is of 13 cases of psychosis (note high **D**, **Pa**, and **Sc**). (After H. O. Schmidt, Test profiles as a diagnostic aid: The Minnesota Multiphasic Inventory. *J. appl. Psychol.*, 1945, *29*, 115-131.)

men and women answer differently. A profile (Fig. 26) is constructed to show a person's standing on each of the scales. The keys of the MMPI do not measure traits in the usual sense, but pertain to qualities that clinical workers can identify readily because they refer to common patterns of behavior disorder. Both experience and research show that the MMPI is an aid to the differentiation of disturbances of personality. There are differences of opinion concerning the fineness of the diagnoses that the MMPI can make. Some workers have used the profiles to obtain a detailed description of personality,[13] while others have found that the MMPI discriminates only between psychotic, neurotic, and normal groups, without making finer distinctions.[14]

The MMPI is a pool of 550 items which tap almost all features of human adjustment that can be assessed by the questionnaire method. Therefore, it has lent itself readily to the derivation of additional scales by experimental methods. Keys have been constructed to score the MMPI for personality traits such as social introversion, prejudice, and dominance.[15] Other special scales have been shown to correlate with the examinee's degree of manifest anxiety,[16] with a student's academic achievement in high school,[17] and with the likelihood of a client's success in psychotherapy.[18] Among existing questionnaires, the Minnesota seems to offer the greatest potentialities for clinical use.

Factor Analysis in Questionnaire Construction

Factor analysis has been applied to the construction of personality questionnaires. The method is to compile a large number of items representative of many areas of personality, to administer these items to a substantial number of people, and then to study statistically the relationships among all of the item responses. Questions are found to fall into clusters, so that the items within each cluster correlate with one another, but are relatively independent of those making up the other clusters.

In one of the earlier applications of factor analysis to personality measurement, Guilford demonstrated that "introversion-extraversion" is not a trait.[19] By a factor analysis of a large number of questions originally intended to measure introversion-extraversion, he found five separate traits which were not highly related to one another. They were identified as social introversion (shyness), thinking introversion (thoughtfulness), depression, moodiness, and restraint. The results of this study place additional limitations on the use of the concept "introvert." It is necessary to specify the area of introversion; a person who is shy is not necessarily also thoughtful or depressed.

Some questionnaires based on factor analysis have attempted to measure all of the major components of personality. The Guilford-Zimmerman Temperament Survey appraises ten traits, selected as well identified by factorial studies and useful for guidance and clinical practice.[20] Many of the ten factors are comparable to those found by Cattell. The traits are: general activity, restraint, ascend-- ance, sociability, emotional stability, objectivity, friendliness, thoughtfulness, personal relations, and masculinity. The traits iden- tified by the factor analysis studies have normal connotations be- cause they spring from a search for the dimensions of personality along which normal people vary, rather than from comparing nor- mal men with maladjusted ones. The factor analysis method emphasizes the value of discovering the existence of traits experi- mentally, and then naming them according to their nature and content. This method is the opposite of the old speculative approach which started with a dogmatic definition of a trait and then tried to find situations to illustrate it.

Limitations of Questionnaires

A serious limitation of personality questionnaires is that they depend in a considerable degree on the good will of the persons examined, and to some extent on their insight into their own be- havior. This shortcoming is mitigated to some extent by the experi- mental procedures used to validate the better inventories. Two kinds of inferences can be drawn from answers to questions. If we ask a man his age, we make a direct inference that his answer is a true one. On the other hand, if we ask, "Are you the victim of a nation-wide plot of persecution?" a reply of "yes" usually would lead to a conclusion that the man is suffering from a delusion rather than that he is really persecuted. Such indirect inferences are basic to the value of many techniques for personal appraisal. Further- more, experimental methods of validation relieve somewhat the dependence on logical truthfulness. Conclusions are based on dem- onstrated findings, such as that hypochondriacs do say, "I often feel just miserable," rather than on the subjective assumption that they should say so.

The situation in which a questionnaire is administered has much to do with its validity. Screening techniques proved to be sur- prisingly effective in the military service in World War II for detecting men with psychiatric disqualifications.[21] One analysis of the reason for this validity has pointed out that well-adjusted men generally wanted to give favorable pictures of themselves so as to get into the service, while maladjusted ones generally wanted to be released. The men's motivation and their real mental health were therefore pulling together; the healthy men concealed their faults, and the unstable men exaggerated theirs. As a result, the validity of the questionnaires was inflated. It is true that questionnaires have not been as successful for screening students, or applicants for employment in industry, as they were in the military situation.

When a person comes to a clinic seeking help, he ordinarily is in a frame of mind to disclose his troubles. It is therefore relatively easy to elicit his full cooperation in answering a questionnaire. In fact, his attitude may be so self-depreciative that he tends to give responses unfavorable to himself and to yield a profile that looks even more maladjusted than he really is.

Several of the most fully developed inventories have special devices to detect people who are not able to respond candidly. The MMPI, and some other scales contain items of this type, "Have you ever been late for an appointment?" Almost every reasonably truthful person would have to say "yes," but one who has an over-intense need to defend himself and not reveal any weaknesses will answer "no." Too high a score on such items indicates that the other ratings on the questionnaire are probably invalid. There are other methods for detecting people who are too self-defensive or, on the other hand, too self-critical. Research studies show that it is easy to detect a malingered questionnaire on which a normal person has tried to fake maladjustment.[22] On the other hand, in spite of the precautions used, many maladjusted persons can fake normality successfully, often with no baser motivation than the quite normal urge to keep one's faults to oneself.

RATING METHODS

The rating of personality is a systematization of the method of "asking others" about a person's traits. Many varieties of rating have been used, among which *rating scales* and *sociometric methods* are distinct and significant enough to warrant describing them briefly.

Rating Scales

A rating scale is a device for expressing one's observations or opinions about a person in a uniform manner. Ratings may be

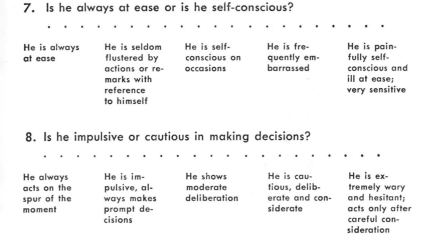

7. Is he always at ease or is he self-conscious?

| He is always at ease | He is seldom flustered by actions or remarks with reference to himself | He is self-conscious on occasions | He is frequently embarrassed | He is painfully self-conscious and ill at ease; very sensitive |

8. Is he impulsive or cautious in making decisions?

| He always acts on the spur of the moment | He is impulsive, always makes prompt decisions | He shows moderate deliberation | He is cautious, deliberate and considerate | He is extremely wary and hesitant; acts only after careful consideration |

Figure 27. Rating Scale Items

The rater checks above the statement most descriptive of the person rated, or between descriptions if appropriate. Each rating is turned into a numerical value by dividing the rating line into nine equal parts, corresponding to the spaces above and between the statements. (Adapted from the Carnegie Institute of Technology Rating Scale.)

made by teachers or other supervisors, or by peers such as classmates or fellow employees. There are also "self-rating" scales, but these are merely questionnaires in multiple-choice form. Two items from a graphic type of rating scale are shown in Figure 27. The scale is used by placing a check mark above the most descriptive answer, or between alternatives if the rater believes that the subject's best description is between the steps given. The rating is quantified by giving each step a numerical value, as from 1 to 5, or by measuring the distance of the check mark from one end of the line.

Since a rating scale is not really a measuring device, but only a method for communicating and recording opinions, it is obvious that it can be no better than the observations on which it is based.

Teachers can rate the "scholarship" of their pupils more reliably[*] than their "persistence" or "impulsiveness," probably because they have more definite observations on which to base judgments in the case of the first trait.[23] Studies in the military service showed that a man's leadership can be rated more validly by his fellow-soldiers (so-called "buddy ratings") than by his superior officers, again because of more opportunities for extensive and realistic observation.[24] In almost all situations, single ratings have been found seriously lacking in reliability. The remedy for this defect is to combine the scores of several raters; the average of about eight qualified raters gives a reliability equal to that of a satisfactory test. Another shortcoming of rating methods is the "halo effect," a tendency to rate a man high on all traits or low on all traits because of a general impression of his degree of merit. "Halo" can be overcome in part by rating all of a group of people on one trait, then all of them on another trait, and so forth, in order to minimize the influence of one rating on another.

Sociometric Methods

With the increasing recognition of the importance of social factors in personal adjustment, techniques have been used to study the social structures of groups and the place of an individual in his group. A *sociogram* (Fig. 28) is a graphic representation of the relations that exist among members of a group. Although it is most applicable to problems of social psychology, a sociogram also tells much about individual adjustments. To construct a sociogram, the first step is to obtain each person's choices of others within the group with whom he would prefer to have some defined relation-

---

[*] The term *reliability* has a technical meaning with respect to tests, ratings, and the like. The reliability of a measure is its degree of consistency or reproducibility. It can be measured by giving the test on two occasions, by giving two forms of the test, or by comparing the score on one half of the test with the score on the other half when the test can be separated into two suitable halves. The reliability of a rating generally means the goodness of its agreement with that made by another rater. Reliability is expressed by a coefficient of correlation, which varies from .00 for no agreement to 1.00 for perfect agreement. That a measure is reliable or consistent does not necessarily mean that it is true, or good for the intended purpose. The *validity* of a measure, which was discussed informally in connection with questionnaires, is its trueness, or its value for predicting some intended outcome. The validity of a measure can often be expressed by a coefficient of correlation between the test and an independent criterion.

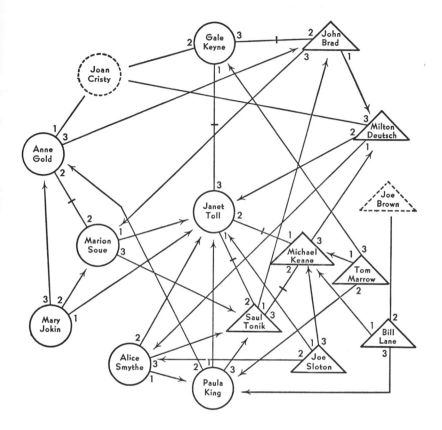

Figure 28. A Sociogram of a School Class

In the figure, the girls are represented by circles, the boys by triangles. Absent members of the group, who were chosen but who had no opportunity to choose, are shown in broken-line symbols. An arrow indicates a one-way choice, and a line between two symbols a mutual choice. Typical social structures include a "star" (Janet Toll), an "isolate" (Mary Jokin), and a "triangle" (Janet, Michael, and Saul). (Helen H. Jennings, *Sociometry in group relations.* Washington: American Council on Education, 1948.)

ship.[25] In a school class accustomed to work on joint projects, each child might write his first, second, and third choice of another child to serve with him on a committee. The choices are tabulated and then represented on the graph. In Figure 28, Janet Toll is a "star," a child often chosen by the others. Janet, Michael, and Saul are a "triangle" of interlocking mutual choices. An "isolate," illustrated by Mary Jokin, is a person not chosen by anyone. One can see clearly that this group presents quite different problems and opportunities of adjustment for Janet than for Mary. The sociometric method can be used to study adults as well as children if the group members are well enough acquainted.

PROJECTIVE TECHNIQUES

People reveal their personalities by the ways in which they perceive their environments. An anxious person sees threats when none exist; a suspicious man perceives hostility when none is intended. Methods of personal appraisal that make use of perceptual responses are called *projective techniques,* the name implying that they involve the mechanism of projection.[26] In projection (p. 179), a person sees his own unacknowledged motives and traits in other people. In a projective personality test, the examinee organizes his response to neutral or ambiguous stimuli in accordance with his own characteristics.

The Rorschach

In 1921, Hermann Rorschach, a Swiss psychiatrist, introduced a projective method destined to become the most widely used instrument of its kind, and also to arouse an unprecedented amount of controversy.[27] The material consists of ten inkblot figures on cards, of which five are in black and grays, two are black, gray, and red, and three are entirely in colors (Fig. 29). The inkblots are "unstructured," that is, they do not represent objects with clear, socially determined meanings, but are so ambiguous that they can be perceived in many ways. Each card is handed to the examinee with instructions that give him great freedom. He is asked what he sees, what it might be, what it makes him think of. There is no time limit, and an examinee may make as few or as many responses to each inkblot as he wishes. His responses are recorded verbatim. After the examinee has responded to all ten figures, the examiner

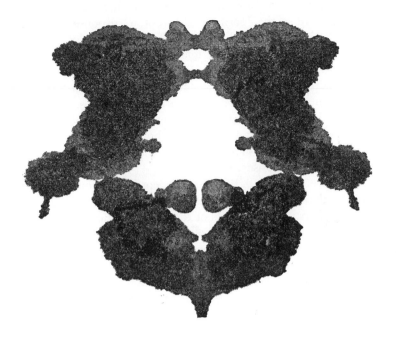

Figure 29. An Inkblot Figure

A figure with characteristics similar to those of the uncolored Rorschach figures. What do you see in it?

goes through the series a second time asking him to point out just where on the blots he saw each object reported.

Each distinct response is scored according to three main characteristics:

Location. Was the response based on a perception of the whole blot, of a large usual detail, of a small detail rarely used, etc.?

Determinant. Was the response suggested by the form of the blot, by its color, by both form and color, by shadings of grays, by movement, etc.? Movement is scored when figures are seen in human-like action, as "two cooks carrying a pot."

Content. Was the thing seen a human figure, a part of a figure such as a head, an animal, a dissected anatomical detail, a landscape, a plant, a man-made object, a map, etc.?

Several other characteristics of responses are also scored. An important attribute is the "form quality" of a response, whether it accurately interprets a real shape to be found in the blot or is vague and farfetched. Responses that many people make are scored as "popular," rarer ones as "original." After each separate response has been scored, the results are tabulated for the entire record, yielding the number of responses referring to wholes, to forms, to movement, to color, to human figures, and the like. Several scores are expressed as percentages of the whole number of responses, and some ratios are calculated, such as the ratio of movement responses to color responses.

The interpretation of a Rorschach record is a complex process that can be done only after extensive specialized training. It is no task for amateurs. Some aspects of the interpretation come from the separate scores. A large number of whole responses of good quality is said to indicate a capacity for organizing one's thinking in general terms. Many small detail responses may mean a constrained or compulsive person. Movement responses are related to fantasy or introversion, and color to the open expression of emotion. Anxious people are said to make responses determined by the black-to-gray shading. Good form quality and good original responses are among the indicators of high intelligence. Most of the interpretation, however, does not assume a one-to-one relationship between scores and traits. Rorschach workers place much emphasis on studying the record as a whole, and on the mutually modifying influences that the scores have on one another. To give one simple example, "good" whole responses go with intelligence, but many feebleminded persons also give records consisting mainly of simple unelaborated wholes such as "a bat," "a bird," and "a bug." Therefore it is impossible to correlate the crude "whole" score with intelligence without taking other features into account.

Does the Rorschach "work"? Is it valid? These crucial questions are not decided to everyone's satisfaction. There are pros and cons. Except for the general theory of projection, the technique is not derived from a comprehensive theory or based on the kind of controlled studies that usually characterize psychological research. It is a product of clinical experience. The interpretations of scores and patterns of scores were worked out by Rorschach and elaborated by his successors by testing many persons, normal and disturbed, and noting rather informally what kinds of responses seemed to

characterize people with various personalities. To prove the validity of the test, Rorschach workers place dependence on "matching"
experiments in which a group of Rorschach records and of independent personality descriptions are studied in the attempt to
match each test record with the correct person's description. Another type of study uses "blind analysis," in which an expert
Rorschach worker makes a diagnosis based on the test alone, which
can be checked against a patient's diagnosis obtained by other
methods. Such experiments have tended to give positive results.
The studies have been justifiably criticized, however, because most
of them are based on small numbers of extreme cases, and because
they have neglected certain precautions which careful research
workers believe essential.[28]

The bulk of the evidence seems to show that the Rorschach is
an aid in diagnosing most cases of psychoneuroses and of the more
serious mental disorders. Whether it is valid in the borderline cases
in which it would be needed most, as in differentiating between a
bad neurosis and an early schizophrenia, cannot be tested adequately because of the absence of good independent criteria against
which to compare it. There is also some evidence that the Rorschach may be used as a screening device to detect maladjustment
in general. There is yet no conclusive proof, however, that it can
yield a detailed and valid description of the personality of a normal
person, as its supporters claim. Within the area of its validity, the
Rorschach is a most desirable technique because of its subtleness.
Good, poor, or diagnostic responses are not evident to naive examinees. Future research will probably clarify the limitations of the
Rorschach, tone down the exaggerated claims of some enthusiasts,
and establish the boundaries of its usefulness.

Picture-Story Tests

Next to the Rorschach, the most commonly used projective technique is one that requires the examinee to make up a story based on
a picture. The pictures are more "structured" than the inkblots, for
they represent actual people in situations that may suggest common
adjustment problems, but they are still sufficiently ambiguous to
permit various interpretations. For example, a picture may represent a boy looking out of a window. One examinee may say that
the boy is daydreaming of his future, another that he is ill and can-

Figure 30. The Thematic Apperception Test

A picture used to evoke a story which sheds light on the motives and thwartings of the examinee. What is happening? How are the people thinking and feeling? How does the story come out? (Reprinted by permission of the publishers from Henry A. Murray, *Thematic Apperception Test*, Cambridge, Mass.: Harvard University Press. Copyright, 1943, by The President and Fellows of Harvard College.)

not go out of doors, a third, that he is being kept inside by his parents as a punishment. It is reasonable to suppose that the interpretation tells something about the person's motives, aspirations, conflicts, and adjustments. Figure 30 shows a typical picture used on such a test.

Murray's Thematic Apperception Test — familiarly, the "TAT" — is the best known of the picture-story projective methods.[29] Twenty pictures are presented in succession to the examinee. Sometimes the stories are written; if they are told orally the examiner records them as completely as possible. The subject may be asked what led up to the event shown in the picture, what is happening, what the people in the picture are thinking and feeling, and how the story comes out. The first step in interpreting a TAT story is to distinguish the "hero," the character in the story with which the examinee is believed to identify himself. An inventory is then made of the hero's "needs" — his motives, strivings, and aversions — and of his "press" — the forces of the environment which act on him significantly. Some typical needs scored by Murray are those for achievement, for aggression, for dominance, for self-blame, and for aid or consolation. Representative "press" are aggression (against the hero), dominance (over him), inducement, protection, and physical danger. The outcome of each story is studied in a number of ways, as by noting whether the ending is happy or unhappy, successful or frustrating. Several indicators are summed for the twenty pictures. The interpretation of the TAT does not come mainly from the score tabulations, however, but from viewing the stories in their entirety as evidence concerning the motives, conflicts, and adjustments typical of the person's life. Interpreting the TAT requires more than a knowledge of the technique; it depends on a broad understanding of human personality.

Because so many kinds of material can evoke projection, their potential variety is almost unlimited. Sets of pictures have been prepared which are especially suitable for use with young children,[30] and sets which suggest the major problems of adolescents.[31] One picture-story test supplies backgrounds and movable cut-out figures so that the examinee can make his own picture and then tell a story about it.[32] The TAT and other picture-story tests are not used for measurement or survey purposes, but as aids to a full clinical study of a person. The findings should be regarded as working hypotheses, to be investigated further by a study of a person's life history, by interviews, and in connection with psychotherapy.

Word Associations

The word association test, an older method of personality study with a long history, is now recognized as a projective technique.[33] The method of administration is to read a list of words, one at a time, to the examinee who responds by saying the first word that occurs to him as quickly as he can. The list is usually repeated, since giving a different response to a word on its second presentation is believed to indicate an area of disturbance. A record is made of each response, and of the time taken to react. The word association test is projective because a word is a rather unstructured stimulus which permits many possible responses. To the stimulus word "house," one subject quickly responds "home," which is the most common response. Another examinee after a perceptible delay says "dark." These responses probably give us glimpses into the private lives of the examinees.

Numerous lists of association words have been compiled for experimental and clinical use. Two early and typical lists, which were guided by somewhat different intentions, are those of Jung and Eder, and of Kent and Rosanoff.[34] Each consists of 100 words, the first 20 of which are given in Table 5.

Table 5

Examples of Free-Association Words

Jung and Eder List	Kent and Rosanoff List
1. head	1. table
2. green	2. dark
3. water	3. music
4. sing	4. sickness
5. dead	5. man
6. long	6. deep
7. ship	7. soft
8. make	8. eating
9. woman	9. mountain
10. friendly	10. house
11. bake	11. black
12. ask	12. mutton
13. cold	13. comfort
14. stalk	14. hand
15. dance	15. short
16. village	16. fruit
17. pond	17. butterfly
18. sick	18. smooth
19. pride	19. command
20. bring	20. chair

Jung's words were designed to call up individual experiences, and hence to detect sources of anxiety or other significant attitudes. Unusual responses ordinarily are followed up in an informal interview and yield clues of diagnostic value. An especially important indicator of an emotionally tinged response is an excessively long reaction time, which the client may report as due to a "blank mind," to competition between several responses occurring simultaneously, or to a need to conceal the first word recalled. A tendency to give long reaction times to many words has been used as an indicator of general maladjustment. Other signs of disturbance include failure to respond, making an irrelevant response, misunderstanding the stimulus word, giving a different response on a second trial than on the first, repeating a response previously made, saying a sentence rather than a word, wanting to change one's response after it has been given, and also laughing, gasping, fidgeting, and other external signs of emotion or embarrassment.

The Kent-Rosanoff method emphasized another aspect of word

association, the classification of the kind of response given. Their list avoided words of strong emotional significance, a procedure opposite to that of Jung. By administering the list to 1,000 normal persons, the authors compiled tables of "common responses," as it was found that most people gave one of a limited number of response words to each stimulus. About 92 per cent of the responses of normal subjects were common, while 247 psychotic subjects gave only 71 per cent of common words. The difference between the normal and disordered groups is striking and significant, but not large enough to be of diagnostic value in individual cases. Another approach to the test classifies the responses according to their logical relationships to the stimuli. Some people have consistent tendencies to prefer one type — opposites, synonyms, part-whole relationships, etc. — but these do not seem to pertain to any important personality differences. Jung himself identified "objective" responses such as "snake-frog," that referred to external things, and "subjective" responses such as "snake-poisonous," that concerned the individual's personal evaluation of the stimulus. Jung related the objective and subjective association patterns to his extravert and introvert types. Today, the qualitative use of the word association test to reveal areas of conflict predominates over its quantitative or formal use.[35]

Sentence Completions

The sentence completion test is a verbal projective technique which can be given economically to groups of examinees. As the sample items in Table 6 show, each sentence begins with an inten-

Table 6
Items from an Incomplete Sentences Test

1. I like	21. I failed ....
4. Back home	28. Sometimes ....
8. The best	34. I wish ....
13. My greatest fear	35. My father* ....

* Sample responses to the item *"My father. . . ."* that have been assigned quantitative score values follow. The negative values indicate poorer qualities of adjustment; the positive values better adjustment. (—3) . . . was a fool; (—2) . . . is stern; (—1) . . . never had much of a chance; (0) . . . is home; (+1) . . . is an excellent mechanic; (+2) . . . is a good man; (+3) . . . is a swell guy. (From J. B. Rotter, Janet E. Rafferty, and Eva Schachtitz, Validation of the Rotter incomplete sentences blank for college screening. *J. consult. Psychol.*, 1949, *13*, 348-356.)

tionally vague stem, which the subject completes in any way he wishes in order to make a whole sentence.[36] Two uses have been made of the sentence completion method. By scoring each response according to the general quality of adjustment shown, a quantitative measure can be obtained which will differentiate better adjusted from more poorly adjusted people.[37] The responses are also studied qualitatively to discover areas of sensitivity and conflict. One method of interpretation analyzes the responses for "needs" and "press" according to the scheme used for the Thematic Apperception Test.

OBJECTIVE METHODS
IN PERSONALITY STUDY

One fundamental method for studying personality is to observe an individual's conduct. Psychological research has not done away with this common-sense approach, but has only refined it to make it a more dependable instrument for appraising persons. Everyone observes the behavior of his fellow men, but the conclusions drawn are often faulty because of failure to take certain essential precautions. Improved methods of observing have developed into two somewhat overlapping techniques, which may be designated as the *directed observation* and the *test*.

Directed Observation

The errors of everyday observation spring from many sources: failure to control or to record all of the conditions that influence the behavior being observed, confusion resulting from an attempt to observe too many complex variables at once, unreliability due to trying to remember and report observations without an immediate record, and the tendency to draw conclusions from general impressions without a detailed analysis of the data. Modern improvements in methods of observation have tried to remedy all of these defects. Two important principles of directed observation are to make a full record of the behavior at the moment that it is being observed, and to analyze the results systematically and quantitatively. It is also important to avoid drawing conclusions and interpretations while the observations are in progress, so as not to contaminate the findings with one's own preconceptions and prejudices.

A classic example of an observation technique applied to a personality problem is Olson's study of certain "nervous habits" in normal children.[38] Olson observed children for five-minute and ten-minute periods daily, for ten to twenty successive observations. Thumb-sucking, nail-biting, hair-twisting, and the like, were tabulated objectively. The methodological findings were important: that many short samples of behavior, obtained systematically, give the most reliable results. It was found that "nervous habits" are consistently characteristic of an individual, run in families, and are influenced by fatigue, but are unrelated to available measures of personality.

Technical resources developed in recent years have provided means for making better controlled observations. Sound-recording devices preserve interviews and other verbal materials for detailed analyses. Check lists of activities synchronized with automatic time recorders increase one's precision in observing and reporting a sequence of a series of actions, and the time devoted to each. One-way-vision windows conceal observers and keep them from becoming participants in the scenes that they are recording. Such aids to observation have been used in many research studies: on the social development of children from age to age,[39] on the personal interactions within groups of people who are working together to solve a problem,[40] and on the processes of psychotherapy with adults and with children.[41]

Directed and recorded observations provide a precise record of behavior in relatively unrestrained situations in which a person is free to "be himself." The method is therefore of great value for research. Because the simultaneous efforts of several observers and technicians are usually required, it is not often practicable for individual appraisal.

Intellectual Tests

A test imposes one more step of control than does a directed observation. In addition to the careful recording and numerical treatment of the results, a test controls the situation presented to the person being studied. Tests were first successfully developed in the area of intellectual behavior. Although they lack perfection and are sometimes misinterpreted or misused, "intelligence tests" represent one of the striking achievements of modern psychology.

"Intelligence" is sometimes considered as if it were something different from "personality"; indeed, laymen often contrast the two. This is a serious misunderstanding, for intellectual traits are components of a total personality, and important ones. No psychological clinic would attempt to study or treat a maladjusted person without giving consideration to whether he is bright, or average, or stupid. Mental tests, appropriately used and interpreted, provide the most effective means for making this judgment. The field of psychological testing is so extensive that at least a whole volume would be required to give an introduction to it. We can mention here only a few common principles, and a few precautions which must be observed in interpreting test results.

The three main kinds of mental tests are individual verbal tests, individual performance tests, and group tests. In the individual verbal test a standard series of tasks is presented, mainly by oral questions. A current example is the Revised Stanford-Binet Test, which evolved from the work of Alfred Binet early in the present century.[42] Its questions demand that the examinee remember, discriminate, judge, and reason, which are typical intellectual tasks. By trying the items experimentally, each task is assigned to an age level, which identifies the age at which the average child can answer it successfully. This standardization process underlies the concept of Mental Age (M.A.). If a given child can just perform the ten-year tasks but no more, he has an M.A. of ten, regardless of his chronological age. The extent to which a child's Mental Age falls above or below the expectation for his age is indicated by his Intelligence Quotient (I.Q.), which is found by dividing his M.A. by his age and multiplying by 100. Obviously, I.Q.'s over 100 indicate intellectual ability that is above average in various degrees; those below 100 are below the absolute average.

Research shows that verbal intelligence tests have decided value for certain applications, but it also reveals their limitations. The tests predict success in school fairly accurately, and also are related to the aspects of clerical and professional occupations which involve the use of language, numbers, and abstract concepts. In the early days of mental testing, overenthusiastic proponents of the method incorrectly ascribed delinquency, poverty, and maladjustment to lack of mental ability, allegations not supported by later and better evidence. One of the chief shortcomings of verbal tests is that they depend on literacy, and hence are greatly influenced by schooling and environmental opportunity. This type of test cannot be interpreted validly for a person who was reared in a culture or schooled in a language different from that in which the test was prepared. Tests given to adults who are not accustomed to verbal or numerical work in their occupations — factory or farm workers, or fishermen, for example — are likely to yield results markedly below other proper estimates of the men's real abilities.

Attempts to minimize the influence of language on the measurement of intelligence have led to the development of performance tests. In these tests, basic intellectual attributes such as discriminating, perceiving relationships, and solving problems are evoked by nonverbal materials. The test instructions may be given by signs and gestures, and the responses made by moving blocks, marking or arranging pictures, placing inserts in form or picture boards, finding the way through mazes, or other performances that do not use language. Performance tests are standardized by experimental trials similar to those employed for verbal tests, and numerical scores such as I.Q.'s can be obtained. Studies show that performance tests have achieved their intended objective only imperfectly; their results are still somewhat dependent on cultural background, although less so than in the case of the verbal tests. They are an invaluable adjunct to the study of a person whom we want to understand comprehensively.

Some individual intelligence tests use both verbal and performance materials. The Wechsler tests for children and for adults are organized as series of subtests, half verbal and half nonverbal.[43] The verbal section includes tests of information, comprehension, memory for digits, similarities, arithmetical reasoning, and vocabulary; the performance tests involve picture arrangement, picture completion, block designs, object assembly, and symbol code learning. A separate Verbal I.Q. and Performance I.Q. may be calculated, in addition to the "full scale" I.Q. The division of the Wechsler scales into subtests, each of which is scored independently, permits a richer analysis of each person's abilities, as in comparing verbal with nonverbal ability, or linguistic with numerical. Attempts have also been made to relate particular patterns of subtest scores to certain kinds of mental disorders.

On group mental tests, the intellectual tasks are presented in printed form, and the examinee answers by checking or by writing numbers or other brief symbols. Group tests are validated experimentally, usually against the criterion of success in school. They may be standardized in terms of the average scores made by children of various ages, or in terms of the rank of an adult in some defined group such as college students or army recruits. Such tests have all the shortcomings of other verbal tests, and the additional fault that they depend greatly on speed and skill in reading. The same factors that cause low scores in group tests are likely to be handicaps in school, and they are therefore good practical indicators of school success. One cannot depend on them for broader appraisals of human abilities.

Factor analysis has been applied to tests of intellectual abilities, resulting in the identification of such factors as perceptual ability, number ability, verbal ability, visual space ability, memory, inductive thinking, and deductive reasoning.[44] These factors are not completely independent, but show some positive correlation with one another. For example, persons who are good in verbal ability tend to be good in number ability also, but the correlation is not high, so that there are numerous exceptions. Most psychologists agree that there is a "general factor" in intelligence, and that the better intelligence tests approximate a measurement of this broad trait. There are also "group factors," that is, components of intellect that are more highly correlated within each cluster than between clusters.

Even in the limited area of the intellectual traits, there are many instruments of measurement, some of which are suited for one purpose and some for other applications. No one test can satisfy all requirements. When an intelligence rating is given in a case history, it is of great importance to know the nature of the test from which it was obtained. Not all tests are equally appropriate, and an "I.Q." of unspecified origin is sadly lacking in meaning as an item of information about a personality.

Personality Indicators in Intelligence Tests

An individual's performance on a psychological test is affected by his whole personality, not by his intellect alone.[45] Although standard tests mainly tap a person's intellectual qualities, his other attributes may influence the results in an appreciable degree. If a really able person is full of anxiety, or if he has an unjustly low estimate of himself, he may become confused by tasks that he could accomplish if he were calm, or may give up too soon when he meets a difficulty. Such considerations have led psychologists to be alert to objective test findings that may reveal broader facets of personality. Some research studies have also contributed to our understanding of the relationships between abilities and other personal qualities. The studies are fragmentary, and only suggest, rather than prove, the nature of predispositions to maladjustment.

One widely explored problem is whether psychoneurotic persons differ in intelligence from normal people. The results are mainly negative. Psychoneurotic men in the armed services do tend to have a slightly lower average intelligence score than normal men, but the difference is small and of no value for diagnosis.[46] Civilian studies sometimes find that psychoneurotic clients of clinics have a higher average intelligence than the total population, probably because more able and better educated people seek professional help for their troubles. On the whole, maladjustment is not limited to any range of the intellectual scale, but can strike the dull or the bright.

Research studies in both World War I and World War II found significant differences in ability between two groups of psychoneurotics — those suffering from anxiety, and those with conversion hysteria. Hollingworth, in 1918, found that "neurasthenics" had a median mental age of 13.0 years (that of the entire native white draft was 13.32 years), while the hysterics averaged only 11.5, a significantly lower figure. It was also noted that hysterical forms of adjustment were more prevalent among the enlisted men. The officers, who on the whole were more intelligent, better educated, and from more favorable cultural levels, tended toward nonadjustive reactions with visceral and anxiety symptoms predominating. In studies of British soldiers during World War II, Eysenck obtained similar results. In the high range of an abstract intelligence test, there were twice as many anxiety cases as hysterics; in the low range, twice as many hysterics as men with anxiety. Although there is much overlapping between the groups, with some cases of anxiety and some of hysteria at every level of ability, these data tend to confirm the clinical evidence (p. 282) that at least some people of superior culture and education lapse into anxiety states because they reject the less rational means for tension reduction such as hysterical symptoms.

A common clinical observation is that maladjusted or "emotionally unstable" people are likely to be erratic in their achievements. At one time or under one set of conditions, they do well; at other times they are unable to make full use of their real capacities because they are inhibited or confused by anxiety. Interpreted in terms of standard mental tests, this observation gave rise to the hypothesis that maladjusted or neurotic persons show excessive *scatter* in their test performances. Scatter means irregularity of achievement, passing some items that most people find difficult and failing some that are usually easy. On an age-level test such as the Stanford-Binet, scatter is shown by a wide range between the lowest failure and the highest success on the scale. In tests that are divided into subtests, as are the Wechsler tests, irregularity in subtest scores constitutes scatter. If, on the six verbal tests of the Wechsler, one man scores 15, 15, 14, 14, 13, and 13, and another's record is 18, 17, 15, 13, 12, and 9, the two have equal average scores, but the second man has greater scatter. Extensive research has not confirmed the clinical hypothesis fully. Many neurotic people show excessive scatter but others do not, and scatter is by no means absent from the test records of clinically normal persons.

A further hypothesis concerning the test behavior of maladjusted and mentally disordered persons is that they can be identified by particular kinds of scatter, that is, by being generally able on some tested functions and performing poorly on others. For example, the hypotheses have been advanced that schizophrenics do relatively well, in relation to their own average scores, on the vocabulary subtest of the Wechsler Scale, but poorly on the object-assembly and symbol-learning tests; psychoneurotics are said to do well on information and comprehension and poorly on picture arrangement and immediate memory for digits.[47] Even more specific assertions have been advanced, such as that a very poor score on the digit-memory test shows the presence of anxiety. This last hypothesis is based on logical analysis and on selected cases that are strikingly affirmative. The test of memory for digits requires sustained attention, a function with which anxiety often interferes. And certainly, every experienced clinician has examined some anxiety-ridden patients who have fallen down badly in this task. Research studies on large numbers of cases, however, do not support such hypotheses. There is no entirely uniform pattern of test scores characteristic of schizophrenia,[48] and digit-memory test scores do not correlate with rated degrees of anxiety.[49] Further analysis of the reasons for failure on a subtest clarifies the experimental findings. A low digit-memory score is certainly due to anxiety in some cases. But it can be caused by other influences as well: inattention not associated with anxiety, inefficiency in immediate learning, poor hearing, or aversion to working with numbers. The test is a psychologically complex task, and more than one influence can make for excellence or defect in its performance. Another relevant finding is that the short subtests of an intelligence scale are not sufficiently reliable to permit stable comparisons of one subtest with another.[50] The sum of the subtests gives a suitable measure of intelligence-in-general, but each subtest is too small a sample of behavior to be used by itself. A regular test performance does not exclude the possibility of maladjustment, and an irregular one does not always indicate it.

Very often a person's manner of response to a test question reveals more about his personality than does the mere rightness or wrongness of his answer. The unsocial attitude of a delinquent, the obsession with detail of a compulsive person, or the self-reference of the suspicious or anxious, tend to shape the quality of their behavior. W. A. Hunt has given a good illustration:

> In response to the question, "How far is it from Paris to New York?" a subject may answer "About 3,000 miles"; but I have had another subject say "Unfortunately I cannot be as exact as I would like to. No, I don't know exactly. For an approximation — about 3,000 miles. Sorry I can't answer more definitely." Both these answers are correct and count the same in the scoring system, with the numerical symbols concealing the diagnostic richness of the second answer. In response to the question, "Where is Egypt?" a subject may answer "In South America"; but I have had a schizophrenic answer "In a manner of speaking it may be said to be in an oasis — plenty surrounded by sand." Both answers are wrong and in scoring are represented by the same symbol, zero. Not only is the pathological significance of the second answer lost, but I would submit that a real difference in intelligence is overlooked.*

Competent clinical workers constantly watch for personality-revealing responses when they are administering intelligence tests.

---

* W. A. Hunt, The future of diagnostic testing in clinical psychology. *J. clin. Psychol.*, 1946, 2, 311-312.

The qualitative observations made during testing often make a greater contribution to understanding a person than do the test scores themselves.

Social Development

The measurement of intellectual abilities in terms of maturity or age units has suggested that developmental standards can also be applied to other features of personality. Children who present problems of adjustment are often retarded, in comparison to other children of the same age, in socialization and in performances which require self-help and self-direction.

One useful scale for measuring social development is the Vineland Social Maturity Scale, standardized by E. A. Doll.[51] The 117 items of the scale describe steps of social maturation from below the level of the one-year-old infant to above that of the average adult. To permit some analysis of areas of development, the items are divided into a number of categories: self-help (*SH*), locomotion (*L*), occupation (*O*), communication (*C*), self-direction (*SD*), and socialization (*S*). Here are a few sample items, with their approximate age levels and categories:

Age 2: 35. Asks to go to toilet (*SH*)
       36. Initiates own play activities (*O*)
Age 4: 52. Washes face unassisted (*SH*)
       53. Goes about neighborhood unattended (*L*)
Age 6: 60. Is trusted with money (*SD*)
       65. Goes to bed unassisted (*SH*)
Age 8: 72. Does routine household tasks (*O*)
       73. Reads on own initiative (*C*)
Age 10: 78. Writes occasional short letters (*C*)
        80. Does small remunerative work (*O*)
Age 12: 83. Is left to care for self and others (*SD*)
        85. Plays difficult games (*S*)
Age 14: 88. Engages in adolescent group activities (*S*)
        89. Performs responsible routine chores (*O*)

The scale defines each developmental accomplishment by a precise description of the behavior which receives credit. The information is sometimes obtained by direct observation, more often by a skillful interview with a parent. A Social Age is obtained by noting the number of items passed, and a Social Quotient may be com-

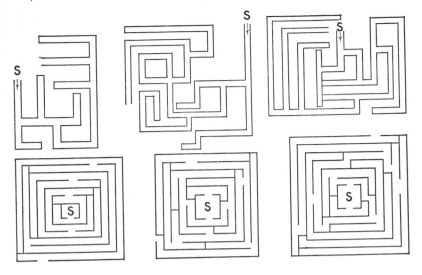

Figure 31. Porteus Maze Tests

The maze tests standardized at the mental age levels 8, 9, 10, 11, 12, and 14 are reproduced. The printed forms used for testing are larger; for example, the 14-year maze shown at the lower right of the figure is 4¼ inches square. The examinee starts at **S** and finds his way out. The moment that his pencil enters a blind alley he is stopped and a failure recorded for that trial. (Courtesy of S. D. Porteus and of the C. H. Stoelting Co.)

puted by dividing a child's Social Age by his life age. Social development depends, of course, on age, intelligence, physique, and opportunities for experience. It is also influenced by the personal adjustments which a child makes to his parents and peers.

Impulsiveness and Control

Although general intelligence tests have not proved very serviceable for the diagnosis of maladjustment, a number of special testing techniques have given promise of making a greater contribution. One common observation concerning maladjusted personalities is that they tend to be impulsive and to lack foresight and control. A psychometric approach to this quality has been made by the Porteus Maze Test, which is a series of printed mazes through which the examinee must find his way with a pencil (Fig. 31).[52] In the first place, the mazes are age-level performance tests which yield mental age scores somewhat comparable to those of the Binet. The method of administration of the Porteus Mazes, however, places a high premium on foresight, planning, and the avoidance of impulsive acts. The subject is not permitted to solve the maze by trial and error, but fails a given trial the instant he enters a blind alley. A person who acts before he looks and thinks is severely penalized. The writer has examined a number of young adults who have secured normal or superior ratings on other tests, but who have scored only from the eight- to the eleven-year level on the mazes. Invariably, these have been persons whom case study characterizes as impulsive, unstable, and anxious. An informal clinical observation must be verified by solid research, however. Numerous research studies have supported the hypothesis that a specific element of personality enters into the maze tests. They will predict "social adaptability" in various groups of examinees more validly than will Binet-type tests.

The usefulness of the Porteus Maze Test has been extended by the introduction of "qualitative scoring," which is based on how the examinee performs rather than solely on the number of mazes that he can complete successfully. The qualitative scoring penalizes inferior work such as making errors in the easier parts of maze paths, cutting corners, crossing lines, lifting the pencil from the paper contrary to instructions, and drawing with irregular or wavy lines rather than direct and clear ones. This score differentiates between delinquent and normal youths and adults.

Persistence and Fatigue

Several studies suggest that maladjusted persons are characterized by a lack of "will power," "strength of character," or persistence in continuing a fatiguing and discomfort-producing task. While the techniques used to measure this quality have varied in detail, they have much in common: seeing how long the examinee can stand with his heels slightly raised from the floor, or sit with one leg extended horizontally, or hold a pair of dumbbells at arm's length.[53] Contrary to one's first impression, these tests have been shown to depend, not primarily on physical strength, but on willingness to endure discomfort in order to make a good rating. Earlier studies found significant differences between normal youngsters and

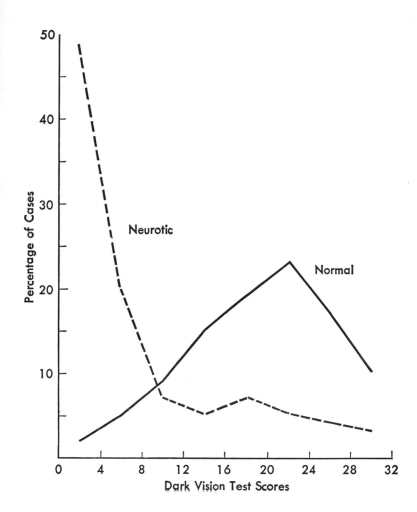

Figure 32. Dark Vision Adaptation Test Scores of Normal and Neurotic Soldiers

The score indicates the quality of dark vision after adaptation. Men making higher numerical scores could see smaller or more faintly illuminated figures in the dark. As the graphs show, 77 per cent of neurotics scored 10 or below; only 17 per cent of normals performed that poorly. (H. J. Eysenck, *Dimensions of personality*. London: Kegan Paul, 1947.)

maladjusted or delinquent boys and girls. The most recent research, using neurotic British soldiers of World War II, showed that hysterics had markedly less persistence than men with anxiety. Tests of this type take too long to administer to be of much use clinically, but the research findings are important.

Two studies suggest that a maladjusted person's lack of persistence may have a somewhat deeper basis than merely a conscious unwillingness to undergo discomfort. A British study found that psychoneurotic soldiers had strikingly poorer dark-vision adaptation than normal men.[54] As Figure 32 shows, the separation between the groups is as great as that achieved by any technique. In simple terms, the test measures how faint a light a person can see, after his eyes have been adapted to a darkened room. The neurotics could not perceive as dim a light as normals. Dark adaptation also decreases with fatigue and age; the neurotics tested as if they were "tired and old" before their time. Similar results were suggested by a small study of American soldiers returned from combat who were normal or who suffered from anxiety reactions. The "flicker fusion frequency" of each man was tested: the speed of flashing of an intermittent light at which it seems to fuse into a continuous glow.[55] The neurotics required a faster alternation of light and dark before the stimulus fused into a constant light without appearing to flicker. Again, their reaction was like that of older persons, fatigued persons, or persons with lower metabolism. These findings imply that a neurotic person is genuinely fatigued. Presumably, his energy is too much used up by the chronic emotional reaction of his anxiety.

Reactions to Stress

An outstanding feature of the real-life behavior of maladjusted persons is that they do not retain a good degree of integration when under stress. They may get along well enough when everything is calm, but become anxious and confused when pressures are exerted upon them. Such behavior is reflected in their performances on some tests.

One early observation arose from the administration of two different versions of the Binet test: the Stanford revision and the Kuhlmann revision.[56] Both were constructed on similar principles as age-level tests of intelligence. It was found that normal children made almost identical scores on the two tests, but that for maladjusted persons, the Kuhlmann M.A. ran 10 per cent or more below the Stanford. For example, a neurotic young woman secured an I.Q. of 88 on the Stanford, but only of 64 on the Kuhlmann.[57] She was notably unstable in behavior, with temper outbursts, quarreling, and threats of suicide. The discrepancy is most probably due to the speed factor in the Kuhlmann tests. The Stanford contains few items in which the examinee is timed, in which he feels that he has to do his best very quickly. In the Kuhlmann tests, in contrast, no fewer than 14 of the 25 different subtests at the nine-year level and above involve conspicuous timing with a stop watch. The observation suggests that an emotionally unstable person is unable to work under the pressure of speed. He "breaks down" when rushed.

Essentially the same results have been secured by a quite different technique. In examining a large group of factory workers in England, a "dotting-speed test" was used, at first as a test of motor skill.[58] This test employs a revolving disk that brings a succession of small, irregularly placed circles to view in a slot. With a pencil, the examinee aims at each circle as it appears. The speed with which the circles appear is constantly accelerated so that the subject has to work faster and faster. The score is the number of circles dotted before "breakdown," which is defined as missing five circles in succession. A significant average difference was found between normal workers and those independently diagnosed as suffering from anxiety. Persons with obsessive symptoms, however, made better scores than normals, possibly because of their tendency to narrowly concentrated attention. As Figure 33 shows, the test is not individually diagnostic because the scores overlap too much, but the average differences are informative. Not every speed test, however, separates normal and neurotic persons. Speeded group intelligence tests made up of printed verbal materials do not discriminate.[59] Individual tests, in which an interpersonal relationship is established between the examiner and examinee, seem better suited to establish the "speed pressure" that neurotics endure poorly.

A closely related finding was obtained from a study that compared two methods of administering the Revised Stanford-Binet Test to well-adjusted and poorly adjusted children.[60] One method administered the items in an invariable routine order, the other "adaptive" method alternated easy and hard items and always gave

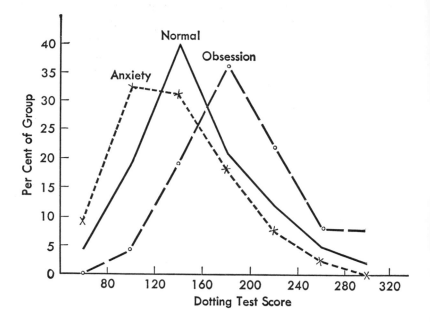

Figure 33. Reactions of Neurotics to Speed Pressure

The horizontal axis indicates the maximum speed attained before "breakdown." Persons with obsessional symptoms made the best scores, normal people next best, while those with anxiety symptoms were, as a group, less able to speed up their performances. (Drawn from data given in M. Culpin, *Recent advances in the study of the psychoneuroses.* London: Churchill, 1931.)

an easy task immediately after a child had failed a hard one. The well-adjusted children scored no differently by the two methods; the poorly adjusted ones performed better when the test was given "adaptively." They needed the additional reassurance of periodic successes in order to control their anxieties and thereby to show their real capability.

Other experimental studies have shown that neurotic people make poor responses to various kinds of stress. In a "mirror-tracing test," subjects trace a geometric figure such as a star which they can see only in a mirror. This task is a frustrating experience for anyone, perhaps because it seems so easy but is really difficult.

Maladjusted persons typically react badly to this stress, take much longer to complete the tracing, and make many more errors.[61] It has also been found that neurotic persons, both children and adults, show more pronounced physiological evidence of emotion when subjected to stress experimentally.[62] As compared to normal people, they tremble more, their hands perspire, and their breathing is more disrupted. Frustration and conflict arouse anxiety, which is shown directly by the physiological studies, and indirectly by its effect on mental and motor performances.

Studies of "Character"

Extensive studies have been made of the segment of personality that comes within the popular definition of "character." One large-scale research project directed by Hartshorne and May in the nineteen-twenties, and other subsequent studies, developed objective methods to test cheating, stealing, and lying, and also self-control, persistence, and helpfulness, among normal children.[63] One aspect of cheating, for example, was measured by allowing children to score their own test papers. A secretly obtained carbon copy of a child's answers permitted the measurement of his degree of honesty in marking and reporting his own performance. Helpfulness was measured by various unselfish acts for which opportunities were offered. Self-control was judged by measuring persistence at unpleasant tasks, and by noting the degree of resistance to attractive distractions while working to make a good score.

One important conclusion of these studies is that "honesty" is not a consistent general trait. Knowing whether a child will steal pennies is of little aid in predicting whether he will cheat in school. Each situation has its own particular determiners of behavior. The finding that honesty is not a trait does not prove, however, that there are no character traits at all.[64] Honest or dishonest acts may arise from different causes in different persons, and yet be consistent in each case with the individual's personality. One child may steal to show off; another, to get money to support a hobby; a third, to express aggression against the person from whom he steals. Each child reveals his personality, but does not have a clear-cut trait that can be labeled "dishonesty."

The chief purpose of research on character has been to discover the sources of the kinds of behavior measured. Cheating in school has been found highly related to intelligence. Brighter children cheat less in the classroom, probably because they do not have to do so to succeed. Cheating in games and sports has little relationship with mental ability. One factor that is significantly correlated with many evidences of "character" is the quality of the child's home background and the example set by his parents. This conclusion agrees with observations from clinical studies of personality development. Little influence on "character" was exerted by less central environmental factors — church and Sunday School attendance, religious or nationality group membership, or motion picture attendance. These researches have been of value in disposing of a number of unfounded beliefs about the origins of character, and in showing how an objective attack can be made on the measurement of some very subtle aspects of personality.

Normal and Deviant Personalities

The description of personality obtained from objective tests and experimental studies is incomplete as yet, but offers worth-while glimpses into the natures of people who suffer from difficulties of adjustment. Conversely, the evidence also helps us to describe the normal personality more explicitly. A maladjusted person is revealed as impulsive, and lacking in foresight and self-control. He cannot persist in tasks and becomes fatigued too readily. He is unable or unwilling to endure personal discomfort in order to meet social expectations. He reacts poorly to stress, and shows decrements of performance when subjected to frustrations and conflicts. Not every inadequate personality shows all these characteristics, of course, and further research may show that some of them are less clearly distinguishing factors than they appear to be at present. The picture is a consistent one, however, and is probably a true representation of at least some of the traits of people who do not adjust integratively.

The observations confirm with objective data an expectation that can be deduced from the theory of adjustment. In the main, the people whom we call "maladjusted" have lowered thresholds for anxiety. Their anxiety is evoked by lesser conflicts, and is aroused in greater degree, than that of normal people. They are over-motivated to escape or to defend themselves, and hence are unable to devote attention and energy to some socially oriented tasks that offer little trouble to normal people. Their resulting behavior is poorly integrated in that it fails in some degree to meet their long-term needs. Some studies suggest the existence of a general factor of quality of adjustment which varies in amount along a single scale of measurement from well-integrated to poorly integrated behavior. If such a trait exists, anxiety is most probably the basic phenomenon behind it.

Experimental studies tell enough about a normal person to justify an explicit statement of their findings. The ideally well-integrated person is persistent, self-controlled, and foresightful. He is able to endure temporary discomforts and passing frustrations and conflicts for the sake of larger but more remote personal and social rewards. Such desirable characteristics, of course, spring from sources in a person's biological functioning and in his past learning experiences. It is helpful to identify and measure them, but it is more important to trace their origins. The next two chapters undertake the task of tracing the sources and development of the characteristics in which personalities differ.

SUGGESTED READINGS

Chapters 12–15 of Thorndike and Hagen, *Measurement and Evaluation in Psychology and Education,* and Part 2 of *An Introduction to Clinical Psychology,* edited by Pennington and Berg, provide excellent overviews of the problems and techniques of personality measurement. For specific tests, see the monumental volume edited by Buros, *The Fourth Mental Measurements Yearbook.* Burton and Harris, *Case Histories in Clinical and Abnormal Psychology* provides numerous instances of how measuring devices are applied and the useful functions they perform in clinical work.

Part 2 of the first volume of Hunt, *Personality and the Behavior Disorders* discusses various techniques for assessing personality. At more advanced levels, Eysenck, *The Structure of Human Personality* and Cattell, *Description and Measurement of Personality* will richly reward the student who has the statistical knowledge to read them. Projective techniques are presented at a relatively introductory level in Anderson and Anderson, *An Introduction to Projective Techniques.*

CHAPTER 12

Organic Factors
in Personality

Psychology pays most attention to the effects of learning processes and environmental influences upon the development of personality. This emphasis is well justified, for it gives prominence to the aspects of human life which are assigned to psychology in the division of labor among the sciences. No one can afford to ignore, however, the importance of some other influences in shaping a person's adjustments. A human being is first of all a biological organism. His potentialities for behavior are in a large degree determined and limited by his anatomical structure and his physiological functioning.

Common observation notes many instances of the influences of physiological conditions on personality. When a person is fatigued, when he is in pain, or when he is otherwise unwell, his typical adjustments may be modified considerably. A sour and pessimistic attitude toward life is sometimes called a "dyspeptic" disposition, a term which attributes a personality characteristic to the state of one's digestion. People with serious organic defects and weaknesses face life problems quite different from those of people who are well formed and strong.

It is convenient to distinguish two ways in which organic states may influence personality — *primary* or direct, and *secondary* or indirect. The most obvious primary determiners are diseases and injuries of the nervous system which impair a person's ability to perceive, remember, discriminate and plan. They thereby diminish his potentialities for making integrative adjustments. Certain psychoses — severe personality disturbances which ordinarily require hospitalization — are caused by identifiable diseases and defects of the central nervous system. Some endocrine gland secretions, some deficiencies of nutrition, and some drugs also have direct effects upon adjustive behavior. The influence of heredity, of the genetic determination of bodily structures, is also a significant area for investigation. Many organic conditions which affect behavior are imperfectly understood and lie on the frontiers of research, but enough is known about them to justify a brief survey.

In other instances, the effects of organic conditions upon personality are secondary or indirect. A person's adjustments may be affected only by his own perception of his physical disabilities and by the social evaluations that other people place upon them. Many examples have already been described. A puny boy is likely to develop different preferred mechanisms than a strong, healthy child, because he has different experiences. Anxiety provoked by threatening diseases or disabling symptoms may lead to defensive or nonadjustive behavior. In such cases, a person's structure or physiology frustrates his motives, creates conflicts, and shapes the experiences through which he learns his adjustments. The precipitating events are physiological but the adjustive process is psychological. No new principles are involved beyond those which apply to all learnings and adjustments. The primary and secondary effects of organic states are not entirely independent, of course. The two may occur together. In numerous instances, a person who suffers from an organically based defect also has a superimposed anxiety evoked by his distresses and frustrations.

THE ENDOCRINE SYSTEM

Chemical Integration

Organic functions and behavior are coordinated by two principal bodily systems.[1] Most of these integrations are accomplished through the nervous system. The neural impulses from the receptors are coordinated and patterned by the central nervous system so as to arouse effective activities of the muscles and other organs of response. Because the operation of the nervous system is basic to learning, it is fundamental to the process of adjustment.

Another way in which responses are coordinated is through *chemical integration*. A large number of complex chemical substances are secreted by the glands of the body. Some secretions perform the well-known processes of digesting food; others, such as tears and perspiration, serve protective and temperature-regulating functions. Psychology is most interested in still other glandular functions, in which the secretion of one gland evokes that of another, and in which secretions have broad regulatory effects on bodily processes.

Chemical integration is illustrated most simply by the way in which one secretion evokes another in the process of digestion. When food mixed with gastric juices passes from the stomach to the duodenum (the upper part of the small intestine), glands located in the mucous lining are stimulated to produce a small quantity of a substance called *secretin*. The secretin goes to the pancreas through the blood stream, where it stimulates the flow of pancreatic juice essential to the next stage of digestion. It will do so even when all the nerves leading to the area have been cut. Thus a chemical substance may evoke a chemical response without the intervention of the nervous system.

Although the glandular and nervous systems may act independently in some instances, they are often linked. A gland may be stimulated by neural impulses, as when the adrenal medulla is aroused during emotional reactions. There are instances in which a neural and a chemical process can accomplish the same end-result. In emotion, both the discharges through the sympathetic nervous system and the adrenalin in the blood stimulate the heart to beat faster.

The Endocrine Glands

Most glands discharge their secretions into body cavities where they perform limited functions. Familiar examples are the secretions of saliva and of gastric juice that take part in the process of digestion. Another type of glandular action, often more widespread in its effects, occurs when a secretion is absorbed by the blood and carried to all parts of the body. Glands that act in this way are called *endocrine* or "ductless" glands. A specific chemical agent secreted by an endocrine gland is known as a *hormone*. Some glands secrete only one hormone, but it is more common for a

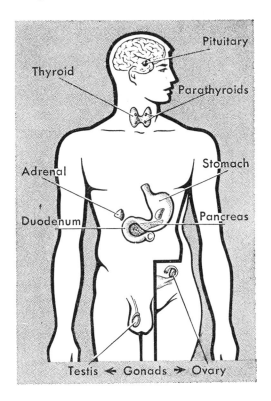

Figure 34. Location of the Endocrine Glands

The figure shows the location of the principal endocrine glands. The parathyroids with the glands of the stomach, duodenum, and pancreas secrete hormones which regulate specific aspects of metabolism. The second type of endocrine is represented by the adrenal medulla, the inner layers of the adrenal glands. The third group of endocrine glands, most important for the general integration of the body, consists of the pituitary, the thyroid, the adrenal cortex, and the gonads.

gland to secrete several, each with a distinct function. The locations of the principal endocrine glands are shown in Figure 34.[2]

The endocrine glands may be classified into three main groups according to the way they function. The first group consists of glands whose hormones regulate specific aspects of metabolism. They operate relatively independently and do not require **neural**

impulses or the secretions of other glands to set them into operation. The *islands of Langerhans* in the pancreas secrete *insulin,* the
hormone which regulates sugar metabolism. A deficiency of insulin causes diabetes, now treated successfully by the administration of the hormone. In addition to its physiological effects, the
high level of blood sugar found in diabetics may give rise to severe
psychological symptoms, ranging from depression to confusion and
disorientation. Another example of the first group is the *parathyroid*
glands, four small bodies embedded in the thyroid but functionally
independent of it. The parathyroid hormone controls the calcium
content of the blood, a serious deficiency of which causes convulsive
seizures and death. The actions of these endocrine glands demonstrate the importance of precise chemical balance within the body
for the maintenance of normal behavior.

Glands of the second type are essentially part of the autonomic
nervous system. The prime example is the *adrenal medulla* whose
hormone, *adrenalin,* participates in emotion as already described
in Chapter 2.

Endocrines of the third group are of great interest to psychology
because of their broad effects on the development and integration
of the body. The key gland of this group is the pituitary, and the
others are the thyroid, the adrenal cortex, and the gonads or sex
glands. The interacting functions of these glands are discussed at
length in the following sections.

Some structures formerly regarded as endocrine glands are now
accorded only a doubtful status. The *thymus* gland in the chest
seems to be a part of the lymphatic system, and the function of the
pineal body, located in the base of the skull, is unknown.

The Thyroid Gland

The thyroid has been understood for a longer time than have
most of the other endocrines, perhaps because its main function is
relatively simple and because its disorders produce severe and
obvious results. The thyroid is a saddle-shaped body which
straddles the trachea in the base of the neck. Microscopically examined, it is seen to consist of many tiny sacs, each lined with
secreting cells and filled with a colloid substance which stores the
secretion. The gland's liberal supply of blood vessels brings chemical materials to it and carries away the product. The hormone,

thyroxin, is a complex organic substance containing about 65 per cent of iodine. Disorders of the thyroid gland are especially prevalent in certain regions whose natural waters are deficient in iodine, such as the Great Lakes region of the United States and some parts of Switzerland. Thyroid deficiency due to a lack of iodine in the diet may be prevented easily by adding a little potassium iodide to table salt. The secretions of all endocrine glands are produced in very small quantities, and low concentrations are sufficient. A normal human thyroid gland, for example, secretes about one milligram every three days, but this minute amount makes a vast difference in the functioning of the body.

Thyroxin is a regulator of metabolism and hence an important agent in maintaining homeostasis (p. 35). It acts as a catalyst — an assisting chemical agent — in controlling the oxidation of proteins, carbohydrates, and fats. Excessive intake of these foods leads to increased thyroid secretion which permits them to be oxidized more rapidly. In contrast, starvation inactivates the thyroid and thereby reduces energy consumption. There is some evidence that the thyroid becomes more active in cold climates and less active in warm ones. All these physiological adjustments help to maintain the constancy of the body's energy level.

Disorders of the thyroid gland interfere with the regulation of metabolism. An underactive thyroid causes a low metabolic rate and results in sluggish behavior and lack of endurance. Too much thyroxin causes oxygen consumption to rise and is accompanied by restless activity and so-called "nervousness." The usual test of the malfunctioning of the thyroid gland is a metabolic measurement. The basal metabolism test determines the rate at which a person uses oxygen while at rest by measuring and analyzing a sample of the air he exhales.

Severe disorders of the thyroid gland have conspicuous effects on growth and behavior. If a baby is born with a seriously defective thyroid, perhaps because of the mother's iodine-deficient diet during pregnancy, he becomes a *cretin*. The growth of a cretin is markedly retarded. A distinctive appearance characterizes the disorder: a flattened nose, a puffy face, short arms and legs, and a protruding abdomen. The skin is dry and the hair scanty. Cretins do not mature sexually. Mental retardation is usually present and many cretins are feebleminded. Fortunately, cretinism can be corrected entirely if treated early in life by thyroid extracts.

Myxedema is a disease resulting from a pronounced thyroid deficiency occurring after birth. In young children it resembles cretinism, in adults it differs because mature growth and mental development have already been attained. An adult with myxedema is likely to be obese because he stores foods which cannot be oxidized. His skin is dry and bloated, and his body temperature is lowered. Mental processes are slowed, with sluggishness of thinking and inability to concentrate. In some most severe cases, withdrawn and bizarre conduct may go so far as to resemble schizophrenia. For reasons that are not well understood, an occasional hypothyroid person may be actively irritable instead of phlegmatic. Myxedema can be treated successfully by administering thyroxin.

Mild cases of thyroid deficiency may go unrecognized. It is quite probable that some persons who suffer from lethargy, chronic fatigue, general lack of vitality, and "hypochondria" are really victims of their underactive thyroids. On the other hand, symptoms of slowness, apathy, and weakness may arise from a number of other causes, either physiological or psychological. The thyroid is not to blame in every case. When hypothyroidism is suspected, the basal metabolism test offers a means for making a fairly secure diagnosis.

The excessive secretion of thyroxin causes an increased tempo of bodily processes, with restlessness and loss of weight. *Hyperthyroidism* can occur without conspicuous physical symptoms, however, and thereby be mistaken for a maladjustment. Its typical psychological correlates are excitability, insomnia, and apparent anxiety. A gross enlargement of the thyroid gland is called a *goiter*, of which there are several kinds. In simple colloid goiter, the gland enlarges in size without secreting excessively. Toxic goiter, also called "exophthalmic" goiter because of the typical protrusion of the eyeballs, involves an excessive or abnormal thyroid secretion. It may be treated with antithyroid drugs to reduce the secretion of thyroxin, or by the surgical removal of a portion of the gland.

All thyroid disorders are complicated by the interacting character of the endocrine system. An apparent thyroid deficiency is often due to a defective secretion of the pituitary hormone which activates the thyroid gland. An overactive thyroid is sometimes a compensation for the undersecretion of a sex hormone. The endocrine system tends to act as a whole, and one glandular disorder often sets off several others.

The Adrenal Glands

The adrenal glands are two small cap-shaped bodies located above the kidneys. Each consists of two functionally distinct parts, the *adrenal medulla* or center layers of cells, and the *adrenal cortex* which makes up the outer layers.

The secretion of the adrenal medulla is a single hormone, *adrenalin* (or *epinephrine*) which was one of the earliest endocrine substances to be identified. Both genetically and functionally, the adrenal medulla is a part of the sympathetic nervous system. During prenatal development, the adrenal medulla comes from the same tissues which form the sympathetic ganglia and nerves. Adrenalin is secreted in strong emotion, and contributes to the interruption of digestion, the raising of blood pressure, and the other "emergency" reactions controlled by the sympathetic system. In fact, recent research shows that the sympathetic nerve endings themselves secrete an adrenalin-like substance. Sympathetic activity, therefore, is carried out entirely by this hormone, locally at the nerve endings, and more generally throughout the body by the secretions of the adrenal medulla into the blood stream. The apparently plausible hypothesis that the secretions of the adrenal medulla help to maintain normal blood pressure and muscular vigor has not been upheld by experimental evidence. Animals deprived of the medullar portions of the adrenals survive in good health. As we shall see shortly, it is the adrenal cortex, not the medulla, which is essential to life.

The adrenal cortex is a complex gland secreting some twenty distinct but chemically related hormones, members of the chemical family of *steroids.* Functionally, the hormones of the adrenal cortex fall into three groups.

The first group of hormones, of which *corticosterone* (sometimes called *cortisone*) is typical, regulates the homeostasis of carbohydrates, especially of sugar.[3] They also perform a function of much wider scope. Their secretion is increased by certain forms of stress such as cold, starvation, physical exertion, and shock arising from infection. The discovery of these functions has led to the use of the hormones, especially corticosterone, as drugs to mobilize the body's resources against rheumatoid arthritis, acute rheumatic fever, and certain eye and skin infections. Corticosterone brings about dramatic and rapid improvement in many cases of these diseases, but treatment must be continued in order to control the illness when it is chronic. Hormones of the corticosterone group have marked psychological effects. Their administration is followed promptly by an exaggerated sense of well-being, often with insomnia and overactivity. Conversely, a long-known disorder involving the destruction of the adrenal glands, *Addison's disease*, has psychological symptoms of exhaustion and depression. These observations suggest that the balance of adrenal cortex hormones may play a part in a normal person's temperament, but such a conclusion is not yet established by experimental evidence.

A second group of adrenal cortex hormones, typified by *desoxycorticosterone*, regulates the retention of sodium salts by the body and their excretion by the kidneys. Deficiency of this hormone leads to abnormal salt-hunger, already discussed as a striking example of homeostasis (see p. 36).

The third identified group of adrenal cortex hormones are chemically identical with the sex hormones secreted by the gonads. Indeed, it is likely that the greater part of the sex hormones found in the blood come from the adrenal cortex and only a minor proportion from the sex glands themselves. Oversecretion of the adrenal sex hormones before birth produces in girls a marked abnormality of the sex organs, tending toward the male type. An excessive secretion in childhood may cause precocious puberty in boys and a change toward masculinity in girls. In adult women, it leads to *virilism*, in which the female sex functions are inhibited, the voice deepens, and a beard appears on the face. The extent to which slight excesses of the adrenal sex hormone may contribute to less marked degrees of masculinity in women is not known. Although adrenal disorders tend to produce changes in the masculine direction, opposite effects can occur. A few cases have been reported in which men have developed feminine secondary characteristics when suffering from adrenal gland tumors.

The Gonads

The sex glands, in addition to their function of developing reproductive cells, secrete hormones which determine the secondary sexual characteristics of bodily form, pitch of voice, and growth of hair. The gonads operate in a complex interlocking system with the adrenal cortex and the anterior lobe of the pituitary gland, which also have profound effects on sex development and functioning.

The male sex hormone, *testosterone*, is secreted in the testes by the interstitial cells, which lie in the tissue supporting the cells that produce the reproductive spermatozoa. If the testes are removed or atrophy before puberty, the secondary sex characteristics do not develop. The shape of the body remains childish or tends toward a distinct type of obesity. The voice is high pitched, and the beard scanty or absent. Loss of the testes by disease or injury in later life after mature male characteristics have been established does not have so extreme an effect. Sexual functions are not entirely abolished by adult castration, perhaps because some quantity of the hormone is supplied by the adrenal cortex, but sex drive and aggressiveness are diminished. It is often observed that men with sex hormone deficiencies tend to be weak, slow, and depressed, characteristics sometimes also seen in older men whose gonads are undergoing involution. How much of these symptoms is due to the primary lack of the hormone and how much to secondary effects of a purely psychological origin has not been determined. Historical evidence indicates that some castrated men, such as the eunuchs of oriental courts, have been able and energetic persons.

The female gonads secrete two types of hormones. One endocrine function is performed by a group of closely related hormones called *estrogens*, contained in the fluid of each follicle, or unit of structure of the ovary. The estrogens are passed to the body in two ways: some amounts are absorbed continuously by the blood as it passes through the ovary; a larger amount is released suddenly once in each ovulation period when a follicle breaks to release an ovum. The estrogens, in a manner analogous to testosterone in the male, maintain the normal primary and secondary characteristics of the female during the period from puberty to the menopause. A second kind of hormone, *progesterone*, is secreted periodically by the *corpus luteum* which consists of cells formed in the follicle of the ovary after the discharge of an ovum. If pregnancy ensues, the corpus luteum continues active for several months, suppressing menstruation and regulating the bodily changes essential to pregnancy. If the ovum is not fertilized, the corpus luteum atrophies in about two weeks and the next menstrual cycle is initiated. Ovarian deficiency involves a lack both of the estrogens and of proges-

terone. The absence of ovarian hormones from birth or from before
puberty results in a sexless creature without the primary or secondary characteristics of womanhood. The effects are not as notice-
able as are those of gonadal deficiency in men, however, perhaps
because women can more easily assume an asexual role in our
culture. Removal of the ovaries after maturity has been reached
does not entirely abolish sexual drives, but often results in a so-
called "nervousness," arising from a general disturbance of endocrine balance rather than directly from the lack of the ovarian
hormones. The effect of lesser shortages of these hormones is not
entirely clear. Hypogonadal women have been described as tending
to be egotistic, resentful, and full of self-pity. This pattern may
well be a defensive reaction to the loss of an esteemed life function, and therefore mainly a secondary effect of the glandular
disturbance.

The Pituitary Gland

Lying in a small depression in the skull at the base of the brain
is the pituitary body, the most complicated and perhaps the most
important of the endocrine glands. The pituitary consists of two
principal parts, the anterior and posterior lobes, which are connected
to the hypothalamic region of the brain by a thin stalk. The anterior
lobe is readily seen under the microscope to be a glandular structure. The posterior lobe, which is derived from the brain in the
course of embryonic development, is not so apparently glandular
but hormones have been traced to it. Each part secretes several
hormones, and the "pars intermedia" between the two lobes also
has an independent endocrine function.

At least six hormones have been identified in the anterior lobe
of the pituitary and there may be more. The best-known is *somatotropin* or the "growth hormone." A deficiency of this hormone
in early life causes dwarfism of a symmetrical type, the individual
becoming an almost perfectly formed miniature adult. Unlike
cretins, most pituitary dwarfs are normal intellectually. An excessive secretion of the growth hormone may cause giantism, with
an especially excessive growth of the long bones and of the hands
and feet. Quite a number of cases have reached authenticated
heights of between eight and nine feet. If somatotropin is secreted
abnormally after mature stature has been reached, the disease of

acromegaly results. Such bones of the body as remain soft — the nose, the chin, the hands, and the feet — show excessive growth, often to the extent of making the person unrecognizable as his former self. Oversecretion of the pituitary is usually due to a tumorous enlargement of the gland.

The anterior pituitary secretes several hormones which have a controlling influence over other endocrine glands. For example, the pituitary's *adreno-cortico-tropic* hormone (ACTH) stimulates the production of the hormones of the adrenal cortex. Therefore preparations of ACTH can be used medicinally in ways analogous to the use of corticosterone, which was described in a preceding section. Similarly, the *thyrotropic* hormone of the pituitary is needed to stimulate the secretion of thyroxin by the thyroid. There are two *gonadotropic* hormones which interact with the sex glands of both males and females. A general pituitary deficiency often affects more than one of its hormones. Thus, a deficiency in the growth hormone is ordinarily accompanied by a defect of the gonadotropic hormones also, so that most, although not all, pituitary dwarfs remain immature sexually. Other known or suspected hormones of the pituitary anterior include regulators of carbohydrate, fat, protein, and water metabolism, and of the secretion of the mammary glands.

The posterior lobe of the pituitary is closely linked with the hypothalamus, a lower brain center which itself controls many basic bodily functions. With the hypothalamus, the posterior lobe contributes to the regulation of blood pressure, the tonus of smooth muscles, metabolism, and the excretion of water.

Because of its psychological implications, one pituitary disorder is of special interest: *adiposogenital dystrophy*, also known as Froehlich's disease. It arises from a complex of pituitary deficiencies probably also involving the hypothalamus. The disorder occurs most commonly among boys. They show great obesity but small bone development, a lack of sexual maturity, and a general lack of endurance. The fat is deposited around the hips and chest in a characteristic way, giving some assistance to diagnosis. The condition is not rare and some cases are to be found in most large schools although, of course, not every fat boy is a "Froehlich." The disorder itself would predispose the youngster to be slow, unaggressive and, in fact, given to abnormal sleepiness. Since they are fat, queer looking, and sissy, such boys are often subjected to ridicule and persecution by their fellows and develop secondary defense mechanisms. As a result, not a few adiposogenital boys become overaggressive behavior problems with symptoms of bullying, cruelty, stealing, and the like. The compensatory social adjustment forced upon them may entirely counteract the primary behavior pattern to which they are predisposed by the endocrine disorder.

Endocrine Disorders in Adjustment

Severe endocrine disorders such as myxedema, toxic goiter, or Addison's disease present problems that are primarily medical rather than psychological. In their early stages some of these diseases may go unrecognized and their symptoms may be ascribed to psychological reactions such as "nervousness" or "neurasthenia." Psychological workers must always be alert to identify the possible signs of endocrine conditions, and should refer suspected cases to appropriate medical specialists for diagnosis and treatment.

Milder forms of endocrine disturbance often underlie adjustive problems that are psychological in all but the predisposing organic factor.

> The history of Louise W. illustrates the interaction of endocrine and psychological factors. Louise was the eldest daughter of an engineer who had attained marked success in his profession. His aims for Louise's education were high and he expected much of her. After a rather undistinguished performance in the upper grades of elementary school, Louise disconcerted her family by repeatedly failing her high school subjects. Enrolled in a classical course of study, she was consistently unable to pass Latin, French, English, and History. At the age of eighteen she had reached only the tenth grade, the work of which seemed beyond her ability. Mr. W. reacted to Louise's failures by lecturing her, by depriving her of privileges, and by trying to ridicule her into better effort. Louise responded alternately with rebellion and with tears, and sincerely threatened to run away from home. The attitude of her father made her loathe her studies and resulted in an even worse school record. A psychologist who was a friend of the family knew of the difficulties, and offered to make a study of the girl's problems.
>
> On an individual mental test which employed few speeded items, Louise made an exactly normal I.Q. of 100, but her responses were unusually slow. A test of reading ability showed

that she scored only at the twelve-year-old level, principally because she was unable to complete the test in the time allowed. Furthermore, Louise presented a very juvenile appearance, looking more like a fourteen-year-old than like a girl of eighteen. She was short and stout in a pudgy way, her face was round with a sagging expression, and her abdomen was markedly protuberant. Louise's slowness and her physique immediately suggested a thyroid deficiency, and it was recommended that she be taken to an endocrine specialist. The physician found a low rate of metabolism and prescribed thyroid treatment. At the same time, the psychologist helped Louise's parents to re-evaluate their attitudes toward her school work. Louise changed to a curriculum that was easier and more interesting to her. Her parents offered support and help in place of scolding. Three years later, Louise was graduated from high school with a creditable record. She married soon afterward and made a successful adult adjustment. The glandular treatment made an irreplaceable contribution to the solution by correcting her slowness and lethargy, but the psychological treatment of the attitudes of Louise and her parents was also essential to the favorable outcome.

The Endocrines in Personality

The value of hormone treatment for the maladjustments associated with endocrine disorders has led to some exaggerated claims about the role of these glands in the formation of normal personality. Because certain pituitary, adrenal, thyroid, and gonadal deficiencies are known to produce slowness, depression, and weakness, it has sometimes been asserted that brilliance of intellect, and dominance or leadership in social behavior, must be due to an uncommon excellence in the functioning of these same glands. An eminent medical authority once made the unsupported statement that hyperthyroid persons readily attain Phi Beta Kappa rank in college! If this were true, thyroid feeding might well be a part of every freshman curriculum. Such extreme claims show the caution that must be exercised in examining the evidence.

The poorest kind of evidence about the endocrines is that based on the apparent results of administering hormone preparations to maladjusted persons. Reports have appeared from time to time indicating that various psychoneurotic conditions have been improved by treatment with the hormones of almost every gland. Few such studies have controlled psychological influences adequately. Regardless of the real merit of any medicine given him, a psychoneurotic person is likely to be helped at least temporarily by suggestion, by a conviction that he is being given a new and powerful treatment, and by the interpersonal relationships incidental to being singled out for special attention. Many alleged endocrine cures are therefore due to a crude kind of psychotherapy rather than to the hormone used. Adequately designed experiments require the use of a control group, which is treated in the same way as the experimental subjects except that it is given an innocuous preparation in place of the hormone. Neither the patients nor the researchers who rate their improvement should know which ones have been given the hormone. So far, no valid experiment has discovered that excellence in any personality trait is due to an identifiable endocrine asset. On the negative side, several careful studies have failed to find an endocrine basis for the psychoses, including schizophrenia.

There is no doubt that endocrine disturbances may have a profound effect on personality in some individual cases. Dysfunctions with respect to several hormones may abnormally decrease or increase a person's metabolic or energy level. The ability to make integrative adjustments is affected at either extreme. Therefore, everyone who is concerned with adjustment problems professionally — psychologists, social workers, teachers, and others — must maintain effective contacts with medical specialists to whom suspected cases can be referred for thorough diagnosis.

Even when endocrine factors have been identified in a particular case, psychological influences remain important. A person who is slow, or fatiguable, or obese because of an endocrine disorder suffers handicaps in his interpersonal relationships. In response to his organically imposed frustrations, he is likely to develop nonintegrative mechanisms of adjustment. He needs psychological treatment as much as medical treatment. Endocrinology and psychology offer supplementary approaches to understanding and helping many people; the two sciences do not replace or refute one another.

OTHER ORGANIC INFLUENCES
ON PERSONALITY

Human beings are complexly integrated organisms whose effective behavior depends on anatomical and physiological integrity. It is therefore not surprising that certain drugs, nutritional deficiencies, and diseases may have a direct effect on the quality of adjustments.

Drugs

From the earliest times of recorded history it has been known that certain drugs have both temporary and more enduring effects on conduct. Alcoholic intoxication, for example, is a familiar temporary behavior disorder. In the early stages of intoxication, most persons become more fluent in language and less inhibited in action. Further ingestion of alcohol has varying effects: some people become elated, others are aggressive, still others weep. There is reason to believe that these changes represent exaggerations of each individual's psychologically acquired characteristics of personality. With still more alcohol, motor coordination fails, discrimination and judgment are affected, and the drunken person lapses into a stupor. Intoxication would be regarded as a serious mental disorder indeed except for the speed with which people recover from it. Chronic alcoholism may be associated with more permanent changes in the nervous system, with an accompanying deterioration of intellectual and social behavior.

In most instances an excessive use of alcohol is a result of personal maladjustment rather than its primary cause. Alcohol provides an escape from the awareness of conflicts and anxieties, serving as a defense mechanism. Most studies now agree that alcoholism is more a response to psychological drives than to physiological cravings. Unassisted medical treatment therefore cannot cure alcoholism entirely. Concurrent psychological treatment is also essential to resolve the conflicts that make a man want to take to drink.

Other more seriously habit-forming drugs such as cocaine, heroin, hashish, and marijuana cause a pleasantly dreamy state while their effects last. After the drug has worn off very severe withdrawal symptoms, including intense anxiety, are experienced.

Psychological factors may play some part in drug addiction, but not in all instances. A few addicts may take drugs because of personal conflicts. Many more are ensnared by cultural and situational factors. A youth may smoke marijuana "reefers" on a dare, or to show his defiance of social norms, or simply for new experience. With continuing use, he builds up a need for the drug in order to escape the severe pangs of withdrawal. Such drugs are more physiologically habit forming than alcohol. Even so, mental hygiene treatment and personal rehabilitation are necessary adjuncts to the medical care of drug addicts.

Nutritional and Vitamin Deficiencies

Clinical observations and experimental evidence show that serious undernourishment may lead to reactions closely resembling psychoneuroses.[4] Starving persons in famine areas and in the concentration camps of World War II often showed striking changes in personality. Much of their distress was due directly to malnutrition, apart from psychological apprehension, as an experimental study of semistarvation has demonstrated.[5] In this experiment, healthy young volunteer subjects were maintained on about half of an adequate diet for six months, and lost an average of 24 per cent of body weight. As their malnutrition progressed the men became increasingly inefficient and undependable. Symptoms of apathy, depression, irritability, and "nervousness" were common among them. Another research study has shown that a chronic deficiency of one essential component of diet can have psychological effects. Salt deficiency gave rise to irritability, depression, and hypochondriacal complaints, which soon disappeared when a normal salt balance was restored.[6]

Lack of vitamins can cause serious deficiencies of tissue nutrition, even when the gross food intake is adequate. One group of vitamins — the vitamin B complex consisting of thiamine, riboflavin, nicotinic acid, pantothenic acid, and pyridoxine — has specific effects on the nutrition of the nervous system. An acute lack of the entire vitamin B complex or of some of its components can precipitate psychological symptoms ranging in severity from mild hypochondria to profound psychosis depending on the degree and duration of the deprivation. *Pellagra*, a disease characterized by skin inflammation, diarrhea, and psychological symptoms, occurs almost entirely among people who have lived on a chronically vitamin-deficient diet. Its mental symptoms vary in intensity from irritability and depression to severe delirium and confusion. Most cases of pellagra can be cured dramatically by large doses of nicotinic acid.

A number of behavior disorders formerly regarded as alcoholic are now ascribed mainly to inadequate vitamin intake. They arise because alcoholic addicts, whose energy needs are supplied by the high caloric value of alcohol, do not eat normally. Vitamin treatment often contributes to the cure of such disorders.

Injuries and Diseases

Injuries and diseases which damage the structural integrity of the nervous system may cause temporary or long-lasting changes in personality. Very profound temporary disabilities, in which psychology has only a minimal interest, often follow acute mechanical or chemical disturbances. Examples are the confusion or unconsciousness resulting from severe blows on the head, and the delirium sometimes accompanying high fever. Modern industrial culture has brought about an increase in head injuries from automobile and factory accidents, but these do not present a serious problem of mental hygiene. The residual effects of head injuries, when any at all persist, are usually limited to specific sensory and motor impairments. A small minority of head-injured persons suffer intermittent attacks of irritability or confusion which interfere with their social adjustments.

Several infectious diseases attack the nervous system specifically. One of the most serious is *general paresis,* a syphilis of the central nervous system. A small proportion of persons with uncured primary syphilis develop paresis some years later, typically when in their forties. The early symptoms of paresis include defects of judgment and tendencies toward alcoholic and sexual excesses which are sometimes mistaken for faults of character. Untreated paresis progresses to sensory and motor disabilities, convulsive seizures, rapid mental deterioration, and delusions. It terminates in death within a few years. Modern treatments are reasonably effective, however, and about four-fifths of cases can be arrested. Paresis can be prevented entirely by prompt and effective treatment of the primary syphilis. It is now only half as common as it was forty years ago, probably because of better and more widespread treatment for primary syphilis. In time, paresis may become a rare disease.

Another brain disease of considerable psychological interest is *epidemic encephalitis,* an inflammation caused by a virus. In most cases, the onset of encephalitis is an acute illness of unmistakable severity. There is intense headache, double vision, pain and rigidity of the neck, and drowsiness or stupor. Encephalitis in childhood is sometimes followed by general disturbances of behavior. Some postencephalitic children are overactive, restless, impulsive, and seriously lacking in emotional control. As a result, these children do not comply with adult-imposed standards of conduct, and their behavior may be interpreted as disobedient, destructive, and "delinquent." Badly disturbed postencephalitic children cannot adjust to a normal home life, but they can sometimes be re-educated to an improved degree of socialization in special schools operated in connection with hospitals.[7] Only a small proportion of delinquents are postencephalitics, but a thorough neurological study of any "incorrigible" child is advisable in order to identify or to eliminate this disease as a possible contributing factor. Encephalitis can also occur in adults, but it then has different sequels. Commonly, a postencephalitic adult may show the "Parkinsonian syndrome" of gross tremors, a mask-like immobility of the facial muscles, and peculiarities of posture and gait. Anxiety, depression, and compulsive and obsessive behavior are also reported.[8]

Old age often brings with it changes in behavior which are correlated with the deterioration of brain structures. Even quite normal elderly people tend to respond more slowly, to remember less well, and to be less flexible in their adjustments to new problems. Individual differences are great, of course. In some persons, age results in only small decrements in ability; in others, the process of aging is accelerated into the pattern known as *senility*. The main physiological basis of senility is the malnutrition of the brain tissues, due to circulatory changes which deprive them of adequate supplies of oxygen and nutrients. If the arteries of the brain become seriously hardened (cerebral arteriosclerosis), the decline tends to be more rapid and to be punctuated by acute episodes of sudden deterioration. The personality characteristics of senile persons vary widely. Some are merely forgetful and confused; others are anxious and depressed; a few are hostile and suspicious even to the extent of having delusions that their relatives are poisoning them or stealing their money. These variations in senile behavior cannot be interpreted solely in terms of the extent or nature of the brain damage. To understand them, it is necessary to seek some broader explanatory principles concerning the interrelationships between organic changes and psychological processes.

Organic and Psychological Interactions

Even this brief survey of the behavior changes associated with organic pathology is sufficient to reveal two of their notable characteristics. First, the effects of various endocrine disturbances, diseases, injuries, drugs, and the like are typically lacking in specificity. Quite different physiological processes can lead to similar behavioral results. Thus, anxiety and depression can accompany drug addiction, nutritional deficiency, brain disease, or senility. Second, the effects of each type of disease or other pathology are extremely variable from one person to another. The behavior of a senile person cannot be predicted just from the fact of his senility. He may be good-naturedly confused, or may be overwhelmed by depression, or may harbor hostile and deluded attitudes against his relatives.

The first of these observations, the nonspecific character of the results of brain damage, is harmonious with what is known about the operation of the cerebral cortex. Although there are some specific sensory and motor areas whose injury causes circumscribed sensory defects or paralyses, most of the cortex is more general in its functioning. The more complex processes of learning, adjusting, and thinking depend on the activity of the cortex as a whole. Extensive damage to almost any part of the brain, caused by whatever agent, leads to a general *incompetence,* rather than to definite behavioral symptoms.[9] The incompetence may vary in character according to whether the damage is sudden as when caused by a blow on the head, or is gradual as when caused by a slowly spreading infection or tumor. Most importantly, the degree of incompetence depends on the extent, severity, and duration of the brain damage.

Since specific behavior defects are not correlated with specific areas or agents of brain damage, other factors must be found to account for the particular symptoms shown. In the main, these other factors are psychological. One determiner of great importance is the developmental stage at which the brain damage occurs. Children may suffer from encephalitis; so may adults, and there is no evidence that the nature or location of the organic damage differs with age.[10] The behavioral sequels of encephalitis, however, are quite different in children than in adults, as we have seen.

Young children are still undergoing a process of psychological development. Their socialization is as yet incomplete, and they tend to act out their impulses. It is not strange, therefore, that an organic process which interferes with a child's ability to comprehend the world and to learn social behavior will result in erratic, impulsive, and unsocial conduct. Identical brain damage in an adult who has already learned his principal social adjustments may give rise to anxiety or depression, but not to antisocial behavior.

The same broad principle is illustrated by some typical characteristics of senility. A senile person is not just a brain-damaged person. He is old culturally as well as biologically. His achievements lie behind him and he lives in a world taken over by younger people among whom he has an insecure and unappreciated status. Senile behavior, therefore, is not merely incapable behavior but consists of relatively handicapped attempts to adjust to life's difficulties. Various elderly persons use various adjustment mechanisms according to the personality traits which they learned in earlier years. The adjustive behavior is determined jointly by the organic condition, the present confronting conflicts, and the past personal history.

PHYSIQUE AND PERSONALITY

Constitutional Types

Since ancient times there has been a tradition that persons of a certain body type, build, or "habitus" show characteristic traits of personality. Thus Shakespeare puts into the mouth of Julius Caesar:

> Let me have men about me that are fat;
> Sleek-headed men, and such as sleep o' nights:
> Yond Cassius has a lean and hungry look;
> He thinks too much: such men are dangerous.

This tradition asserts that the rotund body type indicates the good mixer, the diplomat, and the leader. Thin men are alleged to be moody, introspective, and given to solitude.

Among modern doctrines of body types, that of Kretschmer has evoked the most discussion and research.[11] Kretschmer, a German psychiatrist, distinguished three main types of habitus, and recognized the existence of mixed or "dysplastic" builds. His *pyknic* type is characterized by rounded contours, a full face, a short neck, and a tendency toward stoutness. The *asthenic* or *leptosomic* type is the opposite, thin and angular. The *athletic* type is intermediate in bulk, and notable for the prominence of muscles. By classifying the physiques of patients in mental hospitals, Kretschmer advanced the hypothesis that schizophrenic patients (autistic personality) were mainly of the asthenic type, while manic-depressive (cyclic personality) were predominantly pyknic. Extending these observations to normal people led to the assertion that asthenic persons tend to be autistic or introverted in personality and that pyknics tend to be extraverted or cyclic.

Further research has not confirmed Kretschmer's theories. Average differences between schizophrenic and manic-depressive patients are in the direction proposed by his hypotheses but the overlapping of the groups is great. When exact body measurements are used instead of general impressions, the differences become smaller. Furthermore, schizophrenics tend to be younger than manic-depressives and to be hospitalized for longer periods; both of these factors make for a thinner physique.[12] Kretschmer's body types have no established validity for predicting the personalities of normal people.

Somatotypes and Temperament

Quantitative measurement has clear advantages over qualitative classification. Sheldon introduced a decided improvement in the description of bodily habitus by rating each person on each of three components of physique.[13] Sheldon's components are obviously related to Kretschmer's types, but are used differently. They are:

> *Endomorphy* (visceral-form): degree of prominence of the viscera and of the abdominal region; fatness of the trunk.
> *Mesomorphy* (muscle-form): degree of prominence of muscle and bone structures; appearance of strength, vigor, and erect posture.
> *Ectomorphy* (skin-form): degree of fragility or delicacy, of long, slender, poorly muscled extremities.

An individual's physique is expressed as a *somatotype*, a series of three numerals showing the degree to which he posseses each com-

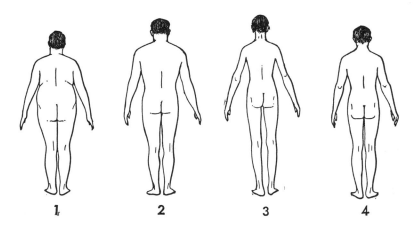

Figure 35. Types of Physiques

The physiques shown are predominantly endomorphic, meso-morphic, ectomorphic, and average. The somatotype of the first physique 1 is 7-1-1½, indicating a maximum of endomorphy, a minimum of mesomorphy, and close to the minimum of ecto-morphy. Physique 2 is 1-7-1½, predominantly mesomorphic. Physique 3 shows the ectomorphic pattern 1½-1½-7. All these extremes occur infrequently. Physique 4 is an average young man whose somatotype is 4-3-4. (After W. H. Sheldon, & S. S. Stevens, *The varieties of temperament.* New York: Harper, 1942.)

ponent. The variables are rated from 1 (low) to 7 (high). As Figure 35 shows, an extreme endomorph is rated 7-1-1, an extreme mesomorph is 1-7-1, and the most extreme ectomorph is 1-1-7. The somatotype 4-4-4 lies at the middle of the scale for each component.

Although the somatotype is a superior method for describing physique, its relation to personality is quite another matter. Shel-don's original investigation hypothesized that there are three main dimensions of temperament, each associated with one of the com-ponents of physique.[14]

> *Viscerotonia* is described as characterized by relaxation, love of comfort, and sociability. It is supposedly associated with the de-gree of endomorphy.
> *Somatotonia* is the characteristic of being energetic, active, and aggressive. It corresponds to mesomorphy.

Cerebrotonia is indicated by restraint, inhibition, intensity, and preference for solitude, and is related to ectomorphy.

Sheldon's original study reported very high correlations between somatotypes and the corresponding temperaments. His results have been criticized severely, mainly because the personality characteristics were rated by clinical case studies in face-to-face relationships without adequate precautions against the rater's possible biases. The interviewer's preconceived faith in the theory may have made it easier for him to perceive "viscerotonic" traits in "endomorphic" subjects. Other studies have failed to confirm Sheldon's results to any great extent. Quantitative measures of personality traits were found to be related to somatotypes by no more than chance expectation.[15] Another investigation found a very moderate degree of correlation between somatotypes and self-ratings of temperament.[16]

The modest correlations so far demonstrated between body build and personality may be understood in terms of learning theory, without a need to hypothesize a direct or innate connection. Physique may well be one of the secondary determiners of personality, because it sets certain limitations to adjustive learning, and influences the social evaluations which a person receives from his fellows. A strong, muscular boy may develop self-confidence because he is successful in athletics, resulting in his acceptance by his schoolmates. A fragile and delicate youngster, under the conditions prevailing in our culture, has a more than average likelihood of learning to withdraw from social contacts. Perhaps all that is significant in the theories of physical habitus is adequately summarized by the old saying that a fat boy has to be good-natured because he can't fight and he can't run.

HEREDITY

Popular opinion regards heredity as a major determiner of personality. Children usually resemble their parents in facial appearance, body build, and color of skin, hair and eyes. Much of this resemblance is hereditary. But children also tend to be like their parents in manner and attitude, and laymen readily ascribe such similarities to heredity, too. Opinions and casual observations, however, do not provide a secure basis for understanding the relationships between heredity and behavior. It is best to look at the evidence.

The Basis of Heredity

Heredity is the contribution to the structure of the organism made by the germ cells. In all species that reproduce bisexually, each individual starts his life as a union of two cells, one from each parent. In the nuclei of these cells are rodlike structures called chromosomes each consisting of a long string of minute particles known as genes. The genes are the bearers of heredity. Human beings have twenty-four pairs of chromosomes, and something like twenty to twenty-five thousand genes. Each gene is about the size of a virus particle, or of ten large protein molecules. The genes interact in determining traits; in only a few instances is there a simple one-to-one correspondence between a gene and a resulting characteristic. For example, the eye color of the fruit fly, *drosophilia*, which has been intensively studied in experiments on heredity, depends on no fewer than fifty pairs of genes.

A popular supposition is that heredity means resemblance to parents, but this concept is inexact and often misleading. The germ cells are not produced by the body cells of the parents and are not modified by the acquisitions, for better or worse, that the parents make in their lifetimes. Parents transmit to their offspring only the traits they themselves received by inheritance. Not all of a parent's germ cells are alike; their cells represent many assortments of determiners derived from the total ancestry. A child may possess a trait quite unlike his parents' which is still due to heredity. Brown-eyed parents usually have brown-eyed children; occasionally they have blue-eyed ones. It cannot be supposed that heredity "works" in the former case and "does not work" in the latter. Both eye colors are hereditary if either is. The simplest principles of genetics, the Mendelian laws, explain quite clearly by the concepts of dominant and recessive traits how children may differ from their parents in a hereditary characteristic, as well as how they may resemble them. The likenesses between parents and children are due to complex causes, partly because both have developed from the same general stock of germ cells, and partly because of environmental influences.

The genes participate only in the development of the structure of an organism. Heredity does not determine function or operation directly, but only through its effect on the organs upon which functioning depends. Theories that human behavior may be inherited as "instincts" or "emotions" have already been explored in Chapter 2, with mainly negative conclusions. When there is a question of the influence of heredity on a dynamic trait of behavior, the first requirement is to identify the structures upon which the characteristic depends. An impaired endocrine gland, or a defect of the number or quality of neurones in the brain, may be as much a matter of heredity as the color of the skin, hair, or eyes. When variation in a behavior trait is clearly associated with a concomitant variation of structure, the probability that it may be affected by heredity is increased.

Heredity and Environments

It is futile to search for traits which are entirely due to heredity and for other traits which are entirely the result of learning processes and environmental agents. No trait is completely uninfluenced by heredity because the very existence of behavior requires an organic structure. All traits also depend in some degree on environment, for they will not develop at all except under reasonably favorable circumstances. Heredity and environment are therefore supplementary, not antagonistic.

Although every trait depends on both heredity and environment for its sheer existence, variations in traits may be unequally affected by these two factors. An issue of great theoretical and practical importance is the relative contribution of hereditary determiners and of specified environmental circumstances upon human traits. The effects of heredity and environment are not constant, but depend upon at least three variables: first, on the trait being considered, second, on the feature of environment which is brought to bear, and third, on the scope and intensity of the environmental forces.

The effects of genetic and environmental influences vary from one trait to another. Some human characteristics are relatively stable, in that they vary only within narrow limits or are affected only by the most catastrophic changes in environment. Other traits are relatively plastic and can be modified substantially by the ordinary variations of environment likely to be encountered in the usual course of life. There is, of course, a continuous gradation from the extreme of stability on the one hand to the extreme of plasticity on the other. Traits can no more be labeled absolutely stable or plastic than they can be designated absolutely hereditary or acquired. An example of a relatively stable trait is the basic skin pigmentation that characterizes a Caucasian, Mongolian, or Negro. It is genetically determined, and seems unmodifiable by ordinary variations in environment. Examples of very plastic traits are numerous. The language you speak, your occupational skills, your likes and dislikes for persons, books, or music, all depend on inherited structures for their sheer existence but are primarily shaped by environmental experiences.

Whether a trait is stable or plastic also depends on the nature and intensity of the environmental influence. Environment is no simple entity; the term "environments" would be more exact. Man encounters many environments. The importance of *prenatal* environment is great, although it is ordinarily very constant. At birth and during the entire course of life, *injuries and diseases* may radically change even the most genetically determined traits. *Physiological* environment — food, warmth, light, exercise, rest, and the like — is an important influence in relation to some traits. In the more psychological sphere, the *intellectual* environment of a person, the literacy level of his home, his parents' interest and participation in intellectual pursuits, and his formal schooling are powerful environmental factors in relation to certain traits. Too often overlooked is what may be called the *emotional* environment. A child who is torn between quarreling parents or who is full of home-grown fears and aversions has been profoundly modified by environmental influences.

The aspects of environments have differential effects on various traits. Nutrition may cause significant variations in height, weight, and resistance to disease but have little effect on literacy, courage, or aesthetic preferences. Aspects of the cultural environment may greatly influence the latter traits while leaving the former ones unchanged. In general, structural characteristics are relatively stable in relation to the usual degrees of environmental variation and are influenced only by circumstances of great intensity. Traits which are more functional, more complex, and less essential to the sheer maintenance of life itself seem usually to be more plastic, susceptible to milder and more usual variations in environments.

EVIDENCE CONCERNING HEREDITY

Many specific questions about the relative effects of heredity and environments are of great theoretical and practical interest to the study of human adjustments. To what extent is one's intellectual ability dependent on identifiable variations in cultural-linguistic environment? In what degree are other dimensions of personality — assertiveness, calmness, stability, vigor — formed or modified by genetic or environmental influences?

Although such questions are ultimately susceptible to objective investigation, serious difficulties stand in the way of designing entirely satisfactory experiments. First, it is usually impossible to control the major variables adequately. The effects of heredity and environments interact so that it is difficult to separate one from the other. Second, studies of heredity depend on the quantitative measurement of the traits which are experimented upon. It is relatively easy to study stature or eye color because these characteristics can be measured or counted readily. Among psychological characteristics, studies of intelligence have the advantage of reasonably satisfactory practical measurement. In contrast, studies of more dynamic personality traits, emotional stability for example, suffer from our relative inability to identify or measure them precisely. It therefore happens that we have considerable knowledge of some traits that are not of the greatest interest to the psychology of adjustment, but lack good evidence about traits of much deeper importance. Still, a number of research studies have made worthwhile contributions.

Studies of Animals

The only true experiments in genetics are performed with lower animals. Laboratory animals may be bred selectively as required for a particular experiment, and their environments may be regulated with considerable precision. Obviously, the ancestry of human subjects cannot be manipulated deliberately, and only imperfect controls can be exercised over their environments. Many of the most crucial experiments on the heredity of bodily characteristics have been carried out with insects, which are ideal subjects because they breed so rapidly and in such great numbers. Experiments on behavior require the use of more complex organisms.

In a now-classic experiment, Tryon showed that maze-learning ability in white rats is greatly affected by heredity.[17] Starting with 142 unselected rats tested for the number of errors they made in learning a maze, Tryon mated together the "brightest" rats within the brightest litters, and the "dullest" rats within the dullest litters, for 18 generations. After 4 generations of selective breeding for maze-brightness or maze-dullness, the error scores of the two groups became clearly distinguishable. By the eighth generation the maze-learning abilities of the two groups did not overlap at all; all the rats in the "bright" group made fewer errors than any of the rats in the "dull" group. Because errors were studied instead of the time required to run the maze, the experiment has been interpreted as demonstrating the inheritance of learning ability, not merely of speed or activity. Other studies with rats have shown that high activity versus low activity, measured by the number of revolutions made by the rats in a revolving-drum cage, can be bred in six or seven generations.[18]

In a study especially significant for the study of personality, Hall succeeded in breeding two strains of rats one of which was designated as "emotional" or "timid," the other as "nonemotional."[19] Emotionality was measured by defecation and urination when placed in a strange situation, a criterion of emotional upset in rats which was well established by earlier observations and studies. Each rat was tested by being placed in a brilliantly lighted circular enclosure 7 feet in diameter, 2 minutes a day for 12 days. Its emotionality score was the number of trials on which it urinated or defecated. The first parent generation of 145 unselected rats made an average score of 3.8. The most emotional rats were then inbred together, and the least emotional ones among themselves, for 12 generations. The nonemotional strain was selected almost at once, the second generation being nearly as free from emotional responses as any subsequent one. The nonemotional rats did not differ very markedly from the unselected parent strain, however, but averaged from about 0.5 to 2 responses, with considerable variability. The emotional rats were selected more slowly, but after 9 generations settled down to a stable average of about 10 responses per 12 trials. The experiment was interpreted as showing that susceptibility to emotional upset can be inherited, and that the genes for nonemotionality are "normal" and dominant over those for emotionality.

A number of other psychological traits of lower animals have been studied in relation to heredity. One of the most interesting is "wildness," the tendency to remain vicious and savage as against being tameable. In spite of many generations of being raised in captivity and being fed and treated identically, the gray Norway rat remains wild in contrast to the easy tameability of the albino. There are many interrelationships between the inherited psychological characteristics of rats. The wild strains tend to be more emotional than the tame ones when tested in the bright-enclosure situation. Tryon's maze-bright rats were more emotionally disturbed in nonmaze situations, but the "dull" rats showed greater emotionality in the maze itself. Nonemotional rats are more dominant or aggressive than emotional ones in attacking strange rats introduced into their cages.

Because heredity can affect only bodily structures, it is important to identify the structural characteristics underlying the inherited behavior traits. So far, no organic differences have been found between maze-bright and maze-dull rats. Their brain weights do not differ, but the variation may reside in subtler microscopic differences in the nervous system. Active strains of rats have a higher rate of metabolism than inactive ones. Hall's emotional and nonemotional breeds differed in their endocrines.[20] The emotional male rats had heavier adrenals and thyroids than the nonemotional, and the emotional females had heavier thyroids and pituitaries, both absolutely and in relation to body weight. If the overweight endocrine glands secrete more hormones, it may be hypothesized that Hall reared a strain of animals with abnormal endocrines which were therefore overemotional.

What are the implications of the animal experiments for an understanding of human heredity? They seem to confirm the hypothesis, also supported by some direct evidence obtained from studies of human beings, that learning ability or general intellectual aptitude is to a considerable degree influenced by genetic determiners. The studies also show, by data obtained under highly controlled conditions, that endocrine abnormalities may be hereditary and may affect the activity level and the emotional lability of organisms.

Two reservations must be made which guard us against drawing excessively sweeping conclusions from the animal researches. First, the behavior of rats is known to be more rigidly set by genetically determined structural factors than is that of mankind. For example, the mating behavior of rats is unlearned and invariable but that of chimpanzees, and surely also of human beings, seems to be acquired by trial-and-error learning (p. 35). Second, substantially the same behavior may originate from structural or from environmental influences. Rats can be taught to be "emotional" or "timid" when confronted with certain stimuli by giving them electric shocks in association with these stimuli (p. 62). When you see an "emotional" rat, you cannot tell whether its behavior is caused by a hereditary endocrine disturbance or by a learned fear reaction. Indeed, the behavior may be the resultant of an interaction between these two factors. Because of the exact controls of both pedigree and environment which animal studies permit, the relative effects of heredity and learning can sometimes be evaluated. Research with human beings does not lead to such definite conclusions.

The Inadequacy of Human Family History as Evidence

Many defects of adjustive behavior run in families. Some years ago several comprehensive studies were made of family lines which showed an excessive incidence of feeblemindedness, psychoses, psychoneuroses, social insufficiency, and crime. These studies contributed greatly to the uncritical popular belief in the potency of heredity.

An early and influential study was that of the Jukes, the descendants of a family of allegedly feebleminded sisters with whom the history begins in the eighteenth century.[21] Of 1258 surviving and traceable descendants, 110 were described as mentally defective and 83 "intemperate," with only 171 considered to be industrious. Equally striking is the history of the Kallikak family.[22] Martin Kallikak, a soldier of the Revolution, is said to have had an illegitimate son by a feebleminded girl. (The evidence of the paternity has been disputed by later scholars.) A total of 480 descendants were traced from the son, among whom 143 were supposedly feebleminded, 292 of uncertain intelligence, 36 illegitimate, 33 prostitutes, 24 alcoholics, 3 epileptics, and 3 criminals, while only 46 were known to be normal. Later, Martin Kallikak married a girl of good family, from which union 496 descendants have been traced. Of the "good" line of descent, only 1 was feebleminded, 1 "sexually loose," 2 alcoholic, and 1 had "religious mania." The remaining 491 were normal, many of them successful business men and eminent members of the professions.

For many years a belief has existed that "insanity" is hereditary. This tradition has been most harmful to constructive mental hygiene because many people, feeling that a shameful "taint" reflected adversely on them, have concealed or denied psychoses in their families instead of securing treatment for the patient. Earlier studies of the heredity of insanity were invalid because of faulty methods of investigation. If a case of mental disorder were found in the family of a patient admitted to a mental hospital, the cause was likely to be ascribed to "heredity." This procedure entirely overlooked the fact that mental disorder is so prevalent that an average individual may have a psychotic person or two among his ancestors or collateral relatives. In recent years, somewhat more sophisticated studies have been carried out. Kallman, for example, traced some 13,000 descendants and relatives of about 1,000 schizophrenics admitted to a German hospital between 1893 and 1902.[23] As compared to an average occurrence of a little less than 1 per cent of schizophrenia in an unselected general population, the incidence of schizophrenia among the relatives of his schizophrenics was 2.6 per cent in first cousins, 3.9 per cent in nephews and nieces, 4.3 per cent in grandchildren, 10.3 per cent in parents, 11.5 per cent among brothers and sisters, and 16.4 per cent in offspring. Although Kallman's methods have been criticized — he sometimes "diagnosed" relatives on report or hearsay, and his data did not always conform to good standards of statistical precision — he seems to have established the finding that schizophrenia runs in families.

The family history studies show that many kinds of personal defects may be familial, but why they have ever been considered as good evidence on heredity puzzles present-day critical thinkers. Those who have put their faith in family histories have tended to ignore the very relevant point that children of Kallikak inheritance were brought up in Kallikak environments, and that parents with psychotic tendencies rear as well as beget their children who may also become psychotic. The observed results may be as much due to familial learnings as to familial heredities. In all probability, both factors contribute to many of the defective traits, to different extents according to the relative plasticity of the traits concerned.

The acceptance of family histories as evidence for heredity illustrates the danger of taking a technique of investigation from one area to another without also taking the appropriate precautions. Valuable information about heredity has been gained from breeding experiments with plants, insects, and lower animals. In such studies, however, heredity has been controlled by planned inbreeding through many generations to produce genetically homogeneous strains, and environments have been regulated precisely. Differences appearing in rats are regarded as hereditary only if they occur systematically in genetically pure lines, and if food, warmth, disease, opportunity to learn, and other pertinent factors are held constant. Human family studies are inconclusive because neither genetic nor environmental conditions can be controlled adequately.

Every clinic which works with practical problems of personal adjustment finds that difficulties are often encountered in successive generations and in many instances are blamed on heredity. Morgan, for example, describes a typical instance.[24]

> A ten-year-old girl was brought to a psychological clinic by her mother with the complaints that she was nervous, overactive, had queer mannerisms, and had run away. Because the family history showed that the mother had suffered a "nervous breakdown" four years previously and had been suspected of having chorea at the age of fourteen, and that the grandmother was nervous as well, the case had earlier been diagnosed as "neurotic tendencies" due to heredity. At the modern clinic, the "heredity" was quickly dismissed. When separated from her mother, the girl acted in every way like a normal child. Further study showed that the girl's supposed instability was due to the experience of being thwarted at every turn by her psychoneurotic mother. One conduct disorder had given rise to another not by inheritance but by the reaction of the child's personality to that of her mother.

Human family histories, then, offer no conclusive evidence as to the relative effects of heredity and environments on intelligence or personality. Familial traits may be hereditary, or may be learned from one generation to another, or may result from the interactions of heredity and learning. The mere fact of running in families does not tell which of these alternatives is correct.

Foster Children

True experiments in genetics ca not be carried out with human subjects, but circumstances sometimes contrive to approximate an experimental design. One such situation arises when a child is reared by foster parents. An adopted child receives his heredity from his biological parents and his environment from his foster parents, thereby permitting some separation of the two influences. Ideally it may be considered that resemblances between foster parents and their foster children are due to environment alone.[25]

Several extensive studies of foster children have been made, but each has had some unavoidable defect which has prevented its conclusions from being unequivocal. Freeman, Holzinger, and Mitchell studied 401 foster children in the Chicago area.[26] Of these, 74 had been tested before adoption at an average age of 8 years and were retested at an average age of 12 years, 2 months. The average I.Q. before adoption was 91.2 and after the four-year interval was 93.7, a gain of 2.5 points. To this gain a perhaps generous correction of 5 points was added, because of defects in the standardization of the Stanford-Binet Scale which made it overestimate the I.Q. of younger children and underestimate that of the older ones. The Chicago study thus concluded that the average gain due to the favorable change in environment was 7.5 points. Other findings were that the children placed in the culturally better foster homes, and the children placed at younger ages, made the greater gains. In the Chicago group were 159 separated siblings, true brothers or sisters placed in different foster homes. Their intelligence test scores showed a coefficient of correlation* of only .25, in comparison to correlations of .50 usually found between siblings reared together. The correlation of children's intelligence scores with those of their foster parents was .37.

Another study, made in California by Burks, traced the develop-

---

* The coefficient of correlation is a measure of the relationship between two sets of paired measures. The measures may be a person's scores on two tests taken at the same time or at different times, or may be the scores made by two defined persons, such as brothers, or twins, or foster parent and foster child. Perfect correlation, or a completely corresponding positive relationship, is indicated by a coefficient of 1.00. The absence of relationship is indicated by .00. Although the interpretation of correlation coefficients depends on the uses to which they are put, the following suggestions are helpful:
.90 — .99 "very high"
.75 — .89 "high"
.50 — .74 "marked"
.20 — .49 "present but low"
.00 — .19 "negligible"
Negative coefficients indicate an inverse relationship, a tendency for one of a pair of scores to be high when the other is low.

ment of 214 children adopted before the age of 12 months, and of a comparison group of 105 children reared in their own homes.[27] The average I.Q. of the adopted children was 107.4. The children were too young to be tested validly before adoption, but on the basis of the occupations of the true parents, Burks estimated an average original I.Q. of 100, and therefore judged that a gain of 7.4 points was due to adoption. The result agrees with that of the Chicago study but perhaps accidentally so, because both researches used somewhat dubious estimates and corrections. The correlation between the intelligence of the foster children and that of their foster parents was .20, a lower figure than found by the Chicago study. The correlation between the intelligence scores of the own children and their parents was the expected .52.

The longest follow-up study of foster children was reported by Skodak and Skeels, who traced an Iowa group of 100 children through a thirteen-year interval.[28] All of these children had been placed in foster homes before they were six months old, and therefore had not been tested before placement. After adoption they were tested at four intervals at average ages of about 2, 4, 7, and 13 years. As Table 7 shows, the children's I.Q.'s did not correlate

Table 7
Correlations of Foster Children's I.Q. with Education of Foster Parents and with Education and I.Q. of True Mother*

		Correlation of child's I.Q. with:†			
Test Interval	Child's average age	Foster father's education	Foster mother's education	True mother's education	True mother's I.Q.
I	2–2	.05	—.03	.04	.00‡
II	4–3	.03	.04	.31	.28
III	7–0	.03	.10	.37	.35
IV (1916 Binet) § ...	13–6	.06	.04	.31	.38
IV (1937 Binet) § ...	13–6	.00	.02	.32	.44

* From Marie Skodak and H. M. Skeels. A final follow-up study of one hundred adopted children. *J. genet. Psychol.*, 1949, 75, 85-125.

† The number is 100, except for the correlations with true mother's I.Q. which are based on 63 cases.

‡ The tests given at age 2–2 correlated poorly with all other data, including the later tests to the same children, probably because of the difficulty of testing children validly at so early an age.

§ The 1916 Revision of the Stanford-Binet Test was used for tests I, II, and III. At the final test IV, both the 1916 Revision and the 1937 New Revised Stanford-Binet were administered.

significantly with the education levels of either of their foster parents, but did correlate substantially with the education of their true mothers. Intelligence tests had been given to the true mothers of 63 of these children. The average I.Q. of these mothers was 85.7; the average I.Q. of their children was 106 when examined with the same test at the age of about thirteen years. This finding shows that the children in the foster homes had higher ability than their true mothers, many of whom had come from culturally deprived backgrounds. However, the children's I.Q.'s correlated significantly with their true mothers' I.Q.'s (Table 7); that is, the brighter children were the offspring of the relatively brighter mothers and vice versa. From this study it may be concluded that a favorable change of environment may raise intelligence appreciably, but that the genetic determiners are still important.

Studies of foster children tend to show that intelligence is a relatively stable trait, neither absolutely fixed by heredity nor wholly plastic. Worth-while, although limited, gains in intelligence result from favorable changes in cultural and social environment.

Because of the difficulties involved in measuring other personality traits quantitatively, there is little exact evidence concerning the effects of adoption on the quality of the children's adjustments. Burks gave a children's version of the Woodworth inventory (p. 323), a screening questionnaire designed to detect maladjustment in general, to a small number of the older adopted and own children in the California study. The foster children's average scores did not differ from those of the own children. Some correlations were calculated between the children's questionnaire scores and ratings of the parents on traits such as "kindness," "tact," and "sympathy," and on the degree of parental supervision of the children. These correlations were as high for the foster parent and foster child relationships as for the own parents and their children. Although the data are based on too few cases to permit sweeping conclusions, they suggest that these personality traits are highly influenced by environment.

Enumerative statistics and case studies offer some evidence about the effects of foster-home placement on personal adjustment, even in the absence of quantitative measurement. Some years ago social agencies placed many children in foster homes as a method for treating personal and social maladjustment. Foster-home placement is not so widely used today. Agencies prefer to work constructively with the child and his parents, and remove the child from the home only only in extreme instances. Still, the older studies of foster-home placement provide data of some value.

A good example is the report by Healy, Bronner, Baylor, and Murphy of the changes produced in 501 children who were placed in foster homes because of conduct and personality problems.[29] In the main group of 339 children, placed by private agencies rather than by state agencies or juvenile courts, the results were judged successful in 74 per cent of the cases. Of 252 children placed because of delinquency, 69 per cent achieved a successful outcome. Of 87 placed for personality or adjustment problems, 89 per cent were judged entirely successful. Among these children, the factors which best predicted success or failure were diagnoses of mental deficiency or of "abnormal mentality or personality," made before placement. Of the children diagnosed as mentally normal, 90 per cent were successful, of those of inferior intelligence, 70 per cent, and of the "abnormal or peculiar" personalities, 45 per cent. Just what was meant by "abnormal or peculiar personality" is not clear. All of the children who presented problems sufficiently severe to warrant placement showed other than normal personality in some degree. The more serious diagnosis seems to have implied a prediction of dubious success in treatment, and it is interesting to note that nearly half of even this doubtful group was satisfactorily readjusted.

The successes of foster-home placement by the social agencies were not due, of course, to "mere environment" in the sense of haphazard change of home. All were carefully studied and were placed under circumstances promising the most hopeful progress. Most of the children received concurrent psychological treatment at an excellent clinic. The most relevant finding of such studies is that traits of conduct and personality can be modified by planned procedures, and are therefore relatively plastic and remediable.

Studies of Twins

Studies of twins throw some further light on the relative influences of heredity and environments. Twins are of two kinds, *fraternal* twins who develop from the simultaneous fertilization of two ova, and *identical* twins who develop from a single fertilized ovum which has divided early in embryonic life to form two individuals. Fraternal twins are no more alike in heredity than are siblings — ordinary brothers and sisters. They may be of the same sex or of unlike sex and commonly show no greater resemblances than do other children of the same family. Identical twins, since they develop from the same germ cells, have identical heredities and are therefore of special significance in the study of heredity. Identical twins are best distinguished by multiple signs: a common chorion or sac at birth, and identity of fingerprints, ear convolutions, color of eyes, color and texture of hair and skin, and the like. No one of these signs is infallible, but the presence of several of them gives a fairly secure diagnosis.

Numerous studies have compared pairs of identical twins to fraternal twins and to siblings.[30] The results of most investigations are similar. In height, weight, and I.Q., identical twins correlate about .90; fraternal twins, .65; and siblings, .50.[31] The interpretation of such data rests, first, on the fact that heredity is identical for identical twins, but is nonidentical and of equivalent weight for both the fraternal twins and the siblings. A further assumption is sometimes made that identical and fraternal twins have equally similar environments because they are of the same age and grow up in the same homes. Siblings have less identical environments. If these assumptions were valid, the difference in the correlations of identical twins and of fraternal twins would be a measure of the effect of heredity; the differences between the correlations of fraternal twins and those of siblings would measure the effect of environment. This rationale has flaws. Identical twins are not only more alike in heredity than are fraternals, but also more alike in environment. Their striking identity of appearance makes other people treat them alike. They often are dressed alike and treated as a unit by their families. The studies of twins reared together in normal homes fails to give conclusive evidence about heredity and environment.

The earlier studies of twins contributed little to our knowledge of the effects of heredity and environment on personality because only crude and unreliable measures of personality traits were available. Anecdotal descriptions have shown that identical twins who are much alike in physique and intelligence may differ greatly in social attitudes and temperament.[32] There are a few quantitative studies. Cattell and Molteno tested 31 pairs of identical and 53 pairs of fraternal twins with objective measures of two aspects of personality: "fluency," or ease of making associations, and "perseveration," or difficulty in shifting from one to another of two conflicting tasks.[33] The identical twins did not resemble one another more than the fraternal twins. Troup gave the Rorschach test (p. 334) to 20 pairs of identical twins.[34] Ten pairs were tested twice at a six-month interval. Expert Rorschach examiners had little trouble in matching an examinee's record with his own later performance. That is, each child tested twice made identifiably consistent responses to the Rorschach. The judges had little success, however, in matching the Rorschach record of a child to that of his twin. To the extent that the Rorschach measures personality, these twins tended to have different personalities. All of these studies seem to support the conclusion that dynamic traits of personality are less influenced by heredity than are physical characteristics or intellectual abilities.

Twins Reared Apart

Identical twins have sometimes been separated at an early age and reared in different homes. Such cases are not common, and only 28 pairs of identical twins reared apart received intensive study in the quarter-century from 1925 to 1950.[35] Of these, 19 were reported in one comprehensive study by H. H. Newman and his colleagues. In anatomical characteristics such as height and head measurements, these twins resembled each other as perfectly as do identical twins reared together. Even in diseases and in glandular disorders there were striking similarities in some cases. The results of intelligence tests give mixed evidence. Among Newman's 19 pairs, 12 showed small differences in I.Q., 3 differed moderately, and 4 had the appreciable differences of 24, 19, 17, and 15 I.Q. points respectively. In each of the extreme instances the higher scoring twin had received marked educational and cultural advantages. The largest difference was between a woman of I.Q. 116 who was a college graduate and a teacher, and her twin of I.Q. 92 who had no schooling beyond the second grade. The educational, social, and health environments of the 19 pairs were rated. Of the traits of physique, only weight was significantly correlated with health environment. But all intelligence and achievement scores had significant correlations with the ratings of educational environment. The average I.Q. difference of all 19 pairs of twins reared apart was about 8 points, in comparison to typical average differences of about 6 between identical twins reared together and of about 10 between fraternal twins or siblings. It is evident from these studies that intelligence test scores may be greatly influenced by extreme variations in cultural environments, even with genetic material held constant.

So far, studies of identical twins reared apart have contributed. no conclusive evidence of the influences of heredity and environment on nonintellectual personality traits. Case studies show both similarities and differences in temperament and adjustive behavior. The earlier studies used some questionnaires and tests of doubtful value. One of the more recent studies gave the Rorschach to three pairs of identical twins reared apart but no substantial conclusions could be drawn from these few cases.

One major trouble with the studies of twins reared apart is that different homes do not necessarily provide radically different environments. The aim of seeing how persons of identical heredity fare under different circumstances is therefore only partly achieved. At present, it is not too difficult to evaluate qualities of physical and cultural environments and therefore to weigh their effects on the characteristics of the twins. The aspects of environment which make for good or poor adjustive behavior are less readily identified, so that the results of the twin studies remain ambiguous in regard to personality traits.

Some Conclusions and Practical Considerations

Although the evidence concerning the relative amounts of variation in human traits ascribable to heredity and to environment is incomplete, it affords some basis for a point of view. There is no doubt of the influence of heredity upon the structure of the human body, although various environmental factors modify even quite anatomical traits within certain limits. Mental ability seems to be a prime example of a characteristic arising from an interaction of heredity and environments. Although intelligence is probably founded on structural properties of the nervous system, favorable cultural environment can improve it somewhat and unfavorable environments can retard it seriously. There is reason to believe that the functional characteristics of personality and adjustment are among the most plastic of human traits. Only when they depend on glandular or other bodily structures are they resistant to formation and change by ordinary environmental influences.

Even if some traits are greatly influenced by heredity, a fatalistic attitude toward them is not justified. "Hereditary" does not necessarily mean "unmodifiable." If a child has hereditary web fingers, parents do not give up but have the defect remedied by surgery. Similarly, no one should ignore the possibility of improving a psychological condition because it is supposedly based on heredity. Even relatively fixed traits can be modified in a worth-while degree if the appropriate environmental influences are brought to bear.

SUGGESTED READINGS

For a general overview of the physiology of behavior, selected chapters of introductory texts such as Munn, *Psychology;* Boring, Langfeld and Weld, *Foundations of Psychology;* and Ruch, *Psychology and Life* will be useful. Textbooks on general physiology also contain material on the endocrines and other organic factors in behavior. Carlson and Johnson, *The Machinery of the Body,* and Stackpole and Leavell, *Textbook of Physiology* are suggested. Chapters 16–19 of Hunt, *Personality and the Behavior Disorders* provide reference material only a little more advanced in character than this text.

On the endocrine glands, see Hoskins, *Endocrinology,* and Beach, *Hormones and Behavior.*

One of the best discussions of heredity is Boyd, *Genetics and the Races of Man.* On specifically psychological problems in genetics, see Anastasi and Foley, *Differential Psychology,* especially Chapter 4, and Woodworth's monograph, *Heredity and Environment.*

CHAPTER 13

Learning and Personality

An individual's personality has been defined as his persistent tendencies to make certain qualities and kinds of adjustments. What are the sources of these tendencies? In the preceding chapter, some evidence was presented to show that structural, physiological, and hereditary factors have some influence upon personality. The next task is to discover how a person's typical adjustive techniques develop through his processes of learning, and to define some of the conditions that determine them.

HOW PERSONALITY IS LEARNED

If we ask how man differs from all other animals, we are likely to think of his upright posture, his use of tools with his hands, and his possession of speech. The capacity for speech and symbolic activities enable him to solve problems in physics and economics, to write poetry, and to think about himself and the world in complex and creative ways. There is little else that separates man's most basic characteristics of personality from the behavior of the rest of the animal kingdom.

Basic Human Characteristics

Even the most basic attributes of upright postures, use of tools, and speech do not appear automatically as a result of man's purely biological nature. There have been a few opportunities to study children who have grown up, like Romulus and Remus, the legendary founders of Rome, in nonhuman environments.[1] Such "wild children" grew up in isolation from other human beings, some surviving apparently through their own efforts, more of them being raised by animals. About forty cases of these children have been described and are of particular importance because of the light they throw on how far characteristically human behavior develops in the absence of ordinary human contact and stimulation.

It appears that all of these wild children were mute and quadrupedal when found. None of them had developed anything resembling speech or language facility of any kind. All of them had adopted some form of locomotion on their hands and feet or hands and knees. Likewise, none showed any disposition to use tools or to employ their hands in the fine movements permitted by their structure.

Other characteristics of these children are noteworthy. Raw meat was the common diet of those raised by carnivorous animals, whereas others seem to have lived on bark, roots, herbs, and wild berries. Their pattern of eating, too, was like that of animals, including the smelling of food before eating, lowering the mouth to the food instead of lifting food to the mouth, and sharpening the teeth on bones and tree bark. They showed no tendency to cover their bodies either because of ordinary human sensitivity to heat and cold or because of any sense of modesty or shame. No crying and no laughter was observed, but the children did seem prone to violent anger and impatience at times. When found, they seemed to fear human company and often to prefer the companionship of lower animals.

Even though these cases are few and sometimes not as well described as we could wish, they strongly suggest that there are virtually no characteristics that belong to man simply by virtue of his biological potentials. These wild children were clearly human in the biological sense, but psychologically they possessed none of the behavioral traits that we associate with human status. Their adjustments were almost completely those of lower animals. An evident conclusion is that our distinctive attributes, even our most fundamentally human qualities, are products of our experience with other human beings. Personality is learned as a result of the events in one's history.

Principles and Conditions of Learning

The proposition that personality is learned may appear to pose an insoluble problem. If personality is the result of experiences, and if the experience of each person differs, how can we arrive at any understanding of personality short of constructing a complete biography of every individual? Even if this impossible task were somehow achieved, would our general understanding be increased or would we simply possess a knowledge of a number of separate people? Would any general principles emerge which could be validly applied to the understanding of new cases? Is there a general psychology of personality, or are there only the individual psychologies of Tom, Dick, and Harriet? The answer to this troublesome question lies in two considerations.

The learning of personality, like all other learnings, is determined by two factors — the general principles of learning which apply to all mankind, and the particular conditions of learning which govern what a specific person learns at a certain time.

While the experiences of all of us are different, the principles in terms of which we learn our adjustments are essentially constant. All of us learn to behave through such processes as reinforcement, generalization, inhibition, and extinction which were described in earlier chapters. These principles provide tools for understanding the effects of events in the lives of specific persons. They suggest what is important to look for in one's past experience in order to understand more fully the determinants of one's present behavior.

Thus, a young man who gets headaches that prevent his taking examinations in college is probably a person whose adjustment by illness has been reinforced through removing him from such anxiety-creating situations as tests. Since the strength of an adjustment is a function of its past reinforcements, we suspect that our young man grew up under conditions where getting sick permitted him to escape trying responsibilities. In examining his history, we are likely to search for instances in which illness led to rewards. Our understanding of his behavior is enlarged when we discover that his mother protected him when he was sick, babied him, excused him from obligations, and appeared to enjoy having him home to care for. The general *principles* of learning — such as reinforcement and generalization — help us to comprehend the particular *conditions* of learning operating in this case. They also help us to decide which of the many possible conditions of learning are most important to examine.[2]

The relationship between principles and conditions also permits us to identify weaknesses in our theories. If we discover, for example, that our hypothesized principles do *not* lead to relevant events in a person's history, then we have an opportunity to revise these theoretical notions and put them to new tests. The psychology of personality develops largely through the process of repeatedly testing proposed principles against actual observations of individual growth and learning.

Another important source of a general understanding of personality is that the conditions of learning themselves, while differing from one life history to another, can be grouped together in useful ways. For example, we can consider rewarding and punishing conditions together even though the exact types of reward or punishment may differ, asking later whether the differences in form affect the adjustment patterns.

> Both Philip B. and Martin W., for example, were noted for their mildness and unaggressive ways although both seemed a prey to sullen withdrawal on frequent occasions. Both were troubled, too, by bad dreams in which they imagined themselves acting aggressively toward loved ones, even killing them in these nightmares. In these respects these two young men had similar personalities, but their upbringings were different. As a youngster, Philip had received severe physical punishment for any show of aggression toward anybody. Martin, in contrast, had never been spanked or beaten, but had had the evils of aggression preached to him by all members of a large fundamentalist family who threatened him with the colorfully depicted torments of hell in the afterworld if he did not behave unaggressively.

Both men had been made afraid of their own aggressive impulses through punishment, although the punishments had differed in form. In this respect, their very similar behavior developed out of similarities in their learning environments, even though these similarities must be identified through the organizing concept of punishment.

Social Conditions of Learning

The events that effect the development of personality may be organized in terms of a relatively small number of concepts. Furthermore, observations show that personality is learned primarily from experiences with other human beings. These two considerations permit an approach to the problem of personality development by considering the effects of group membership on adjustment patterns. Each person belongs to a number of social groups, and each group may affect his behavior in significant ways. Because we are members of the American culture, for example, we speak English, have certain tastes in food and entertainment, tend to put a high value on material success and personal ambition, and think nothing of women going unescorted to restaurants, theaters, and other public places. Many European and Asiatic cultures have quite different customs. In the same vein, our membership in a regional group, a church, or a school shapes our adjustments and influences the contours of our personality through the contact it provides with other people and with their ideas of how we ought to behave.

In short, personality is conceived as a product of social learning. Its development is largely a function of the social conditions under which one grows up. The emphasis on social conditions, however, goes beyond mere abstractions like "the conditions of society." Many social events, such as peace or war, or prosperity or depression, may be important influences on personality. But their importance lies mainly in the effects they have on direct and intimate relationships between people, especially those between children and their parents. The great depression of the nineteen-thirties undoubtedly left its mark on the personalities of many who grew up during that period. In some instances, it had its effect by exposing youngsters to fathers who had lost their self-esteem because they were unable to support their families, or by subjecting people to the intense competition for food and shelter that arises from the threat of poverty. In other cases, the depression probably had integrative effects on some whose fathers provided them with a model of courage and industry during such a trying time, or who were members of a family or a group who banded together cooperatively in a spirit of mutual help to survive long economic hardship. The social conditions basic to personality development are essentially the conditions that are brought to bear on intimate, individual human relationships.

In all descriptions of personality development, special attention is given to the period of childhood. This emphasis is justified but requires clarification. Personality is dynamic, and continues to change with experience from birth to death. It is never completely determined at some point in childhood so as to be unalterable thereafter. On the other hand, children have the most to learn and are more docile learners, and hence acquire many long-enduring reaction patterns. Later learning proceeds against a background of older adjustments that are strong because of effective and frequent reinforcements. Much of later learning therefore involves a modification of adjustment patterns rather than the acquisition of new ones. For these reasons, childhood is a crucially formative period. Just when childhood ends is somewhat indefinite and probably varies from one person to another. At least, it extends well into adolescence. Childhood is important because of the relatively greater amount of learning that occurs then, not because all the adjustment patterns of personality are completely determined by some early age.

Crucial Learnings

Some social learnings are much more important than others in determining the integrative quality of a person's adjustments. The broadest definition of personality includes all traits that distinguish a person as an individual or as a member of a defined group. Therefore, personality may be taken to include the language, food habits, typical diversions, and the like which mark a person as being American, Egyptian, or Balinese. More individually, the total of a man's personality might include whether he habitually prefers to go fishing, play bridge, or solve crossword puzzles. But such features of personality are rarely crucial to a person's happiness and effectiveness.

The personality learnings most crucial to integrative adjustment are those which involve conflict or freedom from conflict. A person whose adjustments are excellently sound is able to make unambiguous responses to his major life activities. He can eat, achieve, enjoy, and love without simultaneously feeling guilty; he can forego a satisfaction when circumstances require without having strong pangs of regret. A little more technically, integrative adjustments require responses that are clearly adient or avoidant, without the contrary impulse being present in undue strength. Conversely, nonintegrative adjustments occur when the social learnings basic to personality have inculcated both the seeking and the avoiding of the same essential life experiences.

Some learnings that breed conflicts can be identified more specifically. One of great scope is the attachment of *fear* to persons and situations commonly met in the course of life, or of strong *anxiety* to one's usual roles or strivings. When fear or anxiety are strongly reinforced by punishments, they tend to generalize to situations beyond the original learning, and therefore to render the person ambivalent and conflicted in many spheres of activity. Another commonly learned nonintegrative attitude is *hostility*, the expectation that other persons are unfriendly and must be combatted. Still another is excessive *dependence*, a learned attitude that comes in conflict with individual, free, and creative adjustments. These habits of personality, and a number of others, are detrimental to effective adjustment because they so often give rise to disabling avoidant-avoidant and adient-avoidant conflicts. Therefore, in a survey of the social situations in which personality is learned, special attention must be paid to the origins of these factors and their integrative opposites — confidence versus fear, self-regard versus anxiety, cooperation versus hostility, and freedom versus dependence.

CULTURE AND PERSONALITY

The largest social unit acting on an individual is his culture. A culture may be defined as the way of life of a people, including their knowledge, beliefs, art, morals, laws, customs, and social organization. Cultures may be geographically contained in large areas like India or small ones like Samoa, or they may be geographically dispersed, as is the case with the Jews. People tend to take their cultures with them when they emigrate to new lands. The refusal of a culture to be restricted to national boundaries is illustrated by the Italian, Polish, or Chinese communities in almost any large American city.

Culture is important to personality because it constitutes the most general patterning of the learning environment for its individual members. Cultures develop institutions which ensure that people accept and behave in accordance with a broadly prescribed set of conduct norms. The process of teaching persons from infancy to act and think in culturally sanctioned ways is *socialization*. Schools, churches, courts, and perhaps most importantly, the family itself, are examples of institutions which make children grow up in harmony with the principles of their culture. All cultures, of course, are susceptible to change. Like individuals, they may be modified by new ideas, inventions, and discoveries. The industrial revolution, for example, represented a very considerable change in our culture, and other more recent changes are apparent as a result of devices for rapid transportation and communication. But cultures retain their identity and set the conditions through which personality is learned. The influence is so pervasive that many agents of the socialization process are hardly aware that they are training others to act like good Americans, Ainus, Scotsmen, or Bedouin Arabs.

Cultural Influences

The scope of cultural influences is dramatically exemplified in the case of Fung Kwok Keung, who arrived in New York as an almost perfect representative of a Mandarin Chinese.[3] His dress, habits, speech, and outlook identified him as Chinese, but his features were Caucasian. Actually, he was born Joseph Rinehart, of American parents on Long Island, New York. Deserted at the age of three, he was adopted by a Chinese who took him to China where he was raised by a Chinese family as one of their own children until he was nineteen. Returning to the United States, he had to go to Americanization classes to learn his "native" language, and to become acquainted with his "native" culture. Apparently, Fung's (or Joseph's) early socialization had been quite complete.

Another instance of the influence of culture on personality, and one more nearly related to the quality of adjustments, may be taken from the Crow Indians.[4] Members of this tribe show many evidences of fear of water. They typically refuse to eat anything that lives in water or is associated with it. They go near water as infrequently as possible and have legends and folk beliefs about dreadful water monsters. Too, the worst shame that a Crow can suffer is to have someone throw water on him. The Crows' behavior toward water seems related to the common practice among Crow parents to pour water down the noses of their children to quiet them when they cry. This experience may condition the Crows' strong fear of water and influence their complex set of attitudes, beliefs, and behaviors toward it.

The illustration from the Crow Indians offers a good opportunity to point out that the relationship between childhood experience and later personality is not a simple one of cause and effect. Rather, it is reciprocal and complicated. While pouring water in the noses of crying babies seems to determine the adult conception of water as a hateful and fearful object, the converse of the proposition must be also considered. What leads Crow parents to use water to punish their children? Punishment, after all, consists in the application of something frightening and hurtful and, among the Crow, few things fit these specifications so well as water. It is doubtful, also, that the isolated incidents of infancy are the sole determiners of the attitude toward water. The Crow child grows up in the Crow culture and has many other opportunities to become indoctrinated in the beliefs of his people.

A third example of a widespread cultural influence on the formation of later personality involves the phenomenon of adolescence. In America, we are accustomed to think of this period as stressful for both biological and social reasons. The maturing of sexual characteristics and the rapid and irregular growth, with their concomitant embarrassments and hidden pride, are considered the source of common adolescent difficulties. Socially, the adolescent considers himself grown up and to a large extent he is, yet he is conflicted between adult injunctions to act maturely and adult restrictions that make him still a child.

Margaret Mead, in a classic study, found that adolescent difficulties do not exist for Samoans.[5] In this island culture in the South Seas, children are regarded as differing in their capacities to learn but gifted with a slowly maturing "understanding." Consequently, although they are urged to learn, work, and behave properly, they are never required to make crucial changes according to an age schedule. A Samoan child is never angrily enjoined to grow up, and Samoan parents seldom compare the ages at which their children are weaned or first accept some responsibility in the household. Since "understanding" develops slowly and at different rates, nobody expects all six-year-olds to do the same things; there is no pressure to "keep up with the Joneses."

On the other hand, Samoan children never have a period of complete freedom from responsibility such as usually marks at least early childhood in our culture. From the time they are four or five, they are given definite tasks graded to their strength and intelligence but of clear importance and meaning in the life of the community. Little boys dig for bait, collect cocoanuts, run errands, and do many other things, depending on their abilities. In the same fashion, little girls sweep the floors, weave mats, help to prepare food, and care for babies. As a result, growing responsibility is readily accepted as a function of growing ability and strength, and work is not regarded as something unfamiliar which is thrust upon one suddenly when he attains adult status.

In such a cultural context, adolescence is unknown as anything except a part of the slow, steady development of the Samoan child into an "understanding" adult. The signs of biological maturity are the same, but there is none of the storm and stress associated with the period in the American culture. The difference seems to lie in the Samoan steadiness, the freedom from pressure to achieve, and the provision for the child both to take responsibility and to enjoy its rewards.

Obviously, the problems of American adolescence cannot be solved by a simple translation of Samoan ways of living into our terms. Samoan culture is essentially simple, a product of a favorable climate, an abundant food supply, a small population, and a well-integrated social system. To achieve the Samoan solution, we would have to give up the advantages of our complex technology and the comforts of modern life. But the comparison of the Samoan culture with our own is instructive in several ways. It affords another example of the determination of personality by the culture in which it occurs, and of the reciprocal interaction between child training practices and adult characteristics. Even as late in the developmental sequence as the period of adolescence, long-enduring conflicts, or freedom from conflict, may be brought about by the conditions of learning.

The Systematic Study of a Culture

The examples given in the preceding section seem to illustrate the effects of culture on personality through its child rearing practices. Still, these examples are anecdotes. Like isolated case studies, they could be exceptional and selected instances and therefore precarious ground for a general theory. The answer to this legitimate skepticism must come from more systematic and better controlled investigations.

An example of a systematic study of a culture is provided by the work of Kardiner, a psychiatrist, which stemmed from the practical problems of a neurotic man who had come to him for psychotherapy.[6]

Kardiner's patient was a thirty-year-old man who complained of difficulties in his relationships with women, a chronic state of anxiety, several phobias including a particularly severe one against making speeches, constant feelings of unworthiness, an inability to compete with others, and a painful sense of failure. After many hours of interviews, Kardiner reconstructed his patient's history in this fashion. His mother had been extremely attentive to him until he was about two, when a change in the family's economic situation demanded that she work in her husband's store. This obligation interfered with her giving the little boy the care she had previously lavished on him and required her to leave him alone for long periods. As a result, he was often hungry and lonely, and his desire for his mother's company and affection went unsatisfied. Out of this experience of desertion and other events following on it, he developed a mistrust of his mother even though he still longed for her care and attention. He grew to think of women as powerful and resourceful but of himself as weak, helpless, and ineffectual. To compensate for these unbearable feelings of insignificance, he developed a habit of dreaming of achievement and success in ways that he could not realistically follow.

From conceptualizing his patient in this way, Kardiner argued that a culture that exposed its children to similar conditions should be populated by adults with personalities similar to that of his neurotic young man. Among the Alorese, these conditions are fulfilled to a very large extent.[7] The women of Alor work in the fields to produce virtually all of the basic foods of the community and, for this reason, care for their babies for only a very short period, usually no more than two weeks, after birth. The mother then returns to the gardens, leaving the child alone. The baby, of course, grows painfully hungry and uncomfortable, and while he may be given pre-chewed food or fondled by anybody who happens upon him, there is no opportunity for him to develop, through repeated and consistent association, any sense of the mother specifically or adults generally as trustworthy sources of relief from tension. His care is too intermittent, and he is allowed to go for too long in a state of unsatisfied need.

Does the neglectful pattern of maternal behavior in Alor, similar in many ways to that of the mother of Kardiner's patient, lead to similar personality characteristics in Alorese adults? The answer seems to be essentially affirmative. The typical Alorese tends to be anxious, mistrustful, and lacking in confidence. Expecting failure, he has little enterprise or initiative and is preoccupied with security in the form of an adequate supply of food. With such an atmosphere of anxiety and mistrust so prevalent, it is not surprising to find that the Alorese culture itself is virtually without art, religion, or science, those institutionalized forms of an avid interest in the world.

Again, the reciprocal relationship between cultural child-rearing practices and adult personality is evident. If the pattern of maternal neglect determines the suspicious anxiety of the adult Alorese, this mistrust and lack of closeness in adult personal relationships also probably acts to perpetuate the inattention and unloving quality that characterizes child care in Alor.

Kardiner's approach has two values. First, it integrates the findings of clinicians and students of culture with respect to the influence of early experiences on personality. Second, it suggests that knowing the type of environment provided for the growing child enables us to predict with some degree of accuracy the adult personality traits most likely to develop. Such conclusions require further confirmation, however, because the one culture of Alor might be unrepresentative.

Cross-Cultural Studies

Confirmation of hypotheses about personality and culture requires the examination of a number of cultures rather than just one. Such a cross-cultural approach permits us to see if a certain personality characteristic tends to emerge in all cultures that have certain customs, and to be absent in cultures that do not have these customs. An example of a cross-cultural study may be drawn from the research of Whiting and Child, who studied records of the customs of seventy-seven primitive peoples who live under a wide variety of social conditions.[8]

Whiting and Child took as an index of personality differences the magical and religious theories of disease held by different tribes. Beliefs about disease are useful cues to personality for several reasons. First, no primitive society has a scientific understanding of disease; therefore rationalizations and fantasies derived from personality tendencies have free rein. Even when the cause of a disability is evident, naturalistic explanations are usually ignored by a primitive group. If a tribesman breaks his leg in a fall from a cocoanut tree, one of his fellows is likely to say, "Yes, he fell from a tree, but a sorcerer must have made him fall." Second, illness is anxiety producing, so theories of disease among primitive peoples should be related to the personality traits which involve anxiety.

Theories of disease held among primitive communities suggest the concerns and fantasies of anxious and maladjusted people in our own culture. A belief that disease is caused by some disapproved or unlawful act committed by the sick person himself is strongly reminiscent of the guilty and self-condemning attitude held by many psychoneurotic persons. In many societies, illness is thought to be the result of eating some forbidden food, violating a sexual rule, or acting aggressively against the prohibitions of the group. These instances imply that sickness is a retribution for wrongdoing. They have familiar analogues in our culture in which many people learn stern rules about food, sex, and aggression and feel guilty when they violate them.

Another primitive theory holds that sickness is caused by sorcerers, by the hostile actions of powerful persons. This idea suggests the suspicious, projecting, or even deluded personality, and reflects the feeling that the source of all woe is that someone "has it in" for the sufferer. Still another theory of disease ascribes it to disobedience or neglect of the spirits, or failure to perform proper religious rituals. This concept has echoes in our own society in the extent to which some of us are dependent on the protection of parents and other authority figures. When we fail to please them we feel uneasy and insecure.

All these primitive theories of disease, then, are bound up with the control of eating, sex, aggression, independence, and the acceptance by the individual of the demands of the group. Such important types of behavior undergo intensive socialization in all cultures. In some, the socialization process may be gentle and gradual, but in others it may be harsh, abrupt, and punitive. If child training is especially severe in one of these areas, then we would expect conflicts and anxieties to develop more in that area than in others. Whiting and Child extended this reasoning to hypothesize that such conflicts would be reflected in a culture's theories of disease.

To test the hypotheses that features of child training are related to concepts of disease, they had judgments made of the severity of such socialization practices as weaning, sex training, toilet training, aggression training, and training for independence in seventy-seven cultures. An illustration of these judgments is the contrast between the Marquesans of Polynesia and the Ontong Java of the East Indies. The Marquesans believe that nursing makes a child hard to raise and not properly submissive to adults. In addition, Marquesan women take great pride in the beauty of their breasts and think that nursing will spoil their attractiveness. In consequence, the nursing period is very short, and the typical way of feeding small babies involves laying them on their backs and filling their mouths with a thin gruel. When, in the course of much crying and choking, the infant has managed to swallow one mouthful, he is given another. Even these rather traumatic feeding times are irregular and dependent on the convenience of the mother, not the hunger of the child. This culture is clearly severe with respect to the weaning process. On the other hand, the Ontong Java wean their children over a long period, gradually substituting solid foods for mother's milk and allowing children to nurse, if they so choose, until they are six years old. This procedure seems to create a minimum of frustration and anxiety in the child and represents a very mild weaning period.

Whiting and Child tested their reasoning by comparing the socialization practices of these cultures with the theories of disease held in them. They predicted several relationships. One hypothesis was that general severity of socialization would produce anxious and guilt-ridden adults, who therefore would be more prone to ascribe disease to their own wrongdoing. More particularly, it was predicted that severe weaning would cause anxiety about food and, therefore, make the people regard illness as a result of violating some rule about eating. Similarly, it was hypothesized that severe toilet, sex, or aggression training would be linked, respectively, with the attribution of disease to excretory, sexual, or aggressive misconduct.

Table 8 shows that most, but not all, of such hypotheses were confirmed from the data. The evidence found a striking relationship between regarding disease as due to the breaking of food or aggression mores, and the severity of socialization in weaning and in the punishment of aggression. Hypotheses about excretion training and

Table 8
Relationships Between Theories of Disease and Child-Training Practices, Investigated in Inter-Cultural Study*

Belief Concerning Cause of Disease	Related Socialization Procedure	Conclusion
1. Wrongdoing by sick person	Severity of socialization	Confirmed
2. Breaking food tabu	Severe weaning	Confirmed
3. Breaking excretion tabu	Severe toilet training	Not confirmed
4. Breaking sex tabu	Severe sex training	Not confirmed
5. Breaking aggression tabu	Severe aggression training	Confirmed
6. Sorcery: Hostility by powerful figures	Severity of socialization	Confirmed
7. Desertion by spirits	Severe independence training	Confirmed

* From J. W. M. Whiting & I. L. Child, *Child Training and Personality.* New Haven: Yale University Press, 1953.

sex training were not confirmed. There was no uniform relation between severe toilet training and ascribing disease to violating rules about excretion, or between severe sex training and regarding disease as due to sexual transgressions. As hypothesized, the belief that disease is due to sorcery or the hostility of powerful persons was related to general severity of socialization. Also, cultures in which children were trained to be independent as early as possible, thereby creating a longing for the security and protection of powerful parent figures, tended to explain sickness in terms of desertion by supernatural beings.

Evaluation of Cultural Studies

The cross-cultural studies seem to show that the relationships between child training practices and personality formation are not fortuitous. Personality develops through processes of learning from an environment largely patterned in cultural terms. The culture defines many of the essential rewards and punishments that the child encounters in the course of growing up. Cultural customs facilitate or prevent his associating the satisfaction of his most urgent needs with certain kinds of experiences with his parents and with other persons.

The results of the cultural patterning of the learning environment are enduring. Adult personality is in some degree predictable from a knowledge of the socialization practices of a culture. Furthermore, those who have been reared under such practices tend to perpetuate them as they achieve adulthood. In general, what seemed right for one's childhood seems right for one's children. There is a reciprocal relationship between cultural child-rearing practices and the process of personality formation. Just as socialization procedures shape a person's adjustment patterns, so his adjustments equip him to carry on the practices of the culture. Thus, strong training for independence may make a man value achievement, and make achievement a dominant theme in his dreams, in the stories he likes, and in the legends he knows. Reciprocally, his telling of these dreams, stories, and legends, becomes a way of urging children of another generation toward early independence.

Within any culture, of course, there are some personalities which deviate from the usual patterns. Great ranges of individual differences exist in all cultures, and an understanding of the dominant cultural pattern of the learning environment, however far it may lead us, does not provide enough information to permit the prediction of every feature of a particular individual in all his complexity. Learning, after all, is a highly individual affair. Every human being learns his personality from his own specific experiences, some of which can be defined in terms of broad culture-determined categories such as "lenient socialization," while others cannot. Cultural studies help to describe some of the most common learning situations with their resultant influences on personality, but they do not attempt to account for all individual differences.

Within their limitations, cultural studies of personality can be used to gain some understanding of the development of individual persons in all cultures, including our own. They suggest, for example, that harsh and punitive socialization in childhood, when other influences are equal, tends to make an adult who is prone to anxiety and guilt and who regards other people as potentially hostile. Abrupt and severe weaning is likely to lead to undue concern about food, and the rigorous suppression of aggression to feelings of guilt about aggressive impulses. Such generalizations give important clues to the sources of individual conflicts.

SOCIAL CLASS AND PERSONALITY

Although the culture provides the most general patterning of the learning environment, smaller but vitally important effects are derived from cultural subdivisions. In India, for example, there is a common culture influencing virtually all Indians. But Indian society is also organized according to *castes,* each of which provides a rather different set of social conditions under which personality develops.[9] The caste system is a classification of people according to the occupation they traditionally follow, the circle within which they must marry, and the group with which they may mingle informally. Birth lays down the caste to which each person belongs, and there is no possibility of his changing to another. Further, each caste has its own rules with respect to what kind of food may be eaten, the manners and rituals to be observed, and with whom and under what conditions a member may engage in personal relationships. Finally, the castes are arranged in an hierarchical manner. Each grade considers those below it as consisting of essentially inferior beings. While the caste system is changing in India, status based on caste is accepted as thoroughly by persons in the lower grades as by those in the higher. The learning environment differs for Indians of different castes, in spite of the similarities deriving from their common membership in the more general culture.

The American Class Structure

American society, too, is organized in an hierarchical fashion but very differently from India's. America's social organization is an *open class system* which varies somewhat from one community or region to another, but is basically similar everywhere.[10] Our class system is "open" because, while it classifies people into higher and lower orders, it does not permanently fix an individual's position. Even though a man is born into the class status of his parents, he may move up or down on the scale in various ways. *Social mobility,* the rise and fall of persons and families, is characteristic of our class system. Mobility tends to be somewhat greater in the more recently developed regions of the west and southwest than in the older and more stable sections of the east and south, but it occurs everywhere.

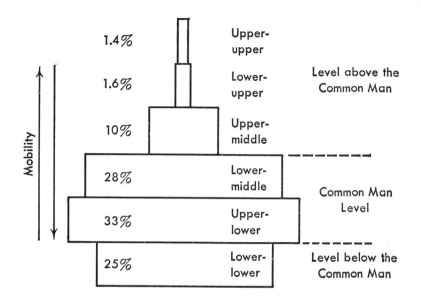

Figure 36. American Social Class Levels

The class levels in American society, with the percentages of the population of "Yankee City," a community studied in a sociological research. The distribution varies somewhat from one community to another. "Jonesville," a Midwestern city, had 3 per cent upper class, 11 per cent upper-middle, 31 per cent lower-middle, 41 per cent upper-lower, and 14 per cent lower-lower. (After W. L. Warner, *American life*. Chicago: Univer. of Chicago Press, 1953. Copyright 1953 by the University of Chicago.)

The American social class system is based on the informal evaluations people make of each other. While there is a direct relationship between economic and social status, social position is by no means entirely determined by income. The wealthy gangster or gambler, to take an extreme example, hardly enjoys the same social status as a member of an aristocratic family that has lost most of its money.

Figure 36 shows the identifiable American social classes and the proportion of the population in each. The vertical arrows at the side represent the open character of the system, indicating that people can move up and down in our social structure.

Each class is defined in terms of the way its members are perceived by people generally. In one program of research, Warner and his co-workers asked persons of all class levels to characterize various families.[11] The upper class was identified by phrases such as "the 400," "the landed gentry," "the people with family and money," "the aristocrats," "people so high up they are social history around here," "the snobs," and "the fancy crowd." Not all of these evaluations are favorable. They share, however, a clear designation of the people in question as being at the top of some kind of social arrangement. The upper class is sometimes further divided into upper-uppers and lower-uppers on the basis of the length of time the people have occupied their position. The upper-uppers are the old families of the community; the lower-uppers are those who have more recently moved to a level where they participate with the top group in their clubs and cliques.

Just below the upper class is the upper-middle, composed of the solid citizens of the community who are its active civic leaders. Warner's informants referred to these people as "a notch or two below the fancy crowd," "people who are in everything in town," "above average but not the tops," "the strivers who are working hard to get into the 400." Upper-middle class people are characteristically "joiners" because they typically belong to the groups and associations which are well known to the public, are given respectful attention by the press, and represent status and position in the community.

The lower-middle class is made up mostly of small businessmen, some highly skilled workmen, and a large number of clerks and other workers in similar occupational categories. Members of this class tend to be conservative and proper. They, too, tend to join various organizations, mainly of the patriotic or fraternal sort. Characteristically, they are careful with their money, anxious about what others think of them, and concerned about their respectability. Typical phrases used by informants included "nobodies but nice," "people with nice families, but they don't rate socially," "good common people," and "the top of the common people."

The upper-lower class level is comprised primarily of the semiskilled workmen and small tradesmen, the "honest workmen" of the community. They, too, tend to be highly respectable even though limited in their outlook and their understanding of the world around them. They were typically characterized as "poor people but honest and fine," "poor people but hard working with nothing the matter with them," and "the little people."

The people of the lowest level, the lower-lowers, are by social reputation either disreputable persons or pitied unfortunates. They often include recently arrived immigrants. The evaluations which define their class position are indicated by such comments as "river rats," "poor whites," "people who live just like animals and aren't worth a damn," "people who scrape the bottom," and "all those folks who live back of the tannery."

These social categories are not sharply set off from one another. By the very nature of an open class system, there are no firm barriers which separate one level from the next. Nevertheless, there is a relatively clear understanding in American communities of the social difference, the values, and the behavior which compose our social organization.

Warner found that the social position of a person or family can be reasonably well identified by an Index of Social Characteristics, which is relatively easy to determine.[12] The Index of Social Characteristics is the sum of the weighted ratings of four social attributes: type of occupation, source (not amount) of income, type of house, and quality of neighborhood. Occupations range from high professionals and proprietors of large businesses down to unskilled workers. The source of income extends from inherited wealth to public relief and disreputable kinds of income. The type of house is scaled from large dwellings in good condition to shacks and shanties; neighborhoods are rated on a continuum from very desirable regions to slums. By summing these ratings, one can arrive at a numerical index which usefully places an individual in his social class. Of course, the characteristics of occupation, source of income, type of house, and neighborhood are only the symbols of the real evaluations, which lie in social perceptions shared by nearly all members of the American culture. We tend to make such evaluations whether we approve of them or not.

Patterns of Socialization in Social Classes

Social class membership, like cultural membership, determines a large part of the child's learning environment. The neighborhood in which one lives and the play groups to which one has access are functions of class status. So are the rewards and punishments to which one is exposed in one's family and in one's peer relationships. The influences playing on the youngster in his most formative period are intimately bound up with the social class into which he is born.

In the *lower class*, the mother is much closer to her baby in many ways than in the middle and upper classes. The period of nursing continues longer, and weaning is far less abrupt than is usual in a middle-class home. Toilet training is also delayed. The typical lower-class attitudes toward bowel and bladder functions regard them as normal physical events, not unclean or filthy, in marked contrast to the standards of most middle-class mothers. The leniency of the lower class during infancy and early childhood extends to virtually all functions associated with the organically based drives. Infantile genital play is not inhibited. As the child acquires loco-motion, he is both permitted greater freedom in his explorations and given more prompt and affectionate attention when he en-counters difficulty.[13] On the other hand, lower-class parents are rather quick to anger. As children grow older, they become more annoying because they get in the way, inconvenience their elders, and get into trouble more frequently. Such annoyance tends to be met in lower-class homes with cuffing, whipping, and other forms of physical punishment or with intense ridicule and shaming.[14]

Ridicule and the rejection it implies assume particular importance in lower-class socialization. Growing up under conditions of eco-nomic privation, children place a high value on belonging to protective groups, including both the family and neighborhood gangs. To retain the favor of such groups is a paramount con-sideration, and disapproval and any threat of loss of membership are greatly feared. One's standing in lower-class groups, however, depends upon criteria very different from those used by the middle class.

The almost perpetual uncertainty of the lower class about such basic matters as food, shelter, and warmth puts a premium on im-mediate gratification.[15] When food is abundant and fuel plentiful, lower-class families tend to overeat and to keep their homes too warm. As a result, they are often considered shiftless, lacking in thrift and foresight, and childishly unwilling to save for a leaner day. But economic and social frustrations, like other thwartings, tend to strengthen the drives for immediate gratification. Because they are generally deprived of money, food, and fuel, lower-class people have a strong urge to make immediate use of them as soon as they are available. The conditions of life which define lower-class membership have much to do with the development of an attitude of seizing upon the pleasures of the moment, letting tomorrow take care of itself.

Part of the lower-class emphasis on immediacy takes the form of a greater freedom of emotional expression than is found in the middle class.[16] Lower-class children and adolescents are much less inhibited in their expression of sex and anger. Fights between children and their father and between husband and wife are frequent. Both older children and the parents themselves teach younger ones to fight with fists or with knives and to hit first. Considerable status is attached to fighting well with no holds barred, and physical cowardice or ineptness in a fight can draw the cruelest torments from both one's family and one's peers. On the other hand, seeking comfort and protection from parents or fellow gang members is regarded as quite appropriate and acceptable, in contrast to the middle-class emphasis on self-reliance.

The formative influences of the *middle class*, unlike those of the lower class, are strongly oriented toward the child's future in the family, the school, the church, and the more informal kinds of relationships.[17] A middle-class youngster is constantly enjoined to improve his position and to think in terms of long-range goals and delayed rewards, not immediate gratifications. Foresight, self-control, and responsible independence are dominant values because they facilitate future achievement. These children, in contrast to their lower-class counterparts, are expected from early ages to assume increasing degrees of responsibility for themselves, and are thereby trained for independence and self-reliance. Early and prolonged experience teaches them that strong impulses must be controlled. Physical aggression must be inhibited except under very specific conditions of provocation, such as personal attack by a bully. Social ostracism among one's peers and sharp physical or symbolic punishment from one's parents follow violations of the code against aggression. What holds true for physical aggression is only slightly less applicable to aggressiveness of language and manner. Similarly, overt sex expression is regarded as essentially improper and indecent except under the delayed and restrictive conditions of marriage. Courtship is regulated by many rules defining right and wrong conduct. While these rules may be violated to a considerable degree, they can seldom be overridden without some experience of guilt and self-recrimination.

Middle-class restraints are intended to facilitate future achievements. The middle-class child wins high rewards by denying impulse gratifications in favor of developing initiative, by learning the social manners and niceties of his group, by acquiring the verbal accomplishments of speaking and writing, and by mastering skills which will later be valuable. Attainment becomes a dominant goal for him, and conversely, failure is a pressing threat. The association of achievement strivings with anxiety is illustrated by the tendency of middle-class college students, often of excellent ability, to fear examinations.

The *upper class* shows a very different patterning of the learning environment. Here the fundamental emphasis is on taste, manners, good form, and the reputation of the family. A child is taught to regard himself as superior, which relieves him of some of the pressure placed upon people of the middle class for upward mobility, but imposes on him the responsibility of the family name. Because his conduct must always bring credit to his class and his family, the upper-class person from childhood on is concerned with questions of honor, etiquette, and discretion. These concerns imply a bond to the family group that is at once sustaining and restrictive. While the secure status of an upper-class member is conferred on him automatically by his family, it can be retained only so long as he does nothing to mark himself as too different or too individualistic.

The family bonds of the upper class and the middle class are almost exactly opposite. The family relations of an upper-class person cannot be readily separated from his individual life, but a mobile member of the middle class must sever nearly all ties with his family if he is to achieve assured status in a higher class. Upper-class young men often bring their brides to live in wings of the family mansion with their parents. Upwardly mobile members of the middle class more often find themselves out of touch with their parents, and experience a visit to their parents' homes as strange and unfamiliar.

Class influences which pattern the learning environment are pervasive and extend over a long period of time. It is not so much a matter of earlier toilet training in the middle class or later weaning in the lower. Social class shapes personality because the developing person, from earliest childhood to late adolescence, is constantly exposed to a particular set of attitudes, values, and concepts about appropriate ways of living. That these approaches to life are often inarticulate and implicit, instead of deliberately formulated and explicitly verbalized, does not miminize their influence. Their force is made felt through the rewards and punishments experienced by the growing child, and by the models of adult behavior that are most intimately and constantly before him in his day-to-day development.

Effects of Social Class Membership

Out of the rather different social worlds defined by social class membership, somewhat different patterns of personality emerge.[18] Middle-class people generally develop achievement needs as an important motive. They tend to work for delayed rewards rather than immediate gratifications, exercise considerable self-control over their emotional impulses, and act with more self-reliance than direct dependence on others. Remote success is highly prized. A college degree is won only after four years of hard work. Advancement in business or the professions demands a long period of work and waiting, often under conditions of little income or prestige. During the climb to some degree of successful attainment, impulsive desires and emotional expression must be controlled. To move upward one must depend primarily on the quality of one's own performance, either in dealing effectively with other people or in technical proficiency. Marriage is delayed in favor of a long education or period of professional training. Outbursts of anger or hostility are generally curbed. Carrying the responsibilities of school or a job becomes one important basis for acquiring a reputation for stability and personal reliability, in one's own eyes as well as in the eyes of others. On the other hand, anxieties and guilt tend to become associated with the expression of impulses and the possibility of failure. Anxiety motivates various mechanisms such as repression, compulsive hard work, or the rationalizations which serve to excuse inadequate performance.

Growing up in the lower class appears to reinforce a different pattern of adjustments. Largely because of the conditions of economic privation typical of this segment of society, immediacy of tension reduction is vitally important, and achievements based on long periods of preparation and work before the rewards are won carry little motivational value. Similarly, the importance of quick gratification gives greater importance to the family and to other tightly knit groups. Middle-class people are "joiners" because membership in the "right" clubs, fraternities, and professional associations represents a fundamental stepping-stone to achievement. Lower-class people, in contrast, belong to more informal groups because they are primary sources of protection against hunger, cold, and the aggression of others. Self-control is far less important, and acting out one's emotional impulses is more strongly rewarded than elsewhere in the social structure.

Differences between the lower and middle classes are well illustrated in criminal behavior.[19] The crime rate, of course, is somewhat higher in the lower class than in the middle group, but it must be remembered that our laws reflect essentially the values of middle-class legislators and are interpreted in our courts by middle-class judges. More revealing than the difference in rate is the difference in types of crimes committed by people from these different levels in American society. Lower-class criminals tend to be convicted of such crimes of violence and passion as unpremeditated murder, assault, wanton destruction of property, and rape. Similarly, they are often guilty of thefts aimed at the gratification of an immediate wish. A car is stolen simply because a group of adolescents wants to go for a ride. A purse is snatched because food must be bought or fuel purchased, or often just because of a desire to go to a ball game. Middle-class criminals, on the other hand, are more typically convicted of offenses which involve planning and are more likely to result in economic gain and the prestige it may buy. Such crimes as embezzlement, forgery, and planned robbery are more frequent in this group. Usually, the motives underlying criminality in middle-class persons seem to be associated with achievement and social position rather than with immediacy of impulse gratification.

A similar class difference is reflected in sexual activity.[20] In lower-class males, sexual relations are begun somewhat earlier, and engaged in more frequently and with a greater number of partners. Less time is involved in reaching orgasm than is the case in the middle class. On the other hand, lower-class sexual activity is not at all without its governing codes.[21] Masturbation, for example, is strongly disapproved and apparently occurs with much less frequency than among middle-class people of all ages. Homosexuality is also opposed by strong sanctions. Unlike the situation in the middle class, flirtatious "teasing" is frowned upon, and such forms of erotic behavior as petting and prolonged kissing are regarded as perversions. Boasting about sexual conquests, however, is quite acceptable and is one way in which lower-class males may exhibit their prowess. The romantic aspects of sexual behavior have less value in the lower class. Sexuality, like many less dramatic forms of behavior, is regarded chiefly in terms of the immediacy of tension reduction it provides. These attitudes contrast sharply with middle-class standards, by which direct heterosexual relations are forbidden except in marriage, masturbation is tolerated to a degree although disapproved, and the more acceptable forms of erotic contact are essentially substitutive and romanticized in character. While this middle-class code is often violated in actuality, it is strong enough to permit few people to break it without a strong sense of guilt and conflict.

Class Differences Shown by Personality Tests

Some evidence about the formative effects of social class on personality comes from studies of personality test responses. Two features of these findings need to be clarified, however, before conclusions are drawn.

First, the results of the studies based on tests show the essential independence of social status and economic status. When status is defined in terms of the amount of income, consistent differences in test responses rarely emerge. When status is measured according to social criteria, as by the Index of Social Characteristics, the resultant differences are reliable and relatively large. This observation reminds us that class membership reflects the way a person is typically treated and evaluated by others, not simply the amount of income he has.

Second, the direction of these differences tends to favor the adjustment of middle-class persons over lower-class ones. While this tendency is expected in view of advantages enjoyed by middle-class children, its interpretation is complicated. The standard of favorable and unfavorable adjustment in terms of which personality tests are constructed are largely determined by the middle-class people who construct them. Such standards are not accepted by lower-class members, and the meaning of the obtained differences is therefore obscured by the unshared criteria of effective adjustment. Also, the meanings of the questionnaire items may differ for middle-class and lower-class subjects. For example, more lower-class high school pupils check as true the statement, "I'm often left out of things the other kids do." It does not follow, however, that this response shows an unwholesome shyness or maladjustment, because lower-class adolescents often are really left out of extracurricular activities, simply because of their inferior social status.[22] On the other hand, consistent exclusion from school affairs may increase inferiority feelings, and evoke defenses against socially aroused anxiety. The life of a lower-class person is complicated by his having to adjust to two social worlds. He must maintain his position in relation to the lower-class people with whom he has his most intimate and continuous contacts and, because compulsory school laws require him to attend schools run essentially by the middle class, he must also work out ways of coping with representatives of a dominant group that is not his own. This situation may provide a fertile ground for the development of conflicts and insecurities.

On personality questionnaires, middle-class subjects appear to achieve higher scores on such traits as self-sufficiency, dominance, and emotional stability, whereas lower-class subjects show greater tendencies toward insecurity and irritability.[23] Among high school students, the scores of middle-class boys and girls suggest greater defensiveness and reserve in regard to personal affairs and problems, more conventional attitudes and manners, and less worry about bodily health than do those of lower-class respondents.[24] Similarly, lower-class pupils answer personality inventories in such a way as to indicate that they like school less, have more nervous habits like nail-biting, experience more trouble in controlling their tempers, are less willing to leave home for a job or college, worry less about being useful to society, and think less about ethical and religious questions.[25] All of these differences are quite understandable in the light of class differences in the socialization process.

Social Class in the Clinic

Practical workers in community mental hygiene clinics must be aware of the influences of social class on personality in order to understand the individual attitudes and problems of clients. Social-class differences in personality are illustrated concretely by two cases, both of whom were evaluated clinically for essentially the same problem in their overt behavior. Kenneth R. referred himself to the clinic because he had struck his wife on two occasions and was severely upset at his lack of self-control, the immorality of his action, and his general aggressiveness. Bill M. was referred to the clinic by the court after the police had been called three times within a month because he was disturbing the peace by beating his wife.

Kenneth R. was a young physician, the older of two sons of an ambitious pharmacist who had wanted to become a doctor himself but who had been unable to go to medical school for financial reasons. He worked hard, devoted himself to giving his boys the chance he had missed, and impressed upon Kenneth the necessity of making the most of the opportunity his father was providing for him. In describing his relationship with his father, Kenneth said that he saw little of him because of the long hours that he worked in the drug store, recalled no good times that he had had with him while growing up, and remembered him chiefly as a man who was seldom home, who was generally tired and irritable, and who seemed pleased only when Kenneth brought home good grades from school, especially in such subjects as biology and chemistry.

When in college, Kenneth had some trouble with his premedical subjects, but he achieved at a sufficiently high level by dint of sheer hard work to be admitted to medical school. In his second year, he married the only girl he had ever dated seriously, and she contributed substantially to the financing of his last two years by working as a secretary. Kenneth felt humiliated and resentful at having to accept financial help from his wife. Following his graduation, he made her quit her job even though his interne's pay was hardly enough for them to live on. The burden of financial responsibility weighed heavily on him, and he was often tempted to resign his internship to take a job, but the knowledge of his father's dreams and sacrifices always dissuaded him. On entering practice with a busy general practitioner in a large city, Kenneth felt the work was more than he could bear. He was never sure of himself with any patient with more than a routine medical problem. To bolster his confidence, he undertook a rather heavy program of study in addition to his work at the office. This step was taken more because of his anxiety and doubt about his own competence than because of any genuine interest in further training. Keeping up with his work and his study required that he neglect his wife, who became bored, dissatisfied, and unhappy. She began to make demands upon his time and finally threatened to leave him. In the course of sharp quarrels, he accused her of interfering with his career and of not caring whether he murdered his patients. Twice, in a mood of uncontrolled panic and fury, he slapped her. After these episodes, Kenneth felt deeply guilty, contrite, and depressed, and he finally sought help because of these discomforts.

Although the behavior of Bill M. had a superficial resemblance to that of Kenneth, his real problem was very different. His social class was a relevant factor.

Bill M., a man of about Kenneth's age, had been one of six children in the home of a semiskilled workman who rarely held the same job for longer than six months at a time. Bill quit school after the seventh grade, worked at many different jobs, and married by the time he was twenty. At the clinic, he described his wife in positive if not affectionate terms, expressed a great deal of resentment toward the police for interfering in his family affairs, and was both bewildered and angered at having been sent by the court for psychiatric evaluation merely because he had been disciplining his wife for her presumed infidelity to him. Such a referral meant to Bill that somebody thought he was crazy for merely acting as a man should. He resented the implication to the extent of making threats against the judge, the police, and the clinic's staff, even though he also expressed great concern about being detained in the hospital and kept from his family.

While oversimplified in the brief accounts, these two cases exemplify major differences in adjustment growing out of different class backgrounds. Kenneth's life had been characterized by striving to get ahead, by great anxiety about the possibility of failure, and by the renunciation of many things in order to achieve the degree of success defined for him by his father. When his success was threatened by his wife's demand that he give some of his attention to her as well as to his profession, he became distressed to the point of breaking the code of gentility toward women and the inhibition of aggressive impulses which had been so fundamental a part of his social learning. The resulting guilt, coupled with an awareness of the strain under which he had been living for some time, led him to seek help on his own responsibility. Bill, in contrast, felt that he had violated no code in striking his wife. To the contrary, he had acted as any vigorous man should when he has reason to believe his wife has been unfaithful. Far from seeking help because of any feelings of guilt, he was enraged at what he took to be interference in his domestic matters, but his anger at this kind of meddling was tempered by his worry about being kept away from home in a strange place.

Kenneth and Bill illustrate very different personalities resulting from very different social class backgrounds. The significance of social classes, like that of cultures, lies in the fact that they represent patterns of experience to which persons are exposed from their earliest ages and for long periods of time. One's social class defines the way one is treated by others, the important stimuli brought to bear, and the kinds of rewards and punishments received. Within the common American culture, we share many important and formative experiences. We also undergo distinctive developmental experiences through growing up in a particular segment of the culture.

The most important of these distinctive developmental experiences are connected with different patterns of family life. Social class membership also defines the neighborhood we live in, the groups with which we play, the occupations with which we become familiar, and to a large extent our material security. But most vitally it determines the range of socialization practices which we encounter in the process of developing from infancy to young adulthood. The people who employ these socialization practices, of course, are primarily the members of the immediate family, especially the parents.

But parents in any one social class do not act with complete uniformity, and it is evident that the generalizations drawn about the typical personality patterns of people in different social classes do not hold for all individuals. Many middle-class people do not have strong achievement needs, nor are they all plagued by a fear of failure. Similarly, self-control is distributed over a wide range of individual differences in middle-class persons, and there is a comparable continuum of differences among them with respect to the ability to work for delayed rather than immediate rewards. In the same way, some lower-class members develop strong achievement needs, learn to curb their aggressive impulses, and come to attach romantic importance to their relations with the opposite sex. Persons in a social class are not all alike; each has his distinctive individuality, determined by his particular learning experiences.

FAMILY STRUCTURE

The importance of the family in child development derives from two considerations. The first is that human infants, unlike the young of all other animals, have such an extended period of immaturity that years must pass before they can act in such a way as to ensure their own survival. Even such relatively highly developed mammals as the great apes are entirely dependent on the care of others for only a brief period. The prolonged state of helplessness of human infants, in contrast, demands that they be fed and protected over a period of years to preserve their very lives. The second consideration arises from the social nature of human life. Children must grow up to become productive and contributing members of their culture. The group's own continuance and survival depends upon the development of children into effective participants in its activities. Whether in a primitive tribe or in a segment of a highly complex society, the family is charged with the two basic tasks of caring for babies for the sake of their own survival and optimal development, and of insuring socialization for the sake of the group.

Types of Family Structures

Although the essential functions of the family are everywhere the same, family structure may vary greatly.[26] In the Trobriand Islands, where the connection between sexual intercourse and childbirth is not understood, the family consists essentially of the mother, her husband who is unknown as the biological father of his children, and her youngsters. This family pattern is very much like our own, in spite of the difference in knowledge about the process of procreation. It is known as the *nuclear family*.

In India, a family includes a man, his sons, his grandsons, and all their womenfolk until the daughters leave to join other families through marriage. Familial authority is vested in the eldest male, and food, religious practices, and ownership of property are shared in common. All income, for example, is held in a common trust similar to "joint" bank accounts in our own culture. Such a pattern of family living is known as an *extended joint family*, the name referring both to the features of common property and common religious observances, and to the family's extension through the generations to all male members of the patrilineal line.

A third example of family structure is provided by the village of *related families*, characteristic of Samoa and the Mojave Indians. Here all adults in small villages of not more than two hundred houses are regarded as related to each other in various degrees. The obligation to care for any child in the village falls almost equally on every adult. The youngster is welcome in virtually any home and consequently grows up in a world populated by "aunts and uncles."

Family Structure and Personality

The structure of the family governs many of the influences brought to bear on the child during his socialization. As one might expect, emotional relationships between parents and children are exceptionally intense in nuclear families. In America, parents and no one else are responsible for many features of the child's welfare and, in consequence, affective ties are strong.

The nuclear pattern of family life has a number of important effects. First of all, it seems to set the stage for strong affective relationships generally. Personal relations have an intimacy and an emotional quality which are not typical of people raised under other patterns of family life. Second, it appears to facilitate a sense of individualistic responsibility. Each person tends to perceive himself as a determiner of the acts in which he engages. He is conscious and proud of the distinctiveness which he recognizes in his own being. Third, the nuclear family is important in activating a sense of guilt, a feeling of wrongdoing that is associated with forbidden acts even in the absence of others. This development occurs because the parents themselves punish their children and accept the responsibility for discipline, even at the risk of incurring the child's resentment and hostility. Also, the parents usually exhibit themselves to their children as representing the virtues they want incorporated in the child's behavior. Parents use themselves, in a context of strong emotionality, as models that the youngster must "live up to." When he fails he is punished, often by the threat of withdrawal of love. Consequently, the child who does not behave in emulation of his parents, especially the parent of the same sex as his own, tends to experience an anticipation of punishment and loss of affection even though the parents are not present to witness his transgression.

The situation is quite different in a village of related families. In a world of relatives, the Samoan or Mojave child develops little dependence on any single pair of adults, and his emotional relationships lack intensity. The death of his biological parents, for example, while a sad event, does not elicit any strong expression of grief. It is not long before the orphaned child in such circumstances fully regains his composure and his sense of secure detachment. On the other hand, such a family structure does not seem to inculcate the individualistic sense of self so common in our own experience, nor does it facilitate the growth of responsibility. With so little intensity involved in personal relationships and with so many people sharing the common life of the village, the rewards for doing little and for relying on the kindness of others are greater than the rewards for asserting oneself and accepting responsibility for one's own welfare.

The extended joint family tends to develop a higher degree of respect for authority, a lack of personal initiative, and a feeling of limited personal control over one's environment. Such outcomes are rather readily understood in view of the dominance accorded the eldest male in the joint family, and the entirely communal nature of family life. The family group under the leadership of the patriarch takes precedence over the individual, and the child learns to act in accordance with this pattern rather than in the interest of his own individuality.

HOME INFLUENCES ON PERSONALITY

Although the nuclear family group exists throughout the American culture, there is still considerable variation from one home to another. Some of the most important factors which shape personality are found in these varying patterns of the behavior of parents toward their children.

Dimensions of Parental Behavior

In studying the effects of parental behavior on child personality, the first step is to develop a method for describing or measuring how parents act toward their children. Countless adjectives have been used to designate aspects of the attitudes and actions of parents — arbitrary, neglectful, rejecting, blaming, neurotic, democratic, stimulating, accepting, rewarding, harmonious, and many others. How can some useful order be injected into this conceptual complexity?

One way in which parent behavior may be analyzed is suggested by studies from the Fels Research Institute.[27] The significant aspects of parent behavior may be conceived as lying along three relatively independent dimensions. One dimension is *acceptance-rejection* or the degree of warmth marking the parent's behavior toward the child. A second dimension is *possessiveness-detachment,* the extent to which the parent protects the youngster, which ranges from inappropriate babying and interfering with his independence and initiative, to neglect and disregard. The third dimension is *democracy-autocracy,* the degree to which the child is permitted some participation in determining family rules and activities, in contrast to a dictatorial method of child government.

The three dimensions were developed from ratings of thirty attributes of parent behavior on the Fels Parent Behavior Rating Scales, made by trained observers who visited the homes periodically.[28] The ratings proved reliable and seemed to provide stable indices of home life. The thirty rated characteristics were reduced to three groups by a "cluster analysis," a statistical method conceptually similar to the procedure of factor analysis which was described in Chapter 11 (pp. 318, 328). A cluster or pattern consists of the features of behavior that tend to occur together. The pattern or dimension of acceptance-rejection, for example, is defined in terms of the ratings of such variables as the child-centered or child-subordinating character of the home, the relative use by the mother of approval or disapproval in relation to the child, the degree of affection or hostility she expresses toward him, and the closeness or distance of the relationship.

Within the framework provided by the three patterns of parent behavior, homes can be described in various ways. For example, two families may be similarly rejectant but differ in the possessive-detached dimension, thus providing very different patterns of experience for the developing child. In one family, the lack of warmth is accompanied by an essentially passive attitude toward the youngster. He is regarded as a burden to be borne dutifully, but is given little attention. The mother is aloof and basically disinterested, more concerned with minimizing the trouble that the child might cause than with either understanding him or guiding his development. Another rejecting home, however, may involve a much more active kind of maternal behavior. The mother, far from being detached and indifferent, tends to be hostile, severe, and restricting. She appears to go out of her way to be frustrating, unfriendly, and strict, seeming to act on the continuous assumption that the child, left to his own devices, will do something irritating to the mother, contrary to the standards of the home, or unnecessarily risky. One such mother constantly showed the expectation that everything her child attempted would be wrong. If her daugh•ter ate an ice cream cone, the mother said caustically, "I suppose you're going to spill that down the front of your dress."[29]

Similarly, homes may be comparable in terms of their democracy but very different with respect to warmth. Both sets of parents may accept the principles of democracy: self-determination of actions, rational discussion of reasons for behavior, and noncoercion of others except through free discussion. In one household, however, the parents may follow this method slavishly, giving little thought to whether it makes sense in concrete situations and paying little heed to the needs and feelings of the child at the moment. Such parents have been called examples of "ideological democracy." In contrast, other parents are equally committed to democratic principles but apply them flexibly, thinking in terms of specific circumstances and what is likely to be best for the child and the family, not solely in terms of democratic abstractions. These homes, in which children are respected as persons and regarded as a source of fun as well as a responsibility, are instances of "warm democracy."

The three dimensions of parent behavior provide useful descriptions of the environments in which children learn. The parental patterns define the balance of the child's experiences between rewards or punishments, protection or isolation, and participation in self-government as against capricious authoritarianism.

Studies of the influence of the home environment have looked for relationships between important segments of children's behavior and the relevant features of their parents' practices. Three crucial areas of child development have already been identified (p. 407) as cooperation versus aggression, anxiety and fear versus self-confidence, and freedom versus dependence. Aggression, anxiety, and dependence are responses especially likely to evoke conflicts which lead to nonintegrative adjustments. A survey of research findings can therefore be organized meaningfully in terms of these three areas of child behavior.

Sources of Aggression

Aggressive or hostile behavior is nonintegrative for the person who shows it and harmful to the social group in which he lives. Hostility seems to be highly subject to learning and is not an entirely inborn characteristic which must always appear and then be harshly suppressed. A child's integrative development is aided when his environment provides him with few incitements to aggression, but reinforces cooperative behavior instead.

The results of one representative study of how parent behavior may influence the development of aggression or cooperation are shown in Table 9.[30] In this investigation, the behavior of children in a nursery school was rated according to the amount of domination displayed and the amount of cooperation demonstrated. By dividing the dominative ratings by those for cooperation, an index of aggression was obtained. High numerical scores indicated that the child was preponderantly aggressive in his behavior toward other individual children and toward the nursery school group as a whole. Low index numbers indicated that the youngster's behavior was primarily cooperative. Parent behavior was rated by means of home visits.

The correlation coefficients in Table 9 show that aggression was positively associated with two features of parental behavior: friction about disciplinary matters and discord in the home. Aggression was related to a *lack* of parental closeness, understanding, responsiveness, and democracy. The findings suggest that socially undesirable forms of aggression are more likely to develop in homes which are frustrating to the child, and which show neglect or isolation, lack of acceptance, and arbitrary discipline.

Table 9
Relationships Between Parental Behavior and Dominance-Cooperation Ratios in Children*

Parent Behavior	Correlation with Child's Dominance-Cooperation Ratio
Disciplinary friction	+.57†
Discord in the home	+.41
Effectiveness of policy	—.65
Closeness of relationship	—.61
Understanding child's problems	—.59
Quickness of approving or disapproving	—.56
Democracy of policy	—.52
Readiness to explain	—.49
Intensity of contact	—.49
Acceptance of child	—.47
Clarity of standards	—.39

* From Charlene T. Meyer, The assertive behavior of children as related to parent behavior. *J. Home Econ.*, 1947, *39*, 77-80.

† Positive correlations show association with dominance. Negative correlations show association with cooperation.

Delinquency is a most disturbing sign of aggressiveness, and indicates an obvious failure of socialization. While the determiners of delinquency are complex and numerous, some factors can be identified in the early home experiences of delinquents which differentiate them from nondelinquent children. In one study by the Gluecks, 500 persistently delinquent boys were carefully matched with nondelinquents who came from comparable underprivileged neighborhoods, and who had similar intelligence levels and ethnic and national backgrounds.[31] When the home lives of these two groups of boys were compared, some striking differences were found in the warmth of their relationships within the family, the degree of supervision and control exercised over them, and the democracy of the disciplinary methods used. The results are shown in Tables 10, 11, and 12.

Table 10

Acceptance in Homes of Delinquent and Nondelinquent Boys*

Rating	Delinquents: Per cent of		Nondelinquents: Per cent of	
	Mothers	Fathers	Mothers	Fathers
Parent's behavior toward the child:				
Overprotective	24.4	—	15.2	—
Warm	47.7	40.2	80.4	80.7
Indifferent	21.2	42.0	3.4	16.0
Hostile	6.7	16.9	1.0	3.3
Child's behavior toward the parent:				
Attached	64.9	32.5	89.8	65.1
Indifferent	4.6	16.5	0.2	5.6
Hostile	2.2	11.8	0.6	2.8
Won't say	28.3	39.2	9.4	26.5

Table 11

Degree of Parental Control over Delinquent and Nondelinquent Boys*

Parental control	Delinquents: Per cent of		Nondelinquents: Per cent of	
	Mothers	Fathers	Mothers	Fathers
Lax	56.8	26.6	11.7	17.9
Overstrict	4.4	26.1	1.6	8.7
Inconsistent	34.6	41.6	21.1	17.9
Firm but friendly	4.2	5.7	65.6	55.5

Table 12

Methods of Home Control with Delinquent and Nondelinquent Boys*

Type of Control	Delinquents: Per cent of		Nondelinquents: Per cent of	
	Mothers	Fathers	Mothers	Fathers
Physical punishment	55.6	67.8	34.6	34.7
Deprivation of privileges	46.5	24.9	45.2	26.2
Threats or scolding	46.9	32.2	37.0	31.5
Reasoning	16.4	11.3	28.2	24.4
Appeal to pride	9.7	3.7	9.4	6.0
Discipline left to other parent ..	3.9	8.8	1.8	12.1

The data show that delinquents come from homes which are less acceptant and warm, and more indifferent and arbitrary, than the homes of nondelinquents. Against this background of rejection, essentially lax supervision, and relatively inconsistent discipline, it is not surprising that the delinquents typically felt unappreciated. They were resentful, suspicious of the motives of others, and defiant or ambivalent in their attitudes toward authority. The continuing frustration at home and the lack of dependable affection seemed to predispose them to anger, mistrust, and hostility. On the other hand, they had fewer feelings of anxiety, insecurity, helplessness, and failure than the nondelinquents. These findings are consistent with the results of another study which discovered that children who manifest early signs of anxiety or other fearful attitudes are less likely to become delinquent than children from comparable backgrounds who lack anxiety.[32]

The delinquent youngster's lack of anxiety is an interesting finding, and is confirmed by many other observations. It is possible that some children refrain from delinquent acts primarily because of a fear of punishment. Such children might be generally more anxious. But most delinquents have had ample experience with punishment and remain unimpressed. The delinquents lack anxiety when, in a

---

* Reprinted by permission of the publishers and The Commonwealth Fund from Sheldon and Eleanor Glueck, *Unraveling juvenile delinquency*, Cambridge, Mass.: Harvard University Press, Copyright, 1950, by The Commonwealth Fund.

sense, they should be anxious because they have done unsocial, punishable deeds. The crucial characteristic of a delinquent is an insufficient internalization of the standards of the culture which, as we saw in Chapter 3 (pp. 83-84), is never attained by punishment alone. Socialization requires social rewards, and therefore depends on the establishment of the close relationships with people which aggressive and delinquent children lack. Children who have experienced closeness to their parents and to other adults are usually socialized although they may also be anxious.

The Development of Anxiety

Considerable evidence shows that anxiety and fearfulness are associated with parental possessiveness and overprotection. David Levy, in a classical research using the clinical method, studied the behavior of children whose mothers were overprotective.[33] The criteria for maternal overprotection included frequent and extended physical contacts with the child, caring for the child like a baby well beyond the age at which such complete care is appropriate, and preventing the development of his independence. In addition, the mother either dominated the child by excessive control or else indulged his whims with little attempt to control him. Thus there are two patterns of maternal overprotection, one *dominating*, the other, *indulgent*. In both patterns oversolicitude was high. The mother insisted that the child stay within sight or call, nursed him overattentively through slight illnesses, and continued to bathe and dress him when he was old enough to assume such responsibilities himself.

The behavior of the overprotected-indulged children was characterized by disobedience, temper tantrums, and excessive demands on other people. In their relations with their peers, the children also tried to domineer and tyrannize. As a result, they had difficulty in making and keeping friends and often became isolated from all persons except members of their families. The indulged children tended to do well in school, partly because of the amount of time spent with the mother who emphasized the value of adult standards of knowledge. Also, their experiences with their peers brought about anxiety and apprehension, so that intellectual pursuits seemed safer and more rewarding than the hurly-burly of social life in grade school.

Anxiety was also common among the overprotected-dominated group of children, but their behavior was otherwise very different. These youngsters were characteristically obedient, submissive to authority, and given to timidity and withdrawal among their peers. The overprotection or possessiveness accounts for their anxiety, whereas the type of parental control determines which mechanism — demanding dependency, or abject submission — the child uses to deal with other people and to control his own fears.

Several factors may account for the similarities found in all over-protected children, and for the differences between the dominated and the indulged. First, parental control in any possessive home is likely to take the form of warnings against danger. "You mustn't cross the street. A car might hit you." "Don't run so much, dear. You might get terribly sick." It is characteristic of overprotective families that much of parental effort is directed toward reducing risks and protecting the child from danger. Consequently, the child learns to perceive the world as a dangerous place where the chances of injury and disappointment are high. When admonitions to be careful are extended to people as well as to things and events, the social as well as the physical world becomes frightening. A mother's refusal to let her twelve-year-old daughter go to a nearby store alone "because a man might get you" illustrates the kind of learning situation likely to lead to an anxious mistrust of others.

Possessive parents not only emphasize warnings, but usually couple them with statements of worry and concern. The mother not only tells the child not to climb the tree in the backyard because he might fall and break his arm; she also says, "It bothers me to see you in such dangerous places." The exposure of a youngster to his mother's anxieties makes him feel responsible for her discomfort. Thus, he learns both to fear the external world, and to feel guilty about causing his mother's anguish. Doing or even wanting to do things that have been called dangerous becomes a cue for anxiety.

The overprotected child's anxiety furnishes the drive to motivate his defenses. The method of parental control determines the reinforcing conditions for two very different defensive patterns in dominated and indulged children. Children of dominant mothers learn to escape or avoid the many dangers of the world by "doing what mother says." By obeying and by exercising as little initiative as possible, they can be protected and safe. On the other hand, children who are possessively indulged seem to learn that protection and safety are won by insistence and demand. Anxiety can be forestalled only by the intervention of some stronger person, but that stronger person must be coerced into his role as a protector by demands and tantrums. Indulged children may appear confident and even aggressive, but their aggressive tendencies amount to little more than a seeking, often desperate in its emotional quality, for the kind of protection provided by an indulgent mother.

A child from a possessive home tends to have less courage than one from a democratic family, or even from a rejecting one. Greater anxiety, and consequent unwillingness to challenge novel situations, are suggested by the finding that possessively held children lack originality, creativity, and curiosity.[34] Such characteristics are particularly evident in possessively dominated children. Strict control, when coupled with the fear-inducing effects of overprotection, suppresses desirable kinds of spontaneous behavior as well as antisocial acts. The dominated youngster cannot think in critically constructive terms about the rules to which he has been subjected.

Parental control does not always lead to anxiety. Under some circumstances a child's anxiety may be aroused by giving him more freedom than he can bear.[35] A child reared in a home which emphasizes socialization is indoctrinated with a sense of his own responsibility. He may then come to fear the results of his own impulses, and welcome the presence of an adult who will control him when he is not sure he can control himself. When a child is asked to wait alone in a room where he must be careful of valuable and fragile objects, he may show his anxiety by the intensity with which he resolves to keep his part of the bargain. When his parents return he is glad the strain is over, and that responsibility for his behavior is again in adult hands.

Dependence

The meaning of dependence has not been defined quite as clearly as have aggression and anxiety. One kind of dependence has already been met in the behavior of the possessively dominated child. He is not only anxious and shy, but he also feels helplessly unable to solve his problems without adult intervention. A dominated child therefore appeals for his mother's help, constantly wants to be reassured, and is in a panic when he is threatened with separation. It is most often the possessively dominated young child who clings to his mother on the first day of school and begs her not to leave him.

Dependence may also be evoked by an almost opposite pattern of parent-child relationship. Parental indifference or detachment often evokes a clinging dependence. One study, for example, found that parents who made the fewest affectionate overtures to their children received the largest number of such advances from them.[36] Such children were insecure and preoccupied with the problem of being cared for and loved. In another research with nursery school children, both severity of weaning in infancy and current frustrations at home were associated with dependent behavior.[37] Children cared for in institutions, and children shuttled from one foster home to another so that they establish no secure relationships, are also described as tense, dependent, and clinging.[38]

At first glance, the dependent behavior of neglected and indifferently treated children seems contrary to a sound interpretation of the principles of learning. If these children's contacts with adults are unrewarding, why do they seek more adult help? In resolving this dilemma, it is important to note that all children do receive rewards from their relationships with adults. Whenever they are fed, bathed, dried, dressed, or otherwise cared for, an adult person ministers to them. The child who is treated negligently or indifferently, but without active hostility, simply receives fewer such reinforcements than other children. But evidence from laboratory studies shows that a response which is reinforced only a fraction of the time — on one-half or even one-tenth of the occasions — may be strongly learned and is actually harder to extinguish than a response reinforced on every trial.[39] Furthermore, the frustration of a once-established response seems to increase the strength of drive (p. 100). These considerations help us to understand how a deprived child comes to have a strong urge to seek the attention, care, and affection of a mother or a mother substitute. Even a neglected child receives enough reinforcement to make him want adult attention and aid, and the accompanying frustrations greatly intensify his demand for such comforts. Dependent attitudes acquired in childhood are often carried throughout adult life. They are seen in adults who always want people to pay attention to them, make their decisions for them, and give them a parent-like degree of affection.

When the deprivation of adult care and affection is unusually severe, as in the case of children raised in negligent or understaffed orphanages, the pattern of overdependence does not emerge. Instead, these exceptionally deprived children are often impulsive, uncontrolled, retarded in development, and unable to establish relationships with people.[40]

Positive Factors in Development

The evidence provides some implications for the development of a normal personality. Social learning in the family can lead to integrative adjustments and creative spontaneity. The warm acceptance of a child, shown by respect for him as a person and the maintenance of understanding communication with him, probably evokes a desire to work cooperatively with people with little need to dominate or to be dependent. The dimension of possessiveness-detachment leads to unfortunate results at both extremes. Moderate indulgence blended with responsibility seems to set the most constructive course. Democratic procedures, when carried out warmly rather than fanatically, promote self-confidence and a respect for others.

A home with a positive basis for integrative development is illustrated by the following case record of the Rampion family.[41] Leonard, the central figure in the study, is eight years old. He has two brothers, Bobby and Bud, and a sister, Carol. The case record is imperfect in telling little about Mr. Rampion, because it was prepared as a part of a study of mother-child relationships. The report is based on the notes of the home visitor.

> The parents themselves are well-adjusted, vital, outgoing; they enjoy children as such, and their own children as individuals. They show a healthy balance between the type of psychological detachment which allows them to appraise the child objectively and a warm emotionality that permits them to exhibit their devotion without embarrassment or artificiality. The child occupies his proportionate place in the household, is a full member of the family group, and is neither catered to nor ignored. . . .
>
> The maturity Mrs. Rampion exhibits in her personal life and in her general attitudes is also displayed, naturally enough, in her behavior toward the children. Respecting them as individuals, she makes a conscious and conscientious effort to maintain an emotional distance, a detachment giving objectivity to her

appraisal of them. An incident which reveals her imperturbability in the area of sex behavior is equally illustrative of her ability in general to see the children's behavior in perspective. . . . Leonard likes to rub himself on a toy horse which the children play on. "He's very sexy," Mrs. Rampion remarked. She had no emotional reaction to it, seemed casual and straightforward about the situation. It is definitely not a problem in her mind.

Her philosophy of non-intervention is further illustrated by the following incident: The three children were playing well together. Once Carol got too near a ladder the boys were balancing. Mrs. R. called out the window for Leonard to watch her. She remarked that she hated to do it, and only resorted to warnings when she could foresee serious injury. . . .

The Rampions . . . have explicit and formalized techniques for expressing their democratic philosophy of child care. Family council is traditional, with full and equal membership being accorded each child as soon as he can meet the requirement of repeating verbatim and explaining the motion before the group. The agenda may consist of matters ranging from the question of who shall wash and who shall wipe the dishes to the decision as to whether Mrs. R. should take a job offered her. The council convenes at the request of any member, and customarily handles the arbitration of all disputes. For example: . . . While Bobby was combing his hair upstairs, Leonard "dibbsed" on the wishbones from two chickens. Bobby was furious when he found what L. had done, said that it was unfair because one could never dibbs on more than his share, that he never had done it, etc. As a matter of fact, Bobby had done it more than any of the others. The two argued far into the night. Both Mr. and Mrs. R. kept out of the argument, hoping, however, that Leonard would stick to his guns and that Bobby's fallacy in argument would be brought out by him. The night of my visit Bob had called a family council to settle the question and said that he would abide by the council's decision. Mrs. R. said that she was going to bring up the fact that Bobby was the prize dibbser unless the other children mentioned it first.

In spite of the formality of democratic family government and in spite of the emotional distance which the Rampions maintain, the home atmosphere is not bleak or forbidding. The warm tone so evident in all the family's relationships characterizes their attitude toward one another. Without a great deal of fondling or other overt symbols of affection, the parents convey to the children their deep devotion.

It should be emphasized that the Rampion home is not "perfect". . . . Mrs. Rampion faces the usual run of disciplinary crises,
feeding problems and general reversals that come to most mothers,
though she handles such situations with more than average patience and understanding. In this democratic atmosphere Leonard
is, at present, making an excellent social adjustment, although his
development in the past has illustrated some of the difficulties
peculiar to such a closely knit and satisfying family structure. On
the one hand, his home background has been so encompassing in
its satisfactions that Leonard found the outside world, by comparison, somewhat dull and uninteresting. His social adjustment
during the preschool years was marked by shyness and withdrawal. At the same time, Leonard has suffered from his failure
to meet the high standards of the Rampion household. He has
been the most irresponsible and lazy of the children and, as a
consequence, he has been subjected to tremendous pressures, not
from the parents as much as from his siblings. As a result, he has
suffered from rather severe feelings of inferiority which have only
been alleviated by his quite remarkable popularity in school.
Under the flattering admiration of his classmates, his talents for
leadership and organization have blossomed until, at present, he
is making a good adjustment.*

Each individual acquires the distinctive ways of behaving which
define his personality through processes of social learning in his
family, his social class, and his culture. Personality is lawfully, if
complexly, determined. To understand its development we need
to know the general principles of learning which apply to all people,
and the particular conditions of learning that govern a person's specific experiences.

SUGGESTED READINGS

Mead's studies of personality in primitive societies have been conveniently collected in one volume entitled *From the South Seas*. Benedict, *Patterns of Culture*, another readable and fundamental contribution
to the understanding of cultural determinants of personality, is available
in a pocket edition. Part 1 of Weinberg, *Society and Personality Disorders* is an introductory discussion of social factors in individual maladjustments, and Fromm, *The Sane Society* is a capably written attempt to

---

* A. L. Baldwin, Joan Kalhorn, & Fay H. Breese. Patterns of parent behavior. *Psychol. Monogr.*, 1945, 58, No. 3 (Whole No. 268). Pp. 49-51.

sketch the outlines of a social order that would facilitate individual happiness.

For the American class structure, see Warner, Meeker, and Eells, *Social Class in America*. *Father of the Man*, by Davis and Havighurst, is a nontechnical discussion of the socialization process in America, and Preston, *The Substance of Mental Health* is a short and easy discussion of the relation of family life to the development of effective adjustments. Whiting and Child, *Child Training and Personality* is a most significant book on cross-cultural studies of personality development. Shaw and Ort, *Personal Adjustment in the American Culture* is centered at a relatively elementary level on the way American culture shapes the learning process. Devereux, *Reality and Dream* is an account of the psychotherapy of an American Indian, giving at once a feeling for the therapeutic process and a considerable insight into the influences of cultural factors on the learning of typical adjustment patterns. The papers collected in Kluckhohn, Murray, and Schneider, *Personality in Nature, Society, and Culture* are bound to interest the student who goes to them.

CHAPTER **14**

Psychoanalysis

Natural events can sometimes be described by more than one system of concepts. Even in the physical sciences, two theories may exist which attempt to account for the same observations. The ultimate aim of a scientific theorist is to reduce the number of conflicting theories, ideally by merging them into one more inclusive formulation.

A system of theory known as *psychoanalysis* deals with the same features of human behavior as does the psychology of adjustment. Psychoanalysis and the psychology of adjustment are not entirely different; indeed they have much in common as this chapter will reveal. But there are also some important distinctions between the two approaches. A student of experimentally-oriented psychology should know something of psychoanalytic theory. Psychoanalysis was an early approach to the problems of troubled people, and a knowledge of it gives historical perspective. Also, psychoanalytic concepts have had a great impact on our entire culture, on literature and art as well as on psychology, so that every liberally educated person needs to know something of them.

It is hard to make a brief presentation of psychoanalysis without superficiality or unfairness. For one thing, it is an intricately developed theory, the subject matter of thousands of books and articles. Another difficulty stems from the variations in psychoanalytic theory which exist even among its orthodox adherents. Every leading psychoanalytic writer differs at least a little from the others. The temporal changes in psychoanalysis are also bothersome, in that earlier writings are often contradicted by later ones. Indeed, one of the chief faults of popularizations of psychoanalysis is the tendency to describe earlier theories of the movement now discarded by its proponents. The term "psychoanalysis" is variously applied to the theory, to the method of investigation, and to the technique of treatment advocated by the psychoanalysts. Confusion sometimes results from a failure to distinguish these aspects. In spite of such difficulties, a useful brief description of psychoanalysis can be presented by adhering to certain limitations.

The account which follows is based mainly on the writings of Sigmund Freud (1856-1939), the founder and universally acknowledged great leader of psychoanalysis.[1] Only briefer attention is given to some other important contributors. Freud's later theories are emphasized without a detailed account of their historical development. Theory is given a central position with only passing reference to practice. For the sake of clarity, the psychoanalytic theories are presented in the next three sections positively and without reservations. Each sentence must be read as if prefixed with the phrase, "According to psychoanalysis. . . ."

FUNDAMENTAL
PSYCHOANALYTIC CONCEPTS

Forces and Energies

Psychoanalysis is a dynamic theory, that is, it emphasizes forces and energies. The moving forces of mental life come from two instincts.* One of them is called *Eros*, the instinct of life and love, which includes love of self, love of others, and the impulses for the preservation of the self and the species. Opposed to Eros is the *destruction or death instinct,* the urge for living organisms to die and return to inanimate matter. The death instinct consists of self-punishing or self-destroying impulses when turned inward, and of cruel and aggressive impulses when directed outward.

The energy of the life instinct or Eros is called libido. Perhaps the most fundamental psychoanalytic concept is that every person has only a limited store of this energy. The strength of libido, its

---

* Freud's German term *Trieb* has uniformly been translated into English as "instinct." It would be fairer, and also more comprehensible to the modern student of psychology, to translate it "impulse," "urge," or even "drive."

nature, and the channels into which it flows are the prime factors in determining personality and in distinguishing between normality and neurosis. The libido is entirely mental or psychic energy, not synonymous with nutrition, appetite, or any physiological, chemical, or physical energy. Although the libido represents all life forces, Freud wrote that most of what psychoanalysis knows about it has been gained from the study of the sexual function. Thus a large and important part of libido is viewed as the force of the sexual urge. The term "sexual" is employed both in a broader and in a narrower sense than in popular speech. It includes all kinds of pleasure-seeking activities and does not apply alone to the genital organs or to the reproductive process. Freud wrote that it includes everything ordinarily understood by the term "love," including self-love, love of parents, and love of mankind. In spite of this broad meaning, libido is also narrowly sexual, its aim being sexual union. The more diffuse manifestations are merely expressions of the narrowly sexual instinctive tendency.

The libidinal vital energy is present from birth and is as important in determining the behavior of infants and children as of adults. In infants, however, it is at first diffusely distributed as will be described later. The libido is dynamic and is constantly flowing and moving. It may flow inward to the self (narcism) or may be directed outward to other individuals or things (object-love). It may be directed to unreal phantasies (introversion). The libido may adhere to infantile love-objects (fixation) or may flow backward to them (regression). It may become restrained or dammed up (repression) or may be directed into altruistic and social channels (sublimation).

The destruction or death instinct is not discussed as fully in psychoanalytic writings. There is no term analogous to libido to designate its force.

Conscious, Preconscious, and Unconscious

The realm of mental life consists of three levels, conscious, preconscious, and unconscious. The concept of a *conscious* mind would have needed little explanation to students of academic psychology a generation or two ago. It comprises the mental content of which the individual is aware at a time. Obviously, it is small in comparison to the other levels of mind and its material is constantly shifting and changing. Some of consciousness comes from the external world; much of it arises from the lower levels of mind. The *preconscious* is the level of mind whose contents can easily be brought into consciousness by the association of ideas. It is the seat of ordinary memory and is on the whole more like the conscious level than like the unconscious. Of course, preconscious ideas vary in the ease with which they can be made conscious, because of strengths of associative processes, but also because of a certain amount of censorship which keeps some painful preconscious ideas out.

The *unconscious* level is the best-known concept in the Freudian theory. It may be thought of as Freud's answer to the inadequacy of the intellectualist consciousness-psychology of the immediately preceding period. Unconscious mental processes comprise the largest part of mind. While unknown to the individual, they have great influence on his thinking and actions. Unconscious material is not verbalized and logically arranged like conscious content. Antagonistic impulses can exist together without conflict. Unconscious processes are spoken of as unintegrated, infantile, and primitive. Emotion, desire and instinct predominate rather than ideas. The unconscious content comes from two sources, that which has been repressed into it from the conscious, and that which never was conscious. The latter aspect, which Jung emphasizes more than Freud, is the racial unconscious consisting of remnants of the mind of primitive man.

Id, Ego, and Superego

The topography of mind is further complicated by the existence of three additional characters: the *id* (*das Es*, the "it"), the *ego* (*Ich* or "I"), and the *superego*. The relationships of these features to the conscious and unconscious levels are represented in Figure 37.

The *id* is the entirely unconscious, striving aspect of personality. It is the original seat of libido and the source of all of the instinct energy of the individual. The id, in keeping with its primitive character, is entirely guided by the "pleasure principle," that is, by the seeking of gratification and the avoidance of pain. It has no contact with reality except through the mediation of the ego. The id is illogical and amoral, and is approximately equivalent to the primitive and animal nature of man.

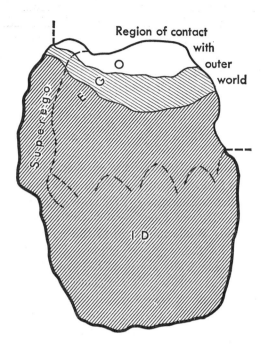

Figure 37. The Psychoanalytic Conception of Personality

The heavily shaded portion is at the unconscious level of awareness, the lightly shaded area is preconscious, and the unshaded portion is conscious. The id is all unconscious, the ego and the superego act at all three levels. (W. Healy, Augusta F. Bronner, and Anna M. Bowers, *The structure and meaning of psychoanalysis,* by permission of Alfred A. Knopf, publisher.)

The *ego* is partly conscious and partly unconscious. In infancy the ego is small and weak, but gradually grows through contact with reality, and by the assumption, through the mechanism of *identification,* of the characteristics of the infantile love objects, notably of the parents. The normal adult ego is governed chiefly by the "reality principle" and is rational and perceptual. In its lower regions the ego is in close contact with the id and acts with it in several ways. The ego is the source of the repression of urges that are pushed back into the id, and in general seeks to control the primitive instincts of the latter. At the same time, the ego grants satisfactions to the id when they are judged to be harmless.

Another structure of personality is the *superego*, which consists partly of inherited moralities and taboos and partly of the moral notions acquired by the child from its parents. The principal function of the superego is criticism. It is largely unconscious and is more aware of the id's amoral impulses than is the ego. Hence, the superego strives to compel the ego to repress the tendencies of the id. As it is sometimes expressed, the superego fights with the id, the ego being the battleground. It is obvious that the superego corresponds to the notion of "conscience."

Dualisms and Conflicts

The psychoanalytic theory uses many dualisms or "polarities," that is, pairs of entities of antagonistic nature. Some of these have already been met as Eros and the death instinct, conscious and unconscious, and the ego and id. In addition there are the opposites of masculine-feminine and love-hate which need no explanation. An important pair is the *pleasure principle* and the *reality principle*. What is done for immediate pleasure or to avoid pain belongs under the first class. This method of determining activity is characteristic of the id, of infants, and neurotics. What is done for expediency or because it is demanded by the external world pertains to the reality principle. In infancy these principles conflict, but the combat is normally compromised by the development of a strong ego that succeeds in reconciling the demands of pleasure with reality. Neurotics are unable to effect this inner peace which, as will be seen later, is an important factor in understanding their condition.

Stages of Personality Development

The core of the psychoanalytic theory is its conception of the development of personality. Development is divided into three principal stages, the infantile period which includes the years up to five or six, the latent period from then until puberty, and the adolescent stage which lasts until eighteen or twenty years of age. The greatest interest and importance is attached to the infantile stage. Development in this early period is characterized by two not unrelated trends, that of the localization of the libido or of the chief

zone of pleasurable sensation, and that of the finding of objects
for the attachment of the libido. Ego development also goes on
simultaneously and is closely related to libido development.

The development of libidinal localization may be described first.
At birth the infant's libido is diffusely distributed, but then in a
brief period of time it comes to be localized in three different body
regions in turn. First is the *oral-erotic* stage in which the libidinal
satisfactions are obtained chiefly from the mouth, at first in nursing
and thumb-sucking, later in biting and chewing. Destructive impulses of infants are ascribed to this later oral ("oral-sadistic")
phase. Then follows the *anal-erotic* stage in which the eliminative
function and organs become the center of satisfaction. In the early
anal phase expulsion is pleasurable, in the later, retention is the
mode of pleasure-finding. The anal stage is displaced by the *phallic*
stage, when the pleasure-giving possibilities of the sex organs are
discovered and utilized. It is distinguished from the genital stage
which is achieved at puberty. Many anomalous conditions among
adults are ascribed to fixation at or regression to one or another
of the earlier infantile stages. For example, cruelty is due to regression to the late oral stage of biting-pleasure, avarice and obstinacy
to the late anal phase of pleasure in retention. The "oral character"
and the "anal character" are thus distinguished in adults. In the
normal course of development the oral-libido is thwarted by weaning and the anal-libido by bowel training. If successfully accomplished these events give the child a better comprehension of the
demands of reality and hence strengthen the ego.

The infantile progress in object-finding passes through three
stages. The first stage is objectless and consists of pure bodily sensation. The libido is not attached, but is gratified only by purely
organic pleasures. As the ego forms, the libido becomes attached
to it, leading to the second state of self-love or *primary narcism*,
named after the legend of Narcissus, who fell in love with his own
reflection in the water. Primary narcism strengthens the ego with
some of the id's energy and persists throughout life, being desirable
if not excessive in degree. The egocentric character results from
fixation at or regression to the narcistic level. At adolescence there
is a second wave of narcism which is a normal event at that time.
The third stage of libidinal attachment is the *object-choice*, the
first adherence of the libido to an external love-object being, naturally enough, directed to the child's parents. It begins at the

same time as the phallic stage of libido localization. Parent attachment introduces the problem of the Oedipus complex.

The Oedipus and Castration Complexes

The course of parental attachment of the *boy* is first directed toward his mother, having already a beginning in the earlier non-genital attachment formed from her relationship to his oral needs. With the development of the phallic phase, the same object-choice becomes more directly sexual and the *Oedipus* complex is formed. Named after the myth of the Theban king who slew his father and married his mother without knowledge of what he was doing, the Oedipus complex represents the boy's unconscious desire for incestuous sexual union with his mother. The unconscious nature of this wish must be emphasized. The child does not become aware of the direct sexual nature of the desire at all. It is manifested only by desire for caresses, for attention, in wanting to sleep with the mother, and in similar attenuated expressions. The earlier psycho-analytic view was that this complex concerned the person of the parent; later it was recognized as carried out almost entirely in unconscious fantasy, a mother-image (or *imago*) in the unconscious being the love-object. The Oedipus complex is not regarded as originating from the mother's affection for the child. It is innate in the boy, a heritage of the racial unconscious. As the sexual love for the mother grows, the father is recognized as a rival for her favors, and hostile wishes including those of death and injury are formed against him.

From his father-hostility comes the second great complex of the boy's infantile period. The boy unconsciously fears that his father will retaliate by physically injuring him, particularly by depriving him of his newly discovered and highly prized penis. This *castration complex* was earlier ascribed to actual parental threats to cut off the genitals when the child was discovered playing with them, and to the discovery that girls apparently lack external genitals and were therefore believed by the boy to be persons on whom the threat had been carried out. Since Freud later believed that he had found evidences of the castration complex in persons who had not had these experiences, the idea was ascribed to an inherited idea, preserved from prehistoric times. The castration complex "explodes" the Oedipus complex. Because of its threat the boy gives up his incestuous desire for his mother. The solution of the Oedipus involves the *sublimation* of the feelings toward the mother into tender affection, and *identification* with the father so that his achievements come to be regarded as the child's own. The superego has its origin in the solution of the Oedipus, the intolerant conscience being formed in the process of the renunciation of the infantile sexual aims.

The parental complex is further complicated by *bisexuality*. Every child has some of the psychic characteristics of the opposite sex. An inverted Oedipus complex is therefore also formed, the boy homosexually loving his father and hating his mother. This process is normal, and with the direct complex constitutes the "complete Oedipus." It is solved by identification and sublimation as is the positive Oedipus complex. If because of psychosexual constitution or circumstantial factors the inverted Oedipus is too strong, a homosexual predisposition will result.

The personality development of the *girl* presents more difficulties than that of the boy. The primary attachment to the mother resulting from nursing must be overcome at the beginning, and the solution at the end is not so clearly defined. In the girl, the castration complex *precedes* the Oedipus complex. The girl discovers what she takes to be her genital inferiority to boys. She blames her lack or deprivation on her mother and hence adopts a hostile attitude toward her. The result is the female castration complex or masculinity complex. Renouncing mother-love because of this hostility, the girl now turns to love of her father and finds in him a compensation for her distressing lack of maleness. Thus emerges the girl's Oedipus complex (sometimes called the Electra complex, after another legend), which often takes the form of the unconscious desire to bear the father a child. The dissolution of the Oedipus complex is slower in the girl than in the boy, since no catastrophic fear brings it to a close. It is eventually solved by identification with the mother and sublimated feelings toward the father. As in boys, the girl's development involves bisexuality, and an inverted Oedipus is also formed. A recurrence of the castration complex may take place at puberty when the first menstruation is attended with fear and shame.

PSYCHOANALYTIC
CONCEPTS OF THE NEUROSES

Normal and Abnormal Development

The course of personality development so far described is deemed to be the normal one. All persons have infantile sexual complexes but in normal development they are solved to a sufficient degree, principally by sublimation and identification. Abnormal development leading to symptoms of varying degrees of severity and to neuroses results when the complexes are inadequately solved. If sublimation is inadequate, a *fixation* occurs, which means that the libido adheres or is fixed to the image of the unrenounced infantile love-object. Two related evils result. First, the fixed libido is not available for dealing with reality, hence the individual with infantile fixations has less energy with which to combat the difficulties of his existence and is more susceptible to emotional shocks and thwartings. Second, a further store of energy has to be used up in repressing the incestuous desires and keeping them from reaching consciousness, which further exhausts his dynamic potentialities. In brief, the psychoanalytic theory holds that the individual's capacity for accomplishment depends on his having an adequate supply of energy available. If too much libido is fixated in infantile wishes, he will be weak and subject to maladjustment and neuroses. Individual differences in the degree of fixation depend upon variations of the constitutional "adhesiveness" or lack of plasticity of the libido, and also upon differences in childhood experiences.

Since all persons cherish remnants of infantile complexes in some degree, all adult behavior shows some peculiarities that are ascribable to fixation. In less numerous cases, behavior is so disturbed as to constitute a psychoneurosis. Healy, Bronner and Bowers enumerated five factors which determine the issue between normality and neurosis.[2] These are: (1) Whether the id is able to disguise the repressed impulses sufficiently so that they are not recognized by the ego or superego. (2) Whether an adequate amount of libido is left unfixed for the use of the ego in facing reality. (3) Whether reality is easy or hard to deal with, that is, whether the adult encounters serious difficulties and frustrations or not. (4) Whether the ego is strong or itself infantile and preoccupied with childhood conflicts. (5) Whether the superego is easy-going or too severe with the expressions of the infantile wishes. If an individual's development is favorable in relation to these matters, he stays normal; if it is unfavorable he develops the symptoms of maladjustment or neurosis.

Mechanisms

In both normal and neurotic persons, mechanisms of thinking and conduct (sometimes called *dynamisms*) are employed to compromise between the forces of the id, both innate and repressed, on the one hand, and the demands of reality on the other. Many of the mechanisms bear names already familiar to the reader, but they are given a somewhat different interpretation in psychoanalytic theory. The mechanisms are regarded as the means by which the ego deals with its three adversaries — the id and superego within and the real world without. Some mechanisms provide outlets for the wishes of the id, others are defenses against the expression of the repressed desires.

Of the mechanisms of defense, *repression* is possibly the most fundamental. The concept of repression arose from the discovery of "resistances" during the process of analysis which are shown in the patient's reluctance or inability to tell of certain wishes and experiences of the past. Repression is a function of the superego, which prevents painful or rejected desires and ideas from appearing in consciousness. *Reaction formation* is another defensive mechanism that operates to negate repressed wishes by the expression of the opposite sentiment. Thus a repressed sexual desire results in a horror of sex as in the form of prudery. In the opposite aspect, a hostile wish toward a parent, the residual of unsolved Oedipus or castration complexes, may show itself by an excessive concern for the parent's welfare. *Rationalization* serves to protect the ego against the necessity of acknowledging the real desires underlying behavior, by substituting socially acceptable reasons for acts really motivated by repressed love or hostility. *Projection* operates by ascribing to the external world the rejected urges of the id. In the extreme of abnormality it is illustrated by delusions of persecution in which the inner destructive impulses of the individual are projected to those about him, causing the patient to believe that others are seeking to harm or destroy him.

The most normal of the fulfillment mechanisms is *sublimation*. By this process the libidinal urges are transformed into interests and activities described as "aim-inhibited," in that their object is no longer sexual. The origins of vocational interests, hobbies, civic activities, and religion are traced to sublimation. Although sublimated activities are in many instances remote from the original urges, they show in other cases their original sexual derivation. *Identification*, already encountered several times, is another useful mechanism, the individual securing outlets by identifying himself with the persons and achievements of others, particularly of his parent of the same sex.

Of the less desirable mechanisms of fulfillment, *regression* is perhaps the most serious. Regression is the retreat of the libido to infantile types of satisfaction. Regression to the oral and anal phases of libidinal localization has been noted as characteristic of certain forms of disorder. Retreat to infantile love-objects is another form of regression. Regressive tendencies are brought about by the weakness of the ego in coping with new developments of reality. This mechanism results in a renewal of infantile conflicts, bringing about the formation of further defenses usually of a neurotic nature.

Repressed urges find easily available outlets in *fantasy*, the wishful character of daydreaming being greatly emphasized by the psychoanalysts. Much distortion occurs in fantasy, and wish-fulfillments of a nonsexual nature are often disguises for fantasied attainments of infantile sexual desires. *Unconscious fantasy* is a further application of the same mechanism, the imagined satisfactions occurring entirely in unconscious processes without ever coming up to awareness. The mechanism of unconscious fantasy was hypothesized by Freud early in his career. His women patients with surprising frequency recalled a childhood seduction by their fathers. Upon ascertaining that these seductions were in many instances not true in fact, Freud ascribed them to a childhood unconscious fantasy of seduction based on the Oedipus complex, which was unearthed in the analysis as an actual occurrence because the child was unable to distinguish effectively between reality and fantasy.

The mechanism of *conversion* denotes the physical expression either of repressed urges or of defenses against them. It is the basis of "conversion hysteria" which is explained as the physical solution of a mental conflict. The desires or defenses are "converted into" the physical symptoms which may be pains, anaesthesias, paralyses, or some other form of sensory or motor impairment. Hysteria is characterized by an excessive sex desire and a strong defense against it. The hysterical symptoms are sexual substitutes, often involving regression especially when the throat (oral region) and bowels (anal region) are involved.

A mechanism of wide application is that of *displacement*, which means the transfer of libidinal energy from one idea to another. Considerable use is made of the concept of displacement in understanding dreams and in the interpretation of all sorts of symbolic behavior. Phobias are explained as examples of the operation of this mechanism. If a person suffers from an irrational fear of a harmless object, such as a fear of enclosed places, it is because the feared object symbolizes or represents, by displacement, some deeper fear. The displacement allows the expression of the emotion while protecting the individual from the necessity of acknowledging the strongly repressed tendency.

Dreams

The theory of dreams has occupied a central position in psychoanalysis since Freud's first book on the subject was published in 1900. Dreams involve a mechanism peculiar to themselves as well as a number of the other dynamisms, and therefore constitute a means of expression for the repressed content of the unconscious. But dreams are much more than just another mechanism to the psychoanalysts, for they have provided the chief means for understanding how unconscious processes operate. The infantile and illogical character of the unconscious parts of the ego, and their preoccupation with direct gratification, were first noted in the study of dreams.

According to psychoanalysis all dreams are meaningful. Not only the dream as a whole but every little element in it has significance that may be interpreted in relation to the dreamer's personality and conflicts. The meaning of a dream is not apparent in the obvious and literal events reported by the dreamer, which are termed the *manifest content* of the dream. The manifest content, consisting chiefly of visual imagery, hides the *latent content* in which the real meaning will be discovered. The latent content consists of unconscious desires and anxieties, which are distorted before being expressed in the actual dream experience. Unconscious impulses strive to make their way upward into consciousness, but are prevented from doing so during waking hours by the vigilance of the ego. In sleep the ego relaxes somewhat and allows the unconscious content to appear. The sleep of the ego is not complete, however, for there remains considerable resistance to the unconscious wishes in the form of the *dream-censor.* The censorship compels the id to disguise the dream to hide its true significance from the ego. If the id impulses appear too strongly or are too thinly disguised the ego shows great anxiety and may awake as a protective measure, the sequence constituting a "nightmare." The process by which the id turns its latent urges into the manifest or apparent content of the dream is the mechanism of *dream-work.*

Fundamentally, dreams are wish-fulfilling devices, but they draw their manifest content from many sources. Part of the dream material comes from the preconscious, repeating or extending experiences of waking life. Other content arises through displacement, one idea assuming the emotional value that properly belongs to another. A special form of displacement is symbolization, which refers to the representation of an idea by means of some sign or substitute. Some symbols appearing in dreams arise through the individual experiences of the dreamer, but others are consistent symbols which always have the same significance for all persons. Among the fixed symbols described by Freud were the following: anything long and pointed as a sword, a whip, or a tree signifies the male; rooms, receptacles, and bags are symbols of the female; going up or down a stairway indicates the sex act; coming out of the water is a symbol of birth. These are only a few samples of fixed symbols, there being many others. Many psychoanalysts have disagreed with Freud on the matter of symbolism, holding that all symbols are the result of the individual experiences of the dreamer.

Neurotic Symptoms

According to psychoanalysis, neurotic symptoms are substitutes for the gratification of repressed urges. They are compromises between the demands of the id and the repressive tendency of the ego. Every symptom represents the fulfillment of some desire that cannot be gained in reality, as seen with special clarity in hysteria, in phobias, and in compulsions. The ego accepts the symptom because it is less shocking than the direct gratification of the wish would be and because it lessens the labor of repression. A compulsion, such as an urge to count one's steps, represents the attainment of a repressed aim and is therefore of value. Anxiety neuroses originate from the castration complex, being the fear of a weak and infantile ego of retaliation from the external world because of the persistence of childish sexual fixations. It is noted that anxiety neuroses are more common among men, the castration fear being characteristic of the male sex. Hysteria is more prevalent among women.

A prominent trait of neurotics is that of *ambivalence* of emotion, love and hate being directed toward the same person. Such ambivalence is characteristic of children at the stage of the Oedipus complex, and is normally outgrown. That neurotics continue to show ambivalence indicates that their infantile complexes have not been solved, a fact already noted in explaining predispositions toward neurotic conditions. The conflict of love and hate constitutes one of the greatest problems of the neurotic and his weak ego attempts to solve it by the inadequate device of repressing one or the other of these tendencies, thus paving the way to symptom formation.

The Aims of Therapy

The psychoanalytic method of treatment is based on the theory that the neurotic suffers from a weakness of internal energy that prevents him from using the superior methods of dealing with the id. His lack of strength is due to the fixation of the libido on infantile love-objects, and to the concern of the ego with infantile anxieties. The aims of treatment are therefore to free the libido from its fixations and to strengthen the ego, thus making the patient capable of dealing with his life problems. The curative procedures of psychoanalysis are based on two concepts, resistance and transference. *Resistance* is shown in the unwillingness and inability of the patient to disclose his real desires and complexes. This phenomenon is, of course, due to repression. The person is quite unaware that the bases of his difficulties lie in infantile attachments and fears, and so is unable to give an account of them to the analyst. The analytic techniques overcome resistances and make the patient conscious of his basic conflicts. When the infantile difficulties are brought into consciousness, the full force of the adult ego can be brought to bear upon them, and a favorable solution can then be secured. The Oedipus complex, unsolved in childhood and since then inaccessible at the unconscious level, is brought out into the light and solved by the now mature ability of the patient.

The concept of *transference* is even more important in psychoanalysis. Because the analyst has a parent-like role and opens up the unconscious content, he becomes a parent substitute for the patient. As analysis proceeds, the patient no longer responds to the analyst as a real and present person, but as the fantasy of an important figure from his childhood. Transference is therefore encouraged, for it enables the patient to re-create, to live again, the emotions which he once directed to his parents. Analyst and patient therefore re-enact the "family romance" of the early years. Like the child's attitudes toward his parents, the emotions of transference are ambivalent. At times the patient loves the analyst and is abjectly dependent on him; at times he is hostile, negativistic, or even hates him. The analyst does not prevent the emergence of these hostile emotions, called negative transference, but uses them to aid the reinstatement of the infantile attitudes. If transference were allowed to continue, the patient would cling to the analyst as he had previously clung to the parent-imago, which would be equally undesirable. The transference must therefore be dissolved by interpreting it to the patient. When the patient understands that he responded to the analyst not as a real person but as a surrogate for a parental fixation, the transference will end. In terms of psychoanalytical dynamics, the libido is transferred from the parent-imago to the analyst, who then gives it back to the patient. The libido so transferred cannot return to its infantile love-objects and so is at the disposal of the ego for dealing with reality. The neurotic condition is thereby cured.

Psychoanalytic Techniques

Psychoanalysis employs several special techniques for discovering unconscious material, which are found useful both for overcoming resistance and for promoting transference. Two principal methods used are those of *free association* and *dream analysis*. These procedures are carried out in combination rather than separately and can only be considered together. The free association method is employed by having the patient lie on a couch and relax, and then relate everything that comes to his mind. The relaxation and the reclining posture tend to minimize the influence of repression through their similarity to the state of sleep. Starting with some idea connected with his difficulties, the patient is made to tell everything that he thinks of, no matter how painful it may be or, on the other hand, how trivial or apparently irrelevant. Psychoanalysts are strict in enforcing the "conditions of free association." Everything must be told, everything is really relevant and meaningful. The associations themselves do not constitute the basic unconscious ideas, being only disguised expressions of the repressed urges. The analyst himself relaxes and lets his imagination play freely on the associations of the patient. Through his training in psychoanalysis, he penetrates the disguises and recognizes repressed material that is unintelligible to the patient himself. When the patient hesitates in the association process or when he protests that the ideas brought up are either too private or too trivial to tell, the presence of resistance and repression is indicated. As transference to the analyst progresses the resistances are broken down and the patient tells the analyst everything.

The dreams of the patient are interpreted in two ways. In some cases the dream content consists of fixed symbols immediately recognizable by the analyst. More frequently, dreams serve as a point of departure for the free association technique. The patient gives an account of his associations to the dream as a whole and to all of its details. The dream and its associations are not interpreted literally, for they constitute only manifest or distorted content. The latent content, discoverable only by the combination of the analyst's knowledge and the patient's associations, is the real meaning sought. In the later stages of the analysis, the physician interprets the associations and dreams to the patient, according to the psychoanalytic theory. This process of *interpretation* plays a large part in the treatment, and may be considered as a third technique of therapy. The object of interpretation is to break down resistances by revealing to the patient their origin in the infantile complexes. Patients are well on the road to recovery when they have assimilated the notion of the childhood causes of their troubles. In using all of the psychoanalytic techniques, the analyst does not guide or instruct the patient to change his traits of behavior. Dependence is placed on freeing the libido and strengthening the ego, after which the patient can solve his problems unaided.

VARIANTS OF PSYCHOANALYSIS

A theory as novel, as challenging, and as dogmatic as that of Freud inevitably called forth a number of variants. Many practitioners and theorists have adopted some of the psychoanalytic structures, rejected others, and added new concepts of their own. Such contributions have varied greatly in their originality and in the extent of their influence. A full account of all varieties of psychoanalysis is beyond the scope of this book. A few demand attention.[3]

Three important contributors — Alfred Adler, Carl G. Jung, and Otto Rank — were closely associated with Freud in the early days of the psychoanalytic movement. They differed with Freud on certain issues and were bitterly denounced by him. Each evolved a fully developed system of theory, attracted a school of partisan followers, and left enduring marks on all subsequent thinking about human maladjustments.

More recent contributions of considerable importance were made by several analytically oriented writers in the United States, among whom Erich Fromm, Karen Horney, and Harry Stack Sullivan may serve as examples. These writers have not constituted a school or group in any formal sense, but they have influenced one another and their theories are harmonious. They have often been labeled the "neo-Freudians" or "neo-analysts."

Individual Psychology

Alfred Adler's school of interpretation assumed the title "individual psychology," as the study of the individual in relation to his environment.[4] Although it grew out of psychoanalysis, Adler's theory is clearly opposed to Freud's on many important points. According to Adler, the principal force of life is a striving for superiority or self-assertion. In normal individuals this urge is adjusted to reality and integrated with social drives, leading to reasonable satisfaction through achievement. In childhood the urge to superiority is thwarted in many directions because of the child's weakness and helplessness and the omnipotence of his parents. The situation may be aggravated by the presence of actual physical defects, imagined defects, excessive parental severity, or other factors. In such circumstances, a person acquires an unconscious *inferiority complex*. The child's place in the family is stressed as contributing to the formation of this feeling. The eldest child is likely to show it least, while the second child, always behind in the race, is more strongly impressed with his inferiority. A pampered child may acquire feelings of inferiority when the spoiling ceases or when he makes contact with other persons than his parents who give him no special consideration. Persons tend to express their striving for supremacy and their contempt for inferiority in symbolic terms. The commonest symbol is masculine-feminine, masculine standing for strong, courageous, and "up," feminine signifying weak, incapable, and "down." The contrast gives rise to the *masculine protest,* a desire to "be a man," characteristic of neurotics of both sexes. According to Adler, sex conflicts are only secondary manifestations of the fundamental drive to superiority.

The inferiority complex evokes *overcompensation.* Organs that are not strong, Adler believed, tend to correct their defect by an excessive activity of some kind. Psychic compensation operates to conceal or to overcome inferiority complexes. So long as an individual's compensations are not antisocial, he is normal; when they become aggressive tricks for subduing others they constitute a neurosis. Another difference between normals and neurotics is in *guiding fictions* or imagined goals. A normal person is oriented to reality and does not set up goals which are impossible to attain. A neurotic pays less attention to reality, being engrossed in his fictions which urge him to an impossible superiority.

As a result of his early experiences which determine the intensity of his inferiority complex, the direction of his compensations, and the nature of his goals, each person adopts a *style of life* which is the core of his character. An overindulged child expects everyone to yield and serve him. A punitively reared child has expectations that people are hostile and must therefore be avoided or attacked. An important source of adult psychoneuroses is a discrepancy between a person's style of life and the demands of social reality. When his style of life is threatened, a person intensifies his compensations in order to maintain it, and thereby develops neurotic symptoms. Hysterical and hypochondriacal reactions, for example, are either ruses to subjugate other people and compel their attention and service, or else excuses to explain away failures by attributing them to illness.

Adler's method of psychotherapy differed considerably from that of Freud. Adler believed that a person's conscious and unconscious urges are directed toward the same goals and are not in internal conflict as Freud hypothesized. Therefore, therapy need not try to uncover unconscious impulses. Resistance is interpreted as an attempt of the patient to get the best of his therapist. An Adlerian therapist seeks to disclose the patient's style of life, his fictional goals, and his compensations. By a gentle educative process, the patient is led to discover and re-examine the bases of his individual strivings. A cure takes place when the patient, through his own thinking, achieves an improved balance between individual aspirations and socialized behavior.

Analytical Psychology

Carl G. Jung was one of Freud's most brilliant collaborators in the early days of psychoanalysis.[5] Before Freud broke with him, he made important original contributions. Jung proposed that psychoanalysis use the word-association method, a variety of free association in which the patient responds to a series of words presented by the analyst by saying the first idea that comes to his mind. Jung also suggested the term "complex," which was readily accepted by Freud. Even after Jung's departure from the orthodox fold, Freud adopted with some delay and modification a number of his novel conceptions. The quarrel between the two men was intense and personal. In his writings, Freud made many derogatory remarks about Jung, and the latter replied in kind. In response to a demand from Freud that he cease calling himself a psychoanalyst, Jung adopted the term "analytical psychology" to designate his theory.

Jung's first break with Freud centered on the nature of libido. As early as 1912, Jung defined libido as a general life urge, while Freud was then describing it as the force of the sexual instinct. The unconscious, Jung wrote, does not consist entirely of animal strivings, but contains in itself a moral or religious principle. Jung described two levels of the unconscious, the *personal unconscious* of repressed individual experiences, and the *collective unconscious* which consists of inherited patterns of neural structure predisposing a person toward archaic ways of thinking like those of modern man's primitive ancestors. On all three of these issues, Freud later veered toward Jung. The concept of the moral nature of a part of the unconscious became the superego and assumed a central place in Freud's theory. The other two features of theory — the libido as a general life urge, and the racial unconscious — were adopted by Freud in his later writings but were never crucial in his thinking. When describing childhood development and neuroses, Freud continued to write as though the libido were a sexual urge. Freud's concept of the racial unconscious could be omitted without damage to the consistency of his system. Both of these points, however, are essential to Jung's approach.

Even more than Freud, Jung made use of inner polarities and conflicts. The conscious, for example, expresses itself in two different ways, by turning outward to the world or inward to the self. The dominance of one of these modes of expression gives rise to the personality types, extravert and introvert, which were described in Chapter 11. Persons also differ in whether their consciousness is dominated by the function of thinking, feeling, sensation, or intuition. All people, whether males or females physically, also have elements of the masculine or feminine in their psychological nature, the masculine characterized by thinking and sensation, the feminine by feeling and intuition. With respect to all these attitudes, if the conscious takes one direction the opposite is present in the unconscious. If the conscious is extraverted, or masculine, or given to thinking, the unconscious is correspondingly introverted, or feminine, or dominated by feeling. An even greater polarity exists between the collective unconscious and the rest of the personality. Responding to the real world, a person becomes divorced from the primitive, archaic side of his nature. The collective unconscious contains the wisdom of the ages represented by primitive urges or instincts and primordial images or archetypes. Important archetypes include the primitive father, the symbol of authority, and the archetypical mother, the symbol of all that is nourishing and protecting. These archetypes do not ordinarily rise to consciousness but appear in dreams, in the delusions of psychotics, and in the myths of mankind.

Psychoneurotic difficulties arise from present conflicts when a person does not have enough strength, enough psychic energy or libido, to deal with his realities. His lack of strength stems mainly from his one-sided development which prevents him from using the resources of the unconscious. Jung's therapy, which he calls "psychosynthesis," therefore consists in restoring man's wholeness. Extensive use is made of the interpretation of dreams as symbols of unconscious forces, especially from the archaic or collective unconscious. A cure is achieved when the patient becomes able to integrate his primitive or irrational nature with his conscious rationality.

Will Therapy

Otto Rank's most distinctive theories stemmed from his concept of the *birth trauma*.[6] At birth, the infant is ejected from complete, nurturing protection of the womb, an experience which causes profound shock and anxiety. In childhood, and indeed throughout life, other threats of separation reactivate the "primal anxiety" of the birth experience. All the years of normal childhood are required to counteract the damaging effects of the birth anxiety. Neurotics are persons who have never overcome it completely, but always feel isolated and separated from other people and hence anxious.

In keeping with his theory of the birth trauma, Rank placed a different interpretation on the stages of child development than did Freud. He viewed the Oedipus complex not as an incestuous sexual love for the mother, but as a desire of the child to incorporate himself in her again and to return to the primal bliss of intra-uterine life.

Rank traced individual development in terms of the emergence of *will*, that is, of separate individuality. In his earliest experiences, an infant is frustrated by the wills of other persons, mainly his parents. He has to accede to their demands to wait for feeding, to be weaned, and to give up his pleasures for their convenience. These experiences evoke the child's "counter will," his negativistic resistance to compulsion. Thereafter, the will may develop through three stages. The first stage consists of the person himself willing what is imposed from without. Thus he lives by authority springing from parents' orders and the codes of the culture. Rank noted that most people do not progress beyond this first stage. In a second stage, the person develops a conflict between the authoritarian will and his own counter will because of his growing need for independence. The outcome is either the evolution of a higher order of will or a neurosis with self-criticism and guilt. The third stage, achieved only by creative persons, is the free, autonomous will of harmonious self-government.

A neurotic person is one who aspires to the third stage of development but fails to reach it. He cannot accept the will of the group, but neither does he develop a creative will of his own. Hence he feels isolated, and suffers from a recurrence of the primal separation anxiety of birth.

Rank called his method of treatment *will therapy*, because it was designed to promote the growth of the mature autonomous will. Others, referring to the means which Rank advocated, have termed it *relationship therapy*. Consistent with his theory that all anxiety arises from a sense of separation, Rank conceived the task of the therapist as the establishment of a close and secure relationship with the patient. Safe in this relationship and no longer feeling himself separated, the patient can overcome his primal anxiety and grow in the direction of autonomous will or self-realization. Rank's theory has a strong appeal because he pictured the goal of therapy reaching beyond a mere restoration of "normality" toward the emergence of a free and creative person.

The Neo-Analysts

The neo-analysts brought cultural anthropology and sociology to bear upon psychoanalysis. Leading "neo-Freudian" writers, including Erich Fromm,[7] Karen Horney,[8] Harry Stack Sullivan,[9] and others, have shared a number of culturally oriented concepts. First, they reject the libido or any other psychic energy as the one source of human urges. Aside from biological wants such as hunger, each person's most important motivations are acquired from his culture, which is represented by the persons with whom he has significant relationships. Second, child development is not seen as an inevitable series of steps centering on the sexual impulse, as Freud held. Instead, the development of personality is a gradual process of socialization which continues through the entire maturing period and is affected by many cultural influences.

Sullivan described personality development in terms of an individual's interpersonal relationships with his *significant others*, the people who most intimately supply the rewards and punishments in his life. A person's conception of his self is derived from the appraisals made by these significant persons. Thus a person can perceive himself as strong and self-respecting if his parents treat him with warmth and respect, or as weak and guilty if they respond to his needs with denial or rejection. Just as a person develops a concept of his self which is learned by experience but not necessarily realistic, so also he may learn distorted perceptions of other people. Intense and convincing learning experiences, unsupported by logic and ill-connected with other perceptions, are called *parataxic* experiences. By such parataxic distortions, a person may come to perceive a mother figure as highly idealized, nurturant, and loving. He may come to perceive all figures of authority as threateningly hostile. As development progresses, many distortions of individual experience are corrected in some degree by *consensual validation*, the sharing of the perceptions made by other people. In understanding a person or in helping him, it is necessary to know how he perceives himself and others.

Psychoneuroses have their roots in anxiety which is acquired mainly from the interpersonal relationships of childhood. Horney saw the origin of anxiety in hostile impulses toward people which conflict with learned dependence and socialization. Such hostile impulses arise when a child's parents are rejecting or lacking in warmth. Sullivan, quite similarly, wrote that anxiety is aroused when a person cannot harmoniously fulfill his biological strivings for satisfactions and his culturally derived needs for security. Although much anxiety comes from childhood experiences, it can be evoked at any stage of life by inconsistencies demanded in a culture. Our own culture has many built-in conflicts, such as its teaching that a person must be competitive and hence aggressive, but must not be hostile toward other people.

In one of her best-known contributions, Horney wrote that people can try to control their anxieties in three main ways, by moving toward people or compliance, by moving against people or aggression, and by moving away from people or detachment. Most persons use these three devices flexibly, but a neurotic may use them rigidly and with self-defeating intensity. Rigid and intense compliance, aggression, or detachment define three *character structures* which may be basic to neuroses. The concept of character structure is similar to Adler's "style of life."

The psychotherapy advocated by the neo-analysts, somewhat like that of Rank, uses a warm and accepting attitude between analyst and patient as a prototype of a good interpersonal relationship which reduces anxiety and hence permits the growth of socialization. Some of Freud's techniques, free association and the analysis of dreams, are used but different interpretations are placed on them. They reveal the patient's self system, his parataxic distortions, and his interpersonal relationships. Childhood experiences are recalled and re-assessed in therapy, but attention to childhood is not enough. Because the patient's conflicts extend into his present life, modifications of his self concept, his perceptions of others, and his social relationships are also needed.

AN APPRAISAL OF PSYCHOANALYSIS

Psychoanalytic theories have been appraised from many viewpoints — practical, scientific, philosophical, social, moral, and religious. These evaluations have ranged from uncritical acceptance to emotionally toned rejection. Here we are concerned with appraising psychoanalysis from only one point of reference, that of science.

Sigmund Freud was without doubt one of the world's authentic geniuses. Few modern men — Newton and Darwin are other examples — have had so broad an influence on the thinking of our culture. Every competent and well-informed person acknowledges psychology's historical debt to Freud and psychoanalysis for some of its problems and concepts. The modern psychology of adjustment sprang from many sources. Experimental psychologists, pioneers in child study, physiologists, anthropologists, sociologists, educators, nonanalytic psychopathologists, and others have contributed to its development. Psychoanalysis is only one of a number of movements which have carried psychology to its present position, but the value of its influence must be acknowledged positively.

Contributions of Psychoanalysis

Perhaps the greatest contribution of psychoanalysis was to make psychology aware of the problems now conceived as personal adjustments. With few exceptions, psychology before 1900 was concerned with sensation, perception, reaction, and intellectual and motor processes in general. While research in these fields was exact, it was far removed from the critical problems of real human life. Although other social movements contributed to the same end, psychoanalysis assisted materially in making psychology aware of the problems of personality and conduct.

Psychoanalysis emphasizes the dynamic or striving aspects of human behavior. Except for some rather mechanical theories of "instinct," psychology paid little attention to the process of *motivation* until it received the impact of psychoanalysis. As you have already seen by comparing Chapters 2 and 3 with Chapter 14, modern psychology does not agree with Freud about the nature and sources of motives. But the historical debt is great. Psychoanalysis presented the challenge and aroused first controversy and then investigation, leading to a better understanding of the principles of human motivation.

Freud's most distinctive concept was of *unconscious* processes, or the nondeliberate determination of behavior. This notion is indispensable to a psychological understanding of personality and adjustment. Psychology does not, of course, support the concept of *the* unconscious as a thing or place, but takes a functional view of the nature of unaware events. So did Freud in his last book, published posthumously, which always refers to unconscious phenomena, never to *the* unconscious.[10] Because of the difference in theoretical interpretation, a strange misunderstanding has arisen that experimentally oriented psychology does not "believe in" unconscious events and pays attention only to consciousness. Nothing could be more false. On the contrary, objective psychology is not much concerned with passing states of conscious awareness, but gives great emphasis to a person's acquired drives and learned responses of which he may be quite unaware. Historically, psychoanalysis spurred psychology to study the motives a person does not know he has, and the blind learning which modifies his behavior without also giving insight.

Another very general concept which psychology shares with psychoanalysis is *causal determinism*. Psychoanalysis from its beginning held that all behavior is the result of discoverable causes, a belief common to all the natural sciences. Even apparently accidental behavior such as slips of the tongue and mannerisms are ascribed to causal motivations and past learnings, not to "error" or "chance." More importantly, maladjustments and behavior disorders are viewed as lawful. Their causes can be traced if we know enough about the person and his past experiences. There are no exceptions to the orderliness of human behavior.

Another bond between psychoanalysis and psychology is the *genetic approach* in understanding personality and behavior. The genetic method was developed independently by psychology, which has always had a concern with development and learning in childhood. On this issue, psychoanalysis contributed more to psychiatry than to general psychology. Pre-Freudian psychiatry attributed mental disorders to two factors, the supposedly hereditary or constitutional predispositions and the recent thwartings and shocks suffered by a patient. Psychoanalysis added another causal factor, the childhood development and experiences of the person. Psychoanalysis made an especially useful contribution in bringing attention to the very earliest years of childhood which, because they are forgotten by adults, were at one time deemed to be of no significance.

Psychoanalytic Therapy

The practice of psychotherapy has been influenced profoundly by the techniques which Freud developed. In its essentials, all psychotherapy uses the pattern of the person-to-person conversation between therapist and client. The therapist listens, tries to think and feel with the client, and never scolds or lectures. The client, on his part, forms a special kind of trustful relationship with the therapist and must talk freely about his troubles and feelings. So much is the almost universal contribution of psychoanalysis to psychotherapy. The more specialized methods of free association and dream analysis are also used by some therapists who do not subscribe to all of psychoanalytic theory, as well as by those who do.

One caution must be observed in appraising the contribution of psychoanalytic therapy. Freud and many other psychoanalysts often wrote that the ultimate proof of the entire psychoanalytic theory is that it "works," that it accomplishes the cure of neurotic patients. This alleged proof is highly suspect for, to the contrary, *that which "works" is not necessarily "true."* A simple illustration will make this dictum clear. Suppose that a child cries in the night. His mother may tell him to stop crying, and that if he does not a bogey-man will come out of the closet and get him. This treatment may "work" and the child ceases his cries. Obviously the effectiveness of the treatment does not prove that there was really a bogey-man in the closet. An orthodox psychoanalyst may interpret a patient's associations and dreams to show that his present anxieties are due to an "unconscious Oedipus complex" which originated in his early childhood. The patient may then give up his symptoms and be "cured," but the cure does not more soundly prove the existence of the Oedipus complex than the preceding anecdote proved the reality of the bogey-man.

Many methods of psychological treatment have been used through the ages, and each one has laid claim to some degree of success. Religious shrines are piled with the crutches of persons cured of lameness by their devotions. In the eighteenth century, Mesmer cured folk by having them touch iron rods which had been energized with "animal magnetism." In our own day, the several varieties of psychoanalysis seem to have helped people through using theories of castration complexes, inferiority complexes, the collective unconscious, the primal anxiety of birth, and faulty interpersonal relationships. The theoretical assumptions which underlie these practices are often in sharp conflict, and not all of them can be "true" at once. There is no present evidence to show that any one current method of psychotherapy is uniformly more successful than other methods.

Eventually, the science of psychology must broaden our understanding of all forms of psychotherapy. In carrying out this task, scientists will not be partisans of one school or another. The goal is to define the conditions and processes which lead to results judged as therapeutic, and to differentiate them from the conditions which do not. In the meantime, practical workers have to use one method or another. But scientific psychologists are unimpressed by anecdotes of successful cures. They demand a sounder foundation for a theory than the crude empiricism of "it works."

Psychoanalysis as Science

Psychoanalysis is an attempted science of personality, but it is relevant to ask how good a science it is. There are some criteria. A good science, among other attributes, presents testable hypotheses, uses clearly defined concepts, and obtains reliable or verifiable data. By such criteria, psychoanalysis is not a very good science.

Freud's language and that of other analytic writers tended to be vivid and literary, full of analogies and metaphors. Such language is pleasing and often convincing, but it lacks the precision demanded for scientific communication. Few if any statements are worded operationally so as to convey testable hypotheses. Let us take one example:

> The sole quality that rules in the id is that of being unconscious. Id and unconscious are as intimately united as ego and preconscious; indeed, the former connection is even more exclusive. If we look back at the developmental history of the individual and of his psychical apparatus, we shall be able to make an important distinction in the id. Originally, of course, everything was id; the ego was developed out of the id by the continual influence of the external world. . . . But during this development the young and feeble ego dropped and pushed back into the unconscious condition certain material which it had already taken in, and behaved similarly in regard to many new impressions which it *might* have taken in, so that these were rejected and were able to leave traces in the id only.*

These lines give Freud's last account of some of the most basic hypotheses of his theory, but how testable are they? By what procedures can one confirm that "the id's sole quality is being unconscious," or define the "young and feeble ego"? Just what operation is meant by "dropped and pushed back into the unconscious condition"? Although the theory seems lively, clear, and stimulating when first read, its terms are too loosely defined and its operations too vague to permit testing.

A scientific proposition must be stated so that any person of competent training can design an experiment to test its generality and its limitations. Take this illustration:

> Whenever an effector activity occurs in temporal contiguity with the afferent impulse, or the perseverative trace of such an impulse, resulting from the impact of a stimulus energy upon a receptor, and this conjunction is closely associated in time with the diminution in the receptor discharge characteristic of a need, there will result an increment to the tendency for that stimulus on subsequent occasions to evoke that reaction.†

The second quotation is Hull's precise statement of the "law of primary reinforcement" which is substantially the same as the

---

* S. Freud. *An outline of psychoanalysis.* New York: Norton, 1949. P. 43.
† C. L. Hull. *Principles of behavior.* New York: Appleton-Century-Crofts, 1943. P. 80.

Law of Effect, or learning by tension reduction (p. 130). A scientific hypothesis is less readable and less interesting, but it is testable because it uses concepts which have been defined precisely — Hull gives the definitions explicitly — and calls for operations which can be verified. A scientific statement is not an ultimate truth, but a hypothesis to be tested, with the aim of producing an increment of knowledge. A theory whose propositions are not testable cannot make such a contribution.

Psychoanalytic theory uses many personified concepts, a device appropriate to literature and art, but less useful to science. Examples are numerous. The "superego battles with the id," the repressed material is "pushed back into unconsciousness" but in dreams it "comes out in disguise." Psychoanalysts use these concepts as if they were real things and forces, rather than mere figures of speech. In doing so they appeal to popular thinking, because unscientific persons through the ages have attributed their behavior to such entities as "will," "soul," "sin," and "conscience," all of which have close analogues in Freud's terminology. All science needs concepts, but psychology has reason to prefer those definable in terms of experimental operations such as *reinforcement, inhibition,* and *adjustment.* It sees the whole man, responding in his social environment and being modified by his experiences, and not a fragmented organism whose "parts" are "in conflict" with one another.

The most serious difficulty with psychoanalysis as science is that its theories are based on a special kind of observation, which is unverifiable and therefore of doubtful reliability. Introspection, even under the best laboratory conditions, has hazards as a method of research. Even less reliable are the methods of free association and dream analysis which psychoanalysis uses. Later recollections of the emotions of earlier life are ambiguous and vague. They are easily given an interpretation which fits the preconceptions of the analyst. Furthermore, these data have generally been obtained from neurotic persons undergoing treatment who are known, from other evidence, to be unreliable and suggestible. To such a person, an analyst may give interpretations of the manifest content of his associations and dreams according to a preconceived theory. If the patient agrees, the theory is proved; if he disagrees he is merely showing his "resistance," which also proves the theory. Such a procedure is a queer method for science.

Leading psychoanalysts have not seen a need for diligent and continued research by more verifiable methods. Freud, writing in 1933, replied to an accusation that psychoanalysis is not an experimental science by citing *one* experiment involving the creation of dreams by hypnosis, which had been reported twenty-one years earlier, in 1912.[11] In short, psychoanalytic theories represent a rich fund of hypotheses about human nature, but the analysts did not subject these hypotheses to any tests acceptable to natural science.

Thoughtful consideration must be given to Freud's contention that psychoanalysis is a unique science, whose data can be obtained only by tapping unconscious processes through associations and dreams and are therefore inaccessible to the ordinary experiments of the laboratory. This defense is plausible. But Jung, Rank, Sullivan, and many others used Freud's very methods for tapping unconsciousness and emerged with quite different conclusions. If the method were unique and scientific, different users would obtain the same findings. In this framework, we can better understand Freud's anger with Adler, Jung, and others who differed from him. Because Freud believed his methods of observation were valid, any conclusions which contradicted his own must have seemed stupidly and perversely wrong.

Judged by the criteria of testable hypotheses, clearly defined concepts, and verifiable data, psychoanalysis must be seen as an inadequate science. How can such a conclusion be reconciled with the appraisal of Freud as a great genius? Perhaps Freud was a great artist, not the scientist he said he was. To an artist, validity is personal and is judged by the experience itself; it cannot be proved by experiments or mathematics. To other men falls the task of sorting Freud's great hunches into the verified and the unverifiable.

Rapprochements

Two trends are closing the gap between psychoanalysis and experimentally oriented psychology. One point of contact is the increasing number of experimental studies whose hypotheses have been derived from dynamic sources, often from psychoanalysis.[12] Many such studies have been cited in the preceding chapters. The concept of conflict, redefined in testable terms, has become invaluable (Chapter 4). Of all Freud's hypotheses, those concerning the mechanisms have been investigated most fruitfully, including regression (p. 103), projection (p. 180), fantasy (p. 205), and repression (p. 231). With respect to infant sexuality, Kinsey's facts have outdone Freud's theories but have not confirmed them. Very young children are indeed capable of sexual experience, as Freud affirmed when he shocked Victorian prudery with the notion. But genital behavior begins earlier than Freud supposed, not waiting until the "phallic stage" at the age of two or three. It reaches no peak in the "Oedipal" ages of four or five, and shows no decrease during later childhood as would be required by Freud's theory of a "latent stage." Much evidence from other sources refutes Freud's hypotheses about the stages of infantile and childhood development. Through such studies, experimental science is beginning to evaluate psychoanalytic hypotheses.

Another promising rapprochement is between psychology and the newer analytically oriented theories such as those of Horney and Sullivan. The concepts of the neo-analysts are more clearly defined in terms of first-hand observations. Some features of Freud's theories which evoked the greatest doubt from experimental psychologists a generation ago are the very things now discarded by the most modern psychoanalysts — the libido as either a psychic force or as a sexual urge, the predestined sequence of child development, and the overwhelming effects of single early experiences such as the Oedipus and castration complexes. The newer analytic theories have drawn heavily upon anthropology and social psychology, counteracting Freud's undue emphasis on innate personal characteristics and his neglect of social influences. As a result of all of these factors, the theories of Horney and Sullivan seem quite close to those of dynamic experimental psychology. In time, psychoanalysis and psychology are likely to grow still closer together until they fuse into one science.

SUGGESTED READINGS

Good secondary sources on psychoanalytic theory are Hall's brief and clear *Primer of Freudian Psychology,* and Healy, Bronner and Bowers's longer *Structure and Meaning of Psychoanalysis.* Shorter summaries are Chapter 2 in Pennington and Berg, *An Introduction to Clinical Psychology,* and Chapter 19 of Murphy, *Historical Introduction to Modern Psychology.* Two excellent summaries of psychoanalytic developments are available in Thompson, *Psychoanalysis: Evolution and Development,* and Munroe, *Schools of Psychoanalytic Thought.*

Many of Freud's writings are not too difficult for students. A suggested sequence is his *Outline of Psychoanalysis*, his *General Introduction to Psychoanalysis*, and then the *Basic Writings*, which is a convenient collection of six of his most influential earlier books.

For a comparison of psychoanalytic theories, see Mullahy, *Oedipus, Myth and Complex*. Single references to several of the important contributors of variants of psychoanalysis would include Adler, *Understanding Human Nature*; Jung, *Modern Man in Search of a Soul*; Rank, *Will Therapy and Truth and Reality*; Horney, *The Neurotic Personality of Our Time*; Fromm, *Escape from Freedom*; and Sullivan, *The Interpersonal Theory of Psychiatry*.

Sears, *Survey of Objective Studies of Psychoanalytic Concepts* reviews evidence from experiments. Blum, *Psychoanalytic Theories of Personality* combines a well presented summary of analytic theories with critical notes. Dollard and Miller, *Personality and Psychotherapy* is a fruitful blending of psychoanalysis with an experimentally based theory of learning.

PART FOUR

Techniques of Mental Hygiene

CHAPTER 15

Approaches to
Mental Hygiene

Mental hygiene is the prevention of nonintegrative adjustments and the restoration to normal living of persons who already suffer from them. Mental hygiene is therefore the practical art which is based on the experimental evidence and theories of the psychology of adjustment. The two aspects of mental hygiene, prevention and cure, overlap to a considerable degree. In general medical hygiene, it is well recognized that the cure of a minor or incipient illness may result in the prevention of a more severe disease. Similarly, the treatment of lesser disorders of behavior may prevent them from reaching serious proportions. Just as public hygiene is concerned with the health of people who are well as much as with the illnesses of those who are sick, so mental hygiene has implications for everyone. In its broadest sense, the aim of mental hygiene is to help all persons achieve fuller, happier, more harmonious, and more effective lives.

THE MENTAL HYGIENE MOVEMENT

Mental hygiene is a product of the twentieth century. It is one part of a broad, almost world-wide social movement toward an increased emphasis on the worth and dignity of individual human beings. Some correlates are seen in the movement in education which pays attention to the child as well as to the subject matter he learns, and the trend in industry which regards the worker as a person instead of merely as the maker of a product.

Although many persons and organizations have contributed to the development of mental hygiene, a conspicuous place is held by the National Association for Mental Health, formerly the National Committee for Mental Hygiene, and its allied state and local organizations. The pioneer mental hygiene society was founded in Connecticut in 1908, closely followed by the establishment of the national organization in 1909. Both of these societies owed their start largely to the efforts of Clifford W. Beers. When a young man, Beers had developed a psychosis which kept him a patient in mental hospitals for several years. Recovering, he wrote *A Mind That Found Itself*, a book which had wide influence, and decided to devote his life to the cause of mental health. The activities of the National Association were first concentrated on improving the condition of patients in mental hospitals. It made surveys of states and localities which disclosed the gap between the extent of mental disorders and the inadequate provisions made for their care. It has supported laws substituting a medical and psychological approach for the older legal one in the admission of patients to mental hospitals. Other early activities of the National Association centered on the improvement of schools for the care and training of the feebleminded, and the re-education of delinquents and prisoners. Because of these efforts, many people formed the misconception that mental hygiene is concerned only with the more extreme departures from normality.

The nineteen-twenties saw a new emphasis on preventative mental hygiene through the establishment of clinics for children. From 1922 to 1927, the National Association for Mental Health and the Commonwealth Fund sponsored and supported child guidance centers in several cities and one rural county. The demonstration of the value of child guidance services was highly successful. Most of the communities took over the support of the clinics when the demonstration period ended, and hundreds of similar centers have since been established. Other recent and continuing activities of the National Association have been the encouragement of research, the improvement of professional education, and the spreading of public information about mental hygiene problems, resources, and needs.[1]

Agencies of the United States government gave great impetus to the development of mental hygiene during the second half of the nineteen-forties. The Veterans Administration established mental hygiene clinics in most major cities, making mental hygiene services available for the first time to a large segment of the adult population, the veterans of the armed forces. To staff its clinics and hospitals, the Veterans Administration found it necessary to carry out graduate training programs in psychiatry and clinical psychology in cooperation with medical schools and universities.

An even broader influence on the progress of mental hygiene resulted from the founding in 1949 of the National Institute of Mental Health, a division of the Public Health Service in the U.S. Department of Health, Education and Welfare.[2] With funds appropriated by Congress, the N.I.M.H. has made grants for research and has supported graduate education programs in all the professions directly concerned with mental health. By distributing funds which are matched by states and localities, the Institute has encouraged and subsidized mental hygiene at its most basic level through community services and public health education.

Mental Hygiene in Public Health

Mental hygiene is everybody's responsibility.[3] Parents, teachers, employers, in fact everyone who has some control or influence over another person, may have either a favorable or an unfavorable effect on that person's adjustments. The practice of positive and constructive mental hygiene cannot, therefore, be limited to professionally trained persons. Improved sensitivity to mental hygiene problems, willingness to do something about them, and skill in making positive contributions can be gained by almost everyone if appropriate educational means are brought to bear. Helping parents, neighbors, teachers, and other people to view behavior problems constructively is a major aim of the mental hygiene movement. A subsequent chapter suggests some of the ways in which mental hygiene may be applied in the course of everyday living.

Public mental health has much in common with other public health enterprises. The public health attack upon tuberculosis, for example, has many facets. The provision of resources for treatment and diagnosis is essential. Research must develop ways to improve these processes, and also discover the conditions, such as those of nutrition, housing and employment, which help prevent tuberculosis. Such professional enterprises are expensive, and the nonprofessional public must have an active concern in order to bring contributions to voluntary organizations and spur legislatures to make appropriations. The requirements for mental hygiene are similar, for without an enlightened public professional activities would come to a standstill.

More than passive support is needed, however. People in general must want to participate in mental hygiene activities. A generation ago, tuberculosis was not only feared but was often regarded as a shameful "taint." Psychological difficulties suffer even more from adverse public attitudes. A community which is well educated with respect to mental hygiene will feel free to consult mental hygiene resources for minor troubles before they become serious, just as it feels free to make use of a mobile unit for chest x-rays. A further mental hygiene objective is for a community to become as intelligently concerned with the favorable psychological development of its children as it is with providing a pure water supply or demanding good standards for housing.

Professional Resources for Mental Hygiene

An important part of a mental hygiene program is studying and helping children and adults who already suffer from the anxieties and defenses which characterize inadequate adjustments. These tasks require special preparation and experience, and are the central concern of the four professions of psychiatry, clinical psychology, psychiatric social work, and psychiatric or mental health nursing.*

A *psychiatrist* is a physician who has specialized in the diagnosis and treatment of deviations of personality and behavior. After obtaining the M.D. degree and serving a general internship, a man or woman who wishes to be a fully qualified psychiatrist undertakes about five years of further training and supervised experience in

---

* In part because of its interdisciplinary history and character, the field of the study and alleviation of psychological adjustment problems suffers from unusual semantic difficulties. The very terms *mental hygiene* and *mental health* are somewhat misleading because they imply that a psychologically maladjusted person is "sick." He is not "sick" in any usual sense, but has difficulties in interpersonal relationships which have come about because of unfavorable learning processes. There is no distinctive term for a person who comes for help concerning his psychological problems. In hospitals and in medically administered community agencies, it is easy to adopt medical terms and call the recipient of help a "patient," his evaluation, a "diagnosis," and the process of helping him, "treatment" or "therapy." Yet these terms are manifestly inappropriate for use by the nonmedical professional people — psychologists in schools and colleges, and social workers in some agencies, for example

psychiatry. Because of the interaction of organic and psychological factors in many maladjustments, medical training is an excellent background for mental hygiene practice. A psychiatrist has two advantages over members of the nonmedical mental hygiene specialties: he can evaluate both the organic and psychological aspects of a person's behavior, and can use medical treatment — sedatives, for example — as an adjunct to psychological treatment when he feels that an advantage will be gained by doing so. Modern psychiatric training pays adequate attention to the recognition and treatment of minor deviations of personality, and often includes a residency in a mental hygiene clinic. Some older psychiatrists are well acquainted only with the serious, hospitalized disorders and may therefore see "nothing wrong" when confronted with a child or adolescent with an incipient maladjustment. Physicians in general practice, because the usual medical curriculum includes scant attention to psychology, are likely to have little or no qualification for dealing with mental hygiene problems.

The standard training of a *clinical psychologist* is a four-year graduate program leading to a Ph.D. degree and including a one-year internship in a clinic or hospital. The curriculum in clinical psychology emphasizes psychological theory, research, psychological appraisal or diagnosis, and psychological counseling or psychotherapy. Because of the nature of his training, the clinical psychologist is often best qualified in theory and research among the mental hygiene specialists, but he lacks the medical training of the psychiatrist. Not all psychologists are clinical psychologists, of course, just as not all physicians are psychiatrists. About one-third of all psychologists have their major interest and training in the clinical field; the remainder teach and carry on research in

---

— who carry out essentially similar processes in helping psychologically maladjusted people. Some compromises of terminology are necessary.

In this chapter and the following ones, the person who comes for help is called a *client* (a term from social work). A professionally trained worker is called a *clinician* with respect to the undifferentiated functions, such as interviewing, which are carried out by all the professions concerned. A *clinician*, then, may be a psychiatrist, psychologist, social worker, or nurse. When the roles of these professions are differentiated, their distinctive names are used. The process of helping a client by psychological means is alternatively called *psychotherapy* (a term from psychiatry) or *counseling* (a term from psychology). No difference of meaning is implied between the words *counseling* and *psychotherapy*. They represent the ameliorative activity carried out with clients by all clinicians.

universities and colleges, or are engaged in applications of psychology to education, personnel work, industry, and other fields.

A *psychiatric social worker* is a graduate of a school of social work, usually with a degree of Master of Social Work requiring two years of graduate study, who has specialized in mental health problems. Psychiatric social work emerged from the basic profession of social work which for many years has helped individuals and families to cope with their distresses. Most psychiatric social workers serve in clinics and hospitals, but some are engaged in preventative mental hygiene activities in other community agencies.

The *psychiatric nurse* in hospitals and clinics and the *mental health nurse consultant* in community public health services are the newest professions to receive recognition as mental hygiene specialists. Training requires from one to three years of advanced study after graduation from a school of nursing. In hospitals, the psychiatric nurse is often the person closest to the patient. The mental health nursing consultant may bring preventative mental hygiene attitudes to bear on situations which other specialists rarely reach, as in parent and baby clinics and visiting nurse services.

Other less specifically qualified professional persons make valuable contributions to mental hygiene. Their professions deal primarily with matters other than mental health, but involve opportunities to work constructively with people in distress. The entire field of social work is alert to the significance of psychological adjustments. An important aim of the mental hygiene movement is to increase constructive participation among pediatricians, other physicians, nurses, law officers, clergymen, school counselors, and teachers.[4]

The minimum organization needed for effective professional work in mental hygiene is a single well qualified person. Many psychiatrists and some clinical psychologists are in private practice and render services of value. Generally, however, the mental hygiene professions work in collaboration.[5] These professions have interacted, and have had considerable influence on one another's concepts and practices. There need be no controversy as to whether psychiatry, or psychology, or social work is best qualified. Each makes its distinctive contribution, and the combined skill of all surpasses the effect of any one alone.

MENTAL HYGIENE CLINICS

Mental hygiene clinics are organizations in which specialists from several professions devote their combined resources to helping people solve their adjustment problems. The first psychological clinic, founded in 1896 by Lightner Witmer at the University of Pennsylvania, was staffed entirely by psychologists and specialized in educational problems. A program of research and service in the prevention of delinquency led to the founding of the second clinic in 1909 by William Healy, a psychiatrist, at Chicago's Juvenile Psychopathic Institute, now known as the Institute for Juvenile Research. Healy's clinic was the first to use a "team" of psychiatrist, psychologist and social worker.[6] The growth of clinics proceeded slowly at first, in spite of the demonstrations supported by the Commonwealth Fund in the nineteen-twenties, and only 83 clinic units were in operation by 1931. The establishment of clinics was retarded as much by the dearth of trained specialists to staff them as by lack of public acceptance and support.

In more recent years, mental hygiene clinics have expanded remarkably. It is almost impossible to make an exact census of mental hygiene resources because of the difficulties involved in counting part-time clinics with fixed locations and traveling clinics which serve several communities. The best estimates made by the Public Health Service indicated that 850 communities were regularly served by clinics in 1947, and 1,280 in 1954. At least 150,000 children were clients of child guidance clinics in 1950. Even this rapid growth does not meet the country's needs for clinical services. There are about 0.8 clinics of all types per 100,000 population, in comparison with an estimated need of at least 2 clinics per 100,000 persons.[7]

A minimum full-time child guidance center or community clinic typically has a staff of one psychiatrist, one psychologist, two social workers, and three or four clerical and secretarial assistants. With this staff, about 300 new cases per year can be accepted, although the number varies with the intensity of the services offered. At 1956 salary and cost levels, such a clinic required a budget of about $60,000 per year, and could usually be supported by a city of 200,000 population. Smaller communities have been served successfully by part-time and traveling clinics.

The administrative organizations of mental hygiene clinics which are out-patient departments of hospitals or general health services are always under medical administration. A psychiatrist is usually the director of a community clinic because he is, in most instances, the most extensively trained and the most highly paid professional staff member. Many smaller clinics, which may have only part-time psychiatrists and other physicians on their staffs, are headed by a full-time psychologist or social worker. Clinics affiliated with colleges and universities are often under the administrative direction of a psychologist or an educator and generally have the part-time services of physicians. It is generally agreed that there is no essential relationship between professional function and administrative responsibility, if the administrator is competent and mature in his own specialty and if he is able to integrate the contributions of the workers in other professions.

Mental Hygiene Problems and Their Sources

Mental hygiene and child guidance clinics try to select cases for consultation and treatment which are likely to profit from the services offered. A typical clinic has twice as many applicants for service as it can accept. In general, the problems presented must be severe enough to warrant the attention of the often overworked specialists. Minor conduct and school problems are often given brief consultation with the way left open for return if the difficulties cannot be handled successfully by parents or teachers. At the other extreme, the problem must not be too unlikely to respond to treatment. Fully developed psychoses are usually referred to mental hospitals, and pronounced cases of mental deficiency to residential schools for the care and training of the feebleminded. When glandular or other organic conditions are prominent, referral is often made to appropriate medical agencies. Genuinely psychological problems are not evaded, however, even though they may arise from physical causes. A child crippled by poliomyelitis may require psychological as well as medical help, because of his anxiety and his disturbed social relationships. His parents may have even greater need for psychological assistance.

An inventory of the problems often encountered by child guidance clinics may be informative. The list is a composite drawn from several sources.[8]

1. Anxious parents of fundamentally normal children who are disturbed by their own feelings of inadequacy in coping with the child's developmental problems. Such parents are not lectured; their anxieties are regarded as needing psychological treatment. Often they also require information about normal child development.

2. Children who have developmental deviations of intellect or physique which interfere with their school or social adjustments. The children and their parents need help with their adjustments, and the children sometimes receive special educational and social assistance.

3. Children who present problems of socially unacceptable aggressive behavior such as disobedience, stubbornness, negativism, rebelliousness and temper. The distraught parents usually want to be told "how to make the child behave," and great skill is required to lead them to an understanding of themselves and of their relationships to the child.

4. Children who are unhappy, anxious, fearful, seclusive, sensitive, timid, and unpopular with other children. Here again, both the child and his parents need the best treatment resources of the clinic.

The sources which refer adults or children to mental hygiene clinics vary greatly from one clinic to another. Clinics operated by school systems naturally receive most of their cases from teachers and are concerned with educational problems. Some clinics have affiliations with courts and therefore receive a large number of problems of delinquency. One clinic may accept many persons who come voluntarily for help, another may refuse all such cases and receive referrals only through established social agencies. Because of the great diversity of practice, averaged statistics on the sources of clients have little value, but each clinic's account of its sources helps to reveal its relationships to the community.

Clinical Procedures

A purely logical analysis of the procedures used in mental hygiene clinics would divide them into two distinct parts: diagnosis and treatment. In actual practice, diagnosis and treatment are not so sharply separated. Even the first and simplest steps of diagnosis may have some remedial values. At the very moment a client enters a clinic he is likely to experience some relief, both from his own decision to come to grips with his problem, and from his feeling that competent professional people are willing to listen to him and respect him as a person worthy of help. Conversely, the "diagnosis" of a client continues throughout the entire process of "treatment." The very nature of psychological counseling makes the client reveal more and more of his attitudes and conflicts as work with him progresses. A deeper understanding of the client's problems is gained by the professional workers and, even more significantly, by the client himself. Because of these intimate interrelationships, the separation of diagnosis and treatment is more defensible as a teaching device than as a principle of procedure. The present chapter concentrates on the appraisal of the client as a person. The following chapter places its emphasis on the ways in which clients are helped to solve their problems.

In the functions of diagnosis, each of the clinical professions has a distinctive responsibility based on its specialized training. As a physician, the psychiatrist is responsible for identifying any organic or physiological factors which may affect the client's adjustments. He may refer clients to other medical specialists for appropriate segments of the diagnosis or treatment, as when a case of suspected thyroid deficiency is sent to a hospital for a basal metabolism test (p. 365). The psychiatrist, especially when he is a full-time staff member and the director of the clinic, usually exercises leadership in making decisions about the nature of the client's difficulties and the remedial steps which are most suitable. The psychiatrist's integrative function is most often carried out at a staff conference in which all of the professions participate.

A psychologist's diagnostic responsibilities in an organized clinic always include the administration and interpretation of such tests and projective techniques as may be judged necessary. The social worker's distinctive role is to evaluate, by interviews and often by visits, the impact of the family and community upon the client. Both psychologist and social worker also have opportunities to listen to the client and to observe him in face-to-face situations, and their conclusions transcend the strict lines of the psychological test and the case history.

An almost universal first step in clinical procedure is the intake interview, an initial contact with the client or with the parent of a child client, usually carried out by a social worker. The intake interview gives an opportunity to hear the client's complaints and his own conception of the problems needing solution. Other information is elicited which throws light on the severity of the problem and the scope of treatment needed. A preliminary decision is reached by the intake worker, alone or in conference with other staff members, as to whether the client should be accepted. When a clinic feels that it should not accept a case, an important function of the social work staff is to help the client to find other resources to meet his needs. A client may be put in touch with family service agencies, psychiatrists or other psychotherapists in private practice, medical specialists or medical clinics, hospitals, or schools.

Clinics vary considerably in the scope of the diagnostic study carried out after the intake interview. Some clinics proceed immediately to treatment, on the belief that the needed insights about the client's nature, conflicts, and background will inevitably emerge in the course of psychotherapeutic interviews. Other clinics do not proceed until an extensive and formal diagnostic study has been completed and the aims and means of treatment decided in a staff conference. A complete diagnostic study includes a case history, medical examinations, psychological examinations, diagnostic interviews, and sometimes other procedures as well. Modern trends favor the flexible use of some explicitly diagnostic processes, but do not support a routinely exhaustive type of case study which sometimes becomes an end in itself.

The diagnostic information gathered about the client of a clinic may be divided conveniently, although somewhat arbitrarily, into two broad classes: the information which is or could be obtained from sources other than the client, and the data which may be obtained only by talking with the person himself or by observing him. The "outside" data are gathered by the techniques of the indirect examination or case history. The "inside" information is acquired by the direct examination, including the interview and its variants, the medical examinations, and the psychological examinations. The two techniques are by no means entirely separate. What a client tells about his past experiences is partly "fact," and partly an expression of his attitudes. An interview with a parent of a child client may provide an indirect examination of the child's background, and also a direct examination of the mother's characteristics. Both kinds of information have substantial value.

INDIRECT STUDY—THE
CASE HISTORY

The Case Study Method

The case history of a person is a description of his development, and of the influences in his environment which have shaped his personality and precipitated his present problems. The method of case study is for the most part a contribution from the field of social work. Toward the end of the last century, social workers began to make systematic investigations of applicants for relief or "charity." At first, these studies were made to determine if the client was "worthy," and if other means for assistance were not available. From this beginning, the case study gradually developed into a method for understanding a person or a family group. Emphasis shifted from external relief to the restoration of self-sufficiency. When psychiatry, psychology, and social work came together in the mental hygiene clinic, social workers naturally fell heir to the task of gathering most of the case histories.

The case study method found ready acceptance among psychiatrists and psychologists, for it offered a practical way to apply the genetic point of view. Psychiatrists and psychologists had recognized the inadequacy of a diagnosis based only on an examination of a person's present characteristics without an inquiry into his development. Personality and behavior are the result of an individual's past experiences and adjustments, on which the case history may throw much light.

Case history data come from a person's reports of his own past, from reports which other people give about him, and from direct observations of home and community influences. The chief sources of information are interviews, not only with the client, but also with parents, other members of the family, employers, teachers, and associates. Records obtained from schools, social agencies, and courts are used when they are relevant and available. Some years ago, the social workers of mental hygiene clinics made many home visits to provide first-hand observations of the family and the neighborhood. More recently, psychiatric social workers have tended to hold office interviews with clients and with significant persons in the clients' lives. The changed procedure is defended on several grounds. It stems in part from an increased emphasis on the attitudes of people in contrast with objective "facts" of observation. Office interviews are also more economical than home visits, and free the social worker's time for increased participation in treatment. Still, some clinical workers feel that a loss is sustained by a failure to obtain the flavor of the home and community by direct observations.

A case study is not a simple compilation of reports and observations. A certain amount of interpretation adds to the significance of the history. For example, the "complaint problem" is an important part of a case history because it defines the behavior symptoms as seen by the client himself or by the referring parent or teacher. Such statements are made by persons with little or no psychological training. They rarely identify the problem which needs treatment and are even less reliably informative about its causes. Thus, in the case of James G. (p. 160), the referral problems were ungovernable behavior in school, bullying, and stealing. Only a more penetrating study revealed that James's underlying difficulties were defensive reactions against a conflict arising from his fear of competing physically with other boys and from his overprotection at home. Discrepancies between various observations and reports often disclose valuable hypotheses concerning a client. A mother may place emphasis on her child's weak and sickly constitution, while other evidence shows that he has average health and strength for his age. The relevant interpretation is not that the child is puny, but that his upbringing has been influenced by his mother's misperception of him as a weakling. Merely to conclude that the mother is "wrong" has little value. To report her attitude as an important factor in the child's development, and an aspect of the mother's personality, is relevant to a psychological understanding.

An Outline for Case Study

A synopsis of the main areas usually covered by a case study is of value in helping to understand the clinical approach. The outline which follows is intended only to suggest the scope of a case history for the benefit of students without extensive backgrounds in any of the mental health disciplines. Professional workers need much more. For the sake of completeness, some data not usually gathered with the social history are indicated, such as the results of the medical and psychological examinations.

A case history outline is not used inflexibly but is adapted to the needs and circumstances of individual clients. The study of a real person cannot be circumscribed by any set scheme. Some instances may require much more detailed information, others less. A modern trend is to prepare a shorter case history, a procedure which is time saving but liable to neglect observations which may become significant as study and treatment progress.

Most of the outline which follows has reference to a child as the client. It requires adaptation for use with adults, but the childhood experiences and earlier parent-child relationships of grown persons are often the most significant features of their histories.

Case Study Outline

A. *Identifying Data*
   Name. Address. Date of report. Date of birth (verify from records). Age. Place of birth. Sex. Race. National origin. Marital status. Occupation. By whom referred.

B. *Statement of the Problem*
   1. *The complaint problem.* Why does the person come for help? How does he conceive his problem? Or, how do parents, teachers, etc., see the problem? Do significant persons see the problem differently? Give in the exact words of the persons quoted.
   2. *Worker's restatement of the problem.* Exactly what distress does the person show which calls for help? What behavior needs modification? To what situations does he so respond? Cite specific examples.
   3. *History of the problem.* When was this behavior first noted? What is its duration? Are there recurring patterns of responses to recurring circumstances?

C. *The Family*
   (Little emphasis is placed on heredity, and much on developmental influences.)
   1. *Persons in the home.* For each of the following persons, give: age; education; health; outstanding characteristics of personality; social behavior; adjustments to one another; and other relevant observations.
      a. Father.
      b. Mother.
      c. Step-parents or foster parents when relevant.

    d. Siblings — ages; position of client in family; comparative health, strength and achievement; any observations of favoritism.

    e. Grandparents — direct effects on the client through home contacts; indirect effects through the formation of the parents' characteristics.

    f. Other relatives, if of direct or indirect influence.

    g. Boarders, servants, other unrelated persons in the home.

    h. Parents' associates, close friends, visitors, in so far as relevant.

  2. *Home attitudes.* What are the attitudes of the persons in the home toward children in general and the client in particular: accepting, indulgent, negligent, restrictive, or hostile; flexible or rigid? What are their attitudes toward the client's problems?

D. *The Culture*

  1. *Culture group.* What is the family's culture group, as defined in terms of socioeconomic status, education, occupation, neighborhood, and residence? What standards and problems of the group are relevant to the client's conflicts and adjustments?

  2. *Cultural deviation and conflict.* Does the family identify with its culture group, or does it have different values or aspirations? Is it upwardly or downwardly mobile? Is the family bilingual? Is there conflict within the group or family between one cultural standard and another, as between old-world customs and newer ones?

E. *Medical Examination and History*

  1. *Medical examination.* When and where made? General description of physique. How do client's development, size, and strength compare with norms? Vision and hearing. Neurological findings. Endocrine findings. Present diseases. Other pertinent assets or disabilities.

  2. *Physical development.* What has been the general course of development? Anomalies of growth. Disease history. Injuries.

  3. *Conditions especially related to adjustment.* Disorders of the nervous system: chorea, encephalitis, etc. Any convulsions, seizures, or "spells." Differential diagnosis of complaints or conditions which might be organic, psychosomatic, or hysterical. Sleepwalking. Nervousness. "Nervous breakdowns."

  4. *Sex development.* Age of puberty. Any other pertinent observations.

F. *Developmental History*
1. *Prenatal period and birth.* Mother's health during pregnancy. Normal, premature, or difficult birth. Birth injuries. Family's attitude toward expected child, toward client in infancy.
2. *Early developmental signs.* Age at which weaned; of teething; holding head erect, sitting, standing, and walking. Age of talking, of learning to read. Control of bladder and bowel. Self-help in eating, dressing, etc. Right or left handed?
3. *Intellectual development.* Results of tests administered at present time. Records of earlier tests. Behavioral signs of intellectual superiority or retardation. Special talents or disabilities.
4. *Speech development.* Speech defects. Their effect on client's social adjustments, on his family's attitudes.
5. *Emotional development.*
   a. Independent-dependent behavior. Initiative and responsibility. Overdependence. To what extent? Upon whom? In what circumstances?
   b. Confident-anxious behavior. Self-confidence and happiness. General fearfulness, shyness. Anxieties, night terrors. Specific fears; experiences which may have led to fears.
   c. Cooperative-hostile behavior. Trust in parents and others, compliance. Tantrums, noncompliance, aggressiveness, cruelty, etc. Toward whom? How often? How strongly?
   d. Emotional balance. Well balanced. Overemotional or apathetic. Elation or depression. Fluctuations of mood.
6. *Social development.* Nature of relationships with persons. Extent of social experiences. Successes or failures in adjustments to groups.

G. *Educational History*
1. *School progress.* Age entered school. Acceleration or retardation. Special classes. Trend of school marks. For adults: grades completed; success in school.
2. *Educational achievement.* Results of educational achievement tests. Comparison with client's marks and reputation. Special abilities or disabilities.
3. *School adjustment.* Attitude toward school. Satisfaction, indifference, reluctance, or hostility. Regarded as conduct or discipline problem? Truancy?

   4. *Educational aspirations and plans.* Plans for education. Are plans consistent with abilities and opportunities?

H. *Economic History*
   1. *Occupation.* Exact description of work. Earnings. Satisfactions. Success or failure in work. Attitude toward occupation.
   2. *Occupational history.* Positions. Dates. Salaries. Success or failure. Reasons for leaving jobs.
   3. *Vocational plans and ambitions.* Aspirations. Plans. Are abilities and opportunities consistent with ambitions, with plans?

I. *Legal History*
   Delinquencies; court records, if any. Exact nature of delinquent behavior. What actions were taken? Effect of experiences on client's attitudes.

J. *The Client's Life*
   1. *Life routines.* Sequences of work, recreation, eating, sleeping. A typical time schedule is sometimes revealing.
   2. *Interests, hobbies, recreations.* What does the client choose to do for pleasure? Are recreations typically social or solitary? Special interests and skills in hobbies. Sports, as participant or spectator. Reading. Interests and preferences in motion pictures, radio, and television.
   3. *Fantasy life.* Wishes, daydreams, and remote or unreal ambitions.
   4. *Sex.* Attitude toward sex functions. Sex interests, knowledge, experience, and outlets.
   5. *Social adjustments.* Has client many or few friends? Typical social contacts and activities. Group affiliations. How does he regard associates? How do they regard him? Leader or follower?

DIRECT STUDY — INTERVIEWS AND EXAMINATIONS

The focus of clinical study is the personality of the individual client. Therefore, data obtained from direct sources, by communicating with the client and by observing him, are of greater value than indirect types of evidence. Apparently catastrophic external events may cause little permanent harm to a child's personal adjustments, but unspectacular, unexpressed conflicts can be much more serious. Because case studies show that children may readjust successfully even after gross neglect, brutality, and sexual assaults, too much emphasis must not be placed on circumstances to the neglect of subtle individual factors.[9]

The interview is the most valuable method for studying a person directly. It is usually the first procedure used when a client enters a clinic, and it merges into the process of psychological treatment. Interviews provide the basis for integrating all of the other findings of the case study. Therefore, a further discussion of interviewing is postponed until after the more formal medical and psychological examinations have been described briefly.

Medical Examination

A general medical examination is an irreplaceable part of the study of a client in a mental hygiene clinic. Approximately half the clients of some clinics suffer from relevant organic conditions, or show symptoms which call for careful medical screening to rule out the possibility of organic involvement.[10] Reports of general medical examinations given by family or school physicians may be used in some instances, but it is better to have the medical examiner relate his task directly to the psychological problems. For this reason, the medical examination is often made by the psychiatrist of a clinic.

A medical examination in a mental hygiene clinic makes the usual observations and tests of the skeletal, muscular, digestive, respiratory, circulatory, excretory, reproductive, and nervous systems. Although the examination is a routine, it should never become perfunctory. Special attention is paid to the possible direct organic causes of maladjustment including diseases and injuries of the nervous system, the effects of drugs, and the functioning of the endocrine glands. Malnutrition, fatigue, glandular disorders, and many diseases may keep a person at a low energy level and hence predispose him to inferior adjustments. Painful or dangerous conditions which arouse anxiety are common sources of persistent nonadjustive behavior. The secondary psychological effects of lack of strength and of injuries have already been noted in several case studies. The medical examination, in combination with other evidence from the study of the person, also distinguishes between symptoms which arise from organic causes and those due to hysterical mechanisms or the visceral effects of emotion. The observations of the client's behavior are often valuable. Is the client unduly reluctant to undress for the medical examination? Is he anxious or confident about his health and strength? The attitudes of the client toward himself and toward the examination may provide valuable insights into his adjustments and personality.

Psychological Examination

All of the diagnostic study carried out in a mental hygiene clinic is a psychological examination, for it is designed to evaluate the functioning of the client as a person. In a more limited meaning, the psychological examination refers to the tests administered by the clinical psychologist. Some clinics use a minimum series of tests routinely, with supplementary tests selected according to the nature of the client's problem. More often, the entire testing program is chosen flexibly. An adult client may be given no tests at all if he has a well-defined problem of personal adjustment which does not involve his intellectual status. In the case of a child whose lack of school progress is a conspicuous complaint, the testing program may be quite elaborate.

A child client is usually tested with an intelligence test suited to his level, such as the Stanford-Binet or the Wechsler Intelligence Scale for Children (p. 344). If a mental ability test is needed for an adult, the Wechsler Adult Intelligence Scale is most often used (p. 345). Performance tests are of value to secure an intelligence rating which is less influenced by cultural opportunities, and to provide an opportunity for watching the client attempt to solve problems. Intelligence is an important part of personality, but too much cannot be expected from test scores alone. They tell something of the resources the client has available for dealing with intellectual tasks, but throw little light on his motivations, attitudes, and conflicts which are of primary concern in adjustment.

Projective techniques (pp. 334-342) are widely used for intensive studies of individual clients. The Rorschach rivals the intelligence test as the most frequently used clinical instrument. Picture-story and sentence-completion tests are fertile sources of hypotheses about the client's strivings and frustrations. Because these methods are subtle, they often suggest the presence of conflicts which the client is unable or unwilling to reveal in the early interviews. Brief screening questionnaires (p. 323) are inappropriate for clinical use; the client has already screened himself by coming for help. Longer diagnostic questionnaires, such as the MMPI (p. 326), have been found valuable in clinics serving adult clients.

The clinical psychologist selects additional tests which are suitable for the particular problems of the client. When school disabilities are prominent, diagnostic tests of reading and other educational skills may be used to help determine whether the child is generally lacking in aptitude, whether he has been unable to profit from the usual methods of group teaching and requires special remedial instruction, or whether his failures are closely related to adjustive conflicts. To cite only one other example, apparently simple tests of copying geometrical figures are valuable aids in the diagnosis of organic brain damage. Hundreds of special tests exist, which are drawn upon flexibly to meet special problems.

Test scores may be used to answer two kinds of questions. First, one may ask how the client compares with other individuals. The answer to this first question is *normative;* it compares a person to norms or averages obtained from groups. A child's Mental Age or Social Age is a familiar way to relate his standing to that of other children. A college student's score may be expressed as his percentile rank in his class — the percentage of persons he excels.

A second question, and often an important one, asks how a person's score on one test compares with his own scores on some other tests. This inquiry seeks *intra-individual* information, how the person varies from one trait to another. For example, if a client scores several years lower on the Porteus Maze Test (p. 351) than on the Stanford-Binet it may be hypothesized that he suffers from impulsiveness or lack of foresight. Both normative and intra-individual comparisons are aided by a systematic tabulation of test scores expressed in comparable units. A *profile* or *psychograph* (Fig. 38) is one way to present the scores so that comparisons can be made readily.

In addition to giving quantitative measurements of some of the client's characteristics, the psychological examination provides a good opportunity to observe him at work and to note many unmeasured features of his behavior. Indeed, the informal observations are often more valuable than the scores. One important issue to judge is whether the person has been tested validly. If a shy

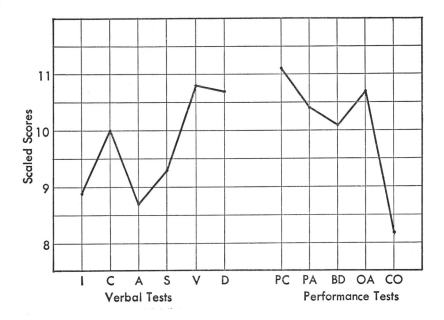

Figure 38. A Profile or Psychograph

The average scores on the subtests of the Wechsler Intelligence Scale for Children of 25 retarded readers of normal intelligence (I.Q. 99). The subtests are information (I), comprehension (C), arithmetic (A), similarities (S), vocabulary (V), digit span (D), picture completion (PC), picture arrangement (PA), block design (BD), object assembly (OA), and coding (CO). The profile, with high PC, PA, and OA, and low I, A, and CO is typical of many retarded readers. The high V is unusual; other studies usually find low vocabulary scores for retarded readers. For another profile chart, see Figure 26, p. 327. (Grace T. Altus, A WISC profile for retarded readers. *J. consult. Psychol.*, 1956, *20*, 155-156.)

child talks little during an intelligence test, it is more than "unfair," it is unprofessional and misleading to give zero scores to his silences and thus assign him a low I.Q. A more constructive procedure is to regard him as untested by the verbal test, and to estimate his ability as closely as possible from his nonverbal performances and from other behavioral evidence.

Skillful observation will often show why a client fails a part of a test, which is more significant than the bare fact of his failing. Habits of work and reactions to frustration may be estimated by seeing how he meets difficulties in the tests. Some tests are used, in fact, which give only qualitative results. The mirror-drawing test, in which the client is required to trace a design that he can see only reversed in a mirror, has no quantitative interpretation. It is valuable for showing whether the client will persevere, give up, appeal for assistance, or show anger in this unfamiliar and frustrating task. The psychologist's report usually describes the client's test behavior in general, and evaluates his speed, accuracy, activity, attention, effort, desire to please, shyness, defensiveness, and other behaviors. Psychological tests are not considered in isolation, but in relation to the whole personality of the client.

The Interview

The interview is the most significant procedure used in a mental hygiene case study. Only from the person himself can a clinician obtain a full and clear picture of the motivations, dependences, hostilities, anxieties, conflicts, and mechanisms which underlie the adjustment problem. Interviews are both diagnostic and therapeutic, in that they serve to determine the nature of the client's difficulties and also to help him correct them. Because every interview is useful for both evaluating and helping, the two aspects of interviewing are inseparable in practice. In fact, the early interviews in a clinic may be regarded as exploratory rather than as strictly diagnostic. If a decision has to be made not to accept a client, the interviews will have served mainly the diagnostic purpose. If the client is accepted for help, the exploratory interviews merge imperceptibly into the psychotherapeutic process.

The diagnostic aim of an interview is to lead the client to express his feelings and attitudes about his problems, and only incidentally to give factual information about his life. The client's ability to communicate is hindered by a number of factors which are called *resistances.* The simplest type of resistance consists of diffidence toward the interviewer and lack of confidence in him which must be overcome at the beginning of the interviews. Another relatively simple resistance is caused by feelings of shame and disapproval with which the client regards his own behavior. A more serious resistance exists when repression has affected the client's ability to express his relevant feelings and to recall events important in the evolution of his maladjustment. Lack of insight is a still more difficult resistance to overcome. In most instances the client is not fully aware of the processes which have shaped his adjustments, because he has learned by blind trial-and-error, or unconscious, learning (p. 140) and cannot identify the drives and the reinforcements which operated. Resistances arising from repression or from blind trial-and-error learning may also be described as due to a lack of integration. The client cannot see his problem as a whole or discriminate significant aspects of it.

The first task of the interviewer is to establish a relationship with the client which makes him feel more free to communicate and thereby lessens his resistances. The ideal clinical relationship, often called *rapport*, is not easily described. From the point of view of the client, rapport is characterized by a warm and positive feeling toward the clinician and a sense of great trust and confidence. These characteristics make the client want to share his feelings and experiences. To secure the rapport of the client, the clinician needs more than techniques. He has to have certain attitudes toward the client, and make these attitudes clear by his own behavior. First, the clinician is attentive and interested. He shows by his facial expression, his posture, and his responses to the client's statements that he regards the client as a worthy human being who deserves his attention. Second, the clinician shows his understanding. He displays by word and gesture that he comprehends what the client is trying to say, or that he is trying his best to do so. A third and very important characteristic of the interviewer is that he does not evaluate. He shows his awareness of the client's feelings and experiences but does not express approval or disapproval. He is never shocked or disgusted or, on the other hand, elated or congratulatory. Fourth, the clinician uses the interview as a strictly one-way communication. In this respect it differs strikingly from a social communication in which there is a reciprocal give and take between the participants. The clinician does not talk about his own affairs or interests; the interview belongs to the client.

The personal characteristics of the interviewer are important in the process of establishing rapport and in the counseling procedures which may follow. The interviewer must be a secure and well-adjusted person himself so that he does not inject his own emotional attitudes into the client's affairs. For example, an interviewer with unresolved feelings of hostility toward his own parents can hardly be warmly but impartially understanding either of a parent or of a child as a client. He is likely to displace his own hostility to the parent, and to identify his own feelings with those of the child, to the detriment of his ability to understand either of them. The qualities which make an effective clinical interviewer are so fundamental that persons have to be selected for this task as well as trained for it.

The opinions of most experienced clinicians, and also a number of experimental findings, favor letting the client tell his own story first, in place of asking him questions. A free, unguided narrative expresses more ideas and is less likely to contain misleading statements than are answers to direct questions. Although he does not question, the clinician does not remain silent while the client tells his story. The interviewer's remarks show that he is listening and that he has gained, or is trying to achieve, a warm nonevaluative understanding. The free narrative adds to rapport for, having told his story, the client feels that the interviewer is an "insider" and has less resistance to subsequent interviews. The interviewer's responses help the client to perceive him as an understanding and unthreatening person, who can be trusted to listen to the most anxiety-arousing thoughts.

The interviewer must master the difficult art of listening. He hears not only the obvious content of the story, but also the client's sensitivities, confusions, and evasions. Any part of the narrative to which the client responds emotionally, or any part in which he finds it difficult to proceed, is likely to be important. The understanding of the client's feelings is of greater value for mental hygiene study than the tabulation of the objective facts of his past experiences.

Questioning is not entirely inappropriate after rapport has been established. The areas of questioning arise from issues suggested by the case history and from the free narrative. Broad, "open-ended" questions are more suitable than detailed or pressing interrogations. Examples are, "Would you care to tell something about your family?" or "Can you tell me more; I'm not sure that I grasp just what you mean?" Professional opinion differs as to the extent of the questioning which should be used in the diagnostic phases of the interviews. Some clinicians explore fully the common precipitating causes of maladjustment such as conflicts involving dependence, hostility, or guilt, and the major predisposing factors including childhood emotional experiences and attitudes toward parents. Other workers prefer to avoid questioning altogether and to tolerate their own ignorance about the client until he feels able to communicate comfortably. All competent clinicians agree that a successful study of a person cannot be done in a hurry. The best clinical practice allows a client to take his own time. Dependence is placed on the development of a relationship which will eventually permit the client to make a full disclosure, rather than on persistent or harassing questioning.

A few pitfalls in diagnostic interviewing, into which the inexperienced and the unskillful sometimes plunge, may be pointed out. The purpose of the diagnostic study is to lay a foundation for helping the client; it is not an end in itself. Therefore any diagnostic step which would impede subsequent psychotherapy must be avoided. It is sometimes all too easy to beguile a client into telling more about his deepest feelings than he is ready to tell. If he feels that the interviewer has tricked him, he may never return to the clinic, or, if he does come back, he is on his guard and not really trustful. In many instances, a skillful clinician deliberately refrains from probing tender spots in the client's adjustments in order to avoid arousing intense anxiety which the client is not prepared to endure. Another pitfall is the temptation to explain the clinician's diagnostic formulations to the client. A well-prepared and secure interviewer does not have to impress the client by showing how erudite he is. His diagnostic role is to listen, think, and help, and he keeps his diagnostic hypotheses to himself.

Diagnostic Studies with Children

Unlike adults, small children can seldom verbalize their adjustive conflicts. The difficulty of communicating directly with young children led psychological workers in earlier years to depend on the external case history for diagnosis and on the manipulation of the environment for treatment. More recently, methods have been developed to help even quite young children express their attitudes toward themselves and toward the adult world, and thereby provide relevant direct observations of their problems of adjustment. These methods are used to carry on psychotherapy with children, but also have values for diagnosis.

One effective method for use with children who are able to talk with some fluency is the *fantasy* approach. After getting some degree of rapport with the child, the worker asks him to make up a story. Sometimes the child will choose his own theme; otherwise he may be given a start from a picture, an uncompleted story, or a situation arising from his play. Children's fantasies, like the daydreams of adults, reveal their motivations, attitudes, conflicts, and trends of personality. The child himself is likely to be the thinly disguised central figure of his imaginative story, and the characters and influences of his immediate environment are also pictured in it. The child's typical responses to his parents, playmates, and school life, and his degree of security, his attachments, and his hostilities may be revealed. With older children, the fantasy may open the possibility of a more direct discussion of problems.

Another approach widely used with children makes use of *play techniques*. The child and the worker are alone in a play room which is provided with resources which help the child express his feelings in play. Sometimes the room has a great variety of toys: a sand box, a sink with water, a work bench, pounding toys, wheel toys, dolls, miniature figures, utensils, toy weapons, and materials for drawing and painting. In other clinics there may be a more limited set of materials, especially when they are used chiefly for diagnostic studies. A miniature house or apartment with rooms, furniture, and small dolls representing all members of a family is perhaps most useful. As with other diagnostic methods, permissiveness and freedom of expression are essential in the play room. The clinician does not prescribe what the child shall do, but participates mainly by making comments which recognize and accept the child's choices of activities and the feelings which he expresses while engaging in them. Diagnostic play techniques merge into play therapy, which is described in the next chapter, just as interviews merge into psychotherapy.

Many diagnostic suggestions may be drawn from watching a child in free play. The play may even contribute to an evaluation of intellectual abilities, as when a child who is too shy to respond to an intelligence test shows by his problem solving that he is not mentally deficient. More often, the observations are used to throw light on the child's personal adjustments. For example, if a child who is playing with a doll family ignores the father doll, gives an authoritarian role to the mother figure, and repeatedly drowns the baby in the bathtub, some hypotheses may be formulated as to how he perceives relationships within his family. The communications of very young children tend to be symbolized only in the activities of play, both in diagnostic studies and in therapy. Some older children will move from play expressions to verbal expressions of their attitudes.

PSYCHOLOGICAL DIAGNOSIS

The sequence of procedures used in the solution of a mental hygiene problem may be compared to the steps of the scientific method. Each person represents an experiment, and therefore requires the collection of data, the formulation of hypotheses, the testing of the hypotheses by further observations, and the drawing of conclusions. The data about each client are gathered from the case history, the examinations, and the interviews. The next step integrates all of the evidence into hypotheses which attempt a comprehensive view of the nature and antecedents of the client's difficulties.

Understanding Adjustments

The general theories of the psychology of adjustment offer many hypotheses about the nature of behavior disorders which may be applied to individual cases. Maladjustments arise as nonintegrative responses to frustrations and conflicts. Subsidiary to this broad generalization are a fund of other hypotheses concerning human motivation, the origins of conflicts, the nature of learning processes, the characteristics of personality, and the typical mechanisms by which people try to resolve their difficulties.

To understand a specific person, however, more detailed and explicit hypotheses are necessary. One has to know the nature of *his* motives, conflicts, and satisfactions, which is a more complex task than to view the operation of these factors in mankind at large. When dealing with a single person, the concept of "cause" must be used with great discretion. A behavior problem is rarely the result of a single experience or conflict. Maladjustments arise from *mul-*

tiple causation, a pyramiding of destructive influences in the formation of the individual's personality and in the environments which have shaped his conflicts. It is impossible to identify all of the factors which have made the person what he is. Clinicians do not attempt this unreasonable task, but try to hypothesize the influences which seem most crucial in the development of the person and which are most relevant to his treatment. The selection is made by evaluating and interpreting the data obtained from the study of the person.

One profitable way to analyze a person's adjustments is to examine the nature of his motivations, conflicts, and satisfactions. One approach to the study of a person's *motivation* is through general psychological study which discovers the common social motives of the individual's culture. A useful method in many cases is to make an inventory of his motivations for approval, recognition, affection, sex, conformity, prestige, mastery, and self-realization. Because the motivations designated by these categories are so common and so strong in our culture, and because they so often come into conflict, they underlie a large proportion of problems of adjustment.

Social motivations are learned forms of behavior, however, and as such vary greatly among individuals. One person may have a much stronger urge for dependence and affection, another for self-assertion and prestige, because of their particular backgrounds of formative experiences. Motivations also differ in various periods of life; those of the infant, the child, the adolescent, and the adult have characteristics peculiar to the circumstances and learning processes of each period. Many nonintegrative adjustments may be traced to the continuation of a kind or degree of motivation into a time of life for which it is no longer appropriate. An overprotected child whose training has prevented him from acquiring independent problem-solving skills will carry an infantile need for attention and dependence into later childhood. when it will come into conflict with other needs and with the expectations of people around him. The drive of anxiety may be very strong in one person and weak in another. These considerations emphasize the importance of a careful study of the motivations of the individual client. His adjustive difficulties may not be due to the impossibility of securing the reduction of mature and usual motivations in his present situation, but to his unattainable demands for certain special kinds of satisfactions.

The study of a person's *conflicts* is closely related to an analysis of his motivations. Here again, general principles of psychology are useful sources of hypotheses, when applied in terms of the experiences and attitudes of the specific client. Conflicts often arise among motives of exaggerated strength, and between such motives and the realistic demands of the world. Especially frequent are conflicts between the common socially-derived motivations for achievement or recognition, and a person's anxious avoidance of social contacts and constructive efforts due to his strongly learned anxiety about his own ability and worth. Also common is a conflict between needs for approval or affection and a client's hostile attitudes against significant persons in his life.

The analysis of a person's *satisfactions* emphasizes the purposive nature of adjustive behavior. The symptomatic behavior of a maladjustment is a means toward an end, which is the reduction of drive tensions. In a nontechnical phrase, a person "gets something out of" his symptoms; they serve as substitute or compromise satisfactions for his particular pattern of motivation. One of the most important concepts in the psychology of adjustment, and one of the most difficult to grasp, is that apparently painful and unrewarding acts are performed because they satisfy motives. Nonintegrative mechanisms such as aggression, withdrawing, hysterical symptoms, and the like are punishing in the long run and fail to fulfill constructive life purposes, but they are maintained only because they give immediate gratifications which the unfortunate child or adult cannot achieve otherwise. Therefore, it is important to understand the value that the client's behavior has for him. He will not give it up easily. Psychological treatment must enable him to achieve greater satisfactions at a better integrated and more mature level, or it cannot be successful.

The Nature of Diagnosis

A summary statement of the antecedents, nature, and course of a client's difficulties is often called a *diagnosis*. In organized clinics, the diagnosis is usually made at a staff conference. Psychiatrist, psychologist, social worker, and other specialists pool their observations and suggestions, which they are better able to evaluate in the light of the information presented by the others. From the integration of all of the data gathered from varied points of view, a tentative conception of the problem as a whole can be obtained. Immediate decisions are whether to accept the client for help or refer him to more suitable resources and, if he is to be accepted, how the treatment is to proceed and who should carry it out.

A psychological diagnosis differs considerably from the familiar type of medical diagnosis which can be stated in a word or two. Still, the objectives of the two kinds of diagnoses are similar.[11] A diagnosis of "measles" identifies the problem, tells its cause, predicts its course, and indicates the treatment. A psychological diagnosis uses more words and, unfortunately, provides less information. The difficulty arises from the different nature and greater complexity of psychological problems. They are not caused by damages or malfunctioning of limited tissues of the body nor by invading microorganisms. Life experiences and learning processes are harder to identify comprehensively.

When a client with a psychological problem also has a medical diagnosis, it may be one of the most relevant facts about him. Injuries and diseases of the central nervous system, disturbances of metabolism, and glandular dysfunctions may call for specific treatments and permit the prediction of the outcome. Even these diagnoses do not tell everything about the affected person, however. A child with an underactive thyroid suffers not only from a chemical and physiological malady; he also has endured conflicts and developed adjustive mechanisms in response to his behavioral incapacities.

Psychological diagnostic labels have limited usefulness. The terms applied to the varieties of adjustive behavior are freely used as concepts, but do not constitute diagnoses in themselves. The value of such designations as "compensation," "negativism," "compulsion," or "hysteria" is that they may serve in place of long descriptions of these forms of behavior. As each may develop from a variety of causes, the terms tell only a small part of the story. They are aids to description, not diagnoses. The psychiatric diagnostic concepts such as "psychoneurosis" or "schizophrenia" have only a little more utility. The latter diagnosis implies a graver disorder, a need for more intensive treatment, and a less favorable probability of good recovery. Still, a clinician needs to know many detailed facts about the life history and present status of a schizophrenic patient, just as he does when dealing with a less severe involvement of personality.

In place of one-word diagnoses, brief summary statements are often serviceable, as "a puny, overprotected boy overcompensates aggressively to maintain his self-esteem and his relations with his peers," or "an immature adolescent girl develops a hysterical paralysis to justify her dependence and maintain the tender attention of her parents." Even such statements fall short of providing a full understanding of a person. The case citations given in the preceding chapters are diagnoses, in a sense, being condensed summaries of the nature of a client and of his problems.

The process of psychological diagnosis does not end with the formal preliminary statement. Throughout the process of psychotherapy the client reveals more and more of himself. The initial diagnostic hypotheses sometimes have to be changed, and almost always grow both in scope and in precision.

SUGGESTED READINGS

On the mental hygiene movement, see the first part of Klein, *Mental Hygiene;* Moloney, *The Battle for Mental Health;* and Chapters 14 and 15 of Coleman, *Abnormal Psychology and Modern Life.* The origin and early history of the mental hygiene movement are in Beers's remarkable autobiography, *A Mind That Found Itself.*

Witmer, *Psychiatric Interviews with Children* illustrates the operation of a child guidance clinic. Lemkau, *Mental Hygiene in Public Health,* Part One, is a survey of mental health in relation to community and professional responsibilities.

Thorne, *Principles of Psychological Examining,* and Menninger, *A Manual for Psychiatric Case Study,* will give the student a sense of the complexity of the diagnostic function and the level of professional training it demands. Rosenzweig, *Psychodiagnosis* shows the use of psychological methods in diagnosis, with illustrative case studies.

CHAPTER **16**

Psychotherapy: Learning New Adjustments

Nonintegrative adjustments are acquired through learning processes. It is no surprise, therefore, that a new learning experience may be helpful to a person whose adjustments have gone awry. When such an experience is provided by a professional clinician, it constitutes psychotherapy. Just as most of our adjustments are products of our social relationships, so psychotherapy serves as an interpersonal relationship from which the client can learn new ways of feeling and thinking about himself and other people, and new responses to his life situations.

Although less is known about the psychotherapeutic process than about many other kinds of human learning, there is nothing mystical about it. When an individual seeks professional help for a personal problem, he essentially engages in a series of very specialized conversations with a skilled clinician. They talk together. In a setting of privacy and confidentiality, the client discusses the things that are bothering him. The therapist helps him to feel differently toward himself and his problems, understand himself better, and develop more constructive ways of acting. The basis for the client's new learnings is his personal interaction with the clinician. Psychotherapy is not a service exclusively for the severely disturbed or psychotic person. People who would be described as neurotic or maladjusted, who feel anxious and ineffective, are likely to find help.

ILLUSTRATIONS OF PSYCHOTHERAPY

One way to gain some understanding of what happens in psychotherapy is to examine a few excerpts from therapeutic interviews. The three brief illustrations which follow are drawn from the practices of two clinicians who represent somewhat divergent "schools" of psychotherapy and one therapist who takes a middle-of-the-road position. Because psychotherapy is still more of an art than a science, its methods are based more on systematic beliefs than on experimentally tested hypotheses. Hence it runs to "schools" but, as we shall see, the adherents of the schools are more alike than different in their actual practices.

The illustrative interviews were electrically recorded and transcribed verbatim. How, you may ask, can real interviews be presented when therapy is such a highly confidential relationship? It is indeed confidential. What transpires between the client and therapist is held in complete trust and is revealed to no one. But there are two well-recognized exceptions to the rule of confidence. First, the therapist may talk about his cases to a supervisor or professional consultant, who also respects the client's confidence. Second, the therapist *with his client's permission* may make a recording of the interviews for his own notes, for research, or for instruction. When such recordings are used for research or teaching, every care is taken to protect the identity of the clients who have permitted their use.

Psychoanalytic Psychotherapy

One example of how a client and his therapist may interact is provided by a brief interchange which occurred as part of a psychoanalysis. The therapist's orientation and method are in agreement with the system of theory presented in Chapter 14. The therapist's responses reveal him as more a modern psychoanalyst than an orthodoxly Freudian one.

The client, an unmarried man of twenty-eight, lives with his widowed mother, whom he cares for devotedly. A quiet, gentle person, he came for help because of strong attacks of anxiety which he could not understand, and a growing sense of futility in his work as an accountant. He has had recurrent nightmares in which he dreamed of himself driving a truck with which he ran down and killed a woman. The following passage is taken from the fortieth hour of his psychotherapy.

Cl. I had another of those dreams last night. I woke up in a sweat and was frightened almost to death.

Th. Tell me about it.

Cl. It's pretty much the same thing. I was driving a big truck along a dark country road at night. I saw a woman walking along it ahead of me, and I could have avoided her easily. But (great agitation) I didn't seem to want to! I just held the truck to the curve of the road on the right side, and I hit her! I hit her! And it was awful! I stopped and went around to her, and she was still alive but dying fast, and she was terribly battered!

Th. Tell me about the woman. Just say whatever comes to mind now. Think about the woman and just say whatever occurs to you.

Cl. Well, she was nobody I've ever known. She seemed small and sort of helpless. She was just walking along the road. It's not always the same woman in these dreams, but they're usually little old ladies like this one. She had dark hair and was terribly, terribly disfigured after the truck hit her. Mother's hair is almost snow white now, but this woman was dark. I've never known anybody like her. (pause)

Th. It seems important to you not to know who this woman was. Go on.

Cl. But I don't know who she was! She was just a little old woman on a dark country road. It was horrible! The accident messed her up so dreadfully! I felt nauseated and revolted by all the mess as well as by the horror of what I had done. But — and this is very strange — I didn't feel any real remorse in the dream, I don't think. I was terrified and sick at the sight but not really sorry. I think that's what wakes me up. I'm not really sorry.

Th. Almost as if you were glad to have got rid of this little old lady. Go on. Just say whatever comes to mind.

Cl. (after a long pause) I guess the horror of the sight is that she was so messy and bloody. Mother, the only older woman that I know really well, is always so neat and clean and well taken care of. This woman in the dream seemed, I don't know, evil somehow in spite of her being so helpless.

Th. Your mother is quite a burden on you at times, isn't she?

Cl. Why, no! How can you say that? She's a wonderful person, and I'm glad to do what I can for her. She means more to me than anybody else.

Th. These things are pretty painful to think about at times, but I'm pretty impressed by your knowing only your mother as a helpless little old lady and your dreaming so repeatedly about killing just such a person. And *you* are the one who dreams it!

It is difficult to convey on the printed page the kindness of the therapist's manner and the understanding quality of his tone of voice. This excerpt suggests the intensity of emotion that is sometimes generated during a psychoanalytic interview, the way in which free association develops in the earlier phases of this type of therapy, and the method by which the clinician attempts to get his client to consider the meaning of his behavior. The therapist is exploring the hypothesis that the client has strong unconscious resentment toward his mother, whose care interferes with his developing a full life of his own. Unable to express his resentment directly, the client appears to reveal it in his dreams, where he acts upon the hostile and destructive impulses which he cannot acknowledge directly because of the anxiety they arouse. The psychotherapist is attempting to bring about a more open recognition of these feelings so that they may be dealt with more straightforwardly as therapy progresses.

Client-Centered Psychotherapy

Another variety of psychotherapeutic interaction is seen in client-centered or nondirective counseling, a method introduced by Carl R. Rogers.[1] This approach, unlike psychoanalysis, does not emphasize the uncovering of hidden impulses or try to direct the client's thinking along particular channels. Rather, it tries to provide the client with an understanding relationship within which he may clarify his feelings. The method is called "client-centered" because it focuses on the client as a present person, and "nondirective" because it believes in a minimum of intervention or direction on the part of the therapist.

The following excerpt is from the case of Robert Winslow Smith, a handsome and bright eighteen-year-old with many worries and insecurities. The passage is from the thirteenth session of counseling.

In his previous statements during the session, the client has said, "I don't want to be inferior in anything." . . . "I try and cover the inferiority up as much as possible." The excerpt begins near the end of the interview.

Cl. Yes, but you can never destroy the things you're inferior in. They always remain where everybody can see 'em, right on the surface. No matter how well you can talk, no matter how well you can dance, no matter how good a time you are to the persons who are with you, you certainly can't wear a veil.

Th. M-hm. It's *looks* again, isn't it? . . . .

Cl. Yeah. I wish I was like my brother. He's dark just as the rest of the family is. Me — I'm light — puny. He's heavier-built than I am, too. Guess I was just made up of odds and ends. I'm too darn light. I don't like my face. I don't like my eyebrows and my eyes. Bloodshot, little cow-eyes. I hate my pimple chin and I detest the way my face is lopsided. One side is so much different from the other. One side, the chin bones stick out further and the jaw bones are more pronounced. My mouth isn't right. Even when I smile, I don't smile the way other people do. I tried and I can't. When other people smile, their mouths go up — mine goes down. It's me; backward in everything. I'm clumsy as the devil.

Th. You feel sort of sorry for yourself, isn't that right?

Cl. Yes, self-pity, that's me. Sure, I know I pity myself, but I got something to pity. If there were two of me I would punch myself right in the nose just for the fun of it.

Th. M-hm.

Cl. Sometimes I get so disgusted with myself!

Th. Sometimes you feel somewhat ashamed of yourself for pointing out all of those physical inadequacies, right?

Cl. Yes, I know I should forget them — yeah, forget them — I should think of something else. And that's — I hate myself because I'm not sure. That's just another thing I can hate myself for.

Th. You're sort of in a dilemma because you can't like yourself, and yet you dislike the fact that you don't like yourself.

Cl. M-hm. I know it isn't natural for a person not to like himself. In fact, most people are in love with themselves. They don't know quite so much of themselves. I've known people like that.

Th. M-hm.

Cl. But not me. (Pause.) I don't see how anybody loves me, even Mom. Maybe it's just maternal love. They can't help it, poor things. (Pause.)

Th. You feel so worthless you wonder how anyone would think much of you.

Cl. Yeah. But I'm not gonna worry about it. I've just gotta make up for it, that's all. I've just gotta forget it. And try to compensate for it.

Th. M-hm. (Pause.)

Cl. I've always tried to compensate for it. Everything I did in high school was to compensate for it.

Th. M-hm. You've never had much reason to think that people really cared about you, is that right?

Cl. That's right. Oh, if you only knew how they —

Th. M-hm.

Cl. Everything anyone ever said or ever did they were just trying to get something out of me. Or else they were —

Th. It sort of made you feel inadequate not having the security of having people show that they cared a lot for you.

Cl. That's right.

Th. M-hm.

Cl. No one ever did. . . .*

This illustration, like the last, indicates the emotional intensity of much of psychotherapy. Further, it demonstrates the important therapeutic dimension of *acceptance*. In spite of the fact that Winslow was characterized as handsome, he is extremely self-conscious and dissatisfied with his appearance. The clinician never contradicts him on this score or opposes a contrary opinion by saying such things as, "I can't understand how you can say such things about yourself. You impress me as an extraordinarily good looking person." Instead, he accepts these self-deprecating remarks by the client as an important *feeling* that Winslow has about himself. It is the feelings that matter. But it should be noted, also, that that acceptance carries neither the implication of approving nor of disapproving what the client says. The therapist responds to these expressions by showing his understanding, and by clarifying the feelings behind them. The client moves from a concern about his appearance to the presumably more important topic of his sense of being unloved and disliked. He may acquire, in the meanwhile, some recognition of his tendencies to pity himself and to wallow in his own misery.

---

* W. U. Snyder. *Casebook of non-directive counseling.* Boston: Houghton Mifflin, 1947. Pp. 82-85.

General Psychotherapy

Many competent psychotherapists disavow any connection with formal "schools" of therapy, and take what they find valuable from many different sources. An example of general or eclectic counseling comes from the case of Diane C., a professional singer in her middle twenties. She entered therapy because she was dissatisfied with music as a career, and because her relationships with men were typically too intense, turbulent, and lacking in permanence to let her feel comfortable about them. Having majored in psychology in college, she has given some thought to graduate study in this field, especially since she began counseling. The excerpt which follows is taken from the thirty-third hour, after a three-week interruption during which she was on tour with a musical troupe. While away she visited a number of universities, including one whose graduate school had refused to admit her because of her erratic undergraduate record.

> *Cl.* Well, I've got loads of good news, but I'm glad to be back here. The trip was fun, and I feel I'm really solid with the show company, but I've got to make up my mind about a lot of things. Smith [a well known singing coach] accepted me as a pupil, and I'm terribly proud and thrilled, only I don't know if I want it. I'd still like to go to graduate school.
>
> *Th.* So this still pulls you in opposite ways and leaves you feeling pretty uncertain about things.
>
> *Cl.* Uh-huh. People were so nice to me at the universities I visited while I was away. Everybody was so warm and encouraging. I learned a real lesson. I'll never apply again unless it's in person. Things go much better then.
>
> *Th.* I get the feeling that you're saying that you made these people so aware of how charming and personable you can be that they were inclined to overlook the weak spots in the record that got you in trouble a while ago.
>
> *Cl.* Y-e-s. (slowly) It's like the audition [for her present job]. I didn't really know the music well and hadn't even sung it over. But I hoped that they would judge me on how well I *could* do it if I practiced and judge me more on things like looks and how well I'd wear period costumes, and it turned out that way. (pause) But I knew I could do the work if they would give me a chance, and I know I can handle graduate school if they would just let me in.

Th. And feeling confident that you could measure up, you rather feel that a very personal kind of appeal is a good way to get in.

Cl. It isn't that! (pause) I guess it is though. I know I can do the work, but I get so scared when I think of people looking at my records and judging me on that basis without knowing *me.* The kind of person you are counts for a lot in clinical psychology, doesn't it? How can they tell if they don't see me and talk to me and give me a chance to meet them?

Th. The main thing is that it's almost unbearable to have these university people thinking slightingly of you when they look at transcripts, is that right? Being thought an unworthy person on the basis of bits of paper is almost more than you can stand.

Cl. Oh, yes. (very softly) And you think that I'm trying to cover up that part of me by charming people and getting them to forget what I did in college.

Th. It's a thought that did occur to me, and I'm rather moved by how important it is to have these unknown people think well of you. They're people like me, too, aren't they?

Cl. Boy, and haven't I thought of that! (laughs) Sometimes I don't know if I'm just trying to be like you, or if I'm just trying to be somebody you'd admire, or if it's the real thing.

Th. Or if being with these people is what you're mostly after.

Cl. (soberly) That's certainly important. I've thought about that a lot. They seem to be so much more genuine somehow than, well, musicians. Music is such a cut-throat profession. . . . And these people at the universities don't seem at all like that. They seem to like people. They were cordial and helpful and reasonable, and I suppose I envied you a little for being one of them.

Th. It's somehow important to be one of my kind of crowd, and that consideration seems awfully important in thinking about school versus music in spite of being so successful with the company.

Cl. Yes, it would be wonderful, I think, to be really liked by you and by people like Dr. X and Dr. Y [whom she had met while on her trip] and to work every day with them. And that way I could have music, too. . . . When you work as a singer, there isn't any time for anything but music while you work. And when you don't, all you can do is worry about your next job.

Th. In a sense, then, you think that psychology would let you keep music but not the other way around; it's the best way to give up the least? And I'm struck by how important this matter of

being liked by me and Dr. X and Dr. Y as an equal is. It occurs
to me that you can't really believe that I do like you unless you're
doing essentially the same things and doing them as well as I am.

Cl. I don't understand. Can you tell me again?

Th. I don't think I'm telling you anything. I'm just kind of
thinking out loud with you about these things. I guess I wondered
if you really feel pretty doubtful about my liking you or about
anybody's liking you unless you're doing the same things and
about as well.

Cl. Oh. (long pause) Yes, I'd agree to that. (long pause)

Th. These are pretty uncomfortable thoughts.

Cl. (nodding) I'm just wondering if I'm trying to compete with
everybody and still cover my tracks so nobody will know if I
lose. . . .

This extract provides a clear illustration of the role that the
client-clinician relationship often plays in psychotherapy. By examining her reactions to her therapist, Diane is developing some
insight into the way she reacts to people in general, and into her
own competitive tendencies. Two other points merit attention.
One is that the counselor shares with the client his impressions of
what her behavior means. By considering these thoughts, the client
moves toward a fuller understanding of herself. A second important feature is that the interview shows the complexity of apparently straightforward human problems. Among other issues,
Diane is concerned with the choice of a career. But the decision
about her occupational problem cannot be considered in isolation.
Because a person's problems are so highly interrelated, the therapeutic process focuses on the client's personal development and
self-understanding much more than on finding specific solutions to
particular difficulties.

COMMON ASPECTS OF PSYCHOTHERAPY

Brief extracts from psychotherapeutic interviews cannot, of course,
demonstrate the changes that take place during a full therapeutic
experience, which often runs into dozens or scores of hours. But
even brief quotations serve several useful purposes. They convey
some of the flavor of a counseling process. They indicate that
counseling is primarily a conversation between client and therapist,

intended to explore the former's feelings, increase his self-understanding, and eventually help him discover new and more effective ways of living. Although the excerpts are drawn from presumably different "schools" of psychotherapy — psychoanalytic, client-centered, and general or eclectic — they suggest that the similarities of these approaches are somewhat greater than their differences. Where differences occur, they are more of degree than of kind. All types of psychotherapy share, in varying degrees, certain common dimensions of the therapeutic process.

Interpretation and Responsibility

One dimension of the counseling process is the degree to which the clinician *interprets* what the client tells him.[2] The therapist's responses may range from merely restating what the client has said, to drawing inferences about his unconscious impulses. A few examples may clarify the continuum of interpretative responses.

The least interpretative reaction, which merely repeats the content of a patient's statement, is illustrated by this interchange:

> *Cl.* I've been awfully nervous and high-strung lately. It's hard for me to get to work and concentrate on what I have to do. I think it's perfectly natural though. I had a pretty big operation not long ago, and I haven't really got my strength back yet.
>
> *Th.* You feel your nervousness and inability to work are just a natural aftermath of your operation.

The therapist has said nothing that the client has not already put into words. Interpretation is at a minimum. Nevertheless, the clinician's response helps to achieve two goals. First, it indicates that the counselor is listening in an attentive, genuinely interested, accepting way, and that the client is quite free to think with him further about his disturbing nervousness. Second, it objectifies the reason that the client gives to explain his uneasiness. It is probable that his recent operation is more a rationalization than an adequate reason for the anxiety that the client feels. But it is more likely that he can consider his own defensive behavior constructively when he hears it expressed by another person than when he hears himself say it, or when someone argues with him.

At the other end of the scale of interpretation are attempts to uncover profoundly unconscious concerns in the client. Usually, the more interpretative the therapist's response, the more it involves the integration of previous statements by the client with his current ones. The clinician is responding not only to what the client says but also to what he has previously said. A suicidal patient in a hospital, for example, has told his therapist about a number of phobias, including fears of crossing streets and bridges. The therapist also knows that the patient attempted to take his own life by drowning, that he was in a panic of anxiety when he did it, and that he suffers from very low self-esteem. The patient says:

> *Pt.* It's got so bad I can't even drive over a bridge any more without feeling so scared it's all I can do not to leave the car and run away.

The therapist responds as follows:

> *Th.* It seems to me that these phobias are all associated with your destructive impulses toward yourself. You think of yourself as a very worthless person and hate yourself for being so inadequate in your own eyes. Streets and bridges symbolize the river in which you could drown this person whom you despise so, and every time you cross them, they arouse this urge to do yourself harm. No wonder you get anxious to the point of panic.

Here the clinician is trying to clarify the patient's behavior by relating his attempted suicide to his lack of self-regard, and by uncovering the unconscious meanings that streets and bridges have for him. Whether such interpretations are helpful may be debatable. The only point with which we are concerned here is the illustration of a highly interpretative response by the psychotherapist.

If we examine the three excerpts on pages 516 to 522, we can readily see that most of the counselor responses are intermediate between the two extremes cited. The client-centered therapist tends to use statements that fall closer to the low end of the interpretative scale; the psychoanalyst tends to work much more interpretatively; the eclectic clinician lies somewhere between. All three, however, vary somewhat in their degree of interpretativeness, depending on the issue the client is discussing and on the extent to which they feel he is ready to consider new interpretations of his behavior. One experimental study, which compared the techniques of analytic and client-centered therapists, showed that the psychoanalysts asked more exploratory questions.[3] The client-centered therapists tended to reflect and clarify the clients' expressions of feeling. The analysts also gave more interpretations, but only 10 per cent of their responses were interpretative.

Another dimension of psychotherapy is the degree of responsibility assumed by the clinician for maintaining and developing the therapeutic relationship. If the therapist asks many questions, determines the topics discussed, advises the client about the decisions he should make in his everyday life, or tells the client to get in touch with him whenever he feels anxious or upset, then he would be rated high on this dimension because he assumes virtually all responsibility for the therapeutic development. On the other hand, the therapist who is primarily an understanding listener, permits the client to choose the topics discussed, encourages the client to think with him about any problems that arise, but offers neither advice nor direction, and essentially limits the client's contacts with him to the consulting room would be rated low because he places most of the responsibility on the client.

It is probable that varying degrees of responsibility are desirable at different points in the therapeutic process. For example, it may be important for the clinician to assume greater responsibility in the earlier stages of counseling than later. Nevertheless, our three excerpts again suggest differences in degree of responsibility assumed by the three therapists. The client-centered counselor listens attentively and reflects feelings sensitively, but he does little to steer the course of the interview. The psychoanalyst, on the other hand, takes full responsibility for instructing his client to associate freely to the elements of his dream. The analyst opens the discussion of the client's possible resentment against his mother. The eclectic therapist is again intermediate, listening carefully and permitting the client to follow her own lines of thought, but often determining the topic to a considerable degree. But the three counselors vary from moment to moment in the amount of responsibility they accept. They seem to overlap in their assumption of responsibility. Their differences are of emphasis, and do not mark them off from one another as representatives of completely independent doctrines.

The Counseling Relationship

Psychotherapy is a *relationship* between two people. In this respect, psychotherapeutic service differs markedly from the service rendered by other professional persons such as general medical practitioners or lawyers. In such instances, one divulges his difficulties and problems in matters of health, or involving some legal issue, and expects that the doctor or attorney will prescribe a course of action which will lead to a solution. While it helps if the physician or lawyer has a pleasant manner and a reassuring way of dealing with people, he is called on primarily for his technical skill and expertness.

In counseling, however, the situation is quite different. Psychological difficulties arise primarily from handicapping interpersonal relations. Their cure understandably lies in an opportunity for new social learning. The personal aspect of the relationship is therefore an integral part of the client's therapeutic experience.

Fiedler has shown that the relationship in psychotherapy is more a function of the experience and expertness of clinicians than of their "schools" or theoretical affiliations.[4] He secured recorded interviews from ten therapists representing psychoanalytic, Adlerian, and client-centered approaches. These recordings were then evaluated by other therapists in terms of how well they approximated an ideal counseling relationship. The findings were that the more expert and experienced clinicians created relationships closer to the ideal than did the nonexperts, and that the relationships created by experts of one school more closely resembled those created by experts of *other* schools than those created by nonexperts of the *same* school. Similarly, expert therapists of different schools agreed better among themselves as to what constituted an ideal counseling relationship than they did with nonexpert members of the same schools.

The psychotherapeutic relationship is characterized by three fundamental attitudes on the part of the therapist.[5] The first of these attitudes may be called *warm concern*. The clinician is genuinely interested in his client as a person and is fully committed to the task of being as helpful as possible. There is no necessary implication of "liking" a client; many psychotherapeutic subjects are not very likeable people, and their unhappy and troubled awareness of this fact is one of the motivations for their entering therapy. All that is meant is that the therapist devotes all his attention during the time he is with his client to understanding the client's feelings as sensitively and as fully as he can. He respects and values the client as a human being and not merely as a "case."

Second, the relationship is characterized by a *nonretaliatory permissiveness*. The clinician gives the client extensive freedom to discuss any topic he chooses, including his reactions to the therapist himself and to the therapeutic situation. Regardless of the topic chosen, the therapist remains calm and unshocked. Even when the client attacks him verbally, he is more interested in understanding the attack than in retaliation or revenge. Consequently, the relationship is a safe one for the client because he is never rejected or subjected to punishment for the behavior he reports or for the attitudes and feelings he verbalizes. On the other hand, the clinician does not express his approval of what the client does or reports. He merely accepts it as an expression of the client's personality and attempts to work with it constructively.

The third hallmark of an effective counseling relationship is *honesty of communication*. The therapist constantly tries to clarify the interaction between himself and his client, and to enlarge his conception of the client's behavior. What is the client really trying to say? How can the client be encouraged to think more clearly about himself? How can the therapist communicate back to the client a clarified understanding of what has been expressed, both intellectually and in terms of feelings? The therapist has to think and feel with the client. At times, the efforts to communicate honestly involve calling painful issues to the client's attention, such as his tendency to feel sorry for himself, his resentment bordering on hatred for his mother, or his competitive tendencies that are destructive of good relations with others. But much of a therapist's skill lies in his ability to combine this kind of honesty and directness with a sensitive understanding of the client's feelings. The therapist may point out personality problems, but he does not condemn them.

Unlike other relationships of comparable intimacy and intensity, the psychotherapeutic one is sharply limited by its utilitarian purpose.[6] The goal of counseling is the improvement of the client's adjustment to a point where the therapist is no longer needed. Consequently, although he accepts the client as a person in difficulty, and is warmly and genuinely interested in him, the clinician gives of himself only insofar as it will help, not please, the client. He limits the relationship to the clinic or consulting room, and generally refrains from any intervention in the client's extraclinical life. The therapist certainly does not become involved with him in informal, extraprofessional ways. The relationship is designed so that it has a termination point, even though the termination point may be indefinite. The relationship is to last only so long as the client needs the therapist's help. Finally, the therapist establishes the relationship in an essentially one-sided fashion. The clinician does not share his own troubles or pleasures with his clients, nor does he usually permit his own personal values or affairs to intrude into the interviews.

The result of these limitations is a considerable amount of anonymity on the part of the therapist. The client knows the clinician primarily in his professional role only, and that role is maintained with a high degree of consistency and integrity. Thus, while the therapeutic relationship develops into one of trust, confidence, and warmth, the distinctive personality of the clinician is decidedly minimized.

The Content of Therapeutic Interviews

The content of psychotherapeutic interviews tends to cut across the lines of the "schools," as do the qualities of interpretation and relationship. Counseling is mainly a series of conversations. Whether the therapy is psychoanalytic, client-centered, or eclectic in orientation, the conversational content is typically concerned with the client's values, motives, and emotions, and with the situations to which he feels they are relevant. These situations may be either current or recollected from his history. One situation of considerable importance is the counseling process and the counseling relationship. Indeed, there is much more focus in psychotherapy on the changing qualities of the client-clinician relationship than in any interpersonal situation outside the clinic walls.

The topics of psychotherapy are often not easy to discuss but the most difficult conversational items are often the most helpful. In one study, for example, forty-three clients judged the therapeutic value of fifteen topics which had been considered in the course of counseling.[7] The clients agreed well among themselves as to the relative value of the topics, and their ratings showed a high correlation between a topic's "helpfulness" and its "disturbing" qualities.

Thus, the topic called "shame and guilt" was judged as extremely upsetting, but the discussion of it in the course of counseling was regarded as highly helpful. When a group of psychologists rated the topics for their "intimacy," their personal significance for clients, the ratings showed a high positive relationship with clients' judgments of helpfulness.

It is not surprising, then, that therapeutic conversations are centered on the client's anxiety, guilt feelings, and feelings of inferiority or inadequacy, and on the occurrences that engender them. Obviously, such topics are precisely the ones that are most difficult for the patient to talk about. One of the hindrances to successful counseling is that it depends on discussing the very things that the client is least inclined to discuss and which are most susceptible to repression. For this reason, psychotherapy is a time-consuming process and often holds many painful moments for the client.

Psychotherapy thus appears to be an interpersonal relationship of great warmth and genuine interest within which the concerns most disturbing to the client are discussed. How does this therapeutic process function? How does the client learn new ways of adjusting to his needs and to his world?

HOW CLIENTS LEARN IN PSYCHOTHERAPY

The function of psychotherapy is to provide a situation in which the client has an opportunity to learn new patterns of responses, which will enable him to live more comfortably with himself and more harmoniously with other people.[8] The therapeutic situation serves as a safe world within which the client can learn new social behavior, and from which he can generalize his learnings to the larger world outside. For descriptive convenience, we can divide the client's learning processes into a number of phases. In actual practice these stages overlap and blend into each other.

The Extinction of Defenses

When a person first comes for psychotherapy, he tends to focus on the clinician essentially the same kinds of response patterns that characterize him in his daily life. He is a bit mistrustful, and a little inclined to expect rejection or hostility. He regards the therapist, as he regards other people, as a figure to be feared, or dominated, or manipulated, or made demands of. Consequently, he typically is rather guarded in his discussion of his problems and is defensive both in the content of his conversation and in his approach to the relationship.

The first task of the therapist is to deal with these defensive maneuvers. Basically, he does two things. First, the therapist avoids punishing comments and moralistic judgments about the client's evasions. He attempts to communicate his real *respect* for the client and his genuine *understanding* of the fact that the client's actions are determined by his discomfort and anxiety, not by wilfulness or perverse impulses. Second, the therapist shows that he recognizes the client's resistive processes. Without insisting or arguing, and without anger, he calmly indicates his awareness of the client's attempts to avoid coming to grips with his problems. This process is illustrated by the following brief exchange from an early interview with a college student who is failing in spite of high academic ability and who has great difficulty in getting along with persons in authority.

> *Cl.* I don't really think I need to come. I can't see how just talking about these things will improve my grades, and the last two times I was here, I felt more upset after I left than when I had come.
>
> *Th.* Sure. Thinking about these things is pretty painful at times, and I suspect that it's particularly hard for you to think about them with me. After all, I'm a part of the university, and I'd guess you'd find it as hard to trust me as you do to trust a lot of the others whom you've talked to.
>
> *Cl.* No, I don't mean — (pause) Well, I — After all, how do I know you won't go to the Dean or make it rough for me like a lot of these guys?
>
> *Th.* I guess you can't find out unless you try. All I can do is tell you that whatever you talk about here is between us and nobody else. I get the feeling that you mistrust a lot of people mostly because you're scared, and that makes it awfully tough for you to talk with anybody about the things that I gather are really worrying you quite a lot.
>
> *Cl.* (nods) I suppose so. I sure feel pretty miserable at times and mad at the whole damn world.

Here the therapist neither presses the client to discuss his anxieties nor punishes him for his recalcitrance. The clinician is not alarmed or angered by the accusation that he has made the client feel worse instead of better. He merely expresses some understanding of the client's resistive tendencies and tries to identify them for what they are. The therapist accepts the client as a person, and accepts his need to act defensively, but is not misled by the defenses.

Such procedures bring about two results. First, the client learns that the therapist, like a good parent, can be trusted to be understanding and nonretaliatory, but that he is unlikely to be deceived by evasions of important topics or distracted by personal attacks and accusations. His gradual learning to have confidence in the therapist is one important basis for the client's later attempts to explore his own personality fully and frankly. Second, the therapist's behavior brings about an *extinction* of the client's defenses in the therapeutic situation. The client's defensive behavior is unrewarded because it does not work. The therapist does not "fall for it." The defensive behavior may even be considered to be mildly punished because the therapist gently calls the client's attention to his evasions and to the functions they serve. As therapy proceeds, defensive and evasive tactics tend to occur with decreasing frequency, giving the client an opportunity to think more straightforwardly about his anxieties and nonintegrative adjustments. The process is analogous to laboratory studies of the extinction of motor responses.[9] Such responses are extinguished more rapidly and efficiently under conditions of simple nonreinforcement or very mild punishment, whereas severe punishment suppresses the response but does not extinguish it (p. 131). The therapist does *not* punish the client's responses strongly by rejecting him as a person, a type of punishment the client has experienced from most other people in his life. The extinction of defenses in the therapeutic situation appears to be one of the early outcomes of counseling.

Verbalizing Anxieties and Problems

Just as the therapist seeks to extinguish defensiveness by not rewarding it, so he seeks to strengthen his client's tendencies to explore his own behavior and to think honestly about himself by reinforcing them. Such reinforcements may take the form of direct expressions of approval of the client's efforts to communicate his anxieties and thwartings. Often the reinforcements are more subtle; the therapist shows his recognition of the difficulties involved in the client's efforts, or gives a heightened degree of participation in the relationship. The following exchange illustrates one way in which self-exploratory behavior is reinforced in counseling:

> *Cl.* (long pause) I really didn't want to come today. I got involved in the same old mess with some of the fellows at the office yesterday, and I'd rather not think about it. I know I ought to talk about it, but I'd rather not.
>
> *Th.* It took real courage to come, knowing that you'd have to face up to some issues that are pretty painful for you.
>
> *Cl.* It was pretty tough. (pause) I just don't understand why I get so damned quarrelsome whenever anybody finds fault with something I do.

Here the therapist speaks warmly of the client's courage in dealing directly with a puzzling and anxiety-producing facet of his own behavior. The client then goes ahead to further explorations, in which he is helped by the therapist's clarifications and interpretations, as shown in the illustrative excerpts. Note that the therapist does not reward or praise a particular explanation or solution proposed by the client. The therapist's function is to reinforce self-explorations of all sorts.

The fruit of the client's exploration is often self-understanding or *insight*. Insight consists primarily of the ability to verbalize one's own motives and goals, and to think about one's behavior in such a way as to control it more effectively in the light of its most probable long-range consequences.[10] In the excerpt from the case of Diane C. (pp. 520-522), the client formed at least the beginning of two such insights. One had to do with her attempts to substitute personal charm for solid accomplishment. The other was concerned with her competitive impulses. Both were troublesome to her because they led ultimately to frictions in her interpersonal relationships and to a considerable degree of guilt. By understanding these tendencies, that is, by relating them to their ultimately punishing effects in her life, Diane was better able to control them in the interest of better social adjustments and a lessened degree of emotional discomfort.

Insight tends to bring past experiences and future consequences into the present by verbalization. As was shown in Chapter 5 (p.

134), insight can lead to more effective learning. Of course, insight is not won quickly. Even after the first verbalizations have been made in therapy, it is usually necessary for the client to consider the same tendencies many times, often in relation to different specific situations in his life, before the learning becomes sufficiently generalized to be of wide utility.

Insight does occur in most therapeutic situations and is ordinarily of value. The concept is a troublesome one, however, for in some cases there is apparent insight without improvement and in others, improvement without evident insight. It is not rare for a client to be able to give an elaborate theoretical account of himself, even a quite correct one, and still be anxious and defensive. In such instances, it is likely that an unskilled therapist has reinforced the wrong responses. The client has learned the technical jargon of a theory instead of having learned to think about his own individual feelings. The opposite effect is seen in some adult clients, and in most children in play therapy, who acquire considerable comfort and security without being able to give a verbal account of themselves. Learning can occur by slow trial and error (pp. 138-140) as well as by insight. Both kinds of cases emphasize the relatively low value of insight alone without the extinction of anxiety.

Learning to Be Secure

In psychotherapy, the client learns to react to his own impulses, and to the situations which formerly troubled him, with security or emotional comfort rather than with anxiety. This change is perhaps the most fundamental one to occur in psychotherapy. Anxiety tends to constrict behavior and to elicit adjustments which immediately reduce the distressing emotion but do nothing to eliminate the conditions which produce it. Thus, the replacement of anxiety by security permits the person to think more constructively about his own behavior, to plan more foresightedly, and to take more fully into account the long-range consequences of his actions. The freedom to think about his own behavior allows the client to discriminate between the situations in which impulses may be expressed and those in which they must be controlled in the interest of greater integration and personal contentment.

Such crucial new learning is brought about essentially in accordance with the principles of conditioning.[11] The therapeutic rela-

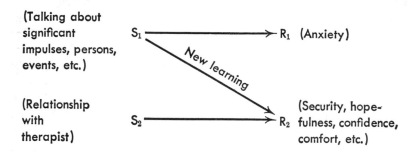

Figure 39. Learning to be Secure

A schematic representation of how security responses are conditioned to previously anxiety-arousing stimuli. Compare to
Figure 12, p. 66, and Figure 10, p. 63.

tionship elicits affective responses of a positive sort. The clinician's
warm concern, his nonretaliatory permissiveness, and his honesty of
communication tend to evoke hopefulness, security, and comfort in
the client. On the other hand, the conversational content of psychotherapy, as we have seen, is focused on the events which produce the
client's anxieties. Since language, like other symbols, calls out some
part of the same response as do the things to which it refers, therapeutic talk amounts to the symbolic reinstatement of those situations
which typically make the client anxious.[12]

When the conversational content and the therapeutic relationship
are skillfully paired, a conditioning may cocur as diagrammed in
Figure 39. This concept of learning in therapy is an application of
the general principle of conditioning (Fig. 12, p. 66), and in a
sense is the converse of the process by which a fear is acquired (Fig.
10, p. 63). When the client discusses the situations which produce
his anxiety (S_1), within the context of the security-eliciting relationship ($S_2 — R_2$), he learns to feel security and confidence (R_2) when
confronted with the formerly anxiety-producing events and impulses. By generalization (pp. 71-73), the response of security
may extend to the world away from the therapist in which the client
lives his daily life. When the process of generalization has been carried to the point at which further reinforcements by the therapist are
unnecessary to keep the response of security in force, the client has
completed his psychotherapeutic experience.

The way that anxiety is removed in therapy resembles the simpler procedure of the reconditioning of a child who feared animals (p. 70). At lunch each day, just as the child began to eat a meal which included his favorite dishes, a rabbit in a cage was introduced into the room. The animal was brought closer each day, until finally the child could eat his meal with one hand while stroking the rabbit with the other.[13] The same pattern of learning appears to hold in psychotherapy, even though the frightening situations are introduced symbolically through the conversational content of the interviews, and the comfort and security are evoked by the client-therapist relationship.

The account of how anxiety is extinguished helps to understand why psychotherapy often takes a long time. Almost all extinction is slow, in contrast to the speed with which fear or anxiety can be acquired. The client's relationship to the therapist must be developed to a point where the security it elicits is stronger than the anxiety evoked by discussing troublesome issues. Otherwise the client may become conditioned in the way opposite to that intended. The therapeutic situation would then become unbearably provocative of anxiety, and the client would have a greater motivation to break off the counseling than to continue. Consequently, the timing of interpretations and the encouraging of self-revealing behavior are matters of importance. Much of therapeutic skill is bound up in the steps of developing a secure relationship, and then evoking the discussion of content which is appropriately uncomfortable for the client, in such a fashion that the most helpful learning takes place.

The Generalization of Psychotherapy

By the steps so far described, the client learns, while in the presence of the therapist, to act less defensively, to feel secure, and to verbalize his anxieties and problems so that he makes new, non-anxious responses to them. How does psychotherapy become generalized outside of the special clinical situation into the client's real life? One important factor is the role played by the clinician. The anonymity of the clinician has already been described (p. 528). Because he is anonymous, the therapist is more a representative of significant people in general than he is an individual.[14] His warm concern and genuine interest imply that the client is worthy of confidence and of positive responses from other people.

The clinician's attitude has important implications for the client's evaluation of himself. G. H. Mead has argued that our conceptions of ourselves are derived basically from the conceptions that others have of us.[15] While growing up we learn to think of ourselves as worthwhile if our parents and other significant people in our lives so conceive us. Conversely, we learn to hold ourselves in low esteem if others regard us as undesirable or unworthy. The therapist, representing the kind of people who are important generally to the client, behaves toward him as if he were a person of worth. Therefore, the client learns to think of himself more positively, and is likely to carry his increased self-regard into his everyday life.[16]

The client's growing sense of his own personal worth has other implications. It seems to be accompanied by a tendency to evaluate other people in more accepting and favorable terms.[17] The client's more positive attitudes toward other people, and his greater freedom from anxiety, tend to elicit more friendly and rewarding responses from the people he encounters in his life outside the consulting room. Their reactions to him, in turn, reward and reinforce his newly learned qualities of feeling secure and behaving cooperatively. In this way, important features of psychotherapeutic learning occur in real life, in the absence of the psychotherapist.

The anonymous role of the therapist has another value. The client does not know him as an individual, but experiences him as the kind of person who is strong, courageous, calm, and responsible. Therefore, the therapist becomes the type of person the client would both like to know and like to be. In consequence, the client may come to take the perceived therapist — the therapist as he is experienced in the counseling process rather than what he is as a person — as a model and try to behave as it is thought he would behave. This identification with the therapist is comparable to the identification of a growing child with his parents. It provides another condition through which the client may learn to feel secure and competent.

The generalization of the client's improvement in psychotherapy, therefore, arises from a number of sources. All of them can be understood by an application of the general principles of learning. The reduction of defenses, the extinction of anxious responses to difficulties, and the increased sense of personal worth, all play a part. The anonymous role of the therapist, which makes the client respond to him as a representative of good people in general, is especially important in the process of generalization.

Evidence from Research Studies

Quantitative research on the processes of psychotherapy was made possible by the development of machines for the accurate recording of interviews. Therapeutic sessions have been recorded verbatim by phonographic, wire, or tape recorders, and then transcribed into a typescript which may be subjected to detailed study. Judges can classify each statement or unit of thought expressed by the therapist and the client according to its nature or content and according to the feelings shown. The largest amount of such investigation has been carried out with client-centered therapy, perhaps because its leaders have been trained and motivated in the research traditions of universities. There have been fewer quantitative studies of psychoanalytic or eclectic therapy but the broadest conclusions from research have considerable applicability to psychotherapy generally, regardless of method or school.

An example of a study of the processes of psychotherapy may be taken from the report by Seeman, who analyzed 60 interviews drawn from the counseling of 10 clients.[18] The sample of psychotherapy may seem small, but the study involved the recording, transcribing, and classifying of 6,570 client statements and counselor responses. Research on psychotherapy is laborious. The clients' statements were classified, using a series of categories developed in an earlier study,[19] into those which expressed problems or symptoms, indicated simple acceptance or acquiescence to the therapists' responses, showed understanding or insight, and discussed or explored plans for the future. Each type of statement was counted for each fifth of the counseling process, so as to reveal differences between the early, middle, and late sessions.

Figure 40 shows that the clients tended to make fewer statements of their problems and symptoms as the psychotherapy progressed. Indications of simple acceptance of the therapists' responses rose from the first to the second fifth and then declined gradually. Especially in the last two-fifths of the counseling process, clients showed an increased understanding of themselves and began to make plans. One index of the clients' changes during therapy was a ratio ob-

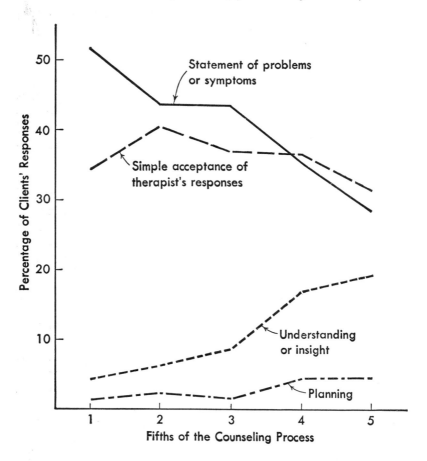

Figure 40. Changes in Clients' Statements During Psychotherapy

The statements of 10 clients were classified into four main categories and counted for each fifth of the series of psychotherapeutic interviews. Statements of problems or symptoms declined, and statements of insights and plans emerged in the later phases. (Drawn from data in J. Seeman, A study of the process of nondirective therapy. *J. consult. Psychol.*, 1949, *13*, 157-168.)

tained by dividing the number of statements of understanding and insight by the total of statements showing understanding and expressing problems. Figure 41 shows the progress, expressed in

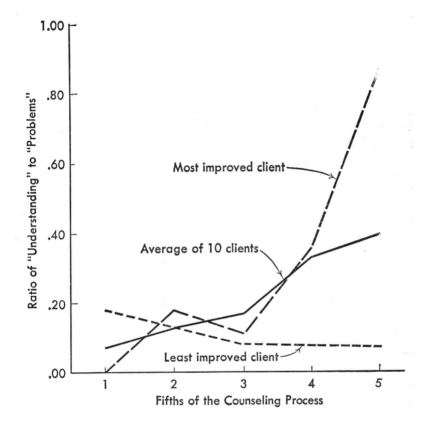

Figure 41. Clients' Statements and Improvement in Psychotherapy

A ratio was obtained by dividing the number of statements showing understanding or insight (U) by the sum of such statements and those expressing problems or symptoms (P). The ratio was therefore: $\dfrac{U}{U + P}$. (J. Seeman, A study of the process of nondirective therapy. *J. consult. Psychol.*, 1949, *13*, 157-168.)

terms of this index of insight, of the average of the ten clients and of the two individual clients whom their counselors rated as having benefited most and least from the psychotherapy.

Further analyses of the same data revealed additional features of the process of psychotherapy. Attitudes which clients expressed

in the present tense tended to become more positive and less negative in feeling as the therapy progressed; attitudes expressed in the
past tense became less positive and more negative.[20] The present
became more secure, the past less rosy. Clients expressed increasingly positive feelings toward themselves and warmer attitudes
toward other people.[21] From the earlier to the later interviews, the
clients' statements tended to report a decrease in current defensive
behavior,[22] and an increase in behavior which was judged as more
mature.[23]

The results of research on the processes of psychotherapy are
harmonious with the account of therapy as an act of social learning.
They show the client expressing his problems and feelings in the
secure atmosphere of the therapeutic situation. The client's feelings
tend to change from anxieties to more positive attitudes toward himself and toward other people. The later phases of psychotherapy see
the gradual emergence of insights and of plans for the future.

SPECIAL FORMS OF PSYCHOTHERAPY

The basic pattern of psychotherapy is the relationship between
an individual client and his therapist, but a number of modifications
of the process have been introduced to serve special purposes. The
two most important special forms of psychotherapy are group
therapy and play therapy with children.

Group Psychotherapy

Group psychotherapy follows the principles that apply to individual counseling, except that one or more clinicians meet with
two or more clients.[24] In group therapy with adults or older children, the participants typically sit in a circle or around a conference
table. The therapist evokes expressions of personal problems or discomforts from the clients, and responds as in individual psychotherapy by acknowledging and clarifying the feelings they express,
by encouraging exploration, and sometimes by making interpretations. The group therapist's role is to be warm, permissive, perceptive, and anonymous. The clients react to one another as well
as to the therapist. One client may acknowledge another's
feelings, show understanding, seek clarifications of what the other

means, or tell a similar feeling of his own. If one group member shows hostile or rejecting attitudes toward another client, as often occurs in the early stages, the therapist accepts the speaker's need to be hostile and sometimes explores why he feels that way.

Group therapy had its inception in the need to provide therapeutic service for larger numbers of people. It developed rapidly during World War II, when psychiatric cases in the armed forces far exceeded the number of therapists available to serve them.

It was soon perceived that group therapy had advantages for some clients quite beyond its economy in reaching greater numbers. Indeed, the primary justification for group psychotherapy stems from the clinical experience that clients who have similar troubles are able to help one another as well as to benefit from a common relationship with a professional therapist.[25]

When a group of four to eight people with relatively homogeneous problems discuss their difficulties with each other and with a skilled therapist, they discover that the anxieties which have seemed to set them apart from others, to make them unhappily "different," are shared. Out of their common experience of anxiety and ineffective adjustment, they tend to develop a degree of emotional kinship. In consequence, their feelings of being isolated and unworthy tend to decline.[26]

Another advantage for certain clients grows out of the typical social ineffectiveness of many people who enter psychotherapy. Since their troubles arise from faulty interpersonal relations, they find themselves unable to form relationships of sufficient intimacy and durability to be satisfying.[27] Accepted by the other members of the group on the basis of a shared misery, they can begin to develop more constructive ways of relating to others. In helping one another, for example, even through no more than listening with understanding and sympathy, they learn how to form friendships and to interact in mutually beneficial ways with people generally. It is not at all unusual for friendships begun in the sessions of group therapy to be retained outside the group.[28]

Group therapy permits the individual participants to feel they "belong," that they have membership in some group where they are valued. The sense of belonging makes individual behavior more meaningful and therefore heightens the motivation to improve individual adjustments. Each person acquires goals to which he can aspire, because of his interaction with other people who are understanding companions. To match the improvement of the group, and to achieve a better level of integration in order to maintain status within the group, become important objectives for each individual member. And since he finds himself accepted and at least potentially approved by people who understand him, each individual tends to develop a rather more positive conception of himself.[29]

Group psychotherapy, however, impresses most clinicians as less effective than individual therapy in helping clients to resolve strong personal conflicts.[30] Further, many seem unable to benefit from group therapy until they have had at least some individual help. Such people are inclined to become too anxious when they reveal their own experiences in a group, or when they hear other group members talk about painful experiences similar to their own. Some are shamed by the therapist's interpretations when made before the other group members. Others become hostile and intolerant of the clinician when he interprets the behavior of other group members because the problems discussed are too much like their own. This degree of aggression toward the therapist interferes with their own gains from the group experience.[31]

Group and individual psychotherapy can be combined. A client will meet with his therapy group and also see a clinician alone at other times. This arrangement is particularly desirable for clients whose primary troubles are associated with isolation from others, but whose personal conflicts are so severe as to make added help mandatory before they can participate with fullest benefit in the interactions of the group.

Group therapy is often a useful adjunct to individual therapy, and is also a way of making therapeutic service available to larger numbers of needful people than would otherwise be possible. Its particular utility, however, lies in the contribution it can make to persons who are lonely, isolated, and socially inept.

Play Therapy with Children

Young children lack the verbal skills needed to participate in conversational psychotherapy. But they presumably are more accessible to therapy than adults because their nonintegrative adjustments are usually less fixed. These two challenges have been met by therapeutic sessions with children in the form of play.

The child therapist meets with the young client under essentially the same conditions of confidence that obtain for adults. The room is usually furnished with a sandbox and a sink for running water, and is equipped with toys which permit the child to engage in activities most likely to express his predominant feelings and concerns. Finger paints, families of dolls made to represent parents, siblings, and the client himself, punching bags, toy guns and knives, and toy cars are representative items.

While therapists differ in their approach to disturbed children, it is usual for the child to be taken to the play room and told, "You may play with any of the things that are here." The clinician then has an opportunity to observe whether the child is hesitant or spontaneous and enthusiastic in beginning his play, whether his play has direction or is aimless, whether it is constructive or destructive, and whether it reflects identifiable anxieties and worries. As with adult clients, the clinician attempts to establish a secure relationship. The therapist interacts with the child by commenting on his play and trying to interpret his feeling or clarify his motivations. He may or may not play actively with the child.

Obviously, the amount of speech involved in play therapy with children is much less than in interviews with adults, but communication is no less important. Children communicate, however, more in symbolic acts than in language, and the clinician must be able to respond to such symbolic behavior with sensitivity and appropriateness.

An example is taken from the therapist's notes on the third play session with Dick, a sullen, withdrawn, five-year-old. During his first session, Dick had not spoken a word, but had played aimlessly in the sandpile or pounded the punching bag most of the time. In the second hour, he had chosen the finger paints, beginning very tentatively at first and then making gigantic scrawls with vivid colors. He had spoken to the therapist, asking about the paints and commenting that finger painting was fun, but again there was little direct conversation between the boy and his clinician.

> When he arrived for his third hour, Dick greeted the therapist in the waiting room, and while walking to the play room asked if the dolls were there. When told that they were, he rather anxiously asked, "Do boys ever play with 'em?" Once in the room, he went straight to the big doll house and began moving the dolls about, muttering rather violently to himself. Noticing that he

was working with two adult dolls, a little boy doll, and a baby doll, and knowing that such was the composition of Dick's own family, the therapist said, "Making a family, Dick?" The boy grunted affirmatively but looked rather furtively over his shoulder at the clinician during the next few minutes of play. The therapist responded to what he took to be some apprehension about the play by saying, "You can play whatever you like here, Dick." Dick's actions again became more violent. Finally, he caught up the mother doll, flung her against the wall of the doll house, shouted "There, you!" at the top of his voice, and then whirled on the therapist, trembling with strong feelings. The therapist said very calmly, "Sometimes you hate your mother very much, don't you, Dick?" Dick burst into tears, came to the clinician, and put his head in his lap.

This example is somewhat more dramatic and specific than many which occur in play therapy. It illustrates well, however, both the magnitude of children's problems, and the way in which a therapist must take his cues more from what the child's actions symbolize than from his direct conversation. The basic processes of therapy, nevertheless, are essentially the same for the child as for an adult. The child, like the adult, comes to perceive the therapist as a warm, calm, and nonpunitive person who accepts his worth and pays attention to him as a person. The child is permitted, even encouraged, to act out and express his anxious or hostile feelings in the presence of his secure relationship with the therapist. As a result the child's anxiety is extinguished and he is able to do without his self-defeating defenses.

RESULTS OF PSYCHOTHERAPY

The evaluation of psychotherapy appears at first glance to be a simple matter. One has only to ask the clients if they feel better as a result of their experience, or ask the therapists if their clients have improved. By and large, such inquiries yield positive results. Most clinicians and most clients seem convinced that the time, effort, and money spent on psychotherapy have been justified by the outcome.

Such answers are unlikely to satisfy scientists who prefer sounder and more stable evidence on which to base an evaluation. The appraisals of both clients and therapists may be warped by wishful perceptions. Social convention presses clients to show their appreciation of the attentions received from a professional person. Consequently, many clients may evaluate their therapists positively out of politeness and personal good will rather than on the basis of verifiable signs of enduring changes in personality.[32] Therapists, in turn, see their clients only in the interviews and have little basis for judging how well the improvement seen in the clinic has generalized to everyday life.[33]

Many studies have tabulated the percentage of clients who seemed to profit from psychotherapy, the improvement usually being judged by the therapists. In spite of their severe limitations, such data have at least a little value. Studies based on over 8,000 cases have shown with considerable uniformity that about two-thirds of the clients were judged to be cured, much improved, or improved; about one-third made little or no improvement.[34] Two small samples have been evaluated under much better controlled conditions. One group was given analytically oriented psychotherapy based on the teachings of H. S. Sullivan (p. 470), and was evaluated by other psychiatrists, not by the clients' own therapists. Of 25 clients, 17, or 68 per cent, were regarded as improved.[35] The other research group received client-centered therapy, and was evaluated by a multiple criterion which included both counselors' ratings and appropriate tests given before and after therapy, and again six months to one year later to appraise the stability of the gains. Here, too, 17 of 25 clients, 68 per cent, were regarded as improved and the remaining 8 as unimproved.[36] The conclusion seems well established that psychotherapy, as practiced by adherents of several different schools of theory, is evaluated as successful about two-thirds of the time.

The most serious shortcoming of the evaluations is the lack of a comparison group of persons who need psychotherapy but do not receive it. Common observations show that at least some neurotic and maladjusted people overcome their problems without professional help. How many? It is almost impossible to tell. Some figures have been cited which might cause psychotherapy to be regarded very pessimistically. Of psychoneurotic patients admitted to mental hospitals in the United States, 66 per cent are discharged as recovered or improved within one year.[37] An insurance company's study of 500 persons claiming disability for psychoneurosis, as diagnosed by general physicians, found that 72 per cent of them were back at work within two years.[38] These two groups of persons were given some care and treatment, but few if any of them received formal psychotherapy. Critics have suggested that these figures cast doubt on the value of psychotherapy.[39] No firm conclusions should be drawn, however, because two important factors are unknown — how severe the maladjustments were, and how strict a standard of improvement was used to define recovery. It is likely that the hospital and insurance cases were more badly maladjusted, and that the standards of recovery were more lax, than is true of clients given psychotherapy in clinics.[40] The same reasoning prevents us from concluding that psychoanalysis and client-centered therapy are equally effective when research studies using the two methods each judged that 68 per cent of its clients had improved.[41] We do not even know the directions of the differences between the groups in the severity of their initial maladjustments or the stringency of the criteria of improvement.

The evaluation of clinical work with children meets the same difficulties. An early but careful follow-up study at a child guidance clinic found that 48 per cent of the cases were successful and 31 per cent partly successful, a total of 79 per cent.[42] In comparison, another clinic made telephone inquiries concerning 72 children who had been on its waiting list for from several weeks to six months.[43] Fifty per cent of the cases were still troubled in some degree, and 24 per cent had secured help of one kind or another elsewhere. For the remaining 19 children, 26 per cent of the group, the parents reported that the problems had cleared up of their own accord or through family efforts.

An experiment for a valid appraisal of psychotherapy seems easy to design but is hard to carry out. Two groups of persons are selected who are comparable in the type and degree of their nonintegrative behavior and who are equally motivated for psychotherapy. One group is given help, the other not. Appropriate evaluative procedures — the person's own appraisal of himself, observations by interviewers and home visitors, and suitable tests — are given before psychotherapy, after its completion, and at follow-up periods for several years. The control group, which has no therapy, receives the same evaluations at the same intervals of time.

Some severe difficulties in executing such a study are apparent at once. If the members of the control group really need help, many of them will get it elsewhere, benefiting themselves but spoiling the experiment. There is a more subtle issue which wrecks the use of a conventional control group in experiments on psychotherapy. In appraising the effectiveness of a vaccine for a disease, for example, some subjects may be innoculated with the vaccine, others with water. The subjects, and the physicians who innoculate them, can be kept in ignorance of whether the vaccine or the water was injected. The situation is quite different for a person who applies for psychotherapy and is denied it. He knows all too well that he has been rejected, and the very rejection may increase his sense of hopelessness and make his nonintegrative behavior worse. It may someday be possible to compare one method of psychotherapy with another, but it may never be practicable to compare the effects of psychotherapy with the effects of "nothing."

In view of the great difficulties which beset a perfect evaluation of psychotherapy through research, studies that are less than perfect deserve attention. Such a study was conducted by C. R. Rogers and his associates at the University of Chicago.[44] One has to agree with the statement made by Rogers himself that it is not a good research in psychotherapy, just the best that there is. The Chicago study did not attempt to have a matched control group, but some useful comparisons were made. The research group was compared on some measures to a group of normal persons not matched for degree of maladjustment, but approximately matched for age, sex, occupation, and social class. A small subgroup of the clients was assessed, waited sixty days, was assessed again, and then began psychotherapy, giving an opportunity to see the changes which took place in two months without therapy after help had been promised. The more successfully counseled cases were compared with the less successful, and those who continued were compared with those who dropped out.

The self concepts of the successfully counseled clients changed in the direction of their own conceptions of an ideal self; the self concepts of unsuccessful cases and control subjects did not. The Thematic Apperception Test (p. 338) was scored for a measure of adjustment in terms of the ability of the central character of the TAT stories to solve his problems, the pleasant or unpleasant nature of the emotions attributed to the characters, the kinds of interpersonal relationships depicted, and the like. The scoring was done "blind," without the scorer knowing whose record he **was** appraising. Before therapy, the research clients were more severely disturbed than the normal persons as judged by the TAT, but they showed significant positive changes during psychotherapy which were maintained through the follow-up period. Two friends of each client rated the maturity of his behavior on a rating questionnaire. These ratings, useful as an entirely external measure unbiased by the clients or their therapists, showed a definite increase in the maturity of behavior of the clients rated as successful, but no increase for the unimproved cases. A large proportion of the clients who did not improve in psychotherapy were those identified by a questionnaire as conventional but hostile and suspicious toward other persons. Depressed, withdrawn, and anxious clients tended to make greater psychotherapeutic gains.

Data on the group which waited two months before beginning therapy led to useful conclusions.[45] At the beginning of the waiting period their scores on a specially devised self-rating technique were markedly inferior to those of the normal comparison group. The scores of these clients did not change during the two-month waiting period, but after therapy they improved considerably, their scores rising to the same level as those of the normal subjects. A six-month period after the end of therapy brought no decrease in their scores. All these findings from the Chicago studies suggest that psychotherapy makes some lasting differences.

Another study was concerned with six applicants for therapy who, after the waiting period, decided that they did not need it.[46] On a self-descriptive technique, these six persons obtained adjustment scores as high as those made by clients who had benefited from psychotherapy. But the ratings of their performance on the Thematic Apperception Test did not confirm their improvement. Most importantly, the self-description items on which they obtained their "good" scores included many — "I am ambitious," "I am superior," "I make strong demands on myself" — which suggested that they had strengthened their nonintegrative defenses by denying their need for help. This finding suggests that many poorly integrated people who seem to improve without therapy may do so by strengthening their defenses, not by reducing their anxieties.

One of the few studies of a therapeutic process which used a real control group was carried out with children in an orphanage.[47] The situation made it possible to match two groups, each of nine children, on several measures of adjustment and on a sociometric rating (p. 332) of how well they were liked by their peers. One group was given ten weeks of play therapy. Both immediately after the play therapy and fifteen weeks later, the adjustment scores and peer ratings of about half of the children who received the therapeutic experience improved. No child in the control group showed a gain.

The experimental investigations of psychotherapy, while suggestive, have shortcomings both in the small numbers of cases studied and in the limited scope of the procedures for evaluation and control. They do not provide strong positive evidence for the effectiveness of psychotherapy. But neither do any studies give clear proof that psychotherapy fails to achieve its goals. Until the issue is settled one way or the other by definitive research, both the available findings and the accumulated experience of clinicians warrant holding the hypothesis that psychotherapy is a useful method for helping people lead happier, more integrative lives. The ultimate test of this hypothesis remains a task for the future.

SUGGESTED READINGS

Introductory discussions of psychotherapy which supplement the present text are to be found in Chapter 18 of Cameron, *The Psychology of Behavior Disorders;* Chapters 17 and 18 of Klein, *Abnormal Psychology;* Chapter 17 of Lehner and Kube, *The Dynamics of Personal Adjustment;* and Chapters 9 and 10 of White, *The Abnormal Personality.*

Perhaps the best way to see what happens in psychotherapy is to read the transcripts of actual cases. Gill, Newman, and Redlich, *The Initial Interview in Psychiatric Practice*, and Snyder, *Casebook of Non-Directive Counseling* are particularly useful on this score. Case excerpts from a number of different kinds of therapeutic approaches are given in most of the chapters of McCary and Sheer, *Six Approaches to Psychotherapy.*

Dollard and Miller, *Personality and Psychotherapy* illustrates its systematic theory of psychotherapy by a running account of a single case. A number of psychotherapeutic theories and research studies are presented in Mowrer, *Psychotherapy: Theory and Research,* a book that is not easy but will prove valuable to serious students.

For more information on play therapy, see Axline, *Play Therapy,* and Moustakas, *Children in Play Therapy.*

CHAPTER **17**

Applications of
Positive Mental
Hygiene

The scope of mental hygiene is not limited to the work of clinics, or to the diagnosis and treatment of persons who are already maladjusted. In a very real sense, everyone is engaged in mental hygiene whether he intends it or not. In this respect, mental hygiene is like other endeavors that are intimately concerned with human welfare. All the fire departments in the country could not extinguish the conflagrations which would ensue if people in general were not careful to prevent fires. Physicians and hospitals could not cope with disease if individuals did not assume responsibility for their own health and that of their communities. If all persons who deal with others, especially parents, teachers, and employers, were governed by the requirements for mental health there would be fewer unhappy and inadequate personalities for clinicians to treat. The constructive measures designed to develop effective personalities are termed *positive mental hygiene*. No unique principles are needed for the positive applications, because the theories developed throughout this book pertain as much to persons who adjust well as to those who adjust poorly.

It is often assumed that only good intentions and common sense are needed to bring about successful outcomes of human problems. This is a half-truth. Many well-adjusted persons lived in the centuries before any scientific study of human behavior began. Such people owed their good fortune to the vague and intuitive formulations of mental hygiene practices that have always existed in folk-lore, religion, and tradition. The need for the scientific study of human problems exists, nonetheless. A century or more ago, sick people were often bled in a vain attempt to cure their illnesses. Modern medicine recognizes that bleeding is generally futile and usually harmful. But children are beaten and scolded even today because parents still in the dark ages of mental hygiene believe that these are effective ways to control their conduct. Some of mental hygiene is as old as the Bible and has existed as long as there have been kind and understanding persons. Other principles of equal importance directly contradict the traditional beliefs of even the wisest of grandmothers.

The layman's role in mental hygiene is exactly analogous to the part he plays with respect to physical health. Parents and teachers do not treat serious physical illnesses, but must know how to recognize their presence in order to call a physician in time. In providing proper food, cleanliness, sleep, and exercise, on the other hand, the parent has a primary responsibility. As far as severe disorders of personality are concerned, laymen need only to know how to recognize them, to regard them with constructive rather than moralistic attitudes, and to seek such expert assistance as may be available. In dealing with the everyday situations in which children learn to cope with their life problems, parents and teachers can contribute directly to the growth of effective personalities. Also, just as parents bind up the child's little wounds of physical injury, so they may give some remedial help to the simpler, more common conflicts and anxieties.

Any attempt to describe all of the applications of mental hygiene to everyday life would be presumptuous, for two reasons. First, we do not know enough about many of the problems of mental health. Recommendations must therefore be tentative until further research has extended the frontiers of knowledge. Second, the problems of the fields of application are complex, and even an account of these problems without their final solutions would require a volume for each field. In a limited space, little more can be done than to suggest some ways in which the psychology of adjustment bears on the problems met by teachers, employers, social workers, and parents. Readers whose interests lie in one of these special fields can obtain further information from books cited in the suggested readings.

MENTAL HYGIENE AND EDUCATION

The aims of education and of mental hygiene are basically the same, namely, the development of persons who can live effective and satisfying lives in society. Public opinion and the judgments of educational philosophers agree that the most significant results of education are the generalized learnings and attitudes that enable a person to attack his life problems more successfully, rather than the specific skills and bits of information that he acquires. The school's responsibility is not limited to intellectual training. The child comes to school as a whole, and it is impossible to separate his intellectual functions from his emotions and his personal and social adjustments. Modern education has had to recognize the greater scope of its task. Years ago, when hours and terms were shorter, there was perhaps more justification for the school limiting itself to verbal learning. The pupil, in a relatively simpler environment, obtained his most important educational experiences out of school. Today the school takes a third or more of the student's waking hours, changed laws and customs make almost every youth attend until nearly an adult, and increasing urbanization makes the school assume many duties formerly carried by the home. The more central place of the school in our society has to be met with an increased concern for the child's general welfare.

The school has two responsibilities for mental hygiene. One task is to rid itself of practices that contribute to pupil maladjustment, and to provide resources to discover and help pupils already in difficulties. The school's duties are not limited to such negative virtues, however. A greater need is to insure that education will be a positive and constructive influence in the life of every student. All functions of the school, including the curriculum, provision for individual differences, the handling of conduct problems, and individual guidance can be made to contribute to these ends.

Mental Hygiene Hazards in School

School experiences sometimes have a detrimental effect on students' adjustments, whereas they should be constructive and integrative. An example familiar to every teacher, whether in elementary school, high school, or college, is the student who seems unable to learn in spite of adequate mental ability. Scoldings, threats of failure, and even well-meaning attempts to help by intensive tutoring, all seem ineffective. Accumulated experience, and the results of some research studies, indicate that three factors contribute to special disabilities in school subjects. The first component is primarily educational. An inflexible school curriculum, which attempts to teach every child in the same way, is not well adapted to individual pupils. A minority of students may fail to learn when taught by methods that are successful, or at least tolerable, for the majority. A second factor is the attachment of anxiety to school in general or to a particular subject because of emotional experiences within the school. A pupil whose initial difficulties with a subject are met by threats or punishments may be overwhelmed by fear whenever he encounters it again. The third component, a severe and common one, is the effect of home-grown anxieties on school work. The three factors are rarely found in isolation. All three are usually present in some degree, but their relative significance varies from one student to another.

When school failure is due primarily to shortcomings of the teaching process, straightforward educational treatment is often successful. Educational psychologists have devised diagnostic tests to determine exactly where the progress of learning has gone astray, and methods for remedial instruction designed to meet individual needs.[1] Such techniques are well developed for the major skills of the elementary school: reading, arithmetic, and spelling. At the high school and college levels some students fail because they do not know how to study or how to solve problems independently. They can be helped by individually planned retraining in study methods, but not by mere exhortation and advice. The cure of school disabilities can be a useful tool for mental hygiene. A youngster who is failing in school suffers a loss of self-esteem, and may be goaded by his teachers and parents and ridiculed by his peers. Relieving his academic difficulties reduces his anxiety and makes him free to undertake more constructive adjustments in other areas of living.

School problems that spring from acquired anxieties are perplexing to teachers and of special interest to mental hygiene. Such anxieties may arise from a large variety of causes. Ridicule and overt punishment, experienced in connection with a subject, are the most obvious sources. Somewhat more subtle are perfectionistic attitudes on the part of teachers or parents. No matter how hard the child tries, he is always reproached for not doing well enough. A parent's anxiety about a child, or a teacher's, may evoke anxiety in the child himself. If the mother is defensive about her own social position, she may have an inordinate need for her son to stand first in his class. Her constant inquiries about his progress and her pressures upon him to work harder make the child doubt his own ability. A well-meaning but inexperienced teacher sometimes sees a child who has a little difficulty in learning to read as a challenge to her professional status. By showing her own anxiety and by going after the pupil with excessive zeal, she intimidates him instead of helping him.

Home conflicts may have similar but often more far-reaching effects. Gates cites an example:

> A boy had been sent to a progressive school on the insistence of the mother and despite the opposition of the father. The mother contended that the progressive school would provide more fruitful education whereas the father predicted that no good would come out of the new-fangled ideas. He maintained in particular that the child would fool around most of the time and not learn to read and write and do his arithmetic. Once the pupil had started going to the progressive school the anxious mother tended to nag him to do well, particularly to read well. The father continually sought for evidence that the boy was doing poorly. The boy thus found himself the center of a conflict between the parents. The boy fluctuated between periods in which he appeared to be learning to read reasonably well and periods when he seemed to have forgotten what he had previously learned and was unable to learn any more. The boy really wanted to please both parents. At first, he alternated from a favorable to an unfavorable attitude and eventually he became confused. The pupil thereafter made uncertain progress and was reported as a reading disability. Fortunately, in this case after studying the motivating conditions in the home and in the school, the examiner discovered the vital factors. When the situation was explained to the parents and all was understood and forgiven, the boy proceeded to learn rapidly and well.[*]

---

[*] A. I. Gates. *The improvement of reading.* (3rd ed.) New York: Macmillan, 1947. Pp. 110-111. By permission of the Macmillan Company.

The effects of the anxiety evoked by a school situation are like those of any strong emotional drive. The anxiety becomes the prepotent motivation, and any response that serves to reduce or control it is reinforced. In a few instances the drive of anxiety may lead to superior school achievement instead of disability, but usually at the expense of fulfilling other motivations. The overdriven student then becomes a perfectionistic scholar at the cost of not being a well-rounded person. More often, the anxiety will be controlled by an avoidance response. If the very sight of the material of a school subject arouses anxiety, the student will naturally try to get it out of the focus of his attention. A student who is "inattentive" or who "cannot concentrate" is almost always escaping from the painful material before him into less disagreeable realms of fantasy. Social pressures and his own aspirations keep him coming back to school, however, and he is caught in the dilemma of an approach-avoidance conflict which keeps him stirred up. In some other cases, a school disability may be more satisfying than punishing. A child who is in rebellious conflict with a dominating parent can retaliate and defeat the parent's aims by becoming a disgraceful failure at school. He also reaps secondary gains from the attention given him as a "poor problem child." Only a thorough solution of the conflict between parent and child is likely to bring about improvement in school.

It is hazardous to generalize about the treatment of disabilities in school subjects. The causes are varied, and each demands its individually planned remedy. Many of the less stubborn cases of reading disability are handled successfully by remedial specialists in school systems and reading clinics. In recognition of the importance of emotional problems in reading, more trust is now placed in a relaxed and permissive atmosphere and less on the remedial drill materials which were popular a few decades ago. The first step is to establish a relationship between child and worker so that the child feels accepted and knows that he will not be punished for failures. When he feels comfortable a youngster will usually make some efforts to read, because the motivation to read is strong in our culture. Easy materials, rewards for small achievements, and the complete absence of threat can get him started. When self-confidence and motivation are established, some students make rapid progress in reading and other school subjects without formal remedial teaching. Others need supplementary help with the aid of materials and devices to counteract their particular handicaps.

When school difficulties are linked to pervasive conflicts or deepseated anxieties, psychotherapeutic approaches are needed. Play therapy for younger children may relieve anxiety and hence, by reducing the drives for defense or escape, make them again free to learn.[2] In a pair of supplementary experiments, R. E. Bills showed that a group of retarded readers with personality problems improved through the use of group and individual play therapy, without the introduction of any remedial reading techniques.[3] A group of "welladjusted" poor readers, in contrast, showed no gain in reading skill after play therapy. Therapy is therefore no panacea for school problems, but must be used discriminatingly with an understanding of the individual student's needs. High school and college students who are failing because of deficiencies in basic reading skills are likely to need psychotherapeutic counseling before they are ready to profit from a direct approach to their educational problems.[4] The most important gain from the therapy is general personal readjustment, but the relief of educational handicaps is a relevant and helpful by-product.

Positive Contributions to Mental Hygiene

Everyone agrees that education should make positive contributions to the personal adjustments of students. The cure or even the prevention of educational difficulties is not enough. School experiences can help students develop attitudes, insights, and skills which enable them to meet life problems more integratively and with a minimum of preventable anxiety. Several modern developments in education have tended to make schools more effective agencies for positive mental hygiene. The changes have been gradual, and much still remains to be achieved.

Among recent trends in education, perhaps the most significant for mental hygiene is an increased emphasis on interpersonal relationships. Teachers pay more attention to students as individuals, are more aware of their needs and personalities, and have more respect for them as persons. These attitudes on the part of teachers are in marked contrast to certain all-too-prevalent customs of the past, in which teachers concentrated on subject matter and were coldly impersonal toward pupils or, even worse, regarded students with a hostile eye as threats to their authority. The ideal of the modern teacher is one who teaches students, not subjects. The attitude of the teacher therefore has some resemblance to that of a psychotherapist. The teacher observes and listens to the students' feelings, and communicates an acceptance of them as worth-while persons. An accepting attitude does not mean, as some mistaken opponents have suggested, that teachers must ignore or reward a pupil's wrong answers to intellectual problems. It is possible to label a student's response as incorrect and help him seek a better one without rejecting the learner himself and labeling him stupid or bad. A warm interpersonal relationship breeds confidence, avoids anxiety, and promotes sounder learning. In a sense, there is nothing new in defining the pupil-teacher relationship as a personally significant one. Great teachers, from kindergarten to college, have always done so, and their sensitivity to interpersonal relationships is the major factor that has made them great. The recent trend is a more explicit recognition of the personal quality of education, and its extension to the work of a greater number of teachers.

Schools can also contribute to mental hygiene by giving attention to the interpersonal relationships of students with their peers. It has been shown throughout this book that personal adjustments are social adjustments, that life's great satisfactions as well as its crucial conflicts come from relationships between persons. Learning to live with other people is therefore one of the major tasks of psychological development. Gaining a friend, being accepted by a peer group or, on the negative side, behaving so as to make all the other youngsters hostile, may have a greater effect on a pupil's life than most of the things he learns from the academic aspects of school.[5] The conventional procedures of the classroom have been modified so as to provide for social learning. The older emphasis on the strictly individual nature of school work regarded any collaboration between students as close to "cheating." Modern education, in contrast, uses group projects, committee work, and class discussions extensively. The self-chosen social groups of pupils, their gangs and cliques, are not regarded as a menace to classroom management but are used as a basis for effective group work. School clubs, athletic teams, and other extracurricular activities, when examined in terms of mental hygiene, are not educational frills but are means for giving students an opportunity to learn interpersonal adjustments.

On the premise that the development of a well-balanced personality is at least as important as the mastery of subject matter, many educators have advocated basic changes in the concept of the school curriculum. At the elementary school level, large units of subject matter, originating from the interests of the pupils and rich in developmental possibilities, have been used to replace a large part of the conventional routine of separate school subjects. In such projects, pupils of the first grade may be found studying community life with emphasis on food supply; a sixth grade may spend a large part of a year investigating the history of how man has made and used written records. Educational tests have shown that pupils gain as thorough a mastery of basic educational skills through such a curriculum as from a conventional one. The chief advantage of the approach, however, is that it teaches children to live by giving them practice in living, in place of the less effective device of making them store up information supposedly for later use. This type of curriculum recognizes that mental hygiene is not an area or subject of school study, but is an aim that permeates all educational activities. At higher educational levels, in secondary school and college, the curriculum can achieve mental hygiene by activities appropriate to the more mature developmental levels. Units of study on community life, personal adjustments, and family living, and the use of home-room or guidance periods for free discussion, can provide opportunities for students to grow as whole persons.

Can a conventional curriculum make direct contributions to mental health? For generations it was believed that the broader aims of education were achieved automatically by the study of traditional school subjects. Reasoning in arithmetic or geometry was supposed to increase the ability to reason in real-life situations. By mastering studies of great difficulty, the pupil was assumed to gain strength of "will," that is, of his ability to tolerate immediate discomforts for the sake of distant rewards. This belief was known as the doctrine of formal discipline. If it were well founded, the gains to mental hygiene through the improvement of "reason" and "will" would be obvious. Experimental studies early in the twentieth century dealt serious blows to faith in formal discipline.[6] It was demonstrated that practice in memorizing does not improve memory in general, that drill in arithmetic reasoning causes little improvement in the ability to solve nonarithmetical problems, and that little relationship exists between the difficulty of a school subject and the general intellectual gain that may result from studying it. Such evidence caused many educators to despair of improving general qualities of character and personality through formal school studies.

The negative findings led to a redefinition of the problem of achieving the wider aims of education. Essentially the issue is one of generalization in learning (p. 71) or of transfer of training, that is, of the extent to which the reinforcement of one response can affect the performance of other responses. Further experiments have tried to discover the conditions which will increase the amount of transfer from specific school learning to broader life problems. Two conclusions seem supported by the evidence. First, in order for transfer to be appreciable students must be taught widely applicable procedures and generalizations as they arise in school studies. Second, they must practice the application of these principles to a great variety of problems so that the generalizations are not perceived as tied only to a particular subject matter. An example may be drawn from one of the early experiments.[7] Pupils were given training in neatness in connection with arithmetic, not merely by insisting on neat work, but by group discussion of the value of neatness in dress, business, the home, and other real-life situations. These students improved in neatness in their other school studies. In contrast, another group of students who were only rewarded and punished for their neatness or lack of it in arithmetic without any attempt to generalize the instruction, showed no improvement in their other subjects. Similar results have been found by experiments on the transfer of reasoning ability from the study of mathematics and science.

Principles governing the improvement of transfer of training have important implications for mental hygiene. School subjects can contribute to mental health when they effectively teach general understandings which are applied to a variety of genuinely relevant situations in the students' lives. The study of literature can give insight into human difficulties and their solutions and can help a student understand the motives and behavior of other people and of himself. History can teach the origins and functions of social institutions that perplex the youngster. Mathematics and science can be made the basis for understanding orderly processes of thinking and the processes of cause and effect. Education in writing and speaking can help a student to express his ideas and feelings more freely and clearly. By proper adaptation to the abilities and needs of students of various degrees of maturity, values such as these can be achieved at all levels of education. But it must be emphasized again that the conventional teaching of subjects for their own sakes does little to advance the growth of healthy personalities. Only when the primary attention is directed to the learner and his needs, and when school subjects are regarded primarily as tools for the development of persons, can education contribute to mental health.

The Hygiene of Individual Differences

A common source of maladjustment is the discrepancy between the achievement of a student and what is demanded of him. Conventional schools require all pupils to study the same curriculum in the same way and apply the same yardstick to their attainments. Even a course of study well adapted to a majority of students will be beyond the comprehension of some of the class and too elementary to excite effort from another portion. While many school disabilities are remediable, as described in a preceding section, there are always students who cannot keep up with the requirements of an inflexible curriculum because of relatively unmodifiable limitations of intellect or because of cultural handicaps beyond the reach of the school. Conventional education has no technique for coping with backward pupils except to fail them and make them repeat grades or subjects.

Failure in school is always frustrating and may evoke intense conflicts. Well-learned social motives for approval and mastery come into conflict with the need to escape from the painful effects of failure. Such conflicts are augmented when there are strong home pressures to excel. Students adjust to school failure by many different mechanisms. The adjustments perhaps least harmful to mental health are made by rationalizing which belittles the value of school and blames failure on the teachers, and by compensating through satisfactions obtained out of school. Such adjustments preserve the integrity of the student's personality to the detriment of his education. In other instances, the adjustments are less fortunate. Withdrawn, self-blaming, and anxious attitudes may be evoked which persist into adult life. Or the pupil becomes hostile and aggressive against the adult-governed world which denies him legitimate satisfactions. Although delinquency is caused by very complex patterns of cultural factors, inflexible schools play their part in its development. Studies consistently show that more than a random share of juvenile delinquents are truant, are retarded in school, or are deficient in tests of achievement. By making these students anxious or defensive, the school has given them positive mistraining in nonintegrative adjustments. While seeking to give them an education, the inflexible school has in reality prevented them from being educated.

The dull are not the only ones who suffer from the discrepancy between abilities and the demands for achievement. Average and even superior students may experience similar conflicts when more is expected of them than they can fulfill. Very bright youngsters are also educationally maladjusted in the conventional school, because a curriculum designed for the average child may not stimulate them to make the most of their abilities. They are less likely to use mechanisms of escape or defense than are dull children, partly because they experience considerable success and praise, and partly because the curriculum retains many features from the past when education was only for the elite. Still, gifted pupils often develop negligent attitudes when they have to sit through boresome lessons, and may escape into daydreaming.

School marks and pressures for competitive achievement are now viewed as hazards to mental health. Praise and encouragement are better incentives than failure or punishment. In an old but still valid experiment, Hurlock compared the achievement of two groups of children in arithmetic, one group being praised daily for good accomplishment, the other scolded.[8] The reproved group gained after one scolding but decreased in achievement thereafter, while continued praise resulted in improvement throughout the entire period of the experiment. The duller children, who in an older moralistic sense "deserved" reproof the most, were most favorably affected by praise.

Many progressive school systems have tried to adapt curricular and administrative procedures to individual differences. Such innovations have usually been justified on the grounds of educational efficiency, but the requirements of mental hygiene provide an even stronger reason for the differentiation of instruction according to abilities. Various methods have been devised to accomplish this end, which are described in detail in books on education. One procedure, widely advocated some years ago, is to place the pupils in sections according to ability which then study the same subject matter at different rates of progress or undertake different curricula

562 *Applications of Positive Mental Hygiene*

suited to the needs of each group. The results of homogeneous grouping have not been entirely satisfactory for several reasons. Most serious for mental hygiene is an adverse effect on child and parent morale. It is almost impossible to conceal which groups are fast and slow, and to be placed in the backward group becomes almost as bad a stigma as failure. Also, groups homogeneous with respect to one school subject, such as reading, may still be widely scattered in capacity for other subjects, such as arithmetic, because abilities in various branches of the curriculum are far from perfectly correlated. The best regarded method at present is for the teacher to give individually differentiated tasks to each child, based on a detailed knowledge of his aspirations and abilities. There remain many school projects in which groups of students can work together for the sake of social learning, with each pupil contributing according to his ability. At the high school and college levels, various programs of study allow for individual directions and standards of attainment. These differentiations are most efficient when personal guidance is available to help a student choose a field in which he can meet his needs successfully. Adequate provisions for individual differences at all levels aid schools to accomplish their primary objective, the development of effective, socialized and well-balanced persons.

The Hygiene of Discipline

The original conception of a disciplined person was one whose actions are controlled and integrated, who is able to exert his efforts purposively and with a self-directed orderliness. This true concept of discipline is substantially identical to integrative adjustment. The development of a truly disciplined person is therefore an important aim both of education and mental hygiene.

Unfortunately, the term discipline has become corrupted to mean an orderliness of conduct repressively imposed by authority, and "to discipline" has even become synonymous with "to punish." The misconception is a survival of an outmoded notion that discipline in the original sense is achieved only through pain and deprivation. This ascetic philosophy has almost disappeared from modern life, yet many schools perpetuate it unwittingly, perhaps because teachers trained in an authoritarian tradition find it easier to suppress pupils than to guide them.

Even in its narrower meaning of orderly conduct, discipline presents many problems of interest to mental hygiene. Misconduct in school is a common basis of interpersonal strife between teacher and student or among students, and hence becomes a source of conflicts. As with many other issues, conduct problems are better understood by an analysis of their various causes. Some arise from faults of the school curriculum and from the attitudes of teachers. A certain amount of disorder in a classroom is healthful. A hard-working group is never entirely quiet, for some moving around and communicating are needed for cooperative work. In well-run schools the bustle of highly motivated activity takes the place of enforced quiet. In a conventional school, the poorly motivated pupil's attention drifts away from tasks he does not understand or like. His activity drives are then evidenced by restlessness, noisiness, and more attractive occupations such as scuffling with a neighbor. The cure for these minor infractions of discipline is not suppression or punishment, but changes in the curriculum and in the teachers' attitudes toward pupils which eliminate some of the petty disorders and ignore the rest.

As perfect a curriculum as can be devised will not eliminate all conduct problems, for some pupils will continue to behave in ways that disrupt constructive educational activities. Such forms of misconduct are symptoms; they are indicators of how the child feels and what he needs.[9] A youngster who is dominating, hostile, or bullying to other children is telling us that he is unsure of himself, that he wants to feel important and does not quite know how to do it. One who clowns, grimaces, throws things, and foments disorder is loudly proclaiming his need to be noticed, perhaps to be appreciated and loved. The truant is saying that school is unbearable and that he must escape it. Teachers who understand the messages these symptoms convey can often help provide the security, appreciation, or satisfaction that the youngster lacks. Merely punishing the disapproved conduct provides no real or lasting solutions. With school conduct problems, as with other nonintegrative adjustments, the underlying conflicts and personality traits have to be treated, not the symptoms.

More serious and persistent conduct problems often need help beyond the resources of a teacher. Some school systems now have psychologists or guidance clinics within their own organizations and others use community clinics. Teachers may do a considerable service for mental hygiene by recognizing maladjustments early in their course of development and by cooperating with clinics in their study and treatment. Teachers are also beginning to recognize the needs for mental hygiene of children who are not troublesome — the unsocial, withdrawn, overdependent, and suspicious.

The Adjustment of the Teacher

The quality of the school's influence for mental hygiene is determined in no small measure by the personal characteristics of its teachers. A teacher who is secure, warm, accepting, and genuinely perceptive of students as persons may have a most favorable influence upon them, even in spite of other shortcomings as an educator. On the unfortunate side, teachers whose personalities evoke anxious or defensive behavior in pupils can wreck the best-planned curricular provisions for mental health. Some teachers are hostile toward pupils, bully them, and have to assert their own authority by physical domination and sarcastic and critical comments. Other teachers are lacking in emotional control, fly into a rage at misdemeanors, or become "nervous" and excessively sensitive to the difficulties of the classroom. Still others may appeal to the class for sympathy, grant special favors to win approval, or shower affection on one or two pupils while neglecting the rest. All of these forms of teacher behavior are harmful to the integrative adjustments of their students.

It must be remembered that teachers are human beings and, like all others, have their own problems of personal adjustment. They are subject to all the common influences that determine the mental health of people in our culture, in childhood development and in the circumstances of adult living. In addition, the teaching profession has its distinctive assets and liabilities. Many features of teaching are conducive to positive mental health. Teaching is socially useful work of which its participants can feel proud; it provides varied and interesting tasks and opportunities for creativeness.[10] Teaching is a relatively continuous and secure occupation, less subject than most others to the ups and downs of economic prosperity. The profession of teaching also has its special hazards. To deal with a classroom full of lively youngsters all day is a difficult and fatiguing task, requiring more intense and sustained attention than almost any other work. Although the teacher's day seems short to laymen, a multiplicity of professional and routine tasks requires many afternoon and evening hours each week. Teachers are often poorly prepared for all the demands made upon them, which creates a need to be defensive. Low salaries, which often have to be supplemented by part-time work out of school, and the often unhonored status of teachers in the community also lower their self-esteem. Unmarried teachers away from home frequently live in rooming houses and lack the integrating influences of family and community life. Women teachers may suffer conflicts about marriage, sex, and their social role, or else if married must assume the dual burden of homemaking and professional work.

Maintaining the mental health of teachers requires that the assets of their profession be used fully and the shortcomings minimized. The morale of teachers is increased, and their professional competence as well, by giving them a full share of responsibility for educational planning. Panels and committees may plan curricula, select instructional materials, and participate in other educational decisions. Such activities emphasize the creative features and the social values of teaching. The opposite effects are produced by arbitrary and authoritative actions on the part of administrators and school boards. When a teacher feels insecure, rejected, or suppressed, he will almost inevitably displace his hostility to the students. Adequate salaries, secure tenure, and integration with the community also bolster mental health. Teachers, like pupils, need to be recognized as persons, and to have someone with whom they can discuss their feelings. It is therefore part of the task of a supervisor or administrator to have an ear for listening and some skill in human relationships. Reprimands and orders are no more effective for an overanxious teacher who has blundered than for an overanxious pupil. Some schools are able to provide consultation services for teachers who need personal help.

Because personal qualifications are so important in education, special attention has to be given to them in the selection and training of teachers. Selection has some value, and at least as much care must be taken to choose sound personalities as to choose good intellects. Well planned vocational guidance can steer some potential misfits away from teaching, for few persons want to enter an occupation for which they know they are poorly qualified. The selection of teachers cannot solve the whole problem, however, for several reasons. Screening methods are imperfect and only the most severely handicapped are likely to be discovered. Also, persons who are tolerably well adjusted when they start teaching may develop difficulties later.

The education of teachers can contribute to their effectiveness as persons. The aims of education for personal development are to guide the students to understand and accept themselves, to gain security and confidence in interpersonal relations, and to develop constructive attitudes toward their future pupils. These purposes cannot be accomplished through conventional lectures and required readings. The most effective methods bear some resemblance to group psychotherapy, involving a permissive atmosphere which makes them free to express their feelings and to solve their problems through the insights developed in group discussion. Attitudes are as important in the education of teachers as are scholarship and skill, perhaps more so. Yet old-fashioned scholars continue to object to the attitude-forming aspects of educational curricula because of a belief, akin to faith in mental discipline, that if teachers were only more profound scholars in their subject fields all other virtues would follow automatically. No one belittles the value of sound scholarship, but the evidence shows that attitudes which facilitate mental health are not invariably associated with it.

Today's teacher has to be a specialist in mental hygiene as well as in subject matter and method. Consequently, schools of education are giving increasing recognition to the place of mental hygiene in the curricula for prospective teachers. One important aim in teacher education is to promote the formulation of attitudes, as already described. But attitudes alone are not enough. Teachers must also develop informed sensitivity and skill to enable them to work constructively with pupils. To be effective, mental hygiene training has to be thorough; a little knowledge leads to a danger against which teachers must be on guard. Every minor classroom problem may become a "case," which is "diagnosed" and "treated" by the partly-trained teacher who possesses more enthusiasm than judgment and skill. Such attitudes may do more harm than good, because pupils and parents become unduly alarmed by the teacher's misguided zeal. Further education and maturity can help teachers to differentiate the transient problems that will take care of themselves, the minor difficulties that are best helped by a warm and simple understanding, and the more serious maladjustments that need referral for professional treatment.

MENTAL HYGIENE IN INDUSTRY

Vocational Adjustment

Almost every adult devotes a major part of his activity and interest to the occupation in which he earns his living. A successful vocational adjustment is therefore a strongly integrative factor in the lives of most men and of many women. Success in a job not only insures one's economic existence, but provides many other satisfactions as well. In the American culture, a man's occupation and his achievement in it are major determiners of his social status and hence of his self-esteem. Socially learned motivations for approval, pre-eminence, and security are satisfied by a good vocational adjustment.

In view of the central position of work in our society, the extent of vocational dissatisfaction is of concern to mental hygiene. Vocational maladjustment is shown in many ways, and no one figure gives a comprehensive appraisal of it. One convenient and objective index that casts some light on the lack of satisfaction of men with their jobs is the amount of labor turnover. In the nineteen-fifties, a period of relative stability, the number of men separated each year from their jobs in manufacturing industries was about 45 per cent of the total number employed.[11] Voluntary separation, in which the men quit their jobs of their own choice, amounted to about 25 per cent annually. The rate of turnover varies, of course, from a much smaller figure in some industries and companies to several hundred per cent in some others. Absenteeism and tardiness at work also express dissatisfaction. About 25 per cent of men in industry are absent at some time each month, and the average loss of working time due to absence is about 10 days a year. Stronger but less quantitative evidence of occupational maladjustment is found in the results of employee surveys which show a large proportion of workers dissatisfied with various features of their jobs, even when they do not quit.

Many workers in business and industry suffer from maladjustments sufficiently severe to be classed as psychoneuroses. An example may be drawn from a careful survey of a sample of 3,000 industrial workers in Great Britain reported by the Industrial Health Research Board.[12] The study found that over 25 per cent of sickness absence was due to neurosis, and that about 10 per cent of the employees examined suffered from disabling neurosis at the time of the survey. The women workers showed twice as high an incidence as the men, probably because of the dual pressures arising from a combination of homemaking responsibilities with industrial jobs. Earlier surveys had revealed a similar state of affairs among department store employees in the United States.[13] From 20 to 25 per cent of the workers suffered from evident symptoms of psychological disturbance. In general, personally maladjusted workers are inefficient workers. Not only are they absent more frequently, but they are rated as less satisfactory by their supervisors, and typically have poorer sales or production records. Psychological distress therefore has implications for the employer as well as for the employee.

The patterns of maladjustment shown by industrial workers are the same as those found among other people. These behaviors have been noted for many years, but their psychological significance has not been recognized. Defensive adjustments are common. Bullying attitudes on the part of executives and foremen are readily recognized as compensations. Personal peculiarities may serve as attention-getting mechanisms. Rationalization is evident in chronic fault-finding and in the blaming of others. Another variety of personnel problem is represented by the overdependent person whose feelings are hurt when he does not receive special consideration, and who constantly worries about his acceptability to others. Daydreamers who escape from frustration into fantasy present special problems of industrial safety and efficiency. The more severe mechanisms of hysteria and the nonadjustive anxiety states account for much illness and absenteeism. The so-called occupational neuroses, described in Chapter 9, are hysterical symptoms closely related to vocational maladjustments. Excessive fatigue, diffuse bodily complaints, and "nervousness" are frequent evidences of the anxiety evoked by unreduced conflicts. Somewhat less common, but sure to be met in any large organization, are delusional beliefs of being spied upon or discriminated against. In short, the entire gamut of maladjustments may be found in a store or factory, just as in a school or community. The whole person comes to work, and it is impossible to separate his purely economic self from the other aspects of his personality.

Sources of Vocational Maladjustment

Vocational maladjustments spring from many sources. Until recent years, it was assumed that all occupational dissatisfaction was due either to something wrong with the job itself or to some fault of the worker's competency. These are indeed factors of great importance. Much job dissatisfaction results from too low wages, from unbearable working conditions, and from fatigue and monotony. The activities of labor unions, Federal and state legislation, and actions by far-sighted employers have done much to ameliorate such conditions. Lack of sufficient ability to fulfill the requirements of a job also accounts for a portion of discontent and turnover. Modern industrial personnel practices, which use interviews, ratings, and tests to match new employees with the requirements of positions, have made constructive contributions. An equally important branch of industrial psychology has given attention to fitting the job to the worker by designing machines better suited to human capabilities, and modifying work procedures to reduce fatigue, hazards, and boredom.

Another important cause of vocational maladjustment, and a remediable one, arises from defects in social organization and interpersonal relations often found in large-scale industry.[14] In the crafts and smaller factories of a few generations ago, working groups were stable and men learned through long apprenticeship to understand the attitudes of their co-workers and to work on common tasks with good morale. The employer, too, was a familiar figure who knew each worker as a person and who was willing to talk with him about human as well as technical problems. In contrast, large-scale industry often ties a man to a machine so that he has little sense of common purpose with his fellow workers. Mobility and technical changes may prevent him from establishing enduring relationships. Management is distant, abstract, and inaccessible to communication. Workers may adjust to the cold impersonality by gaining their greatest satisfaction away from their jobs, and treating their employment as a burden to be endured with only perfunctory effort. In other instances, work frustration evokes hostility which is expressed by absenteeism, low productivity, and turnover. Employees who lack a sense of cooperation and communication are unhappy themselves, uncongenial to their fellow workers, and inefficient in production. They fail to gain the motive satisfactions that creative and socially useful work can supply.

Much vocational dissatisfaction is due to a third cause, the presence of general personal maladjustment. Unhappiness and ineffectiveness in work may not be caused by the vocational situation itself, but by the home-grown conflicts which the worker brings with him. Such adjustive difficulties do not require extended description because they are identical with the nonintegrative mechanisms described throughout this book. A man whose life history has prevented him from establishing secure and warm relationships with other people will respond to the world as a dangerous place. He therefore cannot trust his employer or co-workers, and adjusts to them by cautious withdrawal to protect himself or by defensive hostility. A common cause of vocational difficulty is an overemotional reaction to authority. If a man has never achieved a mature adjustment to his own father he may, by generalization, respond to all authority figures such as employers and foremen with nonintegrative responses ranging from panic to rebellion.

The three varieties of causes of vocational maladjustment do not, of course, act in isolation. All of them may be present in a single worker's experience, and they interact in complex ways. The effect may be cumulative, as when relatively low job aptitude, poor social communication, and pre-existing maladjustment may make unbearable a situation that could have been endured if only one or two of the three factors had been present. Conversely, a favorable work situation may have an integrative influence on the life of a person whose earlier adjustments have been disturbed.

Improving Mental Health in Industry

There are three principal ways in which mental hygiene may be applied to prevent or reduce personal maladjustments in industry. One is the provision of counseling services to which employees may appeal voluntarily to talk about their difficulties within the industry and their personal problems outside of work. A second industrial function that serves mental hygiene is adequate provision for the selection, guidance, and training of personnel. Third, and in many ways more fundamental, is the organization of industry to promote human values and to give recognition to the worth of employees as persons.

Many businesses and industries in recent years have provided the services of counselors whose chief function has been the maintenance of good personal adjustment among employees.[15] An employee counselor uses the same general principles that apply to any other field of counseling. Elton Mayo* has summarized some rules of practice that govern the industrial counselor:

1. Give your whole attention to the person interviewed, and make it evident that you are doing so.
2. Listen — don't talk.
3. Never argue; never give advice.
4. Listen to:
    (a) What he wants to say.
    (b) What he does not want to say.
    (c) What he cannot say without help.
5. As you listen, plot out tentatively and for subsequent correction the pattern (personal) that is being set before you. To test this, from time to time summarize what has been said and present for comment (e.g., "Is this what you are telling me?"). Always do this with the greatest caution, that is, clarify but do not add or twist.
6. Remember that everything said must be considered a personal confidence and not divulged to anyone.

Such counseling is not easily learned by persons with only industrial experience, but requires training in an appropriate profession such as counseling psychology or social work. To maintain the essential confidentiality, the counseling service may be an independent unit in the organization plan of the industry, or may be allied to the medical office, which most workers regard as primarily concerned with their personal welfare. The counselor must have means of communication with central management and the personnel office in order to bring about the correction of general practices that are detrimental to mental health and morale, but any conception of the counseling office as an adjunct to hiring and firing would defeat its purpose.

A counselor is as appropriate in an industry as is a medical service. From a humanitarian standpoint, a counseling service aids workers to maintain happiness and effective living. From a narrower

---

* Elton Mayo. *The social problems of an industrial civilization.* Boston: Harvard University, Graduate School of Business Administration, 1945. Pp. 73-74.

point of view of profit and loss, the service pays its way by reducing inefficiency and turnover due to personal maladjustment. The human and economic features are not in conflict but are highly compatible.

The personal counselor, like the company physician, recognizes that his services have appropriate limitations. Employees who need intensive and prolonged help because of long-standing maladjustments are put in touch with community agencies or psychiatric clinics which can meet their needs. The company counselor does not attempt to solve all problems unaided.

Even when a counseling service cannot be provided in a small establishment, some of its spirit can be applied by employers and supervisors. Every executive, down to foremen, can assist the adjustments of workers by having respect for them as persons, by knowing how to listen with understanding to tales of trouble, and by adapting work procedures to human needs. Training courses in practical human relations have been effective in sensitizing executives to the problems and their solutions. Employers, like teachers and parents, have to be mental hygienists whether they wish to be or not.

Effective methods for selecting, guiding, and training employees can help to reduce maladjustments. Work difficulties, with resultant personal conflicts, often arise when an employee is placed in a position which is too hard or too easy for him, which is uncongenial to his interests, or which brings into prominence a detrimental and relatively unmodifiable feature of his personality. Job guidance does not end with the initial selection and hiring. If a worker fails in one position, his transfer to a more suitable job is both more humane and more profitable than his discharge. Department stores with well-developed counseling and personnel services have found, for example, that a failure as a sales clerk may make a good cashier and *vice versa*.

Other sources of maladjustment cannot be removed by counseling services or personnel procedures, but only by a deeper recognition of the part that the worker as a person plays in the social organization of industry.[16] An illustration may be drawn from an early study reported by Mayo.

> In one department of a company which had a generally enlightened management, efficiency was low and turnover great. Financial incentives in the form of bonuses for higher production

had been ineffective. A counselor, made available to the workers, found many complaints of fatigue, leg pains from long standing, and social isolation due to individual work. Rest periods were introduced, cots supplied for lying down, and teams of three men operating a bank of machines were made responsible for the exact scheduling of their rest periods. Complaints disappeared, efficiency increased from 70 to 85 per cent, and turnover fell from 250 per cent annually to 5 or 6 per cent.

The spectacular solution of the problem was due to no one factor, but illustrates several important principles. The counselor made the workers feel respected as persons. Their stories were worthy of attention, and their complaints of fatigue led to prompt action to meet their expressed needs. The rest periods themselves had value, but the recognition of the workers as a social group which made real decisions was probably of equal importance. The gain in work efficiency was not the most important outcome. The greater social gain was the reclamation of an unhappy group of people who had been preoccupied with pessimistic thoughts all day, and too fatigued to enjoy social evenings after work. In this example, as in later and more elaborate studies of the social psychology of industry, economic and personal gains have been highly compatible. To make employment a creative and integrative experience is the ultimate social aim of mental hygiene in industry.

MENTAL HYGIENE AND SOCIAL WORK

Social Problems as Psychological Adjustments

An adequate description of the applications of mental hygiene in social work would be a review of the entire psychology of adjustment, for the profession of social work, more than any other, deals comprehensively with helping people who are in difficulty.[17] At a first glance the functions of social work seem very diverse. Social workers are concerned with family services, dependency, child welfare, recreation, delinquency, and a score of other human problems. As social work has evolved in the present century, its leaders have recognized that these varied activities have a central problem and that a common essential method, known as *casework*, is used to deal with all of them.

Some areas of social work, such as child welfare, are clearly seen as applications of mental hygiene. In working directly with a child, progressive social agencies use substantially the same approaches as would a child guidance clinic, with or without the collaboration of psychiatrists or psychologists. Parents, too, are regarded psychologically. Neglect or abuse of children by their parents does not arise primarily from ignorance and cannot be regarded moralistically. A parent mistreats a child because of his or her own motivations and adjustments arising from unfortunate features of personality development and integration. To readjust the family is a more constructive approach than to condemn the parents and remove the child. The child may be placed in a foster home for a longer or shorter period of time, but placement is made only when conditions are severe. Even then, work with the parents is continued in the hope of restoring a normal family group.

Some other social problems are less apparently psychological, but may constructively be regarded from a mental hygiene point of view. Family welfare and economic dependency are perhaps the most common problem met by the largest social agencies. The social worker's concern is not only with the relief of the urgent economic distress, but with the remedy of aspects of human relationships which led to the breakdown. In many instances, of course, poverty results from economic displacements, illness, old age, and other factors that are not originally psychological. Many other economic crises, however, are due to failures of adjustment. Dependency may result from the desertion of the family's wage earner who is unable to accept the responsibilities of maturity or who, perhaps, has fled from a complaining and nagging wife he can no longer endure. If so, the social worker's attention is given to the persons, not to their circumstances alone, in an attempt to remove the causes and restore the family as a social and economic unit. Poverty is sometimes caused by the inability of a worker to keep a job because of disadvantageous traits of personality. To label such persons as shiftless and ne'er-do-well does no good. To provide economic relief for them indefinitely is not only an undue burden on the rest of society, but is destructive of the unfortunate person's self-regard. The sounder approach is through the rehabilitation of the potential wage earner through mental hygiene procedures. Many other social problems which seem economic when regarded superficially can be solved only by the psychological consideration of the needs, resources, and remediable shortcomings of persons.

Even when a social problem does not have basically psychological roots, the readjustment of persons is fully as important as the provision of economic aid. When the supporting member of a family dies, for example, the remaining dependents are left in a state of anxiety and confusion. The social worker's role is to remedy these attitudes as well as provide temporary financial assistance, for the reduction of human misery is the socially more important objective. Another member of the family may be prepared to become the wage earner, which requires not only vocational guidance and training, but the development of attitudes of independence and self-confidence. Unemployment due to economic depressions and technological changes is preventable only by broad social and economic measures but, even here, mental hygiene can help maintain the morale of the unemployed. Balancing recreational outlets, a forward orientation, training for a superior kind of work later, and a number of other activities may keep the jobless from developing attitudes which might make them ultimately unemployable. While these steps cannot substitute for economic changes which would remove the causes of unemployment, they help to conserve human values in the face of temporarily unmodifiable circumstances.

Many social workers are engaged in group and recreational work in settlements, clubs, and similar organizations. Although their activities differ greatly from those of workers in family agencies, they, too, are influences for mental health. Guided group activities provide good opportunities for the education of personality. A well-trained group leader is usually far ahead of the typical schoolteacher in recognizing that the aim of educational activity is the development of persons. Many forms of group participation are used, ranging from storytelling and puppets for young children, through athletics and hiking trips for older boys and girls, to dramatics and social dancing for young adults. All may serve to promote a desirable balance between independent initiative and social cooperation, to provide integrative satisfactions for common motives, and to develop attitudes and skills that help people live comfortably with themselves and with one another.

The Social Worker as a Mental Hygienist

For dealing with problems of adjustment and personality, a social worker has to be as well equipped in the understandings and techniques of mental hygiene as does a psychiatrist or a clinical psychologist. Such knowledge is needed not only by psychiatric social workers who are specialists on the staffs of mental hygiene clinics, but by all social workers of whatever branch of the profession. The ideal of the social worker as a mental hygienist is imperfectly realized at present — this is also true of many other professions, especially of teaching. Financial limitations of agencies lead to the employment of staff members whose professional training is incomplete or even entirely lacking. Social work is also handicapped by a misunderstanding of its aims, both by clients and by the general public. Leaders in social work have recognized the primacy of mental hygiene objectives for many years. Still, the public often perceives the family worker as one who investigates facts, doles out relief, and makes further visits to "check up" on the behavior of the client. The persistence of the popular misperception of social work causes much of the distrust with which social workers are sometimes regarded.

Is social case work a form of psychotherapy? The question is much debated within the profession and, in the end, resolves itself into a matter of definition.[18] If psychotherapy is defined narrowly, as intensive long-term treatment of a personality disturbance conducted entirely by interviews, then typical casework is not therapy, although some individual social workers may function, in certain settings, as psychotherapists. If a broader definition is adopted, which sees psychotherapy as an interpersonal process which considers the client's attitudes and conflicts and attempts some modification of them, then all casework entails some features of psychotherapy. The most distinctive characteristic of social casework, in comparison to the therapeutic activities of psychiatrists or psychologists, is greater attention to the realities that the client faces, and a willingness to use environmental resources as aids in resolving his conflicts. Indeed, social workers may legitimately complain that many psychiatrists see the client only as a single person and neglect his role as a social organism in a complex culture. The emphasis on realities and on cultural interrelationships, originating from social work, have had effects on the practice of psychotherapy by other professions.

The most effective tool of the social worker, like that of any psychotherapist, is the relationship with the client. A sensitively perceptive yet objective relationship is developed which recognizes and understands the client's feelings and attitudes. Because a social worker often controls important features of the client's real life, such as financial assistance, the relationship is subject to hazards more severe than those of other professions. Care must be taken not to foster undue dependence on the part of the client, and the worker must avoid authoritarian management. As in the clinic, the relationship between worker and client leads both to diagnostic insights and therapeutic gains. In the early interviews, it is common for the social worker to meet long tales of woe and vehement denunciations of other persons and of the social agency. The worker shows an understanding of such feelings and respects the client as a person without necessarily approving all of his behavior. The interviews thereby serve the purposes of revealing the client's attitudes, opening them to communication, and fostering an opportunity for the client to achieve a better integrated view of himself and his world.

In the professional education of social workers, psychology and mental hygiene are given a prominent place. General courses in psychology, developmental psychology, abnormal psychology, and the psychology of adjustment are commonly studied in the preprofessional undergraduate curricula. Graduate professional subjects include dynamic psychology, psychopathology, and clinical psychiatry. Guided fieldwork practice is given more emphasis in social work education than in most other professional curricula. Courses and seminars in interviewing and casework, as well as supervised practice in agencies, place stress on the role of the social worker as a mental hygienist.

Even when good academic preparation has been given, the mental hygiene functions of social work may be prevented from achieving their full value because of subtle hindrances arising from the worker's own emotional sensitivities and unresolved conflicts. A worker reared in a slovenly home may have reacted with anxiety about its social acceptability and may have erected defensive mechanisms. An ill-kept household, then, may arouse antagonism and an excessive zeal to set things to rights. She may then scold or manage the unskillful housekeeper instead of trying to understand and accept her. A worker who has an overemotional attitude toward mistreated children, due to her own relations to her parents, cannot be effective in family work because she is prevented from feeling the parents' viewpoint and establishing a relationship with them. In general, blaming or resentful attitudes on the part of social workers point to weak spots in their own adjustive equipment. Social work educators in schools, and supervisors in agencies, are fully alert to the need for social workers to be aware of their own attitudes and to take them into account when perceiving clients' problems.

MENTAL HYGIENE IN THE FAMILY

The Adjustments of Husband and Wife

The marriage relationship may have either a positive or a destructive influence on the psychological well-being of the husband and wife. It involves many of the most crucial adjustments in human lives which, if solved integratively, can have a constructive effect on mental health second to no other. To marriage each partner brings the equipment of motives, attitudes, and preferred modes of adjustment which have been learned through previous experiences. These personalities are brought into an intimate and pervasive contact that has unusual potentialities for evoking emotional responses. Some adjustment problems, such as those of school or employment, can be relieved temporarily by evading or ignoring them, but the adjustments of marriage are less escapable. For a successful outcome, the personalities of the partners in marriage must be complementary and harmonious at the outset, or else sufficiently flexible to make new adjustments without undue anxiety or hostility.

The success or failure of a marriage is popularly attributed to the "good" or "bad" character of the husband or wife, interpreted moralistically, or to the fortune of their external circumstances. To psychologists, it is evident that the main determiner of success is the quality of the adjustments that the husband and wife make to each other. The adjustive histories of their childhoods are significant, because the relationships in marriage have much in common with those experienced between a parent and a child. A married person who retains either resentful or dependent attitudes toward his parents readily generalizes them to his spouse. An immature, dependent wife may expect the same kind of indulgence from her husband that she received from her father. She is therefore anxious and "hurt" when she is called upon to assume adult responsibility. On the other hand, a spouse who has developed rebelliously hostile attitudes toward his parents cannot tolerate the inevitable limitations on individual freedom which marriage requires. He always demands pre-eminence and is angry and quarrelsome when his wife's needs prevent the fulfillment of his transient desires. Much of the quarreling of married couples involves issues of no real consequence which are only symbolic of poorly integrated motivations for dominance.

Research on the factors associated with marital happiness has confirmed the impressions gained from clinical observations. Such studies have compared the life histories, attitudes, and personality traits of groups of happily married persons with those of unhappy or divorced couples.[19] More of the happily married had happily married parents, were themselves more happy in childhood, and had fewer conflicts with their parents. Their adult relationships with their parents were more close and warm. As children, they typically received firm and dependable but not harsh discipline. Experiences subsequent to childhood have effects, of course, on marital happiness. Young people who achieved better social adjustment before marriage had more successful marriages. Marital compatibility is related to the tendency of husband and wife to rate the other higher than the self on desirable traits, evidence of a humble and nondefensive attitude.[20]

Symptoms of marital discord may be viewed psychologically as nonintegrative responses to frustrations and conflicts. All the major adjustment mechanisms are identifiable. Family bullying and nagging may be aggressive compensatory defenses. Escape takes many forms, from daydreaming to absorption in clubs and sports. Hysterical and hypochondriacal reactions are common defenses against a hostile spouse or serve to gain recognition otherwise denied. An ailing wife is sometimes motivated by a need for tender consideration and is also rewarded, as a secondary gain, by relief from the monotonies of housekeeping. Hysterical mechanisms are by no means limited to women, but may be used by husbands to evoke consideration or excuse their failures. Such motives are unrecognized by their possessors, of course, as is always true of hysterical reactions. Open anxiety, so-called nervousness, and other persistent nonadjustive reactions are often precipitated by the interpersonal difficulties of marriage, when no type of response is available for reducing tensions.

Sexual compatibility is a significant factor in marital adjustment, but not the all-important one that it was deemed a few decades ago. Studies indeed show that marital happiness is statistically associated with certain evidences of sexual adjustment, such as agreement on frequency of intercourse, infrequent refusal, and a high degree of sexual satisfaction. But satisfactory sexual relations may be either a result or a contributing cause of generally successful marriage. Couples free from anxieties and hostilities are typically as compatible in sex as they are in other spheres of life. In some instances, however, adverse attitudes toward sex acquired in childhood and adolescence may be harmful to subsequent marital happiness. Although considerable changes have taken place in recent years, the taboos surrounding the subject of sex compel many young persons to face this adjustment with less preparation than for any other life problem. Sexual knowledge and skill are not innate, and education is as much needed as in any area. The lack of free communication about sex also prevents the reformulation in more mature terms of acquired attitudes of fear, disgust, or guilt. Because sex is such a highly valued and intimately personal function, failures in sexual adjustment often lead to anxious self-devaluation and hence to generally defensive behavior.

The need for the guidance of marital adjustments has led to the emergence of a new profession, marriage counseling.[21] A competent marriage counselor is prepared to deal both with the realities of marital situations and, more importantly, with attitudes and personal adjustments. The giving of information — social, economic, legal, and sexual — makes a contribution to the solution of some marital difficulties. In the main, however, the marriage counselor uses the general tools of psychotherapy to help couples reduce their anxieties, resolve their conflicts, and attain more integrative adjustments.

The positive mental hygiene of marriage is the same in its essentials as that of any other human undertaking. Each partner in a successful marriage recognizes the motivations of the other and acts so as to fulfill rather than to frustrate them. Each preserves the freedom of the other from petty dictatorship as jealously as his or her own. The discussion of domestic issues is used not only for the joint decision reached, but also as an opportunity for sharing an understanding of attitudes and feelings. The constructive influence of marriage includes factors other than stable home life and sexual adjustment, although the importance of these primary satisfactions must not be minimized. The well-adjusted husband and wife provide a kind of continuous psychotherapy for one another through warmly sympathetic communication about their mutual and individual problems. The close and confidential relationship aids each partner to gain insight into his or her own attitudes, to resolve conflicts integratively, and to feel the strength of a united effort against difficulties.

Parent and Child

The significance of the parent relationship in the formation of the child's personality need not be emphasized again, for it has been a major thesis throughout the study of the psychology of adjustment. Parents determine the behavior of their children by both direct and indirect influences, the latter being less well recognized but more important. Direct education and training occur through conditioning and the more obvious forms of reinforcement. Indirectly, the parents mold a child's personality by subtle rewards and punishments such as the giving or withholding of attention, the power of which is usually unappreciated. By identification, most children adopt many of the attitudes and adjustments of their parents, since from their point of view the conduct of these loved and powerful persons represent rewarded courses of action. In order to rear a child whose potentialities for personal development are fully realized, parents need to live well-integrated adjustments as well as teach them.

Parents should enjoy their children. The finest satisfaction that parents may derive from the development of a well-adjusted child is like that of a creative artist in his work, a satisfaction arising from the value of the product itself, without consideration of more immediate and selfish motives. Parents provide opportunities for a child to grow psychologically and socially as well as physically by letting him undertake tasks that are within his ability to solve successfully. They help a child to avoid some of the most disastrous mistakes, but do not overprotect him from all of the effects of his trial and error, since he learns chiefly through his own independent experiences. While giving him freedom to explore his world, parents maintain a warm and accepting relationship with a child which makes it possible for him to seek their counsel voluntarily when he is in difficulty. Unfortunately, parents may seek some "enjoyments" from their children which are harmful to mental health. Such parental faults have been described in preceding chapters, but a few may be repeated for emphasis. In the American culture, which places a high value on upward social mobility, parents' compensation through their children is all too common. Feeling a lack of mastery and approval in themselves, parents want their children to fulfill their own educational, vocational, and social ambitions. When the parents' motives coincide with the children's interests and abilities, useful drives to achievement may result. In more instances the overdriven child, whose real accomplishments never quite meet his parents' demands, is left anxious, insecure, and distrustful of himself. Another nonintegrative enjoyment is the encouraging of dependency. It is gratifying to be depended upon by a weaker, less mature person who needs and receives protection and care. Babies satisfy such motivations fully. As the child grows older, some parents are unable to give up the satisfactions of dominance but try to maintain an infantile degree of dependence in their children, who are guarded, managed, and prevented from developing independence. The result is an anxious personality which either remains helpless and dominated, or else becomes demanding and ill-tempered. Some overdriven or overprotected children succeed in painfully readjusting themselves later in life, but little credit is due to their parents for the accomplishment.

What it means to *love* a child has perplexed many parents during the past two generations. Love is not an easy concept to discuss with precision, for it is a literary word, not a scientific one. Hence, writers of various schools and periods have defined love differently. In the nineteen-twenties the earlier behaviorists, of whom J. B. Watson was typical, perceived the anxious and troubled lives of overprotected or overdominated children.[22] They saw that such children were often given large amounts of parental attention and were hugged and kissed in a way which was, in a broad sense, sexually satisfying to the parents. Such children often became demanding and were unhappy and whining when not the center of attention. The remedy, thought Watson, was to avoid the "excessive love-conditioning" which made the child so anxious, and to leave him "wholesomely alone" and free so that he could develop independent initiative.

Exactly the contrary argument was popular in the nineteen-forties. Ribble, for example, advocated that children be given large amounts of "mothering," of being held, rocked, and fondled by the mother.[23] She based her recommendations on observations of routinely institutionalized and severely neglected children who, deprived of kindly contacts with adults, often became depressed, emaciated, and backward in development.

Who was right, Watson or Ribble? In a sense they were both right in seeing the causes and remedies of two different problems in child development. And both were also quite wrong in over-generalizing their findings, so that the avoidance of one unfortunate extreme was exaggerated into a universal principle. They based their conclusions on different developmental levels and different types of mistreatment. Babies and children need both security and freedom, not one or the other. Furthermore, the ratio of security to freedom varies with the developmental stage of the child. Babies are inevitably dependent, and a good amount of mothering probably helps them to establish a warm and affectionate bond which forms a basis for later security in interpersonal relationships. Older children also need to progress toward individuality and freedom without being hampered by parental possessiveness. If one may risk defining a hazardous term, "true love" of a child means a genuine acceptance of him as a person, accepting both his need for a degree of secure protection and his equally urgent need for emerging individuality and independence as he grows.

Education for parenthood is an important objective of the mental hygiene movement, but effective communication with parents is impeded by a number of obstacles. First, it usually reaches only a small proportion of parents, mainly the child-conscious ones who perhaps need it least. Second, popular education in lectures, non-technical books, and articles in general magazines is often given by zealous partisans for extreme viewpoints who promote cults, somewhat like those of dietary fadists, and impart little well-integrated wisdom. A sad consequence of some books and lectures is that mothers are made to feel guilty and anxious about their relations with their children because they cannot live up to extremist ideals. The anxious mother then attacks her child's "problems" with misguided zeal, often to his detriment. Third, parents often need something more than factual education. Child rearing is largely a matter of attitudes. Beyond information, parents need to gain insight into their feelings toward their children.

One resource for parent education which is being used with increasing effectiveness is group discussion, governed by evidence from social psychology as to how groups operate. With skillful nonauthoritarian leadership, groups of parents can identify their problems, express their attitudes, come to understand the motivations and conflicts of themselves and their children, and hence clarify their thinking. Decisions made in group discussion are more likely to be put into effect than are recommendations made by an authority. There is hope that the coming generations of parents will make as much progress in the psychology of childhood as the present generation has made in nutrition and the control of disease.

MENTAL HYGIENE FOR YOURSELF

You may legitimately ask psychology if there are not some principles of mental health through which you may attain a fuller, happier, better integrated life. The answer is affirmative. In fact, there is no kind of improvement except self-improvement. Teachers, parents, and counselors can only help to prevent or remedy adjustive difficulties; the real changes must be made by each person for himself. Even a psychotherapist does not "cure" a client, but only provides a situation in which new attitudes and behaviors can be learned. It must be emphasized, however, that there are no easy formulas for attaining integrated adjustment or effective personality. Books which offer oversimplified methods for easy self-improvement are sheer quackery, on a par with get-rich-quick schemes which promise high returns for little investment. Like other worth-while human enterprises, self-improvement is possible but it requires time and effort.

Knowledge and Self-Direction

A first step toward improving adjustments is understanding your own behavior. Almost everyone who studies the psychological principles of adjustment with comprehension emerges with greater insight into his own life. You get a clearer conception of your own motives, of their origins, and how they are satisfied. An examination of the varieties of adjustive behavior helps you to discriminate between your own more integrative mechanisms and the less effective ones. A study of the development of personality may reveal the sources of characteristics that you did not understand in yourself.

One common pitfall has to be avoided. A partial knowledge of psychology can serve as a means for self-deceit and self-justification. Unless used with real understanding, psychological labels may cover up more than they reveal. One student protests his inability to achieve because of his "nervousness" which he seems to be cherishing fondly. Another points out that he is the inevitable product of his heredity and his environment, and so asks how should he be expected to improve! Such statements are rationalizations, not insights. They are not blameworthy, but show that a smattering of psychology has provided the person with a new means for justifying inferior conduct.

More serious damage is sometimes done by people with a little psychology who go about diagnosing and labeling the maladjustments of their acquaintances. Such behavior, of course, is a mechanism for showing off and asserting one's superiority. When you have a truly psychological attitude you keep your guesses at diagnosis to yourself and try to do something simple and helpful. Considerable good may be accomplished by giving a warm friendship to a shy, seclusive person; much harm may be done by summarily labeling him an "introvert." The cure for the abuses of psychology is not to abandon instruction in it, but to teach more and better psychology.

Is a study of your own motivations and adjustments morbid? Not necessarily. A morbid attitude is a nonadjustive one which ends in hopelessness and anxiety. Mental hygiene for yourself must be positive rather than diagnostic. An understanding of your adjustments is only a first step, to be followed by active efforts for improvement.

Some Conditions for Mental Health

To state the conditions for positive mental health is an ambitious task but not an impossible one. The enterprise must be approached with humility because of our present incomplete knowledge of how the strengths of human personality are developed. We know more, alas, about the shortcomings. In spite of the reluctance of scientists to apply knowledge which is admittedly fragmentary, urgent practical needs dictate that we do the best we can. At least, some tentative generalizations may be more serviceable than none at all. It is difficult to state the conditions of good mental health; it is admittedly even harder to apply these concepts to yourself. Principles of positive mental hygiene, however, contain within themselves the germs of their own accomplishment. Following some of the easier ones makes it possible to achieve the others.

Good physical health. The integrative adjustments of your life as a physiological organism and as an experiencing and behaving person are inseparable. Both involve your activity as a whole being. A visit to your physician is therefore a good first step when you feel a need to improve your own psychological state. A number of bodily disabilities, such as glandular disturbances, may affect behavior directly. Many other conditions of poor health may reduce your zest for living and your capacity for enjoyment. Painful and annoying symptoms are tension producing in themselves and make you anxious about your integrity as a person and your continued ability to carry on your life activities. Fearing an unfavorable verdict, you may evade the issue by putting off a medical examination. To prevent a vicious circle between physiological and psychological distress, you have to treat your physical disorders promptly and vigorously. It is all too easy to let real illnesses or hypochondriacal exaggerations become rationalizations for ineffective adjustments. The best counteraction is a positive emphasis on the rewards of good health and an active attitude in dealing with any defects.

Accepting yourself. A simple but important generalization is that a well-adjusted person lives comfortably with himself. To a great extent, self-acceptance is a result of good mental health rather than its cause, but the principle can be applied positively. The first step toward accepting yourself is understanding yourself. First, you need to know how you operate, what your dominant wants are and how you go about satisfying them. Second, you have to recognize your strengths and successes without belittling yourself unduly if you do not immediately reach goals which were perhaps unrealistically high. Third, you should be able to face your limitations without too much need for self-deceit and rationalization. When you understand your own behavior and feelings, you can be honest with yourself and admit your own errors and shortcomings. You can then accept the bad with the good and not be plunged into anxiety at every failure. A serviceable tool for self-acceptance is a sense of humor by which you can smile at your own mistakes and see the ridiculous in your own conduct.

Self-acceptance, like other integrative aspects of life, has to be achieved in balance. It does not mean smug complacency, or the inability to see that any feature of your life might be improved. Neither does self-acceptance mean an overbearing sense of your own superiority over other people. In fact, both of these attitudes indicate lacks of integration, of anxiety-motivated drives to escape unpleasantness by denying it or by bolstering oneself up with over-aggressiveness. The really self-accepting person accepts his own needs and strivings just as he accepts his assets and his liabilities. To accept yourself is in no way incompatible with constructive motivations which can spur you to improvement.

Accepting other people. Understanding other people has an importance for mental health second only to understanding yourself. Understanding is objective; that is, it is guided more by observations than by one's own biased attitudes, distorted perceptions, or defensive needs. When you see people objectively you see them striving to fulfill their own drives; you see their strengths and their shortcomings. You do not see them as hostile to you or as obstacles to the appropriate attainment of your own motives. Objective insight into other people is a good trait, but it is not enough. In fact the word "objectivity" sometimes has a ring of coldness or of calculated advantage. Accepting other people requires objectivity in the sense of understanding and tolerance, but a warm feeling toward them is also needed. When you are comfortable with yourself, and see others as real people and not as fantasied threats, you usually have a warm liking for them as well.

The acceptance of other people does not mean, of course, that you are governed by them. To "adjust" is not to succumb to the pressures of your environment. That would be conformity, which is recognized as a nonintegrative way of life, generally motivated by fear. Individual and creative accomplishments are by no means opposed to the acceptance of others. To the contrary, when you understand and accept other people you have an expectation that they will accept you too, and hence have less need to protect yourself by abjectly conforming behavior. Acceptance of others does not imply a *laissez faire* attitude about social problems. When you feel close to other people you are concerned about people's welfare generally, not solely with your own individual problems.

A confidential relationship. One of the most effective ways to maintain integrative adjustments is to talk about your feelings and problems. Therefore, every person needs someone with whom he can communicate freely with confidence that he will be respected. The maintenance of a confidential relationship with someone lets you discuss anxious and shame-ridden thoughts which you might otherwise repress or contemplate in solitary fantasy. Sharing attitudes and problems gets you out of ruts of thinking and helps you see your situation as a whole. Don't expect much help from your confidant's advice, of course. As in psychotherapy, the gains come from what you say and think, not from what is said to you. The role of an accepting listener is not limited to clinicians but may be shared by parents, husbands and wives, physicians, teachers, and friends.

An active attitude. The maintenance of integrative adjustments does not end with talking. You have to do something about them. Many adjustments involve processes of trial and error, and when you make vigorous attempts to resolve your conflicts you have a greater chance of ultimate success. An active approach to a difficulty may result in overcoming it, thereby solving the immediate adjustment problem. Even when the attempt does not succeed entirely, anxiety is likely to be reduced by the active effort. Of course, mere random muscular activity does not itself maintain integrative adjustment. The active attitude must be correlated with other conditions of mental hygiene, especially with self-understanding and a realistic perception of external situations.

Social participation. Social activity in work or play is more conducive to mental health than is solitary activity. When you are in a group, you tend to be less aware of your own immediate needs and difficulties as you find satisfaction in joint achievement. Group participation lessens fantasy and anxiety because you have to attend to the communications from the others and cannot withdraw to your own reveries. Social contacts also help you to sustain other important hygienic attitudes, of accepting others and of making an active approach to difficulties.

Satisfying work. Another invaluable factor in mental health is constructive work. In your work you accept an obligation to plan and complete tasks that have recognized social value. Such work is intrinsically satisfying to some of the strongest motives that you have learned in your culture. Work has its best hygienic values when it is characterized by freedom and success. You need to be free to choose a task that is most suitable and satisfying to you. You also require the greatest practicable freedom to plan your work and bring it to completion in your own way. The sense of satisfaction and completeness that comes from work well done can be one of the strongest integrating experiences of your life.

Creative experience. Some of the deepest satisfactions come from tasks and experiences that are not labeled "work" and which may, in many instances, have no economic or social values. Such are the experiences in the fine arts: designing, painting, composing, and writing. Their creativity is shared by many avocations such as gardening or building things in the home workshop. What makes these activities creative? One important factor is your great freedom to choose your task and set your goals. The standard of excellence, too, can be your own. If the product is truly art it is good when it pleases you, and cannot be judged by social or economic standards. Such satisfactions are rarely replaceable by others, and make clear why some form of creative experience has a place in every person's plan for full enjoyment.

Using the scientific method. A very general principle of mental hygiene, which includes many of the others, is to use the scientific method for the solution of personal problems. The same approach that serves to unravel the complexities of nature can be used to discover superior solutions for individual difficulties. In applying the scientific method, your first need is for data. You try to define the problem clearly. You gather the evidence about yourself and the situation, including not only objective facts but also the feelings and attitudes of yourself and others, which are important data indeed. You talk of the problem with someone, integrating your own thinking and gaining insights from another person's point of view. A second step is to formulate hypotheses. You consider various courses of action, and weigh the immediate and remote consequences of each. Finally, on the basis of these considerations, you decide what to do and act on your decision at once, vigorously and persistently. A person tests a life hypothesis by action, just as a scientist does by experiment. The criteria of an integrative hypothesis are its personal satisfyingness and its social value. If one plan fails you try another, just as the scientist attempts another theory after one has been rejected.

When you can secure a balanced satisfaction of your motives by planned courses of action, you will have achieved integrated adjustment and satisfying living, which is good mental health.

SUGGESTED READINGS

A number of books on mental hygiene are organized in chapters which deal with the areas of application — childhood and family, courtship and sex, marriage, education, social relationships, delinquency, vocations, religion, maturity and old age. For introductory surveys of such areas, see Lehner and Kube, *The Dynamics of Personal Adjustment;* Lindgren, *Psychology of Personal and Social Adjustment;* Patty and Johnson, *Personality and Adjustment;* and Steckle, *Problems of Human Adjustment.*

Education

Books in mental hygiene which deal primarily with educational applications are Lindgren, *Mental Health in Education;* Redl and Wattenberg, *Mental Hygiene in Teaching;* and Fenton, *Mental Hygiene in School Practice.* Driscoll, *Child Guidance in the Classroom,* contains a wealth of illustrative materials which help teachers understand children as persons. Jersild and Helfant, *Education for Self-Understanding,* and Hymes, *Effective Home-School Relations,* are other useful references. Committee reports which are insightful, clear, and practical are the National Society for the Study of Education's *Mental Health in Modern Education,* and the Association for Supervision and Curriculum Development's *Fostering Mental Health in Our Schools.* Applications at the secondary school level are illustrated in the two volumes by Smith, *Principles and Practices of the Guidance Program,* and *Counseling in the Secondary School.*

Vocations

A good introduction to the problems of choosing a career and of being effective and satisfied in it is Super, *The Dynamics of Vocational Adjustment.* From the employer's point of view, the issues relevant to job morale and adjustment are described in several chapters of Waite, *Personnel Administration.* Mayo, *The Human Problems of an Industrial Civilization,* and Roethlisberger, *Management and Morale,* are pioneer presentations of the concept that human values have an important place in industry. Counseling services in industry are described by Cantor, *Employee Counseling.* Anderson's older *Psychiatry in Industry* is still of value.

Social Work

Readers unacquainted with the scope of social work will be much enlightened by reading Fink, Wilson, and Conover, *The Field of Social Work,* or Stroup, *Social Work: An Introduction to the Field.* The mental hygiene functions of the social worker are described more explicitly in Aptekar, *The Dynamics of Casework and Counseling,* and Hamilton, *Theory and Practice of Social Casework.* Hamilton, *Psychotherapy in Child Guidance,* describes a social agency's intensive work with delinquent and poorly adjusted children.

Family and Children

Books which may enlarge one's understanding of parenthood and family life include Levy and Monroe, *The Happy Family;* Baruch, *Parents Can Be People;* and Beverly, *In Defense of Children.* Parents will find that modern books on child development give emphasis to social adjustments and the growth of personality. Good examples, not too technical for nonprofessional readers, are Almy, *Child Development,* and Strang, *An Introduction to Child Study.* References on marital adjustments are Stone and Stone, *A Marriage Manual,* and Cuber, *Marriage Counseling Practice.*

For One's Self

Self-understanding is often a useful step toward improving one's own adjustments, and most of the books cited throughout the Suggested Readings may contribute to this end. Nontechnical books that help people know about themselves include Hooton, *Young Man, You Are Normal,* and Heath, *What People Are.* Psychologists have a justifiable skepticism about the value of the many popular books published every year which promise personal happiness and social effectiveness at small cost. Some do a little good for people who need a bolstering of their self-regard; some are harmless; some are detrimental because they present distorted views of human nature or lead people to depend on tricks instead of understandings. None of this self-help literature can be recommended. Three valid books which deal with some of the immediate problems of students are Kitson, *How To Use Your Mind;* Morgan, *How To Keep a Sound Mind;* and McKinney, *The Psychology of Personal Adjustment.*

Questions and Exercises for Thinking and Discussion

Chapter 1 • Adjustment

1. What are some typical problems of adjustment that college students have to resolve?

2. Analyze the attitudes of your group toward a person who seems to have an unsolved problem of adjustment. To what extent do modern young people express the equivalent of "moralistic" attitudes? How do these differ from scientific attitudes? Which is more helpful? Why?

3. If everyone had a scientific attitude toward behavior problems, searching for causes rather than placing blame, would standards of conduct improve or would they deteriorate? Why?

4. Using the diagram in Figure 1, try to identify the components of an adjustment problem of your own, or of someone you know. What motivation underlies it? What goals are sought? What blocks the direct satisfaction of the motive? What varied responses are made in an attempt to overcome the thwarting? How is a solution achieved?

5. What are the general steps of scientific method? Can you apply the steps to an issue in some other field of science? To a problem in psychology?

6. Can the general rules of science be applied to a personal problem as well as to a general one? Formulate a personal problem and try to resolve it, following the principles of scientific method.

7. What are some advantages and disadvantages of the clinical research method? Of the experimental method?

8. What is meant by *control* in an experiment? What is its value?

9. What are some advantages and some shortcomings of the use of animals as subjects in psychological experiments?

10. What kinds of training are needed for professional practice which deals with adjustment problems? What can people do who lack such professional training?

11. Vocabulary exercise. Can you give the exact meaning of each of these terms? Adjustment; Social adjustment; Moralistic attitude; Physiological; Psychological; Motive; Thwarting; Response; Solution; Hypothesis; Clinical research method; Experimental method; Experimental group; Control group; Psychoanalysis; Behaviorism; Dynamic; Psychiatrist; Psychologist; Social worker.

Chapter 2 • Motivation

1. What do you want? What do you think some of *your* motives are? Write a list of some of your wants, including both immediate and remote ones.

2. Name a number of older, now discarded concepts once used to explain motivation. What are some of their shortcomings?

3. Identify some stimuli that clearly have motivating characteristics. Name some that do not. Distinguish the main characteristics of stimuli that may motivate adjustive behavior.

4. Distinguish between drives and mechanisms, and give some examples of each. How are these two concepts related to each other?

5. Have you ever felt a general restlessness or stirred-up state the source of which was not easily recognized at first, but which turned out to be based on hunger or on some other physiological drive? Analyze the experience in psychological terms.

6. Are there "abnormal" hungers? What is the physiological meaning of a craving for some particular substances?

7. What is homeostasis? What is the relationship between homeostasis and adjustment?

8. Give several examples of *avoidant* responses of animals or children. Give some examples of *adient* responses. What distinguishes the stimuli evoking them?

9. Describe some instances of strong emotion from your own experience. What is the relation between your emotion and your motivation?

10. How many "emotions" do you have? How many "emotions" does an infant have? How do many emotions develop from few?

11. What part does emotion play in adjustment? Is emotion of any positive value? What about the problem of being "overemotional"?

12. Vocabulary exercise. You should know the meanings of: Instinct; Need; Stimulus; Drive; Response; Mechanism; Endocrine; Hormone; Homeostasis; Tension; Avoidant; Adient; Emotion; Visceral; Anxiety; Autonomic; Cranial; Sacral; Thoracico-lumbar; Sympathetic; Parasympathetic; Adrenalin; Adaptive; Adjustive.

Chapter 3 • Socially Acquired Motivation

1. What seems to be the relationship of "tastes" and "values" to motivation? Do peoples of different cultures or social groups want different things? Why?

2. How does a drive come to be evoked by a stimulus other than the one which originally arouses it? Illustrate the process from experiments with animals. Illustrate it from your own experience; how did you come to feel aversion or disgust for something? What basic psychological principle is involved?

3. Give some examples of learned fears which you have observed in animals or people. In everyday observations, outside of the laboratory, what makes it hard to tell whether a particular fear is a result of conditioning?

4. A college student, ordinarily a pleasant companion, returns to the dormitory after a dispute with his chemistry instructor and snaps at his friends, seeming to be "spoiling for a fight." What psychological processes seem to be involved?

5. From your own experience, illustrate the *gradient of generalization* of an emotional response, such as anger.

6. What is the difference between the *extinction* and the *inhibition* of a response? How are these concepts alike and how are they different?

7. What are some differences between *logical* and *psychological* understandings of behavior? Illustrate the distinction in training animals, in educating children, and in influencing adults by advertising or propaganda.

8. Account for differences in the degree to which different people like to be with others. To what extent are differences related to one's culture, to one's individual experiences?

9. Can cultural differences in motivation be found between persons who live in the same country? What are some typical motivational differences between well educated professional men and farm laborers? How would you account for them?

10. What are some cultural values that you have *internalized?* Can you explain them in terms of a two-step learning process of punishment and reward by your culture?

11. What is the difference between "social approval" motivation and "conformity" motivation? Which is more desirable? Why?

12. Are most people aware that they are strongly motivated by such patterns as social approval, conformity, and mastery? Is it true that they are motivated by these patterns, even though they do not recognize them? What light do these questions throw on unconscious motivation?

13. Show how motives become organized as systems of attitudes.

Illustrate by attitudes toward one's family, toward a political party with which you disagree, toward authority figures such as college administrators.

14. What is your own self concept? How did you acquire it?

15. Vocabulary exercise. How accurately can you use these terms? Conditioned reaction; Reinforcement; Extinction; Spontaneous recovery; Reconditioning; Generalization; Displacement; Gradient; Discrimination; Inhibition; Disinhibition; Unconscious; Culture; Externalization; Internalization; Motive; Attitude; Self concept; Goal; Purpose.

Chapter 4　•　Frustration and Conflict

1. Distinguish between *frustration* and *conflict*. Can you give some examples of each from your own life?

2. Can you illustrate from your own experience, or from observations of other people, the typical effects of frustration — increased motive strength, aggression, and regression?

3. Is regressive behavior in an adult the same as the behavior typical of a child? What are some similarities and some differences?

4. List some typical conflicts experienced by college students. What are some ways in which they are resolved? What resolutions represent good adjustments and what ones are poor adjustments? Why?

5. Classify the examples listed in No. 4 according to the types of conflict they represent. Compare them to examples in the text.

6. Why is an approach-approach conflict usually solved with little difficulty?

7. Under what conditions is an avoidance-avoidance conflict relatively easily resolved? Under what conditions is it hard to resolve?

8. Why does a person not "leave the field" to solve an approach-avoidance conflict?

9. Give an illustration from human life of maladjusted behavior resulting from a conflict between *excitation* and *inhibition*.

10. How is the feeling of helplessness, as an aspect of human anxiety, related to the difficulty of discrimination involved in animal studies of experimental neurosis?

11. Have you ever found mild anxiety to be a useful drive? How? In what way does strong anxiety disturb a person's life adjustments? Compare anxiety to hunger with respect to the effects of weak and strong drives.

12. Vocabulary exercise. Be sure that you can use these terms correctly and precisely: Frustration; Drive strength; Aggression; Regression; Conflict; Valence; Approach-approach; Avoidance-avoidance; Leaving the field; Approach-avoidance; Experimental neurosis; Discrimination conditioning; Excitation; Inhibition; Blocking; Anxiety.

Chapter 5 • Adjustment and Learning

1. Why do studies of the adjustments of lower animals help in understanding human adjustment processes?

2. In so-called "trial-and-error" behavior, what are the "trials"? What determines the behavior that will be tried? How would you define an "error," a "success"?

3. What constitutes the solution of an adjustment problem? Are all solutions "good" solutions?

4. In relation to the effects of an adjustive attempt, how would you define a reward? How would you define a punishment?

5. What is the evidence that reward reinforces responses, but punishment does not extinguish responses? What does punishment do?

6. Cite some instances in which common sense seems to show that an animal or a child learned because of punishment. Analyze an incident psychologically. What was the effect of the punishment? What brought about learning?

7. Compare the *Law of Effect* and the *Principle of Closure* as they apply to adjustive learning. What are the similarities and differences? Show how the two approaches may supplement each other.

8. Why do two main principles of learning seem necessary? What kinds of learning can be explained by effect or reward? What instances of learning cannot be so explained?

9. In what sense may adjustive learning be unconscious? Cite some examples of how people have learned without being aware of what or how they were learning.

10. How do symbols serve as stimuli, as responses? What are some symbols that have stimulated you recently? What are some symbols you have used as responses?

11. Note an instance in which you have suddenly remembered an appointment or an obligation. Try to identify the symbols that served as cues for the recall.

12. Write a description of one or of several dreams. As an aid to dream recall, jot down notes immediately while you are still drowsy. Attempt to account for the dream, in terms of present perceptions, distorted recall of events, and symbolic problem solving.

13. Identify a conflict common among young people (as, between dependence on parents and desire to be independent), and list various adjustments to it made by various persons you know. List the various adjustments made by the same person on different occasions. Which adjustments seem to help in the long run, and which hinder? Can you discover some of the characteristics which differentiate the better and the poorer adjustments?

14. Why do some people continue to make adjustments that are harmful to them in the long run? Explain in terms of principles of learning.

15. Apply the concepts of integrative, nonintegrative, and nonadjustive responses to some of the examples you cited in No. 13.

16. Vocabulary exercise. Are you thoroughly familiar with the technical meanings of these terms? Varied responses; Trial and error; Tension reduction; Law of Effect; Reward; Punishment; Closure; Figure and ground; *Gestalt;* Insight; Unconscious; Blind trial and error; Symbol; Recall; Adjustive; Integrative; Nonintegrative; Nonadjustive.

Chapter 6 • Adjustment by Defense

1. What is an adjustment mechanism? List some of your own typical mechanisms.

2. What are three ways in which adjustments might be classified? What are some difficulties involved in making such classifications?

3. Describe a child or an adult whom you know whose behavior is like that of James G. Do factors similar to those found in James's case seem to underlie the behavior? Different ones? What can you learn from comparing the cases?

4. Do most people show, in some degree, the typical symptoms of an attitude of inferiority? Why? What is the difference between most people and those who are severely handicapped by defensive behavior?

5. Make a list of the kinds of family relationships that might produce unfavorable self-evaluations. What kinds of family relationships might help to establish favorable attitudes toward oneself?

6. Would you expect anxiety about sex, or about aggression, to differ from one culture to another? Can you explain any differences you identify in terms of principles of learning?

7. Do mentally defective persons usually have attitudes of inferiority? How is it possible for a person of normal intelligence to behave as if he were defending himself against a belief in his own intellectual inferiority?

8. Is it easier to detect defense mechanisms in the *varied response stage* or in the *fixed response stage?* In which stage can they more easily be corrected?

9. Give some examples of compensations that are common in the behavior of normal people or those who are only slightly maladjusted. Are compensations always undesirable, or may they sometimes be integrative forms of adjustment?

10. How can attention-getting responses be explained in terms of learning? Do the principles of learning suggest constructive ways to deal with such mechanisms?

11. Go through the newspaper for a week and make a list of crimes that may be understood as defensive behavior. What are the implications of this conception of certain criminal acts for dealing with crime as a social problem?

12. Why do most people attempt to conceal their real motives by rationalization? What would probably happen if people frankly admitted their strongest motives?

13. In what ways are children taught, even compelled, to rationalize? How could this process be avoided?

14. What is the difference between "good" reasons and "real" reasons? Give some examples of widely held "good" reasons and trace their origins in psychological terms.

15. Vocabulary exercise. Check your knowledge of these terms: Adjustment mechanism; Defense mechanism; Attitude of inferiority; Basic anxiety; Attention-getting; Compensation; Identification; Reaction-formation; Rationalization; Sour grapes; Projection; Delusion.

Chapter 7 • Adjustment by Escape

1. Why do withdrawing mechanisms often go undiscovered? Why do laymen frequently think of them as less severe than aggressive mechanisms? Why do psychologists usually regard them as more serious?

2. Trace the development of seclusive and withdrawn behavior in someone you know. How do your observations compare with the account given in the text?

3. Have you heard of a person who was regarded as stupid when in school, but who turned out to be an intellectually successful adult? Will a large proportion of "stupid" pupils turn out this way? How could you explain the few cases in which this seems to be true?

4. In what ways are simple withdrawing and schizophrenia alike? What are some of the main differences?

5. What forms of negativism are more frequent in young children? What forms are more characteristic of adolescents?

6. What can parents do to prevent or minimize negativistic behavior in young children?

7. Compare your own daydreams with those reported in Table 2. How many of the types have you daydreamed? How many of them recently?

8. What functions do your daydreams serve? To what extent do they represent the symbolic fulfillment of your motives? What motives are most frequently involved?

9. How can a daydream be unpleasant, yet satisfying to a person's motivation?

10. Give some examples of regression in children and adults of your own acquaintance.

11. Vocabulary exercise. You should know these terms: Escape; Seclusiveness; Autism; Feeblemindedness; Pseudo-feeblemindedness; Schizophrenia; Dementia praecox; Negativism; Fantasy; Conquering hero fantasy; Martyr fantasy; Regression.

Chapter 8 • Fear and Repression in Adjustment

1. Under what circumstances have you recently felt fear? In what instances was the fear evoked by adequate stimuli, similar to those described in the text? What are the characteristics of situations that evoke fear?

2. Does fear ever have any value for integrative adjustment? Should children be taught to be afraid of anything?

3. Have you ever felt afraid of something without knowing why? Mild phobias are very common. Did you succeed in identifying the origin of your unaccountable fear?

4. In what ways are phobias which arise from conditioned fears like those due to displaced anxieties? What are some of the main differences?

5. How can anything as uncomfortable as a phobia be an adjustment? Why is it more tension-reducing to fear an identifiable situation than to have a vague anxiety?

6. Identify an instance in which you have forgotten a name or an engagement which you should have remembered. By free association, try to trace the causes of your failure to recall.

7. Why are experimental studies of selective forgetting needed, as well as evidence from case studies? What are the values and shortcomings of evidence from clinical sources, from experimental studies?

8. Recall some events of your childhood, as by writing a brief note on each event that you can remember from the year in which you were five years old, and from the year in which you were ten years old. Do pleasant memories predominate? Are you an "optimist" or a "pessimist" in your early memories? How can you account for the recall of unpleasant events as well as pleasant ones?

9. What evidence shows that repressed behavior is inhibited rather than extinguished?

10. To what extent does repression make life happier? To what extent does it lead to distress? Make up arguments on both sides, and draw some conclusions.

11. In terms of the psychology of learning, show how repression and phobias may be acquired.

12. How does the repression of a response hinder its extinction?

13. What are the relationships among phobias, compulsions, and common superstitions?

14. Why are hostility and sex more subject to repression than most other kinds of behavior? What would change this state of affairs? What would be some of the consequences of such a change?

15. Vocabulary exercise. Do you thoroughly understand these concepts? Fear; Anxiety; Phobia; Displacement; Secondary gain; Repression; Extinction; Inhibition; Unconscious; Obsession; Compulsion; Compulsive character.

Chapter 9 • Adjustment by Ailments

1. Can you find traces of ailment adjustments in your own life? Can you cite some instances of an apparent disability which got you out of a distasteful task or helped you to get your own way?

2. A professor once noted that when he forbade making up quizzes missed because of illness, the amount of illness on quiz days suddenly decreased. Explain this effect in psychological terms.

3. In terms of principles of learning, show how hysterical persons acquire their characteristic traits of personality. How, in turn, do these traits cause an individual to use hysterical mechanisms as adjustments?

4. What are some of the relationships between socialization and the predisposition to various types of adjustment mechanisms?

5. What is the relationship between hysteria and malingering? What light does the concept of blind trial-and-error learning throw on this problem?

6. How does punishing a person's hysterical symptom sometimes remove the symptom? Why are punishment and suggestion inadequate methods for treating hysteria?

7. From newspapers or similar sources, cite some examples of alleged miraculous cures. How does the concept of ailment adjustments help to understand them?

8. What is the evidence that occupational cramps and tremors are psychoneurotic symptoms rather than physiologically caused diseases?

9. Observe a person who stutters. Exactly what sounds cause the greatest difficulty? Are they the same in all cases?

10. Vocabulary exercise: Psychoneurosis; Psychasthenia; Neurasthenia; Hysteria; Conversion hysteria; Ailment adjustment; Anaesthesia; Hysterical seizure; Amnesia; Fugue; Multiple personality; Dissociation; Overexclusion; Suggestibility; Consistency reaction; Malingering; Motor psychoneurosis; Occupational psychoneurosis; Stammering; Stuttering.

Chapter 10 • Anxiety and Its Effects

1. What is a baffling difficulty? How does the degree to which a situation is baffling depend on the problem, on the person?

2. Distinguish between an adjustive response and an integrative response; between an adjustive response and a nonadjustive one.

3. What are the three main types of symptoms of unreduced anxiety? Can you illustrate each of these from your own experience?

4. What are some factors in a person's history that predispose him to develop an anxiety state, instead of using mechanisms that are more reductive of tension?

5. What are some common sources of worry among students?

6. When you find yourself worrying about something, apply the practical hints for controlling worry. Do they help? How? Do you have difficulty in using some of the suggestions? Why?

7. How is a hypochondriacal-fatigue response similar to a hysterical mechanism? How do they differ?

8. How do the physical symptoms of a hypochondriacal-fatigue state arise? How should they be treated?

9. How can behavior that is mainly nonadjustive still have some adjustive functions? Can all behavior be classed as either adjustive or nonadjustive?

10. Describe the course of the development of a somatization reaction, such as a peptic ulcer. What is the interaction of physiological and psychological factors?

11. What are the implications of somatization reactions for medical practice? For medical education?

12. What is "nervousness"? What are some psychological factors that cause it? Why is it often mistaken for an organic disorder?

13. What is the popular belief about the relationship between "overwork" and "nervous breakdown"? What is the relationship as understood by psychology?

14. Why are the nonadjustive reactions a highly inappropriate field for diagnosis and treatment by partly trained students of psychology? What are some special hazards met in dealing with these conditions?

15. What are some arguments for and against the use of diagnostic labels in describing varieties of adjustment?

16. Vocabulary exercise: Nonadjustive reaction; Anxiety; Visceral; Asthenic reaction; Hypochondriacal; Depressive; Somatization reaction; Worry; Circular reaction; Balancing factors; "Psychosomatic"; Peptic Ulcer; Hypertension; Effort syndrome; Allergic reaction; Nervous disease (correct usage); "Nervousness" (popular usage); Tic; "Nervous breakdown."

Chapter 11 • Personality Measurement

1. Give examples of different adjustive responses that different people may make to the same conflict or problem. What determines the ways in which people adjust?

2. In several of the case studies cited in the book (James G., ch. 6; Mariana F., ch. 7; Mildred K., ch. 8; Ronald B., ch. 9; Thomas R., ch. 10, etc.) distinguish some of the predisposing factors, some of the precipitating factors.

3. What are some reasons why many people in our culture try to classify persons into "types"?

4. Do you think that you are an "extravert" or an "introvert"? What difficulties do you have in arriving at a decision?

5. Trace personality "types" historically. What are some different words that have been used to designate similar behavior patterns?

6. What are some of the valid objections to classifying people into types?

7. How many personality traits are there? What difficulties arise in trying to answer the question? What is the best way to undertake the selection of a practicable list of traits?

8. What are the four main methods used to assess personality? How may all four be used informally, as in an interview?

9. What are some of the principal advantages and disadvantages of personality questionnaires?

10. How successful are screening questionnaires? How does the value of such a questionnaire depend on the situation in which it is used?

11. Name several methods that have been used to develop more valid questionnaires.

12. What implications for the adjustments of individuals can be drawn from studying the sociogram of a group?

13. What is a projective technique? Name several types of projective techniques, and compare their procedures.

14. What are the main ways in which a test differs from a questionnaire, from a projective technique?

15. Cite some interrelationships between intelligence and other aspects of personality.

16. What are some of the differences between normal and maladjusted persons that have been found by objective methods of testing? In terms of these qualities, describe the typical characteristics of the well adjusted person, of the nonintegratively adjusted person.

17. Vocabulary exercise: Personality; Predisposing factor; Precipitating factor; Personality type; Sanguine; Choleric; Melancholic; Phlegmatic; Rationalist; Empiricist; Autistic; Schizoid; Cyclothymic; Cyclic;

Extravert; Introvert; Ambivert; Trait; Common trait; Individual trait; Factor analysis; Questionnaire; Screening questionnaire; Validation; Criterion; Rating scale; Sociometric method; Projective technique; Rorschach method; Thematic Apperception Test; Unstructured; Word association test; Sentence completion; Intelligence test; M.A.; I.Q.; Performance test; Scatter; Social Age; Dark adaptation; Speed pressure.

Chapter 12 • Organic Factors in Personality

1. Distinguish between primary and secondary effects of organic states on personality.

2. What are the two main systems that integrate behavior?

3. What is an endocrine gland? Describe the three main types of endocrine glands.

4. Make a table of the endocrine glands of the third type, giving name, location, hormone or hormones secreted, functions of the hormones, and associated disorders.

5. Have you observed persons whose appearance and behavior suggested an underactive or an overactive thyroid? What were some effects on their adjustments?

6. Why is it easy to confuse glandular disorders with behavior disorders resulting from conflicts? Give some examples.

7. When a person is given a hormone preparation and his behavior then improves, is it proved that the cause of his disorder was glandular? Explain.

8. How can an addiction to alcohol or to a drug be a result of a maladjustment rather than its cause?

9. Name some diseases of the nervous system and describe the effects of each on behavior.

10. Describe some fat or thin people of your acquaintance who seem to confirm assertions about the relation between physique and temperament, as described by Kretschmer or Sheldon. Note some persons who seem to contradict such theories. Is it easier to notice and remember cases that fit a theory than those that do not?

11. When lower animals are used in the study of heredity, what controls and precautions are observed? What are the implications for the use of human family histories as evidence on heredity?

12. What are three methods by which some valid evidence about human heredity can be derived?

13. What are some practical implications of the evidence on heredity and environment in relation to human personality?

14. Vocabulary exercise: Chemical integration; Endocrine; Hormone; Thyroid; Thyroxin; Cretin; Myxedema; Hypothyroidism; Hyperthyroidism; Adrenal medulla; Adrenal cortex; Adrenalin; Epinephrine; Corti-

costerone; Addison's disease; Gonads; Testosterone; Estrogen; **Progester-**
one; Corpus luteum; Pituitary; Somatotropin; Acromegaly; **ACTH;**
Adiposogenital dystrophy; Pellagra; Paresis; Encephalitis; Habitus; Pyknic; Asthenic; Endomorphy; Mesomorphy; Ectomorphy; Heredity; Chro-
mosome; Gene; Plastic trait; Stable trait; Correlation coefficient; Fraternal
twins; Identical twins.

Chapter 13 • Learning and Personality

1. List the most characteristic personality traits of two people whom
you know well. What kinds of interpersonal experiences probably account for these differences? Try to check your guesses by talking with
the persons involved.

2. Read the biography or autobiography of some important person
who interests you. Try to apply the principles of learning to increase
your understanding of how his experiences shaped his personality.

3. List some recent instances of cultural change. What have been
the probable effects of these changes on the development of personality?

4. Inventory the attitudes of your group about when children should
be weaned and toilet trained, when they should be taught about sexual
functioning, and how their aggressive behavior should be controlled.
What is the range of ideas about socialization represented? What implications does your survey have for parent eduction?

5. Think of some people you know who belong to different social
classes. By what behaviors do you identify them? Compare these observations with the account in the text.

6. What are the basic aims of the socialization process in all cultures?
How were these aims achieved in your own experience? What people
and what institutions figured prominently in making you behave as you
do with respect to anxiety, aggression, and dependency?

7. Draw up a list of criteria for "good family life." Why are these
ideals not realized more often and more completely?

8. Show how experiences in the family can influence political beliefs,
attitudes toward minority groups, and notions about such issues as the
role of women in society. How are such beliefs related to personality?

9. Show how adjustment mechanisms, such as rationalization, develop out of family experience. Analyze your account to identify the
specific social conditions of learning and the general principles of learning that are involved.

10. What adjustment mechanisms are most likely to develop in an
overprotected-indulged child? What role is played in this development
by the processes of reinforcement, generalization, inhibition, and extinction?

11. What are the implications of the discussion in the text for the

control of delinquency? Outline a program to reduce delinquency in your own community.

12. Vocabulary exercise. Culture; Socialization; Dependence; Cross-cultural research; Class; Caste; Social mobility; Nuclear family; Rejection; Overprotection; Neglect; Delinquency; Democracy-autocracy.

Chapter 14 • Psychoanalysis

1. Compare psychological theories of motivation with the psycho-analytic theory of *libido* or *Eros*.

2. What are some similarities of, and differences between, "libido" and "adient drive"?

3. Do psychology and psychoanalysis differ in their recognition of the existence of unconscious events or processes? Do they differ in the way that they explain these observations?

4. How does psychology consider the phenomena that psycho-analysis ascribes to the id, the ego, and the superego?

5. Compare the accounts of the influences on personality develop-ment given in Chapter 13 with the psychoanalytic account. What are some similarities and differences?

6. Discuss the similarities and differences of the psychological de-scription of the adjustment mechanisms (Chapters 6-10) and the psycho-analytic descriptions of them.

7. How does each of the main deviating psychoanalysts — Adler, Jung, Rank, and Sullivan — differ from Freud? In what ways are their theories like that of Freud?

8. What are some of the greatest historical contributions of psycho-analysis to psychology?

9. The proof of a theory is not that it "works." Apply this idea to psychoanalysis; to other types of theory. How does one go about the evaluation of a theory?

10. What are three main criteria of a good science? Discuss psycho-analysis and experimental psychology in relation to each of these criteria.

11. Vocabulary exercise. The special vocabulary of psychoanalysis is very extensive. A few terms of wide importance are: Libido; Eros; Conscious; Preconscious; Unconscious; Id; Ego; Superego; Pleasure principle; Reality principle; Oral stage; Anal stage; Phallic stage; Oedipus complex; Castration complex; Fixation; Regression; Manifest content; Latent content; Resistance; Transference; Inferiority complex; Style of life; Collective unconscious; Birth trauma; Will therapy; Significant other; Parataxic distortion; Consensual validation.

Chapter 15 • Approaches to Mental Hygiene

1. What are the two aims of mental hygiene? How do they overlap?

2. What aspects of mental hygiene must be practiced by every person? What aspects should be practiced only by persons with thorough professional training?

3. Name the professions that are centrally concerned with mental health. What are the training and qualifications of each of these professions? What is the distinctive contribution of each to the mental hygiene team?

4. What kinds of problems are brought to mental hygiene clinics? What are some relationships between the problems of children and those of their parents?

5. How is the method of case study illustrated by the cases cited in Part Two of this book? Compare some of the longer cases with the Case History Outline, noting what information is given and what is omitted.

6. Using the Case History Outline as a guide, write a case history of yourself, or of some child or adult whom you have an opportunity to know and observe.

7. What observations made in the medical examination are especially relevant to a study of a person's adjustments? In what ways does a medical examination contribute to the understanding of personality?

8. Enumerate and briefly describe the procedures used in a psychological examination.

9. Define and compare normative and intra-individual data obtained from psychological tests.

10. Wht is a test profile or psychograph?

11. What is meant by resistance in an interview? What are some causes of resistances, and how are they overcome?

12. Compare a psychological interview with a social conversation. What are the most important differences?

13. What means are used to study children who are too young to interview? How do the aims and results of such procedures compare with those of an interview?

14. What is a psychological diagnosis? In what ways is it like a medical diagnosis? In what ways is it dissimilar?

15. Vocabulary exercise: Mental hygiene; Clinical team; Client; Clinician; Case history; Indirect study; Direct study; Normative; Intra-individual; Profile; Psychograph; Resistance; Rapport; Diagnosis; Multiple causation.

Chapter 16 • Psychotherapy: Learning New Adjustments

1. Ask the members of your group how they would feel if it were recommended that they seek psychotherapeutic help. Compare these attitudes with those toward medical care. How do you account for the differences?

2. Compare the examples in the text of what happens in psychotherapy with the procedures of giving advice or urging troubled people to "get hold of themselves." In terms of the principles of learning, why does the psychotherapist do neither of these things?

3. In the first three excerpts of therapeutic interviews in this chapter, rate the therapist's statements as to their degree of interpretation and responsibility. How do the three clinicians compare? Which statements seem most helpful?

4. Must a clinician know a great deal about you before he can help you? How does the importance of the therapeutic relationship fit into the conclusions you draw?

5. Draw schematic diagrams to show how psychotherapy may reduce anxiety and help a person learn more effective adjustment mechanisms.

6. Why is insight insufficient to produce a change in the effectiveness of a person's adjustments? Can you think of a person who seems to have a good deal of insight but is unable to behave in an integrative fashion?

7. Why are friends unable to perform a psychotherapeutic function? How does a relationship with a friend differ from the relationship described between client and clinician?

8. In terms of the principles of learning, how is an increase in self-esteem related to an increase in regard for others?

9. How can play therapy be conceptualized as a process of social learning when so little conversation is involved? See if you can account for personality changes resulting from play therapy in terms of the diagrams you drew for No. 5.

10. Discuss the statement, "In psychotherapy, the client, not the clinician, is responsible for his own improvement." How does this idea relate to the discussion in the text of the therapeutic relationship?

11. In terms of learning principles, explain why psychotherapy often takes a long time.

12. How would you feel about being a member of a therapeutic group? How do you think these feelings might best be handled in the group?

13. What is the difference between a lack of evidence that psychotherapy helps people and evidence that it does not? Are there other questions in human affairs where this distinction is important?

14. Vocabulary exercise: Psychotherapy; Psychoanalysis; Client-centered psychotherapy; Interpretation; Responsibility; Relationship; Permissiveness; Insight; Defense; Acceptance; Conversational content; Extinction; Generalization; Group therapy; Play therapy.

Chapter 17 • Applications of Positive Mental Hygiene

1. Why does it take more than common sense and good intentions to promote mental health?

2. Cite some principles of mental hygiene that agree with the traditional conception of the good life. Cite some that disagree with tradition.

3. Compare the role of the parent and teacher in mental health to their role in physical health.

4. How are the aims of mental hygiene and of education alike?

5. In what ways may the school be a cause of maladjustments instead of a constructive influence?

6. What are some of the main reasons why pupils may fail to learn in school? With what reasons is mental hygiene most concerned?

7. Suggest activities or materials that may be used in a school subject — English, History, Biology, or Geometry — to make positive contributions to the integrative adjustments of pupils.

8. What developments in the curricula of elementary schools have implications for positive mental health?

9. From the point of view of mental health, discuss various ways of handling individual differences in schools, such as promoting and failing, homogeneous grouping, promoting all pupils every year, giving school marks.

10. Describe a problem of school "discipline" from your own experience or observations. How was it dealt with? What were the effects on the school, on the individual pupil?

11. What are some of the special psychological problems of teachers? What constructive steps can be taken in teacher education, in school administration?

12. What are some of the major causes of the dissatisfaction of workers in industry?

13. How is an employee counselor in an industry like a clinician in a community mental hygiene agency? Are there also differences between the two roles?

14. What implications does the social organization of an industry have for mental health? Name some of the most valuable principles for improving the satisfaction and morale of workers.

15. Prepare an outline of a talk on mental health to be given to the executives and foremen of an industry. Keep in mind the needs, previous training, and probable preconceptions of this audience.

16. Why does social work conceive its main task as that of personal adjustment?

17. What are the main contributions of social work to the concept of mental health? How has psychology contributed to social work?

18. How are psychological problems and practices involved in the main tasks of social workers, such as family casework, child welfare, and group work?

19. How are casework and psychotherapy alike and how do they differ?

20. Describe some married couple of your acquaintance who seem to have difficulties in getting along together. How do concepts of adjustment and personality help in understanding them?

21. What are the constructive contributions that marriage may bring to mental health?

22. How do the parents' love and enjoyment of a child contribute to the child's favorable development? How may some so-called satisfactions that a parent gets from a child be detrimental to the child?

23. Discuss what it means to love a child.

24. How would you plan to hold a group meeting with the parents of a school class? Who should do most of the talking, you or the parents? Why?

25. What attitude should a student of psychology take toward his own problems of adjustment?

26. What should your attitude be toward the problems of other persons? What may be done? What should be avoided?

27. Define an adjustment problem of your own, and plan an application of the principles of positive mental hygiene to it. What do you learn about yourself? What do you learn about psychology?

References

The books and articles indicated by the superior numbers in the chapters are given below. The full citation in each instance may be found in the Bibliography which follows.

Chapter 1

1 Rogers, Kell, & McNeil (510)
2 Postman & Bruner (478)
3 Mowrer & Viek (442)

Chapter 2

1 Mulinos (446), Templeton & Quigley (621)
2 Bulateo & Carlson (77)
3 Cannon (91, 92)
4 Wada (650)
5 Tsang (643)
6 Hoelzel (256)
7 Bash (39)
8 Richter (500)
9 Young (700)
10 Beach (44)
11 Wang (657)
12 Davis (130)
13 Halverson (233)
14 Halverson (232)
15 Kinsey, Pomeroy, & Martin (327), Walker & Strauss (653)
16 Kinsey, Pomeroy, Martin, & Gebhard (328)

17 Beach (43, 44)
18 Beach (42, 45), Bingham (60)
19 Cannon (93)
20 Stagner (592), Dempsey (131)
21 Wilkins & Richter (685)
22 Sanford (528, 529)
23 Franklin, Schiele, Brozek, & Keys (173)
24 Warden (658)
25 Holt (264)
26 Kuhlmann (344)
27 Levy (359, 360)
28 Levy (358)
29 Sears & Wise (548), Davis, Sears, Miller, & Brodbeck (129)
30 Bernstein (54), Orlansky (465)
31 Jersild (293)
32 Bridges (66), Banham (33)
33 Buhler (75), Pratt, Nelson, & Sun (481)
34 Carmichael (97), Gesell (203)
35 Coghill (109)
36 Watson (666)
37 Sherman (562, 563)

38 James (286)
39 Sears & Sears (546)
40 Hebb (251, 252)
41 English (152)
42 Lund (378), Young (701)
43 Dempsey (131)
44 Arnold (22), Gaskill (198), Gaskill & Cox (199, 200)
45 Leeper (353)
46 Cannon (90, 91)
47 Mowrer & Kluckhohn (439), Mowrer (434)
48 Shaffer (552), Wickert (683)
49 Leeper (353)

Chapter 3

1 Belo (50)
2 Klineberg (333)
3 May (394)
4 Miller (416), Brown & Jacobs (74)
5 Tolman (636), Hull (276), Mowrer & Lamoreaux (440), Brown & Farber (73)
6 Pavlov (467, 468)
7 Watson & Raynor (667), Watson (666)
8 Jones (305, 306)
9 Van Ormer (648), Minami & Dallenbach (420)
10 Miller (417)
11 Hovland (272)
12 Miller (417)
13 Bass & Hull (40), Hovland (272)
14 Switzer (612)
15 Jones (301, 302)
16 Darrow & Heath (122)
17 Cason (99)
18 Menzies (411)
19 Shipley (567)
20 Menzies (411)
21 Cowles (116), Wolfe (692)

22 Scott (538)
23 Lorenz (375)
24 Belo (50)
25 Bateson (41), Mead (402, 403)
26 Erikson (154)
27 Davis (124, 126)
28 Anderson (17, 18), Seward (550)
29 Goodenough (212)
30 Child (104)
31 Woodworth (693)
32 Allport (6)
33 Sherif (561), Edwards (147, 148)
34 Levine & Murphy (357)
35 Allport (7, 8), Raimy (487)
36 Mowrer (433), Rice (499)

Chapter 4

1 Britt & Janus (67)
2 Amsel & Roussel (14)
3 Amsel & Ward (15)
4 Wright (697)
5 Wright (697)
6 Dollard, Doob, Miller, Mowrer, & Sears (138), Miller *et al.* (419)
7 Sears, Hovland, & Miller (545)
8 Hovland & Sears (274)
9 Morlan (428)
10 Barker, Dembo, & Lewin (34)
11 Lewin (366, 367)
12 Masserman (392)
13 Pavlov (467, 468, 469)
14 Cook (113), Karn (318, 319), Kempf (323)
15 Gantt (194)
16 Liddell (368)
17 Jacobsen, Wolfe, & Jackson (285)
18 Brown (72)

19 Bijou (56), Cook (112), Liddell (368)
20 Krasnogorski (340), Razran (494)
21 Freeman (177)
22 Hovland & Sears (273), Sears & Hovland (544)
23 May (395)
24 Mowrer (431)
25 Mowrer (435)

Chapter 5

1 Thorndike (629)
2 Ruger (524)
3 Thorndike (632)
4 Estes (157)
5 Muenzinger (443, 444), Muenzinger, Bernstone & Richards (445), Wischner (687, 688)
6 Peterson (473)
7 Mowrer (431)
8 Hull (275)
9 Koffka (335, 336), Kohler (337, 338)
10 Tolman (637), Tolman & Honzik (639)
11 Mowrer (434)
12 Hull (275), Dollard & Miller (139)
13 Holt (264), Guthrie (225)
14 Schlosberg (505), Skinner (575), Tolman (638), Mowrer (434, 436)
15 Skinner (576)
16 Freud (186)
17 Hollingworth (261)
18 Pressey & Pressey (483)
19 Mowrer (435)
20 Farber (162)
21 Brown, cited by Mowrer (435)
22 Mowrer & Ullman (441)

Chapter 6

1 Carroll (98), Horney (269), Landis & Bolles (348), O'Kelly (461), Snygg & Combs (588), Steckle (594), Symonds (615), White (678)
2 Horney (267)
3 Bagby (28)
4 Mowrer (432)
5 Morgan (425)
6 Sears (539, 541, 543)
7 Merrill (412)

Chapter 7

1 Thompson (627)
2 Wickman (684)
3 Terman (623)
4 Kanner (315)
5 Bender (51)
6 Burnham (84)
7 Cameron (88)
8 Jersild (292), Reynolds (497), Rust (526), Caille (87), Levy & Tulchin (363, 364)
9 Buhler (76)
10 Jersild, Markey, & Jersild (296)
11 Green (217)
12 Sherman (564)
13 Mowrer (432), Hamilton & Krechevsky (237), Sanders (527)
14 Watson & Spence (664)
15 Dudycha & Dudycha (142), Waldfogel (652)
16 Morgan (425)

Chapter 8

1 Shaffer (551)
2 Dollard (137), Shaffer (551), Stouffer *et al.* (601)

3 Jones & Jones (304), Jersild (293)
4 Jersild & Holmes (295)
5 Rivers (501)
6 Blakiston's (61)
7 Bagby (28)
8 Crider (118)
9 Masserman (393)
10 Prince (485)
11 Freud (180)
12 Bingham (59)
13 Crider (118)
14 Maslow & Mittelmann (391)
15 Bartlett (37), Sears (540, 542), Ray (493), Clark (106), McGranahan (387), Lanier (350), Edwards (149), Shaw (555), Glixman, (206), Rapaport (492), Belmont & Birch (49)
16 Summaries are given by Meltzer (405), Gilbert (204), Pintner & Forlano (474), Zeller (702), and Blum (62). For additional studies, see O'Kelley & Steckle (463), Lanier (351), Rosenzweig (515), Wallen (655), Gould (216), Shaw (554), Steckle (593), Shaw & Spooner (557), Alper (12), Glixman (207), Korner (339)
17 Meltzer (404, 406, 407)
18 Alper (13)
19 Stagner (591)
20 Wallen (655), Shaw (554), Shaw & Spooner (557)
21 Shaw (554)
22 Postman, Bruner, & McGinnies (479)
23 McCleary & Lazarus (383)
24 Hamilton (234)
25 Morgan (424)
26 Maslow & Mittelmann (391)
27 Bagby (28)

Chapter 9

1 Cameron (88)
2 Taylor & Martin (620)
3 Cameron (88)
4 Janet (288), Babinski & Froment (27)
5 Eysenck (159)
6 Hollingworth (262), Carter (100)
7 Clendening (107)
8 Janet (288)
9 McDougall (386)
10 Grinker & Spiegel (219, 220)
11 Culpin (121)
12 Travis (640), Van Riper (649)
13 Travis (640)
14 Froeschels (192)
15 Fletcher (171)
16 Eysenck (159)
17 Johnson & Knott (300), Wischner (689)
18 Fletcher (171), Hahn (227), Rotter (519), Johnson (297, 298), Van Riper (649), Froeschels (191)
19 Froeschels (192)
20 Johnson (297)
21 Froeschels (191)

Chapter 10

1 Hamilton (234)
2 Kierkegaard (326), Freud (184), May (395)
3 U. S. Army (645)
4 Hastings, Wright, & Glueck (241)
5 Symonds (614)
6 Grinker & Spiegel (220)

7   Landis & Bolles (348)
8   Eysenck (159)
9   Pressey & Pressey (483)
10 Dunbar (144), Weiss & English (674)
11 Wolf & Wolff (691)
12 Mittelmann, Wolff & Scharf (421)
13 Sullivan & McKell (606)
14 Metzger (413)
15 Hamilton (234), Culpin (121)

Chapter 11

1   James (287)
2   Jung (310)
3   Allport & Odbert (10), Allport (6)
4   Cattell (101)
5   Cattell (101, 102)
6   Franz (174), Woodworth (694)
7   Shaffer (553), Wickert (683)
8   Weider *et al.* (672)
9   Shipley, Gray, & Newbert (568)
10 Wallen (656)
11 Allport & Allport (9), Allport (5)
12 Hathaway & McKinley (243, 244)
13 Hathaway & Meehl (245)
14 Wheeler, Little, & Lehner (676)
15 Cottle (115)
16 Taylor (619)
17 Gough (214)
18 Barron (36)
19 Guilford & Guilford (223), Guilford (221)
20 Guilford & Zimmerman (224)
21 Ellis & Conrad (150)
22 Hunt (278), Gough (215)

23 Symonds (613)
24 Wheery (677)
25 Jennings (290)
26 Anderson & Anderson (19), Bell (47), Frank (172)
27 Rorschach (514)
28 Cronbach (119), Schneider (537), Zubin *et al.* (703)
29 Murray *et al.* (455), Murray (454)
30 Bellak & Bellak (48)
31 Symonds (616, 617)
32 Shneidman (569, 570)
33 Jung (307)
34 Jung (309), Kent & Rosanoff (324)
35 Rapaport (491), Rosenzweig & Kogan (517)
36 Rohde (512)
37 Rotter, Rafferty, & Schachtitz (521)
38 Olson (464)
39 Thomas (626)
40 Bales (32)
41 Rogers *et al.* (511)
42 Terman & Merrill (625)
43 Wechsler (668, 669, 671)
44 Thurstone (635)
45 Wechsler (670), Jastak (289)
46 Hollingworth (260), Eysenck (159)
47 Wechsler (668)
48 Carfiold (196)
49 Shoben (572), Warner (659)
50 Derner, Aborn, & Canter (133)
51 Doll (135)
52 Porteus (476, 477)
53 Bronner (68), Fernald (165), Eysenck (159)
54 Eysenck (159)
55 Krugman (342)

56 Plant (475), Terman (622), Kuhlmann (344)
57 Wells (675)
58 Culpin (121)
59 Eysenck (159), Guilford (222)
60 Hutt (282)
61 Peters (472)
62 Sherman (565), Sherman & Jost (566)
63 Hartshorne & May (238), Hartshorne, May & Maller (239), Hartshorne, May, & Shuttleworth (240)
64 Allport (6)

Chapter 12

1   Dempsey (131)
2   Hoskins (271), Turner (644)
3   *Cortone* (14)
4   Landis & Bolles (348)
5   Keys, Brozek, Henschel, Mickelsen, & Taylor (325), Franklin, Schiele, Brozek & Keys (173)
6   Saphir (530)
7   Lurie, Greenebaum, Leichtentritt, & Rosenthal (379)
8   Maslow & Mittelmann (391)
9   Cameron (88), Cameron & Magaret (89)
10 Cobb (108)
11 Kretschmer (341)
12 Burchard (78)
13 Sheldon, Stevens, & Tucker (560)
14 Sheldon & Stevens (559)
15 Fiske (170), Smith (585)
16 Child (105)
17 Tryon (642)
18 Rundquist (525)
19 Hall (229)
20 Yeakel & Rhoades (698)

21 Dugdale (143), Estabrook (156)
22 Goddard (209)
23 Kallman (313)
24 Morgan (425)
25 Woodworth (695)
26 Freeman, Holzinger, & Mitchell (176)
27 Burks (80)
28 Skodak & Skeels (578, 579)
29 Healy, Bronner, Baylor, & Murphy (248)
30 Woodworth (695), Jones (303)
31 Newman, Freeman, & Holzinger (459)
32 Burnham (83)
33 Cattell & Molteno (103)
34 Troup (641)
35 Muller (448), Saudek (531), Newman, Freeman, & Holzinger (459), Gardner & Newman (195), Burks (81), Stephens & Thompson (595), Burks & Roe (82)

Chapter 13

1   Singh & Zingg (574)
2   Dollard & Miller (139)
3   Scheinfeld (533)
4   McAllester (380)
5   Mead (400)
6   Kardiner (317)
7   DuBois (141)
8   Whiting & Child (680)
9   Wallbank (654)
10 Warner & Lunt (661)
11 Warner (660)
12 Warner, Meeker, & Eells (662)
13 Davis (125), Whyte (682)
14 Maccoby, Gibbs, & staff (382)
15 Warner (660)

16 Davis & Havighurst (127)
17 Havighurst & Taba (247)
18 Warner (660)
19 Sutherland (611)
20 Kinsey, Pomeroy, & Martin (327)
21 Whyte (681)
22 Hollinshead (263)
23 Hoffeditz (257), Brown (70)
24 Gough (213)
25 Auld (24)
26 Honigmann (265)
27 Baldwin, Kalhorn, & Breese (30), Roff (506), Lorr & Jenkins (376)
28 Baldwin, Kalhorn, & Breese (31)
29 Baldwin, Kalhorn, & Breese (31)
30 Meyer (414)
31 Glueck & Glueck (208)
32 Hathaway & Monachesi (246)
33 Levy (361)
34 Baldwin, Kalhorn, & Breese (30)
35 Jersild (292)
36 Lafore (346)
37 Sears, Whiting, Nowlis, & Sears (547)
38 Fischer (169)
39 Humphreys (277)
40 Goldfarb (210, 211)
41 Baldwin, Kalhorn, & Breese (30)

Chapter 14

1 Freud (179, 181, 182, 183, 184, 185, 186)
2 Healy, Bronner, & Bowers (249)
3 Blum (62), Woodworth (696), Mullahy (447)
4 Adler (1, 2, 3)

5 Jung (308, 310, 311, 312)
6 Rank (488, 489, 490)
7 Fromm (187, 188)
8 Horney (267, 268, 269, 270)
9 Sullivan (607, 608, 609)
10 Freud (186)
11 Freud (182)
12 Sears (543), Blum (62)

Chapter 15

1 Root (513)
2 U. S. Public Health Service (647)
3 Lemkau (355), Felix (164), Stevenson (597)
4 Langford (349)
5 Krugman (343), Robinson (502)
6 Levy (362)
7 Pennell, Cameron, & Kramer (470), U. S. Department of Health, Education, and Welfare (646)
8 Stevenson & Smith (598), Louttit (377), Brewer (65)
9 Bender & Grugett (52)
10 Levy (362)
11 Kanner (314)

Chapter 16

1 Rogers (507, 508)
2 Collier (111)
3 Strupp (605)
4 Fiedler (166, 167)
5 Shoben (573)
6 Weinberg (673)
7 Talland & Clark (618)
8 Shoben (573)
9 Estes (157)
10 Mowrer & Ullman (441), Dollard & Miller (139)
11 Shoben (571)

12 Mowrer (438)
13 Jones (306)
14 Sullivan (607), Magaret (390)
15 Mead (399)
16 Raimy (487)
17 Sheerer (558)
18 Seeman (549)
19 Snyder (586)
20 Seeman (549)
21 Sheerer (558), Stock (599)
22 Haigh (228)
23 Hoffman (258)
24 Hobbs (255)
25 Powdermaker & Frank (480)
26 Schilder (534)
27 Slavson (580)
28 Klapman (330)
29 Schilder (534)
30 Menninger (410)
31 Slavson (581)
32 Hathaway (242)
33 Strang (602)
34 Eysenck (160)
35 Barron (35)
36 Rogers & Dymond (509)
37 Landis (347)
38 Denker (132)
39 Eysenck (160)
40 Rosenzweig (518)
41 Rogers & Dymond (509), Barron (35)
42 Lee & Kenworthy (352)
43 Morris & Soroker (429)
44 Rogers & Dymond (509)
45 Dymond (145)
46 Dymond (146)
47 Cox (117)

Chapter 17

1   Gates (201)
2   Axline (25)
3   Bills (57, 58)
4   Ephron (153)
5   Association for Supervision and Curriculum Development (23)
6   Gates, Jersild, McConnell, & Challman (202), Slight (582), Winch (686), Thorndike (631)
7   Ruediger (523)
8   Hurlock (281)
9   Hymes (283)
10 National Education Association (457)
11 Waite (651)
12 Fraser (175)
13 Anderson (20)
14 Mayo (398)
15 Cantor (94), McMurry (389)
16 Mayo (398), Roethlisberger & Dickson (505), Roethlisberger (504), Waite (651)
17 Kasius (320), Emerson (151), Fink, Wilson & Conover (168), Hamilton (236), Stroup (604)
18 Garrett (197), Kasius (320)
19 Terman (624), Burgess & Cottrell (79), Locke (374)
20 Kelly (322)
21 Cuber (120)
22 Watson (665)
23 Ribble (498)

Bibliography and Index of Authors

The numbers in italics show the page or pages of this book on which each reference is cited or used. In many instances the authors' names do not appear on these pages, but their writings are basic to the studies or theories presented.

1. Adler, A. *The neurotic constitution.* New York: Moffat, Yard, 1917. *465*
2. Adler, A. *Understanding human nature.* New York: Greenberg, 1927. *465, 480*
3. Adler, A. *The practice and theory of individual psychology.* (Rev. ed.) New York: Harcourt, Brace, 1929. *465*
4. Alexander, F., & French, T. M. *Studies in psychosomatic medicine.* New York: Ronald Press, 1948. *306*
5. Allport, G. W. A test for ascendance-submission. *J. abnorm. soc. Psychol.*, 1928, *23*, 118-136. *325*
6. Allport, G. W. *Personality, a psychological interpretation.* New York: Holt, 1937. *92, 317, 357*
7. Allport, G. W. The ego in contemporary psychology. *Psychol. Rev.*, 1943, *50*, 451-478. *95*
8. Allport, G. W. Effect: a secondary principle of learning. *Psychol. Rev.*, 1946, *53*, 335-347. *95*
9. Allport, G. W., & Allport, F. H. *Ascendance-Submission Reaction Study and Manual.* Boston: Houghton Mifflin, 1928. *325*
10. Allport, G. W., & Odbert, H. S. Trait names: a psycho-lexical study. *Psychol. Monogr.*, 1936, *47*, No. 1 (Whole No. 211). *317*
11. Almy, Millie. *Child development.* New York: Holt, 1955. *591*
12. Alper, Thelma G. Memory for completed and incompleted tasks as a function of personality: an analysis of group data. *J. abnorm. soc. Psychol.*, 1946, *41*, 403-420. *231*
13. Alper, Thelma G. Task-orientation vs. ego-orientation in learning and retention. *Amer. J. Psychol.*, 1946, *59*, 236-248. *232*

13*a*. Altus, Grace T. A WISC profile for retarded readers. *J. consult. Psychol.*, 1956, *20*, 155-156. *503*

14. Amsel, A., & Roussel, Jacqueline. Motivational properties of frustration: I. Effect on a running response of the addition of frustration to the motivational complex. *J. exp. Psychol.*, 1952, *43*, 363-368. *100*

15. Amsel, A., & Ward, J. S. Motivational properties of frustration: II. Frustration drive stimulus and frustration reduction in selective learning. *J. exp. Psychol.*, 1954, *48*, 37-47. *100*

16. Anastasi, Anne, & Foley, J. P., Jr. *Differential psychology.* (Rev. ed.) New York: Macmillan, 1949. *400*

17. Anderson, E. E. The externalization of drive. I. Theoretical considerations. *Psychol. Rev.*, 1941, *48*, 204-224. *83*

18. Anderson, E. E. The externalization of drive. II. The effect of satiation and removal of reward at different stages in the learning process of the rat. *J. genet. Psychol.*, 1941, *59*, 359-376. *83*

19. Anderson, H. H., & Anderson, Gladys L. (Eds.) *An introduction to projective techniques.* New York: Prentice-Hall, 1951. *334, 359*

20. Anderson, V. V. *Psychiatry in industry.* New York: Harper, 1929. *568, 591*

21. Aptekar, H. H. *The dynamics of casework and counseling.* Boston: Houghton Mifflin, 1955. *591*

22. Arnold, Magda B. Physiological differentiation of emotional states. *Psychol. Rev.*, 1945, *52*, 35-48. *54*

23. Association for Supervision and Curriculum Development. Fostering mental health in our schools. *1950 Yearbook.* Washington: National Education Association, 1950. *557, 590*

24. Auld, F. The influence of social class on tests of personality. *Drew Univer. Stud.*, 1950, *40*, No. 4. *427*

25. Axline, Virginia M. Nondirective therapy for poor readers. *J. consult. Psychol.*, 1947, *11*, 61-69. *556*

26. Axline, Virginia M. *Play therapy.* Boston: Houghton Mifflin, 1947. *549*

27. Babinski, J. F. F., & Froment, J. *Hysteria or pithiatism.* London: Univer. of London Press, 1918. *257*

28. Bagby, E. *The psychology of personality.* New York: Holt, 1928. *168, 220, 242-243, 245*

29. Baldwin, A. L. *Behavior and development in childhood.* New York: Dryden Press, 1955. *57*

30. Baldwin, A. L., Kalhorn, Joan, & Breese, Fay H. Patterns of parent behavior. *Psychol. Monogr.*, 1945, *58*, No. 3 (Whole No. 268). *434, 442, 444-446*

31. Baldwin, A. L., Kalhorn, Joan, & Breese, Fay H. The appraisal of

parent behavior. *Psychol. Monogr.*, 1949, *63*, No. 4 (Whole No. 299). *434, 435*

32. Bales, R. F. *Interaction process analysis.* Cambridge, Mass.: Addison-Wesley Press, 1950. *343*

33. Banham, Katharine M. The development of affectionate behavior in infancy. *J. genet. Psychol.*, 1950, *76*, 283-289. *46*

34. Barker, R., Dembo, Tamara, & Lewin, K. Frustration and regression: an experiment with young children. *Univer. Iowa Stud. Child Welf.*, 1941, *18*, No. 1. *103*

35. Barron, F. Psychotherapy as a special case of personal interaction: prediction of its course. Ph.D. dissertation, Univer. of California, Berkeley, 1950. *545-546*

36. Barron, F. An ego-strength scale which predicts response to psychotherapy. *J. consult. Psychol.*, 1953, *17*, 327-333. *328*

37. Bartlett, F. C. *Remembering.* New York: Macmillan, 1932. *231*

38. Baruch, Dorothy W. *Parents can be people.* New York: Appleton-Century, 1944. *591*

39. Bash, K. W. An investigation into a possible organic basis for the hunger drive. *J. comp. Psychol.*, 1939, *28*, 109-135. *32*

40. Bass, M. J., & Hull, C. L. The irradiation of a tactile conditioned reflex in man. *J. comp. Psychol.*, 1934, *17*, 47-65. *73*

41. Bateson, G. Cultural determinants of personality. In J. McV. Hunt (Ed.), *Personality and the behavior disorders.* New York: Ronald Press, 1944. Pp. 714-735. *81*

42. Beach, F. A. Central nervous mechanisms involved in the reproductive behavior of vertebrates. *Psychol. Bull.*, 1942, *39*, 200-226. *35*

43. Beach, F. A. Comparison of copulatory behavior of male rats raised in isolation, cohabitation and segregation. *J. genet. Psychol.*, 1942, *60*, 121-136. *35*

44. Beach, F. A. *Hormones and behavior.* New York: Hoeber, 1948. *33, 35, 400*

45. Beach, F. A. Instinctive behavior: reproductive activities. In S. S. Stevens (Ed.), *Handbook of experimental psychology.* New York: Wiley, 1951. Pp. 387-434. *35*

46. Beers, C. W. *A mind that found itself.* (7th ed.) Garden City, N. Y.: Doubleday, 1948. *484, 513*

47. Bell, J. E. *Projective techniques.* New York: Longmans, Green, 1948. *334*

48. Bellak, L., & Bellak, Sonya S. *Children's Apperception Test.* New York: C.P.S. Co., 1949. *339*

49. Belmont, Lillian, & Birch, H. G. Re-individualizing the repression hypothesis. *J. abnorm. soc. Psychol.*, 1951, *46*, 226-235. *231*

50. Belo, J. The Balinese temper. *Charact. & Pers.*, 1935, *4*, 120-126. *60, 81*

51. Bender, Lauretta. Childhood schizophrenia. *Amer. J. Orthopsychiat.*, 1947, *17*, 40-56. *192*

52. Bender, Lauretta, & Grugett, A. E., Jr. A follow-up report on children who had atypical sexual experience. *Amer. J. Orthopsychiat.*, 1952, *22*, 825-837. *500*

53. Benedict, Ruth. *Patterns of culture.* Boston: Houghton Mifflin, 1934. *446*

54. Bernstein, A. Some relations between techniques of feeding and training during infancy and certain behavior in childhood. *Genet. Psychol. Monogr.*, 1955, *51*, 3-44. *42*

55. Beverly, B. I. *In defense of children.* New York: Day, 1941. *591*

56. Bijou, S. W. A study of "experimental neurosis" in the rat by the conditioned response technique. *J. comp. Psychol.*, 1943, *36,* 1-20. *117*

57. Bills, R. E. Nondirective play therapy with retarded readers. *J consult. Psychol.*, 1950, *14*, 140-149. *556*

58. Bills, R. E. Play therapy with well-adjusted retarded readers. *J. consult. Psychol.*, 1950, *14*, 246-249. *556*

59. Bingham, Anne T. The application of psychiatry to high-school problems. *Ment. Hyg., N. Y.*, 1925, *9*, 1-27. *224*

60. Bingham, H. C. Sex development in apes. *Comp. Psychol. Monogr.,* 1928, *5*, No. 1 (Serial No. 23). *35*

61. *Blakiston's new Gould medical dictionary.* Ed. by H. W. Jones *et al.* Philadelphia: Blakiston, 1949. *220*

62. Blum, G. S. *Psychoanalytic theories of personality.* New York: McGraw-Hill, 1953. *231, 465, 478, 480*

63. Boring, E. G., Langfeld, H. S., & Weld, H. P. (Eds.) *Foundations of psychology.* New York: Wiley, 1948. *23, 57, 154, 400*

64. Boyd, W. C. *Genetics and the races of man.* Boston: Little, Brown, 1950. *400*

65. Brewer, J. E. A community program of psychological services. *J. clin. Psychol.*, 1951, *7*, 357-360. *490*

66. Bridges, Katharine M. B. Emotional development in early infancy. *Child Develpm.*, 1932, *3*, 324-341. *45, 46*

67. Britt, S. H., & Janus, S. Q. Criteria of frustration. *Psychol. Rev.*, 1940, *47*, 451-470. *99*

68. Bronner, Augusta F. A comparative study of the intelligence of delinquent girls. *Teach. Coll. Contrib. Educ.*, 1914, No. 68. *352*

69. Brown, C. W., & Ghiselli, E. E. *Scientific method in psychology.* New York: McGraw-Hill, 1955. *23*

70. Brown, F. A comparative study of the influence of race and

locale upon emotional stability of children. *J. genet. Psychol.*, 1936, *49*, 325-342. *427*

71. Brown, J. F. *The psychodynamics of abnormal behavior.* New York: McGraw-Hill, 1940. *252*

72. Brown, J. S. Factors determining conflict reactions in difficult discriminations. *J. exp. Psychol.*, 1942, *31*, 272-292. *117*

73. Brown, J. S., & Farber, I. E. Emotions conceptualized as intervening variables — with suggestions toward a theory of frustration. *Psychol. Bull.*, 1951, *48*, 465-495. *64*

74. Brown, J. S., & Jacobs, A. The role of fear in the motivation and acquisition of responses. *J. exp. Psychol.*, 1949, *39*, 747-759. *64*

75. Buhler, Charlotte. *The first year of life.* New York: Day, 1930. *46*

76. Buhler, Charlotte. The social behavior of children. In C. Murchison (Ed.), *Handbook of child psychology.* (2nd ed.) Worcester, Mass.: Clark Univer. Press, 1933. Pp. 374-416. *201*

77. Bulateo, E., & Carlson, A. J. Contributions to the physiology of the stomach. Influence of experimental changes in blood sugar level on gastric hunger contraction. *Amer. J. Physiol.*, 1924, *69*, 107-115. *30*

78. Burchard, E. M. L. Physique and psychosis, an analysis of the postulated relationship between bodily constitution and mental disease syndrome. *Comp. Psychol. Monogr.*, 1936, *13*, No. 1 (Serial No. 61). *381*

79. Burgess, E. W., & Cottrell, L. S. *Predicting success or failure in marriage.* New York: Prentice-Hall, 1939. *579*

80. Burks, Barbara S. The relative influence of nature and nurture upon mental development. In National Society for the Study of Education, *Twenty-seventh yearbook.* Bloomington, Ill.: Public School Publishing Co., 1928. Part I, pp. 219-316. *394, 395*

81. Burks, Barbara S. A study of identical twins reared apart under differing types of family relationships. In Q. McNemar & Maud A. Merrill (Eds.), *Studies in personality.* New York: McGraw-Hill, 1942. Pp. 35-69. *398*

82. Burks, Barbara S., & Roe, Anne. Studies of identical twins reared apart. *Psychol. Monogr.*, 1949, *63*, No. 5 (Whole No. 300). *398*

83. Burnham, R. W. Case studies of identical twins. *J. genet. Psychol.*, 1940, *56*, 323-351. *397*

84. Burnham, W. H. *The normal mind.* New York: Appleton, 1924. *192*

85. Buros, O. K. (Ed.) *The fourth mental measurements yearbook.* Highland Park, N. J.: Gryphon Press, 1953. *359*

86. Burton, A., & Harris, R. E. (Eds.) *Case histories in clinical and abnormal psychology.* New York: Harper, 1947. *252, 272, 306, 359*

87. Caille, Ruth K. *Resistant behavior of preschool children.* Child

Develpm. Monogr. No. 11. New York: Teachers Coll., Columbia Univer., 1933. *199*

88. Cameron, N. *The psychology of behavior disorders.* Boston: Houghton Mifflin, 1947. *197, 252, 255, 256, 266-267, 272, 306, 379, 549*

89. Cameron, N., & Magaret, Ann. *Behavior pathology.* Boston: Houghton Mifflin, 1951. *123, 186, 213, 306, 379*

90. Cannon, W. B. The James-Lange theory of emotions: a critical examination and an alternative theory. *Amer. J. Psychol.,* 1927, *39,* 106-124. *56*

91. Cannon, W. B. *Bodily changes in pain, hunger, fear and rage.* (Rev. ed.) New York: Appleton, 1929. *30, 56*

92. Cannon, W. B. Hunger and thirst. In C. Murchison (Ed.), *Handbook of general experimental psychology.* Worcester, Mass.: Clark Univer. Press, 1934 . Pp. 247-263. *30*

93. Cannon, W. B. *The wisdom of the body.* (Rev. ed.) New York: Norton, 1939. *35, 38*

94. Cantor, N. *Employee counseling.* New York: McGraw-Hill, 1945. *571, 591*

95. Carlson, A. J., & Johnson, V. *The machinery of the body.* (4th ed.) Chicago: Univer. of Chicago Press, 1954. *400*

96. Carmichael, L. (Ed.) *Manual of child psychology.* (2nd ed.) New York: Wiley, 1954. *58, 97, 123, 154*

97. Carmichael, L. The onset and early development of behavior. In *Manual of child psychology.* (2nd ed.) New York: Wiley, 1954. Pp. 60-185. *46*

98. Carroll, H. A. *Mental hygiene.* New York: Prentice-Hall, 1947. *158*

99. Cason, H. The conditioned pupillary reaction. *J. exp. Psychol.,* 1922, *5,* 108-146. *76*

100. Carter, J. W., Jr. A case of reactional dissociation (hysterical paralysis). *Amer. J. Orthopsychiat.,* 1937, *7,* 219-224. *260*

101. Cattell, R. B. *Description and measurement of personality.* Yonkers, N. Y.: World Book Co., 1946. *318-321, 329, 359*

102. Cattell, R. B. *An introduction to personality study.* London: Hutchinson's University Library, 1950. *319*

103. Cattell, R. B., & Molteno, E. Virginia. Contributions concerning mental inheritance: II. Temperament. *J. genet. Psychol.,* 1940, *57,* 31-47. *398*

104. Child, I. L. Children's preference for goals easy or difficult to obtain. *Psychol. Monogr.,* 1946, *60,* No. 4 (Whole No. 280). *89*

105. Child, I. L. The relation of somatotype to self-ratings on Sheldon's temperamental traits. *J. Pers.,* 1950, *18,* 440-453. *383*

106. Clark, K. B. Some factors influencing the remembering of prose material. *Arch. Psychol., N. Y.,* 1940, No. 253. *231*

107. Clendening, L. *The human body.* New York: Knopf, 1930. *261*

108. Cobb, S. Personality as affected by lesions of the brain. In J. McV. Hunt (Ed.), *Personality and the behavior disorders.* New York: Ronald Press, 1944. Pp. 550-581. *379*

109. Coghill, G. E. *Anatomy and the problem of behavior.* New York: Macmillan, 1929. *46*

110. Coleman, J. C. *Abnormal psychology and modern life.* Chicago: Scott, Foresman, 1950. *123, 213, 513*

111. Collier, R. M. A basis for integration rather than fragmentation in psychotherapy. *J. consult. Psychol.,* 1950, *14,* 199-205. *523*

112. Cook, S. W. The production of "experimental neurosis" in the white rat. *Psychosom. Med.,* 1939, *1,* 293-308. *117*

113. Cook, S. W. A survey of methods used to produce "experimental neurosis." *Amer. J. Psychiat.,* 1939, *95,* 1259-1276. *116*

114. *Cortone (Cortisone, Compound E), a syllabus.* Rahway, N. J.: Merck & Co., 1950. *367*

115. Cottle, W. C. The MMPI: a review. *Kans. Stud. Educ.,* 1953, *3,* No. 2. *328*

116. Cowles, J. T. Food-tokens as incentives for learning in chimpanzees. *Comp. Psychol. Monogr.,* 1937, *14,* No. 5 (Serial No. 71). *78*

117. Cox, F. N. Sociometric status and individual adjustment before and after play therapy. *J. abnorm. soc. Psychol.,* 1953, *48,* 354-356. *548*

118. Crider, B. Phobias: their nature and treatment. *J. Psychol.,* 1949, *27,* 217-229. *222, 225*

119. Cronbach, L. J. Statistical methods applied to Rorschach scores. *Psychol. Bull.,* 1949, *46,* 393-429. *337*

120. Cuber, J. F. *Marriage counseling practice.* New York: Appleton-Century-Crofts, 1948. *580, 591*

121. Culpin, M. *Recent advances in the study of the psychoneuroses.* Philadelphia: Blakiston, 1931. *267, 304, 333-350*

122. Darrow, C. W., & Heath, Lena L. Reaction tendencies relating to personality. In K. S. Lashley (Ed.), *Studies in the dynamics of behavior.* Chicago: Univer. of Chicago Press, 1932. Pp. 59-261. *75*

123. Dashiell, J. F. *Fundamentals of general psychology.* (3rd ed.) Boston: Houghton Mifflin, 1949. *9, 23, 55, 154*

124. Davis, A. American systems and the socialization of the child. *Amer. sociol. Rev.,* 1941, *6,* 345-354. *82*

125. Davis, A. *Social-class influences upon learning.* Cambridge, Mass.: Harvard Univer. Press, 1948. *421*

126. Davis, A. Child rearing in the class structure of American society.

In G. Emerson (**Ed.**), *The family in a democratic society.* New York: Columbia Univer. Press, 1949. *82*

127. Davis, A., & Havighurst, R. J. Social class and color differences in child-rearing. *Amer. sociol. Rev.,* 1946, *11,* 698-710, *422*

128. Davis, A., & Havighurst, R. J. *Father of the man.* Boston: Houghton Mifflin, 1947. *447*

129. Davis, H. V., Sears, R. R., Miller, H. C., & Brodbeck, A. J. Effects of cup, bottle and breast feeding on oral activities of newborn infants. *Pediatrics,* 1948, *3,* 549-558. *42*

130. Davis, Katharine B. *Factors in the sex life of twenty-two hundred women.* New York: Harper, 1929. *34*

131. Dempsey, E. W. Homeostasis. In S. S. Stevens (Ed.), *Handbook of experimental psychology.* New York: Wiley, 1951. Pp. 209-235. *36, 43, 57, 361*

132. Denker, P. G. Results of treatment of psychoneuroses by the general practitioner. A follow-up study of 500 cases. *N. Y. State J. Med.,* 1946, *46,* 2164-2166. *545-546*

133. Derner, G. F., Aborn, M., & Canter, A. H. The reliability of the Wechsler-Bellevue subtests and scales. *J. consult. Psychol.,* 1950, *14,* 172-179. *349*

134. Devereux, G. *Reality and dream.* New York: International Universities Press, 1951. *447*

135. Doll, E. A. *The measurement of social competence.* Philadelphia: Educational Test Bureau, 1953. *350*

136. Dollard, J. *Victory over fear.* New York: Reynal & Hitchcock, 1942. *245*

137. Dollard, J. *Fear in battle.* New Haven, Conn.: Institute of Human Relations, Yale Univer., 1943. *215*

138. Dollard, J., Doob, L. W., Miller, N. E., Mowrer, O. H., & Sears, R. R. *Frustration and aggression.* New Haven, Conn.: Yale Univer. Press, 1939. *101, 123*

139. Dollard, J., & Miller, N. E. *Personality and psychotherapy.* New York: McGraw-Hill, 1950. *97, 123, 136, 154, 245, 404, 480, 532, 549*

140. Driscoll, Gertrude P. *Child guidance in the classroom.* New York: Teachers Coll., Columbia Univer., 1955. *590*

141. DuBois, Cora. *The people of Alor.* Minneapolis: Univer. of Minnesota Press, 1944. *411*

142. Dudycha, G. J., & Dudycha, Martha M. Childhood memories: a review of the literature. *Psychol. Bull.,* 1941, *38,* 668-682. *213*

143. Dugdale, R. L. *The Jukes.* New York: Putnam, 1877. *390*

144. Dunbar, Flanders. *Mind and body: psychosomatic medicine.* New York: Random House, 1947. *292, 306*

145. Dymond, Rosalind F. An adjustment score for Q sorts. *J. consult. Psychol.*, 1953, *17*, 339-342. *548*

146. Dymond, Rosalind F. Adjustment changes in the absence of psychotherapy. *J. consult. Psychol.*, 1955, *19*, 103-107. *548*

147. Edwards, A. L. Political frames of reference as a factor influencing recognition. *J. abnorm. soc. Psychol.*, 1941, *36*, 34-50. *93*

148. Edwards, A. L. Rationalization in recognition as a result of a political frame of reference. *J. abnorm. soc. Psychol.*, 1941, *36*, 224-235. *93*

149. Edwards, A. L. The retention of affective experiences — a criticism and restatement of the problem. *Psychol. Rev.*, 1942, *49*, 43-53. *231*

150. Ellis, A., & Conrad, H. S. The validity of personality inventories in military practice. *Psychol. Bull.*, 1948, *45*, 385-426. *329*

151. Emerson, G. (Ed.) *Social work as human relations.* Anniversary Papers of the New York School of Social Work and the Community Service Society of New York. New York: Columbia Univer. Press, 1949. *573*

152. English, H. B. Three cases of the "conditioned fear response." *J. abnorm. soc. Psychol.*, 1929, *24*, 221-225. *49*

153. Ephron, Beulah K. *Emotional difficulties in reading.* New York: Julian Press, 1953. *556*

154. Erikson, E. H. Observations on Sioux education. *J. Psychol.*, 1939, *7*, 101-156. *81*

155. Erikson, E. H. *Childhood and society.* New York: Norton, 1950. *154*

156. Estabrook, A. H. *The Jukes in 1915.* Carnegie Institution of Washington, Publication No. 240, 1916. *390*

157. Estes, W. K. An experimental study of punishment. *Psychol. Monogr.*, 1944, *57*, No. 3 (Whole No. 263). *131, 132, 531*

158. Evans, Jean. *Three men.* New York: Knopf, 1954. *123*

159. Eysenck, H. J. *Dimensions of personality.* London: Routledge & Kegan Paul, 1947. *257, 270, 289, 347, 352-354, 355*

160. Eysenck, H. J. The effects of psychotherapy: an evaluation. *J. consult. Psychol.*, 1952, *16*, 319-324. *545-546*

161. Eysenck, H. J. *The structure of human personality.* New York: Wiley, 1953. *359*

162. Farber, I. E. Response fixation under anxiety and non-anxiety conditions. *J. exp. Psychol.*, 1948, *38*, 111-131. *149-150*

163. Faris, R. E. L. *Social disorganization.* (2nd ed.) New York: Ronald Press, 1955. *186*

164. Felix, R. H. Mental hygiene as public health practice. *Amer. J. Orthopsychiat.*, 1951, *21*, 707-716. *485*

164a. Fenton, N. *Mental hygiene in school practice.* Stanford, Calif.: Stanford Univer. Press, 1943. *590*

165. Fernald, G. G. An achievement capacity test. *J. educ. Psychol.,* 1912, *3,* 331-336. *352*

166. Fiedler, F. E. A comparison of therapeutic relationships in psychoanalytic, nondirective and Adlerian therapy. *J. consult. Psychol.,* 1950, *14,* 436-445. *526*

167. Fiedler, F. E. The concept of an ideal therapeutic relationship. *J. consult. Psychol.,* 1950, *14,* 239-245. *526*

168. Fink, A. E., Wilson, E. E., & Conover, M. B. *The field of social work.* (3rd ed.) New York: Holt, 1955. *573, 591*

169. Fischer, Liselotte K. Psychological appraisal of the "unattached" preschool child. *Amer. J. Orthopsychiat.,* 1953, *23,* 803-816. *443*

170. Fiske, D. W. A study of relationships to somatotype. *J. appl. Psychol.,* 1944, *28,* 504-519. *383*

171. Fletcher, J. M. *The problem of stuttering.* New York: Longmans, Green, 1928. *269*

172. Frank, L. K. *Projective methods.* Springfield, Ill.: Charles C Thomas, 1948. *334*

173. Franklin, J. C., Schiele, B. C., Brozek, J., and Keys, A. Observations on human behavior in experimental semistarvation and rehabilitation. *J. clin. Psychol.,* 1948, *4,* 28-45. *37, 376*

174. Franz, S. I. *Handbook of mental examination methods.* (2nd ed.) New York: Macmillan, 1919. *323*

175. Fraser, Russell. *The incidence of neurosis among factory workers.* Industrial Health Research Board Report No. 90. London: H. M. Stationery Office, 1947. *567*

176. Freeman, F. N., Holzinger, K. J., & Mitchell, Blythe C. The influence of environment on the intelligence, school achievement, and conduct of foster children. In National Society for the Study of Education, *Twenty-seventh yearbook.* Bloomington, Ill.: Public School Publishing Co., 1928. Part I, pp. 103-217. *393*

177. Freeman, G. L. A method of inducing frustration in human subjects and its influence upon palmar skin resistance. *Amer. J. Psychol.,* 1940, *53,* 117-120. *118*

178. Freud, S. *The psychopathology of everyday life.* New York: Macmillan, 1914. *229*

179. Freud, S. *Collected papers.* 5 vol. London: Hogarth Press, 1924-1950. *449*

180. Freud, S. Analysis of a phobia in a five-year-old boy. (1909) In *Collected papers.* London: Hogarth Press, 1925. Vol. III, pp. 149-289, *223*

181. Freud, S. *The ego and the id.* London: Hogarth Press, 1927. *449*

182. Freud, S. *New introductory lectures on psychoanalysis.* New York: Norton, 1933. *449, 478*

183. Freud, S. *A general introduction to psychoanalysis.* (Rev. ed.) New York: Liveright, 1935. *449, 480*

184. Freud, S. *The problem of anxiety.* New York: Norton, 1936. *275, 449*

185. Freud, S. *The basic writings of Sigmund Freud.* New York: Modern Library, 1938. *230, 449, 480*

186. Freud, S. *An outline of psychoanalysis.* New York: Norton, 1949. *139, 449, 473, 476, 480*

187. Fromm, E. *Escape from freedom.* New York: Farrar & Rinehart, 1941. *470, 480*

188. Fromm, E. *Man for himself.* New York: Rinehart, 1947. *23, 470*

189. Fromm, E. *The forgotten language.* New York: Rinehart, 1951. *213*

190. Fromm, E. *The sane society.* New York: Rinehart, 1955. *446*

191. Froeschels, E. (Ed.) *Twentieth century speech and voice correction.* New York: Philosophical Library, 1948. *270, 271*

192. Froeschels, E. Pathology and therapy of stuttering. In *Twentieth century speech and voice correction.* New York: Philosophical Library, 1948. Pp. 194-210. *269, 270*

193. Fry, C., & Rostow, E. G. *Mental health in college.* New York: Commonwealth Fund, 1942. *23*

194. Gantt, W. H. *Experimental basis for neurotic behavior.* New York: Hoeber, 1944. Also published as *Psychosom. Med. Monogr.,* 1944, No. 7. *116*

195. Gardner, I. C., & Newman, H. H. Mental and physical traits of identical twins reared apart. *J. Hered.,* 1940, *31,* 119-126. *398*

196. Garfield, S. L. An evaluation of Wechsler-Bellevue patterns in schizophrenia. *J. consult. Psychol.,* 1949, *13,* 279-287. *348*

197. Garrett, Annette. Historical survey of the evolution of casework. *J. soc. Casewk,* 1949, *30,* 219-229. *576*

198. Gaskill, H. V. The objective measurement of emotional reactions. *Genet. Psychol. Monogr.,* 1933, *14,* 177-281. *54*

199. Gaskill, H. V., & Cox, G. M. Patterns in emotional reactions: I. Respiration; the use of analysis of variance and covariance in psychological data. *J. gen. Psychol.,* 1937, *16,* 21-38. *54*

200. Gaskill, H. V., & Cox, G. M. Patterns in emotional reactions: II. Heart rate and blood pressure. *J. gen. Psychol.,* 1941, *24,* 409-421. *54*

201. Gates, A. I. *The improvement of reading.* (3rd ed.) New York: Macmillan, 1947. *553, 554*

202. Gates, A. I., Jersild, A. T., McConnell, T. R., & Challman, R. C.

Educational psychology. (3rd ed.) New York: Macmillan, 1948. *558*

203. Gesell, A. The ontogenesis of infant behavior. In L. Carmichael (Ed.), *Manual of child psychology.* (2nd ed.) New York: Wiley, 1954. Pp. 335-373. *46*

204. Gilbert, G. M. The new status of experimental studies on the relationship of feeling to memory. *Psychol. Bull.*, 1938, *35*, 26-35. *231*

205. Gill, M., Newman, R., & Redlich, F. C. *The initial interview in psychiatric practice.* New York: International Universities Press, 1954. *549*

206. Glixman, A. F. An analysis of the use of the interruption-technique in experimental studies of "repression." *Psychol. Bull.*, 1948, *45*, 491-506. *231*

207. Glixman, A. F. Recall of completed and incompleted activities under varying degrees of stress. *J. exp. Psychol.*, 1949, *39*, 281-295. *231*

208. Glueck, S., & Glueck, Eleanor. *Unraveling juvenile delinquency.* Cambridge, Mass.: Harvard Univer. Press, 1950. *437-439*

209. Goddard, H. H. *The Kallikak family.* New York: Macmillan, 1912. *390*

210. Goldfarb, W. Infant rearing and problem behavior. *Amer. J. Orthopsychiat.*, 1943, *13*, 249-265. *444*

211. Goldfarb, W. Psychological privation in infancy and subsequent adjustment. *Amer. J. Orthopsychiat.*, 1945, *15*, 247-255. *444*

212. Goodenough, Florence L. *Anger in young children.* Minneapolis, Minn.: Univer. of Minnesota Press, 1931. *88*

213. Gough, H. G. A new dimension of status: II. Relationship of the St scale to other variables. *Amer. sociol. Rev.*, 1948, *13*, 534-537. *427*

214. Gough, H. G. Factors relating to the academic achievement of high-school students. *J. educ. Psychol.*, 1949, *40*, 65-78. *328*

215. Gough, H. G. The F minus K dissimulation index for the Minnesota Multiphasic Personality Inventory. *J. consult. Psychol.*, 1950, *14*, 408-413. *330*

216. Gould, R. Repression experimentally analyzed. *Charact. & Pers.*, 1942, *10*, 259-288. *231*

217. Green, G. H. *Psychoanalysis in the classroom.* (2nd ed.) New York: Putnam, 1922. *202*

218. Grinker, R. R., & Robbins, F. *Psychosomatic case book.* New York: Blakiston, 1954. *306*

219. Grinker, R. R., & Spiegel, J. P. *War neuroses in North Africa.* New York: Josiah Macy, Jr. Foundation, 1943. *264*

220. Grinker, R. R., & Spiegel, J. P. *Men under stress.* Philadelphia: Blakiston, 1945. *264, 283*

221. Guilford, J. P. *Inventory of factors S T D C R.* Beverly Hills, Calif.: Sheridan Supply Co., 1940. *328*

222. Guilford, J. P. (Ed.) *Printed classification tests.* Army Air Forces Aviation Psychology Program Research Reports, Report No. 5. Washington: U. S. Government Printing Office, 1947. *355*

223. Guilford, J. P., & Guilford, Ruth B. Personality factors S, E, and M, and their measurement. *J. Psychol.,* 1936, *2,* 109-127. *328*

224. Guilford, J. P., & Zimmerman, W. S. *The Guilford-Zimmerman Temperament Survey.* Beverly Hills, Calif.: Sheridan Supply Co., 1949. *328*

225. Guthrie, E. R. *The psychology of learning.* New York: Harper, 1935. *136*

226. Guthrie, E. R., & Powers, F. F. *Educational psychology.* New York: Ronald Press, 1950. *154*

227. Hahn, E. F. *Stuttering, significant theories and therapies.* Stanford, Calif.: Stanford Univer. Press, 1943. *270, 272*

228. Haigh, G. Defensive behavior in client-centered therapy. *J. consult. Psychol.,* 1949, *13,* 181-189. *540*

229. Hall, C. S. The inheritance of emotionality. *Sigma Xi Quart.,* 1938, *26,* 17-27. *388*

230. Hall, C. S. *The meaning of dreams.* New York: Harper, 1953. *213*

231. Hall, C. S. *A primer of Freudian psychology.* Cleveland, O.: World Publishing Co., 1954. *479*

232. Halverson, H. M. Infant sucking and tensional behavior. *J. genet. Psychol.,* 1938, *53,* 365-430. *34*

233. Halverson, H. M. Genital and sphincter behavior of the male infant. *J. genet. Psychol.,* 1940, *56,* 95-136. *34*

234. Hamilton, G. V. *An introduction to objective psychopathology.* St. Louis: Mosby, 1925. *239, 273, 302*

235. Hamilton, Gordon. *Psychotherapy in child guidance.* New York: Columbia Univer. Press, 1947. *186, 591*

236. Hamilton, Gordon. *Theory and practice of social casework.* (2nd ed.) New York: Columbia Univer. Press, 1951. *573, 591*

237. Hamilton, J. A., & Krechevsky, I. Studies in the effect of shock upon behavior plasticity in the rat. *J. comp. Psychol.,* 1933, *16,* 237-253. *211*

238. Hartshorne, H., & May, M. A. *Studies in the nature of character. I. Studies in deceit.* New York: Macmillan, 1928. *357*

239. Hartshorne, H., May, M. A., & Maller, J. B. *Studies in the nature of character. II. Studies in service and self-control.* New York: Macmillan, 1929. *357*

240. Hartshorne, H., May, M. A., & Shuttleworth, F. K. *Studies in the nature of character. III. Studies in the organization of character.* New York: Macmillan, 1930. *357*

241. Hastings, D. W., Wright, D. G., & Glueck, B. C. *Psychiatric experiences of the Eighth Air Force.* New York: Josiah Macy, Jr. Foundation, 1944. *280*

242. Hathaway, S. R. Some considerations relative to nondirective counseling as psychotherapy. *J. clin. Psychol.,* 1948, 4, 226-231. *545*

243. Hathaway, S. R., & McKinley, J. C. A multiphasic personality schedule (Minnesota): I. Construction of the schedule. *J. Psychol.,* 1940, *10,* 249-254. *326*

244. Hathaway, S. R., & McKinley, J. C. *The Minnesota Multiphasic Personality Inventory.* Minneapolis, Minn.: Univer. of Minnesota Press, 1943. *326-328*

245. Hathaway, S. R., & Meehl, P. E. *An atlas for the clinical use of the MMPI.* Minneapolis, Minn.: Univer. of Minnesota Press, 1951. *327*

246. Hathaway, S. R., & Monachesi, E. D. (Eds.) *Analyzing and predicting juvenile delinquency with the MMPI.* Minneapolis: Univer. of Minnesota Press, 1953. *439*

247. Havighurst, R. J., & Taba, Hilda. *Adolescent character and personality.* New York: Wiley, 1949. *422*

248. Healy, W., Bronner, Augusta F., Baylor, Edith M. H., & Murphy, J. P. *Reconstructing behavior in youth.* New York: Knopf, 1929. *396*

249. Healy, W., Bronner, Augusta F., & Bowers, Anna M. *The structure and meaning of psychoanalysis.* New York: Knopf, 1930. *452, 457, 479*

250. Heath, C. W. *What people are.* Cambridge, Mass.: Harvard Univer. Press, 1945. *591*

251. Hebb, D. O. Emotion in man and animal: an analysis of the intuitive process of recognition. *Psychol. Rev.,* 1946, *53,* 88-106. *49*

252. Hebb, D. O. On the nature of fear. *Psychol. Rev.,* 1946, *53,* 259-276. *49*

253. Hilgard, E. R. *Theories of learning.* (2nd ed.) New York: Appleton-Century-Crofts, 1956. *154*

254. Hilgard, E. R. *Introduction to psychology.* New York: Harcourt, Brace, 1953. *57, 154*

255. Hobbs, N. Group-centered psychotherapy. In C. R. Rogers, *Client-centered therapy.* Boston: Houghton Mifflin, 1951. Pp. 278-319. *540*

256. Hoelzel, F. Central factors in hunger. *Amer. J. Physiol.,* 1927. *82,* 665-671. *32*

257. Hoffeditz, E. Louise. Family resemblances in personality traits. *J. soc. Psychol.*, 1934, *5*, 214-227. *427*

258. Hoffman, A. E. A study of reported behavior changes in counseling. *J. consult. Psychol.*, 1949, *13*, 190-195. *540*

259. Hollingworth, H. L. Vicarious functioning of irrelevant imagery. *J. Phil. Psychol. sci. Meth.*, 1911, 8, 688-692. *143*

260. Hollingworth, H. L. *The psychology of functional neuroses.* New York: Appleton, 1920. *347*

261. Hollingworth, H. L. *Psychology, its facts and principles.* New York: Appleton, 1928. *142*

262. Hollingworth, H. L. *Abnormal psychology.* New York: Ronald Press, 1930. *260*

263. Hollinshead, A. deB. *Elmtown's youth.* New York: Wiley, 1949. *427*

264. Holt, E. B., *Animal drive and the learning process.* New York: Holt, 1931. *41, 136, 138*

265. Honigmann, J. J. *Culture and personality.* New York: Harper, 1954. *431*

266. Hooton, E. *Young man, you are normal.* New York: Putnam, 1945. *591*

267. Horney, Karen. *The neurotic personality of our time.* New York: Norton, 1937. *159, 165, 470, 480*

268. Horney, Karen. *New ways in psychoanalysis.* New York: Norton, 1939. *470*

269. Horney, Karen. *Our inner conflicts.* New York: Norton, 1945. *158, 213, 470*

270. Horney, Karen. *Neurosis and human growth.* New York: Norton, 1950. *470*

271. Hoskins, R. G. *Endocrinology.* New York: Norton, 1941. *363, 400*

272. Hovland, C. I. The generalization of conditioned responses; I. The sensory generalization of conditioned responses with varying frequencies of tone. *J. gen. Psychol.*, 1937, *17*, 125-148. *72*

273. Hovland, C. I., & Sears, R. R. Experiments on motor conflict. I. Types of conflict and their modes of resolution. *J. exp. Psychol.*, 1938, *23*, 477-493. *119, 120*

274. Hovland, C. I., & Sears, R. R. Minor studies of aggression: VI. Correlation of lynchings with economic indices. *J. Psychol.*, 1940, *9*, 301-310. *102*

275. Hull, C. L. *Principles of behavior.* New York: Appleton-Century, 1943. *134, 136, 476*

276. Hull, C. L. The problem of intervening variables in molar behavior theory. *Psychol. Rev.*, 1943, *50*, 273-291. *64*

277. Humphreys, L. G. The effect of random alternation of reinforce-

ment on the acquisition and extinction of conditioned eyelid reactions. *J. exp. Psychol.*, 1939, *25*, 141-158. *443*

278. Hunt, H. F. The effect of deliberate deception on Minnesota Multiphasic Personality Inventory performance. *J. consult. Psychol.*, 1948, *12*, 396-402. *330*

279. Hunt, J. McV. (Ed.) *Personality and the behavior disorders.* New York: Ronald Press, 1944. 2 vols. *123, 154, 359, 400*

280. Hunt, W. A. The future of diagnostic testing in clinical psychology. *J. clin. Psychol.*, 1946, *2*, 311-317. *349*

281. Hurlock, Elizabeth B. An evaluation of certain incentives used in school work. *J. educ. Psychol.*, 1925, *16*, 145-159. *561*

282. Hutt, M. L. A clinical study of "consecutive" and "adaptive" testing with the Revised Stanford-Binet. *J. consult. Psychol.*, 1947, *11*, 93-103. *355*

283. Hymes, J. L., Jr. *Teacher listen, the children speak.* New York: State Charities Aid Assn., 1949. *563*

284. Hymes, J. L., Jr. *Effective home-school relations.* New York: Prentice-Hall, 1953. *590*

285. Jacobsen, C. F., Wolfe, J. B., & Jackson, T. A. An experimental analysis of the functions of the frontal association areas in primates. *J. nerv. ment. Dis.*, 1935, *82*, 1-14. *117*

286. James, W. *The principles of psychology.* New York: Holt, 1890. 2 vols. *48, 228-229*

287. James, W. *Pragmatism.* New York: Longmans, Green, 1907. *313*

288. Janet, P. *The major symptoms of hysteria.* (2nd ed.) New York: Macmillan, 1920. *257, 262*

289. Jastak, J. A plan for the objective measurement of character. *J. clin. Psychol.*, 1948, *4*, 170-178. *346*

290. Jennings, Helen H. *Sociometry in group relations.* Washington: American Council on Education, 1948. *333*

291. Jennings, H. S. *Behavior of the lower organisms.* New York: Columbia Univer. Press, 1906. *125*

292. Jersild, A. T. *Child psychology.* (4th ed.) New York: Prentice-Hall, 1954. *199, 442*

293. Jersild, A. T. Emotional development. In L. Carmichael (Ed.), *Manual of child psychology.* (2nd ed.) New York: Wiley, 1954. Pp. 833-917. *46, 58, 216*

294. Jersild, A. T., & Helfant, K. *Education for self-understanding.* New York: Teachers Coll., Columbia Univer., 1953. *590*

295. Jersild, A. T., & Holmes, Frances B. *Children's fears.* Child Developm. Monogr. No. 20. New York: Teachers Coll., Columbia Univer., 1935. *216*

296. Jersild, A. T., Markey, Frances V., & Jersild, Catherine L. *Chil-*

dren's fears, dreams, wishes, daydreams, likes, dislikes, pleasant and unpleasant memories. Child Develpm. Monogr. No. 12. New York: Teachers Coll., Columbia Univer., 1933. *202*

297. Johnson, W. *People in quandaries.* New York: Harper, 1946. *154, 270, 271, 272*

298. Johnson, W. (Ed.) *Speech problems of children.* New York: Grune & Stratton, 1950. *270*

299. Johnson, W. (Ed.) *Stuttering in children and adults.* Minneapolis, Minn.: Univer. of Minnesota Press, 1955. *272*

300. Johnson, W., & Knott, J. R. Studies in the psychology of stuttering. I. The distribution of moments of stuttering in successive readings of the same materials. *J. Speech Disorders,* 1937, *2,* 17-19. *270*

301. Jones, H. E. The galvanic skin reflex in infancy. *Child Developm.,* 1930, *1,* 106-110. *75*

302. Jones, H. E. The retention of conditioned emotional reactions in infancy. *J. genet. Psychol.,* 1930, *37,* 485-498. *75*

303. Jones, H. E. The environment and mental development. In L. Carmichael (Ed.), *Manual of child psychology.* (2nd ed.) New York: Wiley, 1954. Pp. 631-696. *397*

304. Jones, H. E., & Jones, Mary C. Fear. *Childhood Educ.,* 1928, *5,* 136-143. *216*

305. Jones, Mary C. The elimination of children's fears. *J. exp. Psychol.,* 1924, *7,* 382-390. *70*

306. Jones, Mary C. A laboratory study of fear: the case of Peter. *Ped. Sem.,* 1924, *31,* 308-315. *70, 535*

307. Jung, C. G. The association method. *Amer. J. Psychol.,* 1910, *21,* 219-269. *339*

308. Jung, C. G. *Psychology of the unconscious.* New York: Dodd, Mead, 1916. *467*

309. Jung, C. G. *Studies in word association.* New York: Moffat, 1919. *339*

310. Jung, C. G. *Psychological types.* New York: Harcourt, Brace, 1923. *313-314, 467*

311. Jung, C. G. *Contributions to analytical psychology.* New York: Harcourt, Brace, 1928. *467*

312. Jung, C. G. *Modern man in search of a soul.* New York: Harcourt, Brace, 1933. *467, 480*

313. Kallman, F. J. *The genetics of schizophrenia.* New York: Augustin, 1938. *391*

314. Kanner, L. *Child psychiatry.* (2nd ed.) Springfield, Ill.: Charles C Thomas, 1948. *512*

315. Kanner, L. Problems of nosology and psychodynamics of early infantile autism. *Amer. J. Orthopsychiat.,* 1949, *19,* 416-426. *192*

316. Kapp, F. T., Rosenbaum, M., & Romano, J. Psychological factors in men with peptic ulcers. *Amer. J. Psychiat.*, 1947, *103*, 700-704. *294*

317. Kardiner, A. *The psychological frontiers of society.* New York: Columbia Univer. Press, 1945. *411*

318. Karn, H. W. Experimental neurosis in infrahuman animals — a bibliography. *Psychol. Rec.*, 1940, *4*, 35-39. *116*

319. Karn, H. W. The experimental study of neurotic behavior in infrahuman animals. *J. gen. Psychol.*, 1940, *22*, 431-436. *116*

320. Kasius, Cora (Ed.) *Principles and techniques in social casework.* New York: Family Service Association of America, 1950. *573, 576*

321. Katz, B., & Lehner, G. F. J. *Mental hygiene in modern living.* New York: Ronald Press, 1953. *23*

322. Kelly, E. L. Marital compatibility as related to personality traits of husbands and wives as rated by self and spouse. *J. soc. Psychol.*, 1941, *13*, 193-198. *579*

323. Kempf, E. J. (Ed.) Comparative conditioned neuroses. *Ann. N. Y. Acad. Sci.*, 1953, *56*, 141-380. *116*

324. Kent, Grace H., & Rosanoff, A. J. A study of association in insanity. *Amer. J. Insanity*, 1910, *67*, 37-96, 317-390. *339*

325. Keys, A., Brozek, J., Henschel, A., Mickelsen, O., & Taylor, H. L. *The biology of human starvation.* Minneapolis: Univer. of Minnesota Press, 1950. *376*

326. Kierkegaard, S. *The concept of dread.* First published in Danish, 1849. (Trans. by W. Lowrie) Princeton, N. J.: Princeton Univer. Press, 1944. *275*

327. Kinsey, A. C., Pomeroy, W. B., & Martin, C. E. *Sexual behavior in the human male.* Philadelphia: Saunders, 1948. *34, 425*

328. Kinsey, A. C., Pomeroy, W. B., Martin, C. E., & Gebhard, P. H. *Sexual behavior in the human female.* Philadelphia: Saunders, 1953. *35*

329. Kitson, H. D. *How to use your mind.* (4th ed.) Philadelphia: Lippincott, 1951. *591*

330. Klapman, J. W. *Group psychotherapy: theory and practice.* New York: Grune & Stratton, 1946. *541*

331. Klein, D. B. *Mental hygiene.* New York: Holt, 1944. *23, 123, 186, 213, 245, 513*

332. Klein, D. B. *Abnormal psychology.* New York: Holt, 1951. *272, 549*

333. Klineberg, O. Emotional expression in Chinese literature. *J. abnorm. soc. Psychol.*, 1938, *33*, 517-520. *60*

334. Kluckhohn, C., Murray, H. A., & Schneider, D. M. (Eds.) *Per-*

sonality in nature, society, and culture. (2nd ed.) New York: Knopf, 1953. *97, 447*

335. Koffka, K. *The growth of the mind.* New York: Harcourt, Brace, 1925. *134*

336. Koffka, K. *Principles of gestalt psychology.* New York: Harcourt, Brace, 1935. *134*

337. Kohler, W. *The mentality of apes.* New York: Harcourt, Brace, 1925. *134*

338. Kohler, W. *Gestalt psychology.* (Rev. ed.) New York: Liveright, 1947. *134*

339. Korner, I. N. Experimental investigation of some aspects of the problem of repression: Repressive forgetting. *Teach. Coll. Contr. Educ.,* 1950, No. 970. *231*

340. Krasnogorski, N. I. The conditioned reflexes and children's neuroses. *Amer. J. Dis. Child.,* 1925, *30,* 753-786. *118*

341. Kretschmer, E. *Physique and character.* New York: Harcourt, Brace, 1925. *380*

342. Krugman, H. E. Flicker fusion frequency as a function of anxiety reaction: an exploratory study. *Psychosom. Med.,* 1947, 9, 269-272. *354*

343. Krugman, M. (Chm.) A study of current trends in the use and coordination of professional services of psychiatrists, psychologists and social workers in mental hygiene clinics and other psychiatric agencies and institutions. *Amer. J. Orthopsychiat.,* 1950, *20,* 1-62. *488*

344. Kuhlmann, F. *A handbook of mental tests.* Baltimore: Warwick & York, 1922. *41, 354*

345. LaBarre, W. *The human animal.* Chicago: Univer. of Chicago Press, 1954. *154*

346. Lafore, Gertrude G. Practices of parents in dealing with preschool children. *Child Develpm. Monogr.,* 1945, No. 31. *443*

347. Landis, C. Statistical evaluation of psychotherapeutic methods. In L. E. Hinsie, *Concepts and problems of psychotherapy.* New York: Columbia Univer. Press, 1937. Pp. 155-169. *545*

348. Landis, C., & Bolles, M. Marjorie. *Textbook of abnormal psychology.* (Rev. ed.) New York: Macmillan, 1950. *158, 272, 289, 306, 376*

349. Langford, W. S. *et al.* The professional person — a mental hygiene resource. *Ment. Hyg., N. Y.,* 1950, *34,* 262-286. *488*

350. Lanier, L. H. An experimental study of "affective conflict." *J. Psychol.,* 1941, *11,* 199-217. *231*

351. Lanier, L. H. Incidental memory for words differing in affective value. *J. Psychol.,* 1941, *11,* 219-228. *231*

352. Lee, P. R., & Kenworthy, Marion E. *Mental hygiene and social work*. New York: Commonwealth Fund, 1929. *546*

353. Leeper, R. W. A motivational theory of emotion to replace "emotion as disorganized response." *Psychol. Rev.*, 1948, 55, 5-21. *55, 57*

354. Lehner, G. F. J., & Kube, Ella. *The dynamics of personal adjustment*. New York: Prentice-Hall, 1955. *23, 186, 549, 590*

355. Lemkau, P. V. *Mental hygiene in public health*. (2nd ed.) New York: McGraw-Hill, 1955. *485, 513*

356. Leonard, W. E. *The locomotive-god*. New York: Appleton-Century-Crofts, 1927. *245*

357. Levine, J. M., & Murphy, G. The learning and forgetting of controversial material. *J. abnorm. soc. Psychol.*, 1943, 38, 507-517. *93*

358. Levy, D. M. Fingersucking and accessory movements in early infancy. *Amer. J. Psychiat.*, 1928, 84, 881-918. *42*

359. Levy, D. M. Experiments on the sucking reflex and social behavior of dogs. *Amer. J. Orthopsychiat.*, 1934, 4, 203-224. *42*

360. Levy, D. M. On instinct-satiation: an experiment on the pecking behavior of chickens. *J. gen. Psychol.*, 1938, 18, 327-348. *42*

361. Levy, D. M. *Maternal overprotection*. New York: Columbia Univer. Press, 1943. *440*

362. Levy, D. M. Critical evaluation of the present state of child psychiatry. *Amer. J. Psychiat.*, 1952, 108, 481-494. *489, 500*

363. Levy, D. M., & Tulchin, S. H. The resistance of infants and children. *J. exp. Psychol.*, 1923, 6, 304-322. *199*

364. Levy, D. M., & Tulchin, S. H. The resistant behavior of infants and children. II. *J. exp. Psychol.*, 1925, 8, 209-224. *199*

365. Levy, J., & Munroe, Ruth L. *The happy family*. New York: Knopf, 1938. *591*

366. Lewin, K. *A dynamic theory of personality*. New York: McGraw-Hill, 1935. *104, 123*

367. Lewin, K. Behavior and development as a function of the total situation. In L. Carmichael (Ed.), *Manual of child psychology*. (2nd ed.) New York: Wiley, 1954. Pp. 918-970. *104, 123*

368. Liddell, H. S. Conditioned reflex method and experimental neurosis. In J. McV. Hunt (Ed.), *Personality and the behavior disorders*. New York: Ronald Press, 1944. Pp. 389-412. *116, 117*

369. Lindgren, H. C. *Psychology of personal and social adjustment*. New York: American Book Co., 1953. *23, 186, 245, 590*

370. Lindgren, H. C. *Mental health in education*. New York: Holt, 1954. *590*

371. Lindner, R. *Prescription for rebellion*. New York: Rinehart, 1952. *23*

372. Lindsley, D. B. Emotion. In S. S. Stevens (Ed.), *Handbook of experimental psychology.* New York: Wiley, 1951. Pp. 473-516. *58*

373. Lindzey, G. (Ed.) *Handbook of social psychology.* Cambridge, Mass.: Addison-Wesley Press, 1954. *97*

374. Locke, H. J. *Predicting adjustment in marriage.* New York: Holt, 1951. *579*

375. Lorenz, K. S. The companion in the birds' world. *Auk,* 1937, *54,* 245-273. *79*

376. Lorr, M., & Jenkins, R. L. Three factors in parent behavior. *J. consult. Psychol.,* 1953, *17,* 306-308. *434*

377. Louttit, C. M. *Clinical psychology.* (Rev. ed.) New York: Harper, 1947. *490*

378. Lund, F. H. *Emotions: their psychological, physiological and educative implications.* New York: Ronald Press, 1939. *51*

379. Lurie, L. A., Greenebaum, J. V., Leichtentritt, B., & Rosenthal, Florence M. Late results noted in children presenting post-encephalitic behavior. *Amer. J. Psychiat.,* 1947, *104,* 171-179. *378*

380. McAllester, D. Water as a disciplinary agent among the Crow and Blackfoot. *Amer. Anthropologist,* 1941, *43,* 593-604. *408*

381. McCary, J. L., & Sheer, D. E. (Eds.) *Six approaches to psychotherapy.* New York: Dryden Press, 1955. *549*

382. Maccoby, Eleanor E., Gibbs, Patricia K., & Staff. Methods of child-rearing in two social classes. In W. E. Martin & Celia B. Stendler (Eds.), *Readings in child development.* New York: Harcourt, Brace, 1954. Pp. 380-396. *421*

383. McCleary, R. A., & Lazarus, R. S. Autonomic discrimination without awareness: an interim report. *J. Pers.,* 1949, *18,* 171-179. *237*

384. McClelland, D. C. *Personality.* New York: William Sloane, 1951. *97*

385. McClelland, D. C. (Ed.) *Studies in motivation.* New York: Appleton-Century-Crofts, 1955. *58*

386. McDougall, W. *Outline of abnormal psychology.* New York: Scribner's, 1926. *263*

387. McGranahan, D. V. A critical and experimental study of repression. *J. abnorm. soc. Psychol.,* 1940, *35,* 212-225. *231*

388. McKinney, F. *The psychology of personal adjustment.* (2nd ed.) New York: Wiley, 1949. *591*

389. McMurry, R. N. *Handling personality adjustment in industry.* New York: Harper, 1944. *571*

390. Magaret, Ann. Generalization in successful psychotherapy. *J. consult. Psychol.,* 1950, *14,* 64-70. *535*

391. Maslow, A. H., & Mittelmann, B. *Principles of abnormal psychology.* (Rev. ed.) New York: Harper, 1951. *227, 267, 378*

392. Masserman, J. H. *Behavior and neurosis.* Chicago: Univer. of Chicago Press, 1943. *112, 113*

393. Masserman, J. H. *Principles of dynamic psychiatry.* Philadelphia: Saunders, 1946. *222-223*

394. May, M. A. Experimentally acquired drives. *J. exp. Psychol.,* 1948, *38,* 66-77. *61, 62*

395. May, R. *The meaning of anxiety.* New York: Ronald Press, 1950. *121, 275, 306*

396. May, R. *Man's search for himself.* New York: Norton, 1953. *23*

397. Mayo, E. *The human problems of an industrial civilization.* New York: Macmillan, 1933. *590*

398. Mayo, E. *The social problems of an industrial civilization.* Boston: Harvard Univer. Graduate School of Business Administration, 1945. *569, 571, 572-573*

399. Mead, G. H. *Mind, self, and society.* Chicago: Univer. of Chicago Press, 1934. *536*

400. Mead, Margaret, *Coming of age in Samoa.* New York: William Morrow, 1928. *409*

401. Mead, Margaret. *From the South seas.* New York: Norton, 1939. *446*

402. Mead, Margaret. Social change and cultural surrogates. *J. educ. Sociol.,* 1940, *14,* 92-110. *81*

403. Mead, Margaret. Research on primitive children. In L. Carmichael (Ed.), *Manual of child psychology.* (2nd ed.) New York: Wiley, 1954. Pp. 735-780. *81, 97*

404. Meltzer, H. Individual differences in forgetting pleasant and unpleasant experiences. *J. educ. Psychol.,* 1930, *21,* 399-409. *231*

405. Meltzer, H. The present status of experimental studies on the relationship of feeling to memory. *Psychol. Rev.,* 1930, *37,* 124-139. *231*

406. Meltzer, H. The forgetting of pleasant and unpleasant experiences in relation to intelligence and achievement. *J. soc. Psychol.,* 1931, *2,* 216-229. *231*

407. Meltzer, H. Sex differences in forgetting pleasant and unpleasant experiences. *J. abnorm. soc. Psychol.,* 1931, *25,* 450-464. *231*

408. Menninger, K. A. *Love against hate.* New York: Harcourt, Brace, 1942. *154*

409. Menninger, K. A. *A manual for psychiatric case study.* New York: Grune & Stratton, 1952. *513*

410. Menninger, W. C. *Psychiatry in a troubled world.* New York: Macmillan, 1948. *542*

411. Menzies, R. Conditioned vasomotor responses in human subjects. *J. Psychol.*, 1937, *4*, 75-120. *76, 77*

412. Merrill, Maud A. *Problems of child delinquency*. Boston: Houghton Mifflin, 1947. *183, 186*

413. Metzger, F. C. Emotions in the allergic individual. *Amer. J. Psychiat.*, 1947, *103*, 697-699. *297*

414. Meyer, Charlene T. The assertive behavior of children as related to parent behavior. *J. Home Econ.*, 1947, *39*, 77-80. *436-437*

415. Miller, N. E. Experimental studies of conflict. In J. McV. Hunt (Ed.), *Personality and the behavior disorders*. New York: Ronald Press, 1944. Pp. 431-465. *123*

416. Miller, N. E. Studies of fear as an acquirable drive: I. Fear as motivation and fear-reduction as reinforcement in the learning of new responses. *J. exp. Psychol.*, 1948, *38*, 89-101. *64*

417. Miller, N. E. Theory and experiment relating psychoanalytic displacement to stimulus-response generalization. *J. abnorm. soc. Psychol.*, 1948, *43*, 155-178. *71, 72*

418. Miller, N. E. Learnable drives and rewards. In S. S. Stevens (Ed.), *Handbook of experimental psychology*. New York: Wiley, 1951. Pp. 435-472. *97*

419. Miller, N. E., et al. The frustration-aggression hypothesis: symposium. *Psychol. Rev.*, 1941, *48*, 337-366. *101*

420. Minami, H., & Dallenbach, K. M. The effect of activity upon learning and retention in the cockroach. *Amer. J. Psychol.*, 1946, *59*, 1-58. *70*

421. Mittelman, B., Wolff, H. G., & Scharf, M. P. Emotions and gastroduodenal function: experimental studies on patients with gastritis, duodenitis and peptic ulcer. *Psychosom. Med.*, 1942, *4*, 5-61. *294*

422. Moloney, J. C. *The battle for mental health*. New York: Philosophical Library, 1952. *513*

423. Morgan, C. T., & Stellar, E. *Physiological psychology*. (2nd ed.) New York: McGraw-Hill, 1950. *57, 58*

424. Morgan, J. J. B. *The psychology of the unadjusted school child*. New York: Macmillan, 1924. *240*

425. Morgan, J. J. B. *The psychology of the unadjusted school child*. (Rev. ed.) New York: Macmillan, 1936. *176-177, 213, 392*

426. Morgan, J. J. B. *The psychology of abnormal people*. (2nd ed.) New York: Longmans, Green, 1936. *192*

427. Morgan, J. J. B. *How to keep a sound mind*. (Rev. ed.) New York: Macmillan, 1946. *186, 591*

428. Morlan, G. K. A note on the frustration-aggression theories of Dollard and his associates. *Psychol. Rev.*, 1949, *56*, 1-8. *102*

429. Morris, D. P., & Soroker, Eleanor P. A follow-up study of a guidance-clinic waiting list. *Ment. Hyg., N. Y.*, 1953, *37*, 84-88. *546*

430. Moustakas, C. E. *Children in play therapy.* New York: McGraw-Hill, 1953. *549*

431. Mowrer, O. H. A stimulus-response analysis of anxiety and its role as a reinforcing agent. *Psychol. Rev.*, 1939, *46*, 553-565. *122, 133*

432. Mowrer, O. H. An experimental analogue of "regression" with incidental observations on "reaction-formation." *J. abnorm. soc. Psychol.*, 1940, *35*, 56-87. *176, 211*

433. Mowrer, O. H. The law of effect and ego psychology. *Psychol. Rev.*, 1946, *53*, 321-334. *95*

434. Mowrer, O. H. On the dual nature of learning — a re-interpretation of "conditioning" and "problem-solving." *Harvard educ. Rev.*, 1947, *17*, 102-148. *56, 135, 136*

435. Mowrer, O. H. Learning theory and the neurotic paradox. *Amer. J. Orthopsychiat.*, 1948, *18*, 571-610. *122, 148, 151*

436. Mowrer, O. H. *Learning theory and personality dynamics.* New York: Ronald Press, 1950. *97, 136, 154*

437. Mowrer, O. H. *Psychotherapy: theory and research.* New York: Ronald Press, 1953. *549*

438. Mowrer, O. H. The psychologist looks at language. *Amer. Psychologist*, 1954, *9*, 660-694. *534*

439. Mowrer, O. H., & Kluckhohn, C. Dynamic theory of personality. In J. McV. Hunt (Ed.), *Personality and the behavior disorders.* New York: Ronald Press, 1944. Pp. 69-135. *56, 154*

440. Mowrer, O. H., & Lamoreaux, R. R. Fear as an intervening variable in avoidance conditioning. *J. comp. Psychol.*, 1946, *39*, 29-50. *64*

441. Mowrer, O. H., & Ullman, A. D. Time as a determinant in integrative learning. *Psychol. Rev.*, 1945, *52*, 61-90. *151, 532*

442. Mowrer, O. H., & Viek, P. An experimental analogue of fear from a sense of helplessness. *J. abnorm. soc. Psychol.*, 1948, *43*, 193-200. *18*

443. Muenzinger, K. F. Motivation in learning: I. Electric shock for correct response in the visual discrimination habit. *J. comp. Psychol.*, 1934, *17*, 267-277. *133*

444. Muenzinger, K. F. Concerning the effect of shock for right responses in visual discrimination learning. *J. exp. Psychol.*, 1948, *38*, 201-203. *133*

445. Muenzinger, K. F., Bernstone, A. H., & Richards, L. Motivation in learning. VIII. Equivalent amounts of electric shock for right and wrong responses in a visual discrimination habit. *J. comp. Psychol.*, 1938, *26*, 117-186. *133*

446. Mulinos, M. G. The gastric hunger mechanism. IV. The influence of experimental alterations in blood sugar concentration on the gastric hunger contractions. *Amer. J. Physiol.*, 1933, *104*, 371-378. *30*

447. Mullahy, P. *Oedipus, myth and complex.* New York: Hermitage Press, 1948. *465, 480*

448. Muller, H. J. Mental traits and heredity. *J. Hered.*, 1925, *16*, 433-448. *398*

449. Munn, N. L. Learning in children. In L. Carmichael (Ed.), *Manual of child psychology.* (2nd ed.) New York: Wiley, 1954. Pp. 374-458. *154*

450. Munn, N. L. *Psychology.* (3rd ed.) Boston: Houghton Mifflin, 1956. *23, 52, 57, 154, 400*

451. Munroe, Ruth L. *Schools of psychoanalytic thought.* New York: Dryden Press, 1955. *479*

452. Murphy, G. *Historical introduction to modern psychology.* (Rev. ed.) New York: Harcourt, Brace, 1949. *479*

453. Murphy, G. Social motivation. In G. Lindzey (Ed.), *Handbook of social psychology.* Cambridge, Mass.: Addison-Wesley Press, 1954. Vol. 2, pp. 601-633. *97*

454. Murray, H. A. *Thematic Apperception Test.* Cambridge, Mass.: Harvard Univer. Press, 1943. *338*

455. Murray, H. A. *et al. Explorations in personality.* New York: Oxford Univer. Press, 1938. *338*

456. Nadel, S. F. *The foundations of social anthropology.* Glencoe, Ill.: The Free Press, 1951. *186*

457. National Education Association. The status of the teaching profession. *Res. Bull.*, 1940, *18*, No. 2. *564*

458. National Society for the Study of Education. Mental health in modern education. *Fifty-fourth yearbook*, Part II, 1955. *590*

459. Newman, H. H., Freeman, F. N., & Holzinger, K. J. *Twins: A study of heredity and environment.* Chicago: Univer. of Chicago Press, 1937. *397, 398*

460. Noyes, A. P. *Modern clinical psychiatry.* (2nd ed.) Philadelphia: Saunders, 1939. *213*

461. O'Kelly, L. I. *Introduction to psychopathology.* New York: Prentice-Hall, 1949. *158*

462. O'Kelly, L. I., & Muckler, F. A. *Introduction to psychopathology.* Englewood Cliffs, N. J.: Prentice-Hall, 1955. *97*

463. O'Kelly, L. I., & Steckle, L. C. The forgetting of pleasant and unpleasant experiences. *Amer. J. Psychol.*, 1940, *53*, 432-434. *231*

464. Olson, W. C. *The measurement of nervous habits in normal children.* Minneapolis, Minn.: Univer. of Minnesota Press, 1929. *343*

465. Orlansky, H. Infant care and personality. *Psychol. Bull.*, 1949, *46*, 1-48. *42*

466. Patty, W. L., & Johnson, Louise S. *Personality and adjustment.* New York: McGraw-Hill, 1953. *590*

467. Pavlov, I. P. *Conditioned reflexes.* (Trans. by G. V. Anrep) London: Oxford Univer. Press, 1927. *66, 115*

468. Pavlov, I. P. *Lectures on conditioned reflexes.* (Trans. by W. H. Gantt) New York: International Publishers, 1928. *66, 115*

469. Pavlov, I. P. *Conditioned reflexes and psychiatry.* (Trans. by W. H. Gantt) New York: International Publishers, 1941. *115*

470. Pennell, Maryland Y., Cameron, D. C., & Kramer, M. Mental health clinic services for children in the United States, 1950. *Publ. Hlth Rep.*, 1951, *66*(48), 1559-1572. *489*

471. Pennington, L. A., & Berg, I. A. (Eds.) *An introduction to clinical psychology.* (2nd ed.) New York: Ronald Press, 1954. *359, 479*

472. Peters, H. N. The mirror-tracing test as a measure of social maladaptation. *J. abnorm. soc. Psychol.*, 1946, *41*, 437-448. *357*

473. Peterson, J. Learning when frequency and recency factors are negative and right responses are painful. *Psychol. Bull.*, 1931, *28*, 207-208. *133*

474. Pintner, R., & Forlano, G. The influence of pleasantly and unpleasantly toned words on retention. *J. soc. Psychol.*, 1940, *11*, 147-149. *231*

475. Plant, J. S. The psychiatric value of the Kuhlmann tests. *Arch. Neurol. Psychiat., Chicago*, 1926, *15*, 253-259. *354*

476. Porteus, S. D. *The Porteus maze test and intelligence.* Palo Alto, Calif.: Pacific Books, 1950. *351*

477. Porteus, S. D. *The maze test: recent advances.* Palo Alto, Calif.: Pacific Books, 1955. *351*

478. Postman, L., & Bruner, J. S. Perception under stress. *Psychol. Rev.*, 1948, *55*, 314-323. *17*

479. Postman, L., Bruner, J. S., & McGinnies, E. Personal values as selective factors in perception. *J. abnorm. soc. Psychol.*, 1948, *43*, 142-154. *237*

480. Powdermaker, Florence B., & Frank, J. D. *Group psychotherapy.* New York: Commonwealth Fund, 1953. *541*

481. Pratt, K. C., Nelson, A. K., & Sun, K. H. The behavior of the newborn infant. *Ohio State Univer. Stud., Contr. Psychol.*, 1930, No. 10. *46*

482. Pressey, Luella C. *Some college students and their problems.* Columbus, Ohio: Ohio State Univer. Press, 1929. *207-209*

483. Pressey, S. L., & Pressey, Luella C. *Mental abnormality and deficiency.* New York: Macmillan, 1926. *147, 290*

484. Preston, G. H. *The substance of mental health.* New York: Farrar & Rinehart, 1943. *447*

485. Prince, M. *The unconscious.* (2nd ed.) New York: Macmillan, 1921. *223*

486. Prothro, E. T., & Jeska, P. T. *Psychology: a biosocial study of behavior.* New York: Ginn, 1950. *245*

487. Raimy, V. C. Self reference in counseling interviews. *J. consult. Psychol.*, 1948, *12*, 153-163. *95, 536*

488. Rank, O. *The trauma of birth.* New York: Harcourt, Brace, 1929. *469*

489. Rank, O. *Modern education.* New York: Knopf, 1932. *469*

490. Rank, O. *Will therapy, and truth and reality.* New York: Knopf, 1945. *469, 480*

491. Rapaport, D. *Diagnostic psychological testing.* Vol. I & II. Chicago: Year Book Publishers, 1946. *341*

492. Rapaport, D. *Emotions and memory.* (2nd ed.) New York: International Universities Press, 1950. *231, 245*

493. Ray, W. S. The relationship of retroactive inhibition, retrograde amnesia, and the loss of recent memory. *Psychol. Rev.*, 1937, *44*, 339-345. *231*

494. Razran, G. H. S. Conditioned responses in children. *Arch. Psychol., N Y.*, 1933, No. 148. *118*

495. Redl, F., & Wattenberg, W. W. *Mental hygiene in teaching.* New York: Harcourt, Brace, 1951. *590*

496. Reymert, M. L. (Ed.) *Feelings and emotions.* New York: McGraw-Hill, 1950. *58*

497. Reynolds, Martha M. Negativism of preschool children. *Teach. Coll. Contr. Educ.*, 1928, No. 288. *199*

498. Ribble, Margaretha A. *The rights of infants.* New York: Columbia Univer. Press, 1943. *583*

499. Rice, P. B. The ego and the law of effect. *Psychol. Rev.*, 1946, *53*, 307-320. *95*

500. Richter, C. P. Biology of drives. *J. comp. physiol. Psychol.*, 1947, *40*, 129-134. *32*

501. Rivers, W. H. R. *Instinct and the unconscious.* Cambridge, Eng.: Cambridge Univer. Press, 1920. *220*

502. Robinson, J. F. Current trends in child-guidance clinics. *Ment. Hyg., N. Y.*, 1950, *34*, 106-116. *488*

503. Robinson, J. H. *The mind in the making.* New York: Harper, 1921. *186*

504. Roethlisberger, F. J. *Management and morale.* Cambridge, Mass.: Harvard Univer. Press, 1941. *572, 590*

505. Roethlisberger, F. J., & Dickson, W. J. *Management and the worker.* Cambridge, Mass.: Harvard Univer. Press, 1939. *572*

506. Roff, M. A. A factorial study of the Fels parent behavior scales. *Child Develpm.*, 1949, *20*, 29-45. *434*

507. Rogers, C. R. *Counseling and psychotherapy.* Boston: Houghton Mifflin, 1942. *517*

508. Rogers, C. R. *Client-centered therapy.* Boston: Houghton Mifflin, 1951. *517*

509. Rogers, C. R., & Dymond, Rosalind F. (Eds.) *Psychotherapy and personality change.* Chicago: Univer. of Chicago Press, 1954. *545-548*

510. Rogers, C. R., Kell, B. L., & McNeil, Helen. The role of self-understanding in the prediction of behavior. *J. consult. Psychol.*, 1948, *12*, 174-186. *16*

511. Rogers, C. R., *et al.* A coordinated research in psychotherapy. *J. consult. Psychol.*, 1949, *13*, 149-220. *343*

512. Rohde, Amanda R. Explorations in personality by the sentence completion method. *J. appl. Psychol.*, 1946, *30*, 169-181. *342*

513. Root, O. Basic aims of the National Association for Mental Health. *Ment. Hyg., N. Y.*, 1951, *35*, 1-4. *484*

514. Rorschach, H. *Psychodiagnostics.* (2nd ed.) Berne, Switzerland: Verlag Hans Huber, 1942. *334*

515. Rosenzweig, S. III. Need-persistive and ego-defensive reactions to frustration as demonstrated by an experiment on repression. *Psychol. Rev.*, 1941, *48*, 347-349. *231*

516. Rosenzweig, S. An outline of frustration theory. In J. McV. Hunt (Ed.), *Personality and the behavior disorders.* New York: Ronald Press, 1944. Vol. 1, pp. 379-388. *123*

517. Rosenzweig, S., & Kogan, Kate L. *Psychodiagnosis.* New York: Grune & Stratton, 1949. *341, 513*

518. Rosenzweig, S. A transvaluation of psychotherapy — a reply to Hans Eysenck. *J. abnorm. soc. Psychol.*, 1954, *49*, 298-307. *546*

519. Rotter, J. B. The nature and treatment of stuttering: a clinical approach. *J. abnorm. soc. Psychol.*, 1944, *39*, 150-173. *270*

520. Rotter, J. B. *Social learning and clinical psychology.* New York: Prentice-Hall, 1954. *154*

521. Rotter, J. B., Rafferty, Janet E., & Schachtitz, Eva. Validation of the Rotter incomplete sentences blank for college screening. *J. consult. Psychol.*, 1949, *13*, 348-356. *341-342*

522. Ruch, F. L. *Psychology and life.* (4th ed.) Chicago: Scott, Foresman, 1953. *23, 57, 154, 400*

523. Ruediger, W. C. The indirect improvement of mental function through ideals. *Educ. Rev.*, 1908, *36*, 364-371. *559*

524. Ruger, H. A. The psychology of efficiency. *Arch. Psychol., N. Y.*, 1910, No. 15. *126*

525. Rundquist, E. A. Inheritance of spontaneous activity in rats. *J. comp. Psychol.*, 1933, *16*, 415-438. *388*

526. Rust, Metta M. *The effect of resistance on intelligence test scores of young children.* Child Develpm. Monogr. No. 6. New York: Teachers Coll., Columbia Univer., 1931. *199*

527. Sanders, Marjorie J. An experimental demonstration of regression in the rat. *J. exp. Psychol.*, 1937, *21*, 493-510. *211*

528. Sanford, R. N. The effects of abstinence from food upon imaginal processes: a preliminary experiment. *J. Psychol.*, 1936, *2*, 129-136. *37*

529. Sanford, R. N. The effects of abstinence from food upon imaginal processes: a further experiment. *J. Psychol.*, 1937, *3*, 145-159. *37*

530. Saphir, W. Chronic hypochloremia simulating psychoneurosis. *J. Amer. med. Ass.*, 1945, *129*, 510-512. *376*

531. Saudek, R. A British pair of identical twins reared apart. *Charact. & Pers.*, 1934, *3*, 17-39. *398*

532. Saul, L. J. Physiological effects of emotional tension. In J. McV. Hunt (Ed.), *Personality and the behavior disorders.* New York: Ronald Press, 1944. Vol. 1, pp. 269-305. *123*

533. Scheinfeld, A. *You and heredity.* Garden City, N. Y.: Garden City Publication Co., 1939. *408*

534. Schilder, P. Results and problems of group psychotherapy in severe neuroses. *Ment. Hyg., N. Y.*, 1939, *23*, 87-99. *541, 542*

535. Schlosberg, H. The relationship between success and the laws of conditioning. *Psychol. Rev.*, 1937, *44*, 379-394. *136*

536. Schmidt, H. O. Test profiles as a diagnostic aid: the Minnesota Multiphasic Inventory. *J. appl. Psychol.*, 1945, *29*, 115-131. *327*

537. Schneider, L. I. Rorschach validation: some methodological aspects. *Psychol. Bull.*, 1950, *47*, 493-508. *337*

538. Scott, J. P. Social behavior, organization and leadership in a small flock of domestic sheep. *Comp. Psychol. Monogr.*, 1945, *18*, No. 4 (Serial No. 96). *79*

539. Sears, R. R. Experimental studies of projection: I. Attribution of traits. *J. soc. Psychol.*, 1936, *7*, 151-163. *180*

540. Sears, R. R. Functional abnormalities of memory with special reference to amnesia. *Psychol. Bull.*, 1936, *33*, 229-274. *231*

541. Sears, R. R. Experimental studies of projection: II. Ideas of reference. *J. soc. Psychol.*, 1937, *8*, 389-400. *180*

542. Sears, R. R. Initiation of the repression sequence by experienced failure. *J. exp. Psychol.*, 1937, *20*, 570-580. *231*

543. Sears, R. R. *Survey of objective studies of psychoanalytic concepts.*

Bulletin 51. New York: Social Science Research Council, 1943. *180, 478, 480*

544. Sears, R. R., & Hovland, C. I. Experiments on motor conflict. II. Determination of mode of resolution by comparative strengths of conflicting responses. *J. exp. Psychol.*, 1941, *28*, 280-286. *119*

545. Sears, R. R., Hovland, C. I., & Miller, N. E. Minor studies of aggression: I. Measurement of aggressive behavior. *J. Psychol.*, 1940, *9*, 275-294. *101*

546. Sears, R. R., & Sears, Pauline S. Minor studies of aggression: V. Strength of frustration-reaction as a function of strength of drive. *J. Psychol.*, 1940, *9*, 297-300. *49*

547. Sears, R. R., Whiting, J. W. M., Nowlis, V., & Sears, Pauline S. Some child-rearing antecedents of aggression and dependency in young children. *Genet. Psychol. Monogr.*, 1953, *47*, 135-236. *443*

548. Sears, R. R., & Wise, G. W. Relation of cup feeding in infancy to thumb-sucking and the oral drive. *Amer. J. Orthopsychiat.*, 1950, *20*, 123-138. *42*

549. Seeman, J. A study of the process of nondirective therapy. *J. consult. Psychol.*, 1949, *13*, 157-168. *537-540*

550. Seward, J. P. Note on the externalization of drive. *Psychol. Rev.*, 1942, *49*, 197-199, *83*

551. Shaffer, L. F. Fear and courage in aerial combat. *J. consult. Psychol.*, 1947, *11*, 137-143. *214, 215*

552. Shaffer, L. F. Fear and courage in aerial combat. In F. Wickert (Ed.), *Psychological research on problems of redistribution.* AAF Aviation Psychology Program Research Reports, No. 14. Washington: U. S. Government Printing Office, 1947. Pp. 122-136. *57*

553. Shaffer, L. F. Psychological studies of anxiety reaction to combat. In F. Wickert (Ed.), *Psychological research on problems of redistribution.* Army Air Forces Aviation Psychology Program Research Reports, No. 14. Washington: U. S. Government Printing Office, 1947. Pp. 93-121. *324*

554. Shaw, F. J. Two determinants of selective forgetting. *J. abnorm. soc. Psychol.*, 1944, *39*, 434-445. *231, 233, 234*

555. Shaw, F. J. A stimulus-response analysis of repression and insight in psychotherapy. *Psychol. Rev.*, 1946, *53*, 36-42. *231*

556. Shaw, F. J., & Ort, R. S. *Personal adjustment in the American culture.* New York: Harper, 1953. *23, 97, 154, 213, 447*

557. Shaw, F. J., & Spooner, Alice. Selective forgetting when the subject is not "ego-involved." *J. exp. Psychol.*, 1945, *35*, 242-247. *231, 233*

558. Sheerer, Elizabeth T. An analysis of the relationship between acceptance of and respect for self and acceptance of and respect for

others in ten counseling cases. *J. consult. Psychol.*, 1949, *13*, 169-175. *536, 540*

559. Sheldon, W. H., & Stevens, S. S. *The varieties of temperament.* New York: Harper, 1942. *382*

560. Sheldon, W. H., Stevens, S. S., & Tucker, W. B. *The varieties of human physique.* New York: Harper, 1940. *381*

561. Sherif, M. *The psychology of social norms.* New York: Harper, 1936. *93*

562. Sherman, M. The differentiation of emotional responses in infants: I. Judgments of emotional responses from motion picture views and from actual observation. *J. comp. Psychol.*, 1927, *7*, 265-284. *47*

563. Sherman, M. The differentiation of emotional responses in infants: II. The ability of observers to judge the emotional characteristics of the crying of infants, and of the voice of an adult. *J. comp. Psychol.*, 1927, *7*, 335-351. *47*

564. Sherman, M. *Mental hygiene and education.* New York: Longmans, Green, 1934. *203*

565. Sherman, M. The frustration threshold. *Amer. J. Psychiat.*, 1947, *104*, 242-246. *357*

566. Sherman, M., & Jost, H. Frustration reactions of normal and neurotic persons. *J. Psychol.*, 1942, *13*, 3-19. *357*

567. Shipley, W. C. An apparent transfer of conditioning. *J. gen. Psychol.*, 1933, *8*, 382-391. *76*

568. Shipley, W. C., Gray, Florence E., & Newbert, Nancy. The Personal Inventory — its derivation and validation. *J. clin. Psychol.*, 1946, *2*, 318-322. *325*

569. Shneidman, E. S. *Make a Picture Story (MAPS) Test.* New York: Psychological Corp., 1949. *339*

570. Shneidman, E. S. Manual for the Make a Picture Story method. *Proj. Tech. Monogr.*, 1952, No. 2. *339*

571. Shoben, E. J., Jr. Psychotherapy as a problem in learning theory. *Psychol. Bull.*, 1949, *46*, 366-392. *533*

572. Shoben, E. J., Jr. The Wechsler-Bellevue in the detection of anxiety: a test of the Rashkis-Welsh hypothesis. *J. consult. Psychol.*, 1950, *14*, 40-45. *349*

573. Shoben, E. J., Jr. A theoretical approach to psychotherapy as personality modification. *Harvard educ. Rev.*, 1953, *23*, 128-142. *526, 529*

574. Singh, J. A. L., & Zingg, R. M. *Wolf-children and feral man.* New York: Harper, 1942. *402*

575. Skinner, B. F. *The behavior of organisms.* New York: Appleton-Century-Crofts, 1938. *136*

576. Skinner, B. F. "Superstition" in the pigeon. *J. exp. Psychol.*, 1948, 38, 168-172. *137*

577. Skinner, B. F. *Science and human behavior.* New York: Macmillan, 1953. *23*

578. Skodak, Marie, & Skeels, H. M. A follow-up study of children in adoptive homes. *J. genet. Psychol.*, 1945, 66, 21-58. *394-395*

579. Skodak, Marie, & Skeels, H. M. A final follow-up study of one hundred adopted children. *J. genet. Psychol.*, 1949, 75, 85-125. *394-395*

580. Slavson, S. R. *An introduction to group therapy.* New York: Commonwealth Fund, 1943. *541*

581. Slavson, S. R. Differential dynamics of activity and interview group therapy. *Amer. J. Orthopsychiat.*, 1947, 17, 293-302. *542*

582. Sleight, W. G. Memory and formal training. *Brit. J. Psychol.*, 1911, 4, 386-457. *558*

583. Smith, G. E. *Principles and practices of the guidance program.* New York: Macmillan, 1951. *590*

584. Smith, G. E. *Counseling in the secondary school.* New York: Macmillan, 1955. *590*

585. Smith, H. C. Psychometric checks on hypotheses derived from Sheldon's work on physique and temperament. *J. Pers.*, 1949, 17, 310-320. *383*

586. Snyder, W. U. An investigation of the nature of non-directive psychotherapy. *J. gen. Psychol.*, 1945, 33, 193-223. *537*

587. Snyder, W. U. (Ed.) *Casebook of non-directive counseling.* Boston: Houghton Mifflin, 1947. *519, 549*

588. Snygg, D., & Combs, A. W. *Individual behavior.* New York: Harper, 1949. *158*

589. Spence, K. W. Theoretical interpretations of learning. In S. S. Stevens (Ed.), *Handbook of experimental psychology.* New York: Wiley, 1951. Pp. 690-729. *154*

590. Stackpole, Caroline E., & Leavell, Lutie C. *Textbook of physiology.* New York: Macmillan, 1953. *400*

591. Stagner, R. The redintegration of pleasant and unpleasant experiences. *Amer. J. Psychol.*, 1931, 43, 463-468. *232*

592. Stagner, R. Homeostasis as a unifying concept in personality theory. *Psychol. Rev.*, 1951, 58, 5-17. *36*

593. Steckle, L. C. Again — affect and recall. *J. soc. Psychol.*, 1945, 22, 103-106. *231*

594. Steckle, L. C. *Problems of human adjustment.* New York: Harper, 1949. *158, 590*

595. Stephens, F. E., & Thompson, R. B. The case of Millan and George, identical twins reared apart. *J. Hered.*, 1943, 34, 109-114. *398*

596. Stevens, S. S. *Handbook of experimental psychology.* New York: Wiley, 1951. *57, 58, 97, 154*

597. Stevenson, G. S. The mental-health program in perspective. *Ment. Hyg., N. Y.,* 1951. *35,* 5-9. *485*

598. Stevenson, G. S., & Smith, G. *Child guidance clinics.* New York: Commonwealth Fund, 1934. *490*

599. Stock, Dorothy. An investigation into the interrelations between the self concept and feelings directed toward other persons and groups. *J. consult. Psychol.,* 1949, *13,* 176-180. *540*

600. Stone, Hannah M., & Stone, A. *A marriage manual.* (Rev. ed.) New York: Simon & Schuster, 1952. *591*

601. Stouffer, S. A., *et al. The American soldier.* II. *Combat and its aftermath.* Princeton, N. J.: Princeton Univer. Press, 1949. *215*

602. Strang, Ruth. Criteria of progress in counseling and psychotherapy. *J. clin. Psychol.,* 1947, *3,* 180-183. *545*

603. Strang, Ruth. *An introduction to child study.* (3rd ed.) New York: Macmillan, 1951. *591*

604. Stroup, H. H. *Social work: an introduction to the field.* New York: American Book Co., 1953. *573, 591*

605. Strupp, H. H. An objective comparison of Rogerian and psychoanalytic techniques. *J. consult. Psychol.,* 1955, *19,* 1-7. *525*

606. Sullivan, A. J., & McKell, T. E. *Personality in peptic ulcer.* Springfield, Ill.: Charles C Thomas, 1950. *294*

607. Sullivan, H. S. *Conceptions of modern psychiatry.* Washington: William Alanson White Foundation, 1947. *470, 535*

608. Sullivan, H. S. *The interpersonal theory of psychiatry.* New York: Norton, 1953. *470, 480*

609. Sullivan, H. S. *The psychiatric interview.* New York: Norton, 1954. *470*

610. Super, D. E. *The dynamics of vocational adjustment.* New York: Harper, 1942. *590*

611. Sutherland, E. H. *Principles of criminology.* (5th ed.) Philadelphia: Lippincott, 1947. *425*

612. Switzer, S. A. Disinhibition of the conditioned galvanic skin response. *J. gen. Psychol.,* 1933, *9,* 77-100. *75*

613. Symonds, P. M. *Diagnosing personality and conduct.* New York: Century, 1931. *332*

614. Symonds, P. M. *The psychology of parent-child relationships.* New York: Appleton-Century, 1939. *282*

615. Symonds, P. M. *The dynamics of human adjustment.* New York: Appleton-Century, 1946. *158*

616. Symonds, P. M. *Symonds Picture-Story Test.* New York: Teachers Coll., Columbia Univer., 1948. *339*

617. Symonds, P. M. *Adolescent fantasy.* New York: Columbia Univer. Press, 1949. *339*

618. Talland, G. A., & Clark, D. H. Evaluation of topics in therapy group discussion. *J. clin. Psychol.,* 1954, *10,* 131-137. *528*

619. Taylor, Janet A. A personality scale of manifest anxiety. *J. abnorm. soc. Psychol.,* 1953, *48,* 285-290. *328*

620. Taylor, W. S., & Martin, Mabel F. Multiple personality. *J. abnorm. soc. Psychol.,* 1944, *39,* 281-300. *256*

621. Templeton, R. D., & Quigley, J. P. The action of insulin on motility of the gastro-intestinal tract. II. *Amer. J. Physiol.,* 1930, *91,* 467-474. *30*

622. Terman, L. M. *The measurement of intelligence.* Boston: Houghton Mifflin, 1916. *354*

623. Terman, L. M. *Genetic studies of genius.* Vol. I. *Mental and physical traits of a thousand gifted children.* Stanford, Calif.: Stanford Univer. Press, 1926. *191*

624. Terman, L. M. *Psychological factors in marital happiness.* New York: McGraw-Hill, 1938. *579*

625. Terman, L. M., & Merrill, Maud A. *Measuring intelligence.* Boston: Houghton Mifflin, 1937. *344*

626. Thomas, Dorothy S. *Some new techniques for studying social behavior.* New York: Teachers Coll., Columbia Univer., 1929. *343*

627. Thompson, C. E. The attitudes of various groups toward behavior problems of children. *J. abnorm. soc. Psychol.,* 1940, *35,* 120-125. *188-189*

628. Thompson, Clara M. *Psychoanalysis: evolution and development.* New York: Hermitage House, 1950. *479*

629. Thorndike, E. L. Animal intelligence. *Psychol. Rev. Monogr. Supp.,* 1898, *2,* No. 4 (Whole No. 8). *125, 126, 129*

630. Thorndike, E. L. *Educational psychology.* Vol. II. New York: Teachers Coll., Columbia Univer., 1913. *130*

631. Thorndike, E. L. Mental discipline in high school studies. *J. educ. Psychol.,* 1924, *15,* 1-22, 83-98. *558*

632. Thorndike, E. L. *Human learning.* New York: Century, 1931. *131*

633. Thorndike, R. L., & Hagan, Elizabeth. *Measurement and evaluation in psychology and education.* New York: Wiley, 1955. *359*

634. Thorne, F. C. *Principles of psychological examining.* Brandon, Vt.: Journal of Clinical Psychology, 1955. *513*

635. Thurstone, L. L. *Primary mental abilities.* Chicago: Univer. of Chicago Press, 1938. *346*

636. Tolman, E. C. The determiners of behavior at a choice point. *Psychol. Rev.,* 1938, *45,* 1-41. *64*

637. Tolman, E. C. Cognitive maps in rats and men. *Psychol. Rev.,* 1948, *55,* 189-208. *135*

638. Tolman, E. C. There is more than one kind of learning. *Psychol. Rev.,* 1949, *56,* 144-155. *136*

639. Tolman, E. C., & Honzik, C. H. "Insight" in rats. *Univer. Calif. Publ. Psychol.,* 1930, *4,* 215-232. *135*

640. Travis, L. E. *Speech pathology.* New York, Appleton, 1931. *269*

641. Troup, Evelyn. A comparative study by means of the Rorschach method of personality development in twenty pairs of identical twins. *Genet. Psychol. Monogr.,* 1938, *20,* 461-556. *398*

642. Tryon, R. C. Genetic differences in maze-learning ability in rats. *Yrbk. Nat. Soc. Stud. Educ.,* 1940, *39* (I), 111-119. *388*

643. Tsang, Y. Hunger motivation in gastrectomized rats. *J. comp. Psychol.,* 1938, *26,* 1-17. *32*

644. Turner, C. D. *General endocrinology.* Philadelphia: Saunders, 1949. *363*

645. U. S. Army. Office of the Surgeon General. Psychiatric disorders and reactions: definitions and manner of recording. *War Dept. tech. med. Bull.,* 1945, No. 203. Also in *Ment. Hyg., N. Y.,* 1946, *30,* 456-476. *276*

646. U. S. Department of Health, Education, and Welfare. Public Health Service. *Listing of outpatient psychiatric clinics in the United States and territories, 1954.* Washington: U. S. Government Printing Office, 1954. *489*

647. U. S. Public Health Service. The National Institute of Mental Health. *Publ. Hlth Publ. Ser. No. 20, Ment. Hlth Ser. No. 4 (rev.),* 1950. *485*

648. Van Ormer, E. B. Retention after intervals of sleep and of waking. *Arch. Psychol., N. Y.,* 1932, No. 137. *70*

649. Van Riper, C. *Speech correction, principles and methods.* (2nd ed.) New York: Prentice-Hall, 1947. *269, 270*

650. Wada, Tomi. An experimental study of hunger in its relation to activity. *Arch. Psychol., N. Y.,* 1922, No. 57. *31*

651. Waite, W. W. *Personnel administration.* New York: Ronald Press, 1952. *567, 590*

652. Waldfogel, S. The frequency and affective character of childhood memories. *Psychol. Monogr.,* 1948, *62,* No. 4 (Whole No. 291). *213*

653. Walker, K., & Strauss, E. B. *Sexual disorders in the male.* (3rd ed.) Baltimore: Williams & Wilkins, 1948. *34*

654. Wallbank, T. W. *India in the new era.* Chicago: Scott, Foresman, 1951. *417*

655. Wallen, R. Ego-involvement as a determinant of selective forgetting. *J. abnorm. soc. Psychol.*, 1942, *37*, 20-39. *231, 233*

656. Wallen, R. Food aversions of normal and neurotic males. *J. abnorm. soc. Psychol.*, 1945, *40*, 77-81. *325*

657. Wang, G. H. The relation between "spontaneous" activity and oestrous cycle in the white rat. *Comp. Psychol. Monogr.*, 1923, 2, No. 1 (Serial No. 6). *34*

658. Warden, C. J. *Animal motivation.* New York: Columbia Univer. Press, 1931. *38, 39*

659. Warner, S. J. The Wechsler-Bellevue psychometric pattern in anxiety neurosis. *J. consult. Psychol.*, 1950, *14*, 297-304. *349*

660. Warner, W. L. *American life.* Chicago: Univer. of Chicago Press, 1953. *418-420, 421, 424*

661. Warner, W. L., & Lunt, P. S. *The social life of a modern community.* New Haven, Conn.: Yale Univer. Press, 1941. *417*

662. Warner, W. L., Meeker, Marchia, & Eels, K. *Social class in America.* Chicago: Science Research Associates, 1949. *420, 447*

663. Watkins, J. G. *Hypnotherapy of war neuroses.* New York: Ronald Press, 1949. *252*

664. Watson, G., & Spence, R. B. *Educational problems for psychological study.* New York: Macmillan, 1930. *211*

665. Watson, J. B. *Psychological care of infant and child.* New York: Norton, 1928. *582*

666. Watson, J. B. *Psychology from the standpoint of a behaviorist.* (3rd ed.) Philadelphia: Lippincott, 1929. *46, 67*

667. Watson, J. B., & Raynor, Rosalie. Conditioned emotional reactions. *J. exp. Psychol.*, 1920, 3, 1-14. *67*

668. Wechsler, D. *The measurement of adult intelligence.* (3rd ed.) Baltimore: Williams & Wilkins, 1944. *345, 348*

669. Wechsler, D. *Wechsler Intelligence Scale for Children.* New York: Psychological Corp., 1949. *345, 501, 503*

670. Wechsler, D. Cognitive, conative, and non-intellective intelligence. *Amer. Psychologist,* 1950, *5,* 78-83. *346*

671. Wechsler, D. *Wechsler Adult Intelligence Scale.* New York: Psychological Corp., 1955. *345, 501*

672. Weider, A., *et al. Cornell Index* and *Manual.* New York: Psychological Corp., 1948. *324*

673. Weinberg, S. K. *Society and personality disorders.* New York: Prentice-Hall, 1952. *446, 527*

674. Weiss, E., & English, O. S. *Psychosomatic medicine.* Philadelphia: Saunders, 1943. *292*

675. Wells, F. L. *Mental tests in clinical practice.* Yonkers, N. Y.: World Book Co., 1927. *355*

676. Wheeler, W. M., Little, K. B., & Lehner, G. F. J. The internal structure of the MMPI. *J. consult. Psychol.*, 1951, *15*, 134-141. *328*

677. Wheery, R. J. Buddy ratings: popularity contest or leadership criteria. *Personnel Psychol.*, 1949, *2*, 147-159. *332*

678. White, R. W. *The abnormal personality.* New York: Ronald Press, 1948. 158, 186, *213, 549*

679. White, R. W. *Lives in progress.* New York: Dryden Press, 1952. *123*

680. Whiting, J. W. M., & Child, I. L. *Child training and personality.* New Haven, Conn.: Yale Univer. Press, 1953. *412-415, 447*

681. Whyte, W. F. A slum sex code. *Amer. J. Sociol.*, 1943, *49*, 24-31. *425*

682. Whyte, W. F. *Street corner society.* (2nd ed.) Chicago: Univer. of Chicago Press, 1955. *421*

683. Wickert, F. (Ed.) *Psychological research on problems of redistribution.* Army Air Forces Aviation Psychology Program Research Reports, No. 14. Washington: U. S. Government Printing Office, 1947. *57, 324*

684. Wickman, E. K. *Children's behavior and teachers' attitudes.* New York: Commonwealth Fund, 1928. *189*

685. Wilkins, L., & Richter, C. P. A great craving for salt by a child with cortico-adrenal insufficiency. *J. Amer. med. Ass.*, 1940, *114*, 866-868. *36*

686. Winch, W. H. The transfer of improvement in reasoning in schoolchildren. *Brit. J. Psychol.*, 1923, *13*, 370-381. *558*

687. Wischner, G. J. The effect of punishment on discrimination learning in a non-correction situation. *J. exp. Psychol.*, 1947, *37*, 271-284. *133*

688. Wischner, G. J. A reply to Dr. Muenzinger on the effect of punishment on discrimination learning in a non-correction situation. *J. exp. Psychol.*, 1948, *38*, 203-204. *133*

689. Wischner, G. J. Stuttering behavior and learning: a preliminary theoretical formulation. *J. Speech Hearing Disorders*, 1950, *15*, 324-335. *270*

690. Witmer, Helen L. (Ed.) *Psychiatric interviews with children.* New York: Commonwealth Fund, 1946. *513*

691. Wolf, S., & Wolff, H. G. *Human gastric function: an experimental study of a man and his stomach.* (2nd ed.) New York: Oxford Univer. Press, 1947. *293*

692. Wolfe, J. B. Effectiveness of token-rewards for chimpanzees. *Comp. Psychol. Monogr.*, 1936, *12*, No. 5 (Serial No. 60). *78*

693. Woodworth, R. S. *Dynamic psychology.* New York: Columbia Univer. Press, 1918. *92*

694. Woodworth, R. S. *Personal data sheet (psychoneurotic inventory).* Chicago: C. H. Stoelting Co., 1919. *323, 395*

695. Woodworth, R. S. *Heredity and environment.* New York: Social Science Research Council, Bulletin 47, 1941. *393, 400*

696. Woodworth, R. S. *Contemporary schools of psychology.* (Rev. ed.) New York: Ronald Press, 1948. *23, 465*

697. Wright, H. F. The influence of barriers upon strength of motivation. *Contr. psychol. Theory*, 1937, *1*, No. 3. *100, 101*

698. Yeakel, E. H., & Rhoades, R. P. A comparison of the body and endocrine gland (adrenal, thyroid and pituitary) weights of emotional and non-emotional rats. *Endocrinology*, 1941, *28*, 337-340. *389*

698a. Yerkes, R. M., & Morgulis, S. The method of Pavlov in animal psychology. *Psychol. Bull.*, 1909, *6*, 257-273. *65*

699. Young, P. T. *Motivation of behavior.* New York: Wiley, 1936. *58*

700. Young, P. T. The experimental analysis of appetite. *Psychol. Bull.*, 1941, *38*, 129-164. *33*

701. Young, P. T. *Emotion in man and animal.* New York: Wiley, 1943. *51, 58*

702. Zeller, A. F. An experimental analogue of repression. I. Historical summary. *Psychol. Bull.*, 1950, *47*, 39-51. *231*

703. Zubin, J., *et al.* Symposium: statistics for the clinician. *J. clin. Psychol.*, 1950, *6*, 1-76. *337*

Index of Subjects

book

in psychoanalytic theory, 459
values of, 206-207
Fatigue: in psychoneurosis, 352-354
reaction, 287-291
Fear: acquired, 67-71
in adjustment, 214-244
conditioned, 67-71, 215-216
development of, 46-50
effects of, 18, 48-49
and maladjustment, 217
in military aviation, 214
and motivation, 87-88
normal, 214-217
of school, 553-554
of sex, 238-240
socially learned, 216-217
stimuli for, 46-49, 215
Feeblemindedness: apparent, 192-195
and heredity, 388, 390-391
Field: leaving the, 109, 120
psychological, 28
Figure and ground in learning, 134
Fixation, psychoanalytic concept of, 457
Flicker fusion, 354
Food Aversion Test, 325
Forgetting: of names, 228-230
and regression, 213
and repression, 228-241
Formal discipline, 558-559
Foster children, 392-396
Fraternal twins, 396
Free association in psychoanalysis, 463-464
Freedom: of child, 583
and experimental neurosis, 117
Frigidity, 238-239
Froehlich's disease, 371
Frustration: and aggression, 101-102
and conflict, 111-112
definition of, 99
effects of, 17, 99-103
experiments on, 17, 100-103
and motive strength, 100-101
and regression, 102-103
resolution of, 124-128
weaning as, 42
Fugue, 255
Functional autonomy, 92

Gain, secondary, *see* Secondary gain
Galvanic skin response, conditioning of, 75-76

Generalization: of conditioned stimulus, 71-73, 78
of conflict, 114, 116, 118, 121
of drive, 72-73, 78
gradient of, 72
in psychotherapy, 534-537
in school learning, 559-560
Gestalt interpretation of learning, 134-135
Giantism, 370
Gland, endocrine, *see* Endocrine gland
Goals, 95-96
Goiter, 366
Gonadotropic hormone, 371
Gonads, 368-370
"Good" reasons, 177
Gregarious behavior, 79
Grief, 50
Ground and figure in learning, 134
Group: identification with, 175
psychotherapy, 540-542
work, 575
Growth hormone, 370

Habit and motive, 91-92
Habitus, 380-383
Halo in rating, 332
Hand washing, 243
Handedness and stuttering, 269, 271
Hashish, 375
Hate, attitude of, 93
Hay fever, 297
Headache, hysterical, 251
Health, physical, and mental health, 586
Hebephrenic schizophrenia, 196
Helplessness and fear, 18
Heredity, 383-400
animal studies of, 387-390
basis of, 384-385
of emotionality, 388-389
and endocrine glands, 389
evidence on, 387-399
and environments, 385-386
and family histories, 390-391
foster child studies of, 392-396
of intelligence, 388, 393-395, 397
of personality, 388-389, 391, 392, 395-399
of psychosis, 391
of schizophrenia, 391
twin studies of, 396-399
Hero worship, 204-205